OZ CLARKE'S

WINE GUIDE 1994

TENTH EDITION

Contributors to *Oz Clarke's Wine Guide 1994*

Nicholas Faith is a financial journalist and the author of books on Champagne and Cognac as well as the classic study of the Bordeaux wine trade, *The Wine Masters*. **Michael Schuster** is a writer and lecturer on wine and runs courses at his wine school, Winewise. He is the author of *Understanding Wine*. **Andrew Williams** is a freelance wine writer. **Harry Eyres** is the wine correspondent for *Harpers and Queen*; his books include *Wine Dynasties* and *Cabernet Sauvignon*. **Giles MacDonogh** is the author of *The Wine and Food of Austria*, and *Syrah, Grenache, Mourvèdre*; he also writes on food and drinks for the weekend *Financial Times* and is the author of *A History of Prussia*. **Jim Ainsworth** writes on wine and food for magazines in Britain and abroad, and wrote the Mitchell Beazley pocket guides to *Red Wines* and *White Wines*. **Stephen Brook** is the wine correspondent for *Vogue* and the author of *Sauvignon Blanc & Sémillon* as well as two recent travel books, *LA Lore* and *The Claws of the Crab: Georgia and Armenia*. **Tim Atkin** is the award-winning wine correspondent for *The Guardian* and the author of *Chardonnay;* he is currently writing a book on southern French wines. **David Gleave MW** runs the Italian specialist merchant Winecellars and is the author of *The Wines of Italy*. He is currently writing a book on Tuscan wines. **John Radford** is a wine writer with a particular interest in Spain. **Richard Mayson** has written a book on *The Wines of Portugal* and **Joanna Simon** is the award-winning correspondent of *The Sunday Times* and the author of a forthcoming book, *Discovering Wine*.

Reviews of previous editions

'Packed with insider information and opinion, and worth every penny.' Derek Cooper

'...the guide gets better with every vintage. Clarke writes with enthusiasm virtually steaming off the page. Here is someone who loves wine.' *The Guardian*

'If you haven't bought a copy, there is little hope for you.' *The Sunday Telegraph*

'An enthusiastic, opinionated and entertaining survey of the world's wines and a price guide to wines on the shelves of Britain.' *The Sunday Times*

'... typically up-to-date, irreverent but informative.' *The Independent*

'Scholarly, funny and thought-provoking.' Robert Parker

'*Webster's Wine Guide* is both passionate and quite unpretentious, in true Oz Clarke fashion.' *The Newcastle Journal*

OZ CLARKE'S

WINE GUIDE 1994

TENTH EDITION

'WEBSTER'S'

THE COMPLETE WINE BUYER'S HANDBOOK

WEBSTERS
MITCHELL BEAZLEY
LONDON

The information and prices contained in the guide were correct to the best of our knowledge when we went to press, and the impression of relative price *and* relative value *is almost certainly still accurate even if a particular price has changed.*

Although every care has been taken in the preparation of the guide, neither the publishers nor the editors can accept any liability for any consequences arising from the use of information contained herein.

Oz Clarke's Wine Guide *is an annual publication: we welcome any suggestions you may have for the 1995 edition.*

Editorial Director Sandy Carr
General Editor Margaret Rand
Art Editor Jason Vrakas
Price Guides Editors Anne Cochrane, Lorna Bateson
Editorial Assistants Gemma Hancock, Matthew Barrell
Designer Victor Ibañez
Art Director Douglas Wilson
Editorial Consultant Rosemary George
Database Consultant Alexandra Boyle
Indexer Naomi Good
Cover photograph James Merrell

Created and designed by
Webster's Wine Price Guide Limited,
Axe and Bottle Court, 70 Newcomen Street,
London SE1 1YT
in association with Mitchell Beazley
International Limited, Michelin House,
81 Fulham Road, London SW3 6RB

ISBN 1 85732 165 0

Printed and bound in the UK by
Cox & Wyman, Reading

CONTENTS

INTRODUCTION

Oh my God. The tenth edition of the *Wine Guide*! I haven't been doing this for ten years, have I? When my publisher proudly announced that this was the tenth edition, I had a serious sense of humour failure/mid-life crisis/*déjà-vu*/'is that all there is?' attack all rolled into one. As he proudly talked about sales figures and profitability, I dashed to the bathroom and surveyed the gaunt and haggard hulk gazing at me from the mirror. I leant forward to prod the crows' feet round my eyes, the grey hairs lapping against my temples. All I'd ever wanted to be was an *enfant terrible*, to be the rock and roller of the wine world for a year or two and then move on to something else before any kind of legitimacy caught up with me. And here I am.

Luckily my publisher has a human heart beating away inside his carefully tailored pinstripe suit. After applying a little Clinique eye mask to my crows' feet and a dab of Grecian 2000 to my temples, he got out all the *Guides* we've done together. So I thought about what times in the wine world were like then and what they're like now, what we set out to achieve ten years ago and what has been achieved. Well, I don't want to admit it, but I didn't feel so bad after all. Older we may be. Establishment fogeys, lickspittle lackeys of the capitalist system we certainly ain't.

And as long as this *Guide* keeps going, we never will be. At the end of my first introduction I wrote, 'And finally, I will have fun. There's no point in wine if it doesn't give me fun. If it doesn't make my eyes shine and my heart happy. At £2 or £20 a bottle, that's the only objective.'

Ten-year-old teeter

That may seem like stating the obvious now, but, I tell you, it wasn't then. Ten years ago we were just teetering on the edge of the Wine Revolution which has to a large extent swept away the idea of wine-drinking as a minority activity. The attitude of 'this is what we make, and if you don't like it, that's your problem' was still prevalent. Our preferences, our views on what we were offered to drink were not generally regarded as important. How times have changed, and I hope we've helped those times to change.

A year or two later we were exhorting everybody to try Australian and New Zealand wines, and I was widely regarded as a total weirdo for championing what are now some of the most exciting and most popular wines in Britain. We raged against the methanol and anti-freeze scandals that rocked Italy and Austria and Germany, and the illegal sugaring scandals that shook Burgundy to the core. We raised the banner for a consumer's army, in fact. We asked the consumer to pay a fair price for a fair product, arguing that endless bargain basement pressure forced producers into cutting corners, increasing yields and into giving up on quality. And we were urging that same consumer to have courage, to speak out for what he or she liked and to refuse to be browbeaten either on price or quality.

Have we gone far enough? Have we gone too far? I'd answer yes and no to both those questions. Our enthusiastic reception for wines that taste good regardless of where they come from sets the modern British market apart from almost every other wine market in the world. From being nervous of wine and prey to every social insecurity it can bring, we have become fearless adventurers, demanding only that we enjoy ourselves.

This is all wonderful, but there are dangers here. The 'Australian' style of soft, ripe, spicy whites and round, rich, juicy reds is spreading to other parts of the world. This could lead, say its critics, to an 'internationalization' of taste. The logical result is that any grower wanting to sell his wines in an increasingly competitive market is forced to make the same styles and flavours as everyone else, because that is what sells. Yes, I agree it could lead to that. But just remember, if you can, the quality only ten years ago of the basic wines of southern France, of Chile, of Portugal, Hungary, Bulgaria or Moldova. The Aussie style is the first base of wine – attractive flavours, consistently achieved at a decent price. Let's spread this base quality far and wide; then we'll worry about 'internationalization'. Personally I have no doubts that within five years we'll be seeing more individual, original flavours than ever before on the world stage, as well as a basic level for ordinary wine that could not have been dreamt of just a decade ago.

Chardonnay for beginners

We have shown that we love Chardonnay, Cabernet Sauvignon, Merlot and Shiraz (or Syrah), Sémillon and Sauvignon Blanc. Will this lead to an 'internationalization' of taste? Again, I don't think so. As more and more Chardonnay and Cabernet Sauvignon is planted, it may come to mean that these grapes are increasingly regarded merely as decent white and red, and that we demand nothing more from them, forgetting that they make some of the world's greatest wines as well as some of the best basics. The makers of high-priced Chardonnays and Cabernets may suffer because we can't immediately perceive why we should be paying extra for their wines. Then it is up to them to persuade us that we should pay the extra, by making the difference in quality clear in the glass – extra concentration, extra depth, extra subtlety, extra excitement. Then sure, we'll be happy to pay.

Indeed the only tyranny that I foresee in the next few years is the tyranny of price. Now that the well-known grapes are so widely planted, and the wines made from them at every price level are so astonishingly good, we may, each time one country or region raises its prices, merely slip across a border to a new source of Chardonnay or Cabernet that doesn't break the previous £2.99 or £3.99 price barrier. I hope this won't be the case. As the recession eases, I hope people feel it is worth paying more to explore the greater complexities and thrills of the ever-increasing number of high quality wines.

But if they don't I can't entirely blame them. There is no need, now, for any wine, however low its price, to be less than fresh, fruity and clean. That, in a nutshell, is the result of the wine revolution. What may happen now is that winemakers at the higher end of the market will start to suffer because of the fine quality to be found at the base.

Ten years ago, I could never have said that. Ten years ago we were struggling for our rights as consumers not to be served swill and be told to like it or lump it. Ten years ago the Old Classics reigned, now the New Classics rule. We've all come a long way in ten years.

And what about another ten years, another twenty? Can you be an *enfant terrible* on a bus pass?

100 BEST BUYS

These are the best of the best: our pick of this year's *Guide*. What's more, they're all under a tenner. If you see certain regions missed out, this might be because the wines are good value across the board (like Bulgarian reds) or because (as in the case of Beaujolais) we think there's better value to be found elsewhere. In some regions you can get terrific value for between £3 and £4 (Spain and Portugal, for instance); but remember that by paying a bit extra you can get really super quality. Happy drinking!

Red Bordeaux
1983 Carruades de Lafite (BIB) £9.30
1988 Ch. Fombrauge (EL) £7.81
1988 Ch. Fourcas-Hosten (HIG) £8.42
1990 Ch. Patache d'Aux (BUT) £7.77
1985 Ch. Rahoul (BUT) £8.97
1990 Ch. Sénéjac (TAN) £6.78
1990 Ch. Canon de Brem (MV) £7.64
1989 Ch. de Haut-Sociondo (SUM) £4.95
1990 Ch. Thieuley (SOM) £4.40

White Bordeaux
1992 Ch. de Sours (MAJ) £5.89
1990 Doisy-Daëne Grand Vin Sec (OD) £8.95
1989 Ch. de Berbec (WHG, OD) £5.95-9
1989 Ch. Mayne des Carmes (OD) £ 5.99

Red Burgundy
1990 Bourgogne Pinot Noir Fûts de Chêne, Cave de Buxy (WHG) £4.95
1988 Bourgogne Pinot Noir, Parent (CV) £7.05
1991 Chorey-les-Beaune, Tollot-Beaut (JU) £9.90
1988 St-Aubin Sentier du Clou, Prudhon (BIB) £9.98
1988 Bourgogne Irancy Ste-Claire, Brocard (BEK) £6.49

Sparkling Burgundy
Crémant de Bourgogne Cave de Lugny (WAI) £6.25
Crémant de Bourgogne Rosé (SAI) £6.45

Rhône Red
1990 Crozes-Hermitage Dom. de Thalabert, Jaboulet (NI) £6.69
1990 Côtes du Rhône Parallèle 45, Jaboulet (NI) £4.60
1988 Côtes du Rhône, Guigal (HAY) £4.95
1990 Gigondas, Dom. Raspail (HA) £5.48
Châteauneuf-du-Pape, Dom, de Nalys (WW) £8.61
Châteauneuf-du-Pape, Dom. de Mont-Redon (BR) £8.45

Loire
1992 Muscadet de Sèvre-et-Maine sur lie Carte d'Or, Sauvion (BEK) £ 3.94
1992 Sauvignon du Haut Poitou, Cave Co-op (WAI) £ 3.95
1992 Touraine Rosé Noble Jouée, Clos de la Dorée (AD) £4.95
1991 Gamay du Haut Poitou, Cave Co-op (WAI) £3.79
1989 Bourgueil la Hurolaie, Caslot-Galbrun (TES) 4.99

Alsace
1992 Pinot Blanc Cave Co-op, Turckheim (BOT) £4.49
1991 Riesling Cave Co-op, Turckheim (VIC) £4.99
1988 Tokay-Pinot Gris, Sipp (GRG) £4.99

Germany
1990 Binger Scharlachberg Riesling Kab., Villa Sachsen (TES) 5.49
1989 Wachenheimer Rechbachel Riesling Kab., Bürklin-Wolf (ASD) £5.99
1983 Oestricher Doosberg Riesling Kab., Schönborn (GA) £5.79
1985 Schloss Bockelheimer Kupfergrube Riesling Spät., Staatliche Weinbaudomane (RAE) £7.95
1992 Graacher Himmelreich Riesling Kab., Kesselstatt (ASD) £5.99

The codes given in brackets after the wine names indicate the merchants stocking the wines at these prices in the summer of 1993. The same codes are used in the price guides which begin on page 257. The key to the codes will be found on page 254.

Italy
1990 Dolcetto d'Acqui, Viticoltori dell'Acquese (VIC) £3.59
1988 Inferno, Nino Negri (HOG) £5.15
1990 Valpolicella Classico Superiore, Masi (DI) £4.99
1992 Molinara, Quintarelli (BIB) £ 5.98
1989 Recioto di Soave Capitelli, Anselmi (OD) £8.49
1991 Rosso Conero San Lorenzo, Umani Ronchi (NI) £ 3.79
1990 Chianti Rufina, Villa di Vetrice (SOM) £3.65
1990 Parrina Rosso, La Parrina (OD) £4.49
1988 Montefalco Rosso d'Arquata Adanti (OD) £4.89
1991 Carmignano Barco Reale, Capezzana (SOM) £5.40
1988 Chianti Classico, Isole e Olena (SOM) £6.70
1980 Chianti Rufina, Riserva Selvapiana (WCL) £6.95
1991 Vermentino di Sardegna, CS di Dolianova (WCL) £3.59
Corvo Colomba Platino Bianco (HOG) £5.74

Spain – Table Wine
1990 Rioja, CVNE (CV) £4.58
1988 Rioja, Montecillo Viña Cumbrero (BOT, THR, WR) £4.99
1988 La Rioja Alta Vina Alberdi (WAI) £ 5.65
1985 Rioja, Bodegas Riojanas Monte Real Reserva (BY) £6.45
1981 Rioja, Campo Viejo Gran Reserva (AUG, OD) £ 6.99
1986 Rioja, CVNE Imperial Gran Reserva (LAY) £8.95
1985 Rioja, Coto de Imaz Gran Reserva (DAV) £8.95
1985 Rioja, CVNE Vina Real Gran Reserva (PIP, CV) £8.20-47
1982 Rioja, Faustino I Gran Reserva (HOG) £8.10
1987 Rioja, CVNE Reserva Blanco (PIP, CV) £5.81-88
Don Darias (TES,SAF) £2.69
1990 Farina Colegiata (MAJ) £3.99
1989 Chivite Gran Feudo (DI) £3.99
1987 Felix Solis Viña Albali Reserva (BOT, THR) £3.55
1989 Raimat Abadia (TES, SAI) £4.99
1988 Ochoa Tempranillo (HOG) £4.99
1984 Senorio de los Llanos Gran Reserva (MAJ) £4.99
1988 Scala Dei Priorato (SOM, MOR) £5.45-75
1980 Felix Solis Viña Albali Gran Reserva (GA) £5.49

Sherry
Manzanilla de Sanlúcar, Barbadillo (OD) £4.75
Fino de Sanlúcar, Barbadillo (SUM, PIP, HAY) £5.10-25
Lustau Old East India (HOG) £7.34

Portugal
Sainsbury's Arruda (SAI) £2.85
1990 Dão, Grão Vasco (DAV) £3.99
1986 Pasmados JM da Fonseca (WAI) £3.95
1992 Douro, Quinta de la Rosa (GE) £4.25
1989 Tinto da Anfora João Pires (WAI, OD) £4.95-9
1980 Bairrada, Frei João (GE) £4.40
1984 Garrafeira Particular, Caves Alianca (DI) £5.75
1991 João Pires Branco (SAI) £4.49

United States
1989 Robert Mondavi Cabernet Sauvignon (VIC) £5.09
1992 Cá del Solo Big House Red (MV, AD) £6.90-7.20
1990 Jade Mountain Mourvèdre (MV) £9.90
1989 Renaissance Riesling (AD) £6.50

Australia
Angas Brut (SOM) £5.00
1990 Penfolds Kalimna Shiraz Bin 28 (PIP, OD) £5.57-99
1991 Charles Melton Nine Popes (SOM) £7.75
1990 St Halletts Old Block Shiraz (SOM) £7.95
1992 Hill-Smith Old Triangle Riesling (ASD) £3.99

New Zealand
1991 Redwood Valley Late Harvest Rhine Riesling half (FIZ) £5.95
1992 Jackson Estate Marlborough Sauvignon Blanc (WHI, CV, JU, WAI) £6.49-95

South Africa
1989 Backsberg Pinotage (HOG) £3.95
1990 Rustenberg Dry Red (HOG) £4.30

Other Regions
1990 Nemea, Boutari, Greece (OD) £3.85
1985 Château Carras, Côtes de Meliton, Greece (CV) £5.88
1987 Negru de Purkar, Moldova (BU) £3.99
1986 Tamaioasa, Romania (TES) £3.39

FRANCE'S BRAVE NEW WORLD

Right, answer me this one. What does the south of France have in common with Australia? And this: why are the grand *appellations contrôlées* of France increasingly being left out on a limb? And this: why I am feeling so happy at the moment?

The south of France ten years ago was a nightmare of a place. The *vin de pays* movement, designed to encourage growers in their attempts to make quality wines rather than spew out dreadful plonk that nobody wanted, was making only spasmodic progress. There were a few *appellations contrôlées*, but they weren't much good. The vast vinelands of France's far south were basically reservoirs of swill destined for Europe's bulging wine lake.

What a change in a decade. What was a vinous wilderness has become what I believe is France's most exciting and imaginative wine area, one that should strike terror into the heart of the numerous producers in Bordeaux, Burgundy, Beaujolais and the Loire who sit back on their *appellations contrôlées* and vainly hope that consumer cowardice will continue to support their lifestyles.

It was an area crying out to be the subject of this year's tasting. But, let's face it, not all of it is wonderful. There are still areas that are underperforming, where a mindless adherence to tradition is producing wines that are traditionally dull, traditionally fruitless, traditionally tired. Well, I wasn't looking for tradition in this tasting. I was looking for innovation.

Vins de pays – your flexible friends

The first place to look was in the *vins de pays*. That's where most of the action is: that's where the more flexible rules allow adventurous winemakers to plant the vines they want, in the places they want them. I was in half a mind not to allow in any *appellation contrôlée* wines at all – and how wrong I'd have been. They comprised around a third of all the wines sent in for the tasting, and about the same proportion of my top 30 – but it's not the highly-praised ACs like Coteaux des Baux-en-Provence or Bandol that came up trumps, it was the usually despised Coteaux du Languedoc. It was Collioure, too, and St-Chinian. Look at Château Pech-Celeyran. Look at Les Vignerons de la Carignano. I kept writing words like 'exciting' and 'brilliant' and 'gorgeous'. And of the *vins de pays*, which area is it that is specializing in producing fruit and flavour and excitement? The Vin de Pays d'Oc. Precisely. Same part of the South, same sense of adventure.

The point is that it's precisely the places that can't command high prices, where the tourists don't sip overpriced rosé on the beach, where there have never been refugees from Paris or Bordeaux determined to make good wine and where wine-making has traditionally been aimed at the lowest common denominator – these are the places that have to improve or die. There's nothing in between. Not these days.

Which brings us to the Australians. They had been drifting in and out of southern France's wineries ever since Tony Laithwaite of the Sunday Times Wine Club started employing them in his 'Flying Winemakers' scheme. They began by making wines that were perfectly correct, if rarely interesting. However, word got back to Australia about the opportunities to be found in the vast unexplored wineland of the Midi – whose production is five times that of

Australia and 55 times that of New Zealand – for trying out all the techniques they'd learnt in remarkably similar conditions in Australia. Opportunities that carried no risk whatever, because the wines simply had to be better than anything that had gone before.

The difference was one of state of mind. The New World winemakers weren't producing a dietary staple consumed for generations out of sheer necessity; they were competing in terms of enjoyment with beer and Coca Cola. They also knew that new international grape varieties were not going to be the death of the Midi's individuality – most of the vineyards didn't *have* any individuality. No, they would transform Languedoc-Roussillon from being a swill pit to being the most value-for-money, high-quality vineyard region in the world – with the vital added cachet of being able to put 'Produce of France' on the label.

If we look at the incredibly rapid spread of quality wines in the Midi, the threat to many of France's better known regions becomes evident. There was no Chardonnay or Sauvignon Blanc in the South at the beginning of the 1970s nor was there any Merlot or Cabernet. By the end of the '70s there were 99 hectares of Chardonnay, 5 of Sauvignon Blanc, 2260 of Merlot and 1420 of Cabernet. By 1992 there were 3100 hectares of Chardonnay, 1700 of Sauvignon, 12,500 of Merlot and 7000 of Cabernet, as well as 19,000 hectares of the crucially important Syrah.

That's more, in nearly all cases, than Australia had. In 1991 Australia could boast just 978 hectares of Sauvignon Blanc, 609 of Merlot, 5083 of Cabernet and 5449 of Merlot, though she did have 4849 hectares of Chardonnay. New Zealand had 486 hectares of Chardonnay and 343 of Sauvignon Blanc.

And in my top 30? Well there are some Chardonnays, and there's a Sauvignon Blanc; there's even a dry Muscat of which many a more northerly winemaker could be proud. But what this tasting showed above all is that it is red wines that are the South's strength. At the moment, anyway. Things are changing so fast there that the whites that this year are still a little too neutral, too correct and too 'manufactured'-tasting could, in just two or three years' time, be challenging Australia for sheer verve and style. It's as well to remind ourselves that most of the Australian Chardonnay we so gaily glug down is grown in areas that are supposedly much better suited to beefy reds. Yes, modern technology in vineyards and wines – as well as a vision of the flavour you want to produce – can triumph over climate.

Stay cool, Aussie-style

Domaine Virginie, for instance, which makes the excellent two-starred Tanners Chardonnay as well as our only starred Sauvignon Blanc, employs an Australian winemaker, and has learnt the value of things like purchasing grapes from different microclimates to add structure to the flavours, and like using mechanical harvesters to pick between 2am and 10am so that the grapes come to the winery cool. They have learnt how to use skin contact – they leave a proportion of the grapes, skins and juice all mixed together for a few hours to extract flavour and aroma. They de-oxygenize the grape must before fermentation to reduce the need for sulphur dioxide additions. They keep the fermentation really cool and clean, and maybe they'll leave the wine lying on its lees for a while to gather some more flavour, and maybe they'll age it for a bit in new oak barrels to give it some sweetness and spice. And when they bottle it, their bottling line will be spotlessly clean. Nothing mysterious – well, maybe they add a little cocktail of yeast strains to get a bit more of the Chardonnay fruit we all like so much – but this kind of wine-making goes on every day in the New World. From now on the New World runs from Avignon round to Perpignan too.

Several of our winning reds are indeed from the grand old regions of Minervois, Corbières and Collioure, though not, interestingly enough, from the trendy region of Fitou that seems to be suffering from over-popularity at the moment. Domaine la Combe Blanche uses the same traditional grape varieties, but the vines are pruned right back, yields are really low and you get a great wodge of thick, satisfying, unsubtle country flavours.

However, four of the six three-star wines are totally different. Three rely on the Syrah grape, and one on the red Bordeaux varieties. Look at Domaine des Barthes, or the varietal Syrahs from Les Vignerons de la Carignano or Domaine de la Condamine l'Evêque for the former, or Château des Festes for the latter. Some use new oak, some use the Beaujolais method of vinifying – carbonic maceration – but all of them strike out proudly, bravely, inspirationally, for flavour, for freshness, for the thrilling mixture of richness and flavour, herbs and perfume – and individuality. That is the mark of the new breed of red wines in the South. If producers in Bordeaux, Beaujolais and the southern Rhône were to taste these wines against their own, they'd be wetting themselves with trepidation.

Crisis and prices

Not that all these wines are cheap. Well, not dirt cheap. Most of them will give you change from a fiver, but don't rely on it for your bus fare home. Do I mind about that? No, I don't. When I first saw the prices I thought – hang on, these are *vins de pays* we're talking about – but then I tasted them. These wines are fairly priced. Which is something you could say about very few of the grander and more famous regions further north.

Because there's no question that France's wine producers are in crisis at the moment – but that crisis isn't in the far South; it's in Champagne, the Loire, Burgundy, Beaujolais and Bordeaux. These are the areas where prices have been pushed too high. These are the areas where far too few producers have taken advantage of the modern methods of cultivating their vines, the available up-to-date techniques of retaining freshness and fruit in their wine. These are the areas where it is still possible to hide behind the the sheltering shroud of their *appellations contrôlées*, many of which, if quality matters were to the fore, would be disbanded this very minute.

But the South is not in crisis. It has been through its crisis. It has seen demand slump for its wines. It has seen the French government finally admit that the system of excessive subsidy was crippling its own exchequer, not just that of Brussels. It has stared in the face the bankruptcy that now threatens many more pampered names. And it has realized there was no alternative but self-help or ruin.

How the winemakers of the South must bless the fact that grandees of the old *appellations* further north used to despise them so. Oh, but they needed the South's wines up there: most of the more northerly *appellations* were more than happy to turn to the South when their own vintage had failed to produce anything of colour, structure or flavour.

How lucky the Midi is, in retrospect, to have avoided the dead hand of *appellation contrôlée.* Despite the protestations of the French national body in charge of *appellations contrôlées* that *terroir* is everything – that it is the potent combination of soil, microclimate and exposure alone that the public wants to buy – we all know that this is just bunkum. The public wants flavour, and the public wants value for money. If the *appellation contrôlées* gave good flavour at a fair price – I'm not asking for a cut price, I said a fair price – then I'm sure we'd drink them much more than we do.

But we have been woefully served by so many of France's *appellations* during the 1980s and early '90s. Do the growers in Beaujolais wonder why we don't want their wines any more? Do the winemakers of Muscadet, of Sancerre, of Bordeaux red and white ask themselves *why* we've stopped buying their wines?

No flavour, and too much money. What a simple equation. And how negative. Northern Europe is experiencing an unprecedented wine boom at the moment, and it's based on young people who are discovering wines for the first time, and on other people transferring allegiances. What's turning them on? Loadsaflavour. Change from a fiver.

If the big sprawling *appellations* like Beaujolais, Muscadet and Bordeaux (the catch-all appellation, not specific ones like Pessac-Léognan or Pauillac) can't provide flavour at a fair price, they should rip out their vineyards and plant something else. I wouldn't mind seeing great swathes of basic Bordeaux, basic Burgundy, basic Beaujolais, Champagne and Muscadet ripped up and the land given over to potatoes. Then we could all appreciate the genuinely good wines from these areas without their reputations being sullied by the dross their *appellation* committees shamefully allow to be sold. And where could we go for flavour and value? To the South. To the golden South.

A sense of place

But are these wines true to their regional identity? OK. Let's stop right there. The grapes are grown in the region, and they grow well. The wines are made in the region and they are well made. The producers live in the region, are passionately committed to making products that cause the nape of my neck to tingle with pleasure, make me dash to the wine store, money in hand, to say, 'Please give me another bottle. Here's the money – I'm happy to pay, because the wine makes me happy.'

Ruining regional traditions? Internationalizing our palates, homogenizing flavours, making all wines taste the same? That's what the traditionalists will say. What claptrap. Let's get some of the Mâcon Blanc-Villages producers to taste the Domaine Virginie or the Hugh Ryman or the Fortant de France Chardonnays. Let's get Bordeaux red and white producers to taste the Château de Festes red, the Domaine la Croix Belle rouge or the Domaine Virginie Sauvignon. Let's get Beaujolais producers and Côtes du Rhône producers to taste the Coteaux du Languedoc wines from the Carignano co-operative, the Corbières from the Mont Tauch co-operative or the Domaine la Croix Belle rosé. We would be right to be worried if all the wines of the South tasted like second-rate Beaujolais or Bordeaux, Mâcon Blanc or Muscadet. But if a vast number of the growers in the supposedly superior *appellation contrôlée* areas want a few ideas as to what their wines *could* taste like – well, there are 30 suggestions waiting for them just as soon as they turn the page.

OZ CLARKE'S TOP THIRTY

WINE	RATING	SAMPLE PRICES
Coteaux du Languedoc Cépage Syrah, Les Vignerons de la Carignano	★★★	£3.99
1992 Domaine Barthes Syrah, Coteaux du Languedoc	★★★	£4.59
1992 Domaine la Condamine l'Evêque, Cépage Syrah, VdP des Côtes de Thongue	★★★	£3.95
1991 Château des Festes, Côtes de la Malepère (red)	★★★	£3.68
1989 Château Pech-Celeyran, Coteaux du Languedoc	★★★	£4.65
1990 Domaine la Combe Blanche, Minervois	★★★	£5.29–£5.99
1991 Château Russol, Cuvée Emilie, Minervois	★★	£4.12
Corbières	★★	£2.85
1990 La Cuvée Mythique, VdP d'Oc (red)	★★	£4.95
1992 Domaine la Croix Belle, VdP des Côtes de Thongue (red)	★★	£3.99
1991 Château de Jau, VdP des Côtes Catalanes (red)	★★	£2.89
Tanners Chardonnay, VdP d'Oc	★★	£4.99
1992 Chardonnay, VdP d'Oc, HDR Wines	★★	£4.99
1991 Chardonnay des Rives de l'Argent Double, Vin de Pays d'Oc	★★	£6.49
1990 Chardonnay, Fortant de France, VdP d'Oc	★★	£6.95
1992 Domaine Virginie Sauvignon, VdP d'Oc	★	£4.69
1991 Chardonnay, Fortant de France, VdP d'Oc	★	£5.49
1990 Philippe de Baudin Chardonnay, VdP d'Oc (under Chais Baumière label in SAI)	★	£3.99–£4.49
1991 Domaine du Bosc Cépage Muscat Sec, VdP de l'Hérault	★	£4.60
1992 Domaine la Croix Belle, VdP des Côtes de Thongue (rosé)	★	£3.69
1990 Les Clos de Paulilles, Collioure	★	£6.49
1992 Château la Dournie, St-Chinian (red)	★	£3.59
1990 Gilbert Alquier Cuvée Speciale, Faugères	★	£7.54
1990 Domaine Grand Bourry, Costières de Nîmes (red)	★	£3.99
1992 Coteaux du Languedoc, Les Vignerons de la Carignano	★	£3.79
1990 Domaine d'Aupilhac, VdP du Mont Baudile (red)	★	£4.95
1991 Domaine la Condamine l'Evêque Cépage Syrah, VdP des Côtes de Thongue	★	£4.05
1990 Cuvée de l'Arjolle, VdP des Côtes de Thongue	★	£4.76
1991 Domaine des Fontaines Cépage Merlot, VdP d'Oc	★	£2.99
1991 Domaine de la Fadèze Syrah, VdP d'Oc	★	£5.39

Prices are as supplied to us by merchants in June 1993. Vintages may change.

SOUTHERN FRENCH WINES

TASTING NOTES	STOCKISTS
Bursting with blackberry, loganberry and damson fruit, a streak of Wright's Coal Tar and a splash of violets.	OD
Chocolate and raspberry; grassy freshness, a hint of plimsolls – well, I liked it!	THR, BOT, WR
Purple red colour, and a joyous riot of bramble, raspberry, chocolate and smoke.	WS
All strawberry-bananas, leather and plum, this could wallop Beaujolais.	BEK
Exciting pine needles attack sweetened by ripe plum and raspberry fruit.	BER
Traditional red; jammy loganberry fruit, dust, herbs; appetizingly savoury.	WCL, BYR
Sturdy, aggressive, but ultimately ripe, rich, herby red.	BEK
Gluggable strawberry, peach and pepper flavours.	Co-op branches
Strange but delicious: cooked strawberries, eucalyptus – and plimsolls again!	SAF
Delightfully easy-going wine – creamy pears and bananas, followed by cherry and smoky raspberry. Beaujolais should be making this.	OD
Attractive soft cherry/strawberry flavours flecked with pine and powder.	OD
Soft Chardonnay made from slightly neutral fruit. Class winemaking.	TAN
Soft and creamy, slightly better depth and balance than the previous wine.	SAI, SAF, MAJ
Fatter, fuller, toasty, bacony style of Chardonnay with full, soft, creamy fruit.	OD
Soft, toast and grilled nuts mixture, good balance.	Ring 071-736 7009
A nice fresh, almost spritzy Golden Delicious, apple-and-peardrops flavour.	LAY
Toasty, soft, a hint of marmalade, though slightly empty at the core.	SAI
Very dry wine with a hint of hardness, but it's saved by soft honey and nuts.	WAI, GA, NA, LO, SAI
Mildly crunchy, gently dry Muscat made in the Alsace style.Very attractive wine.	WS
Attractive fresh fruit with lots of good creamy strawberry and apple flavour to it.	OD
Big but brawny old-timer, all black treacle and chocolate and prunes.	OD
Grassy freshness fattened up with meat and herbs, raspberry and plums.	THR, BOT, WR
Beefy old-style red, chocolate and plums and herbs with a peppery rasp.	EY
Almost Burgundian, ripe strawberry and gentle toasty oak.	SAI
Strong, enticing flavours of burnt strawberry jam, caramel and tannin – but it's good.	BEK
Strong, overripe but attractive goulash of cherry, chocolate, sweet plums.	AD
Brusque but pleasant style: spicy strawberries combined with a good lick of tannin.	TAN
Unusual raw blackcurrants, eucalyptus leaf and lime. Attractive red.	TAN
Raspberry, earth and ground coffee – like a Mediterranean Chinon.	WAI
Deep, smoky, farmyardy Syrah with black chocolate and black plum fruit.	LAY

For a key to stockists and codes, see page 256. (Shipments may vary.)

IDEAL CELLARS

The trouble with me is, I'm mean. I've been handing out cheques to wine merchants and the odd writer for ten years now, and have I increased their budgets by a single penny? I have not. But then I figure I don't need to – not while they keep coming up with goodies like these. These are my kinds of wine: bags of flavour, bags of value, and bags of change from a tenner.

MARTIN BROWN

THE GRAPE SHOP

Choosing these wines at British prices, at the back of my mind was the sneaky thought of how much more I would have to play with if I were buying from The Grape Shop in Boulogne. (Same company, same list, different prices...) Why not deprive the Chancellor and take a trip?

£100

Everyday, ready-to-drink wines from around the globe make up the £100 cellar. Given the range available, this was not an easy selection to make.

Hungarian Pinot Blanc *Light, dry, fragrant wine which shows off the skills now at work in Eastern Europe.* **6 for £17.70**

Chardonnay Domaine de la Bergerie *All the wonderful character of the Chardonnay grape without the influence of oak – quite a change these days, and a pleasant one. The result is a clean, dry finish.* **6 for £25.50**

Dry Plains Red *An Aussie 'laboratory' wine, this is great value and full of flavour – and cheaper than Jacob's Creek.* **6 for £18.90**

Far Enough Pinot Noir *If you like red Burgundy, this is a must. Bottles can be variable but it's worth the risk – you may be rewarded with a brilliant wine for the price, and if not you can always have* Boeuf Bourguignon *for dinner.* **6 for £22.50**

Champagne Georges Gardet *Every cellar should have at least one bottle of Champagne for emergencies. Georges Gardet is especially good in halves, which means I can have two.* **2 halves for £15.90**

Total cost £100.50

£500

£500 allows me to choose a selection of wines to keep and wines to drink, as well as indulging myself with a dessert wine.

1989 Corban's Winemaker's Reserve Chardonnay *Wonderful use of oak and a full, intense flavour. This delicious wine is ready for drinking now.* **12 for £93.60**

1991 Pouilly Fumé Domaine Chatelain *This crisp, dry wine is textbook stuff. As a reminder of how good Sauvignon can be, this is worth every penny.* **12 for £107.40**

1988 Mercurey Château de Chamilly *This is not cheap even for a red Burgundy, yet I always regret not buying enough. It will be drinking superbly in a couple of years' time and should outclass many Côte d'Or wines.* **12 for £119.40**

Mount Helen Cabernet/Merlot *A big, rich, intense Australian with heaps of fruit and flavour. Drinking now, but will keep to 1996.* **12 for £90.00**

1990 Château Vieux Malveyren *Intensely-flavoured Monbazillac, full of botrytis. Drink with or without pudding.*
12 for £107.40

Total cost £517.80

£1000

Pure luxury here, with plenty of scope for me to indulge my passion for Champagne. You may want to keep this cellar to yourself.

1989 Pouilly Fuissé Vieilles Vignes Domaine Vincent *When I tasted this wine from tank, there were two different* cuvées, *both superb. M. Vincent blended the two. The result is stunning.* **12 for £275.40**

Champagne Vilmart Grand Cellier *Has been described as a 'poor man's Krug' – at a third of the price. I will age this one for a year or two.* **12 for £227.40**

1988 Beaune Cent Vignes Domaine Bescancanot Mathouillet *Everything you could want from a red Burgundy. Age for three to five years and don't share it with anyone.* **12 for £227.40**

1985 Château Rausan Ségla *This was my first ever* en primeur *claret purchase: quite a worrying experience. I don't regret it – in fact, if you know where I can find some more, please let me know.* **12 for £227.40**

Champagne Vilmart Grand Cellier d'Or *I've nearly enough left for two bottles of really decent Champagne – one for me and one for the wife.* **2 for £55.00**

Total cost £1012.60

MIKE CONOLLY

SAINSBURY'S

It's ten years since my predecessor, Allan Cheesman, made his first selection of wines for *Webster's*. How times, and Sainsbury's, have changed – of his choice, all were European, and only four weren't French. I cover 19 wines and seven countries. But it's good to see that André Brunel's Châteauneuf-du-Pape is as satisfying to me as it was to Allan.

£100

Sainsbury's Manzanilla Pasada *Close your eyes and imagine yourself in southern Spain with a plate of prawns in front of you. Preprandial perfection.*
6 halves for £20.70

Sainsbury's Do Campo Branco *Made to an exacting specification by Portugal's favourite Australian, Peter Bright. Crisp and lip-smacking.* **6 for £17.94**

Sainsbury's Australian Chenin/Chardonnay *The Chenin in this blend gives it a nice touch of acidity, but it's still unmistakably an Oz wine. Full of flavour.*
6 for £21.90

1989 Suhindol Cabernet Sauvignon Reserve, Bulgaria *Quite simply the best value red in the whole Sainsbury's range at the moment. Beautifully integrated fruit and oak, and a lovely long finish.*
6 for £17.94

1990 Château la Voulte-Gasparets, Corbières *Wizard Midi winemaker Marc Dubernet has a guiding hand in producing this rich-flavoured red wine, carefully vinified from a blend of traditional local grapes. An example of the good things that are happening in the South.* **6 for £28.14**

Total cost: £106.62

From Fonseca Successores comes the excellent **Alentejo 1989**.

Also exclusive to Sainsbury's, this is a mature, full-bodied red from the most rapidly developing and innovative table wine region in Portugal.

Another talented Australian is Peter Dawson, chief winemaker for BRL Hardy at Beziers in southern France.

We stock four of his superb Chais Baumière wines, with one of the best being the **Cabernet Sauvignon 1990**. A classic of its kind, it comes replete with blackcurrant nose and plummy flavour. You'll find it will benefit from being allowed to breathe before drinking.

Kym Milne is a renowned New Zealand winemaker. At the moment however he's working in Eastern Europe. And working well, as a taste of his delicious **Chapel Hill Chardonnay 1992** will testify.

The ripe Chardonnay fruit flavours, balanced with a certain crisp acidity and a subtle hint of American oak, give this wine body and style.

In Spain we found a Frenchman. Jacques Lurton is a leading wine expert who, in conjunction with the Hermanos Lurton winery in the Rueda region of northern Spain, has made a single varietal wine from Sauvignon Blanc grapes.

What makes this wine remarkable, is that you would not expect such distinctive Sauvignon Blanc characteristics to come from such a hot climate as Spain.

For this to happen, the grapes have to be hand-picked very early in the morning while it is still cool.

Fermentation then lasts for two months at very low temperatures.

We stock their **Rueda Sauvignon Blanc 1992**; a wonderfully clean and crisp wine with a style typical of a New Zealand Sauvignon Blanc, but so very untypical of a Spanish wine.

Finally, what do you get if you put an Englishman based in France with a team of Australian winemakers in Hungary?

Gyongyos Estate Wines.

Hugh Ryman and his team have, between them, produced one of the Hungarian wine industry's more unusual success stories. Their **Sauvignon Blanc Gyongyos Estate 1992** is a delightfully light and refreshing wine with just a hint of summer flowers.

Good wine costs less at Sainsbury's.

ARGER STORES ONLY. BY LAW WE ARE NOT ALLOWED TO SELL ALCOHOLIC PRODUCTS TO PERSONS UNDER 18.

£500

Sainsbury's Manzanilla *In Spain again, and with enough to share.* **12 for £51.48**

Sainsbury's NV Champagne *A blend that consistently wins praise. Look for that slightly nutty finish.* **12 for £143.40**

1992 Matua Valley Sauvignon Blanc, NZ *You almost need a spoon for the gooseberries in this one.* **12 for £63.00**

1992 Penfolds Koonunga Hill Chardonnay *Classic Aussie Chardonnay – tropical fruit with oak – delicious.* **12 for £59.88**

1987 Viña Herminia Reserva *The sort of Rioja we all fell for in the '70s. They can still do it when they focus on the wine, not the short-term profit.* **12 for £79.08**

1989 Château La Vieille Cure *Stunning claret from a new* chai *in slightly unfashionable Fronsac.* **12 for £83.88**

1992 Sainsbury's Sancerre, les Beaux-Regards *Subtle Sauvignon that makes you realise you'll never forsake the Loire.* **12 for £93.00**

1992 Tasmanian Chardonnay, Pipers Brook *Tasmania's cool, damp climate produces a wine with all the fruit you expect of Australia, and leaves you wanting more.* **12 for £95.88**

1991 Fleurie La Madone *Gamay at its best – light, fruity, elegant.* **12 for £77.40**

Total cost £480.72

£1000

1988 Sainsbury's Vintage Champagne *This is a seriously serious Champagne, and ridiculously cheap. I think it's at its best with food.* **12 for £167.40**

1989 Castello di San Polo in Rosso Chianti Classico Riserva *An intense, complex wine that needs to be open for a good few hours before you drink it.* **12 for £94.20**

1990 Châteauneuf-du-Pape André Brunel *Rich and robust. M Brunel delivers the goods year after year.* **12 for £101.40**

1988 Pavillon Rouge du Château Margaux *No need to describe the wine, so all I have to add is tell you to hang on to it for a couple of years – if you can bear it.* **12 for £173.40**

1978 Fonseca Guimarens *Absolutely at its peak. Buy some good cheese and call up three really good friends.* **12 for £188.64**

Total cost £991.32

PHILIP EYRES

PHILIP EYRES

The last ten years have been remarkable for the rise and rise of the New World.

Now, however, those wine merchants that survive Mr Lamont's attempts to extinguish them may look towards Italy, where improved wine-making and a weak currency offer great opportunities – and grape varieties other than Chardonnay and Cabernet Sauvignon.

£100

Four European wines from grape varieties which do not lend themselves to successful imitation elsewhere.

1992 Cortese dell'Alto Monferrato, Araldica *Wonderfully fresh and lively: for palates bored with Chardonnay.* **6 for £25.50**

1991 Dr Loosen Riesling QbA *The Mosel's star young grower, Ernst Loosen, has produced a delicious quaffing Halbtrocken.* **6 for £35.10**

1991 Chénas, Château de Chénas, Eventail *Sensational Beaujolais; excellent value from an underrated* cru. **6 for £32.10**

Manzanilla La Gitana, Hidalgo *Both the perfect apéritif and an ideal match for a variety of fish dishes.* **3 halves for £7.95**

Total cost: £100.65

£500

An all-German selection drawn from the three splendid vintages of 1988, 1989 and 1990. Variety is provided by one wine being red and another being from the unusual Scheurebe grape.

1989 Niederhäuser Hermannsberg Riesling Spätlese, Staatliche Weinbaudomänen *The Nahe State Domaine excelled itself in this vintage. Just ready.* **12 for £88.92**

1990 Grosskarlbacher Burgweg Scheurebe Spätlese Trocken, Lingenfelder *Scheurebe, made dry, couldn't have a better advocate than this glorious perfumed and intense wine from the Rheinpfalz.* **12 for £99.60**

1990 Erdener Treppchen Riesling Kabinett, Dr Loosen *Acidity and sweetness in perfect harmony.* **12 for £101.52**

1988 Deidesheimer Hohenmorgen Riesling Spätlese, Bassermann-Jordan *Sufficiently dry to be appealing with fish and chicken.* **12 for £106.92**

1989 Spätburgunder Tafelwein, Lingenfelder *Excellent Pinot Noir character on nose and palate, from the Rheinpfalz. Now drinking beautifully.* **12 for £100.08**

Total cost: £497.04

£1000

With £1000 to spend we are up to Auslese and Beerenauslese level for the German choices, while the reds include a First Growth claret.

1990 Wehlener Sonnenuhr Riesling Auslese, Dr Loosen *My first vinous enthusiasm was for the middle Mosel, and what better example could one find than this? Drink from 1994.* **12 for £171.60**

1988 Maximin Grünhäuser Herrenberg Riesling Auslese, von Schubert *Perhaps only the Ruwer could produce such a combination of delicacy, sweetness and acidity.* **12 for £182.52**

1988 Schlossböckelheimer Kupfergrube Riesling Beerenauslese, Staatliche Weinbaudomänen *With its amazing concentration of flavour and richness, this Riesling is strictly for post-prandial consumption.* **6 halves for £177.42**

1989 Carignano del Sulcis Riserva Rocca Rubia, Cantina Sociale Santadi *My most recent enthusiasm is for the wines from this Sardinian co-operative. This is Carignan with a little Cabernet; the first impact on the palate is almost New World in its immediacy, but layers of flavour subsequently emerge.* **12 for £90.12**

1987 Don Melchor Cabernet Sauvignon, Concha y Toro *Chilean Cabernet Sauvignon doesn't, in my experience, come any better than this. Decant about an hour before serving.* **12 for £94.32**

1978 Château Haut-Brion, Graves *Of all the 1978 clarets, Haut-Brion is surely one of the best for current drinking. In its richness and overall character it is reminiscent of the 1961, although less intense.* **6 for £312.48**

Total cost: £1028.46

ROSEMARY GEORGE MW

My theme this year is New Zealand. Its Sauvignon Blanc has been one of the great success stories of the last ten years, but now the reds are getting better and better every vintage. And as for the fizz...

£100

I thought I'd choose three simple whites for everyday drinking.

1992 Montana Marlborough Sauvignon *There's nothing better than fresh, pithy NZ Sauvignon.* **6 for £30.00**

1992 Collards Chenin Blanc *From one of the few producers to take this grape variety seriously.* **6 for £30.00**

1992 Stoneleigh Sauvignon Blanc *Well, I like NZ Sauvignon.* **6 for £30.00**

Total cost: £90.00

£500

A chance to broaden the vinous horizons and explore all the new tastes that New Zealand is producing.

1991 Waipara Springs Pinot Noir *Illustrates the potential of cool climate Pinot Noir with appealing raspberry fruit and a hint of chocolate.* **12 for £96.00**

1992 Collards Rhine Riesling *A delicious example of a sadly underrated grape variety: a lovely combination of slatey Riesling fruit and acidity.* **12 for £72.00**

1990 Hunter's Chardonnay *Elegant and stylish (and fashionable).* **12 for £114.00**

1991 Redwood Valley Chardonnay *A slightly riper, more buttery style, but with a good balance of acidity.* **12 for £98.40**

1992 Jackson Estate Marlborough Sauvignon Blanc *A ripe, juicy Sauvignon with bags of fruit.* **12 for £84.00**

Daniel le Brun NV *Since I know Oz will not return my change, I'm going to spend it on three bottles of one of New Zealand's best sparklers.* **3 for £29.85**

Total cost: £494.25

£1000

Okay, for £1000 I could go there, but instead I'll splurge it on some of the real stunners that New Zealand now produces.

1991 Morton Estate Black Label Chardonnay *Richly flavoured, with some nutty fruit.* **12 for £96.00**

1990 Te Mata Coleraine Cabernet Merlot *Just to show how good Cabernet Sauvignon from Hawkes Bay can be.* **12 for £180.00**

1991 C J Pask Gimlett Road Cabernet Sauvignon Merlot *A stunning Bordeaux lookalike from one of Hawkes Bay's most talented winemakers.* **12 for £100.00**

1991 Martinborough Vineyards Pinot Noir *A terrific example of this temperamental grape variety.* **12 for £123.00**

1991 Ata Rangi Pinot Noir *Yet another wonderful Pinot Noir.* **12 for £180.00**

1991 Redwood Valley Late Harvest Riesling *Ripe honey and apricot fruit, with balancing acidity.* **24 halves for £144.00**

Montana Deutz Marlborough Cuvée NV *Some deliciously creamy, delicately yeasty bubbles.* **18 for £180.00**

Total cost: £1003.00

HAROLD HECKLE

J MORENO (WINES) & CO LTD.

Narrowing down the wines of the world for these cellars was not difficult: we are Spanish specialists, and my predilection is for Spanish wines. For one thing, they are made from grapes other than French varieties; and for another, they bring back such good memories.

£100

Condé de Caralt Cava Brut, Catalonia *Bottle fermented Cava is the perfect celebration wine.* **6 for £31.50**

Armonioso Vino Joven Blanco, Bodega Los Llanos, Valdepeñas *The humble Airén is the most widely planted grape in the world. Thanks to modern technology, now it can taste good as well.* **6 for £25.50**

1986 Palacio de León Tinto Crianza *How can anyone resist this?* **6 for £16.14**

1988 CVNE Viña Real Tinto Crianza, Rioja *CVNE produce wonderful Riojas. This is soft and lingering.* **6 for £29.94**

Total cost: £103.08

£500

Recent archaeological evidence indicates that Spain was drinking wine since well before the Phoenicians, making it one of the world's oldest wine cultures. Even so, such diversity and richness is surprising.

1992 Lagar de Cervera Albariño, Galicia *The rediscovery of the Albariño grape is one of the great success stories of recent years.* **12 for £96.00**

1987 Contino Tinto Reserva, Rioja *Wine of stunning intensity. This is one to cellar, but when it wakes up...* **12 for £120.00**

1981 Marqués de Caceres Tinto Reserva *Smooth and aromatic Rioja.* **12 for £135.50**

Barbadillo Manzanilla Pasada Solear **12 halves for £51.50**

Gonzalez Byass Matusalem Oloroso **6 for £100.00**

A Spanish cellar without sherry would be impossible, but as neither Manzanilla nor Oloroso improve in bottle I'm going to cheat and have six of each. The Manzanilla is the driest and most delicate of sherries; and nothing can prepare you for the orgasmic delight of the Oloroso.

Total cost: £503.00

£1000

I've been extravagant here: £600 for one case? Still, it's my money... Ask me nicely and you might get an invitation to dinner.

1962 Marqués de Murrieta Castillo Ygay Blanco, Rioja Gran Reserva *If they drink white in Heaven this is it. Rare, but I know where to get some.* **12 for £600.00**

1982 CVNE Viña Real, Gran Reserva, Rioja *CVNE makes two whoppers, one from the Rioja Alavesa, the other from the Rioja Alta. This is the Alavesa one, and a year to dream about.* **12 for £155.50**

1987 Bodegas Alejandro Fernandez Pesquera Tinto Cosecha Especial *Despite all the hype, this is impressive.* **6 for £71.00**

1982 CVNE Imperial Tinto Gran Reserva *CVNE's Rioja Alta masterpiece. Austere and dignified, it demands starched napkins and silver candelabra.* **24 halves for £167.70**

Total cost: £994.20

ALASTAIR LLEWELLYN-SMITH

FULLER SMITH & TURNER PLC

Whichever of the following three cellars you choose, you can be sure of delicious drinking over the next year or so. Or you could buy all three, and prolong the pleasure even longer.

£100

Fino Quinta Sherry, Osborne *Bone-dry with a delightfully salty tang, this makes the perfect apéritif.* **6 for £41.94**

1992 Château de Sours, Bordeaux Blanc *Made by Esmé Johnstone (who used to own Majestic Wine Warehouses) and the ubiquitous Hugh Ryman, this is what white Bordeaux ought to be like – crisply dry, with mouthfilling fruit and a well-judged hint of oak.* **6 for £32.94**

1989 Gran Fuedo Crianza, Navarra *Well-structured, with bags of ripe brambly fruit, this is drinking well now, but will certainly develop further – if you can resist it for long enough.* **6 for £23.94**

Total cost £98.82

£500

With £500 to spend it's worth buying in full cases – which if you buy at Fullers means you get even more wine since we throw in a 13th bottle with every unmixed case.

1991 Chardonnay de Beaujolais, Domaine des Terres Dorées *First-class Chardonnay from southern Burgundy. Ripely buttery with pleasing acidity, for when you get tired of Australia.* **12 for £77.88**

1990 Château du Cèdre, Cahors *Concentrated blackberries and a firm grip make this a deeply satisfying wine.* **12 for £56.28**

1988 Barbaresco Cascina Morassino *Rich, chewy, tarry fruit and great length: well-balanced, well-made wine.* **12 for £64.20**

Château de Boursault NV Brut *Fine Champagne this, with yeasty, toasty flavours on the palate and a crisp, clean finish. Our house fizz.* **12 for £173.88**

1991 Saintsbury Garnet Pinot Noir *Real silky Pinot Noir raspberry and farmyard flavours – but this is from Carneros in California, not from traditional Burgundy.* **12 for £101.88**

And to bring me up to the £500 mark:

1989 Chapoutier's Crozes Hermitage La Petite Ruche *If this is the small beehive, I'd love to taste the big one.* **4 for £23.16**

Total cost: £497.28

£1000

This sum should guarantee you a treat or two I've deliberately gone for quality not quantity. These are all classic regions – Bordeaux, Burgundy, Alsace and Madeira – but sometimes the appeal of the classics is hard to resist. Especially if money is hardly any object. Any one of the following wines should remain in your memory long after the bottle's been dropped in the bottle-bank.

1988 Château Palmer, Bordeaux *A magnificent vintage for claret, and a great château. Try it at the turn of the century;* it *will have been worth the wait.* **12 for £348.00**

1990 Chablis Grand Cru Moutonne Long-Depacquit *A perfect balance of steely Chardonnay and well-judged oak.* **12 for £227.88**

1989 Chambolle-Musigny, G Roumier *Ripe raspberry fruit on the palate, and great length.* **12 for £203.88**

1990 Gewürztraminer Grand Cru Hengst, Cave Vinicole de Turckheim *Why don't more people drink Alsace of this quality? The scent of attar of roses, and mouthfilling fruit.* **12 for £131.88**

And to finish:

1845 Bual Solera Madeira *This solera was started in the same year as Fuller's, and both are still going strong. It is a rich, concentrated wine with hints of toffee-apples and crême brulée.* **2 for £80.00**

Total cost £991.64

JAMES NICHOLSON

JAMES NICHOLSON

I've stacked my three cellars with wines from all over the world. The criterion I set for this vinous globetrotting (and it's the cheapest, most painless way of travelling I know) is value for money – which is why the famous names don't always make the grade.

£100

1992 Domaine de Juzan, Vin de Pays de Côtes de Gascogne *Where better than Gascony for good, clean-tasting, value-for-money white? Winemaker Gilles Lhoste gets the best out of the local Colombard, Ugni Blanc and Gros Manseng grapes.* **6 for £22.14**

1991 Domaine Amblard, Côtes de Duras *Real Sauvignon Blanc flavour that's extremely easy on the pocket.* **6 for £23.34**

1991 Château de Cabriac, Corbières *Investment from Bordeaux's Château Chasse-Spleen and the skill of winemaker Jean de Cibens has produced a stunner.* **6 for £23.34**

1989 Pinotage Fleur du Cap *One of the best value South African reds available.* **6 for £29.94**

Total cost: £98.76

£500

Okay, I have overspent by £1.66. Just insist on the discount.

1990 Coudoulet de Beaucastel, Château de Beaucastel *The wonderful skill of the Perrin brothers shows us what the southern Rhône should be about. Full and delicious.* **12 for £83.40**

1991 Quinta de la Rosa *Unfiltered, rich and wonderful red table wine from Portugal's Douro Valley. Worth putting down for a year or two.* **12 for £57.00**

1986 Condé de Valdemar Rioja Reserva *The Riojas of Martinez Bujandas continue to grow in stature.* **12 for £69.60**

1992 Château Tour de Mirambeau *The new-wave white Bordeaux that will give you faith in the whites of the region.* **12 for £59.88**

Chardonnay Oxford Landing, Yalumba *This exotic fruit cocktail with a twist of oak is one of Australia's best bargains.* **12 for £57.48**

1989 Wehlener Sonnenuhr Riesling Kabinett, JJ Prum, Mosel *Too often we forget how good the best of Germany can be – real class.* **12 for £115.80**

Vouvray Pétillant, Société Huet *No-one gets elegance and richness into Vouvray quite like Huet.* **12 for £58.50**

Total cost: £501.66

£1000

1992 Sauvignon Blanc Cloudy Bay *Not a great vintage in Marlborough country – supposedly.* **12 for £95.88**

Louis Roederer Brut *I still think this is the best NV Champagne.* **12 for £239.88**

1990 Château Climens, 1er cru Sauternes *One of the best vintages ever. But wait for seven or eight years at least.* **12 for £285.00**

1990 Château d'Angludet, Cru Bourgeois Margaux *Will reward the patient collector around the year 2000.* **12 for £116.33**

1989 Hermitage la Chapelle, Paul Jaboulet *A Rhône for the next century. It should prove to be one of the best wine-making efforts of the decade.* **12 for £262.80**

Total cost: £999.89

ALEXANDER SCOTT

GELSTON CASTLE

Ten years ago, when *Webster's* first appeared, wine was a fringe interest. Even today I think we sometimes miss the point, which is that wine is made to go with food.

£100

No room for extras, just the essentials to get through a month or so (or longer, if you're more abstemious than I am.)

1992 Domaine de Lacquy, Vin de Pays des Terroirs Landais, Gascony *Sprightly and quaffable white.* **6 for £22.20**

1992 Château Haut-Rian, Bordeaux Blanc *Supremely versatile white: great with plain pork chops or salmon.* **6 for £27.00**

1991 Montepulciano d'Abruzzo, Canaletto *Bouncy and juicy red, with that refreshing Italian twist of bitter cherry.* **6 for £19.50**

1991 Coteaux du Languedoc, Mas Champart *An elegant red with the richness to cope with sauces. A rare beauty in its class.* **6 for £28.50**

Total cost: £97.20

£500

Now we can begin to explore a bit: there's room for a sparkler, a sweetie and even a German. All are ready to drink, but will also keep. For the reds we stay in the south of France, my passion of the moment.

Vouvray Méthode Champenoise Demi-Sec, Foreau *This is quite dry enough, thank you – I'm no masochist. Just starting to develop; drink it now as an apéritif.* **12 for £99.00**

1990 Château Saint-Genès, Entre-Deux-Mers *Subtly unlike other Bordeaux whites. Try it with chicken.* **12 for £63.00**

1991 Saint-Véran, Auvigue *The inexpensive answer to salmon. The classic one must wait until the next cellar.* **12 for £75.00**

1987 Kallstadter Steinacker Kabinett, Koehler-Ruprecht *This, barely off-dry, is a treat with the Chicken Tikka from M&S.* **12 for £75.00**

1991 Saint Chinian, Mas Champart *Matthieu Champart makes wines with great clarity of definition.* **12 for £60.00**

1984 Bandol, Domaine Tempier *Surprising finesse for a Provençal wine; could even stand in for claret with lamb. Ten years old, just mature.* **12 for £99.00**

1991 Tanunda Creek Late Harvest Muscat, South Australia *Light, zesty and not at all cloying. Uses up my last £29, too.* **6 for £28.50**

Total cost: £499.50

£1000

Some finer wines from classic regions and a wider variety, as well: I'd like to have something in the cellar for every occasion. I probably haven't managed that, but then I've hardly looked at half of France yet, let alone further afield.

Champagne Robert Driant *Classic, long-term stuff, from now to 2005. Australia, eat your heart out.* **12 for £165.00**

1990 Sancerre, Domaine de la Mercy-Dieu *Austere in youth, ages well. Perfect with goat's cheese. Now to 1996.* **12 for £90.00**

1990 Domaine la Grave, Graves Blanc *Unique flavours that are perfect with roast pork. Drink from now until 1996.* **12 for £93.00**

1988 Meursault Tillets, Jean Germain. *At last, the perfect match for that poached salmon. 1996 to 2010.* **12 for £144.00**

I'll permit myself a split German case:

1990 Enkircher Batterieberg Spätlese, Immich *Essence of slaty Mosel Riesling. Don't touch it until 2000.*

1989 Hochheimer Hölle Kabinett Trocken, Künstler *Punchy, dry, developing smoky depth with age.* **6 of each for £97.50**

1992 Beaujolais à l'Ancienne, Domaine des Terres Dorées *Piquant and refreshing, and ideal with cold ham.* **12 for £69.00**

1989 Clos des Galevesses, Lalande de Pomerol *Ripe, succulent claret, like essence of Merlot. With lamb or beef, plus the Christmas turkey.* **12 for £90.00**

1990 St-Joseph, Jean Marsanne *Perfumed Syrah from the original slopes of St-Joseph; marvellous with game.* **12 for £102.00**

1990 Chambolle-Musigny, Pierre Bertheau *Red Burgundy from probably the top grower in Chambolle. Hard to resist now, but will keep until 2000.* **12 for £177.00**

Total cost: £1027.50

RICHARD TANNER

TANNERS

What a change in ten years. When I put together some Ideal Cellars for the first edition of *Webster's* even the least expensive cellar contained some classic regions, and for £1000 one could stock up with some of the world's best. Today, with the same budgets, these are out of reach; but in compensation wonderful wines have emerged from elsewhere, including, believe it or not, Mexico.

£100

These four should be in everyone's cellar. They're good value and exceptionally stylish.

1988 Petite Sirah, LA Cetto, Mexico *Not related to the Rhône Syrah, but lots of peppery, spicy fruit from an unlikely source.* **6 for £28.30**

1992 Domaine La Condamine l'Evêque, Cuvée Harmonie, Bascou, Vin de Pays des Côtes de Thongue *Superbly made blend of Cabernet, Merlot and Syrah.* **6 for £24.30**

1992 Cépage Colombard, Producteurs Plaimont *Zippy, fresh and fruity from the fine Plaimont co-operative.* **6 for £24.90**

1991 Quinta da Folgorosa Branco, Torres Vedras, Carvalha, Ribera & Ferreira, Portugal *Delicious honeyed fruit, excellent freshness and balance.* **6 for £21.72**

Total cost: £99.92

£500

I make no excuses for including so many of our own label wines here. They really do offer a wonderful quality/price ratio at this level.

Tanners Claret, Bordeaux *Soft, attractive fruit but with structure and backbone. Enjoy now, or better, still in six months' time.* **12 for £53.88**

Tanners Chardonnay, Domaine Virginie, Vin de Pays d'Oc *A cross between French and Australian styles with good fruit and balance and a touch of oak.* **12 for £59.88**

1991 Château du Grand Moulas, Côtes du Rhône-Villages, M Ryckwaert *Half Grenache and half Syrah, with wonderful depth, spice and herbs.* **12 for £70.68**

Tanners Sauvignon, Vin de Pays d'Oc *Crisp, fruity, elegant, plenty of Sauvignon character.* **12 for £58.20**

Mariscal Manzanilla, Hidalgo *Zippy apéritif, light, fresh and with a salty tang.* **12 for £71.88**

1990 Schlossböckelheimer Kupfergrube Riesling QbA State Domaine Nahe *Peachy fruit, wonderful balance.* **12 for £69.12**

1991 Domaine Comte de Margon, Vin de Pays des Côtes de Thongue, L M Teisserenc *A delicious claret-style Cabernet/Merlot from another of the south of France's leading winemakers.* **12 for £52.56**

1990 Paradyskloof Pinotage, Vriesenhof, South Africa *Elegance here is allied with rich, ripe berried fruit. The red Pinotage grape is a speciality of the Cape and makes its most typical and distinctive wines.* **12 for £69.24**

Total cost: £505.44

£1000

As always, it is the expertise of the individual winemaker which makes this selection special; it is the honing of this expertise that has been the hallmark of the last decade.

1986 Duval Leroy Champagne *Superbly elegant vintage Champagne for less than the price of a NV* Grande Marque. **12 for £203.88**

1992 Marlborough Chardonnay, Jackson Estate *New Zealand Chardonnay tends to be much better balanced than Australian, and not dominated by that ubiquitous taste of oak.* **12 for £86.04**

1989 Remélluri Crianza, Rioja Alavesa *Fuller and richer than many Riojas, but with elegance and the capacity to age well too.* **12 for £107.88**

1990 Crozes-Hermitage La Petite Ruche, M Chapoutier *This wine has complexity, body and a delicious, lingering aftertaste.* **12 for £90.00**

1990 Givry, La Grande Berge, G Mouton *What real Pinot Noir should be about: farmyards on the nose, raspberries on the palate.* **12 for £117.96**

1991 Sancerre Cuvée C M Jean Max Roger *Elegance, complexity, flavour and length. This should dispel the growing belief that all flavoursome Sauvignons come from New Zealand.* **12 for £110.64**

1990 Château Durand-Laplagne, St-Emilion *Every serious cellar should have a claret from the wonderful 1990 vintage. It will be a legend in years to come. This is well-structured and full of concentrated fruit.* **12 for £89.40**

1990 Trittenheimer Apotheke Riesling Spätlese, F W Gymnasium *Top quality German Riesling from the Mosel in a top quality vintage. Wine-drinking heaven.* **12 for £99.84**

1989 Pinot Blanc, Rolly Gassman, Alsace *Aromatic, clean, with wonderful fresh, concentrated fruit flavours. Alsace at its best.* **12 for £100.20**

Total cost: £1005.84

RICHARD WHEELER

LAY & WHEELER

Ten years ago my ideal cellar for the first edition of *Webster's* contained few bottles from the New World. It is a measure of how much things have changed that today there are a number of Australian and California wines really worth laying down.

£100

These are the wines I drink every day. The two whites show just what modern wine-making can achieve at only just above table-wine price.

1990 Château Penin, Cuvée Cellier, Bordeaux Supérieur *M. Carteyron's wine was a chance find. He is doing everything right, on a small scale – and not far from his cellars is the best* Routiers *restaurant in France.* **6 for £35.70**

1992 Buiten Blanc, Buitenverwachting, South Africa *Good Cape whites are reminiscent of the Loire, only with much more mouthfilling fruit. This is delicious, but don't try to pronounce the name!* **6 for £29.94**

1992 Sauvignon Blanc Domaine Virginie, Vin de Pays d'Oc *Quite simply stunning. If there are any more wines like this in the Midi, then Australia and New Zealand had better watch out.* **6 for £28.14**

Total cost: £93.78

£500

This is the cellar that really measures a merchant's worth, with wines of real quality and distinction at sensible prices. I've taken advantage of the super Burgundy vintages of the last few years.

1987 Château Saransot-Dupré Cru Bourgeois, Listrac *Yves Raymond's half-Merlot blend has a delightful, fleshy style. This is real claret at a sensible price.* **12 for £83.28**

1990 Bourgogne Rouge, Gérard Potel *This wine's humble* appellation *disguises a beauty of a wine grown within the grounds of the famous Volnay domaine of La Pousse d'Or.* **12 for £115.80**

1988 Cabernet Sauvignon, Cyril Henschke, Henschke Winery, South Australia *This has the potential to go on and on. Delicious now, but I'm keeping a few bottles for the next century.* **12 for £127.80**

1990 Riesling Cuvée Reserve, Schleret, Alsace *A brilliant wine, a brilliant winemaker, a brilliant vintage from a brilliant region.* **12 for £95.88**

1992 Mâcon-Vergisson, Gilles Guerrin *1992 was a superb year for white Burgundy, but Guerrin is a new discovery. He manages to combine subtlety with breadth of palate.* **12 for £73.80**

Total cost: £496.56

£1000

This cellar celebrates the fabulous vintages that we've enjoyed in the last five years, vintages which will form the backbone of wine collections for many years to come.

Lay & Wheeler Extra Quality Brut Champagne *This must be the height of luxury – to be able to select one's own Champagne* cuvée. *Lay & Wheeler Brut is not our cheapest label – quality and a degree of bottle age are much more important.* **12 for £176.28**

1989 Château Léoville-Barton, 2ème cru St-Julien *Antony Barton's wine seems to get better with every vintage, and this is one of the stars of a spectacular year. It is so ripe and voluptuous you could almost drink it now.* **12 for £191.28**

1989 Chardonnay Jordan Winery, California *Californians make fabulous Chardonnay. I serve this wine in my garden on special occasions with barbecued fresh lobster.* **12 for £187.80.**

1988 Cabernet Sauvignon Rust-en-Vrede, South Africa *The Cabernet Sauvignon here particularly appeals. It has a mature bouquet after five years and an authoritative structure. You could even mistake it for a decent Pauillac.* **12 for £143.88**

1983 Quinta da Agua Alta, Churchills Port *This single quinta has the hallmarks of the year, exuding swirling aromas and deep fruit flavours. I love it.* **12 for £188.28**

1991 Muscat, Charles Schleret, Alsace *Muscat is little heard of these days, and the plantings are falling. A pity, for I can think of no more mouth-watering apéritif, or no more successful accompaniment to asparagus.* **12 for £111.48**

Total cost: £999.00

OZ CLARKE

Dear oh dear. I'm beginning to repeat myself. My first reaction, thinking about my £100 cellar for this year's *Websters* was – I want fruit, fruit and more fruit! Sounds familiar, I thought. That's exactly what I said last year. So should I change my rallying cry, just for the sake of it? Hell, no. So here I go.

£100

1992 Slovakian St Laurent
A wonderfully rich concoction of damsons, loganberries and black cherries. **6 for £18**

1992 Bulgarian Vatted Merlot
1992 Bulgarian Vatted Cabernet
At last, the pure blackcurrant fruit that Cabernet and Merlot have when young. These are gorgeous, juicy reds – once you try them you'll come back to them again and again. **6 of each for £34**

1992 Hungarian Mecsekaljai Special Reserve Chardonnay *The East Europeans are finally learning how to do whites as well. This is lovely, fresh, clean-tasting Chardonnay* **6 for £18**

1992 Lindeman's Cawarra *But of course Australia still leads the way in cheap crowd-pleasers. Brilliant, soft and spicy.* **6 for £21**

1987 Sparkling Shiraz, Seppelt *And this is one of my most enduring obsessions...* **1 for £9**

Total cost: £100

£500

I thought I'd trade up a bit here – by all of 50p a bottle. Well, it seems silly to spend tons more money when there's brilliant drinking to be done at not much more than £3 a bottle.

1992 Pinotage, Kleindal
1992 Pinotage, Simonsvlei
1992 Pinotage, Oak Village
The South Africans will soon be rivalling Bulgaria and Hungary as a source of brilliant, affordable red wine. These are full of damsons and cherries with the exotic perfume of smoky marshmallows.
6 of each for £66

1991 Zinfandel, L A Cetto, Mexico *A gorgeous, fruit-filled gobsmacker.*

1991 Petite Syrah, L A Cetto, Mexico *More fruit, same country – from the Pacific coast.*

1988 Tannat, Castel Pujol *A deep, ripe purple mouthful of concentrated power from northern Uruguay.*
6 of each for £84

1992 Sauvignon Blanc, Oxford Landing
The best fair-priced Sauvignon that Australia has yet come up with.

1992 Brown Brothers' Tarrango *Puts Beaujolais Villages to shame.*
12 of each for £57

1992 Sauvignon Blanc, Allan Scott *This and the next are two of the best Sauvignons in the world, from New Zealand's South Island.*

1992 Sauvignon Blanc, Jackson Estate
Shows that Cloudy Bay has got some competition on its hands – and at a much fairer price. **6 of each for £88**

1991 Henschke Sémillon, Australia
Barossa Valley Semillon: altogether more traditional and old-fashioned.

1989 Rockford Local Growers Sémillon, Australia *Fabulous old-time flavours from one of Australia's most original winemakers.* **6 of each for £94**

1990 Green Point Brut *Superb fizz from Moet & Chandon in Australia.*

NV Daniel le Brun Brut, NZ *It would cost me twice as much to match these flavours in Champagne itself.* **6 of each for £101**

1990 Sparkling Shiraz, Charles Melton *I wonder if Charlie Melton would let me have a bottle of this for my last tenner? I think he might – if I promise to share it with him.* **1 for £10**

Total cost: £500

£1000

When people ask me what I want to spend my £1000 on, I feel like counting the whole lot out in £10 notes to remind myself that we're talking about a lot of money here. So indulge. Indulge!

1988 Petaluma Red, Australia *Brilliant deep, ripe-flavoured red, from all that succulent New World fruit.*

1988 Carmenet Red, California *This owes a lot to the top wines of Bordeaux, and even more to the inspired vision of the New World.* **6 of each for £137**

1988 Château Cos d'Estournel, St-Estèphe *Austere but perfectly crafted classicism, from a Bordeaux grower who cares passionately about wine and wine-drinkers.*

1990 Château Lynch-Bages, Pauillac *A hedonistic riot of flavour. Jean-Michel Cazes of Lynch-Bages doesn't just offer pleasure with his wines – he guarantees it.* **6 of each for £210**

1990 Fixin en Tabelliou, Philippe Rossignol *The 1990 Burgundies give me so much pleasure. Philippe Rossignol doesn't have the best land in Burgundy, but he has the best attitude.*

1990 Gevrey-Chambertin Vieilles Vignes, Philippe Rossignol *I put single bottles of tip-top Burgundies in last year's cellar. Well, this year I'll have a bit more.* **6 of each for £159**

1990 Barolo Brunate, Voerzio *An inspiring vintage ran headlong into an inspired winemaker here.*

1990 Barbaresco Montestefano, Prunotto *The whole of Europe swims in this brilliant vintage, but even so this wine is remarkable.* **6 of each for £201**

1989 Goldwater Estate Cabernet/ Merlot, New Zealand *Outstandingly richly textured; almost claret-like.*

1991 Morton Estate Black Label Chardonnay, New Zealand *Deliciously toasty and hedonistic.* **6 of each for £191**

1990 Fleur du Cap Noble Late Harvest, South Africa *Time for some sweet wines. First I thought of all those '88, '89 and '90 Sauternes. Lovely. But unless the prices come down... In the meantime, go south young man. Far south.*

1991 Yalumba's Pewsey Vale Autumn Botrytis, Australia *Lovely, delicate angelica-and-peach rich wine.*

1989 Lindeman's Padthaway Botrytis, Australia *Another sweet wine, packed with strawberry-and-peach richness flecked with salt, of all things.* **A mixed half-dozen for £62**

NV Sparkling Black Shiraz, Rockford, Australia
1987 Sparkling Shiraz, Seppelt, Australia
1990 Sparkling Shiraz, Charles Melton, Australia *Okay, I know I said I don't want to repeat myself from last year, but...* **1 of each for £40**

Total cost: £1000

FRANCE

However you look at it, it's a masterpiece of timing. This is the year in which varietal wines from the south of France – made with the aid of Australian expertise, as often as not, and designed as France's answer to the cheap and tasty New World threat – have made their presence felt in a big way on the shop shelves and on our tables. And then what happens? France goes and bans them.

Well, not all of them. What the French powers-that-be have decided to abolish is the labelling of *appellation contrôlée* wines as varietals. Varietals are not traditional and they are not what *appellation contrôlée* is about – so goes the argument. Soil and climate and so on are at least as important to the character of an AC French wine as is the grape variety, it continues: if everybody made nothing but varietals, *appellation contrôlée* would cease to have any meaning, and there would be nothing to distinguish France from the New World.

Still, there are exceptions to the new ban. Alsace is one, where varietal labelling is traditional for AC wines; much of the Loire is another, where the grape variety can be part of the AC name, as in Cabernet d'Anjou. Vins de Pays , happily, are excepted *en masse*. And the new rules do not say that AC wines may not be made from a single grape variety; only that they may not be labelled as such.

How earth-shattering this will be is open to doubt. At the moment between five and ten per cent of AC wine is believed to be labelled as a varietal; some producers, particularly in the South, may opt out of AC altogether. Other areas may be covered by the exceptions. In any case, there will be a delay of at least two years before the change comes into effect.

QUALITY CONTROL

The French have the most far-reaching system of wine quality control of any nation. The key factors are the 'origin' of the wine, its historic method of production and the use of the correct grape types. There are three defined levels of quality control – AC, VDQS, and *Vin de Pays*.

Appellation d'Origine Contrôlée (AC, AOC) To qualify for AC a wine must meet seven requirements:
Land Suitable vineyard land is minutely defined. **Grape** Only those grapes traditionally regarded as suitable can be used. **Degree of alcohol** Wines must reach a minimum (or maximum) degree of natural alcohol. **Yield** A basic permitted yield is set for each AC, but the figure may be increased or decreased year by year after consultation between the growers of each AC region and the Institut National des Appellations d'Origine (INAO).
Vineyard practice AC wines must follow rules about pruning methods and density of planting. **Wine-making practice** Each AC wine has its own regulations as to what is allowed. Typically, chaptalization – adding sugar during fermentation to increase alcoholic strength – is accepted in the north, but not in the south. **Tasting and analysis** Since 1979 wines must pass a tasting panel.

Vin Délimité de Qualité Supérieure (VDQS) This second group is, in general, slightly less reliable in quality. It is in the process of being phased out. No more *vins de pays* are being upgraded to VDQS but there is still no news on when existing ones will be upgraded to AC (or downgraded to *vin de pays*).

Vin de Pays The third category gives a regional definition to France's basic blending wines. The rules are similar to AC, but allow a good deal more flexibility and some wonderful cheap wines can be found which may well surprise. Quality can be stunning, and expect fruit, value and competent wine-making.

Vin de Table 'Table wine' is the title for the rest. No quality control except as far as basic public health regulations demand. *Vins de pays* are always available for approximately the same price, and offer a far more interesting drink. Many Vins de Table here are dull and poorly made.

RED BORDEAUX

In the end (you will be glad to hear) the Bordelais did not waste the excessive profits they made from their wines during the 1980s: much of it was invested in brand-new wine-making equipment and in hiring increasing numbers of well-qualified technicians. Both proved essential in 1991 and 1992 when only a combination of science and rigorous discipline, plus even more severe selectivity, saved Bordeaux's reputation. Twenty or even ten years ago both vintages would have been disasters. Yet they produced what seemed to me light and elegant wines, both rather similar in style, that at their worst are diluted, and at their best fit that old (but still useful) description, 'light luncheon clarets'.

Most of the necessary technical equipment was pretty standard stuff: proper temperature-controlled stainless steel vats have become commonplace in the Gironde since Jean-Bernard Delmas first introduced them at Haut Brion over 30 years ago. But they have now been complemented by the many ways used to counter over-dilute juice: these range from simple bleeding of the vats – running off over-pale juice to enable the rest to gain more colour during fermentation; the juice that is run off can make delicious rosés – to 'cold concentration under vacuum' and 'reverse osmosis', phrases covering some advanced equipment to do the same thing more scientifically.

Lead balloon wines

And by God they needed every last bit of help they could get last year. If 1991 had been dramatic – the year of the Great Frost – 1992 was just miserable, rubbing in Nature's cruel ways and proving that all the talk of great and permanent droughts on account of the ozone layer was, well, if not hot air, then more like a cold, damp wind. Nevertheless, after all their efforts, the growers ended up with the biggest crop in history, larger even than in 1989 and 1990. The wines were not remarkable, however, and are currently largely unsaleable even though prices *en primeur* have dropped by over 30 per cent – the 1992 First Growths opened this spring at between FF130–150, roughly their 1987 level, and found some takers, but lesser wines dropped like a lead balloon. Château Cos d'Estournel sold at a mere FF58, which is the sort of price not seen for a decade. Whether this means the end of the famous *en primeur* market for ever or merely until people cheer up and are tempted by the next small, fine vintage (due by my reckoning sometime between here and 1995) remains to be seen. But despite the problems at Lloyds – which have led to gallons of wines being auctioned from anonymous cellars, mostly in Hampshire for some unknown reason – I believe that the Bordeaux market, which has kept itself going this past quarter of a millennium, isn't finished just yet.

For the moment it remains what the French call *morose*: not dead, just schizophrenic. Sales of basic Bordeaux and Bordeaux Supérieur are pretty healthy thanks to the small 1991 vintage and steady demand from the French themselves – and the market sold a fifth more wine in the eight months from September 1992 to April 1993 than in the same period two years earlier. Peter Sichel of Château Palmer remarked that the market 'though saturated, has not collapsed as it did in the last crisis nearly 20 years ago.'

The trouble lies in the better wines. And here the British drinker is helpless, caught between two larger forces: French banks and French supermarkets – with the foreign exchange market adding its own twist. Since growers never seem to go in for marketing, they simply maintain their prices until they're forced to dump their wines. If the banks get stroppy they can ensure that great quantities of fine wine get dumped – over a million bottles of Châteaux Talbot and Gruaud-Larose were sold recently at prices which will enable British drinkers to enjoy themselves for years. According to Peter Sichel, there is 'more high quality wine available at low prices in Bordeaux today than at any time in history.'

Expect the French supermarkets to hoover up the '89s – many of which are

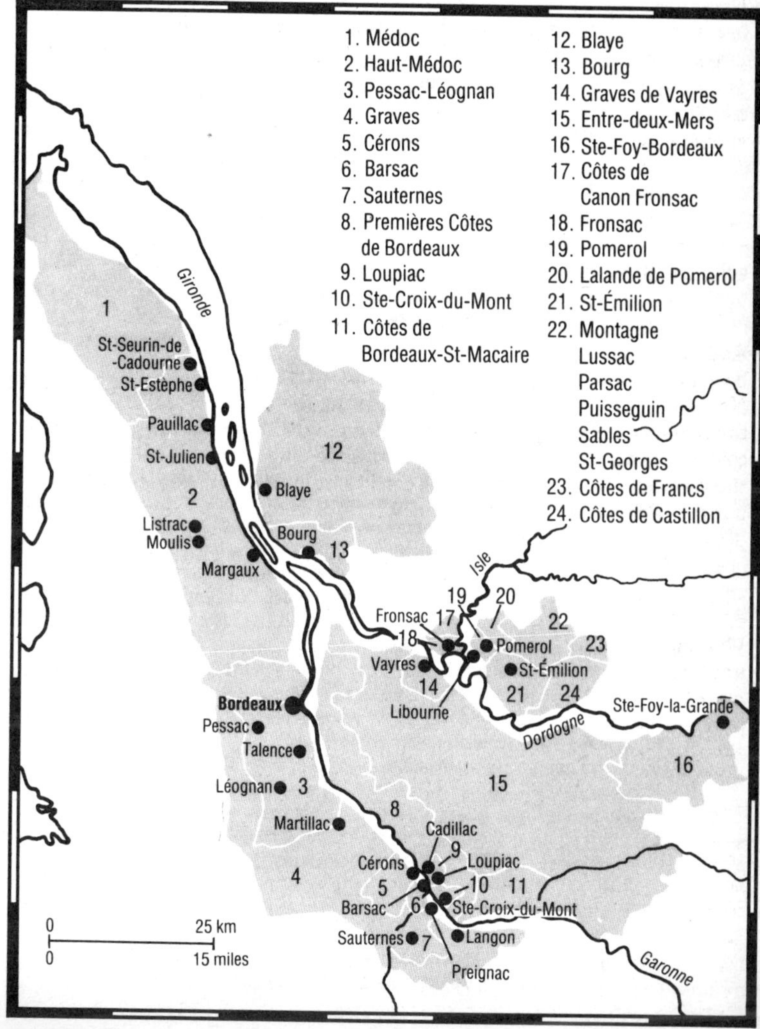

ready to drink, by French standards anyway – the way they did with the '87s. You have to remember that the French like drinking their claret young; they don't appreciate the new dimensions claret gains with age. As a result the '88s are already on many a French wine-list, with even the Classed Growths on offer in the best restaurants.

Waiting for bargains

Even without any dramatic bankruptcies, the present depression – and the increasing power of the French supermarket chains – is putting an unprecedented strain on the structure of a market which dates back to the early 18th century. Increasingly the *négociants* are being bypassed, or treated simply as brokers. This is simplifying the historic route by which claret has been imported into Britain. In the meantime consumers in Britain have a choice: wait for the franc to fall and more growers and merchants to dump their stocks, or take advantage of the bargains which are already around.

One of the results of the *morosité* is that there's nothing to gossip about in Bordeaux. At the time of writing, none of the much-forecasted bankruptcies had come about and not a single major estate has changed hands – largely because the owners can't bring themselves to accept how far prices have fallen (the classic case is Latour, still on the market, but, unsurprisingly, without takers at a rumoured price of around FF150 million). As a result the fear that there wouldn't be more than a handful of family-owned major estates left in the Gironde by the year 2000 has (for the time being, at least) gone the way of similar attacks of hysteria in the past.

NICHOLAS FAITH

BUYING CLARET *EN PRIMEUR*

Throughout much of the eighties, buying claret and fine white Bordeaux *en primeur* was a good way of getting the wine you wanted, at a lower price than you would have to pay if you waited until the wines were bottled and shipped. The system is simple: each spring following the vintage the château proprietors announce an opening price for their new wines. Customers buy the wines through their wine merchant, pay in advance and sit back and wait until the wine is delivered, after bottling, 18 months or so later.

The slump in the Bordeaux market has partly removed the price advantage in buying *en primeur*. It is still a way of being certain of particular châteaux, but potential buyers should be aware that prices can fall after opening offers as well as rise. Anybody thinking of buying this way should choose their wine merchant in Britain very carefully. They should make quite sure that they have written title to the wine, and that their name is on every single case of wine that they have bought, while it is in the merchant's warehouse. If one has paid for the wine, one should then be able to prove to the Official Receiver that one has a right to it, in the event of the wine merchant going bust.

But of course it is not always as simple as that. A wine merchant's contract is usually with a Bordeaux négociant, not with a château; if a négociant goes under, the wine merchant will not get the wine. A less-than-honest wine merchant might also take your money and not use it to buy the wine you want. And even when the wine has been safely delivered to a wine merchant's British cellars, a dishonest merchant who is about to go under might in theory still raid your cases and sell your wine without your knowledge. No piece of paper exists that will get you your wine if your wine merchant is not honourable.

All this amounts to is advice to choose a solvent, honest wine merchant and ask some searching questions. An honest merchant will deal with you honestly: it is as simple as that. And if it means you pay a few pounds more: well, isn't it worth it for the peace of mind?

GRAPES & FLAVOURS

Fine claret has the most tantalizing and unlikely combination of flavours of any red wine. There's the blast of pure, fragrant blackcurrant essence of the basic fruit, and then the exotic, dry perfumes of lead pencil shavings, fresh-wrapped cigars and the intense smell of cedar resin to weave an endlessly fascinating balance of sweet and dry tastes. Increasingly nowadays this is also blended with the buttersweet overlay of new oak barrels.

Bordeaux's vineyards are so poised on the knife-edge of being able to ripen their grapes or failing to do so that every vintage is fascinatingly, absorbingly different. The relatively temperate air in this coastal region is a crucial factor in the quality of the wine. In all but the very hottest years, the sunshine is tempered by cool breezes off the Atlantic. If the year nevertheless gets too hot, as in 1959 and 1976, and in some cases 1982, 1989 and 1990, the flavour can be rich, strong and burnt, more like the Californian or Italian attempts at claret. If the summer rains and autumn gales roll in off the Bay of Biscay and the grapes can't ripen, then the taste may be thin and green, resembling the Cabernets of the Loire valley. But in the years of balance, like 1966, '70, '78, '83, '85, '86, '88, '89 and '90 those astonishing sweet and dry, fruity and tannic flavours mix to produce the glory that is claret.

CABERNET SAUVIGNON It comes as a surprise that this world-famous Bordeaux grape covers only a fifth of the vineyard area. In the Médoc and Pessac-Léognan, however, more than half the vines are Cabernet Sauvignon, and the grape has a greater influence on flavour here than elsewhere in Bordeaux. Crucially, a wine built to age needs tannin and acidity, and the fruit and extract to keep up with them. Cabernet Sauvignon has all these in abundance. It gives dark, tannic wine with a strong initial acid attack, and a stark, pure blackcurrant fruit. When aged in new oak, it can be stunning. It's the main grape of the Haut-Médoc, but other varieties are always blended in to soften it and add a further dimension.

CABERNET FRANC A lesser Cabernet, giving lighter-coloured, softer wines than Cabernet Sauvignon, sometimes slightly earthy but with good, blackcurranty fruit. It's always blended in Bordeaux. In St-Émilion and Pomerol it can give very fine flavours and is widely planted. Château Cheval Blanc in St-Émilion is two-thirds Cabernet Franc.

MERLOT Bordeaux has more Merlot than Cabernet Sauvignon. It covers almost a third of the vineyard, and is the main grape in St-Émilion and Pomerol, whereas in the Médoc and Graves it's used to soften and enrich the Cabernet. It ripens early and gives a gorgeous, succulent, minty, blackcurrant- or plum-flavoured wine, which explains why Pomerols and St-Émilions take less effort to enjoy than Médocs. It also makes less long-lived wine than Cabernet, and is likely to peak and fade sooner.

MALBEC A rather bloated, juicy grape, little seen nowadays in Bordeaux, though it appears in some blends, especially in Bourg and Blaye. In Bordeaux it tastes rather like a weedy version of Merlot, soft and low in acidity. Upriver in Cahors it has real style, which probably explains why there's lots of it in Cahors and little in Bordeaux.

PETIT VERDOT A dark, tough grape with a liquorice-and-plums taste, and a violet perfume, used for colour. Little planted in the past but on the increase now because it adds quality in a late, ripe year.

WINES & WINE REGIONS

BORDEAUX ROUGE, AC Unless qualified by one of the other ACs below, this is the everyday wine of Bordeaux, either from co-ops, from properties in undistinguished localities, or wine disqualified from one of the better ACs. It can come from anywhere in Bordeaux. Still reasonably priced, for drinking young, it is a delicious, appetizing meal-time red when good, and a palate-puckering disappointment when bad.

BORDEAUX SUPÉRIEUR, AC Similar to Bordeaux Rouge but, in theory, a bit more interesting. It must have more alcohol and be produced from a slightly lower yield. The same comments on quality apply, but from a good estate the wines can be delicious – and age for a number of years. Best results increasingly are from properties producing white Entre-Deux-Mers and from the Premières Côtes on the right bank of the Garonne river. Best châteaux: *Brethous, Cayla, Domaine de Terrefort, Fayau, la Gabory, le Gay, Grand-Moüeys, Gromel Bel-Air, Jalousie-Beaulieu, Jonqueyres, du Juge, Lacombe, Méaume, Peyrat, Pierredon, Reynon, la Roche, Tanesse, Thieuley, de Toutigeac, de la Vieille Tour.*

CÔTES DE BOURG, AC A reasonable-sized area across the river to the east of the Médoc, with its best vineyards looking directly across the Gironde to Margaux. Their rather full, savoury style is backed up by sweet Merlot fruit and occasionally a touch of new oak. As Médoc and St-Émilion prices spiral, Bourg wines are slowly coming into their own. Best châteaux: *de Barbe, du Bousquet, Brûle-Sécaille, la Croix, Dupeyrat, Grolet, Guionne, Haut-Guiraud, Haut-Rousset, de Millorit* and wines from the co-op at *Tauriac*.

CÔTES DE CASTILLON, AC and **CÔTES DE FRANCS, AC** Two small regions east of St-Émilion on the road towards Bergerac, which are turning out an increasing number of exciting wines. They can be a little too earthy, but at their best they combine a grassy Cabernet Franc freshness with a gorgeous, juicy, minty Merlot sweetness, even honeyed in the best châteaux. Best châteaux: *Beau-Séjour, Belcier, Brisson, Canon-Monségur, Ferrasses, Fonds Rondes, Grand Taillac, les Hauts-de-Grange, Lessacques, Moulin-Rouge, Parenchère, Pitray, Rocher-Bellevue*. On the extreme eastern edge of the Gironde is the department's latest rising star. The scions of a number of well-known wine-making families are producing fruity, light, delicious wines to drink early, using a lot of Cabernet Franc. Best châteaux: *la Claverie, de Francs, Lauriol, du Moulin-la-Pitié, la Prade, Puygueraud.*

CÔTES DE FRONSAC, AC (now usually called simply Fronsac) with the (in theory) superior **CANON-FRONSAC, AC**, is a small area just west of Pomerol. The wines can be a bit grassy and tannic, but they can also be excellent, often having the sweet fruit of St-Émilion, the mineral depth of Pomerol, and a slightly cedary perfume. Nevertheless the general standard has been increasing recently, greatly helped by the interest shown by the firm and family of *Jean-Pierre Moueix*, the best merchants in Libourne. Best châteaux: *Canon-de-Brem, Canon-Moueix, Cassagne Haut-Canon, Dalem, de la Dauphine, Fonteuil, Mayne-Vieil, Mazeris, Moulin Haut-Laroque, Plain Point, la Rivière, la Truffière* (super since 1985), *Toumalin, la Valade.*

GRAVES, AC Since 1987 the Graves, the vast region south of Bordeaux town, has been deprived of its most prestigious properties, the ones nearest the city, and

The price guides for this section begin on page 257.

now grouped in a separate AC, Pessac-Léognan. The southern two-thirds had a bad reputation as a semi-sweet white area, which it has taken a decade to overcome. These efforts have been intensified by the lopping off of Pessac-Léognan.

Red Graves run the gamut of claret flavours, and are less easy to sum up than others. There are various soils, and though the Cabernet Sauvignon is the dominant grape in the North, as in the Médoc, there's less stress on Cabernet, more on Merlot, so slightly softer wines. They tend to have some of the blackcurrant and cedar of the Médoc, but without the sheer size of, say, Pauillac: they have some of the full, plummy richness of St-Émilion yet it never dominates; and there is a slightly gravelly quality in many of them, too. The less well-known châteaux are cheapish, and pretty good. Local merchant Pierre Coste has developed a style of young-drinking Graves which is deliciously drinkable (available in Britain at Adnams, Haynes, Hanson & Clark, Tanners and others).

HAUT-MÉDOC, AC Geographically, the prestigious southern part of the Médoc, nearest Bordeaux – from Blanquefort in the South to St-Seurin de Cadourne in the North. The AC covers the less exciting vineyards in between because there are six separate ACs within the region where the really juicy business gets done. These are Margaux, St-Julien, Pauillac, St-Estèphe, Listrac and Moulis. Even so, the AC Haut-Médoc has five Classed Growths including two superb ones – *Cantemerle* and *la Lagune* – and an increasing number of fine *bourgeois* properties like *Beaumont, de Castillon, Cissac, Hanteillan, Lamarque, Lanessan, Liversan, Pichon, Sociando-Mallet* and *la Tour-du-Haut-Moulin* – plus lots of lesser properties, such as châteaux *Bernadotte, Cambon-la-Pelouse, Coufran, le Fournas, Grandis, du Junca, Larose-Trintaudon, Malescasse, Maucamps, Moulin de Labarde, Quimper, Sénéjac* and *Verdignan*.

LALANDE-DE-POMEROL, AC Pomerol's northern neighbour, a region as tiny as Pomerol itself, is often accused of being overpriced, but since it can produce rich, plummy wines with a distinct resemblance to those of Pomerol at a distinctly less painful price, this criticism is not entirely justified. The best châteaux are *Annereaux, Bel-Air, Belles-Graves, Bertineau-St-Vincent, Clos des Moines, Clos des Templiers, la Croix Bellevue, la Fleur St-Georges, Grand Ormeau, Haut-Ballet, les Hauts-Tuileries, Lavaud-la-Maréchaude, Siaurac, les Templiers, Tournefeuille*.

LISTRAC, AC One of the less prestigious communes of the Haut-Médoc, just to the west of Margaux. Grown on clay-dominated soils, the wines contain a higher proportion of Merlot. They are generally tough, rather charmless, only slightly perfumed wines, lacking the complexity of the best villages, but the meteoric rise in quality amongst the *bourgeois* wines since the '82 and '83 vintages has made its mark, though without quite the same show of fireworks. But some properties rise above this such as *Clarke, la Bécade, Cap-Léon-Veyrin, Fonréaud* (since 1988), *Fourcas-Dupré, Fourcas-Hosten, Fourcaud, Lestage* and the *Grand Listrac* co-op.

MARGAUX, AC Of the famous Haut-Médoc communes, this is the nearest to Bordeaux, covering various villages making rather sludgy, solid wines at one extreme, and at the other extreme the most fragrant, perfumed red wines France has yet dreamed up. The great wines come from round the village of Margaux itself. People pay high prices for them and still get a bargain. The best châteaux include: *d'Angludet, la Gurgue, d'Issan, Labégorce-Zédé, Margaux, Monbrison, Palmer, Prieuré-Lichine, Rausan-Ségla, du Tertre*. Among the next best are châteaux *Durfort-Vivens, Giscours, Marquis d'Alesme-Becker, Marquis de Terme, Siran* and *la Tour-de-Mons*.

MÉDOC, AC This name covers the whole of the long (80km) tongue of land north of Bordeaux town, between the Gironde river and the sea, including the Haut-Médoc and all its famous communes. As an AC, it refers to the less regarded but important lower-lying northern part of the area, traditionally known as the Bas-Médoc. AC Médoc reds, with a high proportion of Merlot grapes, are drinkable more quickly than Haut-Médocs and the best have a refreshing, grassy, juicy fruit, backed up by just enough tannin and acidity. Easily the best property is *Potensac*, where Michel Delon of Léoville-Las-Cases makes wine of Classed Growth standard. Other good wines are *le Bernadot, Cardonne, Cassan d'Estevil, David, d'Escot, la Gorce, Greysac, Grivière, Haut-Canteloup, Lacombe-Noaillac, Noaillac, Ormes-Sorbet, Patache d'Aux, la Tour-de-By, la Tour-St-Bonnet, Loudenne, Vieux-Château-Landon*. Most of the co-ops – especially *Bégadan, Ordornac* and *St-Yzans* – make good fruity stuff.

MOULIS, AC Another lesser commune of the Haut-Médoc next door to, and similar to, Listrac, but with more potentially outstanding properties and a softer, more perfumed style in the best which can equal Classed Growths. Best are *Bel Air Lagrave, Brillette, Chasse-Spleen, Duplessis-Fabre, Dutruch-Grand-Poujeaux, Grand-Poujeaux, Gressier-Grand-Poujeaux, Maucaillou, Moulin-à-Vent, Poujeaux.*

PAUILLAC, AC The most famous of the Haut-Médoc communes, Pauillac has three of the world's greatest red wines sitting inside its boundaries, *Latour, Lafite* and *Mouton-Rothschild*. This is where the blackcurrant really comes into its own. The best wines are almost painfully intense, a mixture of blackcurrant and celestial lead pencil sharpenings that sends well-heeled cognoscenti leaping for their cheque books. Best: *D'Armailhacq (*formerly known as *Mouton-Baronne-Philippe), Grand-Puy-Lacoste, Haut-Bages-Avérous, Haut-Bages-Libéral, Lafite-Rothschild, Latour, Lynch-Bages, Mouton-Rothschild, Pichon-Baron, Pichon-Lalande*. Next best: *Batailley, Clerc-Milon-Rothschild, Duhart-Milon, Grand-Puy-Ducasse, Haut-Bages-Monpelou.*

PESSAC-LÉOGNAN, AC An AC in its own right since September 1987 for the area traditionally the Graves' best and containing all the *crus classés*. The AC covers ten communes but only 55 châteaux. In recent years the growers have fought back with increasing success against the tide of suburbia, replanting and improving their wines, above all the whites which, at their best, offer a depth surpassed only by the best Burgundies. The reds have a biscuity, bricky warmth. Best: *Carmes-Haut-Brion, Cabannieux, Cruzeau, Domaine de Chevalier, Domaine de Gaillat, Domaine la Grave, Ferrande, de Fieuzal, Haut-Bailly, Haut-Brion, Haut-Portets, la Louvière, Malartic-Lagravière, la Mission-Haut-Brion, Pape-Clément* (since 1985), *Rahoul Rochemorin, de St-Pierre, Smith-Haut-Lafitte* (since 1988), *Roquetaillade-la-Grange, la Tour Martillac, Tourteau-Chollet*.

POMEROL, AC Tiny top-class area inland from Bordeaux, clustered round the town of Libourne. The Merlot grape is even more dominant in Pomerol than in St-Émilion, and most Pomerols have a deeper, rounder flavour, the plummy fruit going as dark as prunes in great years, but with the mineral backbone of toughness preserving it for a very long time. Pomerol has no classification, but it harbours the world's greatest red wine, *Château Pétrus*. Any vineyard that has been picked out by Jean-Pierre Moueix or influenced by oenologist Michel Rolland can be regarded as being of good Classed Growth standard. Best châteaux: *le Bon Pasteur, Bourgneuf-Vayron, Certan-de-May, Certan-Giraud, Clinet, Clos René, Clos du Clocher, Clos l'Église, la Conseillante, la Croix de Gay, l'Église Clinet, l'Évangile, le Gay, la Grave-Trigant-de-Boisset, Lafleur, Lafleur-Gazin,*

La Fleur Pétrus, Lagrange à Pomerol, Latour-à-Pomerol Petit-Village, Pétrus, le Pin, Trotanoy, Vieux-Château-Certan.

PREMIÈRES CÔTES DE BLAYE, AC There is a shift to red in this historically white area across the river from the Médoc. The wines are too often a little 'cooked' in taste and slightly jammy-sweet. They're cheap, but have a lot more improving to do. Good names: *Bas Vallon, Bourdieu, Charron, Crusquet-Sabourin, l'Escadre, Fontblanche, Grand Barail, Haut-Sociando, Jonqueyres, Peybonhomme.*

PREMIÈRES CÔTES DE BORDEAUX, AC This long, south-facing slope stands opposite Bordeaux town and slides down the river Garonne to about opposite Barsac. In spite of its rather grand name, its only claim to fame until recently has been the production of rather half-baked Sauternes lookalikes. But it is now producing some very attractive reds. The 1985, '88 and '89 vintages produced numerous wines with a surprising amount of soft fruit and durability. Best châteaux: *de Berbec, Brethous, Cayla, Fayau, Grands-Moüeys, du Juge, Lamothe, de Lucat, Peyrat, la Roche, Reynon, Tanesse.*

ST-ÉMILION, AC Soft, round, and rather generous wines, because the main grape is the Merlot, aided by Cabernet Franc and Malbec, and only slightly by Cabernet Sauvignon. St-Émilions don't always have Pomerol's minerally backbone, and the sweetness is usually less plummy and more buttery, toffeed or raisiny. Top wines add to this a blackcurranty, minty depth. It's a well-known name, yet with few famous châteaux. It has its own classification, but is very sprawling, and has two top châteaux, *Cheval-Blanc* and *Ausone*, plus a dozen excellent ones. Some areas also annex the name, like St-Georges-St-Émilion or Puisseguin-St-Émilion. They're often OK, but would be better value if they didn't trade greedily on the St-Émilion handle.

Best in satellites: *St-Georges, Montaiguillon, Tour du Pas St-Georges* (St-Georges-St-Émilion); *Haut-Gillet, de Maison Neuve* (Montagne-St-Émilion); *Bel Air, la Croix-de-Berny* (Puisseguin-St-Émilion); *Lyonnat* (since 1983) (Lussac-St-Émilion). Best châteaux: *l'Angélus, l'Arrosée, Ausone, Balestard-la-Tonnelle, Beauséjour-Duffau-Lagarosse, Canon, Canon-la-Gaffelière, Cheval-Blanc, Clos des Jacobins, la Dominique, Figeac, Fonroque, Larmande, Magdelaine, Pavie, Pavie Decesse, Soutard, Tertre-Rôteboeuf, Troplong-Mondot.* Next best: *Belair, Cadet-Piola, Berliquet, Cap de Mourlin, Cardinal Villemaurine, Carteau, Côtes Daugay, Clos Fourtet, Corbin-Michotte, Couvent des Jacobins, Destieux, de Ferrand, Trappaud, Fombrauge, Franc-Mayne, la Gaffelière, Grand-Mayne, Gravet, Villemaurine, Magnan-la-Gaffelière, Mauvezin, la-Tour-du-Pin Figeac, Monbousquet, Pavie-Macquin, Rolland-Maillet, Tour-des-Combes, Trottevieille.*

ST-ESTÈPHE, AC This northernmost of the great Haut-Médoc communes is a more everyday performer. There aren't many famous names, and most are relatively cheap. Best: *Calon-Ségur, Chambert-Marbuzet, Cos d'Estournel, Haut-Marbuzet, Lafon-Rochet, Marbuzet, Meyney, Montrose, les Ormes-de-Pez, de Pez.* Next best: *Andron-Blanquet, Beausite, du Boscq, Cos Labory, le Crock, Lavillotte, Phélan-Ségur.*

ST-JULIEN, AC There are two main styles. One is almost honeyed, a rather gentle, round, wonderfully easy-to-love claret. The other has glorious cedar-cigar-box fragrance mixed with just enough fruit to make it satisfying as well as exciting. Best châteaux to look for: *Beychevelle, Ducru-Beaucaillou, Gruaud-Larose, Lagrange* (in recent vintages especially), *Lalande-Borie, Langoa-Barton, Léoville-Barton, Léoville-Las-Cases, St-Pierre, Talbot.* Next best: *Branaire-Ducru, Gloria, Hortevie, Léoville-Poyferré* and *Terrey-Gros-Caillou.*

THE 1855 CLASSIFICATION

This is the most famous and enduring wine classification in the world – but it was never intended as such, merely as a one-off guide to the different Bordeaux wines entered for the Great Paris Exhibition of 1855, made up by various local brokers and based on the prices the wines had obtained over the previous century or so. Those brokers would be dumbfounded if they returned today to find we still revered their rather impromptu classification.

An interesting point to note is that the wine name was classified, not the vineyard it came from. Some of the vineyards that make up a wine are now completely different from those of 1855, yet, because the name got into the lists, the level of classification remains. There are endless arguments about the quality ratings, but the only change so far occurred in 1973, when Mouton-Rothschild got promoted from Second to First Growth level after 50 years of lobbying by its late owner. In general, those properties which are classified do deserve their status, but that's never yet stopped anyone from arguing about it.

First Growths (1ers Crus)

Latour, *Pauillac*; Lafite-Rothschild, *Pauillac*; Margaux, *Margaux*; Haut-Brion, *Pessac-Léognan* (formerly *Graves*); Mouton-Rothschild, *Pauillac* (promoted in 1973).

Second Growths (2èmes Crus)

Rausan-Ségla, *Margaux*; Rauzan-Gassies, *Margaux*; Léoville-Las-Cases, *St-Julien*; Léoville-Poyferré, *St-Julien*; Léoville-Barton, *St-Julien*; Durfort-Vivens, *Margaux*; Lascombes, *Margaux*; Gruaud-Larose, *St Julien*; Brane-Cantenac, *Cantenac-Margaux*; Pichon-Longueville, *Pauillac*; Pichon-Longueville-Lalande (formerly Pichon-Lalande), *Pauillac*; Ducru-Beaucaillou, *St-Julien*; Cos d'Estournel, *St-Estèphe*; Montrose, *St-Estèphe*.

Third Growths (3èmes Crus)

Giscours, *Labarde-Margaux*; Kirwan, *Cantenac-Margaux*; d'Issan, *Cantenac-Margaux*; Lagrange, *St-Julien*; Langoa-Barton, *St-Julien*; Malescot-St-Exupéry, *Margaux*; Cantenac-Brown, *Cantenac-Margaux*; Palmer, *Cantenac-Margaux*; la Lagune, *Ludon-Haut-Médoc*; Desmirail, *Margaux*; Calon-Ségur, *St-Estèphe*; Ferrière, *Margaux*; Marquis d'Alesme-Becker, *Margaux*; Boyd-Cantenac, *Cantenac-Margaux*.

Fourth Growths (4èmes Crus)

St-Pierre, *St-Julien*; Branaire-Ducru, *St-Julien*; Talbot, *St-Julien*; Duhart-Milon-Rothschild, *Pauillac*; Pouget, *Cantenac-Margaux*; la Tour-Carnet, *St-Laurent-Haut-Médoc*; Lafon-Rochet, *St-Estèphe*; Beychevelle, *St-Julien*; Prieuré-Lichine, *Cantenac-Margaux*; Marquis-de-Terme, *Margaux*.

Fifth Growths (5èmes Crus)

Pontet-Canet, *Pauillac*; Batailley, *Pauillac*; Grand-Puy-Lacoste, *Pauillac*; Grand-Puy-Ducasse, *Pauillac*; Haut-Batailley, *Pauillac*; Lynch-Bages, *Pauillac*; Lynch-Moussas, *Pauillac*; Dauzac, *Labarde-Margaux*; d'Armailhacq (formerly Mouton-Baronne-Philippe), *Pauillac*; du Tertre, *Arsac-Margaux*; Haut-Bages-Libéral, *Pauillac*; Pédesclaux, *Pauillac*; Belgrave, *St-Laurent-Haut Médoc*; de Camensac, *St-Laurent-Haut-Médoc*; Cos Labory, *St-Estèphe*; Clerc-Milon-Rothschild, *Pauillac*; Croizet-Bages, *Pauillac*; Cantemerle, *Macau-Haut-Médoc*.

__Webster's__ is an annual publication. We welcome your suggestions for next year's edition.

CHÂTEAUX PROFILES

These properties are valued according to how they are currently performing; a five-star rating means you are getting a top-line taste – not just a well-known label. Some big names have been downgraded, some lesser-known properties are promoted – solely on the quality of the wine inside the bottle. A star in brackets shows that the wine can achieve the higher rating but does not always do so.

The £ sign shows which are offering particularly good value – that does not mean any of these wines will be cheap but look for recessionary price reductions.

L'ANGÉLUS *grand cru classé St-Émilion* ★★★★ One of the biggest and best known *grands crus classés*. A lot of Cabernet in the vineyard makes for a reasonably gutsy wine, although rich and soft. Since 1979 new barrels have helped the flavour. The 1985 and 1986 are, by a street, the finest yet, with excellent '87, '88 and '89.

D'ANGLUDET *cru bourgeois Margaux* ★★★ £ *Bourgeois* easily attaining Classed Growth standards. Owned by Englishman Peter Allan Sichel, the wine has much of the perfume of good Margaux without ever going through the traditional lean period. Fairly priced. Tremendous value. The 1980s have seen Angludet on a hot streak. The '83 and '90 are the finest *ever*, and the '85, '86, '88 and '89 are big and classy.

D'ARMAILHACQ *5ème cru classé Pauillac* ★★★(★) (Formerly known as Mouton-Baronne-Philippe) A wine of very good balance for a Fifth Growth, with the perfume particularly marked, this obviously benefits from having the same ownership as Mouton-Rothschild. 1986 and '83 are very good, with '82 not bad either.

AUSONE *1er grand cru classé St-Émilion* ★★★★(★) The phoenix rises from the ashes. For many years people referred to Ausone as they would to a slightly mad aunt, who then marries the most popular boy in town. The boy in question is Pascal Delbeck, who has been at the château since 1976 and has worked at returning Ausone to its proper position as one of St-Émilion's two First Growths. Potentially great wine at its best. The 1985, '86, '89 and above all the '90, should be especially good.

BATAILLEY *5ème cru classé Pauillac* ★★★ £ Batailley's reputation has been of the squat, solid sort rather than elegant and refined, but recently the wines have performed that extremely difficult Pauillac magician's trick – they've been getting a lot better, and the price has remained reasonable. Drinkable young, they age well too. The 1983, '85, '86, '88, '89 and '90 are excellent, available – and affordable.

BELAIR *1er cru classé St-Émilion* ★★★ The arrival of Pascal Delbeck at Ausone had a dramatic effect on Belair too, since it's under the same ownership. It looked as though it was rapidly returning to a top position as a finely balanced, stylish St-Émilion, but some recent bottles have been strangely unconvincing.

BEYCHEVELLE *4ème cru classé St-Julien* ★★★★ Certainly the most expensive Fourth Growth, but deservedly so, since traditional quality puts it alongside the top Seconds. It takes time to mature to a scented, blackcurranty, beautifully balanced – and expensive – wine. At the end of the 1970s and beginning of the 1980s the wines were rather unconvincing, but the sale of the château (to a civil servants' pension fund) in 1985 dramatically improved matters through greater selectivity. 1989 and 1990 are sublime.

BRANAIRE-DUCRU *4ème cru classé St-Julien* ★★★ Used to be soft, smooth wine with a flavour of plums and chocolate, gradually achieving a classic, cedary St-Julien dry perfume in maturity. The 1981, '82, '85 and '86 are good. But the 1980s have been very erratic, with rather dilute flavours and unclean fruit. '82, '85 and '86 were clean and fruity, but '83, '87 and '88 were strangely insubstantial. 1989 and '90 saw a welcome return to form, thanks to a change of ownership, with wine of sturdy fruit and backbone.

BRANE-CANTENAC *2ème cru classé Margaux* ★★ A big and famous property which has been underachieving when most of the other Second Growths have been shooting ahead. It has had chances in the last eight years to prove itself, but remains behind the rest of the field. Even its supposedly inferior stable-mate Durfort-Vivens has produced better wine in recent years.

CALON-SÉGUR *3ème cru classé St-Estèphe* ★★★(★) The château with the heart on its label. This is because the former owner, Marquis de Ségur, though he owned such estates as Lafito and Latour, declared 'my heart belongs to Calon'. An intensely traditional claret, it's certainly good on present showing, but doesn't set many hearts a-flutter. '86 and '88 were promising though.

CANON *1er grand cru classé St-Émilion* ★★★★(★) Mature Canon reeks of the soft, buttery Merlot grape as only a top St-Émilion can. Recently, it has been getting deeper and tougher, and although we'll probably miss that juicy, sweet mouthful of young Merlot, the end result will be even deeper and more exciting. The wines seem to get better and better; marvellous 1982s and '83s were followed by a stunning '85 and a thoroughly impressive '86. 1988 was excellent. '89 and '90 are keeping up this high standard.

CANTEMERLE *5ème cru classé Haut-Médoc* ★★★(★) For some years after 1983 the Cordier company controlled this Fifth Growth and the wine is now often up to Second Growth standards, although sometimes a little light. The 1988 and '89 are the best recent vintages by a long way, and the '83 was really good, but though the '85, '86 and '90 are beautifully perfumed, they are a little loose-knit. Interestingly, the perfumed style quite suits the '87.

CHASSE-SPLEEN *cru bourgeois Moulis* ★★★(★) A tremendously consistent wine, at the top of the *bourgeois* tree, and a prime candidate for elevation. It already sells above the price of many Classed Growths. The wines were impressive, chunky and beautifully made right through the 1980s, except for a rather 'over-elegant' 1985. Choose 1982 and '86, followed by lovely '87 and tip-top '88. The 1989 is a bit fierce, but the '90 is first class, with lots of blackberry fruit backed by a firm structure. Even the '91 and '92 are impressive.

CHEVAL-BLANC *1er grand cru classé St-Émilion* ★★★★★ The property stands on an outcrop right next to Pomerol, and seems to share some of its sturdy richness, but adds extra spice and fruit that is unique, perhaps due to the very high proportion of Cabernet Franc. Good years are succulent. Lesser years like 1980 can be successes too, and only 1984 and 1987 haven't worked. The 1982 is unbelievably good, and the '81, '83, '85 and '86 are not far behind. '88 is one of the top wines of the vintage, but '89 and '90 are not quite of the intensity I would want.

CISSAC *cru grand bourgeois Haut-Médoc* ★★★ £ Traditionalists' delight! This is one of the best known *bourgeois* growths, dark, dry and slow to mature with lots of oak influence, too – the oak perhaps a little more apparent than the fruit. It is best in richly ripe years like 1982 and '85, and can be a little lean in years like '86. '88, '89 and '90 were very good indeed.

COS D'ESTOURNEL *2ème cru classé St-Estèphe* ★★★★★ £ The undoubted leader of St-Estèphe, this has much of the fame of the top Pauillacs. The wines are dark, tannic and oaky: classically made for long ageing despite a high percentage of Merlot. A 'super-second' but less expensive than its rivals – the 1992 is a real bargain. The quality was so good in '85, '88 and '89 that they are probably undervalued. Even the '91 is decent. Second label Château Marbuzet is good.

DOMAINE DE CHEVALIER *cru classé Pessac-Léognan* ★★★★(★) The red and white are equally brilliant. The red has a superb balance of fruit and oak, and the white is simply one of France's greatest. You have to book ahead even to see a bottle of the white but you might find some red. Buy it. It's expensive and worth every penny. The hottest years are not always the best here, and despite an impressive richness in 1982, the '81, '83, '85, '86 and '88 may yet turn out better. 1987 is a resounding success in a light vintage, as is 1984. 1989 and 1990 were classy in an area of Bordeaux where results seem uneven.

DUCRU-BEAUCAILLOU *2ème cru classé St-Julien* ★★★★ One of the glories of the Médoc. It has now distanced itself from most other Second Growths in price and quality, yet the flavour is so deep and warm, and the balance so good, it's still worth the money. With its relatively high yields, it has a less startling quality when young than its near rivals Léoville-Las-Cases and Pichon-Lalande, but if the balance is right, the wine can age beautifully. 1982, '85, '86, '88, '89 and '90 are all top drawer and marvellously complex, while '81, '79 and '78 are also remarkably good and fit for the long haul.

L'EVANGILE *Pomerol* ★★★(★) Top-line Pomerol, lacking the sheer intensity of its neighbour Pétrus, but perfumed and rich in a most irresistible way. Output isn't excessive, demand is. 1982, '85, and '88 are delicious, with first-rate '87 too. '89 is packed with multi-layered, firm, luscious fruit, and '90 is another blockbuster.

DE FIEUZAL *cru classé Pessac-Léognan* ★★★★ One of the stars of Pessac-Léognan, the white only just behind Domaine de Chevalier, the red well ahead. The red starts plum-rich and buttery, but develops earthiness and cedar scent allied to lovely fruit. It made one of the finest 1984s, outstanding '85s and '86s as well as lovely '87s and thrilling '88s. '89 was top-notch, the '90 very good. The white, though unclassified, is scented, complex, deep and exciting. Even the '92 is worth buying.

FIGEAC *1er grand cru classé St-Émilion* ★★★★ Figeac shares many of the qualities of Cheval-Blanc (rare gravelly soil, for a start) but it's always ranked as the – ever-reliable – star of the second team. A pity, because the wine has a beauty and a blackcurranty, minty scent uncommon in St-Émilion. High quality. High(ish) price. Figeac is always easy to drink young, but deserves proper ageing. The excellent 1978 is just opening out, and the lovely '82, '85 and '86 wines will all take at least as long. '89 and '90 are already seductive.

LA FLEUR-PÉTRUS *Pomerol* ★★★★ This wine is in the top flight, having some of the mineral roughness of much Pomerol, but also tremendous perfume and length. Real class. We don't see much of this in the UK since the Americans got their teeth into it, but the 1982 and '89 are without doubt the best recent wines; the '85 and '86 seem to lack that little 'extra' class.

GAZIN *Pomerol* ★★★ This can produce the extra sweetness and perfume Nenin usually lacks. Although fairly common on the British market, it wasn't that great up to about 1985. Now controlled by Moueix, '87 and '88 are an improvement, and '89 and '90 are really very fine, so we can all start buying it again.

GISCOURS *3ème cru classé Margaux* ★★★ This property excelled right through the 1970s and into the '80s, and made some of Bordeaux's best in years like '75, '78 and '80. But something's gone wrong since 1982. Although 1986 is good, and '87 reasonable for the year, '83, '85 and '88 are not up to par. 1989 and '90 showed a return to form.

GLORIA *cru bourgeois St-Julien* ★★(★) Owing to the high-profile lobbying of its late owner, Henri Martin, Gloria became expensive and renowned. The quality of this quick-maturing wine has not always been faithful to the quality of the rhetoric. 1986, '88 and '89 show some signs that the wine is becoming worthy of the price.

GRAND-PUY-DUCASSE *5ème cru classé Pauillac* ★★★ £ Every recent vintage has been a success, and, with a price that is not excessive, its slightly gentle but tasty Pauillac style is one to buy. The 1979 is lovely now, and the '82 and '83 are very nice without causing the hand to tremble in anticipation. Since 1984 there has been a discernible rise in tempo and '85 and '86 look to be the best wines yet, but little exciting wine was made in the late 1980s.

GRAND-PUY-LACOSTE *5ème cru classé Pauillac* ★★★★ £ This combines perfume, power and consistency in a way that shows Pauillac at its brilliant best. Blackcurrant and cigar-box perfumes are rarely in better harmony than here. Not cheap but worth it for a classic. The 1978 is sheer class, the '82, '83, '86 and '88 top wines, and the '84, though very light, is gentle and delicious. 1989 is deliciously perfumed with robust fruit – a real star, as is the super 1990.

GRUAUD-LAROSE *2ème cru classé St-Julien* ★★★★(★) Another St-Julien that often starts rich, chunky and sweetish but will achieve its full cedary glory if given time, while still retaining a lovely sweet centre, typical of the wines (like Talbot) formerly owned by the Cordier family. The remarkable run of 1982, '83, '84 and '85 continued with a great '86, an attractive '87, exceptionally impressive '88 and '89 and, keeping up the standards, almost unnervingly juicy, ripe '90.

HAUT-BAILLY *cru classé Pessac-Léognan* ★★★★ Haut-Bailly tastes sweet, rich and perfumed from its earliest youth, and the high percentage of new oak adds to this impression even further. But the wines do age well and, though expensive, are of a high class. 1981, '82, '85, '86, '88 and '89 are the best recently.

HAUT-BATAILLEY *5ème cru classé Pauillac* ★★★ Once dark, plummy and slow to sweeten, this is now a somewhat lighter, more charming wine. In some years this has meant it was somehow less satisfying, but 1989 is the best yet, marvellously concentrated. 1986 and '88 are the best of earlier wines, with '82, '83 and '85 all good, but just a touch too diffuse and soft.

HAUT-BRION *1er cru classé Pessac-Léognan* ★★★★★ The only non-Médoc red to be classified in 1855. The wines are not big, but are almost creamy in their gorgeous ripe taste, deliciously so. If anything, they slightly resemble the great Médocs. Although 1982 is strangely insubstantial, the next four vintages are all very fine and '88 and '89 are outstanding, while the 1990, although worthy of the château, could not quite compete with its predessors. There is also a delicious, if overpriced white Haut-Brion – the 1985 is spectacular.

D'ISSAN *3ème cru classé Margaux* ★★★★ One of the truest Margaux wines, hard when young (though more use of new oak recently has sweetened things up a bit), but perfumed and deep-flavoured after ten to 12 years. Fabulous in 1983, '88 and '90, first rate in '85 and '86, with a good '87 too. 1989 has excellent fruit, while 1990 is a star, rich and concentrated, with lots of liquorice fruit on the palate.

LAFITE-ROTHSCHILD *1er cru classé Pauillac* ★★★★★ The most difficult of all the great Médocs to get to know. It doesn't stand for power like Latour, or perfume like Mouton. No, it stands for balance, for the elegant, restrained balance that is the perfection of great claret. And yet, till its day comes, Lafite can seem curiously unsatisfying. I keep looking for that day. I keep being unsatisfied. 1990, '89 and '88 are undoubtedly the best recent vintages, followed by 1982 and '86, and this fabled estate seems to be dishing up fewer fairy tales and more of the real stuff that dreams are made of.

LAFLEUR *Pomerol* ★★★★★ This tiny property is regarded as the only Pomerol with the potential to be as great as Pétrus. So far, they couldn't be further apart in style, and Lafleur is marked out by an astonishing austere concentration of dark fruit and an intense tobacco spice perfume. The 1982 almost knocks you sideways with its naked power, and the '83 and '85 are also remarkable. 1989 is superbly fruity and displays tremendous finesse already.

LAFON-ROCHET *4ème cru classé St-Estèphe* ★★★(★) Since the 1970s, an improving St-Estèphe, having as much body, but a little more perfume than most of them. 1982, '83 and '85 are all good, though none of them stunning, while '86, '87, '88, '89 and '90 show some class and a welcome consistency of style.

LAGRANGE *3ème cru classé St-Julien* ★★★(★)Until its purchase by the Japanese Suntory whiskey group in 1984, Lagrange had always lacked real class, though '82 and '83 were reasonable. But the vineyard always had great potential, even when the wine was below par, and investment is making its presence felt; '85, '86, '88, '89 and '90 are impressive and '87 was good too. Another bandwagon is rolling. Make sure you concentrate on more recent vintages.

LA LAGUNE *3ème cru classé Haut-Médoc* ★★★★ Certainly making Second Growth standard wine, with a rich, soft intensity. It is now becoming more expensive, but the wine gets better and better. The 1982 is a wonderful rich, juicy wine, with '85 and '88 not far behind, and '83 not far behind that. 1986 is burly but brilliant stuff, as is '89. 1987 is more delicate but good.

LANESSAN *cru bourgeois Haut-Médoc* ★★★ 'Grand Cru Hors Classe' is how Lanessan describes itself. This could be a reminder of the fact that a previous owner felt it unnecessary to submit samples for the 1855 Classification, so its traditional ranking as a Fourth Growth was never ratified. Nowadays, the wine is always correct, if not distinguished. But this may be because the owner resolutely refuses to use new oak and therefore his wines are more discreet when young. The '82 and '83 are both exhibiting classic claret flavours now, '88 looks set for the same path and '90 is a wine of balance and depth.

LANGOA-BARTON *3ème cru classé St-Julien* ★★★★ £ This wine is very good. It is in the dry, cedary style, and although sometimes regarded as a lesser version of Léoville-Barton, this is patently unfair since the wine has exceptional character and style of its own, and is reasonably priced. '82 and '85 are exciting, '86 and '87 very typical, but the '88 may be the best for 30 years. The '89 almost matched Léoville for elegance and the '90 was fully its equal.

LASCOMBES *2ème cru classé Margaux* ★★★ Lascombes made its reputation in America, and that's where it still likes to be drunk. Very attractive early on, but the wine can gain flesh and character as it ages. It's been a little inconsistent recently, but the 1985 and '83 are good, and the '86 is the most serious effort for a long time. '87 is also good, but '88 is so light you'd think they'd included every grape on the property. The '89 and '90 are more hopeful.

LATOUR *1er cru classé Pauillac* ★★★★★ This is the easiest of all the First Growths to comprehend. You may not always like it, but you understand it because it is a huge, dark, hard brute when young, calming down when it ages and eventually spreading out to a superb, blackcurrant and cedar flavour. It used to take ages to come round, but some recent vintages have seemed a little softer and lighter, yet usually retaining their tremendous core of fruit. Let's hope they age as well as the previous ones, because the 1984 was more true to type than the '85! And though the '82 is a classic, both '83 and '81 are very definitely not. '86 and '88 seem to be back on course, and '89 looks splendidly powerful. With the '89 and '90 the new management showed that power and richness were part of their inheritance. The '91 and '92 are the best wines of their years. The second wine, Les Forts de Latour, is getting better and better, while the third wine, Pauillac de Latour, is now made in most years to preserve the quality of the two greater wines.

LÉOVILLE-BARTON *2ème cru classé St-Julien* ★★★★★ £ The traditionalist's dream. Whoever described claret as a dry, demanding wine must have been thinking of Léoville-Barton. Despite all the new fashions and trends in Bordeaux, Anthony Barton simply goes on making superlative, old-fashioned wine for long ageing, and resolutely charging a non-inflated price for it. All the vintages of the 1980s have been attractive, but the 1982, '83, '85 and '86 are outstanding, the '87 delicious, and the '88 and '90 are two of the best wines of the Médoc. 1989 keeps up the standard. All are *wonderfully* fairly priced.

LÉOVILLE-LAS-CASES *2ème cru classé St-Julien* ★★★★★ Because of the owner's super-selectivity, this is the most brilliant of the St-Juliens, combining all the sweet, honeyed St-Julien ripeness with strong, dry, cedary perfume. The wine is justly famous, and despite a large production, the whole crop is snapped up at some of the Médoc's highest prices. The 1982 is more exciting every time a bottle is broached, and all the vintages of the 1980s are top examples of their year. The second wine, Clos du Marquis, is better than the majority of Classed Growths, if only because Michel Delon puts into it wines which any other owner would put into his *grand vin*.

LÉOVILLE-POYFERRÉ *2ème cru classé St-Julien* ★★★(★) The Léoville that got left behind, not only in its unfashionable reputation, but also in the quality of the wine, which until recently had a dull, indistinct flavour and an unbalancing dryness compared with other top St-Juliens. Things are now looking up with new investment and new commitment and I feel more confident about this property with every vintage. The 1982, '85, '86 and even the '87 are considerable improvements, and '88, '89 and '90 continue the progress, but it still has some way to catch up in terms of power and concentration with its peer group.

LOUDENNE *cru bourgeois Médoc* ★(★) The château is owned by Gilbey's and the wine is seen a lot in such chains as Peter Dominic. The red has a lot of Merlot and is always fruity and agreeable, but a little too soft to lay down for long.

LYNCH-BAGES *5ème cru classé Pauillac* ★★★★★ This château is so well known that familiarity can breed contempt, and its considerable quality be underestimated. It is astonishingly soft and drinkable when very young, and yet it ages brilliantly, and has one of the most beautiful scents of minty blackcurrant in all Bordeaux. The most likely to show that character are the 1986 and '83, and, remarkably, the '87, but for sheer exuberant starry-eyed brilliance, the '88, '85 and particularly the '82 are the ones. '89 is unusually big and powerful, while the '90 is more restrained and classic.

MAGDELAINE *1er grand cru classé St-Émilion* ★★★★ A great St-Émilion, combining the soft richness of Merlot with the sturdiness needed to age. They pick very late to maximize ripeness, and the wine is made with the usual care by Jean-Pierre Moueix of Libourne. Expensive, but one of the best. 1982 and 1985 are both classics, '88 and '89 tremendously good.

MALARTIC-LAGRAVIÈRE *cru classé Pessac-Léognan* ★★★ £ While its near neighbour, Domaine de Chevalier, hardly ever produces its allowed crop, this property frequently has to declassify its excess. Even so, the quality is good, sometimes excellent, and while the white is very attractive young, the red is capable of long ageing. 1987, '86, '85, '83 and '82 are all successful, with '88 and '89 the finest yet, but the '90s are disappointing.The red, in particular, is rather wishy-washy.

MALESCOT-ST-EXUPÉRY *3ème cru classé Margaux* ★★(★) A property which seems to have lost its way. Traditionally it started out lean and hard and difficult to taste, but after ten years or so it began to display the perfume and delicate fruit only bettered by such wines as Palmer and Margaux. Yet after tasting and re-tasting the wines of the 1980s, the conclusion is that they are made too light and lacking in depth for this thrilling scent ever to develop. The 1990 may prove me wrong. I hope so.

MARGAUX *1er cru classé Margaux* ★★★★★A succession of great wines have set Margaux back on the pedestal of refinement and sheer, ravishing perfume from which it had slipped some years ago. The new Margaux is weightier and more consistent than before, yet with all its beauty intact. 1978 and 1979 were the harbingers of this new 'Mentzelopoulos era', the '80 was startlingly good in a tricky vintage, and '82, '83 and '86 are just about as brilliant as claret can be, while the '88 may well be the wine of the vintage. The deep, concentrated '89 doesn't seem to match up to the '88, but the 1990 is as fragrant and powerful as the 1986 – which is saying a lot. In '91 and '92 the wines, though not up to Latour's level, were better than most of the First Growths.

MEYNEY *cru bourgeois St-Estèphe* ★★★(★) £ This epitomizes St-Estèphe reliability, yet is better than that. It is big, meaty and strong, but never harsh. Vintages in the 1970s lacked personality, but recent wines are increasingly impressive and although the wine is difficult to taste young, the '82, '83, '85, '86, '88 and '89 are remarkable and the '84, '87 and '90 good.

LA MISSION-HAUT-BRION *cru classé Pessac-Léognan* ★★★(★) La Mission likes to put itself in a class apart, between Haut-Brion and the rest. Yet one often feels this relies more on weight and massive, dark fruit and oak flavours than on any great subtleties. For those, you go to Haut-Brion or Domaine de Chevalier. '82, '85 or '86 are recommendable of recent vintages.

MONTROSE *2ème cru classé St-Estèphe* ★★★★ Traditionally famous for its dark, tannic character, and its slow, ponderous march to maturity. For a wine with such a sturdy reputation, some recent vintages have seemed faintly hollow. 1986 made amends with a really chewy, long-distance number, and '87 was densely structured, if hardly classic, but it's taken until '89 and '90 for the wine really to return to form. The château, which tends to pick rather early, came into its own in '89 and '90, and even made a decent '91 and a better '92. The second wine, Dame de Montrose, has been a bargain these past four years.

MOUTON-ROTHSCHILD *1er cru classé Pauillac* ★★★★★After years of lobbying, Baron Philippe de Rothschild managed to raise Mouton to First Growth status in 1973. Of course it should be a First Growth. But then several Fifths should probably be Seconds. The wine has an astonishing flavour, piling intense cigar-box and lead-pencil perfume on to the rich blackcurrant fruit. The 1982 is already a legend, the '86 and '89 are likely to join '82, and the '85, '84 and '83 are well worth the asking price.

NENIN *Pomerol* ★★ A thoroughly old-fashioned wine. It quite rightly pleases the royal family, who order rather a lot of it. But in fact it is rather chunky and solid and has quite a tough core for a Pomerol, which doesn't always disperse into mellow fruitfulness. The 1985 and '86 aren't bad, but, really, the '82, the '83 and the '88, all good vintages, were pretty feeble.

PALMER *3ème cru classé Margaux* ★★★★ 'Most expensive of the Third Growths?' asks one of Palmer's owners. 'No. Cheapest of the Firsts.' There's (some) truth in that. Until 1978 Palmer used to out-Margaux Margaux for sheer beauty and perfume. And it still can occasionally out-perform some of the First Growths in tastings. It was consistently brilliant in the 1960s and 1970s (excepting '64), but the 1980s have seen it lose some of its sure touch, and the '83 lacks some of its neighbours' class. '87 and '88 are very good too, but are closer in style to out-Beychevelling Beychevelle. '89 is cedary and elegant, rich but tannic, in a year when not all Margaux wines had great depth of fruit. In 1990 Palmer was better than most, but not all, of its neighbours.

PAPE-CLÉMENT *cru classé Pessac-Léognan* ★★★★(★) One of the top properties in Pessac-Léognan, capable of mixing a considerable sweetness from ripe fruit and new oak with a good deal of tough structure. 1975 was great, but then we had a very poor decade until 1985. The last five vintages are outstanding, with the 1990 an example of Pessac-Léognan at its best.

PAVIE *1er grand cru St-Émilion* ★★★★ The biggest major property in St-Émilion, with high yields, too. Until recently good without being wonderful, stylish without being grand. Still, Pavie does have the true gentle flavours of good St-Émilion and recent releases are showing a deeper, more passionate style which puts it into the top flight. 1990, '89, '88, '87, '86 and '85 are good examples of the new, '82 of the old.

PETIT-VILLAGE *Pomerol* ★★★★ A fairly pricy wine, it is not one of the soft, plummy Pomerols, and until recently there was a fair amount of Cabernet giving backbone. The wine is worth laying down, but the price is always high. 1985, '83 and the absurdly juicy '82 are all very good, but the '88 and '89 look likely to be the best yet.

PÉTRUS *Pomerol* ★★★★★ One of the world's most expensive reds, and often one of the greatest. Astonishingly, its fame, though surfacing briefly in 1878, has only been acquired since 1945, and in particular since 1962, when the firm of Jean-Pierre Moueix took a half-share in the property. This firm has given the kiss of life to many Pomerol properties, turning potential into achievement, and with Pétrus it has a supreme creation. Christian Moueix says his intention is to ensure no bottle of Pétrus ever disappoints. 1982 and 1989 were stupendously great. 1985 isn't far off it, nor is '81, and the only example from the last 20 years which seemed atypical is the rather Médoc-like 1978.

DE PEZ *cru bourgeois St-Estèphe* ★★★ One of the most famous *bourgeois* châteaux, the wine is almost always of Classed Growth standard, big, reliable, rather plummy and not too harsh. 1982 and '83 were very attractive, though some prefer the more unashamedly St-Estèphe wines of the 1970s, which saw a bit of a comeback with the excellent '86.

PICHON-LONGUEVILLE *2ème cru classé Pauillac* ★★★★★ (since 1987) Often described as more masculine than its 'sister', Pichon-Longueville-Lalande, this tremendously correct but diffident Pauillac (formerly Pichon-Longueville-Baron) was until 1987 only hinting at its potential. Drier and lighter than Lalande, it was also less immediately impressive, despite aging well. 1987 saw the property being bought by the Axa insurance company and Jean-Michel Cazes of Lynch-Bages being brought in to run it. The '87 was very good, the '88 superb, the '89 *tremendous*, broodingly intense, while the '90 is one of the Médoc's greatest wines.

PICHON-LONGUEVILLE-LALANDE *2ème cru classé Pauillac* ★★★★(★) Pichon-Longueville-Lalande (formerly Pichon-Lalande) produced a stunning 1970, and since then has been making a rich, oaky, concentrated wine of tremendous quality. Its price has climbed inexorably and it wishes to be seen as the equal partner of St-Julien's leading pair, Léoville-Las-Cases and Ducru-Beaucaillou. 1982, '83 and '85 all brim with exciting flavours, and '86 may be even better. '87 doesn't quite reach the same standards, but '88 does, and '89 is elegant and seductively fruity. With the revival of Pichon-Longueville over the road, the rivalry between these properties has produced some stunning twins, notably in 1990, when Longueville triumphed.

PONTET-CANET *5ème cru classé Pauillac* ★★★ The biggest Classed Growth. Famous but unpredictable, and still trying to find its traditionally reliable form. 1985 and '86 are hopeful, '87 and '88 less so, '90 hopeful again as the owners become more selective.

POTENSAC *cru bourgeois Médoc* ★★★(★) £ The most exciting in the Bas-Médoc. It is owned by Michel Delon of Léoville-Las-Cases, and a broadly similar style of wine-making is pursued. This gives wines with a delicious, blackcurrant fruit, greatly improved by a strong taste of oak from once-used Las-Cases barrels. Not expensive for the quality. Beats many *crus classés* every year for sheer flavour.

PRIEURÉ-LICHINE *4ème cru classé Margaux* ★★★ One of the more reliable Margaux wines, and in years like 1970, 1971 and 1975 it excelled. Recently it has been fairly priced and although not that perfumed, a good, sound Margaux. 1983, '86, '88 and '89 are all good, but '90 is the first really exciting wine for some time, and 1991 and '92 continue the improvement.

RAUSAN-SÉGLA *2ème cru classé Margaux* ★★★★(★) Up to and including the 1982 vintage this lovely property, rated second only to Mouton-Rothschild in the 1855 Second Growths, had been woefully underachieving for a couple of generations. But a change of ownership in 1983 saw a triumphant return to quality – in the very first year. 1983, '85 and '86 were triumphs. 1987 was declassified as Château Lamouroux but is still delicious. The '88 is a supreme achievement which the '89 matches and the '90 surpasses.

RAUZAN-GASSIES *2ème cru classé Margaux* ★★ Right behind Rausan-Ségla, but the wine is leagues below most Second and Third Growths in quality, and so far hasn't taken the hint from Ségla that quality pays in the end.

ST-PIERRE *4ème cru classé Médoc* ★★★★ Small St-Julien property producing superb, underrated, old-fashioned wine. Once under-priced, but the image-conscious Henri Martin of Gloria stopped that when he took over in 1982. Still, the quality has been worth it. While the 1970 and '75 were underrated stars, the wines of the 1980s are possibly even better. Martin died in 1991, and the family are carrying on the tradition.

DE SALES *Pomerol* ★★★ £ An enormous estate, the biggest in Pomerol by a street. This vastness shows in a wine which, though it is good round claret, doesn't often excite. The 1985 is very nice, the '83 and '82 are very nice.

SIRAN *cru bourgeois Margaux* ★★★ Sometimes mistaken for a Classed Growth in blind tastings, this property is indeed mostly made up from the land of Châteaux Dauzac and Giscours. The '85 and '83 are the most successful wines of recent years, but all vintages have been good lately. The '88 was a bit clumsy, but the1989 and 1990 vintages are showing well.

TALBOT *4ème cru classé St-Julien* ★★★★ One of the most carefully made and reliable of the fleshier St-Juliens, suffering only in comparison with its sister château in the former Cordier stable, Gruaud-Larose, and always offering value for money and tremendous consistency. Maybe the name Talbot just lacks the right ring? Whatever the reason, you must seek out the exciting 1986, the super-classy '85, '83 and '82 and the ultra-stylish '84, as well as the lovely '87, the impressive '88 and the big, rich '89. The '90, however, seems to lack something in the way of concentration.

DU TERTRE *5ème cru classé Margaux* ★★★(★) This wine is unusually good, with a lot of body for a Margaux, but that weight is all ripe, strong fruit and the flavour is direct and pure. Funnily enough, it's not cheap for a relative unknown but neither is it expensive for the quality. The '85 is rich and dense and yet keeps its perfume intact, while the '86, '83 and '82 are rich and blackcurranty – already good and sure to improve for ten years more. '88 was not quite so good, for some reason, but '89 was back to normal.

TROTANOY *Pomerol* ★★★★ If you didn't know Pétrus existed, you'd say this had to be the perfect Pomerol – rich, plummy, chocolaty fruit, some mineral hardness, and tremendous fat perfume. It's very, very good, and makes Pétrus' achievement in eclipsing it all the more amazing. The '82 is brilliant, and although the '85 is also wonderfully good, the vintages of the mid and late 1980s haven't been quite as thrilling as have previous examples of this château.

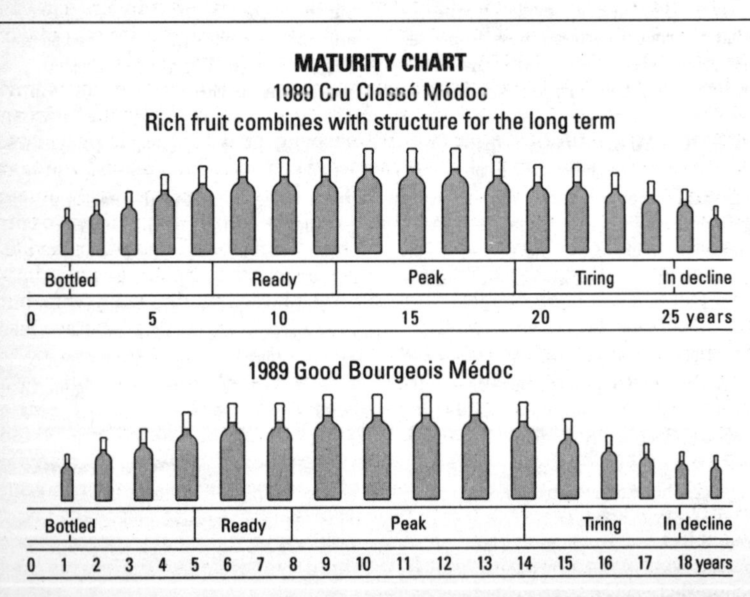

SECOND WINES

The second wines from the major Bordeaux châteaux can be defined, broadly, as wines from the same vineyard as the *grand vin* (the wine with the château name) which, for quality reasons, have been 'selected out' of the top wine. Legally they could be included, but maintaining the quality of the *grand vin* is vital.

These may be the produce of particularly young vines, which won't have the concentration and staying power demanded from an expensive Classed Growth. They may be from sections of the vineyard that, owing to the vagaries of the weather, didn't produce quite the right style, or that are just traditionally less good. Or they may include first-class wine from mature vines and good parts of the vineyard that just doesn't fit into this particular vintage of the *grand vin* style. For example, if the Merlot grape produces an enormous crop and the tougher Cabernet falls a bit short on quantity, then a winemaker may decide to use less Merlot, so as to preserve the balance he wants.

Then there is another form of second wine. Sometimes a major château buys up a lesser property nearby, and begins to use its label for its second wine. Since it is in the same appellation this is perfectly legal. Cos d'Estournel uses the seven-hectare vineyard of Château Marbuzet like this, and Lynch-Bages uses Haut-Bages-Avérous in the same way.

Claret off the peg

If you talk to retailers about the Bordeaux market in Britain, more and more will tell you that sales of remotely ready to drink Classed Growths are gradually becoming almost irrelevant to their business. Apart from a few old-established companies and one or two new up-market specialists, very few retailers now sell more than token amounts of mature *grand vin* claret. But the desire to trade up is as strong as ever. It's just the ridiculous price at which people balk.

And that's where the second wines have made phenomenal inroads during the last couple of years. If we leave out wine such as Pavillon Rouge du Château Margaux and Les Forts de Latour, which are usually priced at the £15 plus mark, the other top Bordeaux properties are mostly able to offer their second wines at between £8 and £10 a bottle. Sure, that is a lot, but given the seemingly innate desire of the British to drink decent claret, and given the fact that at three to four years old, the second wine of a property like Léoville-Barton, Pichon-Longueville, Pichon-Longueville-Lalande, Palmer, Lynch-Bages or, above all, Léoville-Las-Cases can be outstandingly attractive – far less tannic than the main wine, but fleshy and soft and reasonably oaky too. Consumers can really taste the class they are buying. As top properties declassify more and more of their wine to maintain the densely structured, dark, long distance style which is popular with the château owners and the trade at the moment, the second wines will play a bigger and bigger part in our market. In years like '85, '86, '88, '89 and '90 top properties might declassify as much as 40 per cent. Twenty years ago many of them wouldn't declassify at all, and more than ten per cent was very rare. But recently, as prices have risen, the owners have realized that to justify the price, the quality has to be something special. In 1991 and 1992 many conscientious owners went round boasting just how high a proportion of their wine was declassified – often to mere generic status.

We should take immediate advantage. Not only to drink now, but also to lay down. Good second wines do have a ten year life expectancy from the good vintages of the '80s, although there are lighter styles – like some of the AC Margaux properties, and the delicious but delicate wines of a label like Lacoste-Borie (Grand-Puy-Lacoste) which are so good at five years old it seems a pity to wait. But if you've got the wherewithal – try a bottle of the *grand vin* next to a bottle of the second wine. There's no question of not being able to tell them apart. The second wine almost always lacks a little of the drive, a little of the lingering, tantalizing flavour of the *grand vin*. The flavours that shout at you in the *grand vin* are more likely to whisper in the second wine. Well, that's as it should be: if you buy the *grand vin*, that's what you're paying for. But they'll be ready to drink much more quickly, and that is often their chief virtue. They give you a suggestion, within four or five years of the vintage, of the glorious flavours the *grand vin* may take 20 years to achieve.

Just one word of caution. The number of second wines appearing on the market has mushroomed. If you see an unfamiliar name on a bottle with a familiar *appellation contrôlée*, look at the small print on the bottom of the label. If it's a real château it'll just say something like 'Propriétaire M Major et Fils' or something like 'Société Civile' of the main name on the label. But it may also say 'Société Civile' of one of the well-known properties in the AC. In which case it is almost certain to be a second wine of that property. Some proprietors own more than one property in the AC – Jacques Lurton of Brane Cantenac and Durfort Vivens is an example – in which case it may say something like 'Domaine Lurton' on the second wine label.

Second or second-rate?

And another cautionary note. There are a lot of ambitious properties in lesser ACs – like Listrac, Moulis, Haut-Médoc, St-Émilion, Lalande-de-Pomerol, even Côtes de Francs. Many of these are starting to utilize second labels for their lesser *cuvées*. That's fine; the wine can be good and not expensive. But make a rule – don't buy the second wine of a property you don't think is up to much in the first place. It'll just be a worse example of a not very good wine. And, despite the pronouncements of one or two leading Bordeaux figures about '87 being the year for second wines – don't buy second wines from indifferent vintages. To take 1987 as an example, the properties who cared to make fine wine in 1987 did so because they declassified as much as half their wine. Almost all of this would be the unripe Cabernet Sauvignon hit by vintage-time rains. There is nothing less likely to give you drinking pleasure in the short term than unripe, dilute Cabernet Sauvignon. So don't touch it. (The exception I would make is Château Lamouroux, which is declassified Rausan-Ségla – but they declassified all their wine and the result is delicious. And Palmer and Angludet sold some extremely attractive wine to large groups in the UK for drinking at less than two years old which was also a delight.) Anyway, 1987 is the year we can afford to buy the *grand vin* – so whatever the Bordelais try to tell us, what we don't want is their '87 slops. 1985 was basically a year when Merlot and Cabernet both overproduced and the second wines are absolutely lovely for now and to keep. A 1987 Classed Growth *grand vin* should be better than '86 second wine and not necessarily much more expensive, but there should be some good '89s and '90s to look forward to, and '88s to keep us going until then.

RECOMMENDED WINES

Most of these (and we have starred the ones we feel are the best bets) are from the Haut-Médoc, since properties there are larger and the opportunities for selection much greater. But when you buy a second wine, don't feel you're buying a second rate modern invention. Château Margaux produced its first Pavillon Rouge du Château Margaux in 1908, and Léoville-Las-Cases created its second label, Clos du Marquis, in 1904. But the habit faded in the 1930s as the owners rushed to sell everything as *grand vin* simply to survive. Only recently has it been revived.

Haut-Médoc

1st Growth: ★les Forts-de-Latour (Latour), Moulin-des-Carruades (Lafite), ★Pavillon-Rouge-du-Château Margaux (Margaux).

2nd Growth: ★le Baronnet-de-Pichon (Pichon-Longueville), ★Clos du Marquis (Léoville-Las-Cases), ★la Croix (Ducru-Beaucaillou), la Dame de Montrose (Montrose), Domaine de Curebourse (Durfort-Vivens), ★Lamouroux (Rausan-Ségla), ★Marbuzet (Cos d'Estournel), Moulin-Riche (Léoville-Poyferré), Notton (Brane-Cantenac), ★Réserve de la Comtesse (Pichon-Longueville-Lalande), ★St-Julien (Léoville-Barton), ★Sarget de Gruaud-Larose (Gruaud-Larose), ★les Tourelles-de-Pichon (Pichon-Longueville).

3rd Growths: ★Fiefs de Lagrange (Lagrange), ★St-Julien (Langoa), de Loyac (Malescot St-Exupéry), Ludon-Pomies-Agassac (la Lagune), Marquis-de-Ségur (Calon-Ségur), ★Réserve du Général (Palmer).

4th Growths: de Clairefont (Prieuré-Lichine), Connétable-Talbot (Talbot), des Goudat (Marquis de Terme), Moulin-de-Duhart (Duhart-Milon-Rothschild), ★Réserve de l'Amiral (Beychevelle), St-Louis-le-Bosq (St-Pierre).

5th Growths: Artigue-Arnaud (Grand-Puy-Ducasse), Enclos de Moncabon (Croizet-Bages), ★Haut-Bages-Avérous (Lynch-Bages), les Hauts-de-Pontet (PontetCanet), ★Lacoste-Borie (Grand-Puy-Lacoste), ★Villeneuve-de-Cantemerle (Cantemerle).

Good Bourgeois Châteaux: Abiet (Cissac), ★Admiral (Labégorce-Zédé), Bellegarde (Siran), Bory (Angludet), ★Clos Cordat (Monbrison), Domaine de Martiny (Cissac), Domaine Zédé (Labégorce-Zédé), Ermitage de Chasse-Spleen (Chasse-Spleen), Labat (Caronne-Ste-Gemme), Granges-de-Clarke (Clarke), ★Lartigue-de-Brochon (Sociando-Mallet), ★Lassalle (Potensac), Moulin d'Arrigny (Beaumont), Prieur de Meyney (Meyney), Réserve du Marquis d'Evry (Lamarque), ★Tour de Marbuzet (Haut-Marbuzet)' ★Salle-de-Poujeaux (Poujeaux).

Graves, Pessac-Léognan

★Abeille de Fieuzal (Fieuzal), Bahans-Haut-Brion (Haut-Brion), ★Batard-Chevalier (Domaine de Chevalier), ★Coucheroy (la Louvière), ★Hauts de Smith-Haut-Lafitte (Smith-Haut-Lafitte), ★la Parde-de-Haut-Bailly (Haut-Bailly).

St Emilion

Beau-Mayne (Couvent des Jacobins), ★Domaine de Martialis (Clos Fourtet), ★Franc-Grace-Dieu (Canon), Jean du Nayne (Angelus),Grangeneuve-de-Figeac (Figeac), ★des Templiers (Larmande).

Pomerol

Chantalouette (de Sales), Clos Toulifaut (Taillefer), ★Fleur de Clinet (Clinet), la Gravette-de-Certan (Vieux-Château-Certan), Monregard-Lacroix (Clos du Clocher), ★la Petite Église (l'Église Clinet).

Bordeaux Supérieur Côtes de Francs, les Douves de Francs (de Francs), ★Lauriol (Puygueraud).

CLARETS OUT OF THEIR CLASS

Trying to rearrange the Classification of 1855 is a regional pastime. These days there is many a Fifth Growth that should perhaps be a Second or Third, and some Seconds or Thirds that should be Fourths or Fifths.

One of the most exciting things for a claret devotee is to catch a château at the beginning of a revival in its fortunes. While a reputation is being built or re-built, the quality will keep ahead of the price. However, the price will rise – and nowadays you can go from mediocrity to magnificence in two or three years.

The problem for the drinker is complicated by the competitive nature of the growers who, naturally, see price as a yardstick of quality. In the late 1970s, there was a handful of Second Growths – most obviously Ducru-Beaucaillou, Pichon-Lalande and Léoville-Las-Cases – which rose above their peers, in price and quality, while others – notably Cos d'Estournel and Léoville-Barton – kept quality up and prices (relatively) down. The same process was repeated in the late 1980s with the emergence of some excellent but over-priced 'super' *crus bourgeois*. Monbrison, Poujeaux-Thiel, Chasse-Spleen, Sociando-Malet, all got above themselves. Fortunately 1991 sobered them up.

Médoc

Minor châteaux performing like top bourgeois *wines:* Andron-Blanquet, Cartillon, le Fournas Bernadotte, de Junca, Lamothe, Malescasse, Maucamps, Moulin-de-Laborde, Patache-d'Aux, Peyrabon, Ramage-la-Bâtisse, la Tour-de-By, la Tour-du-Haut-Moulin, la Tour-Pibran, la Tour-St-Joseph, Victoria.

Top bourgeois *performing like Classed Growths:* d'Angludet, Brillette, Chasse-Spleen, Chambert-Marbuzet, Cissac, la Gurgue, Hanteillan, Haut-Marbuzet, Gressier-Grand-Poujeaux, Hortevie, Labégorce-Zédé, Lanessan, Maucaillou, Meyney, Monbrison, les Ormes-de-Pez, de Pez, Potensac, Poujeaux, Siran, Sociando-Mallet, la Tour-de-Mons.

Classed Growths outperforming their classification: Camensac, Cantemerle, Clerc-Milon-Rothschild, Grand-Puy-Lacoste, Haut-Bages-Libéral, d'Issan, Lagrange, la Lagune, Langoa-Barton, Léoville-Barton, Lynch-Bages, Marquis d'Alesme-Becker, Rausan-Ségla, St-Pierre, du Tertre, la Tour-Carnet. Since 1987 Pichon-Longueville has been top flight.

Graves

Outperformers: Cabannieux (white), Domaine la Grave (white), Montalivet (red and white), Rahoul (red), Roquetaillade-la-Grange (red and white), Cardaillan.

Pessac-Léognan

Outperformers: Carbonnieux (white), Couhins-Lurton (white), Cruzeau, de Fieuzal (red and white), la Louvière (red and white), Malartic-Lagravière (red and white), Rochemorin, Smith-Haut-Lafitte (white, and red since 1988), la Tour-Martillac.

Pomerol

Outperformers: Bertineau St-Vincent (Lalande-de-Pomerol), Belles Graves (Lalande-de-Pomerol), le Bon-Pasteur, Bourgneuf-Vayron, Certan de May, Clinet, Clos du Clocher, Clos René, L'Eglise Clinet, Feytit-Clinet, la Fleur-St-Georges (Lalande-de-Pomerol), Franc-Maillet, Grand Ormeau (Lalande-de-Pomerol), la Grave-Trigant-de-Boisset, les Hautes-Tuileries (Lalande-de-Pomerol), Latour-à-Pomerol, Lavaud la Maréchaude (Lalande-de-Pomerol), Siaurac (Lalande-de-Pomerol), les Templiers (Lalande-de-Pomerol).

St-Émilion

Outperformers: l'Arrosée, Balestard-la-Tonnelle, Bellefont-Belcier, Berliquet, Cadet-Piola, Cardinal-Villemaurine, la Dominique, de Ferrand, Fombrauge, Larmande, Monbousquet, Montlabert, Pavie-Decesse, St-Georges, la Serre, Tertre-Rôteboeuf, Troplong-Mondot, Vieux-Château-Mazerat.

Sauternes

Outperformers non-classed: Bastor-Lamontagne, Chartreuse, de Fargues, Gilette, Guiteronde, les Justices, Liot, Menota, Raymond-Lafon, St-Amand.

Outperforming Classed Growths: d'Arche, Doisy-Daëne, Doisy-Védrines, de Malle, Nairac.

CLARET VINTAGES

Claret vintages are accorded more importance than those of any other wine; so much so that good wine from a less popular vintage can get swamped under all the brouhaha. We have had a parade of 'vintages of the century', although the fuss more usually starts in Bordeaux itself or on the volatile American market than in more cynical Britain.

Wines age at different rates according to their vintage. They may get more delicious or less so as they mature; some may be at their best before they are fully mature, because, although their balance may not be terribly impressive, at least they've got a good splash of young fruit. Wines also mature differently according to the quality of the property.

The generic *appellations* – like Bordeaux Supérieur – rarely need any aging. So a 1985, for instance, from a *premier cru*, might take twenty years to be at its best, a good *bourgeois* might take ten, and a *petit château* might take five years.

The grape variety is also important. Wines based on the Cabernet Sauvignon and/or Cabernet Franc (many of the Médocs and the Graves) will mature more slowly than wines based on the Merlot (most Pomerols and St-Émilions).

In the following tables, **A** = quality; **B** = value for money; **C** = drink now; **D** = lay down.

1992 This was the wettest summer for at least 50 years and Bordeaux had fewer hours of sunshine than in any year since 1980. The record rainfall in June made the flowering prolonged and difficult and set the tone for the problems to come.

This year a hot spell at the end of July was merely the prologue to torrential rain and hail in August, when there was a record 248mm of rain (over ten inches to you and me). Conscientious growers went through the vineyard again in September to remove some bunches, not, said Peter Sichel, 'with the hope of increasing the concentration in the remaining crop, but primarily to remove those grapes that now had no hope of reaching a decent degree of ripeness.' But there was so much rain that the growers could not keep up with the grapes' production of yet more watery juice.

By then it was clear that there was no hope of decent quality, and although the first part of September was rather cheerier, many of the grapes did not ripen, reaching only a miserable seven or eight degrees of potential alcohol, a mere two-thirds of the level they had reached in 1990. Many owners ensured that the grapes went through a further inspection before they reached the presses.

But only a few managed to bring in their whole crop before the rain set in more seriously and continuously in early October – the only blessing was that the weather was too cold to allow rot, so that the grapes were mostly healthy, if watery. Even in the best estates the wines risk dilution – most obviously with the Merlot, where some of the grapes were as bloated as small plums. And it will be a year in which the winemakers would do well to avoid one modern snobbery: to boast of the amount of new wood used will be counter-productive. The wines will simply not have the character to stand much wood.

But despite the size of the total crop, the market won't be flooded. The selectivity continued into the vats. Every estate worth the name has a second wine, many a third, and most are prepared to declass some of their wine even more completely. The result will be that they will be offering less than half their total as their '*grand vin*'. It has become a matter of pride to insist on how small a percentage of the wine goes into the *grand vin*.

1991 After the Great Frost, a miserable May and June did not help matters, though hopes rose after an August which was the hottest on record. The more optimistic growers started to talk of a repeat of 1961, when a spring frost produced a small but perfectly formed vintage.

Trouble started again in late September, just as the harvest was beginning in the Médoc. Rain fell heavily, and those growers who waited a few days for the grapes to ripen but managed to pick before 14 October stood the best chance of making decent wines. At that point the rain started in earnest and all hope for improvement had to be abandoned. The result was a small and wildly variable vintage, but not as small as has been suggested by merchants anxious to dispose of their stocks of earlier years. As far as red wines were concerned it was less than half the amount made in the two previous vintages, but the region has become so used to record crops that everyone has forgotten how much more wine is now being made than even a few years ago. In fact in 1991 a tenth more claret was made than in 1984, and in the 1970s it would have been considered a perfectly decent crop, at least in size.

This is one of those difficult years (like 1987) when you stick to the very best estates, stars like Margaux, Latour, Pichon-Baron and Léoville-Las-Cases. Montrose also stood out: Jean-Louis Charmolüe is famous for picking early, so he got his grapes in before the onset of the rains. Even his second wine (Dame de Montrose) is good value. Among the *crus bourgeois* reliable estates like Chasse-Spleen and Sociando-Malet came up to scratch. In the Graves a few estates like Smith-Haut-Lafitte and La Tour Martillac made decent wines.

But all the growers faced problems. I agree with merchants Lay & Wheeler that 'the best are fragrant and attractive, but they are not wines to lay down'. In the Libournais the situation was still worse, with nine-tenths of most crops simply wiped out in the frost. Few reputable growers are marketing 1991 wines under their château labels, preferring instead usually to ship the little wine they did make under a generic label, although there were a few more-than-acceptable wines, notably Gazin.

And the prices? Happily, unlike in 1984, they reflect the lower quality of the wine. The first-growths dropped FF40 to a mere FF160 (Haut Brion sold at FF150) and there has been a corresponding 20 per cent drop elsewhere, bringing an excellent wine like Haut-Bages-Liberal down to a mere FF32. But, frankly, stick to the bargains. These will never be great wines. Instead they will be agreeable, light, easier to drink than the 1987s but, like that other vintage which was damned at first, very decent in four or five years' time, if you can find the right wine at the right price.

1990 (AD) For the third consecutive year and for the eighth time in a decade, the harvest was excellent if not superlative. The sum of average temperatures was higher than in any year since 1947 and there were more hours of sunshine than in any year since 1949. There was also a far from contemptible amount of rainfall; albeit chiefly falling in two great bucketfuls at the end of August and in the fourth week of September. August was hotter than in 1989: only those notable scorchers 1947 and 1949 had the edge on it.

The freak weather conditions began even before the buds appeared on the vines. Bordeaux is a hot, dry place; but by anyone's description, 1990 was an exceptionally hot year. As the heat set in, the vines became severely stressed. In these circumstances it is generally the old vines which cope best, as their roots have pushed their way into every nook and cranny where they know water can be found. In a very hot year a water-collecting, clay-based subsoil is an advantage: those vines grown on well-drained pebbles (chiefly Cabernet Sauvignon) were in for a hard time that year.

With some notable exceptions, the Merlot-based wines did better than those primarily made from Cabernet Sauvignon. Some Médoc properties (Latour is unusual in this) have a subsoil of clay.

On the whole the very hot summer and lack of rain during the ripening season meant that the acidity was low and the alcohol high. Some wines may be very good and exceptionally ripe; but they were not made to be stashed in the furthest corner of your cellar or to be laid down for your first-born's 21st.

The quality has been widely reported as uneven. In the very north of the Médoc (the area that used to be called the Bas Médoc), the wines fared well. Also good were St-Estèphes from the most northerly of the Médoc Classed Growths; as you go further south, however, through Pauillac, St-Julien and Margaux, quality is far more variable: some very nice wines, yes, but to be chosen with care. Across the Gironde where the Merlot dominates the mix, the alcohol in the wines tends to be too high to produce wines of the elegance which is meant to typify Bordeaux in a good year.

It is now clear that 1990 was the last of the *'trois glorieuses'* along with 1988 and 1989. Of the three it now seems clear that anyone looking for a classic Bordeaux vintage (albeit a tough and tannic one) should opt for the 1988; the last two vintages having been too unusual to produce wines in the old claret mould, though many were splendid, if richer and fruitier than old-style claret buffs would like. Modern drinkers, immersed in rich Australian reds, will lap them up.

1989 (AD) For those who like to designate a Bordeaux vintage as either a Merlot year or a Cabernet year, this was one in which the Cabernet Sauvignon couldn't fail to ripen well, and in fact most of the Cabernet grapes brought in were deliciously, juicily ripe. Merlot was more of a problem. Grown to add ripeness and fatness to a possibly lean Cabernet, in 1989 the Merlot grapes were in most cases fully ripe at the beginning of September. It became a balancing act, attempting to catch the grapes *before* acidity got too low but *after* the tannins were ripe.

Prices, needless to say, went up, even though this was a gigantic crop and a record for AC reds was reached at nearly five million hectolitres. But the growers claimed that the 1988 First Growths increased in value by 50 per cent within a year of picking; they felt little pressure on them to keep prices down.

So to specifics. In the Haut-Médoc, Cantemerle stood out from others, followed by La Tour de By, Coufran, Citran and Lanessan. Rausan-Ségla in Margaux was back on form. Giscours, d'Issan, du Tertre, Lascombes and Cantenac-Brown were very successful, but overall it may not prove to be a Margaux year.

Elsewhere in the Haut-Médoc the wines seem juicier, fruitier, better constructed for the long haul. In St-Julien, Langoa-Barton, Léoville-Barton, Beychevelle, Gruaud-Larose, Talbot, Branaire-Ducru were all excellent with Ducru-Beaucaillou a notch above. In Pauillac, Haut-Batailley looks back on form, sturdy, rich Pichon-Longueville a lovely counterpoint to the elegance of

Pichon-Lalande, Latour impressively magnificent, combining power with finesse.

In St-Estèphe Montrose attracted attention with a triumphant return to the top, and also successful were Cos Labory, Meyney and Lafon-Rochet.

Over on the right bank, St Émilion and Pomerol defied attempts to call this a Cabernet year by producing Merlot wines of great richness and charm, from First Growths down. Best so far seem to be Canon-la-Gaffelière, Balestard la Tonnelle, Larmande, Cap-de-Moulin, Troplong-Mondot among the good value ranks, elsewhere there is Canon, La Conseillante, Gazin, Clinet, L'Evangile, Clos Fourtet, Pavie, an especially powerful L'Angélus, and a Cheval-Blanc of tremendous concentration and fragrance.

The Graves and Pessac-Léognan produced more uneven levels of quality on the whole, and although Domaine de Chevalier and Pape Clément are as classy as you would hope, only de Fieuzal, La Louvière and Haut-Bailly stood out from the rest.

1988 (AD) A difficult year, saved by a long warm summer – a vintage which could yield the most classically balanced claret of the '80s.

Graves/Pessac-Léognan yielded a remarkable range of wines, and it really showed how they are getting their act together down there. Special efforts from La Louvière, Larrivet-Haut-Brion, de France, Smith-Haut-Lafitte (a joyous return to the top rank), Fieuzal, Olivier (another wine coming out of the shadows), La Tour-Martillac, Malartic-Lagravière, Pape-Clément, Haut-Bailly and Domaine de Chevalier. In the Médoc, La Lagune was good and Cantemerle as good as the inspiring '83. Margaux was less exciting, but there were good wines from Angludet, d'Issan, Tertre, Prieuré-Lichine, Palmer, Durfort-Vivens (at last) and superb efforts from Monbrison, Rausan-Ségla and Margaux. Chasse-Spleen and Poujeaux were the best of the Moulis while St-Julien had beautiful wines from Beychevelle, Gloria, St-Pierre, Talbot, Gruaud, Ducru-Beaucaillou, Langoa-Barton and Léoville-Barton. Pauillac did very well, with Lafite, Grand-Puy-Lacoste, Haut-Bages-Libéral and Pichon-Lalande all excellent, and tip-top Lynch-Bages and the triumphantly resurrected Pichon-Longueville. St-Estèphe made its best vintage for several years, with consistently high quality from Cos d'Estournel, Calon-Ségur, Les Ormes-de-Pez, Meyney, Cos Labory and Lafon Rochet. The northern Médoc was a success too, in particular at Cissac, Hanteillan, Sociando-Mallet, La Tour-de-By, Potensac.

Pomerol made some excellent wines, and should have made more, but overproduction diluted the quality in many cases and they taste rather one-dimensional. Best so far seem to be Clinet, Beauregard, Évangile, Moulinet, l'Enclos, Vieux-Château-Certan, with improved efforts from La Croix-de-Gay and La Pointe. St-Émilion made superb wines, as good as 1985 and '82. Cheval-Blanc and Figeac lead the way, followed by Canon, Pavie, L'Angélus, Larmande, Fonplégade, Canon-la-Gaffelière, Balestard-la-Tonnelle, Couvent-des-Jacobins and Clos des Jacobins.

1987 (BCD) There *are* lean, unbalanced edgy wines from 1987 – often made by the same uninspired proprietors who made mediocre '88s. But the overall style of the vintage is wonderfully soft and ridiculously drinkable, the soft Merlot fruit combining with good new oak to produce light but positively lush reds, totally unlike the other two vintages it tends to be bracketed with, 1984 and 1980. These will happily last up to ten years, but you can start really enjoying them *now*.

1986 (AD) These wines are not in general heavyweight brutes; if anything inclining to the lean and austere in style, but the fruit does seem to be developing a vintage

MATURITY CHART

1986 Cru Classé Médoc
A great vintage that requires patience

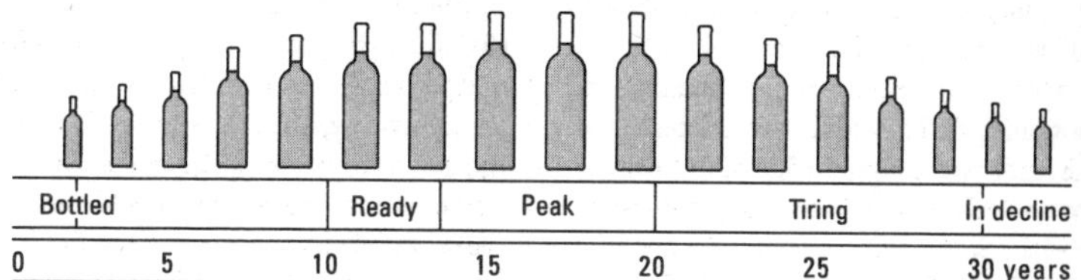

1986 Good Bourgeois Médoc

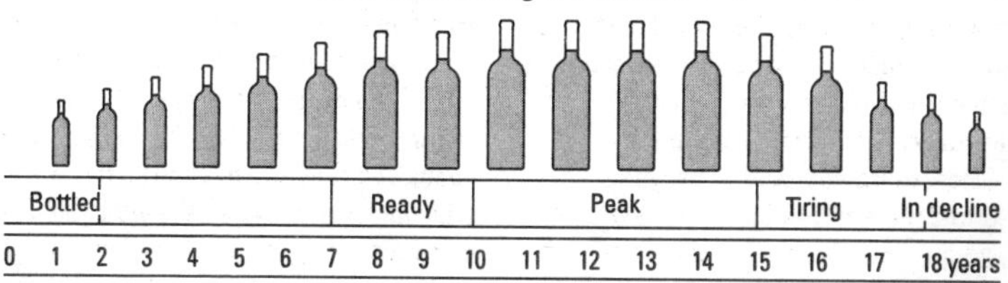

1988 Cru Classé Médoc
Classic Bordeaux vintage destined for a long life

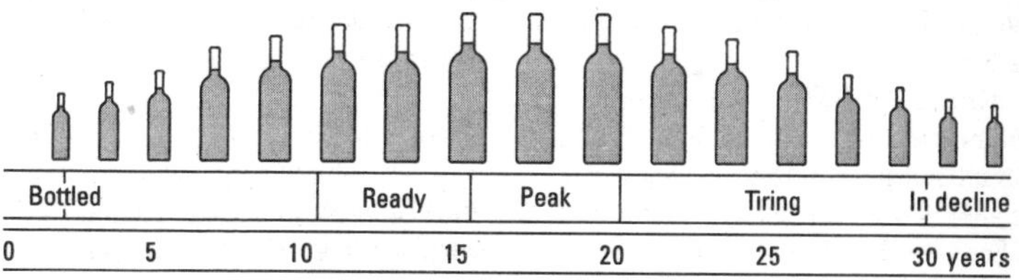

1988 Good Bourgeois Médoc

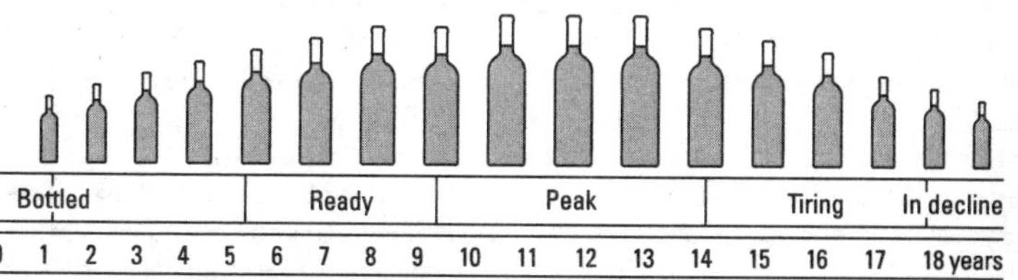

style in a surprising number of wines – and it is rather thick and jammy, allied to a slight rasp like the flavour of the grape skin itself. That said, the wines are good, sometimes very good, and mostly for the 10 to 20 year haul, though some will be attractive in about five years' time. I think you should have some in your cellar, but if I had only one fistful of £5 notes and '86 and '88 to choose between, I'd choose '88.

1985 (ACD) These are so delicious you can drink them now – even the top wines. The top wines will age as long as any sensible person wants to age them – but like, I'm told, 1953, they'll *always* be good to drink. The *petits châteaux* are still gorgeous if you can find them, the *bourgeois* probably the best ever on many properties and most of the Classed Growths and Graves/Pessac-Léognans are soft and deep and ravishing.

1984 I downgrade this every time I drink an example. What seemed to be quite light, dry – and grossly overpriced – Cabernet clarets are, at present, mostly short, fruitless and tough. They *may* improve, but it gets less likely every year.

1983 (ABD) A true Bordeaux classic, still relatively well-priced. Though tannic now, the wines will flower into a lovely dry cedar and blackcurrant maturity – but it'll take another few years. AC Margaux made its best wines for a generation.

1982 (ACD) Fabulous year, unbelievably ripe, fat, juicy and rich. They're going to make great drinking right to their peak in 5 to 10 years' time, although some of the lesser wines, while marvellous now, are not likely to last over five years.

1981 (BCD) Good but not spectacular. Quite light, but classic flavours from top properties which should still age a bit.

1980 (BC) Nice light, grassy claret, which needs drinking up.

1979 (ABCD) Many of these wines demand another five years at least. Keep your top wines, and hurry up and drink the lesser ones.

1978 (ACD) Some of the tip-top wines are a bit tough still, but most Classed Growths are lovely now, and many lesser wines are still good. Graves and St-Émilions are ready, although Graves will hold out for a while longer.

1976 (C) Rather soft and sweet on the whole. Not inspiring, apart from a few exceptions in St-Émilion and Pomerol. Drink it up.

1975 (A) A difficult vintage. The very harsh tannins frequently didn't have fruit ripe enough to mesh with, and the flavour went stale and brown before the wine had time to soften.

1970 (ACD) Now re-emerging with the fruit intact to make lovely current drinking – but the top wines will age a decade yet.

1966 (AC) Some say they're tiring, some say they aren't quite ready yet. I say *all* the wines are ready, with many at their peak now. Yet some lesser wines which seemed to be dying out have taken on a new lease of life.

1961 (AC) Still wonderful. I marvel at how great claret can match richness and perfume with a bone-dry structure of tannin and acidity.

Most other vintages of the 1960s will now be risks; '69 and '67 are basically past it, '64 can still be good, rather big, solid wines, and '62, one of the most gorgeous, fragrant vintages since the war, is just beginning to show the ladders in its stockings. If your godfather's treating you, and offers '59, '55 or '53, accept with enthusiasm. If he offers you '49, '47 or '45, get it in writing before he changes his mind.

WHITE BORDEAUX

In 1991 and 1992 all the winemakers in the Gironde underwent examinations far more rigorous than they had endured for decades. The dry whites, in particular, passed triumphantly. That is not to say that these were good years, full of memorable wines. They weren't. But they did rub in the point that, for the first time in history, the winemakers could produce considerable quantities of decent wines even in unpromising vintages – although in 1991 poor weather meant that the crop was so small that sales slumped and the rhythm of ever greater success was interrupted.

Success had not involved vastly increased sales, since the production of dry white wines has not grown much over the past couple of decades. This is because the growers, as so often happens, completely misread the international market. Despairing of selling their white wines at a decent price, they turned to black grapes just at the very time that the world's thirst for dry white wines was becoming insatiable.

In spite of this, however – and because of the determination of a young, fanatical professor from the Institut Oenologique in Bordeaux, Denis Dubordieu, who convinced the growers that they could make excellent dry whites – Bordeaux has now become respected the world over as a source of such wines. The Sauvignons nowadays offer a half-way house between the pungent grassiness the variety develops in the Loire, and the slight blowsiness, the over-ripe gooseberryness I find so *de trop* in the fashionable examples from New Zealand. The increasing number of more expensive wines from top châteaux naturally include a proportion of Sémillon, a variety which is deceptively light and straightforward in its youth, but which can mature into a complexity and depth found in few other white wines.

Divide and rule

Also critical to the success of dry white Bordeaux in recent years has been the division of the enormous, sprawling region of the Graves into two, separating out Pessac, the heart of the old Bordeaux vineyard, and Léognan, on the outskirts of Bordeaux (together these two areas embrace all the Grands Crus des Graves) from the rest of the region, which stretches down the west bank of the Garonne as far as Sauternes. The result, surprise, surprise, has been to help the rump of the Graves far more than Pessac-Léognan, which continues to rely far more on the famous names of individual estates than on that of the *appellation*. But since the division of the region in 1987 the Graves' winemakers have been 'condemned to do better' as the French neatly put it, and, as and when nature allows them, they are showing why their region was always considered one of the prime sources of fine white wines.

Unfortunately the years since the split have not been kind to them. While 1988 was a splendid year for making crisp, well-balanced dry whites, the very warmth and sunshine which made the two following vintages so remarkable for claret meant that it was extremely difficult to make dry white wines with enough acidity to balance the depth of fruit nature had provided. In 1991 the new-found pride of the winemakers ensured that they released only the tiny quantity of wines worthy of the *appellation*: and in 1992 they were lucky that they, alone of the winemakers in Bordeaux, managed to harvest before the rains and produce perfectly decent, if unmemorable dry wines.

But if science, discipline and selectivity can save dry white wines, they can still do little for the sweet white wines of the Gironde if Nature really puts her nasty little mind to ruining them as she did in both 1991 and 1992. The contrast was the greater because Sauternes has done even more than the Graves to pull itself up by its bootstraps over the past couple of decades. Moreover it has laboured under several disadvantages: it has no obvious *locomotifs*, whether technical, like Dubordieu, technological or commercial. Nor were the commercial advantages of investment as obvious there as they were in Graves: the world was increasingly drinking dry not sweet. Added to that there are the vagaries of noble rot and the tiny yields allowed – a maximum of 25 hectolitres of wine per hectare, less than half the level permitted for red wines, which means that Barsac and Sauternes need high prices if they are to be able to afford to make such high-risk wines.

But, against all the odds, the 1980s saw everything coming right for the Sauternais. Increasingly the French public started to appreciate their wines, which had been profoundly out of fashion for a generation. In addition, it was prepared to pay the proper (high) price for them. Nature smiled on the winemakers; but above all they helped themselves, largely by enduring the discipline involved in making better wines, but above all by eliminating the overwhelming aroma of sulphur dioxide (the winemaker's all-purpose anti-oxidant) and of non-grape sugar which hung over the vast majority of the wines of Sauternes and Barsac until well into the 1980s.

But it's important not to exaggerate the progress made by the Sauternais. Merely eliminating evil influences like sulphur does not automatically result in great wines – as I, for one, have tended to assume in the past. Given the way prices have escalated in recent years, we are entitled to ask for more than a mere absence of obvious flaws in what should be top-class, long-lived wines. Too often we are still not getting the necessary quality: many are only 'correct', too few properly great. It is apparent from blind tastings that not all the owners are taking the risks attached to late harvesting, and not all are selecting the grapes, nor indeed the wines, carefully enough.

Sauternes' big freeze

Lack of concentration can be a problem, even with the 1988s and '90s – which, incidentally, are more consistent than the '89s. But when we come to taste the '91s and '92s we will be grateful even for 'decent' wines in Sauternes. Even the best of the winemakers were struggling against such appalling conditions in those years that they made little if any wine – and those wines they did make were pretty unremarkable. The results showed the limitations of even the most advanced techniques, even the much-heralded cryoextraction. This involves freezing the grapes straight after picking, to a temperature at which the only juice that runs will be desirably full of sugar. It is an expensive business – requiring a specially-built cold room – and is supposed to compensate for those years when the Sauternais have no option but to pick in the rain. And despite whatever its (largely German) critics may say, it does not affect the chemical content of the juice.

Ironically, though, the cryoextraction equipment hasn't been much use to those châteaux that have it in the half dozen vintages since it was installed. The Sauternais didn't need its help in 1988, 1989 or 1990 – and in 1991 not even the most elaborate equipment could have allowed them to produce much wine. In 1992 there simply wasn't enough sun to ripen the grapes, nor, perhaps mercifully, was there much botrytis. An unbotrytized ripe vintage in Sauternes is one thing, but trying to make good Sauternes from unripe grapes is quite another. And botrytis on grapes that have not ripened properly merely serves to concentrate their unripeness.

If classed growth Sauternes is now likely to cost nearly double the price payable for equivalent reds given recent reductions in claret prices, it's increasingly worth the drinker's while to look slightly further afield. During Sauternes' bad years the vineyards the regions on the other side of the Garonne which also make sweet botrytis-affected wine – like Loupiac and Saint-Croix-du-Mont – had an even worse time. Now they have been caught up in the slipstream of their seniors, and are increasingly making lighter wines – not only because they can never have the concentration of a Sauternes (except in 1990 when it was virtually impossible to tell them apart) but because they are allowed, and can often get, much higher yields. But the resulting wines do make the most delightful aperitifs, what the French call '*aperos.*' Why not try one when you next go to what the very same French call a '*resto*'? **NICHOLAS FAITH**

GRAPES & FLAVOURS

SAUVIGNON BLANC There has been a rush to plant more of this fashionable grape in Bordeaux in recent years, but with a couple of exceptions – such as Malartic-Lagravière, Couhins-Lurton and Smith-Haut-Lafitte – Sauvignon by itself here often gives rather muddy, tough wine. Even so, many dry white Bordeaux are entirely Sauvignon, particularly at the cheaper end, and can be fresh and flowery if made by careful winemakers like Mau, Dourthe, Ginestet and Coste. But the best are almost always blended with Sémillon. A little Sauvignon adds acidity and freshness to Sauternes and the other sweet whites of the region, too.

SÉMILLON The most important grape of Sauternes, and very susceptible to noble rot. Sémillon is vital to the best dry wines, too, though it has become sadly unfashionable. With modern techniques one can hardly tell a good dry Sémillon from a Sauvignon, except that it's a little fuller. But ideally they should be blended, with Sémillon the main variety. It gives a big, round dry wine, slightly creamy but with an exciting aroma of fresh apples and leaving a lanolin smoothness in the mouth. From the top estates, fermented cool and aged in oak barrels, the result is a wonderful, soft, nutty dry white, often going honeyed and smoky as it ages to a maturity of between 7 and 15 years. Like this it produces one of France's great white wines, and is an antidote to anyone getting just a little tired of varietals.

MUSCADELLE A very little (up to five per cent) of this headily perfumed grape often goes into the Sauternes blend and has proved particularly good in wines from Loupiac and Ste Croix du Mont. In dry white blends a few per cent can add a very welcome honeyed softness. It is now being produced in small quantities as a single varietal; dry, lean, but perfumed.

The price guides for this section begin on page 284.

WINES & WINE REGIONS

BARSAC, AC (sweet) The only one of the Sauternes villages with the right to use its own name as an official *appellation* (it may also call itself Sauternes – or Sauternes-Barsac for that matter). Barsac has chalkier soils than the other Sauternes villages, and tends to make lighter wines. Even so, wines from good properties are marvellously rich despite a certain delicacy of texture.

BORDEAUX BLANC, AC (dry) This AC covers a multitude of sins. It is the catch-all name for all white Bordeaux, and as such is the label on some of France's dullest medium-to-dry whites, as well as on many fresh, simple, well-made wines. With the sudden surge of interest in Bordeaux's dry whites spurred on by the idiotic pricing shenanigans of its rivals in the Loire and Burgundy, there is simply no excuse for the – happily decreasing – amounts of over-sulphured sludge still coming on to the market. Thank goodness every year sees another surge of good guys beating back the bad. Château wines are usually the best and should generally be drunk as young as possible. Recommended names include: *Birot, Grand-Mouëys, du Juge, Lamothe, Reynon*. Good blends are possible from *Coste, Dourthe, Dubroca, Ginestet, Joanne, Lurton, Mau, Sichel* and *Univitis*. Some classy properties in red areas make good, dry white which is only allowed the AC Bordeaux. Château Margaux's white, for instance, is a simple AC Bordeaux. Many great Sauternes châteaux have started to make a dry wine from the grapes unsuitable for Sauternes. These use the 'Bordeaux Blanc' AC and often their initial letter – as in 'G' of Guiraud, 'R' of Rieussec and 'Y' of Yquem. 'Y' can really be spectacular.

BORDEAUX BLANC SUPÉRIEUR, AC (dry) Rarely used, but requires higher basic strength and lower vineyard yield than Bordeaux Blanc AC.

CADILLAC, AC (sweet) In the south of the Premières Côtes de Bordeaux, just across the river from Barsac; can produce attractive sweet whites, but since the price is low, many properties now produce dry white and red – which do *not* qualify for the AC Cadillac. The AC is in any case so involved that few growers bother with it.

CÉRONS, AC (sweet) Enclave in the Graves butting on to Barsac, making good, fairly sweet whites, but many growers now prefer to produce dry whites, which can sell as Graves. *Château Archambeau* is typical, producing tiny amounts of very good Cérons and larger amounts of good, fresh dry Graves. *Château Cérons* makes splendidly complex sweet whites worthy of the AC of Barsac. Other good names: *Grand Enclos du Château Cérons, Haura*.

ENTRE-DEUX-MERS, AC (dry) Large Bordeaux area between the Garonne and Dordogne rivers. The AC is for dry whites, which are of varying quality, but every vintage produces more examples of good, fresh, grassy whites. Many properties make red, and these can only be Bordeaux or Bordeaux Supérieur. Best: *Bonnet, Ducla, de Florin, Fondarzac, Moulin-de-Launay, Tertre du Moulin, Thieuley, Union des Producteurs de Rauzan*.

GRAVES, AC (dry) Famous, or perhaps infamous area south of Bordeaux, on the left bank of the Garonne. The infamy is the result of the endless turgid stream of sulphurous, flabby, off-dry white that *used* to flow out of the region. However, modern Graves is a dramatic improvement. Even at the level of commercial blends it can be sharply fruity and full in style, while at the best properties, with some oak aging employed, the wines are some of the most delicious dry whites in France. As from the 1987 vintage the wines from the northern Graves bear the *appellation* 'Pessac-

Léognan'. Best châteaux: *Archambeau, Bouscaut, Cabannieux, Carbonnieux, Domaine de Chevalier, Couhins-Lurton, de Cruzeau, Domaine la Grave, de Fieuzal, la Garance, la Garde, Haut-Brion, Landiras, Laville Haut-Brion, la Louvière, Malartic-Lagravière, Montalivet, Rahoul, Respide, Rochemorin, Roquetaillade-la-Grange, Smith-Haut-Lafitte* and *la Tour-Martillac.*

GRAVES SUPÉRIEURES, AC (sweet or dry) White Graves with a minimum natural alcohol of 12 degrees. Often made sweet. Best property: *Clos St-Georges.*

LOUPIAC, AC (sweet) These white wines from the lovely area looking across the Garonne to Barsac are not as sweet as Sauternes, and many properties until recently made dry white and red without the Loupiac AC because of difficulties in selling sweet whites.With rising prices has come a welcome flood of lemony-honeyed Barsac styles. Best châteaux: *Domaine du Noble, Loupiac-Gaudiet, Ricaud.*

PESSAC-LÉOGNAN, AC (dry) The AC for reds and whites declared in 1987 and created out of the best and northernmost part of Graves. Fifty-five estates are involved, including all the *crus classés*, so quality ought to be high. Yields are lower than for Graves and the percentage of Sauvignon is higher (at least a quarter of the grapes used). This might change the style of some estates, but the crucial point is that the new AC will be further motivation for improvement in what is rapidly becoming one of France's most exciting white areas. The best wines start out with a blast of apricot, peach and cream ripeness and slowly mature to a superb nutty richness with a dry savoury finish. Best châteaux: *Bouscaut, Carbonnieux* (from 1988), *Couhins-Lurton, Domaine de Chevalier, de Fieuzal, Haut-Brion, la Louvière, Malartic-Lagravière, Rochemorin, Smith-Haut-Lafitte* and *la Tour Martillac.*

PREMIÈRES CÔTES DE BORDEAUX, AC Some very attractive reds and excellent dry whites from the right bank of the Garonne in the bang-up-to-date, fruit-all-the-way style, as well as some reasonable sweetish wines. The sweet wines can be AC Cadillac, but you still get some under the Premières Côtes mantle, sometimes with their village name added, as in *Château de Berbec*, Premières-Côtes-Gabarnac.

STE-CROIX-DU-MONT, AC (sweet) The leading sweet white AC of the Premières Côtes de Bordeaux. Can be very attractive when properly made. *Château Loubens* is the best-known wine, but *Lousteau-Vieil* is producing better wine every year, and *Domaine du Tich, La Grave, la Rame, des Tours*, and the sadly minuscule *de Tastes* are also good.

SAUTERNES, AC (sweet) The overall *appellation* for a group of five villages in the south of the Graves: Sauternes, Bommes, Fargues, Preignac and Barsac. (Barsac wines may use their own village name if they wish.) Concentrated by noble rot, the

1855 CLASSIFICATION OF SAUTERNES
Grand premier cru Yquem (Sauternes).

Premiers crus Climens (Barsac); Coutet (Barsac); Guiraud (Sauternes); Haut-Peyraguey (Bommes); Lafaurie-Peyraguey (Bommes); Rabaud-Promis (Bommes); Rayne-Vigneau (Bommes); Rieussec (Fargues); Sigalas-Rabaud (Bommes); Suduiraut (Preignac); la Tour-Blanche (Bommes).

Deuxièmes crus d'Arche (Sauternes); Broustet (Barsac); Caillou (Barsac); Doisy-Daëne (Barsac); Doisy-Dubroca (Barsac); Doisy-Védrines (Barsac); Filhot (Sauternes); Lamothe (Sauternes), Lamothe-Guignard (Sauternes); de Myrat (Barsac) (now extinct); Nairac (Barsac); Romer-du-Hayot (Fargues); Suau (Barsac); de Malle (Preignac).

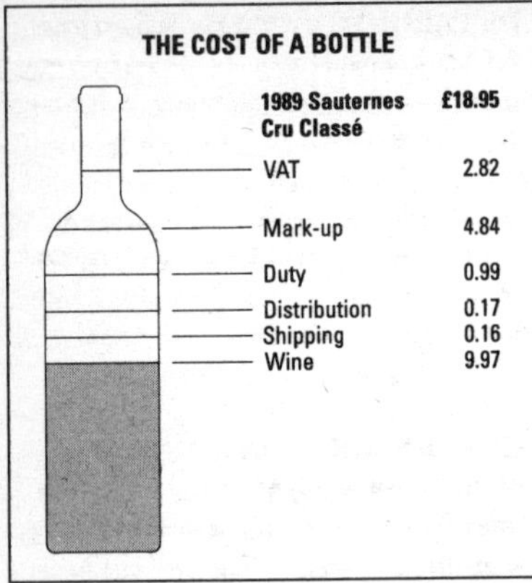

Sémillon, along with a little Sauvignon and Muscadelle, produces at its glorious best a wine that is brilliantly rich and glyceriny, combining honey and cream, pineapple and nuts when young, with something oily and penetrating as it ages and the sweetness begins to have an intensity of volatile flavours, rather like a peach, bruised and browned in the sun, then steeped in the sweetest of syrups. These are the fine wines. Sadly, owing to economic pressures, much Sauternes outside the top Growths used to be made sweet simply by sugaring the juice and stopping the fermentation with a massive slug of sulphur. In recent years the average quality has soared, and the wines are infinitely less turgid and sulphury, as indeed they ought to be given their rising prices. And in bad years those châteaux that can afford it can now practise cryoextraction – which isn't some form of torture but a method of freezing the grapes before fermentation which can increase the richness of the juice pressed out. Best châteaux: *Bastor-Lamontagne, Climens, Doisy-Daëne, Doisy-Védrines, de Fargues, Gilette, Guiraud, Lafaurie-Peyraguey, Lamothe-Guignard, Rabaud-Promis, Raymond-Lafon, Rayne-Vigneau, Rieussec, St-Amand, Suduiraut, La Tour Blanche, d'Yquem.*

CHÂTEAUX PROFILES

I have valued these properties according to how they are currently performing; a five-star rating means you are getting a top-line taste – not just a well-known label. Some big names have been downgraded, some lesser-known properties are promoted – solely on the quality of the wine inside the bottle. A star in brackets shows that the wine can achieve the higher rating but does not always do so.

The £ sign shows which wines are offering particularly good value for money – although that does not mean any of these wines will exactly be cheap.

D'ARCHE *2ème cru Sauternes* ★★★(★) A little-known Sauternes property now beginning to make exciting wine after a long period of mediocrity. 1983, '86, '88, '89 and '90 are particularly good and show great promise for the future

BASTOR-LAMONTAGNE *cru bourgeois Sauternes* ★★★ £ Unclassified property making marvellous, widely available and easily affordable wines, as rich as many Classed Growths. 1981, '82, '83 and '86 epitomize high quality Sauternes at a remarkably fair price.

BROUSTET *2ème cru classé Barsac* ★★(★) A reliable, fairly rich wine, not often seen, but worth trying. The '88 and '90 are especially good, the dry white disappointing.

CABANNIEUX *Graves* ★★★ £ One of the new wave of non-classified Graves which is radically improving its white wine by the use of new oak barrels. The red is good, too. 1986, '88 and '89 show the way.

CARBONNIEUX *cru classé Pessac-Léognan* ★★★(★) This large property used to make decent enough old-style white that aged surprisingly well, but since 1988 they have been using 50 per cent new oak – and can you taste the difference! The 1990 is the best yet.

CLIMENS *1er cru Barsac* ★★★★★ Undoubtedly the best property in Barsac, making some of the most consistently fine sweet wines in France. 1983, '86, '88, '89 and '90 are all excellent. It also makes a delicious second wine called Les Cèdres that is well worth seeking out.

COUHINS-LURTON *cru classé Pessac-Léognan* ★★★★ 100 per cent Sauvignon dry white fermented in new oak barrels, producing a blend of grassy fruit and oaky spice. Recent vintages have been excellent.

COUTET *1er cru Barsac* ★★(★) A great property which in recent years has not been living up to its previous exacting standards.

DOISY-DAËNE *2ème cru Barsac* ★★★(★) A very good, consistent property providing relatively light, but extremely attractive sweet wine. Doisy-Daëne Sec is a particularly good dry white.

DOISY-VÉDRINES *2ème cru Barsac* ★★★★ £ A rich, concentrated wine, which is usually good value. 1980, '83, '86 and '89 are very good.

DOMAINE DE CHEVALIER ★★★★★ (for white). See Red Bordeaux.

DE FARGUES *cru bourgeois Sauternes* ★★★★(★) Small property owned by Yquem, capable of producing stunning, rich wines in the best years.

DE FIEUZAL ★★★★(★) The white is unclassified, but, with its burst of apricot fruit and spice, is one of Bordeaux's leading dry whites. See Red Bordeaux.

FILHOT *2ème cru Sauternes* ★★(★) Well-known Sauternes property producing pleasant but hardly memorable wines, though the 1988 looks a bit more hopeful.

GILETTE *cru bourgeois Sauternes* ★★★★ Remarkable property which ages its wines in concrete tanks for 20 to 30 years before releasing them. Usually delicious, with a dry richness unique in Sauternes thanks to long maturation and absence of wood. The 1955 and 1959 are heavenly, and only just released. Seriously!

GUIRAUD *1er cru Sauternes* ★★★★(★) Fine property owned since 1981 by a Canadian who has revolutionized the estate and brought the wines back to peak, and pricy, form. The wines are difficult to taste when young but are very special, and the 1983, '86, '88, '89 and '90 are going to be outstanding.

HAUT-BRION *cru classé Pessac-Léognan* ★★★★(★) Small quantities of very fine, long-lived wine, also appealing when young. See Red Bordeaux.

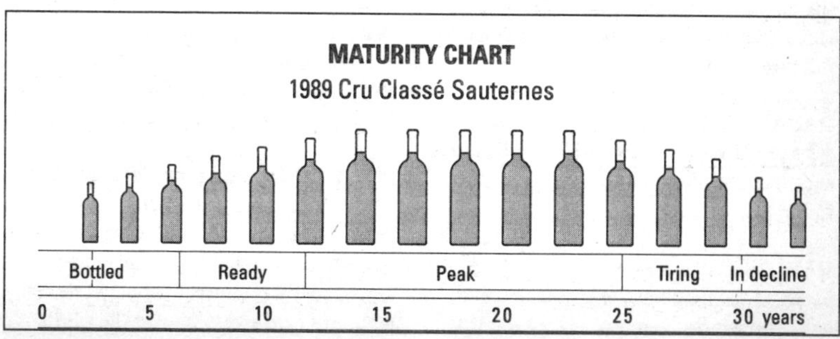

LAFAURIE-PEYRAGUEY *1er cru Sauternes* ★★★★(★) Fine property, returning to top form after a dull period in the 1960s and '70s. Remarkably good in the difficult years of '82, '84 and '85, it was stunning in '83, '86, '88, '89 and '90.

LAMOTHE-GUIGNARD *2ème cru Sauternes* ★★★ Since 1981 this previously undistinguished wine has dramatically improved. 1983, '86 and '88 show the improvement as will '89 and '90.

LAVILLE-HAUT-BRION *cru classé Pessac-Léognan* ★★★★ This should be one of the greatest of all white Pessac-Léognan, since it is owned by Haut-Brion, but despite some great successes, the general effect is patchy – especially given the crazy prices.

LA LOUVIÈRE *cru bourgeois Pessac-Léognan* ★★★★ This property has been making lovely, modern, oak-aged whites since the mid-70s but is only now achieving the acclaim it deserves. Since 1987, the quality has climbed even higher.

MALARTIC-LAGRAVIÈRE *cru classé Pessac-Léognan* ★★★(★) £ Tiny quantities of perfumed Sauvignon; recently more variable.

DE MALLE *2ème cru Sauternes* ★★★ Good, relatively light wine from a very beautiful property set partly in the Graves and partly in Sauternes. It went through a bad patch in the early and mid-'80s when the owner died after a long illness, but since '88 his widow has been making wines fully worthy of the name.

RABAUD-PROMIS *1er cru Sauternes* ★★★(★) At last! The 1986, '88 and '89 are excellent and show a long-awaited return to First Growth quality.

RAHOUL *cru bourgeois Graves* ★★★ A leader of the new wave of cool-fermented, oak-aged whites among the Graves properties, having an effect on all the growers in the region. Also increasingly good red. Ownership changes are worrying, though, and the '88, '89 and '90 were not as special as previous vintages, though still good. Domaine Benoit and Château Constantin also good in the same stable.

RAYMOND LAFON *cru bourgeois Sauternes* ★★★★ Owned by the former manager of neighbouring Yquem, this is fine wine but not quite as fine as the increasingly daunting price would imply.

RIEUSSEC *1er cru Sauternes* ★★★★(★) One of the richest, most exotic Sauternes, and particularly good wines during the 1980s. The 1982 is good, the '83, '86 and '88 really special, the '89 and '90 wonderful.

ST-AMAND *cru bourgeois Sauternes* ★★★(★) £ Splendid property making truly rich wines that age well, at an affordable price. Also seen as Château de la Chartreuse. Since the 1970s each decent vintage has produced a delicious example.

SMITH-HAUT-LAFITTE *cru classé Pessac-Léognan* ★★★★ A late convert to cool fermentation and oak-aging, but since 1985 making superb wines. Also increasingly good, and better-known, reds.

SUDUIRAUT *1er cru Sauternes* ★★★★ Rich, exciting wines, frequently deeper and more intensely perfumed than any other Sauternes – except for its neighbour, d'Yquem, but unfortunately not as reliable as it should be. A remarkable 1982 was followed by a fine '83, a very good '85 but slightly disappointing '86 and ditto in 1988. 1989 was a leap up again though.

D'YQUEM *1er grand cru classé Sauternes* ★★★★★ The pinnacle of achievement in great sweet wines. Almost every vintage is a masterpiece and its outlandish price is almost justified, since d'Yquem at its best is the greatest sweet wine in the world.

SWEET WHITE BORDEAUX VINTAGES

The 1980s brought Sauternes a share in the good fortune that was drenching the red wines of Bordeaux with great vintages. About time too, because 1983 created a much needed surge of interest in these remarkable, super-sweet wines and 1986, '88, '89 and '90 can continue it. The astonishing run of Indian summer vintages that saved red Bordeaux year after year from 1977 was not always so kind to Sauternes. In 1978 and 1981, the botrytis just didn't quite develop, and in 1982 the rains came at exactly the wrong time, diluting potentially perfect grapes. But the vintages of the late 1980s are more than making amends. It's worth remembering that Sauternes can be drunk very young or very old, depending entirely on whether you like the startlingly sweet shock of young wine or the deep, nutty, golden honey of older wines. The best can last a very long time. The *en primeur* prices have the wine merchants listing the best Barsac at around £250 a case and the finest Sauternes at over £300. But you can still find super 1983 and 1986 wines for half that price, so it's worth shopping around.

1992 A handful of châteaux managed to harvest some botrytized grapes in September, but most of the little wine that was made then will not be 'true' Sauternes but *passerillés,* wine made from ripe grapes which have not been attacked by the botrytis. The October rains washed the grapes so thoroughly and ensured that they would never attain the desired degree of over-ripeness. Oh dear.

1991 A very difficult year in Sauternes, as in the rest of Bordeaux. In Sauternes the impact of the frost was greatest on the Sémillon, leaving yet another source of imbalance in an overly high proportion of Sauvignon. Such wines as are being let onto the market are correct or better, but only Climens seems to have produced a stunner.

1990 The most extraordinary year in Sauternes since 1893. The weather was tropical, and the grapes were so ripe that when it rained heavily in late August the botrytis really took off, and there was no stopping it. Almost everybody (including Yquem, the most traditional and cautious of châteaux) started to pick in early September, earlier than in any year since... 1893.

The wines are so big and so varied, even within the same estate, as to be almost impossible to judge young — because no-one, even in Sauternes, has any point of comparison. Whether they will remain too big, rich and heavy to be truly enjoyable is possible, but I doubt it: they should all, the lesser wines as well as the classed growths, be treated as if they were old-style claret, to be left for a decade before being sampled. Then, I believe, they will prove to be the treat (though not, alas, the bargain) of a lifetime.

1989 A vintage that has not developed as in theory it should. The wines are rather dumb and sulky at the moment. Moreover they are turning out to be wildly inconsistent. In theory the growers who picked early – before the rains which set in on October 19 – did best. So stick to the stars – apart from Lafaurie-Peyraguey, which had an off-year.

1988 In 1988 every Sauternes and Barsac château and many in Cadillac, Loupiac and Ste-Croix-du-Mont, had the chance to make the greatest wine in a generation. It was a dry year and patience was needed while botrytis developed. Sadly, one or two leading properties were seen harvesting long before noble rot had run its full course. Many other producers went through the vines again and again, picking only the well rotted grapes: the wines are already destined to be classics.

1987 The rains came far too early this year, long before noble rot could get going on the grapes. Even so some pleasant, light wines were made, especially by those properties who used the cryoextraction method of freezing the grapes to concentrate what sugar there was. But some estates bottled no wine from this vintage.

➤

1986 Another marvellous year, when noble rot swept through the vineyards, and any proprietor who cared to could make great sweet wines. At the moment the best wines seem to be even better than 1983 and 1988 but it is notoriously difficult to judge young Sauternes, so I could well reverse my opinion in a year or two. By which time the '89s and '90s can join the debate.

1985 Quite pleasant lightish wines, but only a handful of outstanding wines from estates with the courage to wait for botrytis in a very dry year.

1983 Superbly rich, exciting wines to be ranked alongside 1986 and 1988, 1989 and 1990. Which vintage will finally turn out best is going to entail a large amount of comparative tasting over the next decade. What a jolly thought.

1981/80/79 Three attractive mid-weight vintages. The 1981s are a touch graceless, but the best 1980s have been underrated and will still improve.

1976 Fat, hefty, rich. Some haven't quite developed as hoped, but lots of 'lanolin' oiliness and lusciousness in those that have.

1975 Another lovely year. Not quite so utterly indulgent as 1976 but perhaps a little better balanced.

1971/70 Two fine years which need drinking up.

DRY WHITE BORDEAUX VINTAGES

Using cool fermentation, and a greater percentage of Sauvignon Blanc, many white Bordeaux are not now being made to age, but all Graves/Pessac-Léognan should be kept for at least two to three years, and the best 10 to 20 years.

1992 The growers in the Graves were lucky. They alone could take advantage of the rare spells of good weather in a generally disastrous year to bring in a decent crop of wines which are generally perfectly pleasant, albeit unremarkable. Unfortunately the French are snapping them up so you can't look for any real bargains. Nevertheless there are some serious well-structured wines, like Fieuzal, La Louvière, Smith-Haut-Lafitte and Domaine de Chevalier, though the latter was still woody.

1991 The April frost that damaged just about the whole of Bordeaux hit the Graves particularly badly, so there simply won't be much dry white from there that year. What there is, though, could be rather good: concentrated by the frost damage, and well-balanced. Try and get somebody else to buy it for you: it won't be cheap.

1990 Even hotter and drier than 1989, and considerably less successful. The Graves seems especially disappointing. No doubt there will be some good wines, but consumers will need to be very selective.

1989 Unlike 1988, the problem was with overripe rather than underripe grapes. Growers who picked early made crisp wines, but those who didn't will provide flabby drinking. In years to come the dry wines will inevitably be overshadowed by the sweet ones.

1988 Some of the 1988 dry whites lack a little oomph. The excessively dry summer retarded ripening and some producers picked grapes which were not totally ripe. Even so, most 1988s from good producers are delicious, and some are outstandingly good.

1987 All the grapes were safely in before the rains arrived. A slight lack of acidity has meant they have aged quite fast and even the top wines are already drinking well, although those from Pessac-Léognan can happily take further aging.

1986 Basic wines now tiring. Top line properties made outstanding wines which will last.

BURGUNDY

With sticky markets worldwide, falling prices and two good vintages or more still unsold in the cellar, the collective Burgundian gaze has this year been lifted from the region of its navel. Two of the most noticeable consequences of this have been a polarization of pricing, and the recognition that with so much good wine elsewhere, Burgundy doesn't sell automatically; you have to get out and market it.

So prices are falling? Well, yes and no. The answer is as fragmented and complex as the region itself. The 1992 Hospices de Beaune sale continued the decline of the previous two years. The 1989 peak prices had had much more to do with boom euphoria than with the inherent quality of the wines, and 1990 saw an overall drop of 25 per cent. In the following year prices slid a further 29 per cent and 1992 saw them fall 23 per cent again, by which time they were back to the levels of 1983. Does that mean we shall see similar percentage drop for bottles on the shelf? If only. Bidding at the Hospices signals a trend, but it is not a realistic guide to cost at the cellar door or on the retail shelf.

That said, many lesser quality Burgundies will be be perceptibly cheaper, for what is emerging from the recession is a much more marked price differential between the best and the rest.

The *négociants*, with considerable stocks left that they needed to move, led the way with significant price reductions at the bottom end of the range, and by November 1992 the price of many basic village wines was down by 50 per cent from the heights of 1989. Inevitably that stimulated sales and prices have moved up somewhat since then. But should you want to buy top quality you won't get away so easily: a 1990 village Meursault of Jobard's will cost you £21. There are now huge differences of price within an *appellation*; really good quality Burgundies have hardly moved in price at all, while the ordinary wines are a lot lower. And that differential is to be welcomed where it reflects and rewards real differences in quality. What used to be as frustrating for a grower committed to quality as for a punter looking for value was when *négociant* Meursault cost £14, a good grower's £17, and yet there was a world of difference between them. That made no sense at all. Unfortunately Britain has lost out on any price reductions of less than 20 per cent or so because of the weakness of the pound.

Vive la difference

More realistic price differentials are a part of the positive fallout from recession. But customers calling for (and producers obliging with) ever cheaper prices is a recipe for disaster. It encourages overproduction and discourages quality – which means that the wine is still seen as overpriced. The result is an image destroyed, and more custom for the New World. If any region should beware of this at the moment, it is the Mâconnais.

Simple pressure on cellar space is also generating a rare spirit of enterprise amongst the Burgundians. All of a sudden Burgundy is promoting itself generically, which is no mean achievement in a region where consensus is a rare commodity. While 1992's regional jollification, *Grand Jours de Bourgogne*, aimed at wooing the wine merchants and journalists, a new initiative this year targets any visiting wine-lover and gastronome. *Restaurants Bourgogne Découverte* will

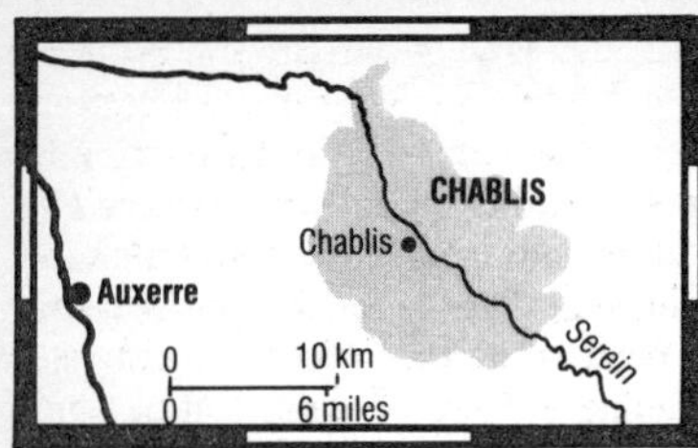

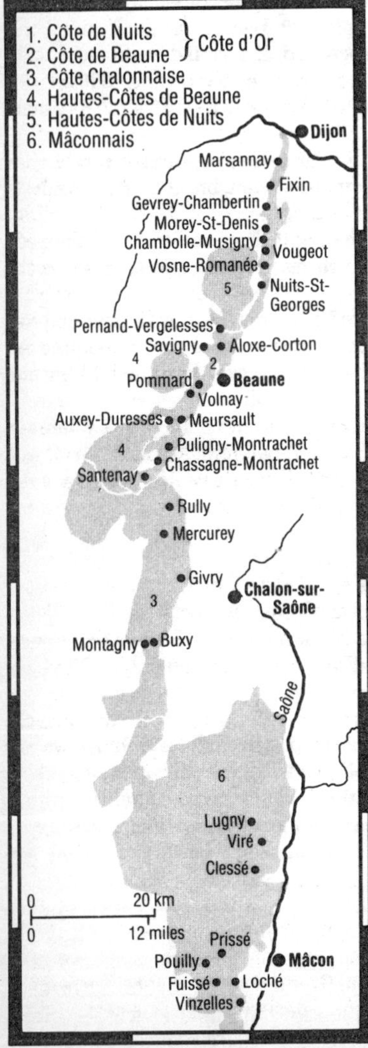

CLASSIFICATIONS

Burgundy has five different levels of classification:

Non-specific regional appellations with no geographical definition, e.g. Bourgogne, which may come from inferior land or young vines.

Specific regional appellations, e.g. Côte de Beaune-Villages, generally a blend from one or more villages. Côte de Nuits-Villages is usually better.

Village commune wines Each village has its vineyards legally defined. The village names are traditionally used for vineyards with no special reputation, which are thus usually blended together under the village name. But there is a growing move towards even relatively unknown vineyards appearing on the label. These unclassified vineyards are called *lieux-dits* or 'stated places'. They can only appear on the label in letters half the size of the village name.

Premier cru It's typical of Burgundy that *premier cru* or 'First Growth' actually means 'Second Growth', because these are the second best vineyard sites. Even so, they contain some of Burgundy's finest wines. They are classified by both village and vineyard names, e.g. Gevrey-Chambertin, Combe-aux-Moines. The vineyard name must follow the village name on the label, and it may be in the same size print. Confusingly, some growers use smaller print, but the appellation should make it clear whether it is a *premier cru* or a *lieu-dit*.

Grand cru These are the real top growths. Not every village has one. The reds are mostly in the Côte de Nuits, the whites in the Côte de Beaune. A *grand cru* vineyard name can stand alone on the label without the village – for example, Chambertin from the village of Gevrey-Chambertin. (By long tradition, a Burgundy village is allowed to tack on the name of its *grand cru* vineyard, and use the compound name for wines that have nothing to do with *grand cru*, for instance Puligny-Montrachet.)

run annually from April to November and the idea is to encourage the 200 or so participating restaurants to offer a red and white village Burgundy for between FF60 and FF100 a bottle (£7 to £12 at current rates) and a Grand Cru wine for FF200 to FF250 (£25 to £30), the producers having supplied their wines at a reduced price to the restaurants. (Details can be had from the B.I.V.B. Beaune; tel 010 33 80 24 70 20.) Chablis has also made itself more accessible to the visitor recently. A few years ago the town seemed closed to the outside world, with both information and producers practically impossible to locate. It is now well worth the detour. Individual producers are extremely well signposted throughout and there is a highly efficient source of information at the new Maison des Vins right in the centre of the town.

Nor are public relations limited to home ground. If a vintage of the quality of 1990 had appeared at the end of the eighties it would have largely sold itself; it is a reflection of hard times not only that it needed promoting, but also that there are still good stocks on merchants' lists.

It is our luck that a sluggish market allied to an unprecedented run of good vintages means there is a comparatively large amount of good Burgundy to choose from at the moment. And 1992 looks like being yet another excellent vintage. The whites, where not overcropped, will be first rate, and the reds promise a great deal of supple, fruity charm. As the vintage in between the excellent 1990 and 1992, 1991 risks becoming something of a cinderella, especially as it was overpriced to begin with. It is an extremely irregular year, but there are some beautiful wines to be had. And then among the reds there are still the exceptional 1990s to be found, 1988s for the long haul and 1989s and some delightful 1987s for the shorter term.

Get hold of the specialist mail order lists: Adnams, Lay and Wheeler, Tanners, Morris & Verdin, Justerini and Brooks, Bibendum, Adam Bancroft and Domaine Direct. British Burgundy lovers have rarely had such a good opportunity to buy.

RED WINES

When it comes to Pinot Noir, Burgundy still has a more or less captive audience. A few strikingly successful Pinot Noirs from New Zealand, California and Oregon do not constitute much of a threat to this particular slice of Gallic pride.

Current consumer thrift, however, doesn't allow for the purchase of much top notch red Burgundy, great vintages notwithstanding, so happily for us we are seeing many more bottles of basic Bourgogne Rouge from top growers. At somewhere between £9 and £12 they may not be exactly bargain basement stuff, but when they are from the likes of Domaine de la Pousse d'Or, Ghislaine Barthod, Denis Bachelet, Lejeune, Patrice Rion and many others they are probably the only affordable way of sampling Burgundy's best wine-making.

In a similar price bracket there are increasingly good wines to be had from dedicated growers in less illustrious *terroirs*. Michel Juillot and Antonin Rodet in Mercurey, Gérard Mouton and Domaine Joblot in Givry, Claude Maréchale, Simon Bize and Jean-Marc Pavelot in Savigny, for example, are making wines of Burgundian Pinot flavour and character at a price that makes such pleasure a much more regular prospect. And for a real bargain (well, a relative bargain: we are talking Burgundy) the Igé cooperative's Bourgogne Pinot Noir, Cuvée Futs de Chêne at under £8 (from Lay & Wheeler) is hard to beat. I am not normally a fan of Pinot from the Mâconnais, but this is intelligent wine-making, with plenty of sweet, cherry fruit there to support the oak; both the 1989 and 1990 were particularly successful.

Leap in the dark

The consultant Guy Accad, much of whose advice on both viticulture and wine-making is uncontroversial, continues to divide Burgundian opinion over his use of long periods of cold maceration and heavy doses of sulphur dioxide before fermentation. The idea is that better quality tannins and aromas are extracted from the skins by water plus sulphur dioxide before they ferment than by alcohol during and after fermentation. When young the Accad wines are very dark in colour and exceptionally sweet on the nose; to many they seem atypical Burgundy, and the same critics have grave doubts as to their quality when mature. The wines are controversial precisely because many of the domaines that use him are of considerable standing (Senard, Grivot, Pernin-Rossin, Confuron-Cotetidot, Château de la Tour) and their owners would not have undertaken to follow his methods lightly. There is no question that Accad has been behind the making of many fine wines, and as he claims to be making wines for the long term I think the final jury will be out until the late nineties.

Meanwhile, some 'returns to form' worth noting are those of the *négociant* Champy, and the two great domaines of Chandon de Briailles and Jacques Prieur. After a long period of indifferent wine-making, new management made splendid 1990s at all three. Long may they continue. **MICHAEL SCHUSTER**

GRAPES & FLAVOURS

PINOT NOIR The sulkiest, trickiest fine wine grape in the world is the exclusive grape in almost all red Burgundies. It needs a more delicate balance of spring, summer and autumn climate than any other variety to achieve greatness, and one Burgundian maxim is that you must have unripe grapes, ripe grapes and rotten grapes in equal parts to achieve that astonishing part-rotted, part-perfumed, and part-ethereal flavour.

It used to be true to say that no other part of the world could produce a Pinot Noir to match those of Burgundy. But isolated growers in Oregon, California, New Zealand, Australia and South Africa are now making very fine examples. Even so, Burgundy is still the only place on earth where fine Pinot Noirs abound. The problem is, awful Pinot Noirs abound too, heavy, chewy and sweet-fruited or thin and pallid. Good Burgundian Pinot Noir should generally be *light*, fragrant, marvellously perfumed with cherry and strawberry fruit, sometimes meatier, sometimes intensely spicy, but, as a rule, *light*. It needs time to mature, but it can be delicious young.

GAMAY Most Burgundy has by law to be 100 per cent Pinot Noir, but the Gamay (the Beaujolais grape) can be used in wines labelled 'Burgundy' or 'Bourgogne' which come from the Mâconnais and the Beaujolais regions, or from elsewhere in Burgundy in wines labelled 'Bourgogne Passe-Tout-Grain', 'Bourgogne Grand Ordinaire' or 'Mâcon'.

WINES & WINE REGIONS

ALOXE-CORTON, AC (Côte de Beaune) Ten years ago, this village at the northern end of the Côte de Beaune was the best of all buys for full-flavoured, balanced Burgundy. Most recent Aloxe-Corton has been pale stuff indeed. Its production is overwhelmingly red, and it has the only red Grand Cru in the Côte de Beaune, Le Corton, which is also sold under various subdivisions like Corton-Bressandes, Corton Clos du Roi and so forth, and is seen on the market rather more frequently than one might expect a Grand Cru to be. Go for *Jadot, Drouhin, Jaffelin* and *Tollot-Beaut*. Also good are the following: *Chandon de Briailles, Dubreuil Fontaine, Faiveley, Juillot, Daniel Senard, Michel Voarick, Bouzerot-Gruère*.

AUXEY-DURESSES, AC (Côte de Beaune) Backwoods village with a reputation for full, but fairly gentle, nicely fruity reds. After a slump in the early '80s there have been excellent wines made recently by a handful of good growers, especially in the years from 1987 to 1990. Look for *Ampeau, Diconne, Alain Gras, Duc de Magenta, Leroy, Roy, Prunier* and *Thévenin*.

BEAUNE, AC (Côte de Beaune) One of the few reliable commune wines, usually quite light, with a soft, 'red fruits' sweetness and a flicker of something minerally to smarten it up nicely. The wines are nearly all red. Beaune has the largest acreage of vines of any Côte d'Or commune, and they are mostly owned by merchants. It has no Grands Crus but many excellent Premiers Crus, for example Grèves, Marconnets, Teurons, Boucherottes, Vignes Franches and Cent Vignes. In general, the 1983s were better than elsewhere, the 1986s a bit light but the 1987s much better and the '88s, '89s and '90s outstanding. The best growers are *Lafarge* and *Morot,* and good wines are made by *Besancenot-Mathouillet, Drouhin, Germain, Jadot, Jaffelin, Morey, Tollot-Beaut*.

BLAGNY, AC (Côte de Beaune) Tiny hamlet on the boundary between Meursault and Puligny-Montrachet. The red wine is usually a bit fierce, but then this is white wine heartland, so I'm a bit surprised they grow any red at all. Best producers: *Leflaive, Matrot*.

BONNES-MARES, AC (Côte de Nuits) Grand Cru of 15.54 hectares mostly in Chambolle-Musigny, with a little in Morey-St-Denis. Usually one of the most – or should I say one of the very few – reliable Grands Crus, which ages extremely well over 10 to 20 years to a lovely smoky, chocolate and prunes richness. Best names: *Domaine des Varoilles, Drouhin, Dujac, Groffier, Jadot, Roumier, de Vogüé*.

BOURGOGNE GRAND ORDINAIRE, AC Très Ordinaire. Pas Très Grand. Rarely seen outside Burgundy, this is the bottom of the Burgundy barrel. It may be made from Pinot Noir and Gamay, and even a couple of obscure grapes, the Tressot and César, as well.

BOURGOGNE PASSE-TOUT-GRAIN, AC Often excellent value, lightish wine made usually in the Côte d'Or or the Côte Chalonnaise from Gamay blended with a minimum of one-third Pinot Noir. In some years it may well be mostly Pinot. *Rodet* and *Chanson* make it well, but as usual, the growers make it best, particularly in the less famous Côte d'Or and Hautes-Côtes villages; *Rion* in Nuits-St-Georges, *Léni-Volpato* in Chambolle-Musigny, *Henri Jayer* in Vosne-Romanée, *Thomas* in St-Aubin, *Chaley* or *Cornu* in the Hautes-Côtes, and many others like them.

BOURGOGNE ROUGE, AC The basic red AC from Chablis in the North to the Beaujolais *crus* in the South. Unknown Bourgogne Rouge is best avoided – much of it is very basic indeed. Most Bourgogne Rouge is made exclusively from Pinot Noir, but Gamay can be used in the Beaujolais (if declassified from one of the ten *crus*) and Mâconnais, and the César and Tressot are permitted in the Yonne around Chablis. Wine from the ten Beaujolais *crus* can be declassified and sold as Bourgogne – and *that* should generally be from the Gamay grape alone. Domaine-bottled Bourgogne Rouge from good growers can be excellent value. Look out for those of *Bourgeon, Coche Dury, Germain, d'Heuilly-Huberdeau, Henri Jayer, Juillot, Lafarge, Mortet, Parent, Pousse d'Or, Rion* and *Rossignol*. Good merchants include *Drouhin, Faiveley, Jadot, Jaffelin, Labouré-Roi, Latour, Olivier Leflaive, Leroy, Rodet, Vallet*. The co-ops at *Buxy* and *Igé* are also good as is the *Caves des Hautes-Côtes*. Their 1987s are still good now; their 1988s and 1989s are better, and their '90s will be best of all.

CHAMBERTIN, AC (Côte de Nuits) Most famous of the eight Grands Crus of Gevrey-Chambertin, this 13-hectare vineyard should make wines that are big, strong and intense in their youth, mellowing to a complex, perfumed, plummy richness as they mature. Good ones need 10 to 15 years' aging. Best producers: *Drouhin, Faiveley, Leroy, Mortet, Ponsot, Rebourseau, Rousseau, Tortochot*.

CHAMBERTIN CLOS-DE-BÈZE, AC (Côte de Nuits) Grand Cru in the village of Gevrey-Chambertin next to Chambertin both geographically and in quality. Can keep ten years in a good vintage. The wines may also be sold as Chambertin. 1988, 1989 and 1990 are tops. Best names: *Drouhin, Bruno Clair, Faiveley, Gelin, Mugneret-Gibourg, Rousseau*.

CHAMBOLLE-MUSIGNY, AC (Côte de Nuits) This village towards the southern end of the Côte de Nuits can make light, cherry-sweet, intensely perfumed, 'beautiful' Burgundy, but sadly most commercial Chambolle will be too sweet and gooey to retain much perfume. The best producer is *Georges Roumier*, with wonderful wines in every vintage since 1985. For other producers the years to go for are 1988 and '90: *Barthod-Noëllat, Château de Chambolle-Musigny, Drouhin, Dujac, Groffier, Hudelot-Noëllat, Rion, Serveau, Volpato-Costaille, de Vogüé.*

CHAPELLE-CHAMBERTIN, AC (Côte de Nuits) Small Grand Cru vineyard (5.4 hectares) just south of the Clos-de-Bèze in Gevrey-Chambertin. Typically lighter and more delicate than the other Grands Crus. But over-lightness – from over-production – is their curse. Best producer: *Jadot.*

CHARMES-CHAMBERTIN, AC (Côte de Nuits) At 31.6 hectares, this is the biggest of the Grands Crus of Gevrey-Chambertin. It can be fine, strong, sensuous wine, but as with all the Gevrey-Chambertin Grands Crus, it can also be disgracefully light. Best producers: *Bachelet, Drouhin, Rebourseau, Roty, Rousseau, Tortochot.*

CHASSAGNE-MONTRACHET, AC (Côte de Beaune) Down in the south of the Côte de Beaune, about half the wine Chassagne-Montrachet produces is red, even though its fame lies in its large share of the white Grand Cru Le Montrachet. The reds are a puzzle. I'm often disappointed by their rather hot plumskins and chewy earth flavours, yet because the price is keen, I keep coming back for more. Best names: *Bachelet-Ramonet, Carillon, Colin, Jean-Noël Gagnard, Duc de Magenta, Gagnard-Delagrange, Albert Morey, Moreau, Fernand Pillot, Ramonet-Prudhon.*

CHOREY-LÈS-BEAUNE, AC (Côte de Beaune) Good lesser village near Beaune, not expensive for soft, fruity reds. Because the village isn't popular, these are some of the few affordable wines in top vintages such as 1988, 1989 and 1990. *Germain* and *Tollot-Beaut* are the best producers.

CLOS DE LA ROCHE, AC (Côte de Nuits) Largest and finest Grand Cru of Morey-St-Denis, on the border with

Gevrey-Chambertin. When not made too lightweight, this can be splendid wine, full of redcurrant-and-strawberry richness when young, but coming to resemble pretty good Chambertin after ten years or so. Best names: *Amiot, Dujac, Leroy,* both *Hubert* and *Georges Lignier, Ponsot, Rousseau.*

CLOS DES LAMBRAYS, AC (Côte de Nuits) A Grand Cru only since 1981, this nine-hectare vineyard in Morey-St-Denis belongs to a single family (*Saier*), unusual in Burgundy. In the 1970s the estate became very run down and the wines were not only very rare but also not very tasty. Wholesale replanting in 1979 means that no real style has yet emerged, but old-timers say that the Clos des Lambrays could potentially make one of Burgundy's finest, most fragrant reds.

CLOS DE TART, AC (Côte de Nuits) Grand Cru of Morey-St-Denis owned by Beaujolais merchants *Mommessin*. At its best Clos de Tart is a light but intense wine which lasts a surprisingly long time.

CLOS DE VOUGEOT, AC (Côte de Nuits) This 50-hectare vineyard dominates the village of Vougeot. Over 80 growers share the enclosure and, while the land at the top is very fine, the land by the road is not. That rare thing, a good bottle of Clos de Vougeot, is fat, rich, strong, thick with the sweetness of perfumed plums and honey, unsubtle but exciting. It is only found in top vintages, like 1988 and 1990. Best names: *Arnoux, Château de la Tour, Jacky Confuron, Drouhin-Laroze, Engel, Grivot, Gros, Hudelot-Noëllat, Jadot, Lamarche, Leroy, Mugneret, Raphet, Rebourseau.*

CLOS ST-DENIS, AC (Côte de Nuits) The village of Morey-St-Denis gets its name from this Grand Cru but the villagers probably should have chosen another one – like the much better known Clos de la Roche – because this small 6.5 hectare vineyard has rarely achieved great heights and is probably the least known of all the Grands Crus. I'd give my vote to *Georges* or *Hubert Lignier,* or *Ponsot,* though *Dujac* is the best known.

LE CORTON, AC (Côte de Beaune) The only red Grand Cru in the Côte de Beaune, on the upper slopes of the famous dome-shaped hill of Corton. Ideally, Corton should have something of the savoury strength of Vosne-Romanée to the north, and something of the mouth-watering, caressing sweetness of Beaune to the south, but the wines labelled Corton have been strangely insubstantial in recent vintages, and wines from subdivisions of Le Corton such as Corton-Pougets, Corton-Bressandes and Corton Clos du Roi more regularly reach this ideal. Best producers: *Chandon de Briailles, Dubreuil-Fontaine, Faiveley, Gaunoux, Laleur-Piot, Maldant, Prince de Mérode, Quenot, Rapet, Ravaux, Reine Pédauque, Daniel Senard, Tollot-Beaut, Michel Voarick.*

CÔTE CHALONNAISE, AC The area immediately south of the Côte d'Or, the full name of which is Bourgogne Rouge (or Blanc) Côte Chalonnaise. The vineyards come in pockets rather than in one long swathe, but the top three villages of Rully, Mercurey and Givry all produce good wines, with a lovely, simple strawberry-and-cherry fruit.

CÔTE DE BEAUNE The southern part of the Côte d'Or, fairly evenly divided between red and white wines. There is a tiny AC Côte de Beaune which can produce light but tasty reds in warm years. Best producers: *Bouchard Père et Fils, René Manuel, J Alexant.*

CÔTE DE BEAUNE-VILLAGES, AC Catch-all red wine *appellation* for 16 villages on the Côte de Beaune. Only Aloxe-Corton, Beaune, Volnay and Pommard cannot use the *appellation*. Rarely seen nowadays and rarely exciting, it used to be the source of much excellent soft red, as many lesser-known but good villages would blend their wines together. Still, it *is* worth checking out the wines of *Jaffelin, Lequin-Roussot* and *Bachelet*.

CÔTE DE NUITS The northern part of the Côte d'Or, theoretically producing the biggest wines. Frequently it doesn't and many of Burgundy's most disappointing bottles come from the top Côte de Nuits communes. It is almost entirely devoted to Pinot Noir.

CÔTE DE NUITS-VILLAGES, AC Covers the three southernmost villages of Prissey, Comblanchien and Corgoloin, plus Fixin and Brochon in the North. Usually fairly light and dry, they can have good cherry fruit and the slightly rotting veg delicious decay of good Côte de Nuits red. Look out for *Durand, Rion, Rossignol* and *Tollot-Voarick*, and especially *Chopin-Groffier*.

CÔTE D'OR The source of Burgundy's fame – a thin sliver of land only 30 miles long, and often less than a mile wide, running from Dijon to Chagny. It has two halves, the Côte de Nuits in the North and the Côte de Beaune in the South.

ÉCHÉZEAUX, AC (Côte de Nuits) Large, (relatively) unexciting Grand Cru of Vosne-Romanée. Best producers: *Domaine de la Romanée-Conti, Engel, Faiveley, Louis Gouroux, Grivot, Henri Jayer, Lamarche, Mongeard-Mugneret, René Mugneret*.

EPINEUIL, AC Tiny region near Tonnerre, producing light but fragrant styles of Pinot Noir.

FIXIN, AC (Côte de Nuits) A suburb of Dijon, Fixin can make some of Burgundy's sturdiest reds, deep, strong, tough but plummy when young, but capable of mellowing with age. Such wines are slowly reappearing. If you want to feel you're drinking Gevrey-Chambertin without shouldering the cost, Fixin from the following producers could fit the bill: *Bordet, Charlopin-Parizot, Bruno Clair, Fougeray, Gelin, Joliet, Moillard, Guyard*.

THE COST OF A BOTTLE

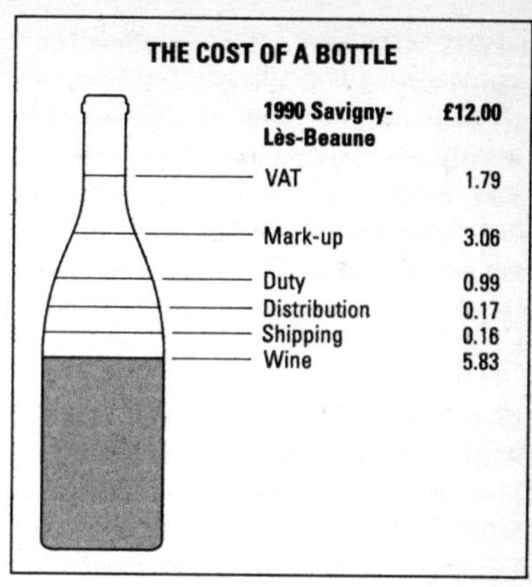

1990 Savigny-Lès-Beaune	**£12.00**
VAT	1.79
Mark-up	3.06
Duty	0.99
Distribution	0.17
Shipping	0.16
Wine	5.83

FLAGEY-ÉCHÉZEAUX, AC (Côte de Nuits) Commune that sells its basic wines as Vosne-Romanée but, in Échézeaux and Grands-Échézeaux, has two Grands Crus.

GEVREY-CHAMBERTIN, AC (Côte de Nuits) The start of the big time for reds. Gevrey-Chambertin has eight Grands Crus, and two of them, Chambertin and Chambertin Clos-de-Bèze can be some of the world's greatest wines. They should have rough, plumskins and damson strength, fierce when young, but assuming a brilliant, wafting perfume and intense, plummy richness when mature. Many of the best wines are made by young growers who do not own as much land in the top vineyards as the larger, old-established estates, but whose commitment to quality shines through. *Bachelet, Boillot, Burguet, Michel Esmonin, Philippe Leclerc, Mortet, Naddef* and *Rossignol* are the names to look out for. Of the old estates, *Rousseau* is best but *Domaine des Varoilles* is also good. Also look out for *Frédéric Esmonin, René Leclerc, Maume* and *Roty*, and for the merchants' bottlings, *Drouhin, Jadot, Faiveley* and *Jaffelin*.

GIVRY, AC (Côte Chalonnaise) Small but important red wine village. At its best, deliciously warm and cherry-chewy with a slightly smoky fragrance but there are too many mediocre bottles around, especially from *négociants*. *Baron Thénard* is the best estate, but *Chofflet, Clos Salomon, Joblot, Lespinasse, Mouton* and *Ragot* are also worth investigating.

LA GRANDE RUE, AC (Côte de Nuits) Wholly owned by the Lamarche family. Elevated to Grand Cru status in 1990, more because of its potential – it is situated between La Tâche and La Romanée-Conti, the two greatest vineyards in Burgundy – than because of the wines it has recently produced.

GRANDS ÉCHÉZEAUX, AC (Côte de Nuits) A slightly second-line Grand Cru, but capable of delicately scented, plum-and-wood-smoke flavoured wine which will go rich and chocolaty with age. Best names: *Domaine de la Romanée-Conti, Drouhin, Engel, Lamarche, Mongeard-Mugneret*.

GRIOTTE-CHAMBERTIN, AC (Côte de Nuits) One of the smallest Grands Crus of Gevrey-Chambertin – 5.58 hectares. Best producers: *Drouhin, Ponsot, Roty*.

HAUTES-CÔTES DE BEAUNE and **HAUTES-CÔTES DE NUITS** A happy hunting ground, this hilly backwater behind the line of famous villages and vineyards on the Côte d'Or. The 28 Hautes-Côtes villages make fairly good, light, strawberry-like Pinot at a decent price. The grapes do not always ripen fully every year, but they had no problems in 1988, '89 or '90. Look out for the Hautes-Côtes de Nuits wines of *Cornu, Domaine des Mouchottes, Jayer-Gilles, Thévenet* and *Verdet* and the Hautes-Côtes de Beaunes of *Bouley, Capron Manieux, Chalet, Guillemard, Joliot, Mazilly* and *Plait*. The *Caves des Hautes-Côtes* is beginning to produce some of the best value reds in the whole of Burgundy.

IRANCY, AC Mostly Pinot Noir from vineyards just to the south-west of Chablis, sometimes with a little of the darker, tougher local grape, the César. Rarely deep in colour, but always perfumed, slightly plummy and attractive, good at two years old and usually capable of aging several years more. It must legally be labelled 'Bourgogne Irancy'. Good producers: *Léon & Serge Bienvenu, Bernard Cantin, André & Roger Delaloge, Gabriel Delaloge, Jean Renaud, Simmonet-Febvre, Luc Sorin*.

LADOIX-SERRIGNY, AC (Côte de Beaune) An obscure village, overshadowed by Aloxe-Corton next door. Worth looking out for though, as *Capitain, Cornu, Prince de Mérode, Chevalier* and *Ravaut* all make decent, crisp wines at very fair prices.

LATRICIÈRES-CHAMBERTIN, AC (Côte de Nuits) Small Grand Cru vineyard in Gevrey-Chambertin and very similar in style to Chambertin though without the power. So long as the producer hasn't pushed the yields too high, it is at its best at 10 to 15 years. Best producers: *Camus, Ponsot, Leroy, Rossignol-Trapet*.

MÂCON ROUGE, AC There's a lot of red wine made in the Mâconnais but it's usually fairly lean, earthy Gamay without the spark of Beaujolais' fruit. If you like that sort of thing, try the wines of *Igé* and *Mancey*, or *Lafarge*'s wine from *Bray*. *Lassarat* is improving things by using new oak, and I'm sure more will follow.

MARSANNAY, AC (Côte de Nuits) This used to produce mostly pink wines, under the name Bourgogne Rosé de Marsannay, but the introduction of an *appellation* for red wines in 1987 has encouraged growers to switch from pink to red. The first results of this new seriousness are most encouraging and some lovely wines are already emerging, usually quite dry and cherry-perfumed, sometimes much more full-blown and exciting. One to watch. Best producers: *Bouvier, Charlopin-Parizot, Bruno Clair, Collotte, Fougeray, Fournier, Geantet-Pansiot, Huguenot, Jadot, Naddef.*

MAZIS-CHAMBERTIN, AC (Côte de Nuits) 12.5 hectare Grand Cru in Gevrey-Chambertin, far more reliable than most of the neighbouring Grands Crus. Mazis wines can have a superb deep blackberry-pip, damson-skin and blackcurrant fruit which gets deeper and more exciting after six to twelve years. Best producers: *Faiveley, Hospices de Beaune, Maume, Rebourseau, Roty, Rousseau, Tortochot.*

MAZOYÈRES-CHAMBERTIN, AC (Côte de Nuits) Grand Cru of Gevrey-Chambertin, rarely seen since producers generally take up the option of using the Grand Cru Charmes-Chambertin instead.

MERCUREY, AC (Côte Chalonnaise) The biggest Chalonnais village, producing half the region's wines. Indeed many call the Côte Chalonnaise the 'Région de Mercurey'. It's mostly red wines, and they are often fairly full, with attractive strawberry fruit and a little smoky fragrance. As with the other Chalonnais reds, Mercurey's problems are infuriating inconsistency of quality, allied to callous exploitation of the name by some *négociants*. *Château de Chamirey, Chandesais, Chanzy, Domaine La Marche, Dufouleur, Faiveley, Jacqueson, Juillot, de Launay, Meix-Foulot, Monette, Antonin Rodet, Saier* and *de Suremain* are all good.

MONTHÉLIE, AC (Côte de Beaune) Monthélie shares borders with Volnay and Meursault, but fame with neither. It's a red wine village, and the wines deserve recognition, because they're full, dry, rather herby or piney, but with a satisfying rough fruit. Often a good buy but beware the insidious growth of *négociants'* labels from firms who never traditionally noticed the AC. Best producers: *Boussey, Caves des Hautes-Côtes, Deschamps, Doreau, Garaudet, Château de Monthélie, Monthélie-Douhairet, Potinet-Ampeau, de Suremain, Thévenin-Monthélie.*

MOREY-ST-DENIS, AC (Côte de Nuits) Once obscure and good value, the wines of Morey-St-Denis are now expensive and in general suffer badly from overproduction and over-sugaring. They should have less body and more perfume than Gevrey-Chambertin, and slight savouriness blending with rich, chocolaty fruit as they age. Most are too light, but there are some outstanding growers. *Pierre Amiot, Bryczek, Dujac, Georges* and *Hubert Lignier, Marchand, Ponsot, Serveau, Charloppin, Perrot-Minot* and *Vadey-Castagnier*. Their 1987s, '88s, '89s and '90s are all excellent.

MUSIGNY, AC (Côte de Nuits) Extremely fine Grand Cru which gave its name to Chambolle-Musigny. All but a third of a hectare of the 10.65 hectare vineyard is red, capable of producing Burgundy's most heavenly-scented wine, but few recent offerings have had me lunging for my cheque book. Best names include: *Château de Chambolle-Musigny, Jadot, Leroy, Jacques Prieur, Georges Roumier, de Vogüé.*

NUITS-ST-GEORGES, AC (Côte de Nuits) When it's good, this has an enthralling decayed – rotting even – brown richness of chocolate and prunes rising out of a fairly light, plum-sweet fruit – quite gorgeous, whatever it sounds like. It used to be one of the most abused of all Burgundy's names and virtually disappeared from the export markets, but is now fairly common, expensive but immeasurably better, and increasingly reliable. From companies such as *Jadot, Jaffelin, Labouré-Roi* and *Moillard*, it's even becoming possible to buy good merchants' Nuits once more. *Labouré-Roi*

The price guides for this section begin on page 290.

is the most consistent merchant, although *Moillard* and *Jadot* are increasingly good particularly at Premier Cru level. The most famous growers are *Robert Chaillon, Gouges, Michelot* and *Daniel Rion,* but excellent wines are also made by *Domaine de l'Arlot, Ambroise, Chicotot, Jean-Jacques Confuron* and the amazing (and amazingly expensive) *Leroy.* There were problems with rot in 1986 and with hail in 1987 so it is best to stick to top vintages such as 1985, '88, '89 and '90.

PERNAND-VERGELESSES, AC (Côte de Beaune) Little-known village round the back of the hill of Corton. Some quite attractive, softly earthy reds, mostly on the lean side. *Besancenot-Mathouillet, Caves des Hautes-Côtes, Chandon des Briailles, Delarche, Dubreuil-Fontaine, Laleure-Piot, Pavelot, Rapet* and *Rollin* are the best producers.

POMMARD, AC (Côte de Beaune) From good producers, Pommard can have a strong, meaty sturdiness, backed by slightly jammy but attractively plummy fruit. Not subtle, but many people's idea of what red Burgundy should be. The most consistently fine wines are made by *de Courcel* and *de Montille,* but also look out for the wines of *Billard-Gonnet, Boillot, Château de Pommard, Girardin, Lahaye, Lejeune, Jean Monnier, Mussy, Parent, Pothier* and *Pousse d'Or.*

RICHEBOURG, AC (Côte de Nuits) Exceptional Grand Cru at the northern end of the commune of Vosne-Romanée. It's a wonderful name for a wine – Richebourg – and, at its best, it manages to be fleshy to the point of fatness, yet filled with spice and perfume and the clinging richness of chocolate and figs. Best producers: *Domaine de la Romanée-Conti, Gros, Henri Jayer, Leroy, Méo-Camuzet.*

LA ROMANÉE, AC (Côte de Nuits) This Grand Cru is the smallest AC in France, solely owned by the Liger-Belair family and sold by *Bouchard Père et Fils*. It is usually adequate, but nowhere near the quality of the next-door vineyards owned by the *Domaine de la Romanée-Conti.*

LA ROMANÉE-CONTI, AC (Côte de Nuits) This tiny Grand Cru of almost two hectares is capable of a more startling brilliance than any other Burgundy. The 7000 or so bottles it produces per year are seized on by the super-rich before we mere mortals can even get our tasting sheets out. It is wholly owned by the *Domaine de la Romanée-Conti.*

LA ROMANÉE-ST-VIVANT, AC (Côte de Nuits) 9.54 hectare Grand Cru in the village of Vosne-Romanée. Far less easy to taste young than its neighbouring Grands Crus and needs a good 12 years to show what can be a delicious, savoury yet sweet personality. Best names: *Arnoux, Domaine de la Romanée-Conti, Latour, Leroy.*

RUCHOTTES-CHAMBERTIN, AC (Côte de Nuits) The smallest Gevrey-Chambertin Grand Cru at 3.1 hectares, with wines of deeper colour and longer-lasting perfumed richness than most of the village's other Grands Crus. Best producers: *Georges Mugneret, Roumier, Rousseau.*

RULLY, AC (Côte Chalonnaise) Village just a couple of miles below Santenay, initially known for its sparkling wine, but gradually gaining a reputation for light but tasty reds and whites. Best producers: *Chanzy, Château de Rully, Delorme, Domaine de la Folie, Duvernay, Faiveley, Jacqueson, Jaffelin.*

ST-AUBIN, AC (Côte de Beaune) Some of Burgundy's best value wines, especially from *Bachelet, Clerget, Lamy, Prudhon, Thomas* and *Roux*. The 1988s, 1989s and 1990s are delicious and reasonably priced.

ST-ROMAIN, AC (Côte de Beaune) Even more out of the way than St-Aubin. Full, rather broad-flavoured, cherry-stone dry reds. On the whole sold cheaper than they deserve. Look for *Bazenet, Buisson, Gras, Thévenin* and *Thévenin-Monthélie*. Go for top vintages such as 1985, '88 and '90.

SANTENAY, AC (Côte de Beaune) Rough and ready red. At its best, with a strong, savoury flavour and good strawberry fruit, though frequently nowadays rather lean and mean. Best producers include: *Belland, Girardin, Lequin-Roussot, Morey, Pousse d'Or, Prieur-Bonnet, Roux*. Even here, there can be a lot of variation.

SAVIGNY-LÈS-BEAUNE, AC (Côte de Beaune) Not renowned, but pretty reliable reds. Rarely very full, but with an attractive earthiness backing up strawberry fruit. Often good quality at a fair price. Look out for *Bize, Camus-Bruchon, Capron-Manieux, Chandon de Briailles, Ecard-Guyot, de Fougeray, Girard-Vollot, Guillemot, Pavelot-Glantenay* and *Tollot-Beaut*. The 1985s, '87s and even some '89s are drinking well now; the '88s and '90s need a while longer.

LA TÂCHE, AC (Côte de Nuits) Another Grand Cru monopoly of the *Domaine de la Romanée-Conti*. As famous as Romanée-Conti, but not so totally unobtainable, since the 6.06 hectare vineyard can produce all of 24,000 bottles a year – that's two bottles each for the world's 12,000 richest people. The wine is heavenly, so rich and heady the perfumes are sometimes closer to age-old brandy than table wine and the flavour loaded with spice and dark autumn-mellow fruits and the acrid richness of dark chocolate.

VOLNAY, AC (Côte de Beaune) Volnay is one of the most perfumed red Burgundies, with a memorable cherry and strawberry spice, but also, in its Premiers Crus, able to turn on a big, meaty style without losing the perfume. The best at the moment are *Lafarge* and *de Montille*. Their 1985s, '88s, '89s and '90s are superb. Other good names: *Ampeau, Blain-Gagnard, Boillot, Bouley, Clerget, Comtes Lafon, Delagrange, Glantenay, Marquis d'Angerville, Pousse d'Or, Vaudoisey-Mutin, Voillot*.

VOSNE-ROMANÉE, AC (Côte de Nuits) The greatest Côte de Nuits village, right in the south of the Côte. Its Grands Crus sell for more money than any red wine on earth, except for Château Pétrus in Bordeaux, and, remarkably for Burgundy, they are dominated by a single estate, *Domaine de la Romanée Conti*. These vineyards make wines capable of more startling brilliance than any other red wine in France, with flavours as disparate yet as intense as the overpowering, creamy savouriness of fresh *foie gras* and the deep, sweet scent of ripe plums and prunes in brandy. You may need to re-mortgage your house in order to experience this though. There are also fine Premiers Crus, and the village wines, though not so reliable as

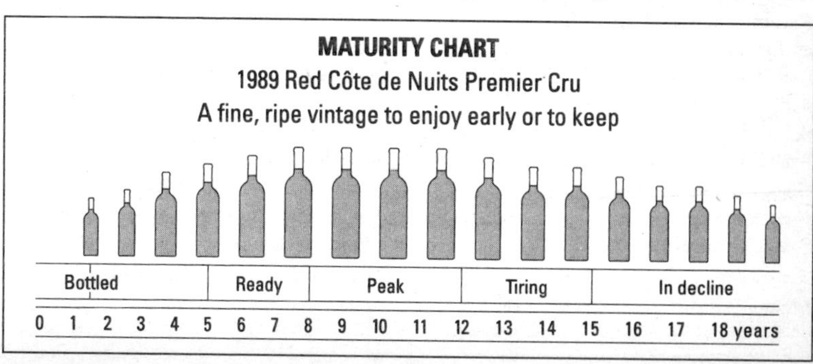

they once were, can sometimes reflect their leaders. The 1987s and '89s are particularly good here; the '85s, '88s and '90s are unutterably great. Apart from the Domaine, good producers include *Arnoux, Sylvain Cathiard, Confuron-Coteditot, Engel, Grivot, Jean Gros, Hudelot-Noëllat, Georges Jayer, Henri Jayer, Henri Lamarche, Leroy, Méo-Camuzet, Mongeard-Mugneret, Georges Mugneret, Pernin-Rossin, Rouget, Daniel Rion* and *Jean Tardy*.

VOUGEOT, AC (Côte de Nuits) A village famous only because of its Grand Cru, Clos de Vougeot, which at its best is plummy and broad. However, there are some decent wines made outside the hallowed walls of the Clos – most notably from the producers *Bertagna* and *Clerget*.

RED CÔTE D'OR VINTAGES

1992 A large vintage of wines with attractive ripe fruit, if not a great deal of concentration and structure. Initial reports suggest most will be pleasing early on, in a style similar to 1989. There may be some first-rate wines from producers who kept their yields low.

1991 A small crop, partly because of hail damage, and spoilt by rain at vintage time. Even so, there were some very good reds made – and with some yields as low as 10 hectolitres per hectare, they can have extraordinary concentration. It's a very patchy vintage, but the good wines will be ones to keep, because of that concentration.

1990 The long, warm summer produced yet another large crop. The 1990s are brilliantly fruity, naturally high in sugars. Most producers now consider this the best of the great trio of '88, '89 and '90. Lesser wines will be ready early; the best are sumptuously rich.

1989 A lot of good wines were made in this warm year, but only a few exceptional ones. They are softer than the 1988s, and some view them as a kind of cross between 1982 and 1985 in style. Though, having said that, there are some superbly concentrated wines, particularly in the Côte de Beaune, destined to rival the 1988s and, dare I suggest it, surpass them in some cases.

1988 There was potential to make great wine in 1988, though it was hardly a textbook year. There was serious drought during the summer, and some may have ended up with grapes rather short on sugar. Those who waited to pick, however, were walloped by the rain. But throughout the Côte d'Or a surprising number of growers did not overproduce, did pick fully ripe grapes before the rains came, and have made delicious wines – more joyously fruity than 1987, and quite a bit deeper and riper than 1986.

1987 It didn't start out with much of a reputation because no-one was enthusiastic about Bordeaux '87s and this impression travelled. The good producers made quite small amounts of well-coloured, concentrated wine which in some cases is better than their 1985s. The best '87s are very good indeed, Côte de Beaune having the edge over Côte de Nuits. Further down the scale the wines aren't as good as '85, but are better than '86.

1986 Over the last year the wines have been shedding toughness, and now exhibit their best feature, perfume. Stick to decent producers, because there was some rot.

1985 When the 1985s were young, they were terrific. Some have gone from strength to strength. Some seem stuck in a 'dumb' phase. Some shot their bolt early.

1983 The best wines display impressive flavour. If you can wait another decade you may have the most impressive old-style Burgundies made in the last 20 years, but I'd avoid Vosne-Romanée, Chambolle-Musigny and Morey-Saint-Denis.

1982 Ridiculously over-praised to start with. The best wines are from the Côte de Beaune and are delicate, perfumed, nicely balanced and need drinking.

WHITE WINES

There is nothing quite like the taste of really good unoaked Chablis: pure, intense, minerally, mouthwateringly keen and refreshing. There is nothing, too, to equal great Premier Cru Puligny-Montrachet: peachy, scented, luscious and lingering, yet always taut and racy at the same time. After a single such encounter we relish the prospect of a continuous love affair with white Burgundy, but for most of us, sadly, the course of this particular affair has become erratic in the extreme.

The figures speak for themselves. In 1991 Britain took 20 per cent less white Burgundy than in 1990, and during 1992 there was a further 12 per cent decrease; a drop of nearly a third in just two years. The consequence of recession, perhaps? Yet New Zealand shipments to Britain were up nearly fourfold during the same period. Most of this was white wine, and plenty of it was Chardonnay. It's not that all of a sudden we've taken against Chablis, Mâcon, Puligny-Montrachet and Meursault – after all, when the flavours and textures are there, so is the passion. What douses the flames is paying high prices for dreary, overpriced insipidity.

Yet it is still possible for a conversation like the following to take place between an English wine merchant and a grower of white Burgundy:

'Are you not worried, Monsieur, by the competition from New World Chardonnay?'

'Ah, *non*! Our fine white wines from the Côte de Beaune are unique and rare; it does not affect them. Chablis, maybe; Mâcon, maybe.'

Possibly only in Burgundy can one still find growers for whom the sub-region down (or up) the road is as much an unknown quantity as a distant continent.

The price of competition

Of course the grower is wrong, and his more cosmopolitan colleagues are beginning to recognize the fact. There are plenty of alternatives to white Burgundy in the £5 to £12 bracket. Recession, unsold stocks, competition and pressure from customers are forcing a more sensible approach to pricing in Burgundy, but as with any commodity the real issue is value. There are plenty of very expensive Meursaults which barely reach the retail shelf because they are snapped up so rapidly year after year: those of Lafon, Jobard and Roulot, for example. Equally there is an abundance of Puligny-Montrachets which cost less but even so sell sluggishly; wines that may be cheaper but are still poor value for money. The fact that some of them sell at all is remarkable. The Puligny-Montrachet name has the most magical ring of any on the Côte de Beaune, but with the exception of a very few star growers its quality-price ratio is absolutely the worst of the lot.

However, white Burgundy is not all gloom and disappointment. There are five good-to-excellent vintages available on merchants' lists at the moment, and there is real value for money to be had, if one looks in some of the less illustrious appellations. Wines from 1988, 1989, 1990 and 1991 are still to be found. With the exception of 1988 (wines that were rather lean and hard early on, but which have now softened considerably) these are all vintages with plenty of ripe fruit, so ripe in fact that one frequently wishes for a bit more acidity to lift the wines and give them greater length. On the whole they are going to be best drunk relatively young, but there is an exciting prospect on the horizon with the 1992 vintage. In spite of a large crop these wines seem to have the combined virtues of ripe fruit, concentration and acidity. Save your pennies (lots of them) in anticipation and taste before you buy more than the odd bottle.

Much white Burgundy remains overoaked. 'Underwined' is perhaps a better way of looking at it: too little flavour (from too generous a crop) to support the oak mask. But there is an increasing appreciation that excess oak is simply in bad taste, in both senses. It is also much more widely understood that actually fermenting in new barrels produces a much more subtle and integrated oak character than fermenting in stainless steel and then just aging in new wood. An intelligent trend, much to be welcomed.

Budget shopping list

There is a new generation of enthusiastic winemakers who are turning out white Burgundies that don't break the bank, and that satisfy one's expectations and prompt the purchase of more than the occasional bottle. They are the producers to encourage, from *appellations* such as Chablis, Pouilly-Fuissé, Mâcon, Saint-Aubin and Auxey-Duresses.

Take Bernard Legland from Chablis (his wines are available, in London and nationwide, from Bibendum). He started the Domaine des Maronniers from scratch just 16 years ago. His father owned *appellation* land but had it planted with cereals; on his death Bernard decided to make Chablis. No inherited tradition to worry about here; he knows what Chablis should taste like, he is a very good winemaker and he charges a fair price for his wine. He doesn't over-fertilize his soil, his yields are low, most of his wines see no wood at all and they restore one's faith in the type: pale to look at, concentrated, vivid to taste and with all stony, minerally imprint of flavour one wants from Chablis and doesn't always find.

He is not the only one. At the southern extreme of Burgundy there are Mâcons and Pouilly-Fuissés that are well made, subtly oaked if oaked at all, and (crucially) worth the asking price. Try the Talmard Brothers' Mâcon-Uchizy at £6 to £7 (Justerini and Brooks, Haynes Hanson & Clark, Tanners of Shrewsbury, Adnams of Southwold), or Olivier Merlin's Mâcon La Roche Vineuse, which has a terrific 1992 vintage on the way (Morris & Verdin) at closer to £8. But if you want inexpensive but reliable, basic, unoaked Mâcon Blanc at under £6, sample that of the Cave de Lugny, currently by far the best of the local cooperatives for white wine, and available from Oddbins.

Pouilly-Fuissé is also restoring its reputation with really stylish wines appearing from the likes of Denogent in Fuissé; Guffens-Heynen, Daniel Barraud, Michel Forest and the Saumaize brothers in Vergisson. These are all winemakers who look after their vines as closely as their barrels, keep their yields low and know what good balance is. And in between these two geographical extremes look out for the whites of St-Aubin (Gérard Prudhon for example) and Auxey-Duresses (Michel Prunier): Côte de Beaune whites of real class in miniature. They are not cheap at £11 to £14, but they are not pretentiously priced either. Support them and spurn the wishy-washy wines, the overpriced dross; for these are the white Burgundies with which to rekindle that cooled love affair.

MICHAEL SCHUSTER

GRAPES & FLAVOURS

CHARDONNAY In a world panting for Chardonnay, Burgundy makes the most famous Chardonnay of all. Even in the decidedly dicky Burgundian climate, it produces a fair to considerable amount of good to excellent wine almost every year. Its flavour depends on where it is grown, and how the wine is made. Chardonnays made without the use of oak barrels for aging will taste very different from barrel-aged wines. A Mâcon produced in stainless steel will have rather appley fruit as well as something slightly fat and yeasty or, in a hot year, a slightly exotic peachiness. Côte Chalonnaise Chardonnay is generally rather taut and chalky-dry, but given some oak, it can become delicately nutty. Chablis, too, generally produces lean wine, but in riper years and with some oak treatment it can get much rounder and mouth-filling. The Côte d'Or is the peak of achievement for Chardonnay, and a top wine from the Côte de Beaune manages to be luscious, creamy, honeyed yet totally dry, the rich, ripe fruit intertwined with the scents of new oak into a memorable and surprisingly powerful wine – from the right producer, the world's greatest dry white. It is this that has so enticed the New World wineries – and quite a few in the Old World, too, outside France – into trying to mimic the success of Burgundian Chardonnay.

ALIGOTÉ Not planted in the best sites – though there are a few vines in Corton-Charlemagne. Aligoté used to be merely sharp, spritzy café wine, but from old vines it can produce a lovely, refreshing wine, scented like buttermilk soap yet as sharp and palate-cleansing as a squeeze of lemon juice.

PINOT BEUROT Known elsewhere as Pinot Gris. Rare in Burgundy, but it produces rich, buttery wine usually blended in to soften the Chardonnay. There is a little unblended Pinot Beurot in the Hautes-Côtes.

PINOT BLANC There is a little of this about in the Côte d'Or – in Aloxe-Corton, for instance, where it makes a soft, rather unctuous, quick-maturing wine. Rully in the Côte Chalonnaise has a good deal and it ripens well in the Hautes-Côtes. There is also an odd white mutation of Pinot Noir – as at Nuits-St-Georges where the Premier Cru La Perrière produces a very savoury white, and in the Monts Luisants vineyard in Morey-St-Denis.

WINES & WINE REGIONS

ALOXE-CORTON, AC (Côte de Beaune) This most northerly village of the Côte de Beaune has one of the Côte's most famous Grands Crus, Corton-Charlemagne. It can be a magnificent, blasting wall of flavour, not big on nuance, but strong, buttery and ripe, which traditionally is supposed to require long aging to show its full potential. Do not expect this sort of quality from the simple village wine, however; recent vintages of Corton-Charlemagne have mostly been strangely disappointing and one is left wondering if they're not trying to produce too much wine.

AUXEY-DURESSES, AC (Côte de Beaune) Tucked away in the folds of the hill rather than on the main Côte de Beaune slope, Auxey-Duresses has never been well known, but has always had some reputation for soft, nutty whites. Recently, though, too many have been disappointingly soft and flabby, but the new confidence of the lesser villages is evident here too and 1990, '89, '88 and '87 have all produced good wine. Producers like *Ampeau, Diconne, Duc de Magenta, Jadot, Leroy* and *Prunier* are still producing pretty decent stuff.

BÂTARD-MONTRACHET, AC (Côte de Beaune) Grand Cru of Chassagne and Puligny lying just below Le Montrachet and, from a good producer, displaying a good deal of its dramatic flavour, almost thick in the mouth, all roast nuts, butter, toast and honey. Exciting stuff, costing rather more than the national average wage – per bottle, that is – in the few restaurants that stock it. Good names: *Blain-Gagnard, Clerc, Jean-Noël Gagnard, Leflaive, Bernard Morey, Pierre Morey, Michel Niellon, Pernot, Poirier, Claude Ramonet, Ramonet-Prudhon, Sauzet.*

BIENVENUES-BÂTARD-MONTRACHET, AC (Côte de Beaune) Tiny Grand Cru in Puligny below Le Montrachet, and inside the larger Bâtard-Montrachet – whose wines are similar though the Bienvenues wines are often lighter, more elegant and may lack a tiny bit of Bâtard's drive. Producers: *Carillon, Clerc, Leflaive, Pernot, Ramonet-Prudhon.*

BOURGOGNE ALIGOTÉ, AC Usually rather sharp and green except for sites near Pernand-Vergelesses where old vines can make exciting wine, but the locals add Crème de Cassis to it to make Kir – which tells you quite a lot about it. Look out for *Coche-Dury, Confuron, Diconne, Jobard, Monthélie-Douhairet, Rion, Rollin.*

BOURGOGNE ALIGOTÉ DE BOUZERON, AC (Côte Chalonnaise) The white wine pride of the Côte Chalonnaise is made not from Chardonnay but from Aligoté in the village of Bouzeron. The vines are frequently old – more crucial for Aligoté than for most other wines – and the buttermilk soap nose is followed by a very dry, slightly lemony, pepper-sharp wine, too good to mix with Cassis. It got its own AC in 1979. It owes its sudden fame to the interest of the *de Villaine* family, who own a substantial estate there making fairly good, oaked Aligoté. *Chanzy* and *Bouchard Père et Fils* are also good.

BOURGOGNE BLANC This can mean almost anything – from a basic Burgundy grown in the less good spots anywhere between Chablis and the Mâconnais to a carefully matured wine from a serious producer, either from young vines or from parts of his vineyard that just miss a superior AC, especially on the borders of Meursault. Best producers: *Boisson-Vadot, Boyer-Martenot, Boisson-Morey, Henri Clerc, Coche-Dury, Dussort, Jadot, Javillier, Jobard, Labouré-Roi, René Manuel, Millot-Battault* and *Buxy* co-op (*Clos de Chenoves*).

CHABLIS, AC Simple Chablis, mostly soft, sometimes acidic, covers the widest area of the *appellation*. Well it would, wouldn't it? They've included most of what used to be Petit Chablis for a start. But at the rate they're now extending the Premier Cru status to virtually anything that grows, maybe Premiers Crus will soon overtake Chablis in acreage. Chablis covers a multitude of sins, with a lot of wine going under *négociants*' labels, and a lot being sold by the co-op – they make most of the *négociants*' stuff too. Some of the co-op's best *cuvées* are outstandingly good, but many of the cheaper *cuvées* are too bland and soft. A good grower is more likely to give you something steely and traditional. Good producers: *Christian Adine, Jean-Marc Brocard, La Chablisienne, Jean Collet, René Dauvissat, Defaix, Jean-Paul Droin, Joseph Drouhin, Jean Durup, William Fèvre, Vincent Gallois, Alain Geoffroy, Jean-Pierre Grossot, Michel Laroche, Bernard Légland, Louis Michel, Guy Mothe, François & Jean-Marie Raveneau, Regnard, Simmonet-Fèbvre, Philippe Testut, Robert Vocoret.*

CHABLIS GRAND CRU The seven Grands Crus (Blanchots, Preuses, Bougros, Grenouilles, Valmur, Vaudésir and Les Clos) come from a small patch of land just outside the town of Chablis, on a single slope rising from the banks of the river Serein. The wines *can* be outstanding, though still unlikely to rival the Grands Crus of the Côte de Beaune. To get the best out of them, you need to age them, preferably after oaking, although *Louis Michel*'s oak-free wines age superbly. The last four vintages have seen a considerable increase in the use of oak by the better producers, and the results are deeper, more exciting wines which may well benefit from six to ten years' aging in bottle.

CHABLIS PREMIER CRU Some 30 names, rationalized into 12 main vineyards. Once upon a time, this used to be a very reliable classification for good, characterful dry white, if less intense than Grand Cru, but again, there has been this expansion mania, meaning that many hardly suitable pieces of vineyard are now accorded Premier Cru status. Given that there is a price difference of £3 to £4 a bottle between Chablis and Premier Cru Chablis, the quality difference should be plain as a pikestaff. Sadly it rarely is. However, since the 1986 vintage there has been a definite move towards quality by the better growers and *La Chablisienne* co-op.

CHASSAGNE-MONTRACHET, AC (Côte de Beaune) Only half the production of this famous vineyard at the south of the Côte de Beaune is white, but that does include a large chunk of the great Montrachet vineyard. The Grands Crus are excellent, but the Premiers Crus rarely dazzle quite like those of nearby Puligny-Montrachet. The Chassagne '86s are mostly at their best now, and should be drunk; the '89s are wonderfully ripe and concentrated and can be drunk now or kept for years. Best producers include: *Blain-Gagnard, Carillon, Chartron et Trebuchet, Colin, Duc de Magenta, Fontaine-Gagnard, Jean-Noël Gagnard, Gagnard-Delagrange, Génot-Boulanger, Lamy-Pillot, Laguiche, Château de la Maltroye, Moreau, Albert Morey, Bernard Morey, Niellon, Fernand Pillot, Ramonet.*

CHABLIS VINEYARDS

Grands Crus

Blanchots, Bougros, Les Clos, Grenouilles, Preuses, Valmur, Vaudésir. La Moutonne, considered a Grand Cru, is from a parcel in Preuses and Vaudésir.

Premiers Crus

Fourchaume (including Fourchaume, Vaupulent, Côte de Fontenay, Vaulorent, l'Homme Mort); Montée de Tonnerre (including Montée de Tonnerre, Chapelot, Pied d'Aloup); Monts de Milieu; Vaucoupin; Les Fourneaux (including Les Fourneaux, Morein, Côte des Prés-Girots); Beauroy (including Beauroy, Troesmes); Côte de Léchet; Vaillons (including Vaillons, Châtains, Séché, Beugnons, Les Lys); Mélinots (including Mélinots, Roncières, Les Epinottes); Montmains (including Montmains, Forêts, Butteaux); Vosgros (including Vosgros and Vaugiraut); Vaudevey.

CHEVALIER-MONTRACHET, AC (Côte de Beaune) Grand Cru vineyard of Puligny, directly above Le Montrachet. The higher elevation gives a leaner wine, but one with a deep flavour as rich and satisfying as a dry white wine can get. Good examples will last 20 years. Best: *Bouchard Père et Fils, Clerc, Jadot, Latour, Leflaive, Niellon.*

CORTON, AC (Côte de Beaune) Corton-Charlemagne is the white Grand Cru here in Aloxe-Corton, but tiny patches of the Corton Grand Cru grow Chardonnay and Pinot Blanc. The finest wine, the *Hospices de Beaune*'s Corton-Vergennes, is all Pinot, and *Chandon de Briailles* makes Corton-Bressandes that is half Pinot Blanc.

CORTON-CHARLEMAGNE, AC (Côte de Beaune) This famous Grand Cru of Aloxe-Corton and Pernand-Vergelesses occupies the upper half of the dome-shaped hill of Corton. It is planted almost entirely with Chardonnay, but a little Pinot Blanc or Pinot Beurot can add intriguing fatness to the wine. Good names: *Bitouzet, Bonneau du Martray, Chandon de Briailles, Chapuis, Dubreuil-Fontaine, M. Juillot, Hospices de Beaune, Laleure Piot, Latour, Rapet.*

CÔTE CHALONNAISE, AC As the ordered vines of the Côte de Beaune swing away and dwindle to the west, the higgledy-piggledy vineyards of the Côte Chalonnaise hiccup and splutter into life as a patchwork of south- and east-facing outcrops. Light, usually clean-tasting Chardonnay predominates among the whites – although at long last the idea of oak-aging is catching on. But the Côte Chalonnaise has one star that cannot be overshadowed by the famous Côte d'Or: the village of Bouzeron makes the most famous, if not quite the finest Aligoté in all France.

CÔTE D'OR This famous strip of vineyard, running south-west from Dijon for 30 miles, sprouts famous names right along its length, with a fine crop of illustrious whites in the southern portion. But in fact it produces only about 16 per cent of Burgundy's white. (Mâconnais is the chief white producer, with the Côte Chalonnaise chipping in a bit.) Price lunacy for whites has become a fairly common phenomenon in all the Côte d'Or villages, as has complete absence of the wines from many British wine-lovers' cellars, including mine.

CRÉMANT DE BOURGOGNE, AC What used to be simple, pleasantly tart Burgundian fizz, based on slightly green Chardonnay and Aligoté grapes, excellent for mixing with cassis, is beginning to sharpen up its act. Competition from other wine-producing regions and from neighbouring countries, added to the increase in Champagne prices, has led to co-operatives, such as the *caves* of Viré or St-Gengoux-Clessé in the Mâconnais, and the *Cave de Bailly* in the Yonne and *Delorme* in Rully, producing excellent, eminently affordable fizz, increasingly from 100 per cent Chardonnay. Crémant de Bourgogne is becoming a wine that no longer needs disguising.

CRIOTS-BÂTARD-MONTRACHET, AC (Côte de Beaune) Tiny 1.6 hectare Grand Cru in Chassagne-Montrachet nuzzled up against the edge of Bâtard itself. Hardly ever seen but the wines are similar to Bâtard, full, strong, packed with flavour, perhaps a little leaner. Best producers: *Blain-Gagnard, Fontaine-Gagnard.*

HAUTES-CÔTES DE BEAUNE, AC and **HAUTES-CÔTES DE NUITS, AC** A lot of reasonably good, light, dry Chardonnay from the hill country behind the Côte de Beaune and Côte de Nuits. Best producers: *Caves des Hautes-Côtes, Chalet, Cornu, Goubard, Jayer-Gilles, Alain Verdet* (organic).

MÂCON BLANC, AC It seemed, a few years ago, that the spiralling price of Pouilly-Fuissé – the region's only white wine star – was acting as a spur for the producers to improve quality. As Pouilly-Fuissé came spinning back to earth – a wiser but better, and cheaper, wine – upping the price of Mâcon to patently unrealistic levels seemed to have been the only effect. Now prices are back down again, and quality has yet to show any great improvement.

MÂCON BLANC-VILLAGES, AC One step up from basic Mâcon Blanc, this must come from the 43 Mâcon communes with the best land. The rare good ones show the signs of honey and fresh apples and some of the nutty, yeasty depth associated with fine Chardonnay. You can expect the better wines from those villages, notably **Viré, Clessé, Prissé** and **Lugny**, that add their own village names (Mâcon-Viré, etc). Full, buttery yet fresh, sometimes spicy: look for that and, if you find it, consider paying the price. You will find it occasionally in the

1989s and 1990s – but only rarely in other vintages. Prices went silly in the mid-1980s but are now merely too high, and have stopped being an insult to our intelligence. Best producers: *Bicheron, Bonhomme, Danauchet, Goyard, Guillemot-Michel, Josserand, Lassarat, Manciat-Poncet, Merlin, Signoret, Talmard, Thévenet-Wicart.*

MERCUREY, AC (Côte Chalonnaise) Village making over half the wine of the Côte Chalonnaise. Most of the production is red – the whites used to be rather flaccid afterthoughts from the less good land, but as the price of white rose in the Côte de Beaune, several producers started making a bigger effort with interesting results. Good examples come from *Chartron et Trebuchet, Château de Chamirey, Faiveley, Genot, Boulanger, M. Juillot.*

MEURSAULT, AC (Côte de Beaune) Halfway down the Côte de Beaune, this village is the first, working southwards, of the great white wine villages. It has by far the largest white production of any Côte d'Or village, and this is one of several reasons why its traditionally high overall standard is gradually being eroded. The wines should be big and nutty and have a delicious, gentle lusciousness, and sometimes even peachy, honeyed flavours. Meursault has more producers bottling their own wine than any other village. These are some of the best: *Ampeau, Pierre Boillot, Boisson-Vadot, Boyer-Martenot, Buisson-Battault, Coche-Debord, Coche-Dury, Comtes Lafon, Gauffroy, Henri-Germain, Jean Germain, Grivault, Jobard, René Manuel, Matrot, Michelot-Buisson, Millot-Battault, Pierre Morey, Prieur, Roulot.*

MONTAGNY, AC (Côte Chalonnaise) White-only AC in the south of the Côte Chalonnaise. In general the wines are a bit lean and chalky-dry, but now that the use of oak is creeping in, some much more interesting wines will appear. Best producers: *Arnoux*, co-op at *Buxy, Latour, B Michel, de Montorge, Alain Roy, Vachet.*

LE MONTRACHET, AC (Côte de Beaune) Finest of fine white Grands Crus in the villages of Puligny and Chassagne. Does it mean most enjoyable, most happy-making? Not really. In fact the flavours can be so intense it's difficult sometimes to know if you're having fun drinking it or merely giving your wine vocabulary an end of term examination. So be brave if someone opens a bottle of Montrachet for you and let the incredible blend of spice and smoke, honey and ripeness flow over your senses. Good producers: *Amiot-Bonfils, Bouchard Père et Fils, Domaine de la Romanée-Conti, Jadot, Comtes Lafon, Laguiche, Pierre Morey, Prieur, Thénard.* Presumably *Leflaive* too, though 1991 was its first vintage.

MUSIGNY, AC (Côte de Nuits) Just 0.3 hectares of this predominantly red Grand Cru of Chambolle-Musigny are planted

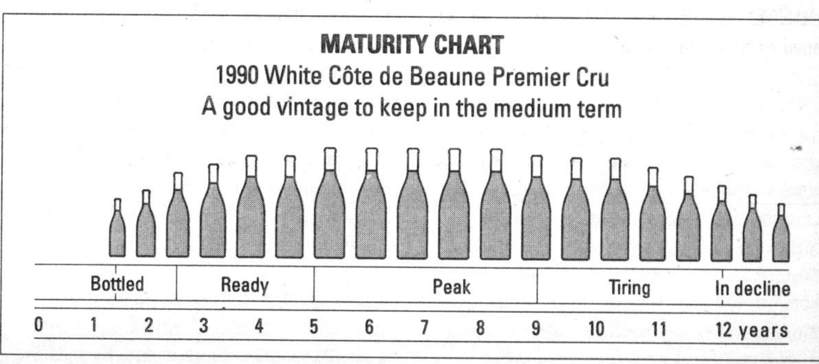

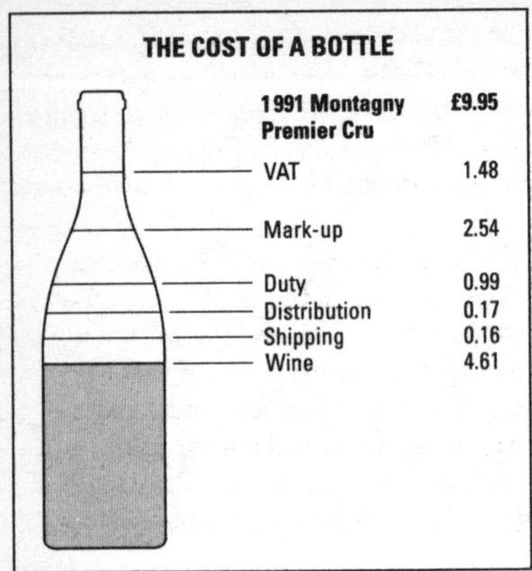

with Chardonnay, owned by the *Domaine de Vogüé*, and most of it seems to be consumed on the premises.

PERNAND-VERGELESSES, AC (Côte de Beaune) The village wines can be good, – with the best Aligoté in Burgundy, while the Chardonnays are generally fairly lean and need time to soften, but can be gently nutty and very enjoyable from a good producer. Can also be very good value. Best names: *Dubreuil-Fontaine, Germain, Laleure-Piot, Pavelot, Rapet, Rollin.*

PETIT CHABLIS There used to be lots of this grown on the least good slopes. But the growers objected that it made it sound as though their wine was a lesser form of Chablis. Nowadays, of course, pretty well the whole lot is called 'Chablis' – so *we* can't tell what's what, *they're* all richer, they're happy, we're not... I give up.

POUILLY-FUISSÉ, AC (Mâconnais) This once ridiculously overpriced white has dropped its price considerably in the last few years. This tumble came about partly because the Americans stopped buying – although they were the ones who made it famous in the first place – and partly because the general quality from this co-op-monopolized, *négociant*-abused AC was a disgrace. Best producers: *Barraud, Béranger, Corsin, Duboeuf's* top selections, *Ferret, M. Forest, Guffens-Heynen, Leger-Plumet, Loron's les Vieux Murs, Manciat-Poncet, Noblet, R. Saumaize, Vincent* at *Château Fuissé*. Adjoining villages **Pouilly-Loché, AC** and **Pouilly-Vinzelles, AC** have borrowed the name and make similar wines at half the price.

PULIGNY-MONTRACHET, AC (Côte de Beaune) The peak of great white pleasure is to be found in the various Montrachet Grands Crus. Le Montrachet is peerless, showing how humble words like honey, nuts, cream, smoke, perfume and all the rest do no honest service to a white wine that seems to combine every memory of ripe fruit and subtly worn scent with a dry, penetrating savouriness. There are several other Grands Crus less intense, but whose wines buzz with the mingling opposites of coffee and honey, and smoke and cream. There are Premiers Crus as well. While 'village' Meursault may be good, it's always worth buying a single vineyard wine in Puligny-Montrachet. Much of the wine is sold in bulk to *négociants* whose offerings vary between the delicious and the disgraceful, but look for the wines of *Amiot-Bonfils, Boyer-Devèze, Carillon, Chartron et Trebuchet, Clerc, Drouhin, Jadot, Labouré-Roi, Laguiche,* both *Domaine Leflaive* and *Olivier Leflaive, Pernot, Ramonet-Prudhon, Antonin Rodet, Sauzet, Thénard.*

RULLY, AC (Côte Chalonnaise) This village gets my vote for the most improved AC in Burgundy. Originally known for fizz, and then for pale, nutty, dull Chardonnay, the use of oak to ferment and age the wine has turned a lot into wonderfully soft, spicy Burgundies of good quality – and low price. Best names: *Bêtes, Chanzy, Cogny, Delorme, Dury, Duvernay, Domaine de la Folie, Jacqueson, Jaffelin, Rodet.*

ST-AUBIN, AC (Côte de Beaune) Some of Burgundy's best value white wines, full and racy, come from this tiny, forgotten

Côte de Beaune village behind the far more famous Puligny-Montrachet and Meursault. Two-thirds of the vineyards are Premiers Crus and it really shows. Starting with '82 it became clear that St-Aubin's Premiers Crus could rival the more famous wines of Meursault and Puligny-Montrachet. The 1986s from *Prudhon, Roux, Albert Morey* and *Jadot* were both delicious and affordable but need drinking. But grab any that you see on sale. The 1989s are better and richer but not such good value. Other good producers in the commune are *Bachelet, Bouton, Clerget, Colin, Delaunay, Duvernay, Jadot, Jaffelin, Lamy, Albert Morey, Prudhon, Roux* and *Thomas*.

ST-ROMAIN, AC (Côte de Beaune) The flinty, dry whites that emerge from this out of the way Côte de Beaune village right up near the Hautes-Côtes are often decent quality and pretty good value. Best are: *Bazenet, Buisson, Germain, Gras, Thévenin, Thévenin-Monthélie*.

ST-VÉRAN, AC (Mâconnais) Pouilly-Fuissé's understudy, capable of simple, soft, quick-maturing but very attractive, rather honeyed white Burgundy. There are some great 1989s but, like their predecessors, they will tire very quickly. Best producers: *Corsin, Dépardon, Dom. des Deux Roches, Duboeuf, Grégoire, Lassarat, de Montferrand, Saumaize, Thibert, Vincent*.

SAUVIGNON DE ST-BRIS, VDQS Wine of undoubted AC quality grown south-west of Chablis that languishes as a VDQS just because Sauvignon Blanc is not a permitted AC grape in the area. Often one of the most nettly, most greeny gooseberryish of all France's Sauvignons, but recent ones have been more expensive and less exciting. Ah well, New Zealand has nice Sauvignon, and Bordeaux Blanc is really tasty now, so perhaps I'll drink those instead. Producers take note. Good names: *Louis Bersan, Jean-Marc Brocard, Robert & Philippe Defrance, Michel Esclavy, André Sorin, Luc Sorin*.

WHITE BURGUNDY VINTAGES

White Burgundy is far less prone to vintage fluctuation than red, and in most years can produce a fair amount of pretty good wine.

1992 A better vintage for the whites than for the reds. The white 1992s have masses of exuberant fruit and seemingly better acidity than their 1991 counterparts. Probably the best white vintage since 1989, but in a less alcoholic, more elegantly balanced style than most 1989s.

1991 Patchy in quality, though without the reds' occasional brilliance. That vintage-time rain did more damage to the Chardonnay than to the Pinot Noir, in terms of rot, and some of the picking had to be pretty hasty. The whites certainly won't match up to the previous three vintages in quality. For early drinking the Mâconnais wines are especially good.

1990 Though the growing season was in many ways similar to 1989 the 1990s have some of the structure of the '88s and some of the richness of the '89s. They are less austere than the '88s and probably won't last as long.The Chardonnay crop was very large, so the whites are likely to be inferior to the reds. A good rather than a great vintage for white Burgundy.

1989 An outstanding year for white Burgundy, in the hands of competent winemakers. Hailed as the best white vintage of the 1980s, almost all the best growers' wines are beautifully balanced, despite their richness. As one Burgundy importer put it: 'a richer version of the structured and seriously undervalued 1985s'. However, a number of wines have worryingly low acidity levels, and some are already showing signs of premature aging.

1988 The fruit was, if anything, a little cleaner and fresher than in 1987. Numbers of Mâconnais wines had a bright, fresh fruit not seen down that way for a few years. Chablis prices went up by 10 to 15 per cent, but you couldn't honestly say that its quality went up in parallel.

1987 Good producers made attractive, quite light wines, sometimes with a slightly lean streak of acidity. Try the exciting new growers in the Côte Chalonnaise and Mâconnais. The Côte d'Or produced wines that were often frankly dull, but Chablis is turning out well.

1986 There's an interesting debate over the relative qualities of '86 and '85. Initially 1986 was given a better reception even than '85 because, whereas the latter seemed to rely on sheer power, 1986 seemed to have finer acidity, a more focused fruit and even a hint of richness. The balance has been redressed a bit now. The good 1985s have proved to be much better balanced than previously thought, and whilst a few '86s have closed up somewhat, others have suddenly started to tire. Chablis had that classic blend of leanness and restrained ripeness which can make it the logical, if not the emotional choice for so many fish dishes. Grands Crus still need several years. The Mâconnais promised much, but few bottles really delivered.

1985 This is on the way back. Along with the strength are increasing signs of a proper acid balance and an outstanding concentration of fruit. Pity nobody waited to find out because most '85s were consumed long ago. If you do see one from a good producer, go for it – well, perhaps not, I've just remembered the price it'll be. Chablis started out with a lesser reputation, but wines from good producers can still improve.

1983 In 1983 there was a serious rot problem and a lot of grapes were also seriously overripe. The result is frequently heavy, rather unrefreshing, soggy-flavoured wines which rapidly lost their fruit. Some rare examples may turn out to be wonderful, but they aren't ready yet.

1982 Easy, outgoing, clean-flavoured wines, almost entirely drunk by now.

BEAUJOLAIS

I must admit to a certain affection for Beaujolais. It was the wine on which I, like many others, cut my vinous teeth. Ripe, foaming, purple Nouveau was something to look forward to each November.

But no longer. Beaujolais has become a victim of its own success. The Nouveau idea was brilliant: it stimulated demand and did wonders for a winemaker's cash flow. Such wonders did it do, in fact, that the temptation was to sell more and more Beaujolais as Nouveau – and to increase yields and reduce quality in order to do so.

Now, with quality down, it is clear that the Nouveau balloon has burst. So where does that leave Beaujolais? What, actually, should it taste like?

Forget the hype. Beaujolais at its best is ripe, gluggable fruit-in-a-bottle. One or two producers, such as Charvet and Brugne in Moulin-à-Vent, may produce a wine of depth and complexity, but for the most part this is quaffing wine.

Unfortunately for the growers of Beaujolais, the Australians have proved more adept and more reliable in producing this style of wine. The overproduction in Beaujolais in recent years has resulted in thin Beaujolais competing with ripe, juicy Australian wines at a fraction of the Beaujolais price. And this is not simply a problem for Nouveau or village wines. Too many of the *cru* wines have become lacklustre in recent years, despite mounting prices.

To buy or not to buy

Prices went through the roof in 1990. There has since been a gradual easing which has brought prices down to a more moderate level. Even so, though... £6.50 for a *cru* Beaujolais? Aren't there quite a lot of wines around that are better value than that? Despite this, we continue to buy. Wine merchant Paul Boutinot attributes this to the production of wines that are suited to modern tastes: 'they are making lighter styles, with less skin contact, and low tannins. Even the *cru* wines are now made to be drunk within the year.' This view is echoed by Kim Tidy of Threshers: 'Gamay is never going to produce wines of world stature. What Beaujolais has going for it is immediate appeal.' Current pricing of Beaujolais, as with all French wines, is in part due to the comparative strength of the French Franc, but to quote Kim Tidy again: 'The base cost of Beaujolais could be reduced. At £2.99 Beaujolais Villages would be good value, but the price is held up by the need to maintain a price gap between *vins de pays* and AC wines.' This, of course, is where Australia, with its more flexibly-structured wine industry, wins: wineries can buy grapes from all over the country and simply truck them to a winery several states away. France, with its prized AC system, cannot do this. And since an unravelling of this system is neither likely nor desirable, France must find some other way of competing.

The first step is to reduce yields. Gamay is a naturally productive vine; left to its own resources it will produce large quantities of grapes. Under the AC rules, in fact, the *crus* can make as much as 60 hectolitres per hectare; the basic appellations can produce even more. Most growers have been happy to take advantage of this profligacy and simply reap the harvest. If, as a result, the grapes are full of water instead of sugar and flavour... well, there's always chaptalization. Adding sugar to the juice increases the alcohol content of the wine, and the extra alcohol makes the wine feel 'fatter' to the taste; but it can also make the wine taste jammy, and certainly detracts from the natural fruitiness of Gamay. The result is unlikely to lure drinkers away from the velvety charms of Australian Shiraz.

Lower yields, less chaptalization, and a general policy of the pursuit of quality are needed if the region hopes to resurrect its reputation. So what are the winemakers doing? Apparently nothing. Their current attitude is a relic of their previous success. Beaujolais has become not so much a drink, more a marketing concept. And, accordingly, the charter for quality that was produced by 144 Beaujolais producers in 1991 has proved little more than another marketing concept. It proclaimed the intention of raising quality and reducing yields, and, not being binding, sank rapidly into oblivion. Last year's crop was prolific, and very few producers made the effort to cut back on yields.

However, all is not lost. There are good wines being produced in the area and some of the *cru* wines do still represent good value. The secret is to look in the less fashionable communes. Fleurie, Morgon and Moulin-à-Vent command a premium; so does St-Amour, because the Swiss like it. Avoid these and go for the less well-known *crus,* Juliénas and Chénas. Both of these communes can produce wines which stand comparison with the best in the region, and often at a fraction of the price.

ANDREW WILLIAMS

GRAPES & FLAVOURS

CHARDONNAY Chardonnay does make some white Beaujolais, and it's usually quite good. Grown in the North, it has a stony dryness closer in style to Chablis. In the South it is much nearer to the fatter, softer, wines of southern Burgundy.

GAMAY The Gamay grape produces pretty dull or tart stuff in most places. But somehow, on these granite slopes, it gives one of the juiciest, most gulpable, gurgling wines the world has to offer. The Gamay has no pretensions. Ideally Beaujolais is simple, cherry-sharp, with candy-like fruit, sometimes with hints of raspberry or strawberry. The wines from the *crus* go further, but in the main the similarity they share through the Gamay grape is more important than the differences in the places they come from. All but the wines of the top villages should be drunk as young as you can find them, although years like 1988, '89 and '91 have produced wines at *cru* levels that are now aging well. 1991s and 1992s still need another year or two for the best wines to come round.

BEAUJOLAIS, AC This covers *all* the basic wines, the produce of the flatter, southern part of Beaujolais, stretching down towards Lyon. Most of the best is now sold as Nouveau. Run-of-the-mill Beaujolais, apart from Nouveau, is likely to be pretty thin stuff, or beefed up illegally with something altogether different. In fact, since you're allowed to re-label Nouveau as 'Beaujolais', some of the best wine in the new year (much appreciated by those who scoff at Nouveau) will be none other than re-labelled Nouveau. Good producers include *Blaise, Carron, Charmet, Château de la Plume,* co-op at *Bully, Duboeuf Bouteille Cristal, Garlon, Labruyère, Loron, Pierre-Marie Chermette* of the *Domaine des Vissoux.*

BEAUJOLAIS BLANC, AC To be honest, Beaujolais Blanc is usually quite expensive and in its rather firm, stony-dry way is rarely as enjoyable as a good Mâcon-Villages. Most of the examples we see come from the North, often bordering on St-Véran in the Mâconnais, so despite being rather closed in, you expect it to blossom sometimes – but it doesn't. I'd plant Gamay instead if I were them. *Charmet* is the most interesting producer, but his vineyards are in the South. *Tête* is good.

BEAUJOLAIS ROSÉ, AC I never thought I'd waste space on this apology for a wine – but a couple of years ago I came across an absolute stunner from *M Bernard* of Leynes – one of the best pinks I'd had all year. The co-op at *Bois d'Oingt* has also shown that it can make exciting Beaujolais rosé.

BEAUJOLAIS NOUVEAU (or **PRIMEUR**), **AC** The new vintage wine of Beaujolais, released in the same year as the grapes are gathered, at midnight on the third Wednesday in November. It is usually the best of the simple wine, and will normally improve for several months in bottle, but in good Nouveau vintages like 1989 and 1991 it can improve for years. I always keep a bottle or two to fool my wine-buff friends – and it always does: they're usually in the Côte de Beaune at about £12 a bottle. I'm sniggering in the kitchen.

BEAUJOLAIS SUPÉRIEUR, AC *Supérieur* means that the basic alcoholic degree is higher. It doesn't ensure a better wine, and is in any case rarely even seen on the label.

BEAUJOLAIS-VILLAGES, AC Thirty-five villages can use this title. They're mostly in the north of the region and reckoned to make better than average wines, with some justification because there are quite major soil differences that account for the demarcation of Beaujolais and Beaujolais-Villages. The wines are certainly better than basic Beaujolais, a little fuller and deeper, and the cherry-sharp fruit of the Gamay is usually more marked. However, look for a wine bottled in the region, and preferably from a single vineyard, because an anonymous blend of

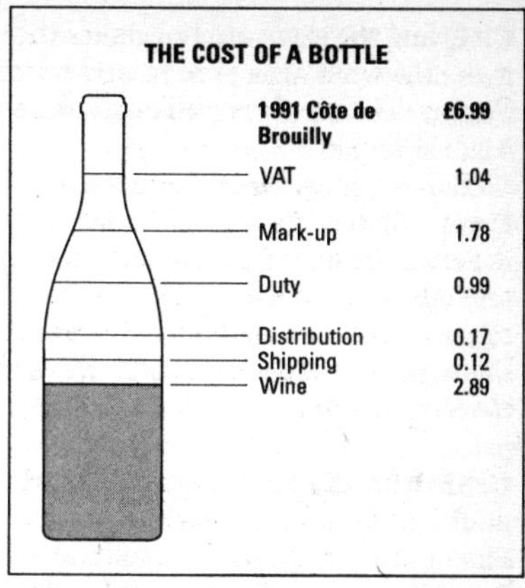

Beaujolais-Villages may simply mean a heftier version of an ordinary Beaujolais. *Noël Aucoeur, Domaine de la Brasse, Domaine de la Chapelle de Vatre (Sarrau), Jacques Dépagneux, de Flammerécourt, Château Gaillard, Gutty Père et Fils, André Large, Château des Loges, Jean-Charles Pivot, Jean-Luc Tissier, Trichard* and *Château des Vergers* are good and local, but most domaines are bottled by one of the merchants in the region. Labelling by the domaine is on the increase.

THE COST OF A BOTTLE
1991 Côte de Brouilly £6.99
VAT 1.04
Mark-up 1.78
Duty 0.99
Distribution 0.17
Shipping 0.12
Wine 2.89

BROUILLY, AC Southernmost and largest of the Beaujolais *crus*, Brouilly has the flattest of the *cru* vineyards, and usually makes one of the lightest *cru* wines. There is some variation in style between the more northerly villages and those in the South where granite produces a deeper, fuller wine, but in general Brouilly rarely improves much with keeping. In fact, it makes a very good Nouveau. A few properties make a bigger wine to age – but even then, nine months to a year is quite enough. Good names include *Château de la Chaize, Domaine Crêt des Garanches, Château de Fouilloux, Hospices de Belleville, Château de Pierreux, Domaine de Combillaty (Duboeuf), Domaine de Garanches, André Large, Château de Nevers. Château des Tours*, although lovely young, can age longer.

CHÉNAS, AC This second-smallest *cru*, from between St-Amour and Moulin-à-Vent, makes strong, dark wines, sometimes a bit tough, that can be drunk a year after the harvest, or aged to take on a Pinot Noir-like flavour. Exceedingly fashionable in France. Look out for the wines of *Louis Champagnon, Charvet, Château de Chénas, Domaines des Brureaux, Domaine Chassignon, Domaine de la Combe Remont (Duboeuf), Pierre Perrachon, Emile Robin.*

CHIROUBLES, AC Another *cru* for early drinking, grown on hillsides south-west of Fleurie, towards the southern end of the Beaujolais *crus*. The wines are naturally light, similar to Beaujolais-Villages in weight, but with a perfumed, cherry scent that makes Chiroubles France's favourite Beaujolais *cru*. Good names include *René Brouillard, Cheysson, Château Javernand, Château de Raousset, Jean-Pierre Desvignes, Duboeuf, Méziat* and *Georges Passot*.

CÔTE DE BROUILLY, AC The slopes in the centre of the Brouilly area make fuller wines than straight Brouilly, since they come largely from exposed slopes and have lapped up the sun. Best producers include: *Château Thivin, Conroy, Claude Geoffray, Jean Sanvers, Lucien Verger, Chanrion.*

CRU The ten *crus* or growths (Fleurie, Moulin-à-Vent, Brouilly, Chénas, Côte de Brouilly, Chiroubles, Juliénas, St-Amour, Morgon, Regnié) are the top villages in the steeply hilly, northern part of Beaujolais. All *should* have definable characteristics, but the produce of different vineyards and growers is all too often blended to a mean by merchants based anywhere in France. Always buy either a single estate wine, or one from a good local merchant like *Chanut Frères, Duboeuf, Dépagneux, Ferraud, Sarrau, Thomas la Chevalière, Trenel.*

FLEURIE, AC Often the most delicious of the *crus*, gentle and round, its sweet cherry-and-chocolate fruit just held firm by a touch of tannin and acid. Very popular in Britain and the US, I used to be prepared to pay, but now the wine has to be *very* special for me to shell out. Try *Château de Fleurie (Loron), Chauvet, Chignard, Colonge, Domaine de la Grand, Grand Pré (Sarrau), Domaine de la Presle, Domaine des Quatre Vents, Duboeuf*'s *la Madone, Bernard Paul, Verpoix,* the Fleurie co-op.

JULIÉNAS, AC Juliénas *can* be big wine, with tannin and acidity, but many of the best more closely resemble the mixture of fresh red fruit and soft, chocolaty warmth that makes for good Fleurie. Good ones include *Château du Bois de la Salle, Domaine des Bucherats, Château des Capitans, Château de Juliénas, Domaine de la Dîme* and *Domaine de la Vieille Eglise*. Also good: *Pelletier* and *Duboeuf*.

MORGON, AC The wines of this *cru* can be glorious. They can start thick and dark, and age to a sumptuous, chocolaty, plummy depth with an amazing cherries smell, not unlike Côte de Nuits Burgundy, and yet still Beaujolais. *Jacky Janodet's* is intense. Look also for *Aucoeur, Château de Pizay, Château de Raousset, Descombes, Desvignes, Domaine de la Chanaise, Domaine de Ruyère, Drouhin, Gobet, Lapierre, Félix Longepierre* and *Georges Vincent*.

MOULIN-À-VENT, AC Enter the heavy brigade. These *cru* wines should be solid, and should age for three to five years, and more from years like 1985 and '91. The best have a big, plummy, Burgundian style,and the toughness of a young Moulin-à-Vent doesn't give you much option but to wait. It rarely resembles anyone's view of straight Beaujolais – it takes itself far too seriously – but quite a few of the 1991s are already very good. *Louis Champagnon's* is good, as

The price guides for this section begin on page 307

is *Brugne, Charvet, Château des Jacques, Château du Moulin-à-Vent, Château Portier, Domaine de la Tour de Bief, Jacky Janodet, Raymond Siffert* and *Héritiers Maillard* (formerly *Héritiers Tagent*). *Duboeuf* is experimenting with new oak barrel-aging.

REGNIÉ, AC Since the 1988 vintage, Beaujolais' tenth *cru*. Makes wine quite similar to Brouilly in ripe vintages but a bit weedy when the sun doesn't shine. *Duboeuf Bouteille Cristal* the best so far.

ST-AMOUR, AC Among the most perfect Beaujolais, this pink-red wine from one of the least spoilt villages usually has freshness and peachy perfume and good, ripe fruit all at once. It isn't that common here (though the French love it), and yet it is frequently the most reliable and most enjoyable *cru*. Sadly, the news has leaked out and prices are leaping up. Look out for *Château de St-Amour, Domaine des Billards (Loron), Buis, Domaine des Ducs, Domaine du Paradis, André Poitevin, Francis Saillant*.

BEAUJOLAIS VINTAGES

With most Beaujolais the rule is, drink it as young as possible. Only the top wines from the best villages will benefit much from aging, although Nouveau can benefit from a month or two's rest.

1992 An above-average crop of below-average wines. Late rains and high yields combined to produce thin, light wines. Moulin-a-Vent and St-Amour suffered hail damage. There will be some decent wines, but only from quality-conscious producers.

1991 Unlike most of France, Beaujolais had an excellent year in 1991. Largely spared the April frosts, the grapes were ripe two weeks before the cold wet weather which set in in the last week of September. Beaujolais from the 1991 vintage has good colour and relatively high tannin levels.

1990 Yet another corker of a vintage – very good quality and plenty of it. The harvest yielded very fruity, typical Beaujolais with rich, authentic Gamay character. Easy-drinking but full flavours reach right across the board, with the ordinary Beaujolais, the Villages and all of the *crus* emerging well. Nouveau prices were high but resistance to the high prices of the other names and widespread slump conditions slowed sales right down and prices began to fall.

1989 Along with other vineyard areas of France, and indeed Europe, the 1989 vintage in Beaujolais was one of the earliest ever. The heat meant that colour was unusually deep, but along with this the aromas were much more pungently fruity than expected after the hot and dusty summer season. But this was the year higher prices really started to bite. In terms of value for money, the less well-known *cru* names like Chénas and Côte de Brouilly were worth a try.

1988 There's no doubt that 1988 was a lovely year in Beaujolais. There is a marvellous quality of luscious, clear, ripe fruit about the best wines. Even the Nouveaus were terrific. I remember a string of delicious Beaujolais-Villages. And some delightful St-Amour and Brouilly. Pressure on supply meant overproduction in some quarters, though. Even so, I'm going to say – 1988 was an exceptional year.

1987 Many are still drinking well, although this was a vintage best enjoyed in its youth. Some of the sturdier *crus* produced wines with the class and stamina to survive – Moulin-à-Vent can be delicious. But the lighter wines are fading already.

1985 No vintage has ever given so much sheer pleasure as 1985 with its riot of fruit and spice. Some of the wines are still excellent – but they've grown up, become serious. Many will be enjoyable, but the days when they made you dance with delight are over.

CHAMPAGNE

The Champenois sometimes remind me of Tory politicians. At their worst, they display a blend of arrogance and incompetence. They preside over (some would say engineer) booms and slumps; they squeeze every last drop out of the former, then assume martyred expressions when the latter follow. There are times when people talk about switching to New World sparkling wines. But when it comes to the crunch the Champenois, like the Tories, somehow scrape through.

Some time in spring 1993 a strange wind could be felt in Champagne. It was caused by a collective letting out of breath, following publication of the export figures for January and February (up 11 per cent on 1992). Champagne, it seemed, had pulled through again; though close reading of the figures revealed that the growth in exports was confined to the bargain basement (the £8.49 or even £7.99 Champagnes, not seen for a couple of years, were back with a vengeance).

With hindsight, it appeared that the nadir of the 1991–1993 Champagne slump had probably been reached in February 1993 when judge Sir Mervyn Davies delivered his magnificently whacky judgment on Thorncroft Elderflower Champagne. He decided that although there had been clear intention to deceive on the part of the English manufacturer of non-alcoholic elderflower bubbly, no-one in their right mind could have been taken in by it. Claude Taittinger spoke of the end of *entente cordiale*; other Champagne producers cast doubt on the judge's sanity. Most disinterested spectators probably hooted with laughter.

By the time the judgment was made, I had already begun to forgive the Champenois for their misdeeds of 1989, 1990 and 1991: the roller-coaster prices and erratic quality. Perhaps the answer is simple: people can only endure so much gloom. Celebratory corks have to start popping again some time.

Pressing for quality

Did the Champenois deserve to be forgiven? How sincere is their often-stated commitment to quality? In 1992-3 we certainly saw some positive developments. New quality regulations were unveiled at Epernay on September 11 1992, the most important of which was probably a small reduction in yield at pressing stage – requiring 160kg of grapes to produce 100 litres of must as opposed to the previous 150kg. This, while not earth-shattering, was welcome. However, reducing the yield at pressing stage is different from controlling the yield in the vineyard, and the latter is better for quality.

A much more significant step was the decision reached by the Comité Interprofessionel du Vin de Champagne or CIVC, Champagne's governing body, in April 1993 to keep yields down to 8500kg per hectare, with a further 1100kg held in reserve, in principle for the next three harvests. This marks a very significant reduction from the 12,500kg per hectare of the late 1980s and has been welcomed by such quality-minded producers as François Roland-Billecart of Billecart-Salmon. The benefits will show in the juice.

Another quality initiative was launched, with surprising boldness, by the ingrainedly conservative house of Bollinger. Bollinger's grandly named Charter of Ethics and Quality (any resemblance to Mr Major's Citizen's Charter is entirely fortuitous) has little to do with ethics (which here seems to mean keeping the name Bollinger for Champagne and using another name for New World sparkling wines) and is in effect a statement of Bollinger's traditional practice: still, no bad thing to have it down on paper. Bollinger have also, more controversially, proposed the setting up of a Club des Grandes Marques which should reaffirm a commitment to quality not always shown by the big names. The Club may eventually comprise between 17 and 20 houses, as opposed to the 28 names currently on the roster of the Syndicat des Grandes Marques.

Pricing into the market

It would be churlish to deny that these developments have some very positive implications for the UK punter. The best news of all may be the stabilization of the price of grapes at reasonable levels: FF24 per kilo of top-quality grapes in 1992, and an estimated FF22 in 1993. 1993 has seen a buyer's market for Champagne: not only lots of cheap wine for sale (FF40 a bottle is not uncommon) but fair quantities of really good wine at attractive prices. Several supermarkets decided to upgrade their own label wine (Tesco, for example, moved to a Premier Cru Brut) and bring in a cheap brand below that. The dramatic change in stock levels (from a low of 2½ years' worth in 1990 to over four years' worth in 1992) in the region has meant that even the cheaper wines are usually palatable.

So is everything in what André Enders of the CIVC calls 'the unique garden of Champagne' rosy? That would be overstating the case. The prolonged economic crisis has undoubtedly hit both the big houses and, probably much more harshly, the small *récoltants-manipulants*. But a genuine, deeply felt commitment to quality is still, I would say, the exception rather than the rule among the big businessmen who run much of Champagne. 'How can you talk about firms being quality-led when they are run by accountants in Paris or New York, rather than true Champenois, and when they make huge vinifications in industrial-sized tanks, and regard Champagne as a mass-produced product like beer or yoghurt?' These are the questions asked by the outspoken François Roland-Billecart.

You could also say that it comes down to a choice between bland mediocrity and individuality. Many of the big houses (Moët & Chandon, to name the most obvious) produce wines which are difficult to fault, but equally difficult to characterize. If you want character, not to mention verve and style, you need to go either to one of the quality-led houses (Krug, Gratien, Billecart-Salmon, Roederer, Bollinger, Laurent-Perrier, for example) or to a *récoltant-manipulant* such as Henri Billiot, Pierre Gimmonet or Albert Beerens. **Harry Eyres**

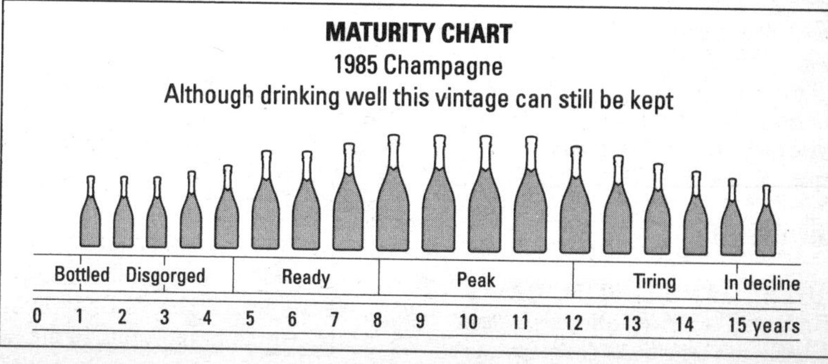

GRAPES & FLAVOURS

CHARDONNAY The grape of white Burgundy fame here tends to produce a lighter, fresher juice, and the resulting Champagnes are certainly the most perfumed and honeyed. They have been criticized for lacking depth and aging potential. Not true. Good Blancs de Blancs have a superb, exciting flavour that is improved by aging, especially those from the southern end of the Côte des Blancs.

PINOT NOIR The grape that makes all the finest red Burgundies also makes white Champagne. Pinot Noir has enough difficulty in ripening in Burgundy, and further north in Champagne it almost never attains any great depth and strength of colour or alcohol, which is fair enough since the general idea here is to produce a *white* wine. Very careful pressing of the grapes in traditional vertical presses is the best way to draw off the juice with as little colour as possible, and the rest of the reddish tinge generally precipitates out naturally during fermentation. Even so, the juice does feel quite big: a Champagne relying largely on Pinot Noir is certain to be heavier and take longer to mature.

PINOT MEUNIER The other black grape, making a softer, fruitier style of wine, important for producing easy wines for drinking young, and crucial for toning down the assertive flavours of Pinot Noir.

WINES & WINE STYLES

BLANC DE BLANCS An increasingly common style from Chardonnay grapes. Usually fresh and bright with a soothing, creamy texture. Many de luxe Champagnes are now labelled Blanc de Blancs, but they rarely have the added nuances the much increased price would suggest. Best producers: *Avize* co-op, *Billecart-Salmon, Henriot, Lassalle, Pol Roger, Louis Roederer, Dom Ruinart, Sézanne* co-op, *Taittinger Comtes de Champagne, Krug Clos de Mesnil, Salon, Charbaut Certificate.*

BLANC DE NOIRS This white style is made from black grapes only and is common throughout the Marne Valley. Few have the quality and longevity of *Bollinger*, but none are even half as expensive. Most are rather solid. *Pierre Vaudon* from the Avize co-op is good; *Barancourt* is more expensive, and beefy; *H.Billiot* is fine.

BRUT Very dry.

BUYER'S OWN BRAND (BOB) A wine blended to a buyer's specification, or more probably, to a price limit. The grapes are of lesser quality, the wines usually younger, and cheaper. *Maison Royale (Victoria Wine), Sainsbury, Tesco, Waitrose* are all pretty consistent, *M&S* less so but can be the best of all.

CM In the small print on the label, this means *co-opérative-manipulant* and shows that the wine comes from a co-op.

COTEAUX CHAMPENOIS Still wines, red or white. Overpriced and generally rather acid. A village name, such as Cramant (white) or Bouzy (red) may appear. *Alain Vesselle*'s Bouzy is one of the few exciting reds.

CRÉMANT A half-sparkling Champagne. If the base wine is good, that's still enough. Among the best are: *Besserat de Bellefon, Alfred Gratien, Abel Lepitre, Mumm Crémant de Cramant.*

The price guides for this section begin on page 310.

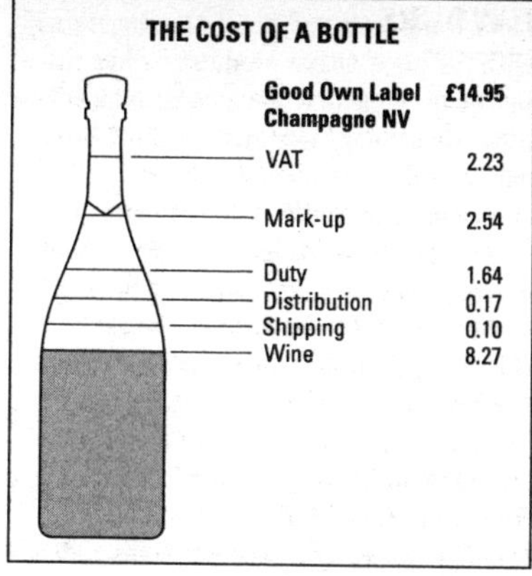

DE LUXE/CUVÉE DE PRESTIGE/ CUVÉE DE LUXE A special, highly prized, highly priced blend, mostly vintage. Some great wines and some gaudy coat-trailers. Most come in silly bottles, and are overpriced, but a few do deliver. In general drunk *far* too young. Most need a good ten years to shine. Best: *Bollinger RD, Dom Pérignon, Dom Ruinart, Krug Grande Cuvée, Laurent Perrier Grand Siècle, Pol Roger Cuvée Sir Winston Churchill, Roederer Cristal, Taittinger Comtes de Champagne, Cuvée NF Billecart, Cattier Clos du Moulin, Philipponnat Clos des Egoïsses, Perrier-Jouët Belle Epoque, Vilmart Grand Cellier.*

DEMI-SEC Medium sweet. Rarely very nice, but *Louis Roederer* is outstanding, and *Mercier* is surprisingly fresh and floral.

DOUX Sweet. *Louis Roederer* is excellent.

EXTRA DRY Confusingly, this is less dry than 'Brut', but drier than 'Sec'.

GRANDE MARQUE Ambiguous term meaning 'great brand'. It was a self-styled group of 28 houses, including the 15 or so best known (recently replaced by the new Club des Grandes Marques, which promises to have fewer members). The term *should* be synonymous with quality – better grapes, older reserve wines and more rigid selection. But the pressure for market share takes its toll.

MA Label code meaning *marque auxiliare*, implying a subsidiary brand or a secondary label. Any Champagne selling for a quid less than you expect is likely to be one.

NM In the code on the label, this means *négociant-manipulant* (merchant-handler) and may show that the wine was bottle-fermented by the house on the label; but buying wine *sur-lattes* is still legal.

NON-DOSAGE Most Champagne has a little sweetness – a 'dosage' – added just before the final cork. A few are sold bone-dry and will have names like Brut Zero, implying a totally dry wine. Best are *Laurent Perrier, Piper-Heidsieck*.

NON-VINTAGE The ordinary, most basic blend. Many houses used to take pride in a house style achieved by blending various vintages. Some would even occasionally go to the extent of not declaring a vintage in a good year if they wanted to use the wine to keep up the standard of their non-vintage. Sadly, this happens far less nowadays. Although a little older reserve wine is added to smooth out the edges when the blend is being put together, most non-vintages are now released 'ready' for drinking, heavily dependent on a single year's harvest of perhaps two or three years' age, and some producers will offer wine not much more than 18 months old. The current blends are based on excellent vintages but are often released much too young to justify fully the scary prices. Best are *Alfred Gratien, Billecart-Salmon, Gosset, Charles Heidsieck, Duval-Leroy, Jacquesson, Henriot, Lanson, Laurent Perrier, Mercier, Bruno Paillard, Pol Roger, Louis Roederer, Veuve Clicquot Vilmart*. All non-vintage Champagnes improve greatly if laid down for even a few months between buying and drinking.

RC A new designation indicating *récoltant-co-opérateur* – for a grower selling wine produced at a co-op. It should stop growers pretending they've made it themselves.

RECENTLY DISGORGED A term used for Champagnes that have been left in the cellars, drawing flavour from their yeast deposits, for much longer than usual before disgorging. The wines can happily rest for 20 to 30 years on the lees but are usually released after seven to ten years. *Bollinger RD* is the most famous; wines also from *Deutz, Alfred Gratien* and *Laurent Perrier*.

RICH The sweetest Champagne.

RM Indicates that the wine comes from a single grower, a *récoltant-manipulant*, literally 'harvester-handler'. Since 1989 RM should indicate a grower who's made his Champagne himself, rather than taking it to the local co-op. Best: *Bara, Beerens, Billiot, Bonnaire, Brice, Cattier, Clouet, Fliniaux, Michel Gonet, André Jacquart, Lassalle, Albert Lebrun, Leclerc-Briant, Legras, Vesselle, Vilmart*.

ROSÉ Traditionally, the pink colour is gained by a short, careful maceration of the black Pinot Noir and Pinot Meunier skins with the juice. Other producers add a little red Bouzy wine to white Champagne before bottling. Ideally rosés are aromatic, fruity wines, with a delicious strawberry or cherry flavour. Sadly, many are virtually indistinguishable from white. Most should be drunk young. Best producers: *Besserat de Bellefon, Billecart-Salmon, Boizel, Bollinger, Charbaut Certificate, Dom Ruinart, Alfred Gratien, Jacquart la Renommée, Lassalle, Laurent Perrier, Moët et Chandon, Louise Pommery, Roederer* and *Roedererer Cristal, Taittinger Comtes de Champagne*. *Krug rosé* is in a class of its own, and so it should be at the price.

SEC Literally 'dry', but actually medium dry.

SR Société de Récoltants. Label code for a family company of growers.

VINTAGE Wine of a single, good year, generally fuller than non-vintage, but almost always nowadays released too young. Best: *Billecart-Salmon, Bollinger, Gosset Grande Millésime, Alfred Gratien, Henriot, Krug, Lanson, Bruno Paillard, Joseph Perrier, Perrier-Jouët, Pol Roger, Louis Roederer, Ruinart, Veuve Clicquot*.

CLASSIFICATIONS

The classification system in Champagne is based on vineyards. The approved areas for vineyards are strictly demarcated and the vineyard land graded according to suitability for black and white grapes, going from 100 per cent for the finest Grand Cru villages through 90–99 per cent for the 41 Premier Cru villages and on to 80 per cent for the least favoured.

If the guideline price is 20 francs per kilo of grapes, a 100 per cent village grower receives the full 20 francs. An 80 per cent grower will receive only 80 per cent – 16 francs – and so on, it's all quite simple. The whole system is now less rigorous than it was 50 years ago, when percentages ranged from 50 to 100.

Champagne houses boast about how high their 'average percentage' of grapes is. Some Champagne labels will say either '100 per cent Grand Cru' or 'Premier Cru' and even a village name as well, Avize, for example, if the wine comes entirely from one single top village.

Hardly surprisingly, no one ever bothers to declare on the label percentages in the 80s or lower 90s, but in actual fact many of the best value Champagnes on the UK market come from these so-called 'lowly' villages. There is no reason why careful vineyard managment and vinification should not produce good results.

CHAMPAGNE HOUSE PROFILES

BILLECART-SALMON ★★★★ Terrifically elegant Champagne from a family-owned house. Very refined, delicate wines and a lovely rosé. Its vintage, Cuvée NF Billecart, is also excellent.

BOLLINGER ★★★(★) Like Krug, makes 'English-style' Champagnes: warm, rich and oaky. Its reputation has been slightly marred in recent years because the wines were released too young. RD, for Récemment Dégorgé, its luxury *cuvée*, is kept on its lees until just before sale. Also Vieilles Vignes. Bollinger has been at the centre of the latest reforms.

ALFRED GRATIEN ★★★★ Serious, oak-fermented wine at a much lower price than Krug. Very long-lived vintage.

KRUG ★★★★★ The classic heavy, serious Champagne. Grande Cuvée, oak-fermented is outstandingly good, and weightier than any competitor. Expensive rosé has an incomparable Pinot Noir cherry-fruitiness. Even more expensive Clos de Mesnil is a delicate, single vineyard Blanc de Blancs.

LANSON ★★★ Until recently had (well-deserved) reputation for excessive acidity. Under new ownership it is aging wine longer, for a light, quaffable style. Classic, long-maturing vintage.

LAURENT PERRIER ★★★★ Possibly the most reliable of all the non-vintage blends. Excellent, reasonably-priced rosé. Prestige brand Grand Siècle is (sensibly) blend of several vintages. Good value.

MOËT & CHANDON ★★(★) Brut Imperial infuriatingly unreliable – sometimes as good as any NV, at other times hardly tasting like Champagne at all. Vintages usually show well but are released far too young.

MUMM ★(★) Traditionally rich wine, but all too frequently unimpressive. Delicate, creamy Crémant from south-facing slopes in Cramant. You can't help wishing its class would rub off on the NV and vintage.

PERRIER-JOUËT ★★★Coasting on its reputation, but can be undistinguished. Best known for Belle Époque in a pretty bottle, all flowery elegance, echoed in fresh, slightly unripe-cherry feel of the wine.

POL ROGER ★★★★ Model family firm, producer of Churchill's favourite fizz. Delicious, delicate Blanc de Blancs. NV, vintage and Cuvée Sir Winston Churchill all top class. New are vintage Blanc de Chardonnay, vintage rosé and a Demi-sec.

POMMERY ★★ Despite ownership changes, Pommery is still rather too bland. The wine can be exciting, when it tries.

LOUIS ROEDERER ★★★★(★) Most famous for Cristal, invented to satisfy sweet tooths of Russian Tsars. Now the most natural of all the prestige *cuvées*, reflecting the quality of individual vintages. Cristal is made (in small quantities) even in theoretically bad years – like 1974 and 1977 – when its almost vegetal sweetness comes through. NV usually one of the best despite needing more maturity. Good Demi-sec and Doux.

TAITTINGER ★★★(★) Splendidly light, modern, Chardonnayish style, carried through in its model Blanc de Blancs, Comtes de Champagne.

VEUVE CLICQUOT ★★★ For a century and a half greatly loved by the British. The NV can still have the rich, warm style first made famous by the formidable Madame Veuve Clicquot-Ponsardin. Prestige *cuvée* La Grande Dame almost chocolate-rich.

CHAMPAGNE VINTAGES

A vintage table for Champagne is not straightforward since so much is blended without vintage designation. Also, vintage wines released and sold very young, while good for laying down, are unlikely to give any more immediate pleasure than good non-vintage. Most Champagne can do with aging; vintage demands it. Historically, a vintage was 'declared' by the houses after an exceptional year, and then released at six to seven years old when reasonably mature. There has been a trend recently for some vintage wine to appear almost every year, and at only four to five years old. Moët is often guilty of infanticide and released its 1985, in particular, far too young. Its excellent '79 is now coming into its own, yet practically all of it has already been drunk. But some of the 1982s, released at only five years old, were immediately delicious.

1992 The fourth-largest harvest ever, gathered in wet conditions. Quality was described by the authorities as 'entirely satisfactory' but rot was a problem.

1991 Like 1986, a vintage declared by a few houses only. A large harvest, despite spring frosts taking their toll. Should be useful for blending non-vintage.

1990 A second, late crop produced the third largest harvest recorded in Champagne, helped by late sunshine. The wines are of fairly good quality, but are unfortunately unlikely to be cheap.

1989 For once an enormous, much-hyped vintage is turning out to be as good as the Champenois thought it would be. But I suppose they'll inevitably release the wines far too young. In fact I've already seen some.

1988 The harvest started on 19 September – weeks before supposedly warmer areas. But the vines had flowered incredibly early – around 12 June – and the grapes were ripe. In ten years' time there could be some memorable bottles of 1988. Try to be patient and not open them until then.

1987 I can say precisely one thing in favour of the 1987 Champagne harvest – there's lots of it. 1987 produced some of the blandest, least memorable wine I can ever remember tasting. What they should have done was to use it to make lots of pleasant, fairly-priced non-vintage. Some hope.

1986 Useful wines of reasonable quality, but the yield was rather spoiled by rot. Mostly good for blending into non-vintage, but the Champagne hounds are all rushing headlong into the more expensive styles and we're already seeing 1986 vintage labels sprouting all over the place.

1985 Well, after all the gloom and despondency when the Champagne guys were wringing their bejewelled hands and crying 'no wine, no wine', 1985 produced a fair amount; much of it good to excellent. All have launched their 1985s, but you could keep them for a few years yet.

1984 A feeble year. Anyone who produced a vintage could probably turn water into wine.

1983 The second of the record-breaking vintages which sent fizz prices plunging in the UK and dramatically increased the amount of Champagne we all drank – remember? There are still some 1983 wines around and they are extremely good, a little leaner than 1982, but high-quality.

1982 Not so long ago I castigated houses like Bollinger and Veuve Clicquot for wantonly releasing their vintage wines at five years old. Well, the '82s were sheer bliss. They were ready at five years old – in fact the Bollinger '82 tasted readier than its non-vintage.

1979 An excellent vintage of beautifully soft, balanced wines still at their peak.

RHÔNE

The Rhône Valley is a simple place. Banish any idea of the sophistication and grandeur of the châteaux of Bordeaux from your mind; even the depths of rural Burgundy will seem suave after a night in Tournon or Ampuis. Apart from a scant handful of rich *négociants* who pride themselves on their ability to re-erect Roman temples in their backyards, the vast majority of growers in the top villages lead very homely lives: they spend their sunlit hours working out in the vines; eat copious meals and while away their evenings in front of the television or browsing through the latest issue of Robert Parker's tasting notes in *The Wine Advocate.* Even if only a few can make any headway with the English, at least they can all read the scores.

Such a world has its charm. And it must be said that in contrast to Champagne or Bordeaux, the wine is still made by hand. No machine could replace man on those steep slopes, and the patches of vines which cover them are so small compared to the rolling hectares of the top estates in the Gironde that each bottle is precious. Making fine wine in the northern Rhône is never easy, and it is hard to begrudge a grower in Côte-Rôtie a price even slightly below the level of a Grande Marque Champagne: the wine is worth far more in sheer sweat and toil.

Occasional winds blow up like the Mistral to ruffle this calm surface. A few years back all the talk was of outside oenologists, and highly-qualified and persuasive men came from Bordeaux to turn local lives upside down with new-fangled ideas about barrels and *pigeage*, or stirring the lees. That is all past now. In Châteauneuf-du-Pape one of the chief exponents of these ideas, Noël Rabon, has become a part of the furniture while in the northern Rhône another erstwhile radical, Jean-Luc Colombo, has joined the establishment – or the establishment has absorbed him. Both Chapoutier and Jaboulet now take part in Colombo's annual tastings in Valence where wine journalists are invited to consider and to measure the changes which can be brought about in the wines by giving a bit more attention to the use of oak. One of the great attractions of this tasting (journalists being journalists) is the slap-up lunch at the three-star Restaurant Pic which crowns the morning.

Cat among the *crus*

Life is at its most sluggish on the granite outcrops which mark the great *crus* of the northern Rhône. There is little land to spare here and only the death or retirement of an aged grower is likely to put the cat among the pigeons. In Côte-Rôtie the current cat is called René Rostaing, an outsider who didn't even possess the pedigree of coming from the market gardens which lie by the riverside at Ampui, and which are somewhat looked down upon by the more elitist producers. He is said to be high-handed with his fellow growers, which puts their backs up. Much to their annoyance, he was able to gain a new chunk of land when Marius Gentaz went into retirement. Gentaz, however, was able to hang on to a small piece of his estate, and not unnaturally he chose the oldest and best vines. Another part went to Alain Bernard. Rostaing got the youngest vines, which were planted in 1975.

Hermitage is even less prone to change than Côte-Rôtie. Here the land is effectively carved up by the big names and the co-operative between them, and the few small producers have to make do with the odd *are*. If you are very canny and lucky you can find some of the wine from these small growers, but quality is frankly variable and quantities can be tiny. The excellent Alain Graillot produces just two casks of Hermitage a year, of which 60 bottles have to be turned over to the owners of the land in the form of rent.

As regards the big names of Hermitage, Chapoutier has made a superb 1991 vintage. Some say that in previous years he was having problems with his choice of oak, but these now appear to have been resolved. Oenologist Jean-Luc Colombo may well have played his part in the changes which have brought Chapoutier's top wines into direct comparison with those of Jaboulet.

Where things really do appear to be happening is in Crozes-Hermitage. The cynical view was that since things could not have got any worse here, improvement was the only thing possible. The recent success of certain growers has emboldened the others; now one by one they are ceasing to sell their wines in bulk to the big merchant houses, or to take their grapes to the local co-operative, and are having a go at bottling them themselves. It is an exciting development to watch. The superiority of Alain Graillot and Etienne Pochon over the rest of the Crozes growers seemed unassailable only a little while ago, and perhaps it still is, but there is now some stiff competition coming from Albert Belle, Stéphane Cournu and Laurent Combier. The latest name to emerge is Gabriel Viale, who also has some vines in Hermitage.

Turning the Cornas

In Cornas Jean-Luc Colombo has benefited from the gradual passing of the valetudinarians. Since 1990, when Guy de Barjac retired, Colombo's Cornas has had the added weight of de Barjac's old vines (although de Barjac continues to make some wine in retirement, much in the manner of Marius Gentaz in Côte-Rôtie). Thierry Allemand has similarly snaffled up half the vineyard land of the fastidious (and now retired) Noël Verset and is increasingly proving the man to watch in Cornas.

Whereas the northern Rhône has (literally) kept its head above water in the last two vintages, the South suffered in both 1991 and 1992 from torrential rains and poor harvests. In 1992 the weather was cold and wet until 14 July, after which there was six weeks of lovely summer weather. Then the rain returned at the beginning of September, albeit briefly. The real storms came with the floods in Vaisons-la-Romaine on 28 September, by which time the lucky ones had brought in their crop.

While the '91s from Châteauneuf-du-Pape have been compared to the '87 vintage, the '92s are being compared to the '84. This may not sound like much of a step up in quality, but believe me, the '84s were better than the '87s. What it really means is that they should not be left lying around too long, and you can happily drink them before you touch the wines you bought from the '88, '89 and '90 vintages.

Apart from that? Well, the big news in Châteauneuf-du-Pape this year is that growers are now allowed to train their Cinsaut, Counoise and other varieties of vine (but not Grenache or Mourvèdre) on wires (as in, say, Bordeaux) as opposed to using the traditional 'goblet' system of training. Didn't I tell you the Rhône Valley was a quiet place? **GILES MACDONOGH**

RED WINES

Northern Rhône reds are really the different manifestations of a single grape variety – the Syrah. It is virtually the only red grape grown in the North, and certainly the only one tolerated for the various *appellations contrôlées*. Syrah can range from light, juicy and simple in the more basic St-Joseph and Crozes-Hermitage offerings, to something rich, extravagant and wonderfully challenging in the top wines of Hermitage, Côte-Rôtie and Cornas.

Southern Rhône reds are usually made from a range of grape varieties, none of which, except the Syrah and very occasionally the Grenache are able to produce wine of dramatic individuality on its own, and that means basic fruit flavours across the whole area are very similar. These are usually raspberry-strawberry, often attractively spicy, slightly dusty, and sometimes livened up with some blackcurrant sweetness or wild herb dryness. The introduction of carbonic maceration – the Beaujolais-type method of vinification – in the Rhône has meant that many wines, even at the cheapest level, can have a deliciously drinkable fruit; but with a certain uniformity of style.

GRAPES & FLAVOURS

CARIGNAN This grape is much maligned because in the far South it used to, and sometimes still does, produce tough, raw, fruitless wines which form the bulk of France's red contribution to the wine lake. Old vines can produce big, strong but very tasty wines that age well, and the use of carbonic maceration can work wonders.

CINSAUT Another gentle grape, giving acidity and freshness but little fruit to the reds and rosés of the southern Rhône.

GRENACHE The most important red grape in the southern Rhône, because it gives loads of alcoholic strength and a gentle, juicy, spicy fruit perked up by a whiff of pepper, ideal for rosés and easy-going reds. So what's the problem? Well, it keeps failing to flower properly which is ruining the crop.

MOURVÈDRE An old-fashioned, highly flavoured wine, low in alcohol, which doesn't always ripen fully, although it does in Châteauneuf (its home base is Bandol, right on the Mediterranean). But it has an excellent, rather berryish taste, and a strong whiff of tobacco spice that is making it increasingly popular with the more imaginative growers.

SYRAH Wine-making in the northern Rhône is dominated by this one red grape variety. Along with Cabernet Sauvignon, Bordeaux's great grape, the Syrah makes the blackest, most startling, pungent red wine in France, and, although it is grown elsewhere, it is here that it is at its most brilliant. From Hermitage and Cornas, it rasps with tannin and tar and woodsmoke, backed by the deep, ungainly sweetness of black treacle. But give it five or ten years, and those raw fumes will have become sweet, pungent, full of raspberries, brambles and *cassis*. Syrah is less prevalent than the Grenache in the southern Rhône, but as more is planted, the standard of southern Rhône reds is sure to rise.

VIOGNIER This aromatic white grape can be used as up to 20 per cent of the blend of red Côte-Rôtie to add fragrance, and it really does: Côte-Rôtie made purely of Syrah lacks the haunting beauty of one blended with Viognier.

WINES & WINE REGIONS

CHÂTEAUNEUF-DU-PAPE, AC The largest of the ACs of the Côtes du Rhône, this can be quite delicious, deep, dusty red, almost sweet and fat, low in acidity, but kept appetizing by back-room tannin. *Can* be. It can also be fruit-pastilly and pointless, or dark, tough and stringy. Thirteen different red and white grapes are permitted, and the resulting flavour is usually slightly indistinct, varying from one property to another. The occasional 'super-vintage' like 1978 gives wines that can stay stunning for ten years and more. Around one-third of the growers make good wine – and as much as two-thirds of the wine sold probably exceeds the permitted yields. So it makes sense always to go for a domaine wine and certainly not to buy one bottled away from the region of production. Good, full Châteauneufs include: *Château de Beaucastel, Château Rayas* and *Clos du Mont-Olivet, Château Fortia, Château St-André, La Nerthe, Chante Cigale, Clos des Papes, Chante-Perdrix, Le Vieux Donjon, la Jacquinotte, Font de Michelle, Font du Loup, Brunel, Quiot, Domaine du Grand Tinel, Domaine de Mont-Redon, Domaine du Vieux Télégraphe, Domaine Durieu, Bosquet des Papes, Lucien Gabriel Barrot, Les Clefs d'Or, Fabrice Mouisset, Chapoutier's La Bernadine* and *Henri Bonnot.*

CORNAS, AC Black and tarry tooth-stainers, from the right bank of the Rhône, opposite Valence. Usually rather hefty, jammy even, and lacking some of the fresh fruit that makes Hermitage so remarkable, yet at ten years old this is impressive wine. There have been quite big price rises in recent years, but then quality seems to improve year by year, too. Excellent blockbusters are made by *Auguste Clape, Robert Michel* and *Noël Verset*. It's also worth looking out for *de Barjac, Colombo, Delas, Juge, Lemenicier, Allemand, Maurice Courbis and Jean Lionnet.*

COTEAUX DU TRICASTIN, AC Constantly improving spicy, fruity reds from this large *appellation* east of the Rhône. Good value. Best producers: *Domaine de Grangeneuve, Tour d'Elyssas* (especially its 100 per cent Syrah), *Producteurs Réunis Ardéchois* (co-op).

CÔTE-RÔTIE, AC The admixture of the white Viognier grape makes this one of France's most scented reds when properly made. But the AC has been extended on to the plateau above the traditional 'roasted slope', and unless something is done to differentiate the two, the reputation of this highly-prized, highly-priced vineyard will be in tatters. At best, from *Gentaz-Dervieux, Jamet, Guigal* and *René Rostaing*, Côte-Rôtie is rare and delicious. Look also for *Gilles* and *Pierre Barge, Bernard Burgaud, Jasmin, Dervieux-Thaize, Vidal-Fleury* and *Delas Cuvée Seigneur de Maugiron.*

CÔTES DU LUBÉRON, AC Upgraded from VDQS in 1987, Lubéron makes some decent reds, usually rather light, but capable of stronger personality. The Val Joanis rosé is one of the best in the South. Try also *Château de Canorgue, Château de l'Isolette, Mas du Peyroulet, Val Joanis* (also to be seen under own label as *Domaines Chancel* or *Domaine de la Panisse), Vieille Ferme.*

CÔTES DU RHÔNE, AC This huge *appellation* covers 80 per cent of all Rhône wines, from Vienne to Avignon. Well-made basic Côtes du Rhônes are quite delicious when young, wonderfully fresh and fruity, like a rather softer version of Beaujolais. Or they can be fierce, black, grape-skins-and-alcohol monsters. Since the label gives

The price guides for this section begin on page 316.

no clue, it's trial and error, or merchants' recommendations. *Coudoulet de Beaucastel* (formerly *Cru de Coudoulet*) is beefy, and many of the weightiest are made by Châteauneuf or northern Rhône producers like *Guigal*. *Château du Grand Moulas* is spicy and attractive, with plenty of body. Also good: *Caves C.N. Jaume, Château de Deurre, Château de Fonsalette, Château de Ruth, Château de Goudray, Clos du Père Clément, Dom de Bel Air, Dom de la Cantharide, Dom de St-Estève, Domaine des Aussellons.*

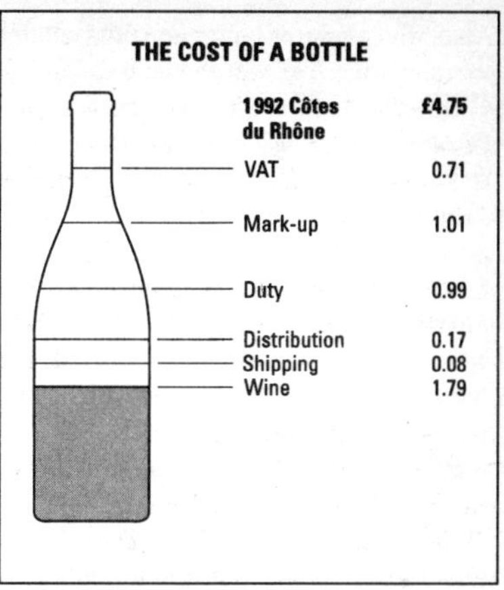

CÔTES DU RHÔNE-VILLAGES, AC One of the best areas for good, full reds that can also age, combining earthy, dusty southern heat with spicy, raspberry fruit. They come from higher quality villages, 17 of which can add their names on the label, including Vacqueyras, Cairanne, Chusclan, Valréas, Beaumes-de-Venise and Rasteau. Good growers: (Laudun) *Domaine Pelaquié;* (Rasteau) *Domaine de Grangeneuve;* (Sablet) *Jean-Pierre Cartier, Château de Trignon, Domaine de Boisson, Domaine St-Antoine, Domaine de Verquière;* (Cairanne) *Domaine de l'Ameillaud, Dom Brusset, Dom l'Oratoire St-Martin, Dom de la Présidente, Dom Rabasse-Charavin;* (St-Gervais) *Dom Ste-Anne;* (Séguret) *Dom Courançonne, Dom de Cabasse;* (Valréas) *Roger Combe, Dom des Grands Devers, Le Val des Rois;* (Vacqueyras) *Château de Montmirail, Clos des Cazaux, Dom la Fourmone, Dom des Lambertins, Le Sang des Cailloux.*

CÔTES DU VENTOUX, AC Rather good area just to the east of the Rhône producing lots of fresh, juicy wine, of which the red is the best. Can occasionally be quite special. Best: *Domaine des Anges, Jaboulet, Pascal* as well as *Vieille Ferme* and *Vieux Lazaret*.

CROZES-HERMITAGE, AC A large AC providing a lot of fairly strong and slightly tough and smoky Hermitage-type wine which at its best has a lovely juicy fruit as well. *Etienne Pochon (Château de Curson), Graillot*'s *La Guérande* and *Jaboulet's Thalabert* brand are outstanding; also good are *Desmeures, Ferraton, Albert Belle, Stephane Cornu, Laurent Combier, Tardy & Ange* and *Gabriel Viale*. The *Tain* co-op is also finally producing some decent stuff.

GIGONDAS, AC Red and rosé from west of Orange. Not the most immediately attractive of reds – a bit ragged at the edges – but consistent, plummy and rather solid. *Domaine de St-Gayan* is very good, as are *Château de Montmirail, Clos des Cazeaux, Château du Trignon, Domaine les Gouberts, Domaine de Longue-Toque, Domaine l'Oustau Fauquet, Domaine les Pallières, Domaine Raspail-Ay*.

HERMITAGE, AC One of France's burliest, grandest reds, from a small, precipitous vineyard area around the hill of Hermitage. Strong and fierily tough when young, it matures to a rich, brooding magnificence. There is always a stern, vaguely medicinal or smoky edge to it, and an unmatchable depth of raspberry and blackcurrant fruit. Although a number of people produce Hermitage of sorts, there have traditionally been only two stars, the marvellously good *Chave*, who produces small amounts of impeccable wine, and the ebullient, export-orientated *Paul Jaboulet*

Aîné, who produces larger amounts of more variable wine. To them should be added *Chapoutier's Le Pavillon*. Also good: *Delas Cuvée Marquise de la Tourette, Desmeure, B. Faurie, Guigal, Sorrel, Belle, Faurie* and *Jean-Louis Grippat*.

LIRAC, AC An excellent, often underrated area just south-west of Châteauneuf whose wines it can frequently equal. The reds are packed with fruit, often tinged with a not unwelcome mineral edge. The rosés are remarkably fresh for so far south. Whites can be first-class if caught young. Best: *Domaine de Château St-Roch, Domaine des Causses et St-Eymes, Domaine les Garrigues, Domaine la Fermade, Domaine de la Tour*.

ST-JOSEPH, AC Almost smooth and sweet compared to their tougher neighbours, these reds, especially those from the hills between Condrieu and Cornas, can be fairly big, fine wines, stacked with blackcurrant in good years. There has been some growth of the AC into less suitable land, but quality is mostly high, and though there have been hefty price rises, the wines *were* undervalued. *Chave, Coursodon, Florentin, Gripa, Grippat, Jaboulet, Maurice Courbis* and *Trollat* are leading names. The co-op at *St-Désirat Champagne* makes 'Beaujolais-type' St-Joseph; not traditional, but lovely.

TAVEL, AC The AC only applies to one colour of wine – pink! The wines are quite expensive, certainly tasty, but too big and alcoholic to be very refreshing. Any of the Rhône grapes will do, but generally it's Grenache-dominated, with the addition of a little Cinsaut. Best producers: *Château d'Aqueria, Château de Trinquevedel, Domaine de la Forcadière, Domaine de la Génestière*.

VIN DE PAYS DES COLLINES RHODANIENNES A usually impressive and expanding northern Rhône area, particularly for inexpensive, strongly flavoured Syrah reds, though Gamay can also be good.

VIN DE PAYS DES COTEAUX DE L'ARDÈCHE This straggly, upland Rhône *département* puts into a nutshell what the *vins de pays* should be trying to achieve. Not content with the usual mishmash of southern grapes, a mixture of go-ahead co-ops and outside influences decided to plant grapes to make wine that would *sell*: delicious Nouveau-style Gamay, first class Syrah, good Cabernet, and they've planted Sauvignon Blanc, Pinot Noir – and Chardonnay. *Louis Latour*, one of the largest sellers of Burgundian Chardonnay, has inspired much of the Chardonnay planting here for his Chardonnay de l'Ardèche. Sixty local growers have planted Chardonnay and are contracted to Latour. That's good news. But the fact that the local co-ops are already producing higher quality wines at far lower prices – without his help – is much better!

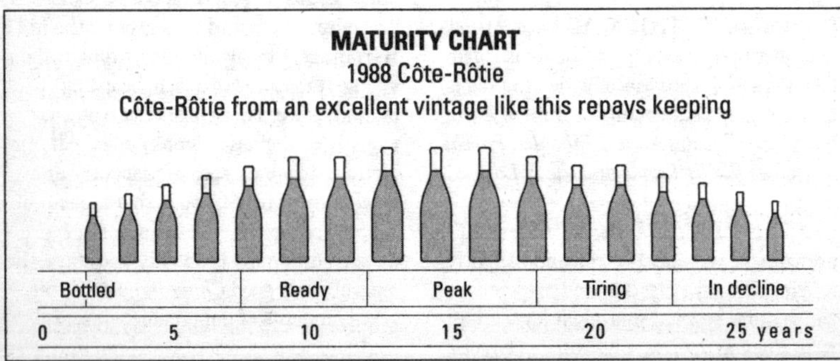

WHITE WINES

The two main styles of northern Rhône white could hardly be more different. The wines based on Marsanne and Roussanne – Hermitage, Crozes-Hermitage, St-Joseph and St-Péray – are in general weighty, strong, initially lacking in perfume and charm, but capable of a great, opulent, even pompous richness, given the decade or so they need to mature. Some modern versions, like those of Jaboulet, are less ambitious but ready within the year. The wines based on the Viognier are heavenly – totally different in style, bursting with the fruit flavours of apricots and pears and a mad, heady perfume like flower gardens in spring. Very special.

The interest in southern Rhône whites is fairly recent because it had always been assumed, with justification, that white wine from the region's non-aromatic grapes, produced on parched vineyards in the baking summer heat, could not possibly be anything but dull and flabby and fruitless. Now that many leading producers have invested in refrigerated equipment,, and adopted cool fermentation techniques, it is quite remarkable what delicious flavours are beginning to appear. The vintage of 1989 was particularly good and 1990 looks like matching that quality – where growers were careful not to overproduce.

GRAPES & FLAVOURS

CLAIRETTE Makes sparkling Clairette de Die, but is a bit dull unless livened up with the aromatic Muscat. In the South it makes rather big, strong whites, sometimes creamy, but more often dull and nutty. Needs careful handling and early drinking.

GRENACHE BLANC A widely planted variety in the southern Rhône producing appley wines with a strong whiff of aniseed. Good, but soft, so drink young.

MARSANNE The dominant of the two grapes that go to make white Hermitage and Crozes-Hermitage, as well as white St-Joseph and St-Péray. Its wine is big and weighty but with a rather good, rich, sweet scent. Further south it makes big, burly wine, fat, lanoliny, but capable of rich exotic peach and toffee flavours, too. A good quality producer.

MUSCAT Used to great effect blended with Clairette to make the sparkling Clairette de Die Tradition, but more famous for Muscat de Beaumes de Venise.

ROUSSANNE Altogether more delicate and fragrant than the Marsanne, but it is inconveniently prone to disease and a low yielder, so it is increasingly losing ground to Marsanne. Found chiefly in Hermitage and St-Péray in the North, though it also makes light, fragrant wines further south in Châteauneuf. Look out for Château de Beaucastel's *Vieilles Vignes* version.

UGNI BLANC Boring workhorse grape planted all over the South to produce basic gulping stuff. The same as the Trebbiano of Italy, where it is hardly more exciting.

VIOGNIER The grape of Condrieu and Château Grillet. It has one of the most memorable flavours of any white grape because it blends the rich, musky scent of overripe apricots with that of spring flowers. The wine is made dry, but it is so rich you hardly believe it. Sweet versions do exist, but in general are to be avoided. The rarest of the world's great white grapes, though interest in planting it is growing, even as far afield as Australia.

WINES & WINE REGIONS

CHÂTEAU GRILLET, AC A single property in the far north-west of the northern Rhône, and the smallest AC in France at only three hectares, excepting a couple of Vosne-Romanée Grands Crus in Burgundy. This wine should have that magic reek of orchard fruit and harvest bloom about it. Sometimes it does.

CHÂTEAUNEUF-DU-PAPE BLANC, AC Only three per cent of the AC is white, but the wines can be outstandingly perfumed with a delicious nip of acidity, leaving you wondering how on earth such aromatic wines could come from such a hot, arid region. Magic or technology; or it might be such delights as the Roussanne, Picpoul and Picardan varieties adding something to the base of Grenache Blanc, Clairette and Bourboulenc. Wonderful wines can be produced in the most unlikely places – and this just happens to be one of them. Although the wine can age, you lose that perfumed rush of springtime madness after a year. Best: *Beaucastel* (their pure Roussanne *Vieilles Vignes* – and the new Viognier white), *Clefs d'Or, Clos des Papes, Font de Michelle, Grand Tinel, Mont-Redon, Nalys, Rayas, Vieux Télégraphe*.

CLAIRETTE DE DIE BRUT, AC Adequate fizz from the Clairette grape grown in the beautiful Drôme valley, east of the Rhône.

CLAIRETTE DE DIE TRADITION, AC Delicious, light, off-dry, grapy fizz made half from Clairette, half from Muscat.

CONDRIEU, AC From a small area at the northern end of the northern Rhône, this is wonderful when made properly, with apricot scent that leaps out of the glass, and an exciting balance of succulent fruit and gentle, nipping acidity. But its sudden popularity has led to great replanting, sometimes by people concerned more with high prices than high quality. Yet the potential quality is so stunning that with luck the *arrivistes* will realize that the real thing is worth striving for. The potential area is 100 hectares, but with only just over 30 planted, there's very little wine; and it's expensive, though less so than Château Grillet. There is some *cépage* Viognier (the grape of Château Grillet), which will show what the fuss is about – at half the Condrieu price. (Yapp has one.) Top names: *Château du Rozay, Delas, Dumazet, Guigal, Multier*, (who, like some others, is using new oak), *Niero Pinchon, Jean Pinchon* and *Georges Vernay.*

COTEAUX DU TRICASTIN, AC Fresh, fruity and quite full-flavoured southerly whites, not as exciting as the reds. Best bet: *Producteurs Réunis Ardéchois.*

CÔTES DU LUBÉRON, AC Usually pleasant and light southern wine but little more, though recent innovations have started to produce much more fragrant, interesting styles at such properties as *Château de l'Isolette, Mas du Peyroulet, Val Joanis* and *Vieille Ferme*.

CÔTES DU RHÔNE BLANC, AC; CÔTES DU RHÔNE-VILLAGES BLANC, AC Increasingly fresh, fruity and gulpable especially from the villages of Laudun and Chusclan. *Domaine Pelaquié* at Laudun is the leading estate, and *Domaine Ste-Anne* at St-Gervais is good.

CROZES-HERMITAGE, AC Generally a rather dull, strong northern Rhône white, but there are good ones from *Desmeure, Fayolle, Jaboulet* and *Pradelle.*

HERMITAGE, AC Often a bit heavy and dull, but curiously it ages tremendously well to a soft, rich nuttiness. Some of the finest is made by *Chapoutier, Chave, Desmeure, Ferraton, Grippat* and *Sorrel*.

LIRAC, AC The whites can be good young, resembling a less exotic Châteauneuf: less exotic flavour; less exotic price.

ST-JOSEPH, AC Northern AC with some fair, nutty white and better red. *Grippat* is good. *Florentin* does an intense old-style headbanging white unlike any other.

ST-PÉRAY, AC Made in the southern bit of the northern Rhône, this was once France's most famous sparkling wine after Champagne. Not any more. It tends to be rather stolid and short of freshness. And the still whites are just dull. The occasional better bottle will come from *Chaboud, Clape, Grippat, Juge* or *Voge*.

FORTIFIED WINES

MUSCAT DE BEAUMES DE VENISE, AC This Côtes du Rhône village is the only place in the Rhône to grow the Muscat grape. The golden sweet wine – a *vin doux naturel* – has become a real fad drink, but for once the fad is a good one, because it's supremely delicious! Grapy, fresh, rich but not cloying. Look for *Domaine de Coyeux, Domaine Durban, Jaboulet* and the *Beaumes de Venise* co-op.

RASTEAU, AC The Côtes du Rhône village of Rasteau also makes a few big, port-like fortified wines – *vins doux naturels* – both red and off-white. Young ones can have a delightful raspberry scent from the Grenache Noir. The whites are made from Grenache Blanc and can be frankly unpleasant. Production is pretty small. Try *Domaine de la Soumade, Co-opérative de Rasteau*.

RHÔNE VINTAGES

1992 A fairly rotten year, but the best growers were able to make something of it. In Châteauneuf and the South a few made decent wines for early drinking. Some 'correct' wines in the North. Buy only from top growers and drink up quickly.

1991 Many northern Rhône growers had their fourth very good year in succession; in Côte-Rôtie at least the wines are generally better than the 1990s. In the South yields were tiny, and the wine only moderately good.

1990 On the whole the North survived the drought best though rain affected picking in Côte-Rôtie. Choose 1990 for the North (though Côte-Rôtie is dodgy); 1989 for the South.

1989 Drought in much of the region, and some poor Hermitage and Cornas was made by growers unable to master it. Small crops meant concentrated Châteauneuf for keeping.

1988 There is certainly *some* great 1988, mostly in Côte-Rôtie, Hermitage and Châteauneuf-du-Pape. There is also a fair amount which is far too tannic for its own good.

1987 Côtes du Rhône reds and northern Rhônes can be good.

1986 A rather joyless vintage for reds. Some very good Châteauneuf and Hermitage but the ambitious Côtes du Rhône names made some of the best. Some white still improving.

1985 Brilliant Côte-Rôtie, St-Joseph and Cornas. Châteauneuf is delicious and juicy.

1983 Outstanding dark, rich, complex Hermitage and very good Côte-Rôtie for keeping. Southern reds are good, but the failure of the Grenache left some a bit tough.

1982 Good, rather simple northern reds; a difficult, hot vintage in the South.

1980 Underrated but high quality in North and South.

1978 The best vintage since 1961. Drink now – if you can find any.

LOIRE

Growers in the Loire must be grateful that meteorological conditions don't follow the long drawn-out example of the economic climate. Nature bounces back more quickly. After the short, sharp ravages of frost in 1991, 1992 was a year in which things more or less got back to normal. It was the kind of vintage that merchants call 'useful'.

The vines recovered well over the winter, flowered early along most of the river, and survived the summer rain which affected most *appellations* except Chinon and Bourgueil. The hail in Sancerre wiped out some vineyards in Bué but, as is the way with hail, left neighbouring ones unaffected.

The overall result was a considerably larger volume than in 1991, with high yields producing some rather dilute wines. The sensational stars of 1989 and 1990 were conspicuous by their absence. It was not a vintage for collectors and hoarders to stash away, just a normal one for everyday drinkers, a modest year for producers to turn over some of the cash that wasn't turned over the year before. In other words, a useful vintage.

Still, there's fizz

Sparkling wine producers were particularly cheered. Stock levels had fallen over the previous three years: in 1991 because of the frost, in the previous two years because potential was so good for still wines that there wasn't much left over to fizz up. Both quantity and reasonable alcohol levels in 1992 were just what Saumur and Vouvray wanted.

Muscadet, knocked about dreadfully in '91, produced some very respectable yields in '92. 'About 100 hectolitres per hectare', admitted one of the region's star producers, adding that he had to chaptalize to reach the 10.5 per cent he felt his wine needed. 'It was common in 1992', he said, a view that was echoed elsewhere. Even though the quality was not wonderful, Muscadet producers were more than happy with a big crop and plenty of drinkable wine, to fill the large empty hole left by the previous year.

In Anjou the '92 reds are very light, lacking the intensity of some of the good '91s, probably because yields in many cases were twice as high. But if the price is right, they will make good value picnic wines.

The Loire's sweet whites enjoyed a tremendous hike in interest following the excellent vintages of 1989 and 1990, but there is a potential problem here. Unless you read the small print, Vouvrays can seem inconsistent. One bottle is sweet, the next dry, in some cases excruciatingly so. Would it not, therefore, be easier if sweetness were standardized, broadly around the *demi-sec* level?

Alexandre Monmousseau at Château Gaudrelle has been making his wine in this compromise '*sec-tendre*' style since the mid-1980s, only deviating from it in years such as 1990 when the temptation to make a *moelleux*, or Réserve Personnelle as he calls it, is overwhelming. So far, however, only a few producers have nailed their Vouvrays to the *sec-tendre* mast. In any case, it would surely be a pity to blur these distinctive styles when the problem for consumers, of not being able easily to divine the style of a wine, could so easily be rectified by writing 'dry' or 'medium' in bigger letters on the label. One of the pleasures of the Loire is its variety. Let us hope that is not prejudiced.

JIM AINSWORTH

WHITE GRAPES & FLAVOURS

CHARDONNAY Increasingly widespread in the Loire and producing lean, light but tangy results in Haut-Poitou, in Anjou as Vin de Pays du Jardin de la France and in Orléans as Vin de l'Orléanais (where it's called Auvernat: *Clos St-Fiacre* is terrific). It also occurs in Muscadet (*Le Chouan* and *Domaine Couillaud* are good) and adds character and softness to Anjou Blanc.

CHASSELAS Makes adequate but dull wine at Pouilly-sur-Loire; it's actually best as a table grape, in a fruit salad.

CHENIN BLANC A grape that cries out for sun and ripens (if that's the word) well after the other varieties. Experiments with allowing the skins to steep in the juice before fermentation, and the quiet addition of a bit of Chardonnay, are beginning to produce outstanding peachy whites.

It also performs superbly on the Loire in a few warm and misty microclimates (especially Quarts de Chaume and Bonnezeaux), where noble rot strikes the Chenin with enough frequency to make it worthwhile going through all the pain and passion of producing great sweet wine, with steely acidity and honeyed, ripe-apple fruit. These wines can seem curiously disappointing when young, but fine sweet Chenin manages to put on weight and become sweeter for perhaps 20 years before bursting out into a richness as exciting as all but the very best from Germany or Bordeaux. And then it lasts and lasts...

MELON DE BOURGOGNE The grape of Muscadet, light and neutral. It's good at producing fresh, surprisingly soft, slightly peppery, dry white wine with a salty tang, generally for drinking young, though a good domaine-bottled *sur lie* can mature surprisingly well.

SAUVIGNON BLANC The grape of Sancerre, and the main white grape of Pouilly and Touraine, with a whole range of fresh, green, tangy flavours that might remind you of anything from gooseberries to nettles and fresh-cut grass, and there's sometimes even a whiff of newly roasted coffee. The wines are usually quite tart – but thirst-quenching rather than gum-searing – and have loadsafruit. Sauvignon can age interestingly in bottle, but the odds are against it, except for the high-priced oak-aged *cuvées*.

WHITE WINES & WINE REGIONS

ANJOU BLANC SEC, AC France's cheapest AC dry white made from the hard-to-ripen Chenin Blanc, grown anywhere in Anjou upriver from the Muscadet region, often tart, sulphured and sour. But it *can* be good, steely and honeyed, especially from Savennières with its two tiny special ACs, Coulée-de-Serrant and La Roche aux Moines, and from names such as *Domaine Richou* who mix Chardonnay with their Chenin, for extra flavour, fruit and body. They are allowed up to 20 per cent Chardonnay or Sauvignon Blanc. Some have planted a little bit more on the side, and it's no bad thing. Other good names: *Mark Angelli (Cuvée Christine) Baranger, Château de Valliennes, Domaine de la Haute Perche, Jaudeau.*

BONNEZEAUX, AC One of the most unfairly forgotten great sweet wines of France. After a long period of decline, this small AC inside the Coteaux du Layon is on the up again. The vineyard area has grown from 42 hectares in 1975 to 157 hectares in 1985 and prices for the lovely noble-rot-affected wines are rising fast. So much the better; they were far too cheap before, and if you don't make it profitable for the growers to indulge themselves in the passion and commitment necessary for great sweet wine, they'll give up and plant apples. Look out for the outstanding wines of *Mark Angelli* (from old vines) and *Jacques Boivin* of *Château de Fesles* as well as *Goizil, Renou* and *Denéchère*.

CHEVERNY, VDQS An up-and-coming Touraine region, of interest as the home of the white Romorantin grape. Attractive Sauvignon (and Gamay) too. *Domaine des Huards* makes fine, delicate wines.

COTEAUX DE L'AUBANCE, AC A rambling *appellation* south of Anjou giving pleasant semi-sweet whites, quite cheaply. Good producers: *Domaine des Rochettes, Jean-Yves Lebreton* and *Domaine Richou.*

COTEAUX DU LAYON, AC A large AC producing varying qualities of sweet white wine, at its best rich and tasty with a taut, cutting acidity that allows the wine to age for a long time. *Château de la Guimonière, Château de la Roulerie, Domaine Ambinois, Domaine du Petit Val, Domaine des Quarres, Domaine de la Soucherie, Domaine de la Pierre St Maurille, Clos Ste-Catherine* and *Ogereau* are worth trying. There are also six Coteaux du Layon-Villages ACs that usually offer higher quality.

CRÉMANT DE LOIRE, AC Sparkling wine AC intended to denote higher quality but not much used. Compared with Saumur AC fizz, the yield must be lower (50 rather than 60 hectolitres per hectare), the juice extract less (150kg of grapes as against 130kg for one hectolitre of juice), and the wine must lie on its lees for 12 months rather than 9 after its second fermentation. The product is usually softer and nicer than the frequently harsh wines of Saumur, but the merchants have built up their brands on Saumur and don't seem inclined to put much effort into Crémant de Loire. Laudable exceptions are the first-rate house of *Gratien & Meyer*, *St-Cyr-en-Bourg* co-op, and the small *Cave des Liards*.

GROS PLANT, VDQS Gros Plant rejoices in being one of the rawest wines in France, and the prosperity of dentists in Nantes is thanks in no small measure to the locals' predilection for the stuff. That said, it *does* go amazingly well with seafood and seems to suit oysters. *Bossard's* is soft and honeyed. *Clos de la Sénaigerie* and *Clos de la Fine* from *Domaine d'Herbauges* are also good. The dentists must be furious.

HAUT-POITOU, AC Produced in an isolated area south of the main Loire vineyards. Chardonnay and Sauvignon from the *Cave Co-opérative du Haut-Poitou* are good but tending to the lean side.

MENETOU-SALON, AC Small, growing AC to the west of Sancerre making pretty good Sauvignons (and some fair reds and rosés). The *Vignerons Jacques Coeur* co-op, which spends most of its time organizing cereal farmers, produces about half the Sauvignon. *Henry Pellé* makes the best in Menetou, followed by *Jean-Max Roger* and *Domaine de Chatenoy*. Prices are lower than for Sancerre, and a top Menetou is always tastier than a mediocre Sancerre.

MONTLOUIS, AC Chenin area to the south of Vouvray. Makes similar wines, but frequently more robust – which, when it comes to the Chenin grape, isn't always a good idea. *Dominique Moyer, Domaine des Liards* and *Jean-Pierre Trouvé* are good, but lots are short on fruit, long on sulphur.

MUSCADET, AC Simple, light, neutral wine from the Nantes area. Straight Muscadet, without any further regional title, is usually flat and boring. But at least it's light – the Muscadet ACs are the only ones in France to impose a *maximum* alcohol level (12.3 per cent).

The price guides for this section begin on page 325.

MUSCADET DE SÈVRE-ET-MAINE, AC The biggest Muscadet area, making the most but also the best wine. A good one may taste slightly nutty, peppery or salty, even honeyed, sometimes with creaminess from being left on the lees, sometimes a chewy apricot-skin taste and sometimes with a slight prickle. It should always have a lemony acidity, and should feel light. Buy domaine-bottled wine only, and check the address, looking out for *St-Fiacre* and *Le Pallet*, two of the best villages.

MUSCADET DES COTEAUX DE LA LOIRE, AC A small area along the banks of the Loire east of Nantes. In quality, it's between Muscadet and Muscadet de Sèvre-et-Maine. *Pierre Luneau* is good.

MUSCADET SUR LIE This is the most important thing to look for on a Muscadet label – even though not all producers use the term honestly. Traditionally indicates that the wine has come straight from the lees (the yeast sediment from fermentation), thus having more character than usual and a slight prickle. In the best cases this is so, but the law only says that the wine must be bottled before 30 June in the year after the vintage – not a guarantee of much, except perhaps freshness. It's best to buy only *sur lie* labelled *mise en bouteille à la propriété / château / domaine*. Some merchants, like *Sauvion*, have portable bottling lines, and bottle properly *sur lie* at the grower's cellar. Its *Château du Cléray* and *Découvertes* range are very good. *Guy Bossard* makes good organic *sur lie*. Also notable: *Domaine de Coursay-Villages, Domaine du Grand Mouton, Pierre Luneau, Domaine de la Montaine, Château de Chasseloir, Clos de la Sénaigerie, Jean-Louis Hervouet, Domaine du 'Perd-son-pain'*, any from *Louis Métaireau* including *Domaine du Grand Mouton, Cuvée LM, Cuvée One,* unfiltered *Huissier* and oddities like *25 August 1989,* the result of a single day's harvest; both *Michel* and *Donatien Bahuaud*'s single domaine wines, *Bonhomme* and *Guilbaud*.

POUILLY-FUMÉ, AC Just over the river from Sancerre and very similar. The wines are said to smell of gunflint because of their smokiness. They can be fuller than Sancerre, and the presence of flint in the soil does give the best a mineral complexity. Top growers include *J C Châtelain, Didier Dagueneau* (Pouilly's most brilliant wine-maker), *Serge Dagueneau, Château Favray, Masson-Blondelet, André Figeat* and the too-expensive *de Ladoucette*.

POUILLY-SUR-LOIRE, AC Made from the dull Chasselas grape which makes good eating but not memorable drinking. *Serge Dagueneau* makes a good example.

QUARTS DE CHAUME, AC A tiny 40-hectare AC in the Layon valley with a perfect microclimate for nobly-rotten sweet wines. They are rare and expensive, not quite as sweet as top Sauternes, but they can be even more intense, with high acid stalking the rich apricot and honey fruit. *Jean Baumard* is superb; also *Château de Bellerive* and *Château de l'Echarderie*.

QUINCY, AC Fairly pungent Sauvignon Blanc wines grown west of Sancerre. *Domaine de Maison Blanche, Pierre Mardon, Jacques Rouzé* and the co-op *Jacques Coeur* make good examples.

REUILLY, AC Light, fragrant Sauvignon Blanc wines from near Quincy, west of Sancerre. *Gérard Cordier* and *Claude Lafond* are the important growers. (There is also some tasty red and rosé.)

SANCERRE, AC Green, smoky, tangy wine from the Sauvignon Blanc grape grown at the eastern end of the Loire. Drunk young when it's at its best, it should be super-fresh and fruity, with a flavour and fragrance like gooseberries or fresh-cut grass, and a brilliant balance between sharpness and ripe, round body. But all too often it smells sulphurous or meaty, and tastes simply flabby. Look for single-domaine wines – especially those of *Pierre Archambault, Joseph Balland-Chapuis, Henri Bourgeois, Francis & Paul Cotat, Lucien Crochet, Pierre & Alain Dézat, Domaine Laporte, Alphonse Mellot, Paul Millérioux, Bernard Noël-Reverdy, Jean-Max Roger, Pierre Riffault, Domaine Vacheron* and *André Vatan*.

SAUMUR, AC Champagne-method wine made from Chenin grapes, sometimes with the welcome addition of Chardonnay, Sauvignon or even Cabernet Franc, any of which can give a bit more roundness to the acid Chenin. Well-made sparkling Saumur (including a little rosé) is lively and appley but too many are just too rough to revel with. Best producers: *Ackerman Laurance, Bouvet-Ladubay, Gratien & Meyer* and *Langlois-Château*.

SAUMUR BLANC, AC White, usually ultra-dry, though it can occasionally be sweet, similar to Anjou Blanc.

SAVENNIÈRES, AC Some of the steeliest, longest-living, diamond-dry white wines in the world come from this tiny Anjou *appellation* just west of Angers. One vineyard, Savennières Coulée-de-Serrant, has its own AC within Savennières, and *Madame Joly*'s wines from the *Clos de la Coulée-de-Serrant* are extremely fine. Look out also for wines from *Yves Soulez* from the *Château de Chamboreau, Clos du Papillon, Jean Baumard (Clos Ste Catherine), Domaine de la Bizolière* and the *Domaine aux Moines*.

TOURAINE, AC Everybody sees Touraine Sauvignon, with some justification, as a Sancerre substitute. The *Confrérie des Vignerons de Oisly-et-Thésée* sell to half the British wine trade, and their wines are good, as are *Paul Buisse, Château de l'Aulée, Domaine de la Charmoise (Marionnet), Château de Chenonceau, Domaine des Corbillières, Domaine Joël Delaunay* and *Domaine Octavie*.

VIN DE PAYS DU JARDIN DE LA FRANCE The general *vin de pays* of the Loire valley. Usually unmemorable, though pleasant, but the results can be impressive, especially when based on Sauvignon and Chardonnay. *Biotteau's Château d'Avrille Chardonnay* and *Domaine des Hauts de Saulière's Chardonnay* have lovely fruit.

VOUVRAY, AC Sparkling wine and still whites ranging from the tangily dry to the liquorously sweet, though usually caught in the middle. In fact Vouvray is best at producing the off-dry *demi-sec* style, and from a good producer this Chenin wine, initially all searing acidity and rasping dryness, over a number of years develops a deep, nutty, honey-and-cream flavour. Most commercial Vouvray is poor. Good producers are: *Daniel Allias, Domaine des Aubuisières, Brédif, Chamalou, Château Gaudrelle, Bernard Fouquet, Château Moncontour, Foreau, Huet, Prince Poniatowski* and *Domaine de Vaugoudy*.

RED GRAPES & FLAVOURS

CABERNET SAUVIGNON This doesn't always ripen too well in the Loire, but even so it adds some backbone to the wines. It is really at its best in the ripest years.

CABERNET FRANC The great quality grape of Anjou and Touraine. All the best reds are based on Cabernet Franc, and the styles go from the palest, most fleeting of reds to deep, strong, proud wines of great character and considerable longevity.

GAMAY This rarely achieves the lovely, juicy glugginess of Beaujolais, but when made by a careful modern winemaker it can have a fair amount of fruit, though always with a tough edge.

PINOT NOIR In and around Sancerre this can, in warm years, produce a lovely, light, cherry-fragrant wine that will be either a rosé or a light red. But really interesting examples are rare in the Loire.

RED WINES & WINE REGIONS

ANJOU ROUGE CABERNET, AC Until a few years ago Anjou Rouge was a byword for raw, rasping red fit to drive a chap to Liebfraumilch. Now it's likely to be light and dry from the co-ops, and spicy, strong and capable of aging from the best domaines. It can rival Bourgueil. Best producers: *Mark Angelli (Cuvée Martial), Château d'Avrille, Château de Chamboureau (Soulez), Clos de Coulaine, Domaine de la Petite Croix, Domaine du Petit Val, Domaine des Rochettes (Chauvin), Logis de la Giraudière (Baumard), Richou, Roussier.*

ANJOU ROUGE GAMAY, AC Rarely more than adequate, but in the hands of someone like *Richou*, the 'rooty' character is replaced by a fresh, creamy fruit that is sharp and soft all at once, and *very* good. *Domaine des Quarres* is also worth a try.

ANJOU-VILLAGES, AC Cabernets Franc and Sauvignon from the 46 best villages in Anjou. Some are labelled 'Anjou-Villages Val-de-Loire'. *Domaine de Montgilet, J-Y& H Lebreton, Domaine Ogereau* and *Richou* are good. Go for the concentrated '90s and '91s rather than the dilute '92s.

BOURGUEIL, AC Some of the best reds of the Loire come from this AC in Touraine. When they are young they can taste a bit harsh and edgy, but give them a few years and they will have a piercing blackcurrant fruitiness, sharp and thirstquenching. They can age remarkably well, developing complex leathery, meaty flavours. Best: *Audebert* (estate wines), *Pierre Breton, Caslot-Galbrun, J-F Demont, Domaine des Forges, Domaine des Ouches, Pierre-Jacques Druet, Lamé-Delille-Boucard.*

CABERNET D'ANJOU, AC (Rosé) There is a reasonable chance of a pleasant drink here, because the Cabernets – mostly Cabernet Franc, but often with some Cabernet Sauvignon in there too – do give pretty tasty wine, usually made a good deal less sweet than simple Rosé d'Anjou. Various estates make it well – *Domaine Baranger, Domaine de Richou, Domaine de Hardières, Château de Valliennes.*

CHINON, AC In a ripe year (1988, '89, '90), Chinon can be delicious, exhibiting from the start a great gush of blackcurrant and raspberry with the acid strongly evident. There's an earthiness too, but it is soft and strangely cooling in its effect, and after a few years it seems to dissolve into the clear, mouthwatering fruit of the vine. Domaine wines are *far* better than *négociant* wines, which can be thin. Best producers: *Bernard Baudry, Jean Baudry, Domaine du Colombier, Domaine du Roncée, Domaine de la Tour, Druet, Gatien Ferrand, René Gouron, Charles Joguet, Alain Lorieux, Pierre Manzagol, Jean François Olek, Jean-Maurice Raffault, Raymond Raffault.*

HAUT-POITOU, AC Fairly 'green' but reasonably enjoyable reds from the Loire hinterland, usually made from Gamay.

ROSÉ D'ANJOU, AC The omnipresent and frequently omnihorrid French rosé. It is based on a pretty feeble grape, the Groslot, and suffers in the main from lack of fruit and excess of sulphur. A few producers like the co-op at *Brissac* can make it fresh and bright.

ROSÉ DE LOIRE, AC A little-made dry rosé from Anjou or Touraine.

SANCERRE ROUGE, AC Pinot Noir, and in general overrated, but occasionally you can find a fleeting cherry fragrance and sweetness of strawberries that can survive a year or two in bottle. Silly prices, though. *Henri Bourgeois, Domaine Vacheron, Pierre and André Dezat,* and *Domaine de Chatenoy* at the nearby Menetou-Salon AC are good.

SAUMUR ROUGE, AC Usually very light and dry Cabernet Franc from 38 villages round Saumur. Light, but the fruit is often marked and attractively blackcurranty. The co-op at *St-Cyr-en-Bourg* is good.

SAUMUR-CHAMPIGNY, AC Cabernet red from the best villages in Saumur. It stands way above other Loire reds thanks to its firm structure and velvety softness, its fruit that is slightly raw and rasping, yet succulent and rich at the same time. Although the term '*vieilles vignes*' is open to wide interpretation it is always the best bet for quality. *Domaine Filliatreau* makes an outstanding one, as well as *Primeur,* for immediate drinking. Also good: *Château de Chaintres, Château du Hureau, Château de Targé, Domaine Dubois, Domaine Lavigne, Domaine Sauzay-Legrand, Denis Duveau, Domaine de Nerleux, Domaine des Roches Neuves, Domaine du Val Brun.*

ST-NICOLAS DE BOURGUEIL, AC These Cabernet reds from an AC within Touraine AC are grown on gravelly soil, so they tend to be lighter and more forward than nearby Bourgueils. They can be good, but stick to warm years. The wines of *Claude Ammeux, Jean-Paul Mabileau* and *Joël Taluau* seem best.

TOURAINE, AC The reds aren't usually very exciting, being rather green and stalky on the whole. They are often Gamay-based but may be made from a variety of grapes, including Cabernet. The *Domaine de la Charmoise (Marionnet)*, and the co-op of *Oisly-et-Thésée* produce fair Gamays. *Château de Chenonceau* is also good.

VIN DE PAYS DES MARCHES DE BRETAGNE These wines from the mouth of the Loire are usually fairly flimsy numbers, but a good grower can use the denomination to produce something unusual and exciting. *Guy Bossard*, for instance, a leading Muscadet producer, makes an amazingly fragrant and fruity red from Cabernet Franc.

LOIRE VINTAGES

Loire vintages are very important, and can be radically different along the river length. In poor vintages, Muscadet is most likely to be OK, while in hot vintages Sauvignon goes dull, but the Chenin finally ripens. The red grapes need the warm years.

1992 A large crop of wines that generally lack concentration. The reds in particular are light, but there should be plenty of sparkling wine.

1991 Devastating April frosts and late September rains meant that in some areas, notably Muscadet, no wine was made at all. Sancerre and Pouilly-Fumé were down by half. Quality was average. Reds were also badly affected. Beware of overpricing, as growers attempt to make up for small quantities.

1990 Another *annus mirabilis,* to the astonishment and delight of all. The sweet white Chenins, again luscious and built to last, may sometimes even exceeed the great '89s. Great reds too. Sancerre and Pouilly can be low in acidity, but the best producers had few problems, and once again late-harvest Sauvignon has given an encore.

1989 An exceptional year, particularly for sweet Chenin Blancs, which are gorgeous, and comparable with the legendary '47s. The reds were ripe, but some dry whites lack acidity. Oddity of the year: sweet, botrytis-affected Sancerre in new oak.

1988 Delicious Sancerres and Pouilly-Fumés, more classic in style than the richer '89s and 1990s. Muscadet was first class and still enjoyable, especially the *sur lie.*

ALSACE

French winemakers love to talk rhapsodically about *terroir*, the way in which the nuances of soil structure and microclimate influence the taste of a wine. But until recently Alsace was an exception to this rule, and to this talk. Here, as in the New World, it was always the grape variety that counted. But the growers always found their own ways of complicating this simple system; and now the establishment of the Grand Cru system (in which the notion of *terroir* is explicit) has thrown in another 50 possibilities.

The growers themselves are deeply aware of the differences between their various plots. At Schlumberger you can learn why they have planted Pinot Gris in the Kitterlé vineyard and Gewürztraminer in the Kessler vineyard rather than in the equally fine Saering. Marcel Deiss routinely produces eight different Rieslings, of which only two are Grands Crus.

Then there are those who prefer to bypass the Grand Cru system. Hugel and Trimbach, both outstanding houses, own large tracts of Grand Cru vineyards, and use no Grand Cru names at all: they argue that their blending skills are a better guarantee of quality than sticking Grand Cru on the label. With some Grands Crus being up to 80 hectares in size, this argument continues, there is no way each parcel can be of uniform quality. Moreover, excessively high yields – a bane of Alsace, even in the Grands Crus – can obliterate the very nuances the system is designed to highlight.

Alsace am Rhein

For most consumers these arguments are largely academic, and the good news is that Alsace remains a highly reliable source of delicious, well-made white wines. Sales, however, have remained consistently underwhelming, as any wine merchant will tell you. The flutes in which the wines are bottled and the Germanic names of the Grand Cru vineyards – names like Altenburg or Hengst still leave many wine buyers with the impression that Alsace is in Germany.

A few years ago, Alsace wines were an even more shrewd purchase. Not only was the standard of wine-making high, but prices were sensible. Not so now: the wine-making is still good, but prices have steadily crept up. The Deiss Rieslings are among the best wines in Alsace, but at those prices so they should be. This is in spite of the fact that, unlike the wines of Bordeaux or Burgundy, Alsace wines are never aged in expensive barriques. It may be expensive to grow grapes of top quality; it is not expensive, in Alsace, to age and bottle the wines.

The Alsaciens could help themselves greatly, it seems to me, if they were to reform their labelling practices, which are a mess. At Kuentz-Bas the basic wine, from bought-in grapes, is called Cuvée Tradition, and wines from the company's own vineyards are called Réserve Personelle. At Hugel, however, the bought-in production carries no quality definition; the next rung up the quality ladder is Cuvée Tradition, and then come the wines from its own vineyards, labelled Réserve Personelle. Or they used to be: now they are called Jubilee. Kuentz-Bas Réserve Personelle wines that have been approved at the blind tasting by the local Confrèrie are additionally labelled Sigillé. At Schlumberger some Pinot Gris is labelled as Réserve Spéciale to signify a wine made from grapes grown in various Grand Cru sites.

In addition, there are the separate bottlings from the Grands Crus, and the bottlings of *vendanges tardives* and the rare *sélection de grains nobles*. Schlumberger, however, doesn't use these terms, preferring Cuvée Christine for *vendanges tardives* and Cuvée Anne for SGN. Kuentz-Bas also uses family names for special *cuvées*. Special names on a Trimbach wine, such as Frédéric Emile, denote top blends from Grand Cru vineyards.

Reserve of confusion

Confused? Me too. Moreover, it is unacceptable that a basic wine should be labelled Réserve. I'm particularly fond of the Trimbach wines, but if you call a wine Réserve, the clear implication is that it is special. In fact it is the most basic of the range.

There is also nothing on the average Alsace label to tell the consumer whether the wine is dry or sweet. There are plenty of ordinary *cuvées* in 1989 and 1990 that have discernible residual sugar – excellent wines, but not ideal with grilled trout. I have encountered *vendanges tardives*, especially from 1983, that are, or that taste, bone dry. The producer says we must let nature take its course as the wine ferments. Fair enough, but let's have the outcome made more apparent.

Nonetheless, the wine in bottle remains of a good overall standard, though some basic *cuvées* can be dilute, and in general you get what you pay for. (And these days you pay more anyway...) A mid-range or Grand Cru wine from a top producer or co-operative can be a splendid wine, packed with fruit and flavour and freshness. Minor varieties such as Sylvaner or Chasselas are disappearing in favour of the far more attractive Pinot Blanc. Gewürztraminer is still popular on export markets, but the Alsaciens prefer the aromatic yet subtle Pinot Gris. Riesling remains the star, and Alsace at its best is as good as any white wine in the world. Whatever the label says. **STEPHEN BROOK**

GRAPES & FLAVOURS

In Alsace wines are generally labelled according to their grape type. Only the cheaper wines (labelled Edelzwicker or Vin d'Alsace) are blends of several grapes. For this reason, recommended producers are listed here under the name of the appropriate grape, for ease of reference.

CHASSELAS Pleasant enough when fresh from the last vintage, but Pinot Blanc and Sylvaner have taken over its role as the backbone of basic blends.

EDELZWICKER or **VIN D'ALSACE** A blend of the less interesting grape varieties, in particular Chasselas, Pinot Blanc and Sylvaner. Usually it is fresh and nothing more. Just occasionally, it is spicy, and then much more enjoyable. Look for *Dopff & Irion, Rolly Gassmann, Klipfel, Maurice Schoech*. Some of the supermarket own-label Vin d'Alsace wines can be good.

GEWÜRZTRAMINER It can be hard to believe that these wines are dry, because they can be so fat, perfumed and spicy. But, with a few exceptions (especially in 1989), dry they are, yet big, very ripe, and with all kinds of exotic fruit tastes – lychees, mangos, peaches – and if you're lucky, finishing off with black pepper. They smell of everything from musk rose to

The price guides for this section begin on page 332.

spice, though poor examples can smell like cheap soap. Best producers: *Becker, Beyer, Blanck, Caves de Turckheim, Dopff au Moulin, Domaine Ostertag, Théo Faller, Gisselbrecht, Heywang, Klipfel, Kreydenweiss, Kuentz-Bas, Muré, Rolly Gassmann, Schlumberger, Trimbach, Zind-Humbrecht.*

MUSCAT Light, fragrant, wonderfully grapy. Imagine crushing a fistful of green grapes and gulping the juice as it runs through your fingers. That's how fresh and grapy a good Muscat should be. Sadly much of what is sold in Britain is already too old. Best producers: *Théo Cattin, Dirler, Dopff & Irion, Gisselbrecht, Hugel, Trimbach, Zind-Humbrecht.*

PINOT BLANC This is taking over from Sylvaner as the basis for Alsace's bright and breezy young whites. It's a much better grape, giving light, appley wine, acidic and sometimes creamy. For some reason, Auxerrois is regarded in Alsace as being synonymous with Pinot Blanc (which it isn't) and wines labelled 'Pinot Blanc' may contain both. Mature Auxerrois can take on a lovely strawberry or white chocolate character. Best producers include: *Becker, Blanck, Gisselbrecht, Heim, Hugel, Humbrecht, Kreydenweiss, Rieffel, Rolly Gassmann* (Pinot Blanc and Auxerrois), *Scherer, Sparr, Trimbach, Zind-Humbrecht.*

PINOT GRIS Still called Tokay locally, though the EC title is Tokay-Pinot Gris. These are fat, musky and honeyed at best, though can run to flab if badly handled. Even the lighter ones are luscious behind their basically dry fruit. The best can age well. Best producers: *Becker, Caves de Turckheim, Éguisheim co-op, Théo Faller, Gisselbrecht, Hugel, Klipfel, Kreydenweiss, Kuentz-Bas, Trimbach, Zind-Humbrecht.*

PINOT NOIR The Burgundy grape makes light reds and rosés with attractive perfume and strawberryish flavour, worth seeking out. Some producers – *Muré, Hugel, Caves de Turckheim, Deiss* – are oak-aging it, and the wines can be delicious. Also good: *Cattin*, the *Éguisheim* co-op and *Zind-Humbrecht.*

RIESLING This is the grape of the great sweet wines of Germany. In Alsace, it is as steely; as it ages, it goes deliciously 'petrolly'. This is Alsace at its most serious. Best names: *Becker, Blanck, Deiss, Domaine Ostertag, Dopff & Irion, Théo Faller, Louis Gisselbrecht, Hugel, Klipfel, Kreydenweiss, Kuentz-Bas, Schaller, Trimbach, Zind-Humbrecht.*

SYLVANER Light, tart, slightly earthy and usually one-dimensional. With age it tastes of tomatoes, for some reason. Best producers: *Beyer, Gisselbrecht, Schlumberger, Seltz, Zind-Humbrecht.*

CLASSIFICATIONS

ALSACE, AC This is the simple *appellation* for the whole region, normally used with a grape name. Thus: 'Riesling – Appellation Alsace Contrôlée'.

CRÉMANT D'ALSACE, AC White fizz, made in the same way as Champagne, but mainly from Pinot Blanc. The few who use a touch of Riesling make more interesting, flowery-fragrant versions and there are one or two good 100 per cent Rieslings worth trying. Look for wines from *Baron de Hoen, Dopff & Irion, Gisselbrecht, Kreydenweiss, Schaller, Wolfberger.*

GRAND CRU Twenty-five historically excellent vineyards were classified as Grand Cru in 1983, and must meet stricter regulations than ordinary Alsace: they can only be planted with Riesling, Tokay-Pinot Gris, Gewürztraminer or Muscat, and notably lower (but still high) yields apply.

They are recognized by the words *Appellation Alsace Grand Cru Contrôlée* on the label. A further 25 vineyards may add the words Grand Cru to the vineyard name on the label, and their AC is, confusingly, *Appellation Alsace Contrôlée, Grand Cru*. They are due for official endorsement in 1993. This will bring the Grand Cru area to 1678 hectares out of the total Alsace plantation of 13,500. In theory, any Grand Cru should be better than ordinary Alsace. But delimitations are generous, and varieties like Sylvaner are excluded from sites where they always did well. In difficult years like 1986 or 1988, the better siting of the Grands Crus was crucial.

RÉSERVE Supposedly used for better wines, but in practice almost worthless.

SÉLECTION DE GRAINS NOBLES The higher of the two 'super-ripe' legal descriptions based on the very high sugar content in the grapes. It only applies to wines from Riesling, Tokay-Pinot Gris, Muscat (very rare) and Gewürztraminer and corresponds to a Beerenauslese. Don't expect German acidity levels, especially not from Pinot Gris or Gewürztraminer.

SIGILLÉ A 'Sigillé' label – a band with a red paper seal – means that blind tasting by a jury has confirmed the wine as a fine example of its type.

SPÉCIAL 'Cuvée Spéciale' or 'Sélection Spéciale' may apply to a producer's best wines. The terms have no legal weight.

VENDANGE TARDIVE The first of the 'super-ripe' categories, made from late-picked grapes. Only applies to Riesling, Tokay-Pinot Gris, Muscat (rare) and Gewürztraminer. They are very full, fairly alcoholic and vary in sweetness from richly dry to dessert-sweet.

ALSACE VINTAGES

1992 An easy vintage after a hot, dry summer. The best producers thinned the crop in the summer to reduce yields. The wines are healthy, and range from dilute to excellent.

1991 Alsace was lucky in the French context this year: unscathed by frost, the main problem, after a splendid summer, was late September and October rains. Careful vinification will have produced fresh, clean wines, but it is not a late-harvest year.

1990 Some of the older growers say 1990 is the best they have ever vinified. With healthy grapes and no noble rot, 1990 was a *vendange tardive* year. The early harvest was already too hot for Muscat. *Coulure* and over-ripening reduced the Gewürztraminer yield by up to half; Rieslings are powerful and will age well, while the Pinots look majestic.

1989 Exceptional weather produced an abundant harvest of very good quality, though not as superb as first reported. Wines are already showing lively fruit, though some are low in acidity. Look for Grand Cru sites and better producers.

1988 Rain at harvest-time made for pleasant, but hardly inspiring wine. Those who waited did better, with Tokay-Pinot Gris and Riesling the most successful.

1987 Not great, but better than first thought. Good single vineyard wines.

1986 The best are at their peak. Good *vendange tardive* and even some *SGN*.

1985 An absolute corker – wonderful wines to drink now but they will keep.

1983 A great year, but only at the top level. These are brilliant – rich, ripe and bursting with character – and will still keep.

1976 Brilliant, deep, late-picked wines bursting with flavour and richness, but still dry.

SOUTH-EAST FRANCE

The highlight of June 1992 was a delightfully eccentric colloquium on Dionysus organized in Beziers by Redmond O'Hanlon (No, not that Redmond O'Hanlon, another one, of University College Dublin). It was a combination of arcane lectures on Greek tragedy, French literature and wine. Between the discussions growers brought in their wines for us to taste. What extraordinary progress has been made in Languedoc-Roussillon. It was no problem mustering a dozen pure Syrahs or Mourvèdres, and they were good too. On the coast in Sète (previously known only for nudists) Robert Skalli is taking on the New World by producing varietal wines on a commercial scale.

Languedoc-Roussillon is not just new-wave, though: a classic style is emerging in areas like the Minervois, Corbières, St-Chinian and Faugères based on low-yielding, hillside Carignan combined with Grenache, Syrah and Mourvèdre. Something of the same can be found on the slopes of the Fenouillèdes in the Roussillon. And on page 10 of this *Guide.*

Where does that leave the super-hyped Provence? There are still good things – such as pure Mourvèdre wines – to be had from Bandol and exciting developments continue in Les Baux, the Coteaux d'Aix and Palette; but in the rest of the region the sun is just a mite too hot and the tourists just a little too gullible to provide the incentive to get the growers off their backsides and into the vineyards to tend the vines.

GILES MACDONOGH

RED & ROSÉ WINES

BANDOL, AC Expensive, but without doubt one of the best Provence reds. These terraced vineyards west of Toulon are the heartland of the Mourvèdre, along with Grenache, Cinsaut and Syrah, and make gorgeous, dark, spicy, soft wine, with sweet fruit and a herby, tobacco edge. Most need five years' aging. Rosé is also excellent, showing soft spice. Best estates: *Château Ste-Anne, Château Vannières, Domaine de la Bastide Blanche, Domaine Terrebrune, Domaine de Pibarnon, Domaine Ray-Jane, Domaine Tempier, Domaine du Cagueloup, Mas de la Rouvière, Domaine le Galantin.*

BELLET, AC The reds from vineyards behind Nice can be pretty dire, but there are a few good ones, deeply coloured with blackberry-like fruit. *Château de Crémat* can be delicious and *Château de Bellet* isn't bad, though the population of Nice deny the existence of the AC altogether.

CASSIS, AC A gorgeous mini-region between Bandol and Marseille, making good but expensive whites, which are surprisingly fresh and fruity for so far south, and stylish rosés. Don't try the reds; they'll bring you to earth with a bump.

COLLIOURE, AC Startling, intense reds from the ancient vineyards cramped in between the Pyrenees and the Med, just north of Spain. *Domaine de la Rectorie, Domaine du Mas Blanc, Clos des Paulilles* and *Mas Casa Blanca* are worth a try.

CORBIÈRES, AC Coarsely fruity, peppery red based on Carignan, Grenache, Cinsaut and others from the welter of mountains stretching from Narbonne towards Spain, and now divided into 11 separate areas. The region is wild and exciting – and the wines are beginning to match. Good wines are emerging from

Château des Colombes, Château de Montrabec, Château Hélène and *Château des Ollieux*. There is increasing use of carbonic maceration (*à la Beaujolaise*) and the results, particularly from some of the co-ops like *Mont Tauch* and *Embres et Castelmaure*, are very encouraging – the peppery bite is still there, but the fruit is enhanced to a really juicy level. New oak is popping up, too. Other names: *St-Auréol, La Baronne, Fontsainte, Villemajou, La Voulte-Gasparets.*

COSTIÈRES DE NÎMES, AC Quite good rosés, and meaty, smoky reds from a large area between Nîmes and Montpellier. I find the meatiness dominates the fruit, and I'd rather it were the other way round. Called Costières du Gard until 1989.

COTEAUX D'AIX-EN-PROVENCE, AC Mostly reds and rosés grown to the south and east of Aix. An increase in Cabernet and Syrah, more careful selection and new oak are rushing some into the top class. They range from light, strawberry-fruited wines, to drink at a great rate and without fuss, to such thought-provoking properties as *Château Vignelaure*, a remarkable Cabernet-based wine that achieves a Provençal-Bordeaux style. Other producers 'worth a detour': *Château de Beaulieu, Domaine de la Crémade, Domaine de Paradis, Domaine du Château Bas, Château de Fonscolombe.*

COTEAUX DES BAUX-EN-PROVENCE, AC For some obscure local political reason Coteaux des Baux-en-Provence only enjoys its own AC as a sub-region of Coteaux d'Aix-en-Provence, though its wines are different – and better. This is a wild, rock-cluttered moonscape of a region, with many of the vineyards literally blasted from the rock. The results are a sensation; as well as producing some very good, soft, fruity whites and some delicious rosés, the reds are the best of the Mediterranean ACs. Based on Syrah, Mourvèdre and Grenache they have an absurdly drinkable deep, ripe, raspberry juicy fruit. The finest property, *Domaine de Trévallon*, can make reds as exciting as almost any in France. In the lunatic way of French officialdom, this is now relegated to *vin de pays* because of the lack of Grenache in the vineyard, but you may still see some wines as AC on the UK market. Perhaps Trévallon should start planting Grenache – and make some rosé out of it. Best wines: *Domaine de Trévallon, Mas du Cellier, Mas de la Dame, Mas de Gourgonnier, Terres Blanches.*

COTEAUX DU LANGUEDOC, AC Usually a pretty solid red. A whole series of former VDQS regions have been re-defined as Coteaux du Languedoc *crus*: Cabrières, La Clape, La Méjanelle, Montpeyroux, Picpoul-de-Pinet, Pic-St-Loup, Quatourze, St-Christol, St-Drézéry, St-Georges-d'Orques, St-Saturnin, Vérargues. ACs Faugères and St-Chinian now come under the Coteaux du Languedoc AC umbrella too. There is a sense of excitement in quite a few spots, like the *St-Georges-d'Orques* co-op where they're starting to use new wood, and at the *Prieuré de St-Jean de Bébian* where the owner says he has the same soil as Châteauneuf-du-Pape and so he's planted all 13 of the Châteauneuf grape varieties.

COTEAUX VAROIS, VDQS Large region recently upgraded. Slightly better than basic reds and rosés, particularly where Syrah and Cabernet are used. A few good estates, like *St-Jean de Villecroze.*

CÔTES DE PROVENCE, AC Sprawling, catch-all AC and a lot of mediocre wine. However, when a grower decides he can do better than provide swill for the sunseekers at St-Trop, these scented southern hills can provide excellent rosé, good, fruity red and fair white. Only a few single domaines are worth seeking: *Château de Pampelonne, Château St-Maurs, Domaine Gavoty,*

Commanderie de la Peyrassol, Domaine de la Bernarde, Domaine des Féraud, Domaine St-Baillon, Domaine du Jas d'Esclans, Château Ste-Roseline and *Domaine de Rimauresq. Domaine Ott* is good, though expensive. The wines of *Les Vignerons de la Presqu'Île de St-Tropez* are widely available and good.

CÔTES DU ROUSSILLON, AC Good, fruity reds, just touched by the hot dust of the south. The Carignan is the dominant grape, mixed with Cinsaut, Grenache and Syrah. Carbonic maceration is being used, as in Beaujolais, to draw out the juicy fruit. Mostly good value, as are the rosés.

CÔTES DU ROUSSILLON-VILLAGES, AC From much the same area as the plain AC, so the Villages wines are generally the best *cuvées*. That juicy fruit and dust mix can be delicious in the best from *Vignerons Catalans* from villages like Caramany, Cassagnes and Rassiguères. Other names: *Cazes Frères, Château Corneilla* and *Château de Jau*. The best two villages have their own separate ACs, Côtes du Roussillon-Villages Caramany and Côtes du Roussillon-Villages Latour de France. One of the best growers, *Vacquer*, refuses to use the AC at all, and sells his wine as very expensive *vin de pays*.

FAUGÈRES Big, beefy wine, but soft with it. A fad in France, so prices have risen, but the quality is there. A few bottles with Faugères AC are still around but it is now sold as a *cru* of Coteaux du Languedoc. Try *Gilbert Alquier, Château de Grézan, Ch. Haut-Fabrègues, Domaine de Fraisse*.

FITOU, AC This is traditionally a fine, rich, old-style red based on at least 70 per cent Carignan, from between Corbières and the plain running south. Should be better and more concentrated than Corbières. The single domaine *Château des Nouvelles* is worth a try. Also usually reliable are the supermarket Fitous.

MINERVOIS, AC Usually lighter than Corbières, with lots of raspberry fruit and pepper, mainly from the Carignan grape. Some juicy, carbonic maceration wines at the co-ops and deeper, wood-aged styles from *Château Fabas, Château de Gourgazaud, Château de Paraza, Château Villerambert-Julien, Domaine Maris* and *Domaine de Ste-Eulalie*.

PALETTE, AC A tiny appellation, hidden in the pine forests near Aix, which makes usually pretty hard and resiny reds that need time to develop. *Château Simone* is virtually the only producer.

ST-CHINIAN, AC A *cru* of AC Coteaux du Languedoc, making spicy, sturdy reds that are becoming fruitier. *Cave de Berlou, Caves de Roquebrun, Château Cazals-Vieil* and *Château Coujan* look good. *Domaine Guiraud-Boyer* is good for rosé.

VIN DE CORSE, AC The overall AC for the island to which one of the local names – Figari, Sartène, Porto-Vecchio, Coteaux du Cap Corse or Calvi – are added. Ajaccio and Patrimonio can use their own ACs. Grenache, Cinsaut, Carignan and other southern grapes are common, but it is the indigenous Nielluccio and Sciacarello which give Corsican wines a distinctive character. The best are warm, spicy, perfumed and rustic, but the huge improvements elsewhere in the Midi seem not to have reached Corsica yet. Best producers: *Cantone, Clos d'Alzetto, Clos Capitoro, Domaine Martini, Domaine Peraldi, Domaine du Petit Fournil* and *Domaine de Torraccia*.

VIN DE PAYS DE L'HÉRAULT All the good guys are experimenting furiously with grape varieties and wine-making styles. Very good 'ordinary' *vins de pays* include *Domaine du Chapître*, made at the institute of oenology at Montpellier, *Domaine de St-Macaire*, and the innovative wines of Pierre Besinet, marketed here as

Domaine du Bosc and *Domaine Cante-Cigale*. (Some of the better *vin de pays* – like Coteaux de Bessilles – carry their own appellation.) *Mas de Daumas Gassac* is a weird and wonderful one-off using mostly Cabernet Sauvignon.

VIN DE PAYS DE MONTCAUME Good reds from around Bandol. The *Bunan* family make a good Cabernet Sauvignon.

VIN DE PAYS DES BOUCHES DU RHÔNE Torrents of reasonable reds and rosés from this departmental zone.

VIN DE PAYS DES SABLES DU GOLFE DU LION Sandy coastal region to the west of the Rhône delta, and the only *vin de pays* to be delineated by its soil, not by administrative boundary. Mostly fairly light wines of all colours. However, the *Listel* operation, based out in the foggy sands of the wild Camargue, produces an astonishing range of every sort, shape and persuasion. It is one of France's foremost experimental wineries, and suggestions that they should upgrade to VDQS status are dismissed, since this would hinder their experimentation, such as growing grapes in a salty swamp.

VIN DE PAYS DU GARD Produces interesting reds and whites from classic 'northern' grapes. It is the smallest of the 'big three' departmental *vins de pays* in the Midi, producing about 30 million bottles. The reds and the rosés are often supposed to have something of a Rhône quality. Most are light and spicy with a gamey earthiness. The rosés are often better.

WHITE WINES

BELLET, AC One of the few pockets of 'special' wines in Provence, just behind Nice. It is a highly unusual, nutty white, expensive and popular with the Nice glitterati. On present experience, they can keep most of them. But the characterful *Château de Crémat* and *Château de Bellet* can be worth seeking out, and the latter improves with bottle age.

BANDOL, AC White Bandol can be the best white of Provence, with a remarkable aniseed-and-apples freshness. Best properties include *Château Vannières, Domaine de la Bastide Blanche* and *Domaine de la Laidière*.

CASSIS, AC No, not the blackcurrant liqueur, though Cassis (AC) and Cassis (Crème de) would mix to a good summer drink. This is a very good but expensive white from a small, dauntingly beautiful vineyard tucked into the bluffs by the Mediterranean between Marseille and Toulon. The grapes are a blend of Clairette, Ugni Blanc and Marsanne (rare this far south), sometimes mixed with a little Sauvignon Blanc. Its cool freshness and fruit is a rare find on this coast, though it has low acidity and needs to be drunk young. Look out for *Domaine du Paternel* and *Clos Ste-Magdeleine*.

CLAIRETTE DE BELLEGARDE, AC Small AC between Arles and Nîmes for dry, still white from Clairette grapes. Unmemorable, a dull old workhorse.

CLAIRETTE DU LANGUEDOC, AC Heavy, alcoholic whites, dry or semi-sweet, mercifully used, for the most part, as a base for French vermouth. Signs of improvement are visible from the likes of *Domaine de la Condemine Bertrand* and *Domaine St-André*.

The price guides for this section begin on page 337.

FORTIFIED WINES

BANYULS, AC (*Vin doux naturel*) Based on at least 50 per cent Grenache, these are red or tawny, sweet or dryish, but always hefty and slightly grapy. Try *Domaine de la Rectorie* or *Domaine du Mas Blanc.*

MAURY, AC (*Vin doux naturel*) 100 per cent Grenache AC for red or rosé wines, quite light and fresh when young but often purposely oxidized to a rather sweet-sour, burnt-caramel flavour. This style is called *rancio* and is done in other ACs too. *Mas Amiel* is the one estate (and the 15-year-old is worth looking out for).

MUSCAT DE FRONTIGNAN, AC (*Vin doux naturel*) The best-known of the fortified Muscats. Rich and raisiny but lacks, surprisingly, any great aroma. The fresher, more fragrant style of *Château de la Peyrade* is a step in the right direction.

MUSCAT DE RIVESALTES, AC (*Vin doux naturel*) Similar to Frontignan, but headier and fatter. With age a rather pungent sweetness not unlike cooked marmalade can develop. It's not the trendiest of styles, so some Muscat is being made as a dry white – which is rather good.

SOUTH-WEST FRANCE

After years in the long shadow of Bordeaux, the wines of the South-West are finally developing a reputation of their own. And with the possible exception of Jurançon, they represent very good value for money, too.

A handful of dynamic figures has transformed the region in the last decade. The Tannats of Madiran, Irouléguy and Saint-Mont are suppler than in the past and frequently aged in new oak; the dry wines of Jurançon show how good the grapefruit-fresh Gros Manseng can taste with the help of new technology; and the same appellation's intensely honeyed sweet wines (made with Petit Manseng) deserve to be ranked among the finest dessert wines in the world.

These are only some of the flavours the South-West has to offer. Buzet, Bergerac and Côtes de Duras can make pretty good claret alternatives, Cahors produces big, beefy wines, predominantly from Malbec, and, in Gascony, Vin de Pays des Côtes de Gascogne is consistently one of France's most appealing cheap whites. One more plus point: after the short, frost-hit harvest in 1991, there was a lot more wine in 1992.

Tim Atkin

RED & ROSÉ WINES

BÉARN Red and rosé from the far South-West. The reds are predominantly from the Tannat grape, but with other local varieties and both Cabernets thrown in. In spite of this they are basically undistinguished but you could try the wines of the *Vignerons de Bellocq* co-op, or the co-op at *Crouseilles.*

BERGERAC, AC An eastward extension of the St-Émilion vineyards, Bergerac is a kind of Bordeaux understudy, but with more mixed results. The rosés are often extremely good, deep in colour, dry and full of fruit, but the reds are more exciting, with the fruit and bite of a good, simple Bordeaux without the rough edges. Like

St-Émilion, it relies on the Merlot grape, with help from both Cabernets and Malbec, but the Bergerac reds are less substantial than St-Émilions. Sadly, most British merchants cut the prices too much for the potential of the area to be seen, so that what we get here is frequently tough, meaty, medicinal and charmless. Bergerac Rouge is usually at its best at between one and four years old, depending on vintage and style. *Château la Jaubertie* is very good and has also produced a wood-aged *'Reserve'*. *Château le Barradis* is also very good, and *Château Court-les-Mûts* makes a delicious rosé and a good red. Most of the wines in the UK originate at the large central co-op, and quality depends on whether someone was prepared to pay a few extra centimes for a better vat.

BUZET, AC Used to be labelled Côtes de Buzet. The most exciting of the claret look-alikes from a region that was historically considered part of Bordeaux. Made from Bordeaux grapes with Cabernet predominant, they can combine a rich blackcurrant sweetness with an arresting grassy greenness. They are for drinking at between one and five years old, depending on vintage and style. Look out for the wines of *Château Sauvagnères*, as well as those of the co-op, which dominates the area and produces a *Château de Gueyze* that is pretty special. The co-op has a real rarity – its own cooper. Almost all the wine spends at least a couple of months in wood, and this contributes massively to Buzet's serious-but-soft appeal.

CAHORS, AC Of all the south-western country wines, Cahors is the most exciting. It's grown on both banks of the River Lot in the region of Quercy, practically due east of Bordeaux (though hotter, because it's well away from the influence of the sea). It's at least 70 per cent Auxerrois (Bordeaux's Malbec), the rest being made up of varying proportions of Merlot and Tannat.

Two hundred years ago, it was one of France's most famous wines, and the 'Black Wine of Cahors' is still held up as an example of how it used to be done. The wine was made black by the simple trick of giving the grapes a quick crushing and then, literally, boiling the must. Just as boiling gets the stain out of a shirt, so it gets the tannin and colour out of a grape skin. Fruit? Er, no, but strength (it was sometimes even fortified) and stability and massive aging potential – yes. Though without fruit, it's difficult to know what age was expected to do.

Adopting modern wine-making methods has added some lovely sweet fruit to the still dark, but now less aggressively tannic wines. There's a clear whiff of fine wine about some of the big, firm products of private growers. With age, they are often almost honeyed and raisiny, with plummy fruit that gets deeper, spicier and darker, often resembling tobacco and prunes. But another sort of Cahors has sprung up, too, lighter and less inspired, for drinking young. It can sometimes be very good. The raw materials for these are quite different: the best, traditional land of Cahors is up in the hills, but most grapes are now grown in easier vineyards on the valley slopes. One third of the wine comes from the co-op, *Côtes d'Olt*, which, after a pusillanimous, fruitless start, is beginning to produce some very good, lightish but proper-tasting wine with real style. Best producers: *Château de Cayrou, Château de Chambert, Château de Haute-Serre, Clos de Gamot, Château St-Didier, Château de Treilles, Domaine du Cèdre, Clos la Coutale, Clos Triguedina, Domaine Eugénie, Domaine de Gaudou, Domaine de Paillas* and *Domaine de Quattre*.

CÔTES DE BERGERAC, AC This is to Bergerac what Bordeaux Supérieur is to Bordeaux: from the same region, but with slightly higher minimum alcohol. It should be better, and often is. Many are still basic Bergerac, although the excellent *Château Court-les-Mûts* now uses the AC.

CÔTES DE DURAS, AC Light, grassy claret lookalikes. *Château de Pilar* and *Le Seigneuret* from the co-op are quite good and cheap, as is a Beaujolais-type *cuvée* which is good quaffing stuff.

CÔTES DU FRONTONNAIS, AC This small area north of Toulouse makes reds largely from the local Négrette grape, plus both Cabernets, Malbec, Syrah, Cinsaut, Fer-Servadou and Gamay. At their best they are silky, plummy and unbelievably soft for red, sometimes with a touch of raspberry and liquorice. The distinctive Négrette grape is wonderfully juicy and tasty and there are now some 100 per cent Négrette *cuvées* from *Bellevue-la-Forêt* and *Flotis*. Great value. Best are *Domaine de Baudare, Château Bellevue-la-Forêt, Château Flotis, Château Montauriol, Château la Palme*.

CÔTES DU MARMANDAIS, VDQS Simple, soft, fruity wines for drinking young, made from the two Cabernets, Merlot, Fer and Abouriou. A few are for more serious aging, but it doesn't suit them.

GAILLAC, AC One of the best known of the south-west wines. There are two styles: Duras plus Fer-Servadou and Syrah, or Duras plus Merlot and Cabernet. Mostly, this is co-op land, but the growers who care make remarkable red. *Domaine Jean Cros* is an especially delicious one. Others are *Lastours, Mas Pignou, Labarthe, Larroze*.

IROULÉGUY, AC A small AC in the Basque country. The co-op dominates, and the wine is mostly roughish, Tannat-based red, though Cabernet is increasing. Try *Domaine Brana* and *Domaine Ilarria*.

MADIRAN, AC Grown near Armagnac, Madiran is often likened to claret, but only rarely shows anything approaching that finesse and excitement. It is generally about half Tannat, along with the two Cabernets and occasionally Fer, with 20 months minimum in wood. It is often rather astringent, and can be toughly tannic. Good ones include *Château d'Arricau-Bordes, Château d'Aydie* (alias *Domaine Laplace*), *Château Montus* (aged in new wood, and the only Madirans I find I really like), *Château Boucassé, Château Peyros, Domaine du Crampilh, Domaine Meinjarre, Laffitte-Teston, Domaine Berthoumieu* and *Domaine Moureou*.

PÉCHARMANT, AC The best red wine of Bergerac from the best slope of the region, east of Bordeaux, this is very good dry red that can take considerable aging, but is deliciously full of quick-drinking blackcurrant fruit when young. Unlike Bergerac, Pécharmant doesn't cut its prices, and shows what could be achieved in other nearby regions if we paid a proper price. *Château de Tiregand* is very good indeed, but *Domaine du Haut-Pécharmant* is even better, resembling a top-line Médoc.

WHITE WINES

BERGERAC SEC, AC A Bordeaux lookalike from east of Bordeaux, planted largely with Sémillon and Sauvignon. *Château Court-les-Mûts* and *Château de Panisseau* are good but the star is *Château la Jaubertie* where tremendous flavour and panache are extracted from a blend of Sauvignon, Sémillon and Muscadelle; this last grape is now being made into a 100 per cent varietal.

BLANQUETTE DE LIMOUX, AC This fizz from near Carcassonne claims to pre-date even Champagne. It's mostly made from Mauzac, with a green-apple bite often softened and improved by Chardonnay and Chenin Blanc. *Domaine de Martinolles* is good. A new AC, Crémant de Limoux, allows nearly 25 per cent of Chardonnay and Chenin in the blend – and is well worth looking out for.

CÔTES DE DURAS, AC Fairly good Sauvignon-based white that can be as fresh as good Bordeaux Blanc, but just a little chubbier. *Château de Conti* is good, as is *Le Seigneuret* from the co-operative.

GAILLAC, AC North-east of Toulouse and south of Cahors, Gaillac makes more white wine than red. It can be *moelleux* (medium sweet), *perlé* (very faintly bubbly) or dry; the dry is usually a little terse, though it can have a quite big apple-and-liquorice fruit if you're lucky. The sparkling wines can sometimes be superb: peppery, honeyed, apricotty and appley all at the same time. From producers like *Boissel-Rhodes, Cros* or *Robert Plageoles*, they are very good value. Other still wine producers to look out for are *Château Larroze, Domaine du Bosc Long* and *Domaine de Labarthe*. The co-op at *Labastide de Lévis* is the main, and improving, force in the area. One to watch.

JURANÇON, AC Sweet, medium or dry (though never *very* sweet or *totally* dry) wine from the Pyrenean foothills. Based on the Petit Manseng, Gros Manseng and Courbu, the dry wines are usually rather nutty and dull, but the sweet wines are not too sweet, and are honeyed, raisiny and peachy, yet with a lick of acidity. New oak is appearing in some cellars. Most wine is from the local co-op, but I'd plump for a grower's wine. The best are *Clos de la Vierge* (dry), *Cancaillaü* (sweet), sweet *Cru Lamouroux, Clos Uroulat* (sweet), *Domaine de Cauhapé, Domaine de Souch, Domaine Bru-Bache* (dry), *Clos Thou* (dry), *Domaine Larredya, Clos Lapeyre, Domaine Castera.*

MONBAZILLAC, AC From east of Bordeaux, south of Bergerac, this is one of the most famous names in the sweet wine world. The occasional true Monbazillac is fine, rich and honeyed, even unctuous, yet never as good as a top Sauternes – more like a good Loupiac or Ste-Croix-du-Mont. Unlike in Sauternes, there are very few quality-conscious single properties prepared to make the real thing. Ones worth seeking out include *Château du Treuil de Nailhac* and *Clos Fontindoule*; and the *Château de Monbazillac* and *Château Septy* of the co-op can be good.

MONTRAVEL, AC Dry to sweet white wine from the Dordogne. The wine is frequently sold as Côtes de Bergerac.

PACHERENC DU VIC-BILH, AC One of France's most esoteric whites, grown in the Madiran area near Armagnac, at its best when dry and pear-skin-perfumed – and sometimes when rich and sweet. Look out for *Château d'Aydie, Château Boucassé* and *Domaine du Crampilh.*

VIN DE PAYS CHARENTAIS As Cognac production declines, table wine production increases, and the Charente produces some good, grassy-fresh whites with fairly sharp acidity, although sometimes the acidity gets the better of the fruit.

VIN DE PAYS DES CÔTES DE GASCOGNE The table wine of Armagnac, and the star of this corner of France. The Ugni Blanc is the major grape, in more abundant supply since the drop in Armagnac sales, and the Colombard adds a definite touch of class. They're trying out the Gros Manseng and Chardonnay too – which should be interesting. The co-op of *Plaimont* supplies many of those on sale in Britain at very reasonable prices, but variable quality. However, the mood of change sweeping the south-western co-ops is evident here too. There are several labels available from the *Grassa* family estates – notably *Domaines de Planterieu* and *de Tariquet*, which are very good, full, dry and acid. Also good are *Domaine St-Lannes, Domaine les Puts, San Guilhem.*

The price guides for this section begin on page 341.

JURA

The Jura produces quite the most idiosyncratic wines of France. The mountainous isolation of the region has ensured that there are grape varieties here that are found nowhere else in France: the white Savagnin, for example, which may be related to Gewürztraminer but certainly does not taste the same, and the red Trousseau and Poulsard. Some Burgundian influence has managed to penetrate the region with some Chardonnay and Pinot Noir.

There are four *appellations* altogether. Côtes de Jura covers most of the region; Arbois, L'Étoile and most distinctive of all, Château-Chalon, are more specific. Château Chalon is the home of *vin jaune*, which is however made in the other three *appellations* as well, and in which a type of flor, not unlike that which gives *fino* sherry its character, develops on the surface of Savagnin wine and imparts a love-it-or-hate-it nutty, almost oxidized flavour. Production is tiny and the wine extremely expensive. Less happily, the taste of oxidation has spread to some of the other white wines of the Jura, which can make them difficult to appreciate, but the better reds have some of the soft velvety flavours of Burgundy.

ROSEMARY GEORGE

WINES & WINE REGIONS

ARBOIS, AC The general *appellation* for wines of all types from the northern part of the Jura around the town of Arbois. Reds are mostly Trousseau and thuddingly full of flavour. Savagnin weaves its demonic spells on the whites, though Chardonnay is sometimes used to soften it. Interestingly there are some attractive light reds and rosés from Pinot Noir or Poulsard which seem positively out of place, they are so delicate. *Henri Maire* is the biggest producer, but the best wines come from the village of Pupillin, where the co-op produces delicious Chardonnay and a fizz.

CÔTES DE JURA, AC These are the wines, of all colours, from the centre and south of the Jura. They are virtually indistinguishable from Arbois wines, though they are sometimes a little less disturbing in their weirdness.

L'ÉTOILE, AC Small area in the south producing whites from Savagnin and Chardonnay and, occasionally, from the red Poulsard, vinified without the colour-giving skins. Also Savagnin *vins jaunes*.

VIN JAUNE The kind of wine of which more than a small glass makes you grateful it is as rare as it is. It grows the same yeasty flor as dry sherry, and its startlingly, painfully intense flavours just get more and more evident as it matures. It seems virtually indestructible, as long as the cork is healthy.

Château-Chalon AC – the 'Montrachet' of *vin jaune*! Well, that's what they think, anyway. This is the most prized – and pricy – of the *vins jaunes*, and is difficult to find even in the region. *Vins jaunes* are sold in small 62cl *clavelin* bottles, which of course the EC tried to ban. That left me in two minds. I felt that 75cl of *vin jaune* would be just too much for anyone to handle, and indeed 37.5cl might be more like it. But I was blowed if the EC was going to destroy yet another great original in the stultifying name of conformity. The EC backed down and the 62cl *clavelin* lives. Actually there *is* a reason for the 62cl size, in that 100 litres of wine, kept in barrels for six years without being topped up, reduces to 62 litres, or 100 bottles. So they can order in nice round numbers.

SAVOIE AND THE BUGEY

In mountainous Savoie the tourists, flocking to the snow in the winter and the mountain air in the summer, get together with the locals to drink nearly all the local wine. Not much Vin de Savoie, therefore, travels beyond the shores of Lake Geneva and the cafés of Chambéry.

Most of it comes under the appellation of Vin de Savoie, but this includes some 15 different *crus*, of which a few exist more on paper than in the bottle. Abymes and Apremont, from an area south of Chambéry, are worth seeking out: the Jacquère grape gives them some lovely fresh, stony flavours. Across the valley, the village of Chignin has a reputation for its appellation of Chignin Bergeron, made from the white Roussanne of the northern Rhône – though how it got here is anyone's guess.

Closer to Lake Geneva, the generally rather neutral Chasselas grape is responsible for Crépy's soft, easy-to-drink white, as well as the *cru* of Ripaille, from the vineyards of a medieval château. There is some, though not much, red, from Pinot Noir, Gamay and the lesser-known Mondeuse, and a little sparkling wine from Seyssel, which links Savoie to the still barely-discovered vineyards of the Bugey.

WINES & WINE REGIONS

BUGEY, VDQS This little VDQS half-way between Savoie and Beaujolais is a rising star in France for its deliciously crisp Chardonnays, although it also uses the other Savoyard grapes for whites and reds. It is one of the most refreshing, zippy Chardonnays in France, and has become a fad wine with some of the local Michelin-starred restaurants. At least that means the growers will keep producing it.

CRÉPY, AC The least interesting Savoie region to the south of Lake Geneva, where the Chasselas produces an even flimsier version of the Swiss Fendant, if that's possible. Drink it very young, very fast, or not at all.

ROUSSETTE DE SAVOIE, AC This can be the fullest and softest of the Savoie whites. It can come from a blend of Altesse and Chardonnay or 100 per cent Altesse (also called Roussette) when it comes from one of the better villages like Frangy or Monterminod. Even at its basic level, it's good, crisp, strong-tasting white.

SEYSSEL, AC and **SEYSSEL MOUSSEUX, AC** The Roussette (sometimes blended with Molette) makes quite full, flower-scented but sharp-edged whites in this zone of the Haute-Savoie and the Ain. Sparkling Seyssel is also good, light but pepper-pungent and available in the UK from *Varichon et Clerc*.

VIN DE SAVOIE, AC Vin de Savoie covers the whole Savoie area, but produces the most interesting results in the South. These alpine vineyards are some of the most beautiful in France and produce fresh, snappy wines. The white, from the Jacquère or the Chardonnay, can be excellent, dry, biting, but with lots of tasty fruit. Avoid aging them for too long. The reds from Pinot Noir are subtly delicious, while the Mondeuse produces some real beefy beauties when the vintage is hot enough. A *cru* name is often tacked on to the best wines. Ones to look out for are Abymes, Apremont, Chignin, Cruet and Montmélian, with Chautagne and Arbin quite important for reds.

VINS DE PAYS

It may sound blasphemous to say so, but over the next decade a good deal of France's most exciting wine is going to emerge not from the famous AC areas, but from altogether humbler origins.

Blasphemous but true. In the Gallic scheme of things, *vins de pays* are supposed to occupy the penultimate rung of the quality ladder, above *vins de table* but some way below VDQS and the supposedly more complex *appellations contrôlées*. Not for much longer, in my view. And why? Freedom to experiment is a large part of the explanation. While the *appellation* laws appear to be set in reinforced concrete, the *vin de pays* regulations allow producers much greater leeway in their choice of grape varieties and production methods. We haven't yet arrived at the ridiculous, and classically Italian, situation where many of the best estates have effectively rejected the wine laws, but we're moving that way.

The greatest concentration of *vins de pays* is to be found in the South, and it is here that the most thrilling advances are taking place. See the tasting results on page 10, for example. Tired old grape varieties like Carignan and Cinsaut have been given new life by temperature controlled fermentation and carbonic maceration, producing fruitier, less tannic reds as a result. And then there's the influx of noble grape varieties from further north. Sometimes these perform in splendid isolation; on others they bring a patrician tone to rustic local varieties.

Accounting for over a quarter of France's total output, *vins de pays* are bound to vary in ambition and quality. What they have in their favour is that they are rarely expensive and often far less disappointing than expensive ACs. My feeling is that we ain't seen nothing yet.

TIM ATKIN

Vins de pays come in three categories:

VINS DE PAYS RÉGIONAUX There are four of these, which between them cover a major portion of France's vineyards. Vin de Pays du Jardin de la France covers the whole Loire basin across almost to Chablis and down to the Charente. Vin de Pays du Comté Tolosan is for the South-West, starting just below Bordeaux, and covering Bergerac, Cahors, the Tarn and down to the Pyrenees, but not including the Aude and Pyrénées Orientales. Vin de Pays des Comtés Rhodaniens includes the Rhône and Savoy; Vin de Pays d'Oc covers Provence and the Midi right down to the Spanish border.

VINS DE PAYS DÉPARTEMENTAUX These are also large groupings, and each one is defined by the boundaries of the *département*. So, for instance, any wine of *vin de pays* quality grown in the *département* of Vaucluse will qualify for the title 'Vin de Pays du Vaucluse'.

VINS DE PAYS DE ZONE These are the tightest-controlled of the categories, and can apply to actual communes or at least carefully defined localities. The allowed yield is lower and there may be more control on things like grape varieties. So, for example, we could have a Vin de Pays de la Vallée du Paradis which is in the Aude, and could also be sold as Vin de Pays de l'Aude, or under the widest, least demanding description, Vin de Pays d'Oc.

GERMANY

Those of us who love German wine are prone to wring our hands at the public disaffection for it in Britain. For while German wine still represents more than 40 per cent of the white wine we drink in this country, we are not drinking the right stuff.

The wine we are drinking is Liebfraumilch and those other, similar brews which sell for way under £3.50 a bottle. Drinking so much of them makes Britain Germany's biggest customer, yet one which obstinately refuses to trade up: one can well understand why the pundits and importers are depressed.

Yet many a shipper and writer works hard at trying to persuade consumers of the virtues of fine German wine. One of these is the writer Stuart Pigott, the evangelist of the Riesling grape. In the spring of 1993 Stuart put on three Riesling tastings in Paris, London and New York, inviting journalists and importers to measure the quality of dry Rieslings from the superlative 1990 vintage. We all expected to be moved, but perhaps not to the extent that we were as beauty after beauty was poured into our glasses. After the London tasting at the Gavroche there was a dinner prepared by Michel Roux Junior: a celery soup with scallops; salmon with dill and mustard, and the restaurant's famous *sablé aux fraises*. From where I was sitting I heard no-one grumble about drinking Riesling with such finely tuned dishes. Riesling is not only good, it is versatile.

Monomaniac seduction

The problem is how to get wine lovers to drink Riesling or the other good German wine varieties when they are increasingly seduced by that monomaniac from Burgundy. The position is not helped by the doubting Thomases within Germany itself – the gastronomic critic of *Die Zeit*, Wolfram Siebeck, for example, who has been hurling around that emotive word 'racialism' not – as you might imagine – to castigate those who would set fire to immigrant hostels, but to attack the German wine authorities who refuse to recognise either Chardonnay or Cabernet Sauvignon as permitted grape varieties for quality wine. This wisdom on the part of the authorities has so far prevented Germany from indulging in the orgy of Chardonnay and Cabernet Sauvignon planting which has beset virtually every other wine-making country in recent years.

The sad truth is that the New World has stolen a march on Riesling and other top German wines by offering so many opportunities to drink big, fruity wines which require the bare minimum of thought and discernment. The British consumer no longer bothers to survey the ever-shortening shelves made over to German wines with their long, poetic labels, and the old connoisseurship which formerly reigned in these islands looks like becoming about as rare as the preprandial glass of sherry or the antediluvian mid-morning tot of Madeira with its accompanying slice of seed cake.

Everyone now agrees that German wines need a rethink, not least the wine-makers themselves. What is less certain is that they are wholly on the right track with their ever greater emphasis on acidity without the balm of balancing alcohol. Nor do I believe that the importers have given the problem all the thought they might. The options seem to lie between aiming at the very bottom of the market where, despite the ever-tightening margins, most wine merchants expect to make a profit from German wines; and the importing of the fine wines of the Rheingau and the Mosel, those great intellectuals among wines which are still best savoured in tranquillity and not necessarily sullied with food.

A rethink of at least some aspects of German wine is however in sight – and seems to be being pushed through the German legislative system at a speed designed to outwit the Eurocrats, who take the view that German wine law, as it stands, does not fit the European single market model. Consultation with interested parties in Germany – the top, quality-conscious growers, the industrial producers of sugar-water and everybody in between – began only in the autumn of 1992. By the spring of 1993 draft proposals were in place, and a new German wine law is scheduled for 1 September 1994. This proves that the German wine authorities can move extremely fast when the EC starts nipping at their heels, but will they move in the right direction?

The proposals affect such matters as yields per hectare, and in the process uncover some of the perfectly legal dodges which were (and still are, until the new law comes into effect) open to producers. Take yields. At the moment they

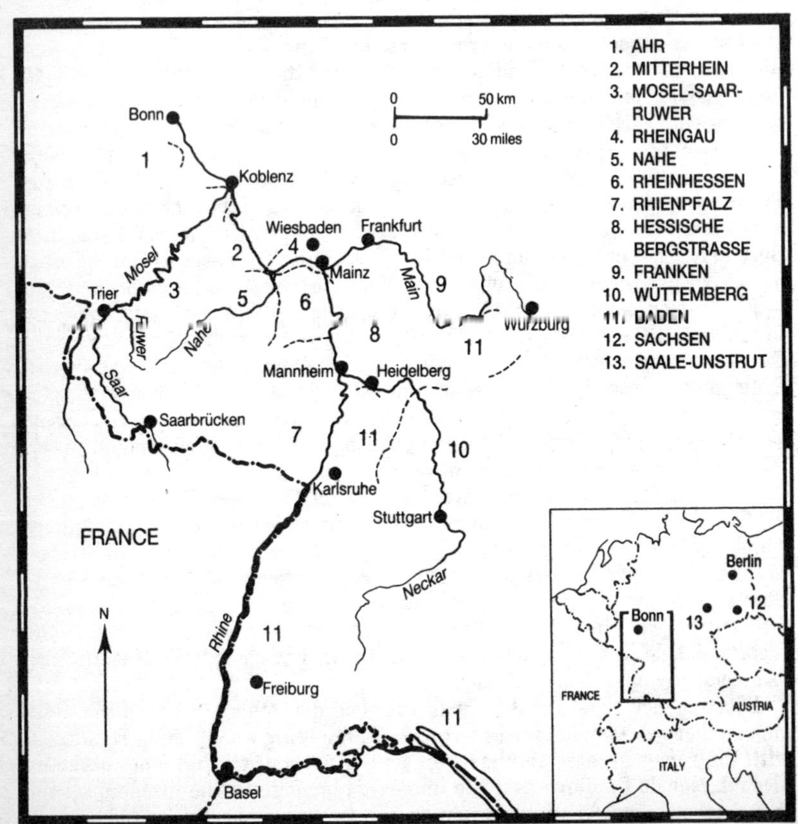

are calculated on the total vineyard surface owned by a producer; the new proposals involve basing them on the total vineyard surface actually in production, and not, for example, on the area being replanted.

The most important of all these draft proposals, however, and the one of most interest to consumers, is the abolition of Grosslagen.

A Grosslage is a collection of vineyard sites: a flock of them, or a herd, like an exultation of larks or a school of whales. The difference is that Grosslagen have legally-defined boundaries and names so confusing that 99.9 per cent of wine drinkers cannot tell from the label whether the wine they are buying comes from a single vineyard (or Einzellage) or from a much larger and less distinguished Grosslage. The lack of distinction between the two is one of the things that the EC doesn't like; and it is certainly one of the problems that must be addressed if we are to start drinking fine German wines again.

What the German wine authorities intend to do about it is less clear. Grosslagen are going to replaced by something called an Ursprungswein-Konzept. Got that? The idea is that district names will be allocated and that the wines from a particular district should have a particular character – all well and good, but not, on the face of it, hugely different from the present situation. Do the Germans really understand why it matters? The district names being bandied about for discussion in the spring of 1993 were potentially just as misleading as the Grosslage names, and one could not help wondering if some sections of the German wine trade positively welcome such confusion if it lends a spurious dignity to inferior wines.

By the time this book appears the proposals will presumably have taken more concrete forms. Let us hope, for the sake of the barely-discovered fine wines of Germany, that they get it right.

North-south divide

I am convinced that whatever the new law does, the best German wines of the future will come from the better vineyards of Rheinhessen, the Pfalz and the other regions to the south of the Main. Can we have some more wines from Baden where they are made with a proper balance of fruit, acidity and alcohol? And while we're about it, some more gutsy Silvaners from Franken please?

Of course, German wine is not just Riesling, although it might be a good idea to forget the majority of those terrible new grapes which the Geisenheim research institute has been churning out since the war. Probably the only one which will achieve classic status is the Scheurebe, which when ripe (when it is unripe it is unbelievably disgusting) can be quite enchanting. We should now be looking to broaden our palette with Grauer Burgunder (Ruländer – the French Pinot Gris) which comes into its own on the right bank of the Rhine. Weisser Burgunder (Pinot Blanc) can also make superb wines which are every bit the equal of the whorish Chardonnay. In years like 1988, 1990, 1991 and 1992 Baden's Spätburgunder (Pinot Noir) distinguished itself; producing wines with 13 to 14 degrees of alcohol without the automatic chaptalization associated with Burgundy. If yields were to be cut in Württemberg something good might even come out of Lemberger (Blaufränkisch), although I despair of Trollinger.

It all requires a little imagination on the part of importers and the general public. In the meantime, all I can do is wring my hands with the best of them and say: make time for German wine. **Giles MacDonogh**

CLASSIFICATIONS

The German classification system is based on sugar levels, and therefore potential alcohol, of the grapes when they are picked. The main categories are as follows:

DEUTSCHER TAFELWEIN Ordinary German table wine of supposedly tolerable quality; low natural strength, sugared at fermentation to increase alcohol, no specific vineyard origin. Deutscher Tafelwein must be 100 per cent German. From a good source, like the major supermarkets, it can be better than many QbAs. The most commonly available are labelled Rhein (or Hock) or Mosel and bear some resemblance to QbAs from the Rhine or Mosel areas. Cheaper wines labelled EC Tafelwein are not worth looking at – they are usually bottled in Germany from very cheap imported wine. However, at the other end of the price spectrum are expensive 'designer table wines', red and white wines from adventurous producers who may age them in oak barriques.

LANDWEIN German *vin de pays*, slightly up-market and drier table wine from one of 20 designated areas. It can be *Trocken* (dry) or *Halbtrocken* (half-dry).

QbA (Qualitätswein bestimmter Anbaugebiete) Literally 'quality wine from designated regions' – the specific areas being Ahr, Hessische Bergstrasse, Mittelrhein, Nahe, Rheingau, Rheinhessen, Rheinpfalz, Franken, Württemberg, Baden, Mosel-Saar-Ruwer, plus two regions in what was East Germany: Saale-Unstrut and Sachsen. QbAs can be mediocre, but are not necessarily so. In modest vintages such as 1987 and 1991 they can be very good indeed, as QbAs may be chaptalized, giving wines of better body and balance than minor Kabinetts. They may also include the products of of prestigious single vineyards, where growers set standards far above those required by the law. These wines can be brimming with class and outstanding value for money.

QmP (Qualitätswein mit Prädikat) Quality wine with special attributes, classified in ascending order according to the ripeness of the grapes: Kabinett, Spätlese, Auslese, Beerenauslese, Eiswein, Trockenbeeren-auslese. Chaptalization is not allowed, and in each category up to and including Auslese, the sugar content may range from almost non-existent to positively luscious. Drier wines may be either Trocken (dry) or Halbtrocken (half-dry). Depending on the vintage conditions, some or all of the following QmP categories will be made.

MATURITY CHART

1990 Mosel Riesling Kabinett

The third great vintage in a row which will repay a few years aging

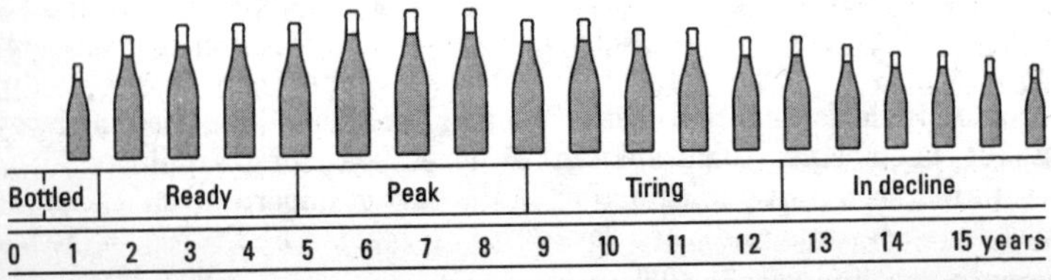

Bottled | Ready | Peak | Tiring | In decline

0 1 2 3 4 5 6 7 8 9 10 11 12 13 14 15 years

KABINETT Made from ripe grapes from a normal harvest. Usually lighter in alcohol than ordinary QbA, and often delicious.

SPÄTLESE From late-picked (therefore riper) grapes. Often moderately sweet, though there are now dry versions.

AUSLESE From selected bunches of very ripe, sometimes late-picked grapes. Often sweet and occasionally with noble rot richness, but many are now fermented dry, giving full wines packed with flavour.

BEERENAUSLESE (BA) From selected single grapes. Not so overripe as TBA, but almost always affected by 'noble rot', a fungus that concentrates the sugar and acidity in the grapes. BA from new, non-Riesling grapes can be dull: Huxelrebe takes to noble rot so easily that you can make a BA before you've even picked Riesling. But Riesling BA, and many a Scheurebe or Silvaner, will be astonishing.

EISWEIN Just that – 'ice wine' – often picked before a winter dawn when the grapes are frozen. They are dashed to the winery by the frost-bitten pickers; once there, quick and careful pressing removes just the slimy-sweet concentrate; the water, in its icy state, stays separate. Eiswein always has a high level of acidity and, say most, needs to be matured for at least seven years in bottle, though you do lose the lovely frosty flavour of youth.

TROCKENBEERENAUSLESE (TBA) 'Shrivelled berries gathered late.' That's a pedestrian translation of one of the world's great tastes. To be TBA, juice has to reach about 22 degrees potential alcohol, and can reach 30 or more. But that stifles the yeasts – so much so that fermentation may hardly get going, and a year later the liquid may have five to six degrees alcohol but 15 to 20 degrees of unfermented sugar. A top Sauternes might be picked with 22 degrees potential alcohol, but end up with about 13 degrees or more, so that TBAs are usually among the sweetest wines in the world. But the tendency is to produce a slightly drier, more alcoholic style. Few growers try to make TBAs because of the risk and the cost. Remember that the vines are making a glass of wine each instead of a bottle, and the weather can easily ruin it all anyway. That's why TBAs are expensive – usually starting at £20 a half-bottle ex-cellars. But, even then, a grower won't make money; it's his pride that makes him do it. And the wines can age for as long as most of us.

GRAPES & FLAVOURS

RIESLING About 90 per cent of the most exciting wines in Germany are made from Riesling. It generally grows on the best slopes in the best villages, and its slow ripening and reasonably restrained yield produce a spectrum of flavours: from steely, slaty, and dry as sun-bleached bones through apples, peaches, apricots, even lychees – more or less sweet according to the ripeness of the grapes and the intentions of the winemaker, and finally arriving at the great sweet wines, which can be blinding in their rich, honeyed concentration of peaches, pineapples, mangoes, even raisins, with an acidity like a streak of fresh lime that makes them the most appetizing of great sweet wines.

MÜLLER-THURGAU The most widely-planted German grape, this cross was propagated in 1882 to get Riesling style plus big yields and early ripening. Well, that's like saying, 'Hey, I've just found a way to turn this plastic bowl into a gold chalice.' You can't do it. Müller is now the workhorse, producing soft, flowery, grapy wines when ripe – and grassy, sharp ones when not. The name Rivaner is used in general for dry wines. By keeping yields down a few growers make good wines.

SILVANER This was the German workhorse before Müller-Thurgau. At its worst it's a broad, earthy wine – dull, fat and vegetal. It is at its best in Franken, where it makes impressive, powerful, earthy wine which develops honeyed weight with age and suits the local porky cookery.

WEISSBURGUNDER or **WEISSER BURGUNDER** The Pinot Blanc is increasingly grown in Nahe, Rheinhessen, Rheinpfalz and Baden to make full dry whites, often as a Chardonnay substitute. It ripens more easily than Chardonnay though and in the right hands can produce soft, creamy wines with a touch of nuttiness. Walnuts, to be precise.

KERNER Another competitor in the 'Riesling-without-the-heartache' stakes. This was recently hailed as 'Riesling in type, but with bigger yields, and earlier ripening.' Is it? Of course not. It does ripen quickly, but the wine ages quickly, too, though with some peachy style.

RULÄNDER The French Pinot Gris. As Ruländer the style is strong, sweetish, rather broad-shouldered, with a whiff of kasbah spice and a splash of honey. When sold as Grauburgunder it is firm, dry, often aged in small oak barriques and can make exciting drinking. Some growers also call it Pinot Gris to help it sell abroad.

SCHEUREBE A tricky grape. When it's unripe, it can pucker your mouth with a combination of raw grapefruit and cat's pee. But properly ripe, it is transformed. The grapefruit is still there, but now it's a fresh-cut pink one from Florida sprinkled with caster sugar. There's honey too, lashings of it, and a crackling, peppery fire which, in the Rheinhessen, Rheinpfalz and even in the Rheingau, produces dry wines as well as sweeter, sometimes outstanding Auslese and Beerenauslese.

SPÄTBURGUNDER The Pinot Noir produces a more thrilling display further south in Burgundy. In Germany they have tended in the past to make gently fruity, slightly sweet, vaguely red wines. Now growers like *Becker* (Rheingau), *Lingenfelder* (Pfalz), *Karl-Heinz Johner* (ex Lamberhurst) and *Joachim Heger* in Baden and *Meyer-Näke* (Ahr) are doing more exciting things. Their wines have good colour and tannin, are dry and often have a spell in oak.

DORNFELDER A red variety grown mainly in the Rheinhessen and Rheinpfalz which at its best produces deep-coloured reds with great fruit concentration combined with firm structure. Made in two styles, either reminiscent of Beaujolais and for early drinking (try *Lingenfelder's*) or aged in barriques for longer keeping. *Siegrist* produces one of the best.

WINES & WINE REGIONS

AHR This small area contrives to be famous for red wines, though the flavour and the colour are pretty light, and its Rieslings are in fact more interesting. The *Staatliche Weinbaudomäne* is the best producer of old-style Spätburgunder. *Meyer-Näkel* represents the new school.

BADEN In the distant, balmy south of the country, Baden makes some red and a lovely rosé in the hills near Freiburg. Dry Ruländer and Weisser Burgunder can be really special – more reliable than the fine examples from Alsace, only ten minutes' drive away. Gewürztraminer is often dense and spicy, and even grapes like Müller-Thurgau and Silvaner can get quite interesting. There's only a little Riesling, but it's good; Spätburgunder is definitely on top. Some good value comes from small co-ops, while the area is dominated by the vast *Badische Winzerkeller*. Top producers: *Karl-Heinz Johner, Dr Heger,* the co-op at *Königsschaffhausen* and *Salwey*.

DEUTSCHER SEKT Often a sure route to intestinal distress and sulphur-led hangover, although Deinhard manages to express the lovely, lean grapiness of the Riesling; *Lila* is especially good, as is *Dr Richter*'s. *Georg Breuer*'s is outstanding, but expensive. Avoid at all costs the stuff made from imported wines, labelled Sekt (not Deutscher Sekt), or worse, Schaumwein.

FRANKEN (Franconia) This is dry wine country. The slightly earthy, slightly vegetal, big and beefy Franken wines in their flagon-shaped 'Bocksbeutel' bottles are usually based on Silvaner or Müller-Thurgau. The quality is, happily, good, but you can often get something much more interesting from elsewhere in Europe for a good deal less money. The best producers are Church and State – the *Juliusspital* and *Bürgerspital* and the *Staatlicher Hofkeller* – though *Johann Ruck* and *Hans Wirsching* at Iphofen are also good. The *Castell'sches Domänenamt* merits a detour.

HALBTROCKEN Half-dry. The general run of German wines used to go from slightly sweet to very sweet, and this 'half-dry' classification was created primarily to satisfy the Germans' own desire for dry wines to drink with food. First efforts were mean and unbalanced but three ripe vintages have shown that producers are learning how to preserve the fruit without oversweetening. At Kabinett and Spätlese level there are some quite good wines – but they're *not* cheap. Riesling Halbtrockens need at least three years to soften.

HESSISCHE BERGSTRASSE A tiny Rhine side-valley running down to Heidelberg, where, presumably, most of its wine is drunk – because it never gets over here. The central town of Bensheim has one of the highest average temperatures of any wine region in Germany, so the wine is worth seeking out. In general the Rieslings are of good quality. The *Staatsweingut Bergstrasse* is the best producer.

LIEBFRAUMILCH Liebfraumilch is a brilliant invention, an innocuous, grapy liquid, usually from the Rheinhessen or Rheinpfalz, that has dramatically fulfilled a need in the UK and US: as the perfect 'beginner's wine', it has broken through the class barriers and mystique of wine. In a way, the rest of German wine has let Liebfraumilch down, since if Liebfraumilch is the base, you should be able to move on to other things – yet many supposedly superior QbAs and even some Kabinetts, for all their high-falutin' names, are *less* satisfying than a good young Liebfraumilch.

MITTELRHEIN The Rhine at its most beautiful, providing all the label ideas for castles clinging to cliffs high above the boats and river-front cafés. It really is like that, and tourists sensibly flock there and just as sensibly drink most of its wine. One grower whose wines have got away is *Toni Jost* – his racy Rieslings are worth trying.

MOSEL-SAAR-RUWER When they are based on Riesling and come from one of the many steep, slaty, south-facing sites in the folds of the river, or strung out, mile upon mile, along the soaring, broad-shouldered valley sides, these northerly wines are unlike any others in the world. They can achieve a thrilling, orchard-fresh, spring flowers flavour, allied to an alcohol level so low that it leaves your head clear enough to revel in the flavour. Most Mosel comes from the river valley itself, but two small tributaries have been incorporated in the designation: the Saar and the Ruwer, with even lighter, perhaps sharper, perhaps more ethereal wines. Some of the best come from *Bischöfliches Konvikt, Bischöfliches Priesterseminar, Wegeler-Deinhard, Dr Loosen, Friedrich-Wilhelm-Gymnasium, Hohe Domkirche, Zilliken, Fritz Haag, von*

The price guides for this section begin on page 345.

Hövel, von Kesselstatt, Karthäuserhof, Egon Müller-Scharzhof, J.J. Prüm, Mönchhof, S.A. Prüm, M.F. Richter, Schloss Saarstein, von Schubert, Selbach-Oster, Bert Simon, Studert Prüm, Thanisch, Vereinigte Hospitien, Weins-Prüm and the *Staatliche Weinbaudomänen* based in Trier.

NAHE Important side-valley off the Rhine, snaking south from Bingen. Many of the best Kabinetts and Spätlesen come from its middle slopes, wines with a grapy taste, quite high acidity and something slightly mineral too. Away from this hub of quality, the wines are less reliable. Top names: *August Anheuser, Paul Anheuser, Crusius, Hermann Dönnhoff, Schloss Plettenberg, Prinz zu Salm Dalberg, Schlossgut Diel* and, a long mouthful to build up a thirst, *Verwaltung der Staatlichen Weinbau-domänen Niederhausen-Schlossböckelheim.*

RHEINGAU This fine wine area spreads north and east of Bingen. It is here, in the best sites, that the Riesling is at its most remarkable – given a long ripening period and a caring winemaker. The Rheingau contains more world-famous villages than any other German vineyard area, and even its lesser villages are well aware of their prestige. It seems a shame to grow lesser grapes here, because the Riesling picks up the minerally dryness, the tangy acidity and a delicious, grapy fruitiness, varying from apple-fresh in a good Kabinett to almost unbearably honeyed in a great TBA. Even Kabinetts have body and ripeness. Around 45 good Rheingau producers have formed the *Charta Association.* The wines, off-dry Rieslings, need four years in bottle, and are recognisable by the embossed arches on the bottle. Top names: *Balthasar Ress, J.B. Becker* (also very good red), *G. Breuer, Deinhard, Knyphausen, von Mumm, Nägler, Schloss Groenesteyn, Schloss Johannisberg, Schloss Reinhartshausen, Schloss Schönborn, Schloss Vollrads, Langwerth von Simmern, Sohlbach, Staatsweingut Eltville, Dr Weil.*

RHEINHESSEN The Rheinhessen, despite having one village as famous as any in the world – Nierstein – is packed with unknown names. Wines from steep river-facing slopes at Nierstein and its unsung neighbours Nackenheim, Oppenheim and Bodenheim can be superb, softer than Rheingaus, still beautifully balanced, flowery and grapy. Otherwise, we're in Liebfraumilch and Bereich Nierstein land, and a great deal of Rheinhessen ends up in one of these two. The village, rightly, feels aggrieved, since its own reputation – traditionally sky-high – is compromised by the mouthwash that oozes out under the Bereich name. Even this is a distortion of Rheinhessen's old reputation, which was built on light, flowery Silvaner. A recent revival of this has seen the emergence of some well-made drier styles from the steep sites on the so-called Rhine Terrace. Top names: *Balbach, Carl Koch Erben, Gunderloch-Usinger, Heyl zu Herrnsheim, Rappenhof, Senfter, Gustav Adolf Schmidt, Villa Sachsen, Guntrum.*

RHEINPFALZ Sometimes known in English as the Palatinate, this has two distinct halves. The northern half clusters round some extremely good villages like Forst, Wachenheim, Deidesheim and Ruppertsberg. There's lots of fiery Riesling; Scheurebe is also excellent. The south is Germany's great success story of recent years, with fewer big names but an astonishing improvement in quality. The Rheinpfalz is now challenging for the Rheingau for the title of top region. Look for *Basserman-Jordan, von Buhl, Bürklin-Wolf, Wegeler-Deinhard, Koehler-Ruprecht, Müller-Catoir, Pfeffingen, Rebholz, Georg Siben Erben, Siegrist* and *Lingenfelder.* There are some good, true-to-type wines from co-operatives.

SAALE-UNSTRUT Three large producers dominate the largest of the wine regions in what we used to call East Germany. The climate is similar to Franken, the grapes are mainly Müller-Thurgau and Silvaner.

SACHSEN Germany's easternmost region in the former GDR, and previously called Elbe Tal. The vineyards are near the banks of the river Elbe, close to the cities of Dresden and Meissen, and are dominated by Müller-Thurgau.They're getting a lot of help from the West now, but there's still a lot to be done.

SEKT bA (Sekt bestimmter Anbaugebiete). Deutscher Sekt increasingly comes from private estates, and is sometimes made by the traditional Champagne method. If the wine comes from one specific quality region it can be labelled accordingly – Rheinhessen Sekt for instance – and is generally a step above Deutscher Sekt. Riesling Sekt bA is especially worth looking out for. (Try *Schloss Wachenheim* or *Winzersekt,* or *Dr Richter's.*)

TROCKEN Dry. The driest German wines. Back in the early 1970s these were painfully, searingly horrid creatures, but things have been improving with a series of warm vintages, and at Spätlese level in particular there are some positively attractive (though pricy) wines.

WÜRTTEMBERG We haven't seen much Württemberg wine here because most has been drunk on the spot. Württemberg's claim to fame – if fame is the right word – is for red, which accounts for half of the production. The most exciting grape is Lemberger, which makes dark, spicy wines suited to oak aging. They're worth trying, especially from *Graf Adelmann* or *Staatliche Lehr- und Versuchsanstalt für Wein-und Obstbau. Schlossgut Hohenheilstein* is also good.

REGIONAL DEFINITIONS

German wine is classified according to ripeness of grapes and provenance. The country is divided into wine regions (alphabetically listed on these pages – Rheingau, Rheinhessen etc, and two in the former East); inside these there are three groupings. The new law, scheduled for 1 September 1994, may make some changes.

Bereich This is a collection of villages and vineyard sites, supposedly of similar style, and grouped under a single name – generally that of the most famous village. So 'Bereich Nierstein' means 'a wine from the general region of Nierstein'. It could come from any one of 50 or more villages, regardless of quality.

Grosslage A group of vineyards supposedly all of similar type, and based on one or more villages. The objective was to try and make some sense of thousands of obscure vineyard names. But it doesn't work. Among the 152 designated names, there are a few good Grosslagen – like Honigberg, which groups the vineyards of Winkel in the Rheingau, or Badstube which covers the best sites in Bernkastel. In these Grosslagen, a blend of several different vineyard sites will produce a wine of good quality and identifiable local character. However, most Grosslagen debase the whole idea of a 'vineyard' identity. Taken to absurd limits, Germany's most famous Grosslage is Niersteiner Gutes Domtal. Gutes Domtal was originally a vineyard of 34 hectares in Nierstein – and not terribly special at that. The Niersteiner Gutes Domtal Grosslage covers 1300 hectares, spread over 15 villages, almost all of which share no quality traits with Nierstein whatsoever.

Einzellage This is a real single vineyard wine, corresponding to a 'cru' in Burgundy or Alsace. There are about 2600 of these, ranging from a mere half hectare to 250 hectares. All the best wines in Germany are from Einzellagen, though only a distressingly small proportion have real individuality. Some growers are using Einzellage names less, and emphasizing their estate and grape names more, or naming QbA and QmP wines simply with the village name, such as Nierstein or Deidesheim. These wines, often from top growers, are likely to be better than many from a Grosslage.

WINERY PROFILES

FRIEDRICH-WILHELM-GYMNASIUM ★★★(★) (Mosel-Saar-Ruwer) Large Trier estate. The best wines are textbook Mosel, but can be inconsistent.

FÜRSTLICH CASTELL'SCHES DOMÄNENAMT ★★★★ (Franconia) Princely estate in the Steigerwald hills which produces excellent Müller-Thurgau, Silvaner, Riesling and as a speciality in top years, wonderfully concentrated Rieslaner.

SCHLOSSGUT DIEL ★★★★ (Nahe) One of the Nahe's top estates. Production is mainly of beautifully balanced dry wines, though sweeter styles from the warm concentrated vintage of 1990 will be well worth waiting for. Impeccably made, barrique-aged dry Grauburgunder.

MÜLLER-CATOIR ★★★★★ (Rheinpfalz) Superbly-concentrated Riesling and Scheurebe. The jewel in its crown, however, is probably the Grauer Burgunder. The dry 1990 won the *Gault Millau* Pinot Gris wine Olympics.

STAATLICHE WEINBAUDOMÄNE ★★★★(★) (Nahe) The State Domaine at Niederhausen is one of the great white wine estates of the world, producing Rieslings which combine Mosel-like flowery fragrance with a special mineral intensity. Prices are very reasonable, considering the very good quality.

VON SCHUBERT ★★★★★ (Mosel-Saar-Ruwer) Exquisitely delicate, fragrant Rieslings are grown on the slopes above the Maximin-Grünhaus, a former monastic property on the tiny Ruwer. The best vineyard at the top of the hill is called Abtsberg, because the wine was reserved for the abbot: the scarcely-less-good middle slope is called Bruderberg, and was kept for the monks. Superlative at every level .

WEGELER-DEINHARD ★★★★ (Mosel-Saar-Ruwer) Koblenz-based shipper with substantial holdings in Rheingau, Pfalz and M-S-R. Wines from all three estates are impeccably made. It has scaled down its operations recently and now bottles only a little under vineyard names. Still makes exquisite Bernkasteler Doctor and Wehlener Sonnenuhr.

WEINGUT BALTHASAR RESS ★★★(★) (Rheingau) Stefan Ress's beautifully fresh, clean Riesling wines have performed consistently well in blind tastings. Highly successful at both traditional-style Spätlesen and Auslesen and off-dry wines under the Charta group label.

MATURITY CHART

1989 Rheingau Riesling Spätlese

Riesling Spätlese develops a more refined character after three years in bottle

WEINGUT DR BÜRKLIN-WOLF★★★★ (Rheinpfalz) Bürklin's wines have an aristocratic elegance which sometimes suggests the Rheingau rather than the Pfalz. Its top Wachenheim wines, from flat vineyards, disprove the theory that great German wines must necessarily come from steep slopes.

WEINGUT LOUIS GUNTRUM ★★★(★) (Rheinhessen) Louis Guntrum wines are always reliable: the top Rieslings and Silvaners from the Oppenheimer Sackträger vineyard are impressively powerful, with a touch of earthiness to their fruit.

WEINGUT HEYL ZU HERRNSHEIM ★★★★(★) (Rheinhessen) An estate that is scandalously underrated in Britain, producing magnificent, traditional-style Riesling Spätlese, ripe yet beautifully balanced, from the red slate vineyards of Nierstein.

WEINGUT LINGENFELDER ★★★★(★) (Rheinpfalz) Dynamic small estate in northern Pfalz, producing excellent Riesling and Scheurebe, both dry and 'traditional' in style, as well as remarkably deep-coloured, full-bodied red Spätburgunder (alias Pinot Noir) and deliciously juicy red Dornfelder.

WEINGUT J.J. PRÜM ★★★★★ (Mosel-Saar-Ruwer) Legendary estate with large holding in the great Wehlener Sonnenuhr vineyard. These are wines for the long haul: often prickly with carbon dioxide when young, and high in acidity, they develop a marvellous peachy richness with time. Wonderful stuff.

VINTAGES

1992 Very good, and already being compared to 1983 and 1989. Like 1989 its problem may be acidity, making for opulent wines which may be short on bite. In the Mosel rain put paid to hopes of making much Auslese, but Spätlese quality should be excellent. Rigorous selection in Sachsen and Saale-Unstrut shows that they may be catching on.

1991 Yields were low, thanks to frost, and gave very good wines in the Saar and Ruwer, and drought led to a preponderance of QbA wines in the Mosel and Rhine. Few wines will reach the heights of the preceding three vintages, but 1991 is not a vintage to write off. It will offer good, well-balanced Rieslings that should give ample pleasure while waiting for the mega-vintages to mature.

1990 The third great vintage in a row and some say the best of all. Some producers committed to dry wine production made their first sweet wines for a decade, saying the acidity was too high to get the balance right for dry wines. A great year for Spätlesen and Auslesen, though with little noble rot. In youth the wines have wonderful ripe fruit flavours but they will need several years for all that acidity to soften.

1989 The vintage to prove the exception – that big can still be beautiful. Some of the wines are proving a little short on acidity now. They should be the first to drink among this trinity of great vintages. From Auslese upwards the wines are luscious.

1988 Wonderful, wonderful wines. Lovely fresh acidity, a beautiful clear, thrilling fruit and remarkable array of *personalities* – you really can see the differences between sites.

1987 A pleasant, dry, not entirely ripe vintage; lots of delicious QbAs from top vineyards.

1986 Not very ripe, not very clean, not very exciting. Buy only from top producers.

1985 Very attractive, fresh-fruited wines overall, without the sheer zinging class of '88, but still drinking well.

ITALY

This has been a difficult year in Italy. Signori Craxi and Andreotti, two of Italy's most influential politicians in the post-war period, have been tainted by the scandal that has seen over a thousand politicians and businessmen jailed for bribery and corruption of one sort or another. Recession has hit the economy hard, bringing the Italians, after the buoyant 1980s, back to earth with a rather unwelcome jolt.

These events and sentiments are echoed in the world of Italian wine. After a decade in which Italian wine had grown up and had become a seemingly unstoppable force on various markets, the past year has forced a number of producers to reassess their marketing, pricing and sometimes even production policies. In other words, after a carefree adolescence in the 1980s, adulthood, with its attendant headaches, finally came to Italian wine last year.

How it copes with these problems will be the making or the breaking of it. Everywhere there is talk of crisis. In the past decade, sales increased at an alarming rate, fuelled by the greater interest shown by the German, Swiss, American and home markets, and prices followed suit, sometimes doubling in the space of five years. Price-sensitive British buyers often had a sceptical reception, especially when they claimed that Italian wines no longer represented good value for money. 'Sales would seem to indicate otherwise,' was the common response, usually accompanied by the sort of chilling smile more usually worn by officials of the British Foreign Office, a smile of self-righteous rectitude.

This smile has now been replaced by a worried frown. Cellars are full, and many prices have tumbled. Those producers who are weathering the storm tend to be those who in the 1980s followed a route of quality at reasonable prices. Their prices trailed behind demand for their wines and were lower than many people were willing to pay, and today they are seen to represent good value for money. Most often, however, and notably in the case of several famous names, the prices that shot into orbit have returned to earth with little fuel left. In some instances, grand producers have been forced to reduce their prices to previously unimaginable levels.

A dividing decade

This can only be healthy. The developments of the past decade have resulted in polarization in the market for Italian wines. They remain strong in the lower price categories, thanks largely to the continuing (though flagging) sales of Lambrusco. Indeed, 85 per cent of all Italian wines sold in Britain sells below £4.50 a bottle. But the past decade has also seen a great increase in the sales of expensive, top-quality Italian wines. Even five years ago, an Italian wine that carried a price tag of over £10.00 a bottle without a name like Tignanello or Sassicaia was more than likely to elicit a puzzled response from a buyer; today, a number at this level are eagerly sought after.

This polarization has left Italy weak in the all-important middle market, where wines sell between £3 and £6 a bottle. This is the most competitive area in the market, and one in which superb value can be found. Because of the wisdom of the Chancellor's philosophy on excise duties (like the wisdom of God, it passeth

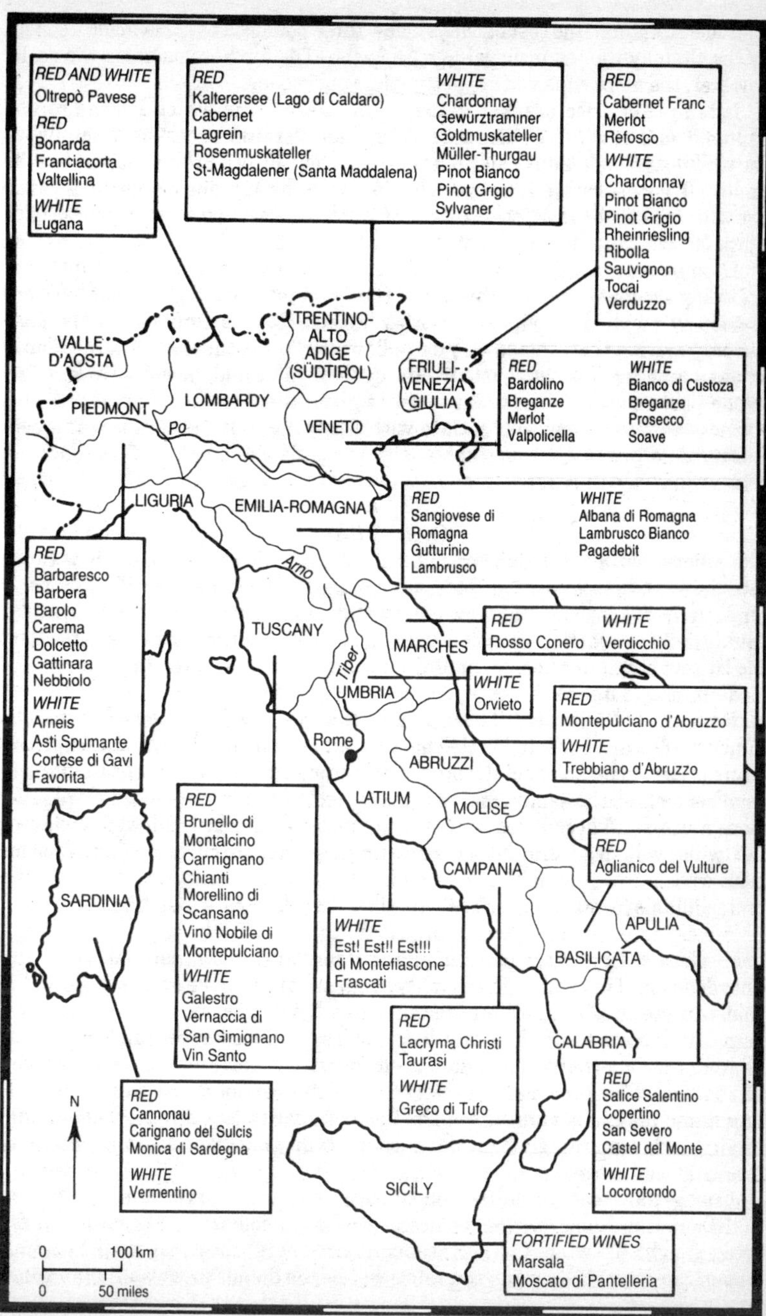
RED AND WHITE
Oltrepò Pavese
RED
Bonarda
Franciacorta
Valtellina
WHITE
Lugana
RED
Kalterersee (Lago di Caldaro)
Cabernet
Lagrein
Rosenmuskateller
St-Magdalener (Santa Maddalena)
WHITE
Chardonnay
Gewürztraminer
Goldmuskateller
Müller-Thurgau
Pinot Bianco
Pinot Grigio
Sylvaner
RED
Cabernet Franc
Merlot
Refosco
WHITE
Chardonnay
Pinot Bianco
Pinot Grigio
Rheinriesling
Ribolla
Sauvignon
Tocai
Verduzzo
VALLE D'AOSTA
TRENTINO-ALTO ADIGE (SÜDTIROL)
FRIULI-VENEZIA GIULIA
PIEDMONT
LOMBARDY
Po
VENETO
RED
Bardolino
Breganze
Merlot
Valpolicella
WHITE
Bianco di Custoza
Breganze
Prosecco
Soave
LIGURIA
EMILIA-ROMAGNA
RED
Sangiovese di Romagna
Gutturinio
Lambrusco
WHITE
Albana di Romagna
Lambrusco Bianco
Pagadebit
RED
Barbaresco
Barbera
Barolo
Carema
Dolcetto
Gattinara
Nebbiolo
WHITE
Arneis
Asti Spumante
Cortese di Gavi
Favorita
Arno
TUSCANY
MARCHES
RED
Rosso Conero
WHITE
Verdicchio
Tiber
UMBRIA
WHITE
Orvieto
RED
Montepulciano d'Abruzzo
WHITE
Trebbiano d'Abruzzo
Rome
ABRUZZI
LATIUM
MOLISE
RED
Brunello di Montalcino
Carmignano
Chianti
Morellino di Scansano
Vino Nobile di Montepulciano
WHITE
Galestro
Vernaccia di San Gimignano
Vin Santo
RED
Aglianico del Vulture
CAMPANIA
SARDINIA
WHITE
Est! Est!! Est!!! di Montefiascone
Frascati
APULIA
BASILICATA
RED
Lacryma Christi
Taurasi
WHITE
Greco di Tufo
CALABRIA
RED
Salice Salentino
Copertino
San Severo
Castel del Monte
WHITE
Locorotondo
N
RED
Cannonau
Carignano del Sulcis
Monica di Sardegna
WHITE
Vermentino
SICILY
FORTIFIED WINES
Marsala
Moscato di Pantelleria
0
100 km
0
50 miles

all understanding), the cost of wines below three pounds a bottle is made up more by tax than by the intrinsic value of the wine. The further you go up the scale, however, the more wine you are getting for your money.

It is in this price bracket that Australia excels, in which France reigns supreme, and in which California and Germany perform almost as miserably as Italy. Unless the Italians can plug this gap, their future in this market will be limited. They are certainly not going to do it with the Tignanellos and Sassicaias, nor with the Lambruscos, so the question must be: where on earth are these mid-range Italian wines to come from?

Here my optimism is restored, for there seem two general areas capable of providing excellent wines at this price. The first consists of regions that have not previously supplied wine in bottle, either because they were unknown or because the only market that existed was for bulk wine. This is the case with the South, where a number of wines of astonishing quality, value and flavour have emerged in the past couple of years. The sun has given them the sort of ripeness and softness we have come to associate with Australia, but flavours are uniquely Italian. And prices are remarkably low, as the Salice Salentino from Taurino, sold by Safeway, illustrates.

Quality lore

The other area involves some crystal ball gazing. It is related to the new Goria law, passed by parliament at the end of January 1992. This law will, if properly implemented, shake up Italian wines by reducing yields and promoting quality. And it is this reduction in yields, and the development of a new classification, which seems to offer the opportunity for creating an interesting selection of medium-priced Italian wines.

From the 1994 vintage, it seems likely that the new *Indicazione Geografiche Tipici* (IGT) will come into effect. This will be the equivalent of the French *vin de pays* and will bring many of the previously errant table wines under some form of legal control. At the same time, maximum yields for DOC wines will be reduced by as much as 25 hectolitres per hectare from those currently allowed. Yields for IGT wines will, in general, be on a par with those that are currently permitted for DOC wines.

If yields are reduced, prices will rise. Well-known wines like Soave and Valpolicella, for instance, which are currently sold largely on price, could find themselves having to compete on quality terms with Australian Cabernets and Chardonnays. They can do it, if quality increases at the same rate as it has in the past five years. The IGTs, on the other hand, will present us with some new names to replace those that have become tired and hackneyed, and could offer exciting new alternatives for the wine drinker. The *vins de pays* have achieved this in France, so I see no reason why the Italians cannot do the same with IGT. The name may lack charm, but the base of quality has already been firmly established, something which was most certainly not the case in the south of France a decade ago.

Changes are afoot in Italian wine. True, the future is uncertain, but no more so than it is in Rome, where replacements for a whole political generation are being sought. In wine, the replacements are there; they just need to be put properly in place. If they are, the 1990s will be the decade in which Italian wines finally come of age.

DAVID GLEAVE

RED WINES

Whereas France has been – and is – the model for all the New World exploits, and although grapes like Cabernet Sauvignon and Pinot Noir are important in Italy, the true glories of Italy are unimitated anywhere else. Red wines from Nebbiolo, Dolcetto, Montepulciano, Lagrein, Sangiovese, Aglianico, Sagrantino and many others are unique expressions of a wine culture which has been too inward-looking for too long. But the jewels are coming out of the woodwork – a mixed metaphor which is entirely apt for the strange delights I'm now lapping up.

GRAPES & FLAVOURS

AGLIANICO A very late-ripening grape of Greek origin, grown in the South. At its most impressive in Aglianico del Vulture (Basilicata) and Taurasi (Campania).

BARBERA The most prolific grape of Piedmont and the North-West. The wines traditionally have high acidity, a slightly resiny edge and yet a sweet-sour, raisiny taste or even a brown-sugar sweetness. But they don't have to be like this: witness some of the lighter but intensely fruity Barberas from the Asti and Monferrato hills. The grape reaches its peak in the Langhe hills around Alba where growers like *Altare, Conterno Fantino* and *Gaja* have used low yields to great effect. Experiments with barrique-aging are also encouraging, and wines like *Aldo Conterno*'s are outstandingly rich. *Alfredo Prunotto*'s *1990 Pian Romualdo Barbera d'Alba* is oaky and rather special.

BONARDA Low acid, rich, plummy reds, often with a liquoricy, chocolaty streak and sometimes a slight spritz. Most common in the Colli Piacentini of Emilia-Romagna where it is blended with Barbera as Gutturnio; also in the Oltrepò Pavese.

CABERNET SAUVIGNON A contentious grape in Italy, because of *tipicità* – local character. Many traditionalists are upset at how this world-class grape is usurping the place of indigenous varieties in the vineyard and also dominating any grape with which it is blended. In fact there has been Cabernet Sauvignon in Italy for well over a century, but Italians have only recently succumbed to Cabernet fever. This is most evident in Tuscany, where Cabernet has added greatly to the fruit of many wines and, aged in small oak barrels, is potentially world class. *Sassicaia* has spawned a host of imitators. There is Chianti with a dollop of Cabernet Sauvignon, though the trend has peaked.

CABERNET FRANC Fairly widely grown in the north-east of Italy, especially in Alto Adige, Trentino, Veneto and Friuli. It can make gorgeous grassy, yet juicy-fruited reds – wines that are unnervingly easy to drink young but also capable of aging.

DOLCETTO Makes good, brash, fruity, purple wine of the same name in Piedmont, ideally full yet soft, slightly chocolaty and spicy, and wonderfully refreshing when young. Try and find the exciting 1992s.

LAGREIN Local grape of the Alto Adige (Südtirol) and Trentino, making delicious, dark reds, strongly plum-sweet when they're young, aging slowly to a smoky, creamy softness. It also makes one of Italy's best rosés, called Lagrein Kretzer.

MERLOT Widely planted in the North-East. Often good in Friuli; provides lots of jug wine in the Veneto but when blended with Cabernet Sauvignon by *Loredan*

Gasparini (Venegazzù) or *Fausto Maculan* (Brentino) achieves greater stature. Other Cabernet/ Merlot blends are produced by *Mecvini* in the Marche and Trentino's *Bossi Fedrigotti* (Foianeghe). *Avignonesi* and *Castello di Ama* in Tuscany are getting promising results.

MONTEPULCIANO A much underrated grape. Yes, it has toughness, but it also has lots of plummy, herby fruit. *Banfi* in Montalcino has high hopes for it. It grows mostly on the Adriatic Coast, from the Marches down to to Puglia.

NEBBIOLO The big, tough grape of the North-West, making – unblended – the famous Barolos and Barbarescos as well as the less famous Gattinara, Ghemme, Carema, Spanna and plain Nebbiolo. This is a surly, fierce grape, producing wines that can be dark, chewy, unyielding and harsh behind a shield of cold-tea-tannin and acidity for the first few years; but which then blossom out into a remarkable richness full of chocolate, raisins, prunes, and an austere perfume of tobacco, pine and herbs. In the past, sloppy wine-making has been all too evident in the wines on sale here but shops are now more willing to fork out for the best. In 1985 modern wine-making allied to a beautiful vintage gave some stunning wines, but prices are pretty high, and anyway there's little left. The 1990s are tremendous. A few growers (*Elio Altare, Clerico, Conterno Fantino* and *Voerzio*) are producing some superb *vini da tavola* by aging their wines in barrique, or blending it with Barbera, or both, as in *Sebaste*'s *Briccoviole* (Tesco).

SANGIOVESE Too much is often asked of this Chianti mainstay. It is extremely good at providing purple-fresh, slightly rasping, herby wines, full of thirst-quenching, acid fruit, to be drunk young. It's not always so successful at providing the weight and personality needed for more 'serious' wines. This is mainly because the clones widely planted in the 1970s were high-yielding ones, rather than the native Tuscan variety. You can make decent quaffing wines from the high-yielders, but wines of real class and substance come only from the Tuscan clone. This makes deeper, plummier wine more suited to aging and is contributing hugely to the improved quality of Tuscan reds.

SCHIAVA Quaffable, light reds with almost no tannin and a unique taste that veers between smoked ham and strawberry yoghurt. An Alto Adige (Südtirol) grape, Schiava is at its best in Kalterersee (Lago di Caldaro Scelto) and Santa Maddalena. The local population, which mostly speaks German, calls it by its German name, Vernatsch.

WINES & WINE REGIONS

AGLIANICO DEL VULTURE, DOC (Basilicata) High up the side of gaunt Monte Vulture, in the wilds of Basilicata (Italy's 'instep'), the Aglianico grape makes a superb, thick-flavoured red wine. The colour isn't particularly deep, but the tremendous almond paste and chocolate fruit are matched by a tough, dusty feel and quite high acidity. What's more, it's *not* very expensive. Two good producers are *Paternoster*, *Fratelli d'Angelo*. D'Angelo's new barriqued *Canneto d'Angelo* is good.

ALTO ADIGE Also called Südtirol as the majority of the population is German-speaking. Although the UK drinks mostly the whites, the attractive light reds made of the Vernatsch/Schiava grape – especially Kalterersee and St Magdalener – have until recently been the most famous offerings. However, Cabernet, Pinot Nero, Lagrein and the tea-rose-scented Rosenmuskateller all make Alto Adige reds – and rosés – with a lot more stuffing and personality to them.

BARBARESCO, DOCG (Piedmont) Toughness and tannin are the hallmarks of the Nebbiolo, Barbaresco's only grape, and they can often overshadow its finer points: a delicious soft, strawberryish maturity, edged with smoke, herbs and pine. The Riserva category (four years' aging) still exists, but most producers these days stick to the minimum two years' aging (one in wood) the law requires. When it works, the Nebbiolo can show more nuances and glints of brilliance than any other Italian grape. Best: *Luigi Bianco, Castello di Neive, Cigliuti, Glicine, Giuseppe Cortese, Gaja, Bruno Giacosa, Marchesi di Gresy, Moresco, Pasquero, Pelissero, Pertinace, Pio Cesare, Produttori del Barbaresco, Roagna, Vietti* and *Scarpa*.

BARBERA, DOC (Piedmont and others) Barbera is Italy's most widely planted red vine, and makes a good, gutsy wine, usually with a resiny, herby bite, insistent acidity and fairly forthright, dry raisin sort of fruit. It is best in Piedmont, where it has four DOCs, Barbera d'Alba, d'Asti, del Monferrato and Rubino di Cantavenna, and in Lombardy under the Oltrepò Pavese DOC; also found in Puglia, Campania, Emilia-Romagna, Liguria, Sicily, Sardinia.

BARDOLINO, DOC (Veneto) A growing number of pale pinky reds with a frail wispy cherry fruit and a slight bitter snap to the finish are appearing from the banks of Lake Garda, along with some lovely Chiaretto rosés and some excellent, *very* fresh-fruited Novello wines. There are also a few fuller, rounder wines like *Boscaini*'s *Le Canne* which can take some aging. As quality has risen, so have the prices. Also *Arvedi d'Emilei, Guerrieri-Rizzardi, Lenotti, Masi* (*Fresco* and *La Vegrona*), *Portalupi* and *Le Vigne di San Pietro*.

BAROLO, DOCG (Piedmont) Praise be – I'm a Barolo fan! Who'd have thought it: only a few years ago I couldn't find *any* I liked. The raw material is still the Nebbiolo grape, a monstrously difficult character that has had to be dragged squealing and roaring into the latter half of the twentieth century. But many growers are trying to stress fruit rather than raw, rough tannins and not only will these wines be enjoyable younger – in five years rather than 20 – they will (according to the basic tenet of the modern school) actually *age better* because you can't age a wine without balance, and balance, too, makes a wine enjoyable young.

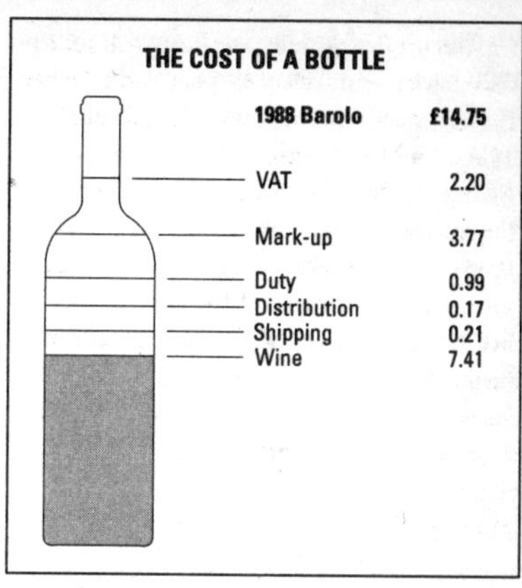

It would be easy to say only expensive Barolo is any good, but the efforts of Asda, Tesco, Sainsbury and Oddbins show that good buyers *can* find bargains. Because the Nebbiolo does have a remarkable, deep, sweet, plum and woodsmoke richness, even blackcurrants and raspberry pips, often a dark, wild maelstrom of chocolate and prunes and tobacco. By shortening fermentation to extract less tannin, or by bending the laws and aging in stainless steel, or bottling early, there are some magical experiences to be had. The 1987s from producers who ruthlessly cut out poor grapes are dry, but delicious. I'm sticking with '87 and '86 (brilliant but in short supply) for the moment until the hefty '85s come round. Some are already displaying delicious perfume, and in the wines from the best sites there's masses of the sweet, supple fruit that you need to stand up to the tannin.

The area of production is small, around 1200 hectares in total, and is divided into five main communes, all with individual styles. La Morra is the largest and makes the most forward and perfumed wines, ripe and velvety from around five years. Barolo itself tends to make wines of more richness and weight, but without the concentration and structure of the wines from Castiglione Falletto, and which need aging. Monforte, the southernmost commune, is known for rich and powerful wines often needing ten years in bottle. To the east, Serralunga is famous for the tough, jaw-locking style which ages more slowly than the others.

Over the last 20 years, producers have been fighting for official classification of the top sites: the new law should do this. Many growers are already citing vineyard names on the label, and, for the moment, the ones to look out for are: Arborina, Monfalletto, Marcenasco Conca, Rocche, Rocchette, Brunate, La Serra and Cerequio (La Morra); Cannubi, Sarmassa, and Brunate and Cerequio (again) which straddle the two communes (Barolo); Bricco Boschis, Rocche, Villero, Bric del Fiasc (Castiglione Falletto); Bussia Soprana, Santo Stefano and Ginestra (Monforte); Marenca-Rivette, Lazzarito, La Delizia, Vigna Rionda, Prapo, Baudana and Francia (Serralunga). The best wines come from producers like *Altare, Azelia, Borgogno, Bovio, Brovia, Cavallotto, Ceretto, Clerico, Aldo* and *Giacomo Conterno, Conterno Fantino, Cordero di Montezemolo, Fontanafredda* (only its *cru* wines), *Bruno Giacosa, Marcarini, Bartolo Mascarello, Giuseppe Mascarello, Migliorini, Pio Cesare, Pira, Prunotto, Ratti, Sandrone, Scarpa, Scavino, Sebaste, Vajra, Vietti* and *Voerzio*.

BONARDA (Lombardy) Delicious, young, plummy red with a dark chocolate bitter twist from Lombardy and Emilia in the central north. *Castello di Luzzano* is particularly good, with great tannic length, the right fruit impact and gently peppery push.

BREGANZE, DOC (Veneto) Little-known but excellent claret-like red from near Vicenza. There's Pinot Nero, Merlot and Cabernet (Sauvignon and Franc) and these Bordeaux grapes produce a most attractive grassy, blackcurranty red, with a touch of cedar. Very good stuff... *Maculan* ages it in new wood, which makes it more exciting.

BRUNELLO DI MONTALCINO, DOCG (Tuscany) A big, strong neighbour of Chianti traditionally better known for its ridiculous prices than for exciting flavours, but slowly coming to terms with a world in which people will pay high prices, but demand excellence to go with them. The reason why the wine can be disappointing is that it can lose its fruit during the three and a half years' wood aging required by the regulations. But in the right hands, in a good, clean cellar, the fruit can hold out, and then the wine can achieve an amazing combination of flavours: blackberries, raisins, pepper, acidity, tannin with a haunting sandalwood perfume, all bound together by an austere richness resembling liquorice and fierce black chocolate. Such wines are a growing minority, scary prices are still the norm. The best wines come from *Altesino, Campogiovanni, Caparzo, Casanova, Case Basse, Il Casello, Col d'Orcia, Costanti, Pertimali, Il Poggione, Talenti* and *Val di Suga*. *Biondi Santi* is the most famous and the most expensive producer but I've never had a bottle that justified the cost.

CAREMA, DOC (Piedmont) The most refined in bouquet and taste of the Nebbiolo wines from a tiny mountainous zone close to Val d'Aosta. *Luigi Ferrando* is the best producer, especially his 'black label', but almost all are good – and need five to six years to be at their best.

The price guides for this section begin on page 352.

CARMIGNANO, DOCG (Tuscany) Although the advent of Cabernet Sauvignon in Tuscany is often talked of as being entirely recent, Carmignano – a small enclave inside the Chianti zone just to the west of the city of Florence – has been adding in 10 to 15 per cent of Cabernet Sauvignon to its wine ever since the nineteenth century. The soft, clear blackcurranty fruit of the Cabernet makes a delicious blend with the somewhat stark flavours of the Sangiovese – the majority grape. There is also some good rosé and some *vin santo*. The zone rose to DOCG status in 1990. *Capezzana* is the original estate and the only one regularly seen over here. Its '85 and '88 Riserva wines are special.

CHIANTI, DOCG (Tuscany) The first few times I had real Chianti, fizzy-fresh, purple-proud, with an invigorating, rasping fruit, I thought it was the most perfect jug wine I'd ever had. It still can be. But following the introduction of DOC in 1963, vineyards expanded all over the place to meet a buoyant demand. Chianti and especially Chianti Classico suffered

NORTH-WEST ITALY VINTAGES

North-West vintages are difficult to generalize about because it isn't always easy to catch them at their best, and a good year for Nebbiolo may not have been a good one for Dolcetto. And vice versa. Also, styles of wine-making may vary from one producer to the next. In general, Dolcetto needs drinking in its youth, Barbera can last but is often at its best young, when the fruit is most vibrant, and although there are Barolo and Barbaresco wines which you can drink after five years or so, the best last for 20 years or more. Whites should be drunk as young as possible.

1992 Quality was diluted by September rains. Until then quality had been promising, after a difficult flowering (which reduced quantity) and a decent summer. The rains meant grey hairs for the producers and lighter, earlier drinking wines.

1991 A very fragmented year. Good wines from grapes picked before the rains that fell during the vintage in Piedmont; Gattinara and Gavi were good. Difficult in Lombardy but good Valtellina and some exceptional whites. Fair to good overall so far.

1990 A fabulous vintage: wines of tremendous colour, richness and perfume, Barolo and Barbaresco for long aging and delicious Barbera. Wonderful Dolcetto again.

1989 Unlike the rest of Italy, Piedmont basked in glorious sunshine in 1989. Dolcetto looks even better than in the last five (excellent) vintages, and the Barbera is very good. Nebbiolo came in early at remarkable levels of ripeness.

1988 Dolcetto and Barbera look really good, a little tough to start with perhaps, but the concentration and fruit are there. Nebbiolo got caught by the rain, but the good growers left the vineyards to dry out and picked healthy ripe grapes.

1987 Very good for Dolcetto and the whites, but patchy Barolo and Barbaresco.

1986 Barbaresco and Barolo are overshadowed by the great '85s but quality is good.

1985 An exciting vintage when more and more growers decided to emphasize fruit and perfume in their wines. We will see some truly great '85s eventually.

1983 All but the best are fading.

1982 Excellent, big ripe reds which have the fruit to age.

1978 Loads of concentrated fruit: a traditionalist's delight, but be prepared to wait.

more than their fair share of investors who cared only about profit and knew nothing about wine.

But Chianti might have stood more chance if the chief grape, the Sangiovese, had not been debased, first by the planting of inferior, high-yielding clones, and second by the traditional admixture of too much white juice from Trebbiano and Malvasia grapes with the red. Growers could at one time legally mix in almost one-third white grapes – yes, white grapes in red wine – and the inevitable result was wines that faded before they even made it into bottle.

Thankfully DOCG regulations now limit the proportion of white grapes to two to five per cent. This seems to have stemmed the flow of thin Chianti, and own-label examples from companies like Asda can be very good indeed.

Another development in the Chianti region has been the emergence of Cabernet Sauvignon as a component of the red wines. Although not really permissible for more than ten per cent of the total, a number of growers use it to delicious effect, though as clonal selection of better Sangiovese develops, there may come a day when this is no longer necessary. The Chianti Classico Consorzio has set in train an operation called 'Chianti Classico 2000' which is intended to ensure that as replanting takes place only top clones of Sangiovese and Canaiolo are used. By 2000 we may well be classing Chianti Classico, at least, as one of the world's great red wines once again.

The Chianti region is divided into seven regions as follows: Classico, Colli Aretini, Colli Fiorentini, Colli Senesi, Colline Pisane, Montalbano and Rufina. Classico and Rufina are almost always marked on the label, where appropriate, but most wines from the other zones are simply labelled 'Chianti'.

CHIANTI STYLES There are two basic styles. The first is the sharp young red that used to come in wicker flasks and just occasionally still does. This starts out quite purple-red, but quickly takes on a slightly orange tinge and is sometimes slightly prickly, with a rather attractive taste, almost a tiny bit sour, but backed up by good, raisiny-sweet fruit, a rather stark, peppery bite and tobacco-like spice. This style is traditionally made by the *governo* method, which involves adding – immediately after fermentation – either a small quantity of grapes dried on racks, or concentrated must, together with a dried yeast culture, so that the wine re-ferments. Apart from the prickle, this leaves the wine softer, rounder and more instantly appealing, but it also makes it age more quickly.

The second type has usually been matured for several years and, in the bad old days before the advent of DOCG, had all the acidity and tannin it needed. Unfortunately the only fruit on show was a fistful of old raisins and a curious, unwelcome whiff of tomatoes. Nowadays there are enough exceptions around to reckon that they are becoming the rule. The Chiantis of top estates, especially in fine vintages such as 1985, 1986, 1988 and 1990 are gaining a range of slightly raw strawberry, raspberry and blackcurrant flavours backed up by a herby, tobaccoey spice and a grapeskinsy roughness that makes the wine demanding but exciting. Top estates include *Badia a Coltibuono, Castellare, Castello di Ama, Castello dei Rampolla, Castello di San Polo in Rosso, Castello di Volpaia, Felsina Berardenga, Fontodi, Montesodi* and *Nipozzano (Frescobaldi), Isole e Olena, Pagliarese, Peppoli (Antinori), Riecine, San Felice, Selvapiana, Vecchie Terre di Montefili* and *Villa di Vetrice.*

DOLCETTO, some **DOC** (Piedmont) At its best, delicious, a full but soft, fresh, and dramatically fruity red, usually for gulping down fast and young, though some will age a few years. Wonderful ones come from *Altare, Castello di Neive, Clerico, Aldo Conterno, Giacomo Conterno, Marcarini, Mascarello, Oddero, Pasquero, Prunotto, Ratti, Sandrone, Scavino, Vajra, Vietti, Viticoltori dell'Acquese* and *Voerzio.*

FRANCIACORTA ROSSO, DOC (Lombardy) Raw but tasty blackcurranty wine from east of Milan. *Contessa Maggi, Bellavista, Ca' del Bosco* and *Longhi De' Carli* are all good.

FRIULI Six different zones (of which Grave del Friuli DOC is by far the most important quantitatively) stretching from the flatlands just north of Venice to the Slovenian border. The wines are marked by vibrant fruit. In particular, 'international' grapes like Cabernet Franc and Merlot have an absolutely delicious, juicy stab of flavour; and Refosco has a memorable flavour in the tar-and-plums mould – sharpened up with a grassy acidity. There is some good Cabernet from *Ca' Ronesca* and *Russiz Superiore*. *La Fattoria* and *Collavini* make excellent Cabernet and Merlot too and *Pintar* in the Collio area makes good Cabernet Franc. *Borgo Conventi*'s reds are very good and worth looking out for.

GATTINARA, DOC (Piedmont) This is good Nebbiolo-based red from the Vercelli hills in Piedmont, generally softer and quicker to mature than Barbaresco or Barolo, but also less potentially thrilling. *Brugo, Dessilani* and *Travaglini* are important producers.

KALTERERSEE/LAGO DI CALDARO, DOC (Alto Adige) Good, light, soft red with an unbelievable flavour of home-made strawberry jam and woodsmoke, made from the Schiava (alias Vernatsch) grape in the Alto Adige (alias Südtirol). It is best as a young gulper. Best producers: *Gries* co-op, *Lageder, Muri-Gries, Hans Rottensteiner, St Michael-Eppan* co-op, *Tiefenbrunner* and *Walch.*

LAGREIN DUNKEL, some **DOC** (Alto Adige) Dark, chewy red from the Alto Adige (Südtirol) with a remarkable depth of flavour for the product of a high mountain valley. These intense wines have a tarry roughness jostling with chocolate-smooth ripe fruit, the flavour being a very successful mix between the strong, chunky style of many Italian reds and the fresher, brighter tastes of France. *Gries* co-op, *Lageder, Muri-Gries, Niedermayr* and *Tiefenbrunner* are good. *Tiefenbrunner* also makes very good pink Lagrein Kretzer.

LAMBRUSCO, some **DOC** (Emilia-Romagna) Good Lambrusco – lightly fizzy, low in alcohol, red or white, dry to vaguely sweet – should *always* have a sharp, almost rasping acid bite to it. Real Lambrusco with a DOC, from Sorbara, Santa Croce or Castelvetro (and it will say so on the label), is anything but feeble and is an exciting accompaniment to rough-and-ready Italian food. But most Lambrusco is not DOC and is softened for the British market for fear of offending consumers. *Cavicchioli* is one of the few 'proper' ones to brave British shelves.

MONTEPULCIANO D'ABRUZZO, DOC (Abruzzi) Made on the east coast of Italy opposite Rome from the gutsy Montepulciano grape, a good one manages to be citrus-fresh and plummily rich, juicy yet tannic, ripe yet with a tantalizing sour bite. Fine wines are made by producers such as *Mezzanotte* and *Pepe*, while the standard of co-operatives such as *Casal Thaulero* and *Tollo* is high. Other good names to look for include *Colle Secco* (from Tollo), *Illuminati* and *Valentini*.

MORELLINO DI SCANSANO, DOC A Tuscan backwater DOC that occasionally comes up with something interesting, like *Le Sentinelle Riserva* from *Mantellassi*. With a similar grape-mix to that of Chianti, its wines have a fine, dry austerity with earthy tannins, deep, ripe fruit, and remarkable, tarry spice.

CLASSIFICATIONS

Only 10 to 12 per cent of the massive Italian wine harvest is regulated in any way at present, and the regulations that do exist are treated in a fairly cavalier manner by many growers. At the same time producers, rebelling against the constraints imposed on their originality and initiative, have often chosen to operate outside the regulations and classify their – frequently exceptional – wine simply as *vino da tavola*, the lowest grade. This situation looks set to change, with up to 60 per cent of Italy's wines becoming subject to the law, and wines like Sassicaia probably getting their own appellation, but for the time being the following are the main categories:

Vino da Tavola This is currently applied to absolutely basic stuff but also to maverick wines of the highest class such as Sassicaia or Gaja's Piedmontese Chardonnay.

Vino Tipico This will apply to table wines with some reference to place, and maybe grape type, but which do not qualify for DOC.

Denominazione di Origine Controllata (DOC) This applies to wines from specified grape varieties, grown in delimited zones and aged by prescribed methods. Nearly all of Italy's traditionally well-known wines are DOC, but more get added every year. In future, the wines will also undergo a tasting test (as DOCG wines do now).

Denominazione di Origine Controllata e Garantita (DOCG) The top tier – a tighter form of DOC with more stringent restrictions on grape types, yields and a tasting panel. First efforts were feeble, but a run of good vintages in 1983, '85, '86, '88 and '90 gave the producers lots of fine material to work with. The revised DOCG should give due recognition to particularly good vineyard sites in future.

OLTREPÒ PAVESE, some **DOC** (Lombardy) This covers reds, rosés, dry whites, sweet whites, fizz – just about anything. Almost the only wine we see is non-DOC fizz, usually Champagne-method, and based on Pinot Grigio/Nero/Bianco. Most Oltrepò Pavese is drunk in nearby Milan, where regularity of supply is more prized than DOC on the label. We see a little red – ideally based on Barbera and Bonarda, which is good, substantial stuff, soft and fruity – though if you happen to drink it in Milan, don't be surprised to find it's fizzy.

POMINO, DOC (Tuscany) A DOC for red, white and the dessert wine *vin santo* in the Rufina area of Chianti. The red, based on Sangiovese with Canaiolo, Cabernet and Merlot, becomes rich, soft, velvety and spicy with age. The only producer is *Frescobaldi*.

ROSSO CONERO, DOC (Marches) A very good, sturdy red from the east coast of Italy opposite Florence and Siena. Combining the tasty Montepulciano grape and up to 15 per cent Sangiovese, Rosso Conero blends herb and fruit flavours; sometimes with some oak for richness. Look for *Bianchi, Garofoli* and *Mecvini*. *Marchetti*, who uses no Sangiovese in the blend, is the best bet.

ROSSO DI MONTALCINO, DOC (Tuscany) DOC introduced in 1984 as an alternative for producers of Brunello who didn't want to age wine for Brunello's statutory four years, or who, like the top châteaux of Bordeaux, wanted to make a 'second wine'. Softer, more approachable and cheaper than Brunello di Montalcino.

ROSSO DI MONTEPULCIANO, DOC (Tuscany) This is to Vino Nobile de Montepulciano what Rosso di Montalcino is to Brunello di Montalcino: for 'lesser' Montepulciano. Pretty much the same style, but lighter and more approachable.

SPANNA (Piedmont) A Nebbiolo-based wine with a lovely raisin and chocolate flavour in the old style. Even cheap Spannas are usually a pretty good bet.

TAURASI, DOC (Campania) Remarkable, plummy yet bitingly austere red grown inland from Naples. To be honest, I'm *not* totally convinced, and am still waiting for a really exciting follow-up to the remarkable 1968. Recent releases haven't had the fruit or, as with the 1983, are impossibly tannic. *Mastroberardino* is the most important producer here.

TORGIANO, DOC and **DOCG** (Umbria) A region south-east of Perugia whose fame has been entirely created by *Lungarotti*. The reds are strong, plummy, sometimes overbearing, usually carrying the trade name *Rubesco*. Single vineyard *Monticchio* and *San Giorgio* Cabernet Sauvignon are exciting. In 1990 Torgiano Rosso Riserva became DOCG. White wines here are also clean and good. Lungarotti also makes a good flor-affected sherry-type wine called *Solleone*.

TRENTINO, DOC Just south of the Alto Adige (Südtirol), making reds either from local varieties such as Lagrein, Teroldego and Marzemino or from international grapes like Cabernet, Merlot and Pinot Noir. Too often their attractive fruit is hopelessly diluted by overcropping; a pity, because lovely Cabernet and Teroldego in particular has come from good producers, such as *Conti Martini Foradori, Istituto di San Michele, Gonzaga, Guerrieri, Pojer e Sandri, de Tarczal* and *Zeni*.

VALPOLICELLA, DOC (Veneto) Uses a variety of local grapes, especially Corvina, Rondinella and Molinara. Valpolicella *should* have delicious, light, cherry-fruit and a bitter almond twist to the finish – just a bit fuller and deeper than nearby Bardolino with a hint more sourness. But it's virtually a forlorn quest searching for these flavours, unless you can find *Tedeschi*'s *Capitel Lucchine*. It's worth going for a Classico or a single-vineyard wine. The Superiore has higher natural alcohol, but these are wines you really must drink young! Producers who can oblige with good flavours are *Allegrini, Boscaini, Guerrieri-Rizzardi, Quintarelli, Le Ragose, Santi, Tedeschi*, *Masi* and *Zenato*.

There are now a few single-vineyard wines appearing, like *Masi*'s *Serègo Alighieri,* which are a street ahead of the 'generic' stuff. The wines cost more, but *Allegrini*'s *La Grola* or *Tedeschi*'s *Ca' Nicalo* may show you what once made Valpolicella great. You might also look for a wine made by the traditional *ripasso* method. In this system, new wine is pumped over the skins and lees of Recioto or Amarone, starting a small re-fermentation and adding an exciting sweet-sour dimension to the wine. The producers *Masi, Quintarelli* and *Tedeschi* all do this very well.

But the wine which can really show you greatness is the weird and wonderful Recioto Amarone della Valpolicella. This is one of those wines that is imitated nowhere else – a true speciality. *Amaro* means bitter, and this huge wine, made from half-shrivelled Valpolicella grapes, *is* bitter, but it also has a brilliant array of flavours – sweet grape skins, chocolate, plums and woodsmoke – which all sound sweet and exotic and, up to a point, they are. Yet the stroke of genius comes with that penetrating bruised sourness which pervades the wine and shocks you with its forthrightness. The good stuff is usually about three times the price of simple Valpolicella, but it's still good value for a remarkable wine. If the label simply says 'Recioto della Valpolicella', the wine will be sweeter and may still be excellent but, to my mind, a little less strangely special. Fine examples come from *Allegrini, Bertani, Masi, Quintarelli, Le Ragose, Tedeschi* and *Tramanal*.

VALTELLINA, DOC (Lombardy) Nebbiolo wine from along the Swiss border, north-east of Milan. I find it a little stringy, but someone must be drinking it because it has the largest output of Nebbiolo of any DOC, including all those in Piedmont.

VINO NOBILE DI MONTEPULCIANO, DOCG (Tuscany) A neighbour of Chianti, with the same characteristics, but more so. Usually, this means more pepper, acid and tannin at a higher price; but increasingly fine Vino Nobile is surfacing, deep wines with a marvellously dry fragrance reminiscent almost of sandalwood, backed up by good Sangiovese spice, and a strong plumskins-and-cherries fruit. Time was when you wouldn't go out of your way to find it, but that's not the case any more. There's also more of it about. The following producers are reliable and good: *Avignonesi, Boscarelli, La Calonica, di Casale, Fassati, Fattoria del Cerro, Fognano, Poliziano* and *Trerose*.

WHITE WINES

It is only a few years since I used to write in my tasting notes, 'dull, sulphured, oxidized, dead – typical Italian'. An entire nation's wines dismissed in the irritated flourish of my pen. Thank goodness it would be impossible to make such a generalization today. The revolution in white-wine-making has been far-reaching. New high-tech methods of wine-making with precise temperature control are now commonplace. In a warm climate like Italy's they are crucial if the fruit character of the grape is to be preserved – although they can lead to an over-emphasis on neutrality. However, the currently favoured practice of cold maceration of juice and skins, and fermentation at slightly warmer temperatures to emphasize fruit and perfume, seem to be overcoming the problem.

A welcome resurgence of traditional Italian varieties has seen exciting grapes like Arneis in Piedmont, Grechetto in Umbria, Tocai and Ribolla in Friuli and Catarratto Lucido in Sicily being given the praise and attention they deserve.

The onward march of Chardonnay and Sauvignon – often in combination with barrel-fermentation and aging in new oak – has already created wines of world-class potential. In Friuli especially, supposedly 'lesser' varieties like Pinot Bianco and Pinot Grigio, made in a rich but clear and precise unoaked style, have risen to new heights and give a lead for the rest to follow.

GRAPES & FLAVOURS

CHARDONNAY The new law should change Chardonnay's DOC status. The typical Italian style is unoaked: lean, rather floral and sharply-balanced from the Alto Adige and usually more neutral, Mâconnais-style from elsewhere. There is exciting, creamy, spicy, barrique-aged wine being made by the likes of *Gaja, Marchesi di Gresy* and *Pio Cesare* in Piedmont, *Zanella* in Lombardy, *Maculan* in the Veneto and both *Caparzo (Le Grance)* and *Avignonesi (Il Marzocco)* in Tuscany. However the best of the 'oak-free' lobby are producing some ravishing stuff by focusing on low yields and picking at the optimum sugar-acid balance. *Zeni* (Trentino) and *Gradnik* (Friuli) make prime examples.

GARGANEGA The principal grape of Soave. Well, it *should* be the major grape, because it is supposed to make up the majority of the blend, and when well made it is particularly refreshing, soft, yet green-apple fresh. However, it has to compete with Trebbiano Toscano in cheaper blends, and often loses. Good producers use Trebbiano di Soave, which is much better, and Chardonnay is permitted from 1992.

GEWÜRZTRAMINER Although this is supposed to have originated in the Alto Adige (Südtirol) village of Tramin, most of the plantings there now are of the red Traminer, rather than the spicier, more memorable Gewürztraminer of Alsace. Gewürztraminer can be lovely, needing some time in bottle to develop perfume.

GRECO/GRECHETTO An ancient variety introduced to southern Italy by the Greeks, it makes crisp, pale and refreshing wines with lightly spicy overtones in Calabria and Campania and, as Grecanico, in Sicily. Grechetto is part of the same family and its delicious, nutty, aniseed character adds dramatically to Trebbiano-dominated blends in central Italy (Orvieto benefits significantly) as well as sometimes surfacing under its own colours in Umbria where *Adanti* makes a splendid version.

MALVASIA This name and the related Malvoisie seems to apply to a range of grape varieties, some not related. Malvasia is found mostly in Tuscany, Umbria and Latium, where it gives a full, creamy nuttiness to dry whites like Frascati. It also produces brilliant, rich dessert wines with the density of thick brown-sugar syrup and the sweetness of raisins, in Sardinia and the island of Lipari north of Sicily.

MOSCATO The Alto Adige (Südtirol) has various sorts of Muscat, including the delicious Rosenmuskateller and Goldmuskateller, making dry wines to equal the Muscats of Alsace and sweet wines of unrivalled fragrance. But it is at its best in Piedmont, where Asti Spumante is a delicious, grapy, sweetish fizz and Moscato Naturale is a heartily-perfumed sweet wine, full of the fragrance of grapes, honey, apples and unsmoked cigars. It is best young, but *Ivaldi*'s Passito from Strevi can age beautifully. It also makes fine dessert wines on the island of Pantelleria, south of Sicily.

MÜLLER-THURGAU This is a soft, perfumy workhorse grape in Germany, but on the high, steep Alpine vineyards of the Alto Adige it produces glacier-fresh flavours; not bad in Trentino and Friuli either.

PINOT BIANCO Produces some of its purest, honeyed flavours in the Alto Adige (Südtirol), and can do very well in Friuli where the best are buttery and full.

RHEINRIESLING/RIESLING RENANO The true German Riesling is grown in the Alto Adige (Südtirol), making sharp, green, refreshing, steely dry wines – as good as most Mosel or Rhine Kabinett in Germany. It can be OK, and slightly fatter, in Friuli and Lombardy. Riesling Italico, nothing to do with real Riesling, is the dreaded Olasz/Laski/Welsch Rizling, which so despoils Riesling's name across Eastern Europe.

SAUVIGNON BLANC Quite common in the North, and gives some acid bite to far-southern blends like Sicily's Regaleali. It can be spicy, grassy and refreshing from the Alto Adige and Friuli, though the style is usually more subtle than New World Sauvignon. *Volpaia* and *Castellare* have started making it in Chianti land as have *Banfi* in Montalcino; others will follow.

SYLVANER Grown very high in the northern valleys of the Alto Adige, at its best this can be chillingly dry, lemon-crisp and quite delicious. But there are still quite a few fat, muddy examples around.

TREBBIANO The widely-planted Trebbiano Toscano is a wretched thing, easy to grow, producing vast quantities of grapes with frightening efficiency. It is responsible for an awful lot of fruitless, oxidized, sulphured blaagh-ness. However, attempts to pick it early and vinify it sharp and fresh are having some effect, and at least its use in red, yes *red* Chianti is now severely restricted. Trebbiano di Soave, the Veneto clone, is much better. Lugana is a Trebbiano DOC of character (*Zenato's* is widely available and good). Abruzzi has a strain which *can* be tasty from producers like *Tenuta del Priore, Pepe* and *Valentini*.

VERNACCIA There are several types of Vernaccia – including some red – but we mostly just see two. Vernaccia di Oristano in Sardinia is a sort of Italian version of sherry, best dry – when it has a marvellous mix of floral scents, nutty weight and taunting sourness – but also medium and sweet. Vernaccia di San Gimignano *can* be Tuscany's best traditional white – full, golden, peppery but with a softness of hazelnuts and angelica. *Fagiuoli, Teruzzi & Puthod*, and *Sainsbury's* own-label show what can be done. Some producers have tried putting it in barrique, but so far *Teruzzi e Puthod is* the only one to understand that you need an abundance of fruit in order to balance the oak.

WINES & WINE REGIONS

ALBANA DI ROMAGNA, DOCG (Emilia-Romagna) I resent putting DOCG against this uninspiring white, which some not particularly cynical people say was made DOCG *(a)* because it was the first to apply, *(b)* because they *had* to have a white DOCG and all the others were too frightful to contemplate and *(c)* because the politicos in Bologna have a lot of clout. What's the wine like? Well, it's dry or sweet, still or slightly fizzy, or very fizzy; you see what I mean. At least these days it's less likely to be oxidized and, at its best, the dry version can be delicately scented with an almondy finish. The only really decent producers are *Fattoria Paradiso* and *Zerbina*.

ALTO ADIGE, various **DOCs** The locals up here by the Austrian border answer more warmly to *grüss Gott* than to *buon giorno* so this area is often referred to as Südtirol. Wines from these dizzily steep slopes are much more Germanic than Italian. Most are red, but this is one of Italy's most successful white regions. The wines are light, dry and intensely fresh, with spice and plenty of fruit. The best are from *Tiefenbrunner*, in his uplifting, aromatic style and *Lageder* who makes fuller, rounder wines. Both are experimenting with barrel maturation to good effect. Also *Haas*, a young producer of promise, *Hofstätter, Schloss Schwanburg, Walch* and *Terlan, Schreckbichl*, and *St Michael-Eppan* co-ops.

ARNEIS (Piedmont) Potentially stunning, apples-pears-and-liquorice-flavoured wines from an ancient white grape of the same name, with high prices to match – but since there's a feel of ripe white Burgundy about the best of them, that's not such a turn-off. Unfortunately it is trendy so some may bear the name and not much more. *Arneis di Montebertotto* by *Castello di Neive* is intense yet subtle. *Bruno Giacosa*'s softer, sweeter one has a taste of hops. *Deltetto, Malvirà, Negro, Vietti, Voerzio* are good.

CENTRAL ITALY VINTAGES

1992 Those who reduced yields have produced decent, light to medium bodied reds that are not up to '91 but will make for good drinking over the next couple of years. An exception is Carmignano, where early picking resulted in wines that are nearly on a par with 1990. The Marches was also fortunate in 1992.

1991 In Tuscany, outstanding wines seem likely, including excellent Brunello. There will be few Riservas, however. Red and white Torgiano from Lungarotti should be very good, from elevated sites that escaped the frost. The Marches overall look good.

1990 Hailed as one of the greatest vintages in living memory in Tuscany. An early harvest yielded deeply-coloured wine of tremendous perfume: rich, strong and built to last.

1989 The spring was good, the summer and early autumn wet. Producers who had the courage to interrupt the harvest and wait for another week will have made the best wines.

1988 Anyone who couldn't make good wines this year ought to give up. Exciting reds.

1987 Reasonable reds such as Carmignano and nice young Chiantis.

1986 Some people are now rating 1986 Chianti Riserva more highly than the 1985s.

1985 Hardly a drop of rain from the Lords Test to the end of the season in September, so some of the wines are positively rich, but this vintage shows what DOCG is made of.

1983 In Chianti, the best '83s have aged well and are better balanced than the '82s.

ASTI SPUMANTE, DOC (Piedmont) It's hard to believe that this frothy, crunchy, fruit-bursting sweet fizzy wine is made next door to beetle-browed Nebbiolo giants like Barolo and Barbaresco. Indeed, some producers make both. It's snobbery that defeats this wine, because it is absurdly delicious, with a magical, grapy freshness, and it's ultra-reliable – a poor Asti is rare. It should be drunk very young, and will be DOCG from 1994. *Fontanafredda, Gancia, Martini* and *Riccadonna* are good, as are *Vignaioli di Santo Stefano* and *Duca d'Asti.*

BIANCO DI CUSTOZA, DOC (Veneto) Thought of as a Soave lookalike, though I wonder if Soave isn't a Bianco di Custoza lookalike. It contains Tocai, Cortese and Garganega, as well as Trebbiano, which helps. But the lack of pressure to make any old liquid as cheaply as possible must be as important. *Gorgo, Portalupi, Santa Sofia, Tedeschi, Le Tende, Le Vigne di San Pietro* and *Zenato* are good.

CORTESE DI GAVI, DOC (Piedmont) Cortese is the grape, Gavi the area. It is dry and sharp, like Sauvignon minus the tang, and fairly full, like Chardonnay without the class. So it should be a refreshing, straight-up gulper at a pocket-easy price. But restaurant chic in Italy coos over it. The only ones I've enjoyed at a reasonable price have been the fresh *Deltetto* and *Arione*, and the atypical oaked *Gavi Fior di Rovere* from *Chiarlo.*

ERBALUCE DI CALUSO, DOC (Piedmont) Half the price of Gavi, with a soft, creamy flavour. Clean-living, plumped-out, affordable white. *Boratto, Ferrando* and *Marbelli* are good; *Boratto* also makes a rich but refreshing *Caluso Passito.*

FIANO DI AVELLINO, DOC (Campania) After numerous attempts to stomach this inexplicably famous wine from near Naples I got hold of a bottle of *Mastroberardino*'s single-vineyard *Fiano di Avellino Vignadora* and found a brilliant spring flowers scent and honey, peaches and pear skins taste. But it may have been a flash in the pan.

FRASCATI, DOC (Latium) True Frascati remains a mirage: most relies on bland Trebbiano or is spoilt by mass production. But with enough Malvasia to swamp the Trebbiano and careful wine-making, it has a lovely, fresh, nutty feel with an unusual, attractive tang of slightly sour cream. Antonio Pulcini is way ahead with *Colli di Catone, Villa Catone* and *Villa Romana;* his *cru Colle Gaio* is very special. *Fontana Candida*'s limited releases are also good.

FRIULI, some **DOC** Some very good fruity and fresh whites from up by the Yugoslav border in the North-East. There's above-average Pinot Bianco, good Pinot Grigio, Chardonnay, better Gewürz, Müller-Thurgau, Riesling Renano, Ribolla and Sauvignon, and the brilliantly nutty and aromatic white Tocai, all capturing the fresh fruit of the varietal for quick, happy-faced drinking. Prices are generally in the mid- to upper range, but they are good value, especially from names like *Abbazia di Rosazzo, Attems, Borgo Conventi, Villa Russiz, Collavini, Dri, Eno Friulia, Volpe, Gravner, Jermann, Livio Felluga, Puiatti, Ronchi di Cialla, Schiopetto, Pasini.* Of the big names *Collavini* is best, but getting pricy. The almost mythical Picolit sweet wine is beautifully made by *Al Rusignul* – who is the *only* producer I've found who took this difficult grape variety seriously.

GALESTRO, DOC (Tuscany) Created to mop up the Trebbiano and Malvasia no longer used in red Chianti. Low alcohol, lemony, greengage taste, high-tech style.

GAVI, DOC (Piedmont) (See *Cortese di Gavi.*) Grossly overpriced, clean, appley white from Piedmont. If it's labelled Gavi dei Gavi, double the number you thought of and add the price of your train fare home: Waterloo-to-Woking for some of the more sensible wine shops, King's Cross-to-Edinburgh for the more poncy restaurants.

LACRYMA CHRISTI DEL VESUVIO, DOC (Campania) The most famous wine of Campania and Naples. It can be red, white, dry or sweet: *Mastroberardino*'s is good.

MOSCATO D'ASTI, DOC (Piedmont) Celestial mouthwash! Sweet, slightly fizzy wine that captures all the crunchy green freshness of a fistful of ripe table-grapes. Heavenly ones from *Ascheri, Dogliotti, Gatti, Bruno Giacosa, I Vignaioli di Santo Stefano, Michele Chiarlo, Rivetti* and *Vietti*. *Gallo d'Oro* is the most widely available.

ORVIETO, DOC (Umbria) Umbria's most famous wine has shaken off its old, semi-sweet, yellow-gold image and emerged less dowdy and rather slick and anonymous. It used to be slightly sweet, rich, smoky and honeyed from the Grechetto and Malvasia grapes. Its modern, pale, very dry style owes more to the feckless Trebbiano. I must say I'm looking forward to Orvieto getting back to its golden days and there are signs that good producers are starting to make this happen. *Scambia* is lovely, peach-perfumed wine and *Barberani* and *Palazzone* are even better. *Decugnano dei Barbi* is good, while exciting wines, full, fragrant, soft and honeyed, come from *Bigi*, whose *Cru Torricella Secco* and *Cru Orzalume Amabile* (medium-sweet) are exceptional and not expensive. *Antinori*'s is a typical over-modern, under-flavoured dry, though its medium is delicious, and a new Chardonnay, Grechetto, Malvasia and Trebbiano *vino da tavola* called *Cervaro della Sala* is outstanding. Sweet, unctuous, noble-rot affected wines (*Antinori*'s *Muffato della Sala* and *Barberani's Calcaia*) are rarely seen but delicious.

PROSECCO, some **DOC** (Veneto) Either still or sparkling, a lovely fresh, bouncy, light white, often off-dry, at its best from the neighbourhoods of Conegliano and Valdobbiadene. *Sainsbury's* does a typical easy-going crowd-pleaser; also *Canevel, Le Case Bianche, Carpené Malvolti, Collavini.*

SOAVE, DOC (Veneto) At last turning from the tasteless, fruitless, profitless mass-market bargain basement to show as an attractive, soft, fairly-priced white. The turn-around in the last few years has been quite amazing. More often than not now an own-label Soave from a good shop will be pleasant, soft, slightly nutty, even creamy. Drink it as young as possible. *Pasqua, Bertani* and *Zenato* are supplying a lot of the decent basic stuff. On a higher level *Anselmi* is outstanding, if expensive (try *Capitel Foscarino*) and *Pieropan*, especially single-vineyard wines *La Rocca* and *Calvarino*, is very good. Other good ones are *Boscaini, Zenato, Costalunga, Bolla's Castellaro, Santi's Monte Carbonare, Tedeschi's Monte Tenda* and the local co-op's *Costalta*. *Anselmi* also makes a *Recioto di Soave dei Capitelli* which is shockingly good in its sweet-sour way, and *Pieropan's* unoaked *Recioto* is redolent of apricots.

TOCAI, DOC (Friuli) Full, aromatic, sometimes copper-tinged, sometimes clear as water, this grape makes lovely, mildly-floral and softly nutty, honeyed wines in Friuli, as well as increasingly good wines in the Veneto. Best: *Abbazia di Rosazzo, Borgo Conventi, Cà Bolani, Livio Felluga, Caccese, Collavini, Lazzarini, Maculan, Schiopetto, Villa Russiz, Volpe Pasini.*

TRENTINO, DOC This northern region, below Alto Adige, can make some of Italy's best Pinot Bianco and Chardonnay, as well as some interesting whites from Riesling, Müller-Thurgau and excellent dry Muscat. But until they stop grossly over-producing we're never going to see the full potential. The tastiest come from the mountainous bit north of the town of Trento. Look especially for *Conti Martini, Gaierhof, Istituto di San Michele, Mandelli, Pojer e Sandri, Spagnolli* and *Zeni*. Trentino also makes fizz from Chardonnay and Pinot Bianco (*Ferrari* and *Equipe 5)*, and fair Vino Santo (equivalent to Tuscan dessert wines) comes from *Pisoni* and *Simoncelli.*

VERDICCHIO, DOC (Marches) Of Italy's numerous whites, only Soave makes more than Verdicchio. It comes from the grape of the same name (with a little Trebbiano and Malvasia) on the east coast opposite Florence and Siena. The wines are reliable rather than exciting – usually extremely dry, lean, clean, nutty with a streak of dry honey, sharpened by slightly green acidity. Occasionally you find fatter styles, and *Fazi-Battaglia's* single vineyard *vino da tavola Le Moie* shows the the area's potential. There is also a Verdicchio fizz. The two leading areas are Verdicchio dei Castelli di Jesi and Verdicchio di Matelica. The rarer Matelica wines often have more flavour. Good producers: *Brunori, Bucci, Fabrini, Fazi-Battaglia, Garofoli, Mecvini, Monte Schiavo, Umani Ronchi, Zaccagnini.*

VERDUZZO, DOC (Friuli and Veneto) Usually a soft, nutty, low acid yet refreshing light white. It also makes a lovely, gentle fizz, and in Friuli Colli Orientali some of Italy's best sweet wines, in particular *Dri*'s *Verduzzo di Ramandolo* and *Abbazia di Rosazzo*'s *Amabile.*

VERNACCIA DI SAN GIMIGNANO, DOC (Tuscany) This can be full, nutty and honeyed, slightly lanoliny in the mouth and perhaps with a hint of pepper, but too much has had all the guts stripped out of it in the headlong pursuit of bland neutrality. Best: *Frigeni, Fagiuoli, Falchini, San Quirico, Teruzzi & Puthod* and *La Torre.*

NORTH-EAST ITALY VINTAGES

1992 As in the rest of Italy, the timing of the rain was vital. The wines picked before the rains are good, with the whites ripe and perfumed if lacking the body of 1991, and the reds medium bodied and forward. Only where yields were low is the quality good.

1991 Veneto blessed its good fortune: good quality and yields up by 20 per cent. It was a more difficult year in Trentino-Alto-Adige, although there were some fine whites and scattered good, if less imposing reds. Some excellent reds and elegant whites were made in Friuli.

1990 Being compared with the legendary 1964. Crop levels were down, but a hot, dry summer was followed by an early harvest of superb quality. Friuli too fared extremely well. The best wines show impressive balance and concentration.

1989 Good, aromatic whites; the reds, though, were less concentrated.

1988 The quantity was reduced, but the quality was tremendous, in particular for reds.

1986 The year provided a good, balanced vintage, but there was too much overproduction for it to be exciting. The good news was that it was superb for Amarone and not bad for Ripasso Valpolicella.

FORTIFIED WINES

The best known Italian fortified wine is Marsala from Sicily. The good examples may be sweet or dryish and have a nutty, smoky character which can be delicious. The off-shore island of Pantelleria produces Moscato which can be even better. Sardinia is strong on fortified wines, particularly from the Cannonau (or Grenache) grape. In general, however, the rich, dessert wines of Italy are made from overripe or even raisined grapes, without fortification.

MARSALA This Sicilian wine has, at its best, a delicious, deep brown-sugar sweetness allied to a cutting, lip-tingling acidity that makes it surprisingly refreshing for a fortified dessert wine. The rare Marsala Vergine is also good – very dry, lacking the tremendous concentration of deep brown texture that makes an old *oloroso seco* sherry or a Sercial Madeira so exciting, but definitely going along the same track. But a once great name is now also seen on bottles of 'egg marsala' and the like. A few good producers keep the flag flying; *De Bartoli* outclasses all the rest, and even makes an intense, beautifully aged, but *unfortified* non-DOC range called *Vecchio Samperi*. His *Josephine Dore* is in the style of *fino* sherry.

MOSCATO PASSITO DI PANTELLERIA From an island closer to Tunisia than Sicily, a big, heavy wine with a great wodge of rich Muscat fruit and a good slap of alcoholic strength.

VIN SANTO Holy Wine? Well, I wouldn't be too pleased with these if I were the Almighty because too much *vin santo* is vaguely raisiny and very dull. It *should* have all kinds of splendid, rich fruit flavours – apricots, apples, the richness of ripe grape skins, the chewiness of toffee, smoke and liquorice. But it's sadly rare and only *Isole e Olena* has provided me with this thrill so far. If you can't get a bottle of that try *La Calonica* or *Avignonesi* in Tuscany or *Adanti* in Umbria.

VINI DA TAVOLA

If I want to find out how exciting the wines can be from the Tuscan hills, I might buy a bottle of Sammarco, or Tignanello, Balifico or Vinattieri. Barolo is the famous name of Piedmont, but I can still learn about the region's capabilities from Il Favot or Vigna Arborina. I'm tired of feeble Valpolicella, but Campo Fiorin or Capitel San Rocco might show me why the region used to be famous.

All these wines have one thing in common – they are not sold with the DOC or DOCG of the area concerned. That none of these wines – and numerous other exciting taste experiences – like Spanna, Moscato di Strevi, Torcolato, Anghelu Ruju, Cuccanea – is produced according to the DOC is a heavy indictment of the present Italian wine regulations. The new law has arrived none too soon. No-one doubts that when the laws were drawn up in 1963 there was a desperate need for them, since Italian wine was rapidly sliding into an abyss. There weren't many winemakers left who clung to quality and when it came to formulating the rules, local politics and laziness triumphed.

One option for a small but determined band of winemakers who cared passionately about quality, was to confront the DOC regulations head-on and say, 'If you force mediocrity on us with your wretched laws then we shall operate outside the law.' Cabernet, Chardonnay and French oak barrels were soon all the rage. But the dust is now settling and the 'me too' philosophy appears to have run its course. In Piedmont, only Chardonnay seems to have a certain future, though barriques may have arrived to stay. Angelo Gaja, who led the revolt there, is the first to concede that his world-class Cabernet Sauvignon Darmagi serves mainly to focus attention back on his Barbaresco. The Piedmontese have an unflinching belief in their own red grape varieties and the other winemakers who took the *vino da tavola* route did so to demonstrate their dissatisfaction with what they saw as the excessive minimum barrel aging required by the law.

The major complaint for many Tuscans however focused on the grape varieties required by law. At first they saw Cabernet as their salvation. Antinori's Tignanello showed that careful techniques can make great wine out of Cabernet/Sangiovese blends and several top 'super' *vini da tavola* are still made from these. In turn this has given rise to a determination to make great wines solely from Sangiovese. Both styles are usually far more exciting than traditional Chianti. For some reason in England we call them the 'super-Tuscans'.

The new wine law, which will be coming into effect over the next few years, should build these super-Tuscans into the system. At the same time, high production figures are likely to become more and more unusual as the new EC viticultural programme for uprooting vines in undesirable areas takes effect. What's more, producers in DOC zones have been warned that future requests to raise yields are likely to be refused. If these plans come to fruition, there could be a serious danger that Italy, at long last, might be about to get it right.

SANGIOVESE AND CABERNET SAUVIGNON

ALTE D'ALTESI A 30 per cent Cabernet Sauvignon, 70 per cent Sangiovese blend from Altesino, aged for about a year in new barrique; first made in 1985. The '86 has good colour, fruit, firmness and elegance.

BALIFICO Volpaia's 'special', two-thirds Sangiovese, one-third Cabernet Sauvignon aged for 16 months in French oak. Exciting, exotic, oaky-rich wine, rather French in its youth, more Tuscan as it ages.

CABREO IL BORGO From Ruffino in Tuscany, vervy wines with variegated flavours: blackcurrants one moment, raspberries and brambles the next.

CA' DEL PAZZO Brunello and Cabernet from Caparzo in Montalcino. Powerful wine behind juicy blackcurrant and vanilla oak.

GRIFI Avignonesi's Sangiovese/Cabernet Franc blend. It's cedary and spicily rich but lacks the class of Grifi's Vino Nobile di Montepulciano. The '85 is the best yet.

SAMMARCO Castello dei Rampolla's blend of 75 per cent Cabernet Sauvignon, 25 per cent Sangiovese. Magnificently blackcurranty, Sammarco is built to last.

TIGNANELLO First made in 1971 by Antinori, when it was Canaiolo, Sangiovese and Malvasia, it is now about 80 per cent Sangiovese and 20 per cent Cabernet Sauvignon. In the late 1970s it set standards that the others could only aspire to. 1982 is rather dull, '85 seems back on form, at a fiendish price.

CABERNET SAUVIGNON

CARANTAN Merlot with both Cabernets, this, from Marco Felluga in Friuli, is big, savoury and tannic. The 1988 still has to come together, but shows terrific promise.

GHIAIE DELLA FURBA Made at Villa di Capezzana from roughly equal parts of both

Cabernets and Merlot, and better each vintage. 1981 is at its blackcurranty peak now. The '83 is even better; the '85 is one of the best of this excellent vintage.

MAURIZIO ZANELLA Both Cabernets and Merlot, from Ca' del Bosco in Lombardy. Expensive but impressive, with roasted, smoky fruit. The '88 is potentially the best, with '89 and '87 not far behind.

SASSICAIA Cabernet (Sauvignon and Franc) from Bolgheri, south-east of Livorno, it has an intense Cabernet character but a higher acidity and slightly leaner profile than most New World Cabernets. It needs about eight to ten years to begin to show at its best; '68 was the first vintage, and remains, with '72 and '82, one of the best, but '85, '88 and '90 are also excellent.

SOLAIA Piero Antinori's attempt to match Sassicaia. A blend of 80 per cent Cabernet Sauvignon and 20 per cent Sangiovese. Sassicaia beats it for beauty of flavour but Solaia does have tremendous rich fruit and a truly Tuscan bitterness to balance.

TAVERNELLE Villa Banfi's 100 per cent Cabernet from young vines at Montalcino. It has good style and varietal character.

SANGIOVESE

CEPPARELLO Very fruity rich wine from Isole e Olena, the oak beautifully blended: one of the leaders of the super-Sangioveses.

COLTASSALA Castello di Volpaia's Sangiovese/Mammolo blend, leaner and less rich than most; lovely, austere wine, needing time to soften and blossom.

FLACCIANELLO DELLA PIEVE Fontodi's Sangiovese, aged in barrique and with a little *governo* used. Cedary, tightly grained fruit, oak and elegance.

FONTALLORO 100 per cent Sangiovese from Felsina Berardenga, fatter and richer than the Flaccianello, with a spicy rather than a cedary oak character, which takes a long time to come out of its tannic shell.

IL SODACCIO 85 per cent Sangiovese, 15 per cent Canaiolo from Monte Vertine. It could have been a Chianti, but was too oaky when young. Elegant; drink young.

I SODI DI SAN NICCOLÒ One of the most distinctive of the new-wave wines first made in the late seventies. A little rare Malvasia Nera alongside Sangiovese adds a wonderfully sweet and floral perfume.

LE PERGOLE TORTE From Monte Vertine, the first of the 100 per cent Sangiovese, barrique-aged wines. It is intensely tannic and oaky when young, and needs at least five years to open up.

PALAZZO ALTESI 100 per cent Brunello, aged for about 14 months in new barrique at Altesino in Montalcino, packed with a delicious fruit and oakiness, and though it needs five years to develop and display its full splendour, its brilliant blackberry fruit makes it drinkable much younger.

SANGIOVETO Made from carefully selected old vines (about 40 years old) at Badia a Coltibuono in Chianti Classico. Yields are minute (15 to 20 hectolitres per hectare) giving tremendous concentration.

VINATTIERI ROSSO Barrique-aged blend of Sangiovese from Chianti Classico and Brunello, getting better each vintage, with the 1985 showing the superb rich Sangiovese fruit and sweet oak of the best of the 'New Classics' in Tuscany.

WHITES

CHARDONNAY In Umbria, Antinori's *Cervaro della Sala* combines Chardonnay with Grechetto for extra-rich fruit and oak. Felsina Berardenga's *I Sistri* is fresh, zingy and grapy with an ice-cream core; Ruffino's *Cabreo La Pietra* is succulent and oaky.

TUSCAN WINERY PROFILES

MONTALCINO

ALTESINO Resurrected by Milanese money in the 1970s and now making an excellent Brunello di Montalcino – called Palazzo Altesi – from Sangiovese partially vinified by carbonic maceration, and also Alte d'Altesi, 70 per cent Cabernet Sauvignon and 30 per cent Sangiovese.

BANFI Oenologist Ezio Rivella's space-age winery in the hills of Montalcino, created with the money of the Mariani brothers, who brought Lambrusco to the USA. Wines include Brunello di Montalcino, Pinot Grigio, Fontanelle Chardonnay, Sauvignon, Tavernelle Cabernet Castello Banfi, a blend of Pinot Noir, Cabernet Sauvignon and Sangiovese, and Moscadello Liquoroso. New versions of Pinot Noir and Syrah will be released soon. The Banfi Spumante is one of Italy's best.

BIONDI SANTI A legendary family making a fabulously priced, but not necessarily legendary wine; however there are indications that quality is improving again, with some modernization in the cellars of its Il Greppo estate. 1988 saw its celebration of the centenary of Brunello di Montalcino.

CAPARZO is one of the new wave of Montalcino estates; investment from Milan has turned it into a serious wine producer of not only Brunello and Rosso di Montalcino, but also oak-fermented Chardonnay called Le Grance, and Ca' del Pazzo, a barrel-aged blend of Cabernet Sauvignon and Sangiovese.

FATTORIA DEI BARBI is owned by one of the old Montalcinese families, the Colombinis. Traditional methods produce serious Brunello and Rosso di Montalcino, as well as Brusco dei Barbi, and a single-vineyard wine, Vigna Fiore.

MONTEPULCIANO

AVIGNONESI An old Montepulciano family, but a relative newcomer to the ranks of serious producers of Vino Nobile, also two excellent Chardonnays: Terre di Cortona, without oak, and Il Marzocco, oak-fermented and aged wine of considerable depth. I Grifi is a barrel-aged blend of Prugnolo and Cabernet Franc.

FATTORIA DEL CERRO Traditional producers of Vino Nobile now experimenting with barriques. Its best wine remains the DOCG Vino Nobile: both 1985 and '86 were excellent and '88 will be even better.

VERNACCIA DI SAN GIMIGNANO

TERUZZI & PUTHOD Commonly acknowledged to be the best producers of Vernaccia di San Gimignano. Most expensive is the oak-aged Terre di Tufo. Also Chianti Colli Senesi and Galestro.

CHIANTI

ANTINORI Indisputably one of the great names of Chianti, boasting 600 years of wine-making. Excellent Chianti Classico from its estates Peppoli and Badia a Passignano; it also initiated the moves towards modern wine-making in Tuscany, with the development of wines like Tignanello, the archetypal barrique-aged Sangiovese, Cabernet blend. Its Orvieto estate, Castello della Sala, is the source of exciting experiments with white grapes.

FONTODI Sleek Sangiovese, in the form of single estate Chianto Classico or *vino da tavola* Flaccianello, mark this out as one of Tuscany's top names. From 1991 it has also been the source of one of Tuscany's best Pinot Noirs.

CASTELLO DI AMA Excellent single-vineyard Chianti Classico: San Lorenzo, La

Casuccia, Bellavista; also a Merlot that had critics raving in 1990. Promising Chardonnay and Pinot Grigio.

FELSINA BERARDENGA Winery very much on the up. Vigneto Rancia is a single-vineyard Chianti, I Sistri a barrique-aged Chardonnay. Fontalloro is a Sangiovese, aged in barrique for 12 months.

FRESCOBALDI The best Frescobaldi estate is Castello di Nipozzano, with a special selection Montesodi, from Chianti Rufina. It is also the producer of some excellent Pomino, including an oak-aged white, Il Benefizio. It also manages the Castelgiocondo estate further south near Montalcino, where it makes Brunello and a good white wine under the new Predicato label. Mormoreto is a fine, Cabernet-style red.

ISOLE E OLENA is rapidly increasing a reputation for fine Chianti Classico. Also Cepparello, a rich pure Sangiovese wine, made from the oldest vines of the estate; outstanding *vin santo* and a superb varietal Syrah.

RICASOLI As well as sound Chianti, Brolio makes a host of other Tuscan wines.

RUFFINO One of the largest producers of Chianti. Riserva Ducale is its best wine.

PIEDMONT WINERY PROFILES

ABBAZIA DELL'ANNUNZIATA (Barolo, La Morra) One of the greats. All the wines are full of excitement, strongly perfumed and develop wonderfully.

ELIO ALTARE (Barolo, La Morra) New wave producer – wines of firm structure and tannin behind perfumed fruit. Highly successful 1984 Barolo. Very good Barbera and Dolcetto and barrique-aged Barbera Vigna Larigi and Nebbiolo Vigna Arborina.

BRAIDA DI GIACOMO BOLOGNA (Rochetta Tanaro) Saw early the potential of Barbera in barrique: *cru* Bricco dell' Uccellone continues to impress with depth, balance and richness. An equally good Bricco della Bigotta. Unoaked, youthful Barbera, La Monella. Good Moscato d'Asti and sweetish Brachetto d'Acqui.

CASTELLO DI NEIVE (Barbaresco, Neive) Impeccable, finely crafted, austerely elegant Barbaresco from Santo Stefano. Barriqued Barbera from single *cru* Mattarello and firm, classic Dolcetto from three sites topped by Basarin. Revelatory Arneis.

CERETTO Known for both Barolo and Barbaresco. Barolo Bricco Rocche Bricco Rocche (yes) and Barbaresco Bricco Asili are legendary with prices to match. Also Barolos Brunate, Prapo, Zonchera, and Faset in Barbaresco. Light Barbera and Dolcetto. Arneis is disappointing.

CLERICO (Barolo, Monforte) Top-notch producer using barrique to fine effect in Nebbiolo/Barbera blend Arte. Barolo from two *crus* (Bricotto Bussia, Ciabot Mentin Ginestra) are among the best moderns.

ALDO CONTERNO (Barolo, Monforte) Great Barolo, traditionally made, slow to mature but worth the wait. Bussia Soprana is very special, Cicala and Colonello quite remarkable. Gran Bussia is made from selected grapes in the best years only. Il Favot (barrique-aged Nebbiolo), powerful Barbera, Dolcetto and Freisa also good.

CONTERNO FANTINO (Barolo Monforte) Guido Fantino and Diego Conterno have earned a reputation for fine Barolo from the Ginestra hillside. Rich but forward, perfumed wines, should age well.

CARLO DELTETTO (Roero, Canale) Good understated, intriguing whites from Arneis and Favorita. Reliable Roero and Gavi.

ANGELO GAJA (Barbaresco, Barbaresco) Uses barriques for most wines, including all Barbarescos: Costa Russi, Sori San Lorenzo, Sori Tildin. In vanguard of Piedmontese Cabernet (Darmagi) and Chardonnay (Gaia and Rey) production. Two Barberas (straight and *cru* Vignarey), two Dolcettos (straight and *cru* Vignabajla), Freisa and Nebbiolo also produced.

BRUNO GIACOSA (Barbaresco, Neive) Traditional wines of, at their best, mind-blowing quality, especially Barbaresco *cru* Santo Stefano and, best of all, Barolo from Serralunga's Vigna Rionda. Outstanding wines: rich, concentrated not overbearing, elegant. Also white Arneis and good fizz.

MARCHESI DI GRESY (Barbaresco, Barbaresco) The leading site, Martinenga, produces Barbaresco, two *crus* – Camp Gros and Gaiun, and a non-wood aged Nebbiolo called Martinenga. Elegant wines; fine '85s.

GIUSEPPE MASCARELLO (Barolo, Castiglione Falletto) Outstanding *cru* Monprivato at Castiglione Falletto. Also Villero from the same commune and other *crus* from bought-in grapes. Barbera d'Alba Ginestra and Dolcetto d'Alba Gagliassi are notable. Good '84 Barolo in a difficult year.

PAOLO CORDERO DI MONTEZEMOLO (Barolo, La Morra) Wines with the accent on fruit. Standard-bearer is *cru* Monfalletto from La Morra; for some the holy of holies. *Cru* Enrico VI is from Castiglione Falletto, refined, elegant scented. Barbera, Dolcetto etc also made.

FRATELLI ODDERO (Barolo, La Morra) Barolo, Barbera, Dolcetto etc from own vineyards in prime sites in the area and Barbaresco from bought-in grapes. Wines of good roundness, balance, style, value.

PIO CESARE (Barolo, Alba) Full spread of Barolo, Barbaresco, Nebbiolo d'Alba, Dolcetto, Barbera, Grignolino and Gavi. Wines are gaining elegance, losing a bit of punch but gaining harmony and balance. Experiments with barriques; also Nebbio (young-drinking Nebbiolo), Piodilei (barriqued Chardonnay).

GIUSEPPE RIVETTI (Asti, Castagnole Lanze) Smallish quantities of magical Moscato d'Asti which sell out in a flash.

LUCIANO SANDRONE (Barolo, Barolo) A small producer making tiny quantities of perfumed Barolo with lovely raspberry and black cherry flavours from the Cannubi-Boschis vineyard. Also excellent Dolcetto.

PAOLO SCAVINO (Barolo, Castiglione Falletto) Hailed locally as one of the emerging masters of Barolo, Scavino makes superb wines which combine purity of fruit with depth and structure. Barolo Bric' del Fiasc' is his top wine; Cannubi and straight Barolo are not far behind. Delicious Dolcetto and Barbera.

VIETTI (Barolo, Castiglione Falletto) Goes from strength to strength. Classically perfect wines of their type, with a punch of acidity and tannin, plus elegance and class. Barolo (straight plus *crus* Rocche, Villero and Brunate) and Barbaresco (*normale* plus *crus* Masseria, Rabajà) are intensely complex wines. Dolcetto and Barbera also very good. Also one of the top Moscato d'Astis. Highly enjoyable Arneis.

ROBERTO VOERZIO (Barolo, La Morra) Ultra-modern approach. Attractive and fine wines, full of fruit and perfume, made with great skill, giving Roberto (not to be confused with brother Gianni) the reputation as an up and coming great. Produces Barolo, Dolcetto d'Alba, Barbera d'Alba, Freisa, and delicious barrique-aged Barbera/Nebbiolo blend Vignaserra, as well as fine Arneis.

SPAIN

Some things never change in Spain, and two things didn't change in 1992: first, the pundits continued to damn Spanish wine with faint praise in the press, and second, Spanish wine sales leapt forward yet again, as wine-lovers voted with their wallets and their palates. Pesky readers; we could have a really good wine-column here, if they didn't keep getting in the way...

Fortunately, the wine trade has a more sanguine approach, and we've seen a wider, better, and more ambitious selection of Spanish wines in the shops in the last 12 months than ever before. There's no substitute for economic forces when it comes to investment, and creaking old Spanish bodegas which had thrown their collective hands up in horror when it was first suggested that they might change their ways, have now learnt that the bottom line is where the action is. I stood on the gantry high above a co-operative winery in Bierzo last year and watched as a bulldozer moved in and smashed the tired old concrete tanks to pieces. Behind it, on the back of a truck from Barcelona, gleaming new stainless-steel tanks pointed the way forward. It could have been a metaphor for the whole business of wine-making in Spain.

To understand Spanish wine, you need to understand how the Spaniards feel about wine. As in France, Italy and Portugal, wine has evolved in Spain over several thousand years as part and parcel of the gastronomic experience: like mint sauce or horseradish or gravy to a Briton, wine was and is simply part of a

meal. Wine as a drink, by itself, just for the pleasure of the flavour, is a relatively new concept. In Britain, however, wine as a drink is a normal idea; hence the popularity of wines from Germany, Australia and New Zealand which have been designed right from the start to fulfil that role. Simple, eh? Well, try explaining it to a horny-handed co-operative member in the wilds of Castilla-La Mancha who has only just been weaned away from brewing his overheated grapes in a giant earthenware jar.

Fortunately, wine-making knowledge has become freely available over the last ten years or so, and Spanish wine is seeing a gentle evolution. In many regions of Spain, you can now buy three quite distinct types of wine: the export stuff, with all its fruit up-front, fermented at low temperatures, elaborated with technological wizardry and bottled young for the northern European market; the local plonk, a headache-in-a-bottle for the uninitiated; and the traditional style of quality wine that often matches the equally traditional foods of its region superbly well. The Spaniards don't see any of these three styles as being necessarily 'right' or 'wrong'. They are different products for different purposes. It's as simple as that.

So, back to Britain. Yet again, in a wine market which isn't going anywhere very fast, Spanish wine sales moved ahead in 1992, with an overall increase of nearly ten per cent in quantity and 27 per cent in cash value over 1991. In other words (and again) we're buying more of the better-quality wines as well as more Spanish wine generally. This in itself is an encouragement to Spanish winemakers to keep improving the quality, and it's been a guiding factor now for quite a number of years.

For the record, the winners in the export stakes have been white wines from Valdepeñas with an increase of 248 per cent, and Navarra whites with 52 per cent – both from a relatively small base, of course. Red Rioja increased by 42 per cent and red Valencia by 28 per cent – both from a very large base indeed. So the message is clear: the world likes the new-style, light fruity reds and crisp dry whites from the space-age wineries, but it still goes on wanting its Rioja.

Growing up, growing older

Rioja is recovering from the crisis of identity it went through in the mid-1980s, when prices shot up and quality drifted down. This slide was arrested with the prospect of promotion to the new super-category of DOC (*Denominación de Origen Calificada*) and by 1989 quite a few bodegas were already starting to remove steel and fibreglass storage tanks and to replace them with oak barriques. The future, they reasoned, lies in Crianza and Reserva styles of wine, and majestic Gran Reservas from great vintages. After all, if you're going to charge a premium price, you might as well have the great wines to go with it. The launch of the Rioja Gran Reserva Club in Britain in 1992, a way of promoting and selling these great wines to enthusiasts, revealed just how good some of them really are – and just how much duff stuff is still lying around waiting to be consumed and (mercifully) forgotten. This is another area that should be addressed by the new regulators of the DOC.

One sector that has lost ground during the last year is basic *vino de mesa*, or table wine, which has been falling steadily for 20 years or more. Not many people will shed a tear at the departure of the old bulk wines – stalwarts of a million student hangovers – which dragged the name of Spanish wine down in the 1960s.

In their place, table wines have taken on a new guise – or two new guises. Today, good *vino de mesa*, like Bodegas Vitorianas' Don Darias, is sold in wine merchants for under £3 a bottle and offers a pleasant, ripe, often mellow and mature style of wine at a very modest price. And then at the other end of the scale, there are a few maverick winemakers like the Marqués de Griñón, who grows forbidden grape varieties (Cabernet Sauvignon and Merlot) in forbidden soil (the province of Toledo) using forbidden methods (California-style drip-feed irrigation). As a consequence he is denied any legal recognition for his wines except that of humble *vino de mesa*. At £10 and more a bottle on the shelf, this worries him sick, of course.

Fast fizz

Cava sales in Britain have remained more or less stable throughout the past year. The actual quantity exported fell by 3.5 per cent, but the total value increased by 1.3 per cent, indicating that, once again, we're buying better quality wines, or more expensive ones at least. This may have something to do with the increased promotional activity for premium and vintage Cavas during the year, but it certainly indicates that there are also better Cavas to buy.

Traditional Cava has a gamey, slightly rooty flavour which Spaniards love and non-Spaniards often do not. Some Cava producers reacted by using greater or lesser amounts of Chardonnay in their blends, and this has achieved some modest success in making wines that are more acceptable to foreign palates. However, there is a new breed of premium Cava coming on to the market which manages to combine the unrestrained Spanishness of the Xarel-lo, Parellada and

Macabeo grapes with a delicious lightness, freshness and cleanliness. It seems to be a matter of picking the grapes very early in the morning while it's still cool, collecting them in small rigid plastic boxes to avoid damage, and getting them to the winery in less than 30 minutes. In this way, no fermentation is allowed to start on the journey, and those naughty, wild-eyed, wild-yeast rogue flavours don't have the opportunity to develop.

If it's innovation you're looking for, the place to be is Navarra, where EVENA, the research establishment at Olite, is doing cutting-edge work on every aspect of viticulture and viniculture – so much so that it hosts regular visits of winemakers from all over Spain, and further afield as well. Experiments include matching every local grape variety with every sort of rootstock in every type of soil in every microclimatic region of Navarra, and then making wine from those grapes in every style. Simple, really. Some winemakers are already taking up EVENA's findings and beginning to put them into practice, perhaps most notably at Bodegas Principe de Viana in Murchante, where winemakers' new ideas include cask-fermented Viura, alternative strains of yeast and a serious investment in new Alliers oak.

There is still work to be done in Spanish vineyards and wineries. There are sleeping giants yet to be awakened, and a large number of old ideas that need to be reappraised, but if the recent past is anything to go by, there are also some very pleasant surprises to come. In the meantime, if Spain can only lay claim to a handful of world-class wines among the many that it produces, it can still say, as a Valdepeñas winemaker said to me last summer: 'we may not make all the best wine, but we make the best wine per peseta.' Quite a lot of people in Britain seem to agree with that.

JOHN RADFORD

CLASSIFICATIONS

Spain has the largest acreage of vineyards in the world, but a relatively small number of demarcated regions. As in every country in the EC, Spain's wines divide into Table Wine (Vino de Mesa), which is allowed only a general regional name, if any, and Quality Wine (Vinos de Calidad Producido en Regiones Demarcadas, or VCPRD). Each of these further subdivides, as follows:

Table Wine

Vino de Mesa is simple table wine, as often as not blended from one or more regions to match a price or quality specification from a buyer. If the producer wants to put a vintage date on it, then it must come from within only one of Spain's 52 provinces, and may carry the provincial name (as long as that name is not already in use for a higher grade of wine): for example Vino de Mesa de Guadalajara, or Vino de Mesa de Toledo.

Vino de la Tierra is roughly the equivalent of the French Vin de Pays, although the 61 wine zones which have this classification are not yet as clearly demarcated as in France.

Quality Wine

Denominacion de Origen (DO) is a classification like the French AC, except that it is administered on a more local level and covers producing zones rather than individual vineyards, rather in the Italian manner. Regulations cover soils, grapes, yields, methods and styles of wine. There are 39 of these.

Denominacion de Origen Calificada (DOC) is the new super-category for wines with a history of quality which are prepared to submit to more stringent controls (although argument still rages as to the precise nature of those controls). Currently only Rioja is so classified (from the 1991 vintage onwards) but sherry is hard on its heels.

RED & ROSÉ WINES

With Rioja's promotion from DO to DOC status, bets are already being placed on the next red-wine zone to go for the gong. Front runners must be Ribera del Duero and Penedés, although if you're looking for quality and value look no further than Navarra (excellent work with the Tempranillo and Garnacha), Valdepeñas (super wines, silly prices) and Valencia (very cheap, very cheerful). And watch out for Somontano, Cariñena, Campo de Borja, Bierzo and Cigales.

A plea here for Spain's rosados: some of the best in Europe, if only people would bother to try them. The best are unquestionably made from macerated (short-term skin-contact) Garnacha in Navarra: big, bold and resolute.

GRAPES & FLAVOURS

BOBAL Good for deep-coloured, fruity red and stylish rosado wines in Utiel-Requena and Valencia. Reasonable acidity and relatively low alcohol keep the wines comparatively fresh and appetizing.

CARIÑENA A high-yielding grape (the Carignan of Southern France) producing dark and prodigiously tannic wine. It is believed to have originated in the region of the same name, south of Zaragoza, but plays no part in the DO wine which carries its name, and the region is now dominated by Garnacha and Bobal. Most Cariñena is grown in Catalonia, mostly as a beefy blender. It is also a minority grape in Rioja under the name Mazuelo. With its high tannin and acidity, and its aroma of ripe plums and cherries, it complements the Tempranillo so well – adding to its aging potential – that, each vintage, the Rioja bodegas fight over the little available.

GARNACHA This is Spain's – and the world's – most planted red grape variety. It grows everywhere, except Andalucía, and makes big, broad, alcoholic, sometimes peppery or spicy wines. The French, who know it as Grenache, moan about its lack of colour; but here in Spain, where burning heat and drought naturally restrict its yield, there's more dark skin in proportion to pale juice, and the wines turn out darker. They don't last well, but they can be delicious drunk young, whether as red, or fresh, spicy rosé. In Navarra the presence of Garnacha is gradually giving way to Tempranillo and Cabernet.

GRACIANO On the verge of extinction, Graciano has been rescued by the DOC upgrade in Rioja, where conscientious winemakers are seeking it out once again for the extra quality it gives to the wine.

MENCIA A grape native to Ribeiro and Bierzo. Believed to have a common ancestor with the Cabernet Franc, it is mainly used in light, fruity young wines, but older examples made in Bierzo before the DO was awarded indicate that it may have a future as a grape for oak-aging.

MONASTRELL Spain's second most planted red variety, used to add body and guts to many Catalonian Tempranillo blends. Produces good crops of dark, tasty, alcoholic reds and rosés right down the eastern seaboard in Alicante, Jumilla, Almansa, Yecla and Valencia – usually dry and stolid but sometimes made sweet.

TEMPRANILLO The fine red grape of Rioja and Navarra crops up all over Spain except in the hot south, but with a different name in practically every region (sometimes it's a slightly different strain too). It's called the Cencibel up on the plains of La Mancha and Valdepeñas, Tinto Fino in the Ribera del Duero; elsewhere it may be Tinto de Madrid, Tinto de Toro, Tinto del País ... It is so highly thought of that it is being introduced into new areas (Cariñena, Somontano, the Rioja Baja...) and is being extended elsewhere. The wines have a spicy, herby, tobacco-like character, along with plenty of sweet strawberry or sour cherry fruit, good, firm acidity and a bit of tannin. Tempranillo makes very good, vibrantly fruity wines for gulping down young, as well as more robust wines for longer aging – and its flavours harmonize brilliantly with oak. It's often blended with other grapes, especially Garnacha.

WINES & WINE REGIONS

ALICANTE, DO Heavy, rather earthy reds made in south-east Spain from the Monastrell grape which are mostly useful as blending wines.

ALMANSA, DO Falling between the high La Mancha plain and the near coastal plains of Alicante and Valencia, up-and-coming Almansa produces strong spicy reds from Monastrell and Garnacha, and even better reds from Tempranillo. The producer *Bodegas Piqueras* makes very good wines under the *Castillo de Almansa* and *Marius* labels.

AMPURDÁN-COSTA BRAVA, DO This part of Catalonia, right up in the North East, is a major supplier to the Costa Brava beaches. Seventy per cent is rosé, catering to the sun-freaks, but it also produces some so-called 'Vi Novell', supposedly modelled on the fresh, fruity style of Beaujolais Nouveau.

CALATAYUD, DO Mainly Garnacha reds, plus some Tempranillo, usually for drinking young. The area supplements neighbouring Cariñena and Campo de Borja, though it (generally) has slightly lower quality.

CAMPO DE BORJA, DO Situated in the heart of Aragón between Navarra and Cariñena. Hefty alcoholic reds made from Cariñena and Garnacha, now making way for lighter reds and very good rosés. *Bodegas Bordejé*, the *Borja* co-op and the *Santo Cristo* co-op look promising.

CARIÑENA, DO A lot of basic red from Cariñena, south-east of Rioja, finds its way as common *tinto* into Spain's bars, but the best co-ops (they make most of it) produce pleasant, full, soft reds. The main grape is the fat, jammy Garnacha, though a certain amount of Tempranillo firms up the better reds. Whites and rosés can be pleasant, but are mostly dull. The reds of the *Bodegas San Valero* co-operative are well made, sold here as *Don Mendo* and *Monte Ducay*.

CIGALES, DO Near Ribera del Duero, famed for Rosados but with some serious reds from Tempranillo/Garnacha mixes.

COSTERS DEL SEGRE, DO A virtual one-producer DO (Raïmat) in the Catalan province of Lérida. It's desert, but has been irrigated to grow cereals, fruit and vines, despite the fact that irrigation is officially banned both in Spain and the EC. But EC wine producers use two let-out clauses: if your vineyard is 'experimental', or if you can claim unusual local conditions, you can turn on the tap. *Raïmat Abadia*, based on Cabernet Sauvignon, Tempranillo and Garnacha and aged in oak, is consistently good, as is *Raïmat Pinot Noir*. The *Raïmat Cabernet Sauvignon* is also very good – ripe but light, blackcurranty-oaky wine. The *Raïmat Tempranillo* isn't so different. *Raïmat Merlot* is plummy and rich.

The price guides for this section begin on page 367.

BIERZO, DO Emergent zone growing the possibly promising Mencía grape. Older wines are pre-DO blends, so the aging potential is pretty unknown.

BINISSALEM, DO Young and Crianza reds from Mallorca, made from the Manto Negro and Callet grapes; young *rosados*.

JUMILLA, DO Usually a palate-buster of a red from super-ripe Monastrell grapes grown in the dust bowls of Murcia. Much of it is sold in bulk for beefing up blends elsewhere. However, French investment is now creating a new fresh-flavoured red style. The *Condestable* brands, *Castillo de Jumilla* and *Con Sello*, are quite good and gentle as is the ripe, plummy *Taja* from French merchants Mahler-Besse. The *San Isidro* co-op is the biggest in Spain.

VINOS DE MADRID, DO Large area split into three parts around the capital: mainly young wines, plus some Crianza from Tempranillo and Garnacha.

LA MANCHA, DO Vast area south of Madrid. Only ten per cent red, most of which is pale semi-red plonk for the bars of Madrid. The reds *can* be enjoyable, yet so far only *Vinicola de Castilla, Cueva del Granero* and *Bodegas Rodriguez & Berger* are proving this with any regularity. *Arboles de Castillejo* from *Bodegas Torres Filoso* is a Tempranillo well worth a try.

MENTRIDA, DO Strong, sturdy reds produced bang in the middle of Spain.

NAVARRA, DO This large region just north of Rioja grows the same grapes, but with more Garnacha. The officially-funded experimental winery here, EVENA, is one of the most impressive in Europe, and its influence is already showing, with Garnacha giving way to Tempranillo and Cabernet.

The best wine is the single estate *Magaña*, which has Cabernet and Merlot, not really DO-permitted varieties. Other potentially good names are *Chivite* and *Bodegas Principe de Viana,* which also uses the label *Agramont*. *Monte Ory* and *Bodegas Ochoa* are now much fresher. *Vinicola Navarra* makes old-fashioned, oaky reds – look for *Castillo de Tiebas* – and the modernized *Bodegas Irache* is producing both fruity and oak-aged styles.

PENEDÉS, DO Catalonia's leading wine region. The example set by Torres and other innovative winemakers is finally starting to filter down to the general run of bodegas, although there is still some way to go. And there are high spots. *Jean León's Cabernet Sauvignon* is one – a superbly weighty, impressively long-lasting red, though sadly lighter since 1980. *Torres* is another, from the rich, rather sweetly oaky basic reds, right up to the exciting Cabernet Sauvignon-based *Mas La Plana* and the 100% Pinot Noir *Mas Borras*. Other names

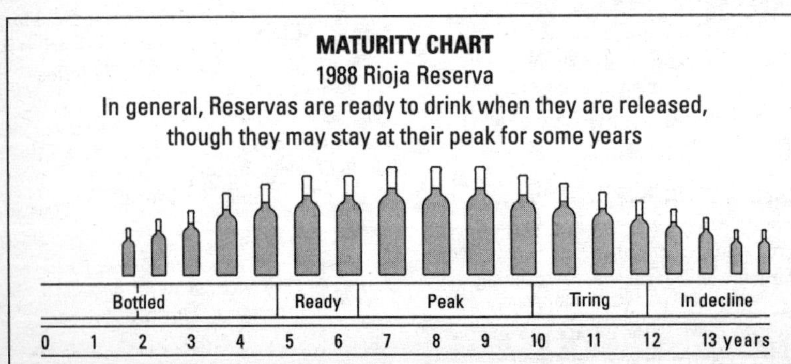

to look out for are *Cavas Hill, Ferret i Mateu, Masia Bach, Mont Marçal, Vallformosa, René Barbier, Jaume Serra.*

PRIORATO, DO You need 13.5 degrees of alcohol here to get your DO! Cool, mountainous region, abutting the west of Tarragona. The reds from Garnacha and Cariñena are renowned – rich and full-bodied in style, and *Masia Barril, Scala Dei* and *de Muller* are worth trying.

RIBERA DEL DUERO, DO 'Ribera' means river bank, and this fine red wine region spreads out over the broad valley of the Duero (Portugal's Douro) and the smaller pine-clad valleys behind. The Tinto Fino grape (alias Tempranillo) is by far the main one, sometimes mixed with Garnacha for drinking young, but used alone for the bigger reds. There's interest in Cabernet for blending into the better wines, too. The wines we see most of are from the *Bodegas Ribera-Duero* co-op at Peñafiel, where a new winemaker has meant improvements. The *joven* (young) reds show the soft fruit of the region.

Vega Sicilia is the famous name, an estate that has grown Cabernet, Merlot and Malbec to blend in with its Tinto Fino since early this century. These wines, which can be horribly expensive, taste like a mix of top Rioja and grand old-style Piedmont, with great concentration. Actually the second wine, *Valbuena*, is often more enjoyable: rich, but with less wood aging – and less of an assault on the wallet. Two other bodegas offer lovely rich, oaked reds at rapidly sky-rocketing prices – a disease that seems to be afflicting this DO. Look out for the unctuous, ripe, but over-oaky *Tinto Pesquera* from *Bodegas Alejandro Fernandez*, whose 1986 is the best recent year; for the delicious *Viña Pedrosa* from *Bodegas Perez Pascuas*; for *Bodegas Victor Balbas*; and for the *Ribera Duero* co-op (the young reds, but not the more dubious Reservas). *Bodegas Monte-Vannos'* Reservas are also good.

RIOJA CLASSIFICATIONS

Rioja is divided into three geographical sub-regions: Rioja Alta, Rioja Alavesa and Rioja Baja: most wines will be a blend from all three. The wine's age, indicated on the label, falls into one of four categories.

Sin crianza Without aging, or with less than a year in wood; wine sold in its first or second year. (The words 'sin crianza' are not seen on the label.)

Crianza With a minimum of 12 months in wood and some months in bottle; cannot be sold before its third year. Whites will have had a minimum of six months in cask before bottling.

Reserva Selected wine from a good harvest with a minimum of 36 months' aging, in cask and bottle, of which 12 months minimum in cask. It cannot leave the bodega until the fifth year after the vintage. Whites have at least six months in cask, and 24 months' aging in total.

Gran Reserva Wine from an excellent vintage (supposedly) that will stand up to aging: 24 months minimum in cask and 36 months in bottle, or vice-versa. Cannot leave the bodega until the sixth year after the vintage. White wines have six months in cask and 48 months' aging in total.

RIOJA, DOC Classic reds that taste of oak and vanilla sweetness. Oak – and in particular American oak, the type liked in Rioja – is full of vanilla, and wine leaches it out, taking up its buttery-vanilla-toffee aromas and flavours. The actual fruit in Rioja is usually rather light, sometimes peppery, with a strawberry jam sweetness.

Practically all the Rioja on sale here comes from firms who make or buy in wine from three distinct parts of the region and different grape varieties, blending and aging them to a 'house style'. Some use more of the more elegant Tempranillo, some more of the fatter, riper Garnacha, perhaps adding a little of the two minority grapes, Graciano and Mazuelo. The Rioja Alavesa region makes more delicate, scented wines; Rioja Alta is firmer, leaner, slower to show its character but slower to lose it too, and the lower, hotter Rioja Baja grows mostly Garnacha, which gets super-ripe and rather lumpish. There is now pressure from the authorities (as well as from the market) to use both new and old wood, both French and American, for aging, and to age for much shorter periods than in the past. The light has finally dawned on some bodegas that their wine actually ages very well in bottle. Best are *Bodegas Riojanas, Campo Viejo, El Coto, CVNE, Faustino, Lopez de Heredia, Marqués de Cáceres, Marqués de Murrieta, Martínez Bujanda, Montecillo, Muga, Olarra, La Rioja Alta Palacio, Campillo, Amerzola de la Mora,* and an improving *Marqués de Riscal.*

There is little credence given, as yet, to the 'estate' mentality, but it will come, as expectations rise and the over-achievers of the area determine to set an individual stamp on their wines. It's already worth trying to search out the wines from *Barón de Ley, Contino* and *Remélluri.*

SOMONTANO, DO The most exciting of Spain's newly demarcated regions in the cool foothills of the Pyrenees, north of Zaragoza. It uses a clutch of grape varieties to make lightly perfumed, attractive reds, whites and rosés, and I've even tasted some pretty good fizz. The *Co-operativa de Sobrarbe* under the *Camporocal* label is encouraging. *Covisa* have been doing well with both Spanish and foreign grapes.

TARRAGONA, DO The largest DO in Catalonia, to the south of Penedés. Originally known for high-strength dessert wines; now making undistinguished and unimpressive reds, whites and rosés.

TERRA ALTA, DO Hefty, frequently coarse red from west of Tarragona. Rather better at producing altar wine – *de Muller* is the world's biggest supplier.

TACORONTE-ACENTEJO, DO Spain's newest DO, on Tenerife. Mostly light reds, from the local Negramoll and Listán Negro.

TORO, DO This can make excellent, cheap, beefy, tannic but richly fruity reds from the Tinto de Toro – yet another alias for the Tempranillo. So far, the only really good wines come from *Bodegas Fariña*, whose *Gran Colegiata*, aged French-style in small oak barrels, is making waves here.

UTIEL-REQUENA, DO The reds, from the Bobal grape, are robust and rather hot and southern in style. The rosés *can* be better – delicate and fragrant.

VALDEORRAS, DO Galician region with young reds only, though good results are promised from the Mencía.

VALDEPEÑAS, DO Until recently the home of soft, unmemorable reds, this DO has latterly much improved When young it is often lightened with the white Airén grape. Crianza and other styles for aging in oak must, however, be made from 100% Cencibel (alias Tempranillo) so that they can turn out deep and herby with good strawberry fruit – and excellent value at very low prices, even for Gran Reservas with a decade's aging. Look for the soft reds, aged in new oak, of *Señorio de los Llanos*, *Viña Albalí* from *Bodegas Felix Solis* and the young, fruity reds of *Marqués de Gastañaga* and *Casa de la Viña.*

VALENCIA, DO Large quantities of red, white and rosé wines; the sort of thing that's fine for the beach. Some low-priced reds from *Schenk* and *Gandia Pla* can be good and the sweet Moscatels can be tasty and good value. *Castillo de Liria,* from *Gandia*, is an attractive red.

YECLA, DO Sandwiched between Jumilla and Alicante, this dry region makes fairly full-bodied reds and more dubious whites. *La Purisima* co-op is the chief label we see.

WHITE WINES

Received wisdom is that there are three contenders for Spain's best white: the cool, crisp wines of Penedés, made with the Catalan grapes Xarel-lo, Parellada and Macabeo, with or without a bit of Sauvignon or Chardonnay to add fragrance; the elegant and stylish Verdejo wines of Rueda, oak-aged or not; and the deliciously fresh and fruity Albariños of Rias Baixas, in Galicia. On sheer quality this last would probably win. The downside is the price, although it is falling: from over £10 to under £8 in the last two years, so on that basis it should be free by the year 2000.

Traditionalists will, however, continue to crown oak-aged white Rioja as the best in the bodega: the 1988 Ardanza Reserva (Safeway £6.99) is, quite simply, sublime.

GRAPES & FLAVOURS

AIRÉN This plain and simple white grape hardly deserves its prominence, but it covers far, far more land than any other grape on earth. It holds sway over Spain's central plateau, where the summers are baking hot, irrigation is banned, and the vines are widely spaced to survive. As a result, the Airén must be a front-runner for another record: the *smallest* producer per hectare. Traditionally, these grapes have yielded tired, alcoholic, yellow plonk to service the bars of Madrid. But new, cool wine-making methods can transform it into some of the most refreshing basic white yet produced in Spain, with a delicious light apple, lemon and liquorice flavour. Most, though, is still the same dull old hooch.

GARNACHA BLANCA A relation of the red Garnacha, and widely grown in the North-East. Like the red, it makes wines high in alcohol, low in acidity and with a tendency to oxidize, so they are usually blended in with wines of higher acidity, like Viura. Good growers are grubbing it up, but its high yields keep it popular, especially in Navarra.

MALVASÍA This interesting, aromatic, flavourful grape is difficult to grow in Spain, as it tends to produce wines of low acidity that turn yellow and oxidize rapidly unless extreme care is taken. It is also low-yielding and prone to rot, so many growers in its traditional homelands of Rioja and Navarra have been ousting it in favour of the less interesting Viura. Only five per cent of Rioja is now planted with Malvasía, although there are hints of new interest from bodegas like *Marqués de Cáceres*. When well made, Malvasía wine is full-bodied, fairly strongly scented, spicy or musky, often with a hint of apricots, and sometimes slightly nutty. It blends well with Viura, which ups its acidity, but more and more wooded white Riojas are now based solely on Viura, which can't meld in oaky softness as successfully as Malvasía. Ten years ago, good white Rioja Reservas really *did* taste like white Burgundy – because of the high proportion of Malvasía in the blend. Still flying the flag for this style are the excellent *Marqués de Murrieta* and *CVNE*, with their *Monopole* and their Reserva.

MESEGUERA Valencia's mainstay white grape, also grown in Alicante and Tarragona, produces light, delicately aromatic and characterful wines.

MOSCATEL The Muscat of Alexandria (Moscatel) is mostly grown in the south of Spain, where it overripens, shrivels and makes big, rich fortifieds. Valencia can make some extremely good, grapy, sweet white from it and *Torres* makes a good, off-dry, aromatic version mixed with Gewürztraminer in Penedés, as does *de Muller* in Tarragona.

PARELLADA Touted as the provider of all the perfume and finesse in Catalonia's whites and in Cava fizz, but Parellada doesn't honestly have a great deal to say for itself, except in the hands of the best producers. *Torres Viña Sol* is refreshing and lemony; other good examples include *Ferret i Mateu* and *Miret*.

VERDEJO This native of Rueda on the River Duero is one of Spain's more interesting white grapes. Nowadays it's used more for table wines than for Rueda's traditional fortifieds, and makes a soft, creamy and slightly nutty white, sometimes a touch honeyed, with good, green acidity and less alcohol than Viura. Not a world-beater, however.

VIURA The main white grape of Rioja, made nowadays apple-fresh and clean and, at best, rather neutral-flavoured; at worst it is sharp and grapefruity. It achieves similarly mixed results, under the name Macabeo, in Catalonia (where it also forms part of the Cava fizz blend). Made in this light, modern style, it's a wine for gulping down young, in its first year. But blended with Malvasía, topped up with a slug of acidity and left to age in oak barrels, the Viura can make some wonderful, rich, almost Burgundy-like white Riojas.

XAREL-LO One of the three main white grapes of Catalonia, heavier, more alcoholic and even less aromatic than the barely aromatic Parellada and Macabeo, with which it is generally blended. Some producers of Cava and still wines like to use it to give extra body and alcohol to their wines, while others scorn it as coarse. It accounts for a third of all white plantings in Penedés. In Alella, it's known as the Pansá Blanca.

WINES & WINE REGIONS

ALELLA, DO Catalonian wine region north of Barcelona, gradually disappearing under the suburban sprawl, whose best wine is from the impressive firm of *Marqués de Alella*. The vines are found on granitic slopes somewhat sheltered from the prevailing easterly wind. Its best-known wine is the off-dry, very fruity Marqués de Alella. Also look out for the light, pineapple-fresh *Chardonnay* and appley *Marqués de Alella Seco*, as well as the sparkling *Parxet*, which beats most of the famous Cavas hands down with its greengagey flavour.

BINISSALEM, DO Mallorca island DO making lightweight, beachfront whites, mainly from Moll, Xarel-lo and Parellada.

CAVA, DO The Spanish name for Champagne-method wine. Around 95 per cent of it comes from Catalonia in the East, not far from Barcelona, and indeed the authorities there have been given the task of supervising the Cava *Denominación de Origen* for the whole of Spain. Various other small vineyard enclaves have been granted the DO, odd little patches of Rioja and Aragon for instance. When Cava was promoted to DO status, several regions lost the right to use the name, and their wines (some, admittedly excellent) must now be called Metodo Tradicional. However, the two biggest outsiders, *Bodegas Inviosa* in Almendralejo (Extremadura) and *Torre Oria* in Valencia have been given (supposedly temporary) permission to continue using the name, even though their grapes do not come from classified Cava vineyards. Their wines are good, and their financial and political clout is probably even better.

However, most Cava comes from the

top right-hand corner of Spain, and it gets criticized in Britain for its earthy, old-fashioned style. There are those who criticize the grape varieties – Xarel-lo, Parellada and Macabeo – and a number of producers add Chardonnay to help the blend, but careful wine-making seems to be a bigger factor, as evidenced by the new generation of Cavas.

Some companies are starting to turn out fresher, less earthy Cavas by better wine-making and less excessive aging, and by including some Chardonnay; *Cavas Hill, Codorníu, Juve y Camps, Mont Marçal* and *Rovellats* look hopeful, though there's a distressing trend to raise prices with the use of Chardonnay. But most are stuck with their grape varieties, none of which will ever be renowned for its perfume or fruit. Most appetizing are *Cavas Hill Reserva Oro Brut Natur, Codorníu Première Cuvée Brut, Mont Marçal Cava Nature* (and *Chardonnay), Parxet, Raïmat, Segura Viudas* and *Rovellats, Freixenet* and its subsidiary company *Condé de Caralt*.

CONCA DE BARBERÁ, DO Ordinary whites and rosés from near Penedés.

CHACOLI DE GUETARIA, DO Basque-country light, white seafood-type wine of mainly local interest (the local spelling is Txacoli de Getaria), made from the (unpronounceable) Hondarribi Zuri grape.

COSTERS DEL SEGRE, DO Raïmat, virtually the only vineyard in the area, makes light, lemony, gently oaked *Raïmat Chardonnay*, as well as a good sparkler, *Raïmat Chardonnay Blanc de Blancs*.

LA MANCHA, DO Long dismissed as the most mediocre kind of base-wine producer, Spain's enormous central plateau – making 40 per cent of all Spain's wine – is now bringing in cool fermentation and is already drawing out unexpected fresh flavours – and still at a pretty rock-bottom price. The traditional wines were light yellow, thanks to creeping oxidation, but this has changed. Some we see here now are the new style, either bland, but fresh and fruity, or else quite surprisingly young and bright-eyed. But you have to catch them *very* young. Best: *Casa la Teja, Castillo de Alhambra, Lazarillo, Señorio de Guadianeja, Viña Santa Elena, Yuntero, Zagarron*.

NAVARRA, DO Navarra's reputation for producing sub-Rioja wines was endorsed by its very ordinary, cool-fermented, neutral Viura wines which died quietly in the bottle on the shelf waiting for someone to buy them. However, young and fresh white Navarra is pleasant and slurpable, and serious work at EVENA and by certain bodegas is producing some new and more exciting wines. New yeast strains, some skin contact in the maceration and a return to tradition is making its mark: look out for *Agramont* from *Bodegas Principe de Viana*, which is barrel-fermented in new Alliers oak. This could be the future.

PENEDÉS, DO There was very little to excite the export market in Penedés until relatively recently. Indifferent wine-making for a voracious and undemanding market in Barcelona gave little incentive to experiment. Then along came pioneers like Miguel Torres and Jean León who found that 'foreign' grape varieties could be made to grow and produce excellent wines in the area. The next step was to apply the same exacting wine-making standards to the native varieties (of which there are 121) and this has been moderately successful in the hands of talented winemakers, like Miguel Torres, who manages to extract a lean, lemony, sharply refreshing flavour from his Parellada. Other good whites from local varieties come from *Cavas Hill, Ferret i Mateu* and *Mont Marçal*. As well as these, *Torres* and *Masia Bach* have Riesling, Chenin, Chardonnay, Sauvignon, and what have you; and *Jean León* makes a delicious oaky, pineappley Chardonnay. Of the new varieties only Chardonnay is officially permitted in wines labelled 'Penedés'.

RIAS BAIXAS, DO Three separate districts make up this DO on the Galician coast, north of Portugal. The Val de Salnes zone around Cambados makes whites from almost pure Albariño – fresh and fragrant when well made. *Martin Codax* is good. Further south, *Condado de Tea* and *O Rosal* make Albariño-dominated wines, sometimes with a dash of Loureiro and Treixadura. As the wines become more fashionable in Spain, the prices are rising. *Bodegas Morgadio, Santiago Ruiz, Granja Fillaboa* and *Lagar de Cervera* are all good and worth a try.

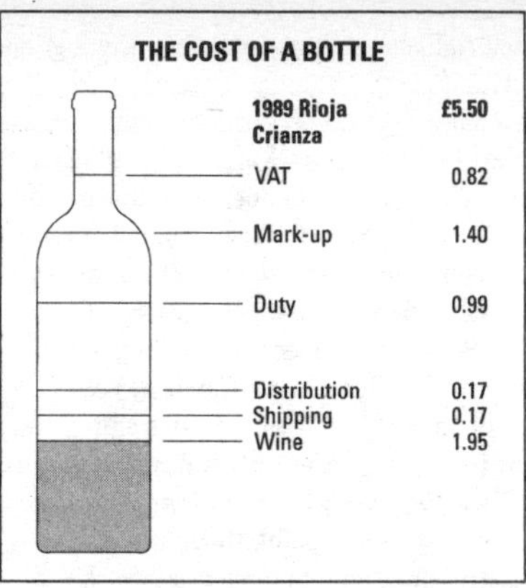

RIBEIRO, DO Since this Galician area was granted DO status, a zone once known for flabby dry whites has been benefitting from investment. Fresh white wines made from Treixadura and Torrontes is a distinct improvement on the old regime, though as in nearby Rias Baixas, demand is causing prices to rise.

RIOJA, DOC The first DO to be upgraded to DOC, though the rules stay the same. Styles vary. White Rioja *can* be buttery and rich, slightly Burgundian in style. It used to be made from a blend of Viura and the richer, more interesting Malvasía, aged for several years in oak. Some were awful, tired and flat; some were wonderful. The style is now starting to make a comeback. *Marqués de Murrieta* still makes a very good example, and so, with rather less oak, does *CVNE* with its *Monopole* and *Reserva,* and *Bodegas Riojanas* with its *Monte Reál*. *Lopez de Heredia* makes an old-fashioned style, while *Navajas, Viña Soledad* from *Franco Españolas* and *Siglo Gold* from *AGE* are all in the oak-aged mould. The best new-wave white Riojas are full of fresh, breath-catching raw fruit, with the acid attack of unsugared grapefruit.

RUEDA, DO This predominantly white wine region lies north-west of Madrid, by the river Duero. Rueda used to be famous, or notorious rather, for its heavy, oxidized, sherry-type wines made from the Palomino grape of Jerez – high on alcohol, low on fruit and freshness. But production of these *vinos generosos* is now really limited to a couple of bodegas, and the rest of the region has switched over to light table wines, picked early and fresh and fermented in cool, modern style. They have a natural advantage here in their local grape, the Verdejo, which makes soft, full, nutty wines, sometimes padded out with the dull Palomino, or sharpened up with a little of the more acid Viura. Most are for drinking young, but there are oaked versions, too. The most interesting Rueda is *Marqués de Griñon*, made by *Bodegas Castilla La Vieja*. Others include *Alvarez y Diez*, who use no sulphur, *Martinsancho* and *Vinos Sanz*. The *La Seca* co-op makes good, clean dry whites.

TACORONTE-ACENTEJO, DO Light wines from Spain's 40th and newest DO, on Tenerife in the Canaries. It produces a small but increasing supply of light young whites for the beach, made from Moscatel and Listán grapes.

VALDEORRAS, DO Galician region with undistinguished whites, fresh and fruity at their best, made from the Palomino and the Doña Blanca, but some useful work being down with the Godello promises well.

FORTIFIED WINES

Spain's most famous and longest-established wine has also turned a corner in the last two years. Sherry had been in decline in export markets since 1979 when all those vicars and bank managers stopped buying bottles of sticky brown stuff to give to their parishioners and visitors. From an all-time high of 1.5 million hectolitres (16.7 million cases) in 1979, exports slumped to 864,000 hectolitres (9.6 million cases) in 1991.

There have been serious ructions in Jerez, with companies being taken over, refinancing deals, grubbed-up vineyards and the sort of worries that the sherry business hadn't known since the Second World War. However, at the end of last year the graph finally turned the other way: there was a modest increase to 922,000 hectolitres (10.24 million cases), but at least it was a pointer in the right direction. And, more importantly, and once again, the wine tends to be of better quality: producers are concentrating more on the fresh, crisp *finos* and *manzanillas* which the Jerezanos enjoy themselves, and the full, dry *amontillados* and *olorosos* which are the masterpieces of sherry wine-making. Surplus grapes also now go to make the light and fresh, if rather neutral table wine, Vino de Mesa de Cádiz. In retrospect, the crisis might turn out to have been the best thing for the quality of the wine.

Accept no imitation

Sherry has, too, finally won back the rights to its own name. From 1 January 1996, the imitations (from Britain, Cyprus and Ireland) will have to find a new name, perhaps more descriptive of their real quality, which is poor and not a patch on the real thing. Britain has settled on 'British Fortified Wine', Irish 'sherry' barely exists anyway and Cyprus is still presumably thinking about it. Suggestions on a postcard?

Montilla is enjoying something of a renaissance, too. After years in the doldrums the Montilla producers have been trying to get their act together to present a united front to the world and shake of the sub-sherry image that has dogged them for so long. They are cashing in on the demand for lower-strength fortified wines by providing everyday quality dry and medium styles at very modest prices, and earnest seekers after truth will be astonished at the quality of some of the older Montillas – they're called '*oloroso*' at home, but the name tends not be used outside Spain to avoid confusion with sherry. Again, surplus grapes go to make table wines for drinking young.

The Condado de Huelva has also made a bit of a comeback, getting into Tesco with its lightly-fortified wines as well as the new young and fruity style of table wine. The main attraction is price, though the wines are pleasant enough. However, the Condado's main export earner will probably continue to be 'sherry' casks for the Scotch whisky industry.

Finally, Málaga has hardly moved at all, which is a great pity though not really surprising. The market for this type of big, hefty, heady, sweet fortified wine was long ago poached by Oporto, and with decreasing production and increasing prices, Málaga probably isn't going to get it back. But if you've never tried it, seek it out, if only the once: you may be very pleasantly surprised. Who knows, you may even want to buy a second bottle. **JOHN RADFORD**

GRAPES & FLAVOURS

MOSCATEL Almost all Spanish Moscatel is the second-line Muscat of Alexandria rather than the top-quality Muscat à Petits Grains. Even so, it makes a lot of good wine – mostly rich and brown in Málaga, or fresh and grapy in Valencia. The Muscat de Chipiona from *Burdon* is wonderfully rich and peachy, and is sold here in half bottles. Moscatel is also planted in Jerez to provide sweetening for cream sherries.

PALOMINO This is the dominant grape of the sherry region, making up all of the dry sherries, and an increasing proportion of the others. Although it produces a great style of fortified wine it is not considered to be a great grape, though it thrives in Jerez. It plays a minor role in Montilla-Moriles. As a table wine grape, it produces dull, fat stuff, but reacts brilliantly to the flor yeast which imparts to *fino* that characteristic bone-dry, stark-sour nose.

PEDRO XIMÉNEZ In decline in Jerez, where it used to be the chief component of sweet sherries, and still makes a startlingly rich wine essence for flavouring called 'PX'. It is sometimes made into dessert wine, deeply coloured and thick. It constitutes 95 per cent of the nearby Montilla-Moriles vineyards, as well as providing richness in Málaga; otherwise used extensively for rather dull dry white wines in the south of the country.

WINES & WINE REGIONS

CONDADO DE HUELVA, DO Faces Jerez across the Guadalquivir river in Andalucia and has broadly similar climate and soils. Wines resembling Montilla are made and have been mostly drunk locally, though some now reaches these shores. Tesco's *Tio Cani* is the sort of thing.

MÁLAGA, DO We don't see much Málaga here – in fact no-one sees much anywhere because Malaga's wine industry is beset by encroaching tourism. However, in the last century, Málaga was very popular and signs of revival have been noted. Málaga is usually full, brown and sweet in a raisiny, but not a gooey way and is slightly smoky too. There is some dry Málaga, but you'll have to take a long weekend on the Costa del Sol to see much. *Solera 1885* from *Scholtz Hermanos* is intense and raisiny while *Lagrima 10 Años* is sweet – and neither are expensive. *Bodega Lopez Hermanos is* also good.

MONTILLA-MORILES, DO Montilla wines are usually thought of as lower-priced – and lower-strength – sherry look-alikes but there is a great deal of fine wine made in Montilla-Moriles; the problem is getting any UK retailer to ship it. In general the dry wines, from Pedro Ximénez grapes, do not quite have the bite of really good sherry, but some of the mediums and sweets can outshine all but the best. In 1992 the Montilla exporters' association launched a campaign to the UK to try and interest people in their wine. If they have any sense, they'll go for the British Fortified Wine market with a vengeance.

SHERRY (JEREZ-XÉRÈS-SHERRY, DO) There are two basic sherry styles, *fino* and *oloroso*, each with sub-divisions. *Fino*, from Jerez or Puerto de Santa Maria, should be pale and dry, with an unnerving dry austerity. The tang comes from a layer of natural yeast, called flor, that forms on the surface of the wine in the barrels. The lightest, freshest wines are selected for *fino*, and they are less fortified than the heavier *oloroso* wines. *Fino* is usually drunk cool and fresh, often as an apéritif.

Manzanilla is a form of *fino* matured by the sea at Sanlúcar de Barrameda. It can be almost savoury-dry, and you might even imagine a whiff of sea salt – if you catch it young enough. Best: *Barbadillo, Caballero, Diez-Merito, Don Zoilo, Garvey, La Guita, Hidalgo, La Ina, Inocente, Lustau, La Riva, Sanchez Romate, Tio Pepe*. Good Puerto *fino* comes from *Burdon* and *Osborne*.

On the UK market there is a problem with freshness, and even good brands can suffer from tiredness. Lesser brands and most own-labels are usually a disgrace (*Sainsbury's* half-bottles are an exception), softened and sweetened so that they don't resemble real *fino*, and whatever it is they *do* resemble, I don't want it down my throat. Most dry *fino* strengths have been reduced from 17.5 per cent to 16.5 or 15.5 per cent.

Real *amontillado* also began life as *fino*, aged in cask until the flor dies and the wine deepens and darkens to a tantalizing, nutty dryness. In the natural state, as drunk in Spain, it is *completely* dry, and a proper *amontillado* will usually say *seco* ('dry'), on the label. But we've adulterated the word in English to mean a downmarket, bland drink of no interest. Most sold here may have little or no real *amontillado* in it. But look out for *almacenista* sherries, unblended wine from small stockholders which can be wonderful.

Look out also for *Principe* and *Solear* (a *manzanilla pasada*) from *Barbadillo*, *La Goya Manzanilla Pasada* and *Amontillado Fino Zuleta* (*Delgado Zuleta*), *Amontillado del Duque* (*Gonzalez Byass*), *Hidalgo Manzanilla Pasada*, *Sandeman Bone Dry Old Amontillado*, *Valdespino*'s *Amontillado Coliseo* and *Don Tomás*. (*Manzanilla pasada* is an old *manzanilla* beginning to take on *amontillado* characteristics.)

Real *olorosos*, made from richer, fatter wines without any flor, are deep and dark, packed with violent burnt flavours – and usually dry, though you may find *oloroso dulce* (sweet) in Spain. In Britain most are sweetened with wine from Pedro Ximénez or Moscatel grapes. They usually come as 'Milk', 'Cream' or 'Brown'. Pale Creams are sweetened (inferior) *fino*, and are some of the dullest drinks around. For the real, dry thing, once again, look for *almacenista olorosos* from *Lustau*. There are a few good, concentrated sweetened *olorosos* around, including the fairly sweet *Matúsalem* from *Gonzalez Byass*, *Solera 1842 (Valdespino)*, *Apostoles Oloroso Viejo* from *González Byass*. Dry: *Barbadillo*, *Don Zoilo*, *Sandeman*, *Valdespino Don Gonzalo*, *Williams & Humbert Dos Cortados*. Most are under a tenner, making these intense old wines one of today's great bargains.

WINERY PROFILES

ANTONIO BARBADILLO (Sanlúcar de Barrameda) ★★★★(★) Best *manzanilla bodega*. Principe is tangy, nutty, well-aged.

CAMPO VIEJO ★★★(★) Decent Riojas and soft, traditional Reservas.

VINICOLA DE CASTILLA (La Mancha) ★★★ Up-to-date producer turning out 14 million litres a year, including white and oaky red Señorio de Guadianeja. Soft red Castillo de Alhambra is good value.

CODORNÍU (Penedés) ★★★ Giant Cava company, owned by the Raventos family, making some of the most likeably reliable fizzes. Good soft and honeyed Anna de Codorníu fizz, and a very good, creamy Chardonnay Cava.

CONTINO (SOCIEDAD VINICOLA LASERNA) (Rioja) ★★★★(★) Excellent, single-vineyard wine made from an estate half-owned by CVNE, half by private investors. Vines are predominantly Tempranillo, planted in one 45-hectare vineyard in prime Rioja Alta land. Big, plummy and spicily complex, Contino is made only as Reserva and Gran Reserva. If you see any '82, snap it up.

CVNE (Rioja) ★★★★ Old-established, traditionally-inclined; the initials stand for Compañía Vinícola del Norte de España. Blanco Viura is one of the best modern white Riojas, and Monopole has nice oak. Best of the reds are the rare Imperial range (especially the '81). Try the Reserva white for a taste of good traditional Rioja.

DOMECQ (Jerez)★★★★★One of the oldest and most respected sherry houses, with top *fino* La Ina, Botaina *amontillado* and Rio Viejo *oloroso*. Also makes Rioja.

FAUSTINO MARTÍNEZ (Rioja) ★★★ A huge, family-owned bodega which makes good reds. Look out also for the new Campillo bodega.

FREIXENET (Penedés)★★★High-tech Cava firm best known for Cordon Negro, but also making good value Carta Nevada, Vintage Brut Nature which includes some Chardonnay, and upmarket Brut Barroco.

GONZÁLEZ BYASS (Jerez)★★★★★Huge, family-owned company, producers of the best-selling *fino* Tio Pepe. GB also makes an impressive top range of wines, and a Rioja, Bodegas Beronia.

CAVAS HILL (Penedés) ★★(★) Table wines as well as fresh, clean Cava Reserva Oro Brut Natur. Look out for Blanc Cru and Oro Penedés Blanco Suave whites, and Rioja-style reds, Gran Civet and Gran Toc.

JEAN LEÓN (Penedés) ★★★★ Jean León makes some of Spain's most 'Californian' wines: super-oaky, pineapple-and-honey Chardonnay, and soft, blackcurranty Cabernet Sauvignon.

JULIAN CHIVITE (Navarra)★★★ One of the most export-minded and state-of-the-art bodegas in Navarra, making a clean white from Viura, attractive *rosado* from Garnacha, and a good Tempranillo-based red, all under the Gran Feudo label.

LOS LLANOS (Valdepeñas) ★★★ The brightest spot here: wonderfully soft, oaky reds. 1978 Gran Reserva is especially good.

LÓPEZ DE HEREDIA (Rioja) ★★★★ Rich, complex whites, Viña Tondonia and Viña Gravonia, and delicate, ethereal reds, Viña Cubillo and Viña Tondonia.

LUSTAU (Jerez) ★★★ 'Reviving Traditional Sherry Values' with their wonderful range of *almacenista* wines.

MARQUÉS DE CÁCERES (Rioja) ★★★(★) Enrique Forner, who started this bodega in the mid-70s, trained in Bordeaux. Whites are cool-fermented and fresh, and reds have less wood aging than usual, but still keep an attractive style.

MARQUÉS DE GRIÑON (Toledo) ★★★★ Carlos Falco, the Marqués de Griñon, makes very good Cabernet in his irrigated, wire-trained vineyard, aided by advice from Professor Emile Peynaud from Bordeaux.

MARQUÉS DE MURRIETA (Rioja) ★★★★ A remarkable, ultra-traditional winery built into a hill outside Logroño. Red, rosés and whites are oak-aged far longer than in any other Rioja bodega; the Etiqueta Blanca wines, the youngest sold, spend at least two years in barrel, and are richly oaky, pungent and lemony. The red is soft and fruity-oaky, while the Reservas are deep and complex. The best wines of the very top years are sold as Castillo Ygay, and may sit in barrel for 40 years.

MARTÍNEZ BUJANDA (Rioja) ★★★ Wine is produced only from the family's own vineyards, and is very well made, from the super-fresh and lively Valdemar white to the strongly oaky Reserva and Gran Reserva Condé de Valdemar.

MONTECILLO (Rioja) ★★★★ Since 1973, this has belonged to Osborne, the sherry company, who built a new winery to turn out an aromatic white Viña Cumbrero, a raspberry and oak red, Viña Cumbrero Crianza, and a Reserva, Viña Monty.

MUGA (Rioja) ★★★(★) This has a sternly traditional image. For reds, it does nothing but good, and the Crianza is fragrant and delicate, while the Prado Enea Reserva or Gran Reserva is more complex, but still subtle and elegant. It's not cheap, though.

VIÑA PESQUERA (Ribera del Duero) ★★★★ Prices have shot up since American wine writer Robert Parker likened this to Château Pétrus. Made from Tinto Fino and Garnacha, it's good but not *that* good, oaky and aromatic, with rich savoury fruit.

PRINCIPE DE VIANA (Navarra)★★★(★) Innovative bodega which used to be a co-op, and became known as Bodegas Cenalsa. Agramont is its best-known UK brand, and look out for new Bodegas Guelbenzu, a Cabernet/Tempranillo estate in Cascante.

RAÏMAT (Costers del Segre) ★★★ The Raïmat Chardonnay Cava is honeyed, with grassy acidity. Abadía is an oak-enhanced blend of Cabernet, Tempranillo and Garnacha. Also: Cabernet Sauvignon, Pinot Noir and Merlot.

LA GRANJA REMÉLLURI (Rioja) ★★★★(★) Single-estate wine; the Rodriguez family have completely rebuilt the winery, installing stainless steel fermentation tanks instead of the old wooden vats, and now make a fine, meaty Reserva, barrel-aged for two to three years.

LA RIOJA ALTA (Rioja) ★★★★(★) A traditional bodega, firm believer in long barrel-aging: over half the wines qualify as Reserva or Gran Reserva. Even the Viña Alberdi Crianza has a delightfully oaky flavour. They make two styles of Reserva, the elegant Viña Arana and the rich Viña Ardanza. In the best years, they make exceptional Gran Reservas.

RIOJANAS (Rioja) ★★★(★) One of the few still using the open *lagar* method of semi-carbonic maceration. Best reds are the Reservas: the light, elegant, plummy Viña Albina and the richer, more concentrated Monte Reál. White Monte Reál Crianza is soft and peachy, with just enough oak.

MIGUEL TORRES (Penedés) ★★★★(★) The best range of table wines in Spain. Viña Sol is a super-fresh modern white. Gran Viña Sol is half-and-half Parellada and Chardonnay, fresh and pineappley, enriched with hints of vanilla oak. Gran Viña Sol Green Label pairs Parellada with Sauvignon Blanc, like oakier Sancerre. The superstar white is Milmanda Chardonnay. Recent red additions are a Pinot Noir, Mas Borras, and a Merlot, Las Torres. Viña Esmeralda is Gewürztraminer and Muscat d'Alsace. Mas la Plana is Torres' top red, a Cabernet Sauvignon. Viña Magdala is equal parts of Pinot Noir and Tempranillo, Gran Sangredetoro is mainly Garnacha, and Coronas – a savoury Tempranillo – is the least exciting.

VALDESPINO (Jerez) ★★★★★ Another family-owned bodega making a range of top-class, dry sherries. Inocente is one of the last traditional *finos* at 17.5 degrees. Their Pedro Ximénez Solera Superior is one of the few examples of sherry's great sweetening wine bottled by itself. *Amontillados* and *olorosos* from here are about as good as you can get.

BODEGAS VEGA SICILIA (Ribera del Duero) ★★★★(★) Makers of Spain's most famous and expensive red wine. Vega Sicilia Unico, the top wine, is sometimes kept in barrel for as long as ten years. Younger wines, called Valbuena, offer a cheaper glimpse of Vega Sicilia's glories.

VINCENTE GANDIA(Valencia) ★★★ Perhaps this DO's most go-ahead producer. Fresh white Castillo de Liria and juicy red and *rosado* from Bobal.

PORTUGAL

Portuguese growers have never been very good at figures. Ask a farmer how many hectares of this or that grape variety are planted in his vineyard and he will probably shrug his shoulders. It's not that he is being coy or secretive; he really won't know. In Portugal vines have traditionally been planted in a haphazard manner with different grape varieties mixed up together on the same pocket-sized plot. Few records have been kept. Bookkeeping has never been accorded a high priority by grape growers who would rather be drinking the fruits of their labours down at the local café.

Now that the EC has a say in the matter, Portugal's wine industry is being brought under control. The torrent of cash flowing from Brussels to Lisbon has to be backed by facts and figures in order to satisfy the bureaucrats. Money is beginning to force the previously unruly Portuguese into quiet submission.

This year's annual report from the Instituto da Vinha e do Vinho (IVV) – the government body controlling Portugal's vines and wines – makes unusually interesting reading. For the first time it is crammed with vital statistics that paint a picture of Portugal's wine industry over the last five years.

They tell us that Portugal, the world's seventh largest wine-producing country, made 9.6 million hectolitres of wine in 1991 and estimate that because of the drought in 1992, production fell to 7.2 million hl. Of this over 60 per cent falls into the common or garden table wine category and just 35 per cent is worthy of 'Quality Wine' status. These proportions have not changed significantly since Portugal joined the EC in 1986. This is surprising because an extra 31 supposedly quality wine regions have been superimposed on the map, taking the total number of *Denominacão de Origem Controlada* (DOC) and *Indicaçao de Proveniência* (IPR; similar to France's VDQS) regions to 44.

Ex-colonial thirst

It is only when you turn to the export statistics that you discover what has really been happening. Angola, a Portuguese colony until a revolution toppled the Lisbon government back in 1974, has returned like a phoenix from the ashes to become Portugal's largest single export market for wine. In 1991 Angola bought nearly 300,000 hectolitres of Portuguese wine: four times the amount she imported in 1986 when Portugal joined the EC.

In fact, happily for Portugal's grape growers, Angola has made up for declining popularity of wine at home. Consumption which peaked at 100 litres per head in the 1960s has slumped by half. In the seven years that have elapsed since Portugal joined the EC, per capita consumption has fallen by 15 litres as the Portuguese have persuaded each other to drink less but better. Portugal is now the fifth largest consumer of wine in the world whereas 30 years ago it vied with France and Italy for first place in the league of tipplers.

This has put pressure on the Ribatejo and Oeste; two adjoining regions immediately north and east of Lisbon which together account for nearly 40 per cent of Portugal's wine production. This is co-operative country where thousands of small growers have traditionally sold fat, over-ripe grapes to giant wineries to be made into fairly unpalatable wine. As Portuguese punters increasingly turn to beer, co-operative cellars like Torres Vedras and Almeirim (two of the largest wineries in the country) have had to find new outlets for their products.

Apart from Angola, which is hardly the most reliable market, the recession-ridden UK has also made the most of declining consumption in Portugal. Wine imports from Portugal increased by a staggering 67 per cent in 1992, just eight per cent less than the increase in imports from Australia. However, translated into escudos, the increase in the value of wine imports from Portugal was a meagre three per cent. (Compare that with Australia, where the comparable increase in value amounted to 40 per cent.)

This disparity can largely be attributed to recession-beating wines like Lezíria, made by the Almeirim co-op, which came from nowhere to sell 200,000 cases last year. The £1.99-£2.29 price tag undoubtedly attracted the bargain hunters who found that the soft, spicy, cherry-and-plum taste of the red was more than a match for the cost. Arruda, Cismeira, Borba and Redondo complete the list of Portuguese dime-store reds which have caught the imagination as well as the pockets of hard-pressed Britons over the last 18 months.

But it's not all cheapness and light. The Alentejo, which still only produces three per cent of Portugal's wine, continues to command attention worldwide. With wines like Peter Bright's remarkable smoky-spicy Tinto da Anfora it is not difficult to see why. But Bright is no longer alone. Fellow Aussie David Baverstock has been coaxed away from the cosy port business to revitalize the vast Esporão estate at Reguengos de Monsaraz in the heart of the Alentejo. Keep a look out for some exciting new flavours bottled under the Esporão and Monte Velho labels over the next 12 months. In the meantime Bright's inexpensive Do Campo wines, made exclusively for Sainsbury's, should help as we stagger out of recession. The white, made from Fernão Pires and Rabo de Ovelha, is fresh and peachy, the Periquita-based red warm and spicy.

Son of Mateus

Progress in the north of Portugal has been slower but Sogrape, the country's largest and most innovative winemaker, is leading the way forward in Dão, Bairrada and the Vinho Verde region by focusing on Portugal's eclectic mix of indigenous grapes. The company that, 40 years ago, turned Mateus into a household name has recently launched a serious, delicate, dry Bairrada rosé called Nobilis. Sogrape (which also owns the port shipper Ferreira) continues to make the most of its strength in the Douro where port production has been cut substantially to match supply with demand. Ferreira's Esteva and a new wine called Cismeira, made by a Belgian-owned company, are among the best examples of the Douro's new generation of supple, value-for-money reds.

But perhaps the most unexpected development in Portugal in recent years is the joint venture between a remote co-operative in the Douro and leading US sparkling winemakers Schramsberg. Not to be upstaged by the trans-Atlantic exchange between Champagne and California, Schramsberg settled on Portugal as the ideal base for their new European project. Not surprisingly they met their first hurdle in the Douro's muddled vineyards. But by marking individual vines with a splash of whitewash, they managed to separate the three most suitable native varieties out of over 50 growing in the region. Schramsberg took over four years to sort things out but the result is a crisp, lacy fizz called Vertice. It may be the shape of Portuguese things to come.

RICHARD MAYSON

WHITE WINES

Portugal is often thought of as being red wine territory. There used to be good reasons for this, unless you happened to enjoy flat, fruitless and probably oxidized dry whites. But it's amazing what a bit of cool fermentation and a dash of stainless steel can do for a wine – especially if it's made from some of the most unusual and promising grape varieties in Europe.

In the Vinho Verde region, Loureiro and Alvarinho make delicate, scented dry whites that are worlds away from the heavy-handed commercial blends. In the Douro the Viosinho and Gouveio grapes appear in Sogrape's peachy-smoky Reserva. Bairrada boasts the spicy Maria Gomes which crops up in the South as Fernão Pires. Sogrape, José Maria da Fonseca and JP Vinhos are the producers showing the most dexterity.

WINES & WINE REGIONS

ALENTEJO This region in the south deserves to feature in the white section for the first time. EC backing means that stainless steel and temperature control are now the norm. The Roupeiro grape has been singled out as the best and *Esporão*'s Aussie winemaker, David Baverstock, is making the most of its tropical, guava-like flavours. The *Redondo* co-op is also producing some good peachy whites.

BAIRRADA, DOC Some increasingly good dry whites from the Maria Gomes grape. *Sogrape*, maker of *Mateus Rosé*, has done the most to freshen up flavours. Try the crisp, floral *Quinta de Pedralvites*. Also very good: peachy *Sogrape Bairrada Reserva* and *Caves Aliança*'s inexpensive dry white.

BUCELAS, DOC Popular in Wellington's day, this dry white was almost extinct, with *Caves Velhas* left as the sole producer. However, two new winemakers have appeared. Look out for *Quinta da Romeira* under the *Prova Regia* label.

DÃO, DOC White Dão was traditionally (and mostly still is) yellow, tired and heavy. But a few companies are now making a lighter, fresher, fruitier style, and now that the co-ops are losing the upper hand with production, others look set to follow suit. White *Grão Vasco*, now made in *Sogrape*'s shiny new winery at Quinta dos Carvalhais is a significant departure from tradition with its crisp lemon-zest appeal. Sadly, local regulations insist that the wine should be at least six months old before bottling, so it pays to catch the wine young. Look out for oak-aged Reservas in future.

DOURO, DOC Nearly all the best table wines are red, though the *Planalto* white from *Sogrape*, the Mateus-makers, is full and honeyed and good, as is its oaked *Douro Reserva*, and *Esteva* from *Ferreira* is clean and crisp. *Quinta do Valprado* Chardonnay, made by the Seagram-owned *Raposeira* fizz company near Lamego, is honeyed and mouth-filling.

SETÚBAL PENINSULA The whole peninsula is now the first Vinho Regional area, with the name of Terras do Sado. The best wines are produced on the limestone soils of the Arrábida hills where Peter Bright makes an oak-aged Chardonnay, *Cova da Ursa*. The *João Pires Muscat* is also good. *José Maria da Fonseca* prefers local grapes, though Chardonnay gives a lemony lift to the white *Pasmados*, and *Quinta da Camarate* boasts Riesling, Gewürztraminer and Muscat.

VINHO VERDE, DOC *Verde* here means youthful-green, immature-green, un-aged, not the colour of a croquet lawn. Ideally, these wines are extremely dry, positively tart, and brilliantly suited to the heavy, oily Portuguese cuisine. But we almost always get them slightly sweetened and softened, which is a pity, although it is in its peculiar way a classic wine style.

Most wines come from co-ops or are sold under merchants' brand names, but there is an increasing tendency for the larger, grander private producers to bottle their own. And some of the big firms are beginning to make characterful single-quinta Vinhos Verdes alongside their big brands. *Palacio da Brejoeira*, made from the Alvarinho grape, is more alcoholic and full bodied, and expensive, for that matter, than the general run. Vinho Verde can be made from a variety of grapes, but there's often a higher proportion of Loureiro in the single-property wines. Indeed, there's quite rightly a lot of interest in Loureiro, with its dry, apricotty, Muscaty aroma and taste. It is more attractive than the much-praised Alvarinho, and it gives the wines a much more tangy but fruity character. *Solar das Bouças* and *Quinta de Tamariz* are almost entirely Loureiro. *Quinta de Franqueira*, *Casa de Sezim* and *Terras de Corga* are also on form at the moment. From the large companies *Gazela* is just off-dry, reliable and good. *Aveleda* also makes some good ones, including one made entirely from the Trajadura grape. Its best is called *Grinalda*, a perfumed blend of the Loureiro and Trajadura varieties.

RED WINES

The rise and rise of Portugal's red table wines is revealing flavours that most of us never knew existed. If you want Cabernet or Merlot then Portugal is not the place to look, but if you want originality and adventure then just start at the Douro and work south. Portugal is blessed with a treasure trove of native grapes, but it's only with the advent of modern technology (heavily funded by the EC, and since that means you and me, we might as well enjoy the benefits) that they've been vinified in such a way as to keep their qualities right up to the glass. They used to be severely injured by the wine-making, and then aged until they were dead; no longer. The grapes, traditionally, used to be so mixed up in the vineyards that even their mothers couldn't identify them; they still are, but they are showing signs of getting sorted out. Grapes like Alfrocheiro, Aragonez, Baga, Castelão Frances and Touriga Nacional may not exactly roll off the tongue yet, but then nor did Cabernet Sauvignon until we all got to know it.

WINES & WINE REGIONS

ALENTEJO Unfettered by Portugal's legendary bureaucracy, the Alentejo comes on in leaps and bounds. With EC help the co-ops are showing more initiative here than anywhere else in the country. *Borba* led the way but *Redondo* is now living up to its name and producing some round, fruity reds. Roseworthy-trained David Baverstock deserves another mention, having left his job in the port trade to revitalise the vast *Esporão* estate at Reguengos de Monsaraz. The large *José Maria da Fonseca* company, a leading innovator, has invested a lot of time and energy in the region. Apart from *Fonseca*'s blends, and the *Tinto Velho* from the *JS Rosado Fernandes* estate, which Fonseca now owns, the best wines are from various co-ops. The reds from the *Redondo* co-op, with their big, brash grapy fruit show the potential waiting to be tapped. The upfront rich damson-and-raspberry fruit of the *Paço dos Infantes* from Almodovar shows the same marvellously untamed excitement. The *Borba* co-op, *Cartuxa, Esporão* and *Reguengos de Monsaraz* are producing reds with terrific fruit. Look also for *Quinta da Anfora*, which is a blend of reds from the region. The Rothschilds have bought a share of *Quinta do Carmo,* near Estremoz, and other foreign investors are looking.

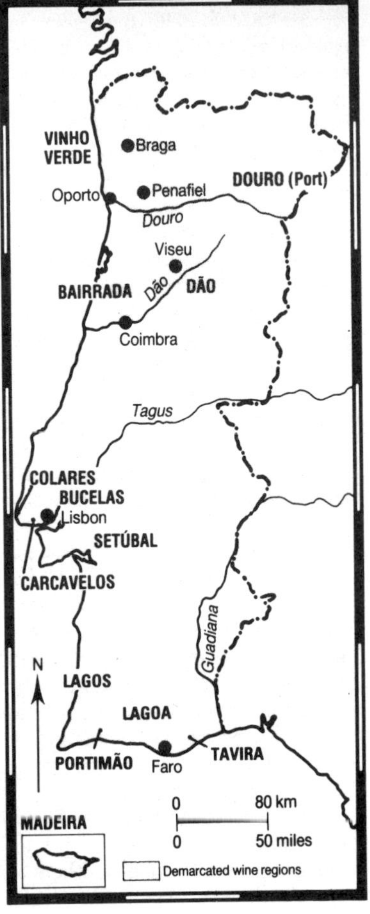

ALGARVE The south coastal strip of the country, making undistinguished wines – mostly alcoholic reds. Once an *Região Demarcada*, it has now been split into four *Denominaçõs de Origem Controlada,* Lagos, Portimão, Lagoa and Tavira. All deserve demotion from DOC status. Among producers, the *Lagoa* co-op is the best bet.

BAIRRADA, DOC In the flat land down towards the sea from the hilly Dão region, vineyards mingle with wheatfields, olive trees and meadows, and the wines frequently overshadow the more famous Dão reds. The wines are apt to be tannic, often the result of fermenting the wine with the grape stalks, but the Baga grape, the chief one in the blend, gives a sturdy, pepper, plum-and-blackcurrant fruit to the wine which can often survive the over-aging, and at ten years old, although the resiny bite and peppery edge are apparent, a delicious, dry fruit is more in command. The best Bairrada wines age remarkably well. Some growers, like *Luis Pato*, are experimenting with blending in a dollop of softening Cabernet Sauvignon.

Some Portuguese merchants will tell you that their own Garrafeira wines are based on Bairrada, though the label won't say so. That's probably true, because of the traditional Portuguese approach to high quality reds – buy where the grapes are best, blend and age at your company's cellars, and sell the 'brew' under your own name. Since 1979, however, the Bairrada region has been demarcated and bulk sales have been banned, and the challenging, rather angular, black fruit flavours of the wines now sport a Bairrada label. *São João* produces wine of world class, though increasingly hard to find. *Aliança* and *Sogrape* (look for its *Nobilis*) are good. The best co-op is *Vilharino do Bairro*, and *Cantanhede* and *Mealhada* aren't bad. Encouragingly, single-estate wines are emerging, with *Luis Pato* the leader so far. He must be good because he's already had some of his wine turned down by the *Bairrada Região* as untypical because he'd used new oak instead of old.

COLARES, DOC Grown in the sand dunes on the coast near Lisbon from the doughty but scented Ramisco grape. Almost all the wine is vinified at the local Adega Regional, stalks and all, aged in concrete tanks for two to three years, then sold to merchants for further maturation and sale. The young wine has fabulous cherry perfume but is *numbingly* tannic. As it ages it gets an exciting rich pepper-and-bruised-plums flavour, but the 1974s are only just ready. The Adega no longer has a monopoly on Colares, but only *Carvalho, Ribeiro & Ferreira* shows interest in exploiting the new freedom, and it may be too late to save the region from extinction.

DÃO, DOC This upland eyrie, ringed by mountains, reached by steep, exotic, forest-choked river gorges, makes Portugal's most famous, if not always her most appetizing reds. They are reputed to become velvet-smooth with age. My experience is that they rarely achieve this and could do with less aging in wood and more in bottle. They are made from a mixture of six grapes, of which the Touriga Nacional is the best, and they develop a strong, dry, herby taste, almost with a pine resin bite.

The protectionist rules that allowed companies to buy only finished wine, not grapes, from growers, and that forbade firms from outside the region to set up wineries there, have been abolished and *Sogrape*, with its own winery in the region, is now making the most of it. Among the others, *Caves São João* deserves an honourable mention along with *Caves Aliança* and *José Maria da Fonseca* for its brand, *Terras Altas*. Other firms are persuading their co-op suppliers to leave the grape stalks out of the fermentation vats and make cleaner, more modern wines, but there's still a long way to go.

DOURO, DOC The Douro valley is famous for the production of port. But only a proportion of the crop – usually about 40 per cent – is made into port, the rest being sold as table wine. There is a glut of grapes for table wine at the moment and *Sogrape* (which owns *Ferreira*) is busy making the most of it. The other port companies are less keen to put their weight behind table wines, though behind the scenes one or two are trying them out based on Touriga Francesa, Touriga Nacional and Tinta Roriz; one producer is working with Cabernet Sauvignon. The flavour can be delicious – soft and glyceriny, with a rich raspberry and peach fruit, and a dry perfume somewhere between liquorice, smoky bacon and cigar tobacco. Look out for *Quinta da Cismeira, Quinta do Côtto, Quinta de la Rosa, Sogrape; Barca Velha, Reserva Especial* and *Esteva* from *Ferreira*.

OESTE Portugal's largest wine area, north of Lisbon (and largest wine area, full stop, in terms of volume) is dominated by huge co-ops, some of which are just beginning to do something about quality. *Arruda* makes strong, gutsy reds, *Alenquer* makes softer, glyceriny wine, while the *Obidos* reds are drier, more acid, but good in a cedary way. *Torres Vedras'* reds are lighter than Arruda, with a climate more influenced by cool Atlantic air. Single-estate *Quinta de Abrigada* makes light, creamy whites and stylish damson and cherry reds, and *Quinta das Pancas* has some Chardonnay and some Cabernet. These two are the only private estates doing much so far, though *Paulo da Silva*'s *Beira Mar* and *Casal de Azenha* are both good Oeste blends. The region sub-divides into six IPR regions: Arruda, Alenquer, Óbidos, Torres Vedras, Alcobaça and Encostas d'Aire.

RIBATEJO Portugal's second largest region, in the flat lands alongside the Tagus, provides the base wine for some important brands and some of Portugal's

The price guides for this section begin on page 377.

best Garrafeira wines – in particular the *Romeira* of *Caves Velhas. Carvalho Ribeiro* and *Ferreira,* recently bought by Costa Pina, a subsidiary of Allied Lyons, also bottles some good Garrafeiras, and with multi-national backing its wines are likely to improve.The co-op at *Almeirim* markets good wine under its own name, including the price-busting *Lezíria*, and the *Torre Velha* brand isn't bad. The *Margaride* estate is the Ribatejo's leading estate. The wines are sold as *Dom Hermano, Margarides* and under the names of their properties, *Casal do Monteiro* and *Convento da Serra*. The wines are patchy, but can be very good. The region is being split up into six IPRs (*Indicação de Proveniencia Regulamentada*) the six being Almeirim, Cartaxo, Chamusca, Santarém, Tomar and Coruche.

SETÚBAL PENINSULA One of the most important wine regions in Portugal, and one with plenty of technical expertise at its disposal. *JP Vinhos* and *José Maria da Fonseca* are the leading lights, for reds and whites. Imports like Cabernet Sauvignon and Merlot are made as varietals and used in blends with local grapes like Periquita.The area around Setúbal is now a Vinho Regional called Terras do Sado.

VINHO VERDE, DOC Sixty per cent of all Vinho Verde produced is red, made from four different grapes, of which the Vinhão is best. The wine is wonderfully sharp, harsh even, is hardly ever seen outside the country and goes a treat with traditional Portuguese dishes like *bacalhau*, or salt cod. Adnams have the red from the *Ponte da Lima* co-op, for anybody feeling brave.

FORTIFIED WINES

Fashion has been unkind to fortified wines over the last few decades. Setúbal and Carcavelos have been driven close to extinction and Madeira, that most long-lasting of wines, has lurched between boom and crisis.

Madeira received a much-needed shot in the arm six years ago when the Symington family of Dow, Graham and Warre port fame took a controlling stake in the Madeira Wine Company, the largest producer on the island. But it has taken the EC to put a stop to the absurd situation whereby a wine could call itself Sercial yet contain no Sercial grapes; the same was true of Bual, Verdelho and Malmsey (or Malvasia), these four being the island's best varieties and the ones that have given their names to the styles of wine. In reality, since they were so little grown, most Madeira, certainly at the cheaper end, was made from the inferior Tinta Negra Mole grape.

Three cheers for the EC: Madeira's eight wine exporters have been obliged to remove any varietal designation unless the wine is made from at least 85 per cent of the stated grape. The words 'Rich', 'Medium Rich', 'Medium Dry' and 'Dry' will replace the traditional varietal description except of course for those wines that manage to break the 85 per cent barrier.

In the meantime the government is running a campaign to return the island's vineyards to noble varieties, but with 4000 growers farming an estimated 1800 hectares of land it will be a long time, perhaps decades, before the results are seen on the labels of all but the best Madeiras.

Back on the mainland, after an unprecedented gap of six years, the 1991 port vintage has been widely declared. The shippers have hummed and ha'ed about the wisdom of a declaration coinciding with a worldwide slump in the market for vintage port, but the wines are good and the quantities small.

GRAPES & FLAVOURS

Eighteen different grape varieties are used to make red and white ports, and of these the most important in terms of quality and flavour are the Roriz, Barroca, Touriga Francesa and Touriga Nacional among the reds, and the Malvasia Dorada and Malvasia Fina in the whites. The Moscatel is chiefly grown in Setúbal just south of Lisbon, where it makes a famous, but not particularly thrilling, sweet fortified wine.

WINES & WINE REGIONS

CARCAVELOS, RD Just when Carcavelos looked as if it was about to disappear for ever, along comes a new vineyard. *Quinta dos Pesos* is making a good, nutty, fortified rather like an aged Tawny port.

MADEIRA, RD Each Madeira style is supposedly based on one of four grapes, Malmsey (Malvasia), Bual, Verdelho and Sercial, though at the moment only the more expensive Madeiras really live up to their labels – the cheaper ones, up to 'five-years-old', are almost all made from the inferior Tinta Negra Mole. The EC is enforcing a rule that 85 per cent of a wine labelled with a grape variety should be made from it, so the cheaper Madeiras are likely to start calling themselves, more honestly, 'Pale Dry', 'Dark Rich', and so on.

The Malmsey grape makes the sweetest Madeira, reeking sometimes of Muscovado sugar, dark, rich and brown, but with a smoky bite and surprisingly high acidity that makes it positively refreshing after a long meal. The Bual grape is also rich and strong, less concentrated, sometimes with a faintly rubbery whiff and higher acidity. Verdelho makes pungent, smoky, medium-sweet wine with more obvious, gentle fruit, and the Sercial makes dramatic dry wine, savoury, spirity, tangy, with a steely, piercing acidity. To taste what Madeira is all about you need a ten-year-old, and, frankly, really good Madeira should be two or three times that age.

The move into Madeira by the Symington family (of port fame) should herald new investment – and better wines.

SETÚBAL, DOC Good, but always a little spirity and never quite as perfume-sweet as one would like, perhaps because they don't use the best Muscat. It comes in a six-year-old and a 25-year-old version, and the wines do gain in concentration with age – the 25-year-old does have a lot more character and less overbearing spiritiness – but the sweetness veers towards the cooked marmalade of southern French Muscats rather than the honeyed, raisined richness of the Australian versions. You can still occasionally find older wines like *José Maria da Fonseca*'s *1934,* or its intense, pre-phylloxera *Torna Viagem,* with a powerful treacle toffee character balanced by a sharp acidic tang.

PORT (DOURO, DOC) The simplest and cheapest port available in Britain is labelled simply 'Ruby' and 'Tawny'. Ruby is usually blended from the unexceptional grapes of unexceptional vineyards to create a tangy, tough, but warmingly sweet wine to knock back uncritically. It should have a spirity rasp along with the sweetness. Cheap Tawny at around the same price as Ruby is simply a mixture of light Ruby and White ports, and is almost never as good as the Ruby would have been, left to itself.

Calling these inferior concoctions 'Tawnies' is very misleading because there's a genuine 'Tawny', too. Proper Tawnies are kept in wooden barrels for at least five, but preferably ten or more years to let the colour leach out and a gentle fragrance and delicate flavour of nuts, brown sugar and raisins develop. Most of these more expensive Tawnies carry an age on the label, which must be a multiple of 10: 10, 20, 30 or even 40 years old, but the figure indicates a style rather than a true date: a 10-year-old Tawny might contain some 6-year-old and some 14-year-old wine. Lack of age on a Tawny label – however often it says 'Fine', 'Old', and so on – is a bad sign and usually implies a cheap Ruby-based blend, though there are some good brands like *Harvey*'s *Director's Bin Very Superior Old Tawny* or *Delaforce His Eminence's Choice*. Most Tawnies reach their peak at somewhere between 10 and 15 years, and few ports improve after 20 years in barrel, so don't pay inflated prices for 30- and 40-year-old wine. Try *Cockburn 10-year-old*, *Ferreira 10-* and *20-year-old*, *Fonseca 10-* and *20-year-old*, *Harvey*'s *Director's Bin*, *Sainsbury*'s *10-year-old*. *Colheitas* – single-vintage Tawnies – are increasingly available, usually from Portuguese houses, and can be really delicious. *Calem* and *Niepoort* are good.

VINTAGE PORTS are the opposite of the Tawnies, since the object here is to make a big, concentrated rather than delicate mouthful. Vintage years are 'declared' by port shippers when the quality seems particularly good – usually about three times a decade. The wines are matured in wooden casks for two years or so, then bottled and left to age for a decade or two.

The final effect should have more weight and richness than a Tawny of similar age, since the maturation has taken place in the almost airless confines of the bottle, which ages the wines more slowly. There should also be a more exciting, complex tangle of flavours; blackcurrant, plums, minty liquorice, pepper and herbs, cough mixture and a lot more besides. Vintage port you get animated and opinionated about, while Tawny is more a wine for quiet reflection.

If you want a peek at what Vintage port can be like, buy Single-Quinta wine. Single Quintas (or farms) are usually from the best vineyards in the less brilliant years, but instead of being bottled and shipped after only two years or so, they are bottled after two years, stored for up to ten years, and shipped ready to drink. They are usually extremely good. Look for *Taylor*'s *Quinta da Vargellas*, *Dow*'s *Quinta do Bonfim*, *Warre*'s *Quinta da Cavadinha*, *Fonseca*'s *Quinta do Panascal* and *Quinta de la Rosa*.

Another good-value Vintage lookalike is Crusted port. This is a blend of wines from two or three vintages, shipped in cask and bottled slightly later than Vintage, at about three years old, so they retain the peppery attack of the top wines and also keep a good deal of the exotic perfumed sweetness of real 'Vintage'. They are called Crusted because of the sediment that forms after three or four years in bottle. More and more houses are producing Crusted ports, though the current collapse of the Vintage market means that both Crusted and Single Quinta look less good value when you can find the real thing for not much more.

Two other types of port like to think of themselves as vintage style. Vintage Character and Late Bottled Vintage are bottled four to six years after the harvest. Ideally, this extra time maturing in wood should bring about an effect similar to a dozen years of bottle-aging. Bottled at four years, and not too heavily filtered, it still can, but most VC and LB ports are too browbeaten into early decline and have as much personality as a pan of potatoes. The best, labelled with the year of bottling, are from *Fonseca*, *Niepoort*, *Smith-Woodhouse*, *Ramos-Pinto* and *Warre*. They are delicious, but can throw a sediment in the bottle, and may need decanting.

There are two styles of White port, dry and sweet. In general, the flavour is a bit thick and alcoholic, the sweet ones even tasting slightly of rough grape skins. But there are a few good dry ones, though I've never felt any great urge to drink them anywhere except in the blinding mid-summer heat of the Douro valley when they're refreshing with a few ice-cubes and a big splash of lemonade or tonic.

MATURITY CHART

Vintage Ports

1970 and 1977 are top-quality vintages for the long-term.
The 1970 has always been the more forward

1970

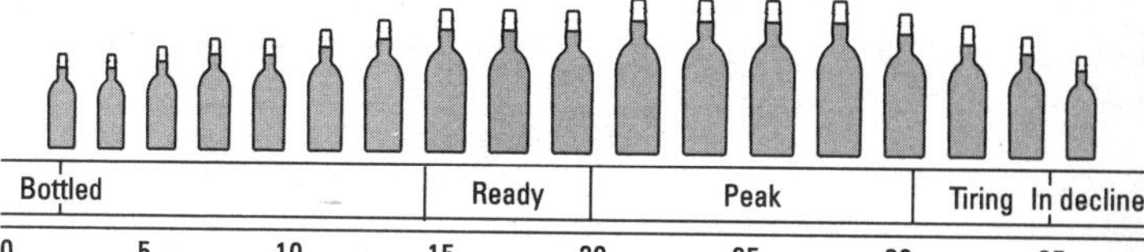

1977

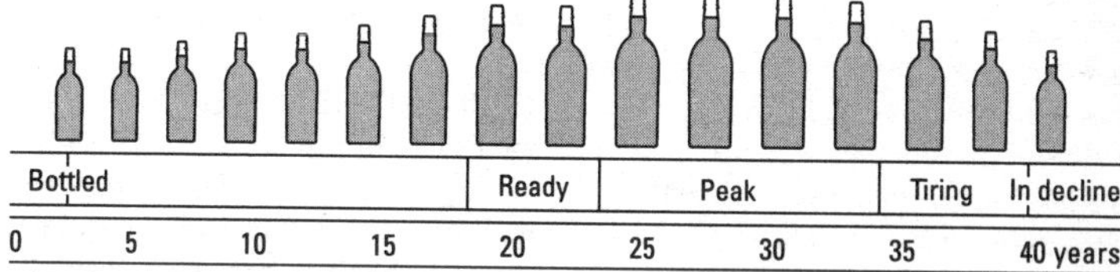

1983 and 1985 are both classic long-lived vintages
with 1985 showing somewhat more fruit

1983

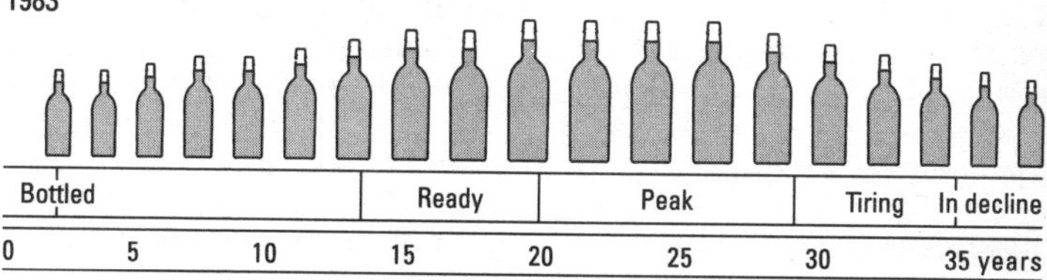

1985

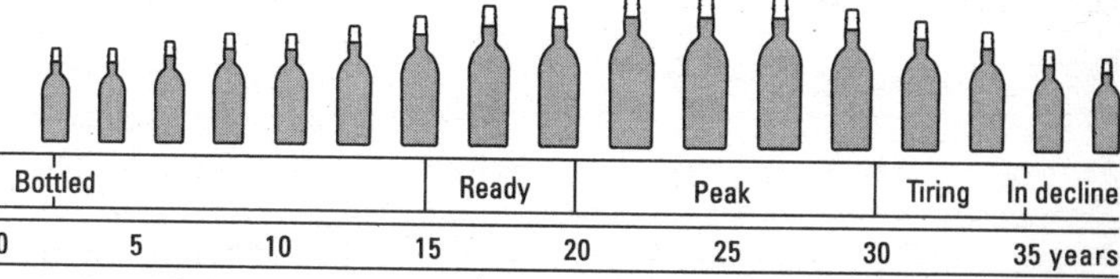

PORT SHIPPER PROFILES

CÁLEM ★★★★ Important Portuguese shipper founded in the last century and still family owned. Cálem produce excellent 10, 20, 30 and 40-year old Tawnies, good Colheitas, and good Vintage port from the spectacular Quinta da Foz at Pinhão.

CHURCHILL GRAHAM ★★★(★) Established in 1981, the first independent port shipper to be founded in more than 50 years. John Graham is establishing a reputation for intense, concentrated wines which are made to last.

COCKBURN ★★★★ Shippers of the best-selling 'Fine Old Ruby' and 'Special Reserve'. At the forefront of research into viticulture in the Upper Douro. Recent Vintage ports have been stunning.

CROFT ★★(★) Quinta da Roêda near Pinhão forms the backbone of its Vintage wines, but many wines are over-delicate.

DELAFORCE ★★(★) The Tawny, His Eminence's Choice, is its best-known wine.

DOW ★★★★★ Quinta do Bomfim at Pinhão produces the backbone of Dow's firm-flavoured, long-living Vintage and has also been launched as a Single Quinta.

FERREIRA ★★★★ One of the best Portuguese-owned shippers, making elegant, early-maturing Vintages and two superb Tawnies; 10-year-old Quinta do Porto and 20-year-old Duque de Bragança. Bought by Sogrape in 1988.

FONSECA GUIMARAENS ★★★★★ Family-run shippers belonging to the Yeatman side of Taylor, Fladgate and Yeatman. Fonseca's wines are sweeter and less austere than Taylor's. The Vintage ports are often outstanding, and the quality of its commercial releases is reassuring.

GOULD CAMPBELL ★★★★ The name is used mainly for Vintage ports which tend to be ripe and mature relatively early.

GRAHAM ★★★★★ Graham's ports tend to be rich and sweet. Quinta dos Malvedos is released as a Single-Quinta wine in lesser vintages. Fine Vintage styles.

NIEPOORT ★★★★★ Tiny firm run by the fourth and fifth generations of a Dutch family who share a total commitment to quality. Aged Tawnies, Colheitas, traditional LBVs and long-lasting Vintage.

OFFLEY FORRESTER ★★★(★) Famous for 'Boa Vista' Vintage and LBV ports. Vintage is mostly based on its own Quinta da Boa Vista and can be insubstantial. Excellent Baron de Forrester Tawnies.

QUINTA DO NOVAL ★★★ A beautiful quinta high above Pinhão as well as a shipper. Noval's Nacional wines, produced from pre-phylloxera, ungrafted vines, are legendary and fetch a stratospheric price at auction. Other Noval wines don't attempt such heights, but are usually good, if light. Noval LB is widely sold, but isn't actually that special; the Tawnies and Colheitas are much better.

RAMOS-PINTO ★★★★ Delicious Tawnies from two quintas – Ervamoira and Bom Retiro. Elegant, nutty and delicate. Now owned by Louis Roederer of Champagne.

REAL VINICOLA ★★ One of the largest port producers, selling ports under seven different names including that of Royal Oporto. They can sometimes be good. Vintage is generally early maturing.

SANDEMAN ★★★ Best at making aged Tawnies and, more recently, improved, quite concentrated vintage wines.

SMITH WOODHOUSE ★★★★ Some delicious Vintage and LBVs. Concentrated Vintage wines which tend to mature early. Full-flavoured Crusted.

TAYLOR, FLADGATE AND YEATMAN ★★★★(★) Very high quality range, but some recent commercial releases have seen standards slip a bit, and their Vintage port is no longer ahead of the field. Quinta de Vargellas is one of the best Single Quintas.

WARRE ★★★★★ The first port company in which the entrepreneurial Symington dynasty became involved. Warre produces serious wines: good LBVs and Vintage, fine 'Nimrod' Tawny. Quinta da Cavadinha has recently been launched as a Single Quinta.

PORT CLASSIFICATION

If you think that Burgundy and Bordeaux make a meal out of classifying their vineyards, just look at how rigidly port is controlled. Nothing is left to chance. The age of the vines is classified on a scale from 0 to 60 points. The level of upkeep of the vines is ruthlessly marked from –500 to +100 points. The objective is to score as many points as possible. The highest possible score would be +1680 points, while the bottom score possible would be a massively embarrassing –3430. The classification, based on points scored, is from A to F, and controls how many litres of juice per 1000 vines can be turned into port. The rest has to be made into table wine, which gives a smaller return.

The Vineyard Calculation

Productivity (Ranging from about 500 litres per 1000 vines to about 2000 litres; the lower the yield the higher the points scored.)
Worst: 0 points Best: +80 points

Altitude (Ranging from a highest allowable altitude of 650 metres to a lowest of 150 metres.)
Worst: –900 points Best: +150 points

Soil (Scored according to type. Schist scores best, granite worst.)
Worst: –350 points Best: +100 points

Geographical position (Predetermined locations score different marks.)
Worst: –50 points Best: +600 points

Upkeep of vineyard (Good housekeeping awards for various factors.)
Worst: –500 points Best: +100 points

Variety and quality of grapes
Worst: –300 points Best: +150 points

Gradient (From 1-in-6 to 1-in-30 – the steeper the better.)
Worst: –100 points Best: +100 points

Shelter
Worst: 0 Best: +70 points

Age of vines (With 5-year-olds scoring 30; up to 25-year-olds scoring 60.)
Worst: 0 Best: +60 points

Distance root to root (The distance from the end of one vine's root to the start of the next root – too close is frowned upon.)
Worst: –50 points Best: +50 points

Nature of land
Worst: –600 points Best: +100 points

Aspect
Worst: –30 points Best: +100 points

THE TOTAL

The experts then add up all these points and classify the vineyards according to score, allowing each group to make a certain number of litres of wine per 1000 vines, as follows:

A (1201 points or more)	600 litres
B (1001–1200 points)	600 litres
C (801–1000 points)	590 litres
D (601–800 points)	580 litres
E (401–600 points)	580 litres
F (400 points or less)	260 litres

PORT VINTAGES

Not every year produces a crop of fine enough quality for vintage-dated wine to be made, and a few houses may not make Vintage port even in a generally good year. It all depends on the quality the individual house has produced, although it is extremely rare for a house to declare two consecutive years. Announcing the intention to bottle Vintage port is known as 'declaring'. Five vintages were good enough in the 1980s, and 1991 looks like being a generally declared year.

1991 At the time of writing it appears that 1991 will be generally declared. A dry summer and an even drier economy mean that quantiites will be small; the Vintage port market is in a poor state at the moment. *Dow*, for example, is declaring half the amount it declared in 1985.

1987 Four shippers, *Ferreira, Martinez, Niepoort* and *Offley*, chose to declare this small but good vintage. Coming so hard on the heels of the nearly universal 1985 declaration, most shippers opted instead for Single Quinta wines for medium term drinking.

1985 Declared by every important shipper. The quality is exceptionally good, and prices have come down, making this a good time to buy (they were extremely high at first). The wines don't quite have the solidity of the 1983s but they make up for this with a juicy ripeness of fruit and unusually precocious signs of perfumes to come. Although *Taylor* isn't as outstanding as usual, several perennial under-achievers like *Croft* and *Offley* are very good, *Cockburn* is very attractive, and *Fonseca* is rich and lush. However, my favourites are *Graham, Warre, Dow, Gould Campbell* and *Churchill Graham*.

1983 Marvellous wine, strong and aggressive to taste at the moment, but with a deep, brooding sweetness which is all ripe, clean fruit. This won't be one of the most fragrant vintages, but it will be a sturdy classic in ten years' time. Again, prices have fallen – buy now.

1982 Not as good as it was at first thought. It begins to look as though those shippers that declared 1982 in preference to 1983 made a mistake. *Croft* and *Delaforce* are already drying out, and most need to be drunk already.

1980 A good vintage, though excessively expensive when first offered. Although they were consequently unpopular, the wines are developing a delicious, drier than usual style. It should be starting to soften now, and will peak about 1995.

1977 Brilliant wine which has hardly begun to mature. The flavour is a marvellous mixture of great fruit sweetness and intense spice and herb fragrance. They will rock you back on your heels if you drink them now, but maybe you like that sort of thing.

1975 These in general don't have the stuffing that a true vintage style demands, but some have surprisingly gained weight and richness and are excellent for drinking now. *Noval, Taylor, Dow, Warre* and *Graham* need no apologies. Most of the others do.

1970 Lovely stuff, but, curiously, only cautiously praised. Fainthearts, take up your corkscrews! This is exceptional, balanced port, already good to drink, very sweet, and ripe with a fascinating citrus flash of freshness. It'll last for ages but it's delicious already. All the top houses are really special – lead by *Fonseca, Taylor, Warre, Graham* and *Dow*, but lesser houses like *Calem* and *Santos Junior* are also excellent.

1966 They didn't rate this at first, but they do now. It's gained body and oomph and is now approaching its best. Doesn't *quite* have the super-ripe balance of the '70 or the startling, memorable character of the '63, but a very good year. *Fonseca* is the star at the moment.

1963 They call it the 'classic' year, and one can see why. It's big, deep, and spicy, with a remarkable concentration of flavours based on any really ripe red or black fruit you can think of washed in an essence of liquorice, mint and herbs. One or two have lost a surprising amount of colour recently, but in the main it's so good that if you decide to see in the millennium with a bottle of *Fonseca, Taylor, Graham, Dow* or *Cockburn*... get my address from *Webster's!*

UNITED STATES

Next time you think you've had an *annus horribilis*, spare a thought for California. They've been having a pretty tricky time for several years now; and it doesn't look like getting any better. Take neo-Prohibitionism, for example. Or rather, don't. Every US winery has to display a warning of the dangers of the demon drink. And now there's phylloxera: the vine disease that destroyed virtually all of Europe's vineyards at the end of the last century, and which was only dealt with by grafting European vines on to resistant American rootstocks, has reappeared in California – and one reason is that the rootstock on which an awful lot of California's vines are planted, called AxR1, is just not resistant enough.

So yes, it's a disaster. Phylloxera has now appeared in 60% of Californian vineyards. There's no cure: the vines have to be uprooted and destroyed, and the land replanted. MKF, the Wine Industry accountants and consultants, believe that production in Napa and Sonoma will fall from the record-breaking crop of 280,000 tons in 1991 to 180,000 tons in 1997. In Napa alone 3700 acres were replanted between 1989 and 1992, and banks will now lend only on current profitability, not future projections. According to the University of California, the cost of replanting is between US$15,000 and $25,000 per acre in the Napa, where the total bill is likely to be in excess of $300 million. When allowance is made for earnings lost while vineyards lie fallow, this figure doubles to $600 million. And it is the smaller producers who will be least able to weather the storm.

However, there is a brighter side to the disaster. With denser plantings and improved viticultural practices, yields from the new vineyards may well be higher after replanting. The range of grape varieties may also broaden, with Rhône and Italian varieties, for so long the preserve of inspired eccentrics like Randall Grahm, now being discovered by growers throughout the state. They are suddenly realising that northern Napa is climatically nearer the Rhône than Bordeaux or Burgundy, so why not grow Syrah?

Merlot goes solo

Even Bordeaux grape addicts are changing their views a little. Merlot, which has always been viewed as an adjunct to Cabernet Sauvignon is now increasingly being given star billing. Some of it is simple, fruity and upfront; some is huge, serious wine of intriguing complexity. Zinfandel, too, has been rehabilitated from the aberration of blush. As ever, Ridge lead the way with this most American of grape varieties, with other good examples coming from Clos du Val and Haywood. And Pinot Noir is becoming firmly established as a rival to red Burgundy. Saintsbury continues to shine, but with strong competition developing from Carneros Creek, Au Bon Climat and Williams-Selyem.

Chardonnay still dominates the white varieties, however. It will take more than phylloxera to separate a California grower from his best-beloved white grape, and Sauvignon Blanc remains very much a secondary variety, although excellent wines are made by Simi. Outside Napa and Sonoma the picture is a bit more varied, though: Mendocino produces excellent Riesling and Gewürztraminer, notably from Handley Cellars and Navarro, and further east in

Yuba County, Renaissance Vineyards produce superb sweet Rieslings. South of San Francisco, Chenin Blanc does well in Monterey County and Rhône varieties like Marsanne, Roussanne and Viognier pop up again. With Randall Grahm turning his sights towards Portugal, who knows what may come next?

In some ways California wine-making is deeply conservative, and the current crisis is challenging that conservatism. For years this has been the home of high-tech wine-making, with wines being produced according to the rules laid down by the oenology department of the University of California at Davis. As it was these academics who recommended the use of the AxR1 rootstock, which lies at the heart of California's current phylloxera problems, it is not surprising that Davis dogma doesn't have quite the cachet it once did. Now, in fact, wineries are increasingly adopting the more traditional methods of the Old World, like the use of wild yeasts, which are less predictable but which can give greater complexity: individuality is increasingly the order of the day.

Despite all its problems California is making progress. Whether the same can be said of other wine-producing regions of the US is another matter. California's main rivals, Oregon and Washington State, both show great promise but still not much more. In the mid-1980s Oregon was viewed as a home from home for Pinot Noir, but the hype was a little premature. Certainly, Oregon can produce excellent wines, but its marginal climate means that the poor vintages outnumber the good ones. Admittedly, the same might be said about Burgundy, but Burgundy has had more practice in coping. Oregon's best Pinot Noirs come from Eyrie, Bethel Heights and, recently, Joseph Drouhin. But by focusing on Pinot Noir Oregon has chosen a difficult path for itself. One can but wish it well. And while Pinot Noir may take all the plaudits, Oregon is also producing excellent Riesling and Pinot Gris.

Washington State is another region with a future but a not terrifically exciting present. The Pinot Noir, Cabernet Sauvignon, Merlot, Riesling, Sémillon and Gewürztraminer from here is all medium-priced and already pretty good; the potential is certainly there. It is just a matter of when Washington will seriously start to perform.

ANDREW WILLIAMS

RED GRAPES & FLAVOURS

BARBERA The Italian variety most grown in California. *Louis M Martini* and *Bonny Doon* are good, as is *Monteviña* with an intense, blackberry-and-black-cherry wine; *Preston Vineyards* (Sonoma County) is also worth a try.

CABERNET SAUVIGNON There was not a single 'bad' vintage in the 1980s. The best vintages of the late 1980s are the '85, '86 and '88, but any of them are good; the '87s are proving very elegant, with subtle, well-balanced flavours and marvellous ripe fruit that often seems to leap out of the glass, which is, of course, the great strength of California Cabernet. Further north in Washington, there are some increasingly good Cabernets, a bit more restrained than California. For serious cellaring, good names are: *Beringer Reserve, Buena Vista, Burgess, Cain, Carmenet Reserve, Caymus, Chimney Rock, Clos du Bois, Clos du Val, Conn Creek, Cuvaison, Diamond Creek, Dunn, Franciscan, Grgich Hills, Groth, Heitz Bella Oaks, William Hill, Inglenook Reserve Cask, Kenwood Artist Series, La Jota, Laurel Glen, Louis M Martini, Robert Mondavi Reserve* and *Opus One, Chateau Montelena, Newton, Raymond Reserve, Ridge Monte Bello, Sequoia Grove, Shafer*

Hillside Select, Stag's Leap Cask 23, Sterling Vineyards Diamond Mountain Ranch, (California); *Ste Chapelle* (Idaho); *Fall Creek Vineyards, Llano Estacado, Messina Hof, Oberhellmann, Pheasant Ridge* (Texas); *Arbor Crest, Hogue Cellars, Chateau Ste Michelle, Staton Hills* (Washington). For a lighter Cabernet quaff, the list is practically endless. Try *Beringer Napa Valley, Caymus Liberty School, Chateau Souverain, Christian Brothers, Clos du Bois, Cosentino, Fetzer, Estancia, Foppiano, Glen Ellen, Kendall-Jackson* (California); *Columbia Crest* (Washington).

MERLOT A lot is blended with Cabernet Sauvignon, and often with Cabernet Franc too. Such Bordeaux blends were christened Meritage (rhymes with heritage) as a sales ploy. Still, there's lots of good varietal Merlot, with that lovely, soft, perfumed fruit. Best are *Cuvaison, Dehlinger, Louis M Martini, Duckhorn, Robert Keenan, Gundlach-Bundschu, Matanzas Creek, Newton, Shafer, Sterling* (California); *Arbor Crest, Leonetti, Hogue, Columbia, Haviland, Paul Thomas* (Washington).

PETITE SIRAH Not the same as the great red Syrah grape of the Rhône or the Shiraz of Australia. It produces big, stark, dry, almost tarry wines – impressive, but usually lacking real style. *Ridge Vineyards* is the exception. In good years *Ridge Petite Sirah* is capable of making real Rhône Syrah blush. The story goes that Gérard Jaboulet of Hermitage carries *Ridge Petite Sirah* to show people the competition.

PINOT NOIR Burgundy's great red grape has not yet made the sea change to the New World with total success. But there are brief flashes of excitement in California and an occasional gleam in Oregon. Good if not great California Pinot Noir comes from the lower cooler reaches of the Russian River Valley in Sonoma County and from Carneros in Napa-Sonoma. But the best is probably in the chalky, dry cliffs of San Benito County (east of Monterey) where *Calera* is located. Other good ones are *Au Bon Climat, Acacia, Bay Cellars* (made from Oregon grapes), *Bonny Doon, Chalone, Carneros Creek, Dehlinger, Iron Horse, Mondavi* (better every vintage), *Rasmussen, Saintsbury, ZD* (California); *Adelsheim, Amity, Chateau Benoit, Robert Drouhin, Eyrie, Forgeron, Knudsen-Erath, Rex Hill, Scott Henry, Sokol-Blosser* (Oregon).

SYRAH/RHÔNE VARIETALS There has been an explosion of interest in the wines of the Rhône in California; they seem in many ways more suited to California's Mediterranean climate than the Bordeaux or Burgundian grapes. Most eyes are on Syrah, but there is also Mourvèdre, Cinsaut, Grenache and Carignan, the last two of which were used in the past in Central Valley jug wines. First results are encouraging, both in public acceptance and in the quality of the wine. Best producers are *Bonny Doon, Duxoup, Kendall-Jackson, La Jota, McDowell Valley, Joseph Phelps Mistral* series, *Qupé, Santino* (California).

ZINFANDEL Its friends keep predicting a surge of interest in red Zinfandel because of the success of the light, sweet white or blush Zins, but so far it hasn't happened. Still, the wine can be good, either in the hearty, almost overpowering style or the lighter 'claret' style. Best of the big Zins are *Cline Cellars, Deer Park, Kendall-Jackson Ciapusci Vineyard, Preston Vineyards Estate, La Jota, A Rafanelli, Ravenswood, Rosenblum, Shenandoah, Joseph Swan.* For a lighter elbow-bender, try *Buehler, Buena Vista, Burgess, Clos du Val, Fetzer, Haywood, Kendall-Jackson Mariah Vineyard, Kenwood, Louis M Martini, Nalle, Quivira, Ridge*. Best for blush are *Amador Foothill, Beringer, Buehler, Ivan Tamas.*

The price guides for this section begin on page 384.

WHITE GRAPES & FLAVOURS

CHARDONNAY Winemakers are learning how to blend different areas for more balanced, rounded wines: offsetting the austerity of Napa Carneros, for example, with the tropical intensity of Sonoma County Russian River (*Louis M Martini*).

American Chardonnay will age, but look for the controlled, balanced fruit of *Acacia, Arrowood, Buena Vista, Beringer, Chalone, Flora Springs, Cuvaison, Dehlinger, Kistler, Mondavi Reserve, Raymond Reserve, Simi, Chateau St Jean* and *Sonoma-Cutrer* (California); *Bridgehampton* (NY); *Prince Michel* (Virginia); *Hogue* (Washington). For more instant gratification, try *Callaway, Clos du Bois, Franciscan, Estancia, Glen Ellen, Matanzas Creek, Kendall Jackson, Morgan, Mirassou, Mondavi non-reserve, Phelps, Monterey, Parducci, Signorello* (yummy), *Wente Bros* (California); *Fall Creek* (Texas); *Chateau Ste Michelle* (Washington).

GEWÜRZTRAMINER Looking up, but California still falls short of Alsace. The problem is that the grape ripens too fast, too soon. A few people are beginning to get it right, making wines with that spiciness that keeps you reaching for another glass. Look for *Adler Fels* (the best New World Gewürz?), *Lazy Creek, Handley Cellars, Rutherford Hill, Obester* (California); *Llano Estacado* (Texas); *Columbia, Chateau Ste Michelle* (Washington).

RIESLING Like Gewürz, most Riesling in California has been planted in the wrong (warm) place. Riesling (in the US called Johannisberg or White) makes a dull wine then; it is the cooler areas of California, Oregon, New York and Washington that are beginning to show what it can do. Best are *Alexander Valley Vineyards, Konocti, Navarro* (California); *Wagner Vineyards* (NY); *Amity* (Oregon); *Chateau Morrisette, Prince Michel* (Virginia); *Hogue Cellars, Columbia Cellars, Chateau Ste Michelle* (Washington).

SAUVIGNON BLANC/FUMÉ BLANC Now being tamed; its tendency to extreme herbal/grassy tastes is now often moulded into complex spicy/appley fruit. If you are a fan of the big, grassy wines, those that smell like a field of new-mown hay, you'll like *Dry Creek Vineyards* Reserve, which carries that about as far as it can go. For more restraint look for *Ferrari-Carano, Hanna, Simi, Robert Mondavi, Newton, Sterling, Chateau St Jean, William Wheeler* (California); *Hargrave* (New York State); *Arbor Crest, Columbia* (Washington).

SÉMILLON Can add complexity to Sauvignon Blanc (*Clos du Val* and *Vichon*, California). For stand-alone Sémillon try *Alderbrook, R H Phillips, Ahlgren, Congress Springs* (California); *Chateau Ste Michelle* (Washington).

MATURITY CHART

1991 Carneros Chardonnay

The best Carneros Chardonnays have the elegance and balance to age well

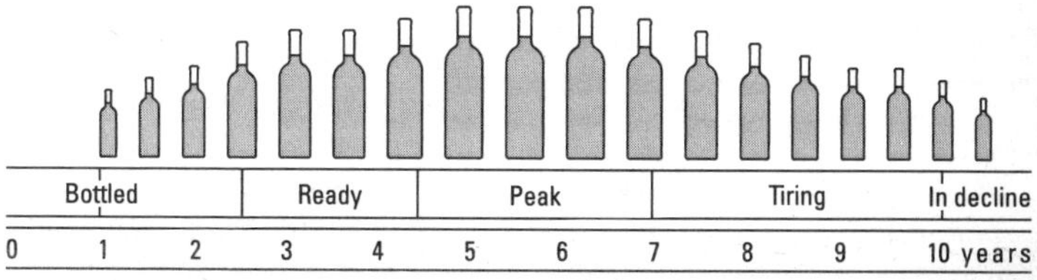

WINE REGIONS

CARNEROS (California) Right at the southern end of the Napa and Sonoma Valleys, snuggled against San Francisco Bay. Breezes from the Bay hold the temperature down and create an ideal climate for Chardonnay and Pinot Noir. Many of California's best Pinot Noirs come from here.

CENTRAL VALLEY (California) Once a vast inland sea, the Central Valley runs from the San Joaquin/Sacramento River Delta in the north to the unappealing flatlands of Bakersfield in the south, from the foothills of the Sierra range in the east to the coastal ranges in the west. It can be 110°F during the day, and hardly cooler at night. It's a brutal life, but with modern techniques there are some decent quaffs.

IDAHO Minor vineyard acreage so far but interesting, promising quality, especially Gewürztraminer, Riesling and Chardonnay. The best hope is for fizz.

LAKE COUNTY (California) Grapes were grown in Lake County (north of Napa County and east of Mendocino County) in the last century; recently there has been a revival of interest with major plantings by *Louis M Martini, Konocti* and *Guenoc*. It's good Cabernet Sauvignon and Sauvignon Blanc territory, with warm days and cool nights, and a very long growing season.

LIVERMORE VALLEY (California) One of California's oldest vine-growing regions, this largely suburban valley, just over the first lap of the Coastal range from San Francisco Bay, has been enjoying a bit of a comeback. It was the first in California to grow Sauvignon Blanc and the century-plus old *Wente Bros* winery in Livermore is increasingly good for that. The region is also proving good for Cabernet. Several small wineries have recently sprung up or been revived; early bottlings are promising.

MENDOCINO COUNTY (California) A rugged, coastal county with one major inland valley north of the Russian River, and several cool east-west valleys running from the interior to the dramatic, rocky coastline. This range of pocket climates makes it possible to grow a range of grapes, with Cabernet Sauvignon at its best in Round Valley in the interior but excellent Riesling, Gewürztraminer, Chardonnay and Pinot Noir doing well in the cool Anderson Valley, where Pacific fog and winds follow the Anderson River inland. This valley is also becoming a leading fizz district, with *Roederer US* making some outstanding bubbly and the tiny *Handley Cellars Brut* one of the best in California.

MONTEREY COUNTY (California) This came late to wine: only in the early '70s did pioneering plantings by *Mirassou* and *Wente Bros* begin to bear fruit. Early Cabernets had a distinct taste of green peppers and other less appealing vegetal smells. Now growers have found more suitable grapes, like Riesling, Chenin Blanc and Pinot Noir. Even Cabernet has made a comeback, on hillsides in the cool Carmel Valley.

NAPA COUNTY (California) There are several important sub-regions within Napa: Calistoga, Carneros, Chiles Valley, Howell Mountain, Mount Veeder, Oakville, Pope Valley, Rutherford, Spring Mountain and Stag's Leap. Some of these are formally designated viticultural regions. This is California's classic wine country. Napa's strong suit is red – Cabernet Sauvignon and Merlot – with Pinot Noir in Carneros.

NEW MEXICO Northern New Mexico grows mostly hybrid grape varieties but some interesting wines are coming from irrigated vineyards in the South. Good producers are *Anderson Valley*, especially for Chardonnay, and a fizz from *Devalmont Vineyards* under the Gruet label.

NEW YORK STATE The big news in New York continues to be Long Island, with outstanding Chardonnay and Pinot Noir. The Chardonnay is very different from those of California, with more austere flavours, a bit like ripe Chablis. There's also decent Chardonnay from the Finger Lakes and the Hudson River Valley. The Lake Erie-Niagara region is lagging behind the other three, with more native grapes. Try *Bridgehampton, Pindar, Brotherhood, Hargrave, Lenz, Le Reve* and *Wagner*.

OREGON Despite all the press attention, Oregon Pinot Noir has never really lived up to its advance notices. The 1987s seemed to be getting on track, but there's still a long way to go. Probably the most successful 'Oregon' Pinots were made by California wineries from Oregon grapes – *Bay Cellars* and *Bonny Doon*. The Chardonnay shows occasional flashes but is, on the whole, a little hard. Oregon's best and most consistent wines so far have been Riesling and Pinot Gris. Good producers for Pinot Gris are *Adelsheim, Eyrie, Knudsen Erath* and *Forgeron*; for Riesling the best are *Amity, Forgeron* and *Oak Knoll*.

SAN LUIS OBISPO COUNTY (California) A Central Coast growing area with the best wines coming from cool regions in canyons opening in from the coast. There are sites here for Pinot Noir, Chardonnay and a few surprising old Zinfandel vineyards. Edna Valley is the chief subregion with a deserved reputation for Chardonnay.

SANTA BARBARA COUNTY (California) This growing region just to the north of Los Angeles is divided into two major subregions, the Santa Maria and Santa Ynez valleys. Both are coastal valleys with openings to the Pacific which means that both day and night are fairly cool. There are some outstanding Pinot Noirs from both regions with some good Sauvignon Blanc and Merlot from the Santa Ynez Valley.

SANTA CRUZ MOUNTAINS (California) Just south of San Francisco, this has lured several people who believe it to be Pinot Noir heaven. Despite some occasional successes, the track record is spotty, but progress is being made. *Bonny Doon, David Bruce, Congress Springs, McHenry* and *Santa Cruz Mountain Winery* have all made Pinot with various degrees of success. Surprisingly, for a cool climate region, some very good Cabernet has been made – notably from *Mount Eden* (not to be confused with Australia's *Mountadam*).

SIERRA FOOTHILLS (California) California's gold country was one of the busiest wine zones in the state in the last century but only a few Zinfandel vineyards survived Prohibition. These are the basis of the area's reputation today, plus good Sauvignon Blanc and Barbera. Sub-regions include Amador County, El Dorado County and Calaveras County. Best are *Amador Foothill Winery, Boeger Winery, Monteviña, Santino* and *Shenandoah Vineyards*.

SONOMA COUNTY (California) On the West Coast, people are beginning to realize that Sonoma's Chardonnay, long in the shade of Napa, need take a back seat to no-one. Sonoma Valley is the main sub-region, but there are many others, in particular Alexander Valley, Chalk Hill, Dry Creek, Knight's Valley, and the Russian River Valley itself (including its sub-region Green Valley). In general, Cabernet and Chardonnay yield the best wines, usually a little fruitier and softer than in Napa.

TEXAS Texas wines continue to amaze. Major regions are the Austin Hills and the Staked Plains region of west Texas, centred around Lubbock. Cabernets from Texas have a drink-me-now rich fruitiness and the Chardonnays and Sauvignon Blancs are looking better every year. In short, it's goodbye Chateau Redneck. Best currently are *Fall Creek, Llano Estacado, Messina Hof, Oberhellmann* and *Pheasant Ridge*.

VIRGINIA Growing good wine grapes in Virginia's hot, humid climate is certainly a man-over-nature drama. Besides the heat and the humidity, there is also the occasional hurricane. Nevertheless, there are some good Rieslings and Chardonnays coming from the state. Top producers are *Chateau Morrisette, Ingleside Plantation* and *Prince Michel*.

WASHINGTON STATE There are those who believe that in the long run, the finest wines from North America may come from Washington State. There is an incredible intensity of fruit right across the board in all varietals that is simply astonishing. When the first serious wines started appearing only about 15 years ago, the best were Riesling and Chardonnay; but most recently, the Cabernets and Merlots can be outstanding, as can the Sauvignon Blanc and Sémillon, varieties which are taken very seriously in Washington. Good wineries: *Arbor Crest, Chateau Ste Michelle, Columbia Cellars, Columbia Crest, Hogue Cellars, Staton Hills.*

WINERY PROFILES

ACACIA ★★★(★) (Carneros/Napa) Acacia continues to produce attractive Pinot Noir and delightfully understated Chardonnay.

ADLER FELS ★★★ (Sonoma) A quirky winery, taking chances that sometimes miss. Outstanding Gewürztraminer and an unusual Riesling fizz that is a treat.

ARROWOOD ★★★(★) (Sonoma) Richard Arrowood was responsible for the great Chateau St Jean Chardonnays of the late 1970s and early 1980s. At his own winery, Cabernet is the best of the range.

AU BON CLIMAT ★★★★ (Santa Barbara) Fine Pinot Noir. The best is soft and approachable, with intense black cherry fruit. Chardonnay can also be impressive.

BEAULIEU VINEYARDS ★★★ (Napa) Beautour label takes up the bulk of production; easy-drinking, stylish 1989 Cabernet Sauvignon is cheap. Top of the range is George de Latour Private Reserve Cabernet, rich, supple and able to age.

BERINGER ★★★★(★) (Napa) This always outstanding performer gets better and better. A fantastic 1986 Cabernet Reserve and 1988 Chardonnay Reserve, but also the low-priced, very drinkable Napa Ridge.

BETHEL HEIGHTS ★★★(★) (Oregon) Impressive, intense Pinot Noirs. The Reserves can be among Oregon's finest.

BONNY DOON ★★★★ (Santa Cruz) Some of the liveliest wines in California. Randall Grahm doesn't make them often enough to polish the edges, but that is part of their appeal. Sometimes he will only make one seat-of-the-pants vintage, and then move on. Buy anything of his, just for fun.

BRIDGEHAMPTON ★★★(★) (New York) A first-class Chardonnay from Long Island vineyards as well as a fresh, light quaffable Pinot Noir and a fruity, forward Merlot.

BUENA VISTA ★★★ (Sonoma/Carneros) A winery that was in the doldrums a decade ago, but is now making well-balanced, elegant wines. Cabernet, Pinot Noir and Riesling can be excellent.

CAKEBREAD CELLARS ★★★ (Napa) Always sound, sometimes outstanding: one of the best Sauvignon Blancs.

CALERA ★★★★(★) (San Benito) The best Pinot Noir in California, according to a lot of critics. It's rich, intense wine. The Jensen Vineyard – named after the family of winemaker Josh Jensen – is the best.

CAYMUS ★★★★ (Napa) The Caymus Cabernets of the early '80s are benchmark California Cab, and later ones show no sign of faltering. Also a good Zinfandel and good value wines under the Liberty School label.

CHALONE ★★★★(★) (Monterey) A reputation for individualistic Pinot Noir and big, buttery Chardonnay. Also some nice Pinot Blanc and Chenin Blanc.

DOMAINE CHANDON ★★(★) (Napa) A producer of consistently good fizz, with the best being Chandon Reserve in magnum. Over-production in the mid-1980s may have hurt, but it seems back on track.

CHATEAU POTELLE ★★★(★) (Napa) Run by two transplanted French wine buffs, Jean Noel and Marketta Fourmeaux. Promising Sauvignon Blanc and Cabernet.

CHATEAU ST JEAN ★★★(★) (Sonoma) A Chardonnay specialist (look for Belle Terre and Robert Young vineyards), with interesting Gewürztraminer, Riesling, Sauvignon Blanc and Cabernet; toying with Mourvèdre, Nebbiolo and Sangiovese.

CHATEAU STE MICHELLE ★★★(★) (Washington) The biggest winery in the North-West makes about half a million cases each of Chateau Ste Michelle and second label Columbia Crest; also owns Snoqualmie winery. Good for Cabernet, Merlot, Chardonnay and Sauvignon Blanc.

CLOS DU BOIS ★★★(★) (Sonoma) Now owned by Hiram Walker-Allied Vintners, Clos du Bois makes consistently good Merlots, Chardonnays and claret-style Marlstone.

CLOS DU VAL ★★★★ (Napa) Bordeaux-trained owner and winemaker Bernard Portet makes silky, elegant, well-balanced reds, with an emphasis on austere fruit. Best wines from this underrated winery are Cabernet Sauvignon and Zinfandel.

COLUMBIA ★★★ (Washington) David Lake's pioneering winery, founded in 1962 by a group of university professors, makes a basketful of varietals including Sémillon, Gewürztraminer, Chardonnay and Riesling (especially Wyckoff vineyard); plus Syrah, soft, peppery Pinot Noir, seductive Merlot (Red Willow vineyard), and surprisingly ripe Cabernet Sauvignon (Otis vineyard).

CUVAISON ★★★ (Napa) Gifted winemaker John Thacher turns first class fruit into elegant, well defined, incisive and balanced wines. The 1990 Chardonnay is a beaut; also good for Merlot, Cabernet Sauvignon and Pinot.

DEHLINGER ★★★★ (Sonoma) Makes one of the best Pinots in North America from cool vineyards along the Russian River Valley County, just a few miles from the Pacific. Also good Cabernets including a good value Young Vine Cabernet.

DOMAINE MUMM ★★★★ (Napa) Early releases of fizz have been outstanding. If quality remains consistent, Domaine Mumm could become one of the best two or three sparkling wines in North America.

DROUHIN ★★★(★) (Oregon) The first few Pinot Noirs have been made with bought-in grapes and are good, but the Drouhin potential will only be seen when its own vines come on stream. The paint is hardly dry at the winery yet.

DRY CREEK VINEYARDS ★★★ (Sonoma) Big, herbal Fumé Blanc loaded with fruit. The reserve bottling ages nicely.

DUCKHORN ★★★ (Napa) Intensely flavoured, deep, rich Merlot and weighty Cabernet.

ELK COVE VINEYARDS ★★★(★) (Oregon) Perhaps the best Pinot Noir in Oregon, with the '86 Estate top of the list.

EYRIE ★★★ (Oregon) David Lett is Oregon's Pinot pioneer. He has spawned a whole industry, and his wines are still some of the best: generally supple, light but flavoursome. Pinot Gris, though, forms the bulk of production.

FALL CREEK VINEYARDS ★★★ (Texas) These wines can hold their heads up anywhere: a delicious Proprietor's Red (Cabernet, Ruby Cabernet, Merlot and Carnelian), a charming Sémillon and a first-rate Cabernet Sauvignon.

FETZER ★★★ (Mendocino) Great value from this large Mendocino producer. Look for Cabernet from Lake County and several different Zinfandels (especially the Ricetti Vineyard). Sundial Chardonnay is tasty.

FLORA SPRINGS ★★★(★) (Napa) Excellent Chardonnay (especially 1990) and a three-way blend of both Cabernets and Merlot called Trilogy. Soliloquy is a creamy, rich, floral white that belies its Sauvignon Blanc base.

FOPPIANO ★★★ (Sonoma) Has been around since the end of Prohibition. In the last ten years it has made outstanding Cabernet Sauvignon and a good if low-key Pinot Noir. Really good Cabernets from Fox Mountain Vineyard.

FRANCISCAN ★★★★ (Napa) Has had a complete turnaround in recent years. Best wines are the rich, lush Cabernets with delicious, forward fruit flavours and complex, barrel-fermented Chardonnay. Estancia is a good value second label.

HANDLEY CELLARS ★★★★ (Mendocino) Very good Chardonnay from family-owned vineyards in Sonoma's Dry Creek Valley and a terrific Brut sparkler that some say is one of the best in the West.

HEITZ ★★★ (Napa) The Martha's Vineyard Cabernet Sauvignon has a devoted following and fetches high prices, but it seems a bit of a dinosaur compared with the elegant, sleek Cabernets of today.

IRON HORSE ★★★★ (Sonoma) Terrific racy, incisive fizz, and now engaged in a joint venture with Laurent-Perrier of Champagne. Very good Pinot Noir and Chardonnay. A Sangiovese/Merlot blend (Mergiovese) is on the drawing board and looking terrific. Second label: Tin Pony.

JORDAN ★★★★ (Sonoma) A rich, ripe Cabernet Sauvignon that ages well and a plausible 'wannabe Meursault' Chardonnay from this French lookalike winery in northern Sonoma. A sparkling wine called J was released in the spring of 1991.

KENDALL-JACKSON ★★★ (Lake) Owns what is probably the biggest Chardonnay vineyard in the world (1200 acres) in Santa Barbara. Chardonnay is smooth, rich, sometimes spicy, invariably seamless; Proprietor's Grand Reserve intense and buttery. Juicy Sauvignon Blanc and rather dense Pinot Noir.

KENWOOD ★★★(★) (Sonoma) A consistent producer of well above-average quality. The Jack London and Artist series Cabernets are outstanding, as is the Zinfandel and Sauvignon Blanc.

LAUREL GLEN ★★★★(★)(Sonoma) Big, fruit-packed Cabernet for long keeping. But Patrick Campbell is no meek follower of Bordeaux orthodoxy, and is contemplating the addition of Syrah, Sangiovese or Mourvèdre for a unique Californian style.

LOUIS MARTINI ★★★★ (Napa) A delightful range, from simple varietals to single vineyards. Sensationally drinkable Gamay Beaujolais; lively, fruity Barbera; very good Merlot; some glorious Cabernet Sauvignons (1985 Monte Rosso) that age well; excellent Petite Sirah; complex Pinot Noir and a rich, ripe Gewürz.

MAYACAMAS ★★★ (Napa) A reputation in the past for big, hard Cabernets that would take decades to come around. There are signs that the reputation is justified, but a lot of people are still waiting.

ROBERT MONDAVI ★★★★(★) (Napa) Mondavi's major strength is in reds: both the straight and Reserve Cabernets are among the best in the world, though Opus One reds seem to lack the Reserve's intensity.

NEWTON ★★★★ (Napa) Excellent, reasonably priced Chardonnay; cedary, cinnamon-spiced Cabernet and increasingly succulent Merlot.

PHELPS ★★★ (Napa) Best here is the Insignia Vineyard Cabernet Sauvignon but exciting things are happening with Rhône grapes, particularly Syrah, released under the Mistral label. Also a nice light touch with that most civilized of wines, Riesling.

PHEASANT RIDGE ★★(★) (Texas) Quite good Chardonnay and Sémillon; promising Cabernet Sauvignon in recent vintages.

RIDGE ★★★★(★) (Santa Clara) Benchmark Zinfandel. The Monte Bello Cabernets are also remarkable, with great balance and long-lasting, perfumed fruit. Petite Sirah from York Creek is brilliant, under-valued and under-appreciated.

ROEDERER★★★★ (Mendocino County) The Champagne house promises to produce California's best fizz.

SAINTSBURY ★★★★ (Napa) A young Carneros winery with a growing reputation for Pinot Noir and Chardonnay. Garnet, from young Pinot Noir vines, is delicious.

SANFORD WINERY ★★★ (Santa Barbara) At its best, Sanford Pinot Noir can be a real treat, with spicy, lush, intense fruit. Good Sauvignon and Chardonnay.

SCHRAMSBERG ★★★★ (Napa) The best fizz in California can still come from here, but the challengers are rapidly gaining ground. The vintage sparklers age beautifully into lush, rich wines.

SHAFER ★★★(★) (Napa) Very good, long-lived Cabernet Sauvignon and Merlot from hillside vineyards.

SIMI ★★★★ (Sonoma) Rich, sometimes voluptuous, always reliable Chardonnay; a touch of botrytis (as in 1989) intensifies the style. Concentrated Cabernets can be drunk young, but really need time. Reserves are excellent, as is Sauvignon Blanc.

SONOMA-CUTRER ★★★★ (Sonoma) Chardonnay from three different Russian River vineyards. The Les Pierres is a restrained classic made to age. Russian River Ranches is more forward and fruity while the Cutrer is rich, full and more in the California tradition.

STAG'S LEAP WINE CELLARS ★★★(★) (Napa) Fine, elegant Chardonnay with lean, appley fruit. The Cabernets, with which this winery made its reputation, seemed to be missing a beat for a few years, but the straight 1987 bottling indicated a welcome turn for the better.

ROD STRONG VINEYARDS ★★★(★) (Sonoma) At this much underrated winery on the Russian River, Rod Strong makes some very fine Cabernet Sauvignon and Pinot Noir from river-terrace vineyards.

TREFETHEN ★★(★) (Napa) Consistently good middle-of-the road Cabernet and Chardonnay. Best is a dry Riesling, one of the state's finest. Best value are the Eshcol reds and whites.

ZD WINES ★★★ (Napa) Cabernet Sauvignon, Pinot Noir and Chardonnay of great intensity and depth. The Pinot Noir, especially, seems to improve each vintage.

AUSTRALIA

It looked as if Australia's luck had run out earlier this year – not in Britain, where sales are still rising at a staggering rate, but in the vineyards themselves, where the vintage was running late absolutely everywhere. And it wasn't just a week here, ten days there: by early March it was five weeks late in some regions. And boy, it was cold for Australia. I was in Melbourne in the second week of March and temperatures were lower than they were in London (admittedly it was unseasonably warm in London, but even so).

It wasn't just the cold either; it had been the wettest season for 20 years and the result was a bad bout of downy mildew. It wouldn't have bothered a French grower, or even a Hunter Valley one, but there were growers and winemakers in South Australia who hadn't ever seen mildew on grapes before. Obviously they didn't have preventative spray programmes, but even those who did found themselves in difficulties when the sprays began to run out throughout the state and simply couldn't be obtained anywhere – not even for ready money.

I could go on with this litany, but the fact is that on the brink of disaster in late March, the grape-ripening sunshine and warmth finally arrived and continued throughout April, especially in key areas of South Australia.

The size of the harvest is down overall, but quality in the Barossa Valley and McLaren Vale is good, sometimes very good, and in Coonawarra, Padthaway and Adelaide Hills it is exceptional, because the reduction in volume and the long, slow ripening concentrated the flavours. Other regions, too, are upbeat: the Hunter has been compensated for its disappointing 1992, with sound quality and average quantities; volumes are down in Western Australia, but quality is top-class; and the Yarra Valley and other southern regions of Victoria (despite my springtime experience) have ended up with fine quality, if not as much of it as they would have liked. And that, in the end, is the hard-luck bit of the story. Almost every region ended up with a smaller crop than it wanted – wanted in order to keep up with rising demand, above all from Britain.

Australia, we love you

Australia has been flavour of the month here for something like 80 months now and there are no signs of any let up: sales are still increasing by 75 per cent a year; Australian wine has overtaken Spanish and, at its current pace, is closing on Italy. That only leaves France and Germany to go – and France, now that its own sales have slipped significantly, has belatedly woken up to the fact. There has been glossy press advertising on behalf of French appellation wines for the first time since 1988, and high-powered delegations have been over from Bordeaux to quiz journalists about where and why their wines are going wrong in the British market.

If they looked at Australia they would know the answer. It's not just that Australia delivers recognizable, pronounceable varietal wines (Chardonnay, Sémillon, Riesling, Cabernet, Shiraz, Pinot Noir *et al*) and bouncy, approachable fizz; it's that Australia delivers reliable quality and bags of flavour every time. You can spend £3 or £12 a bottle, buy a blend, a varietal, a brand of a small estate wine, and know you are not going to feel cheated. Prices progress logically through the range on the shelves and price increases come through in an orderly way. There is none of this shortsighted European business of saying 'Okay, small crop: we're going to double the prices immediately.'

That said, you need to prepare yourself for some price increases this autumn and early in 1994. Penfolds (owner of Lindemans, Wynns, Tollana, Seppelt, Rouge Homme, Koonunga and others) has already put up the prices of some of its premium reds (after three years without an increase) and says it will have 'real problems' supplying wines at under £3 in 1994. (If you didn't know that Penfolds sold wines at £3, look at the small print on some of the supermarket Australian Red and Dry White labels.)

It will be shame to see the end of the £3 Australian bottle; on the other hand, the pressure on supplies is keeping the innovative spirit up. From the consumer's point of view, 1993 has been a year for discovering sensational limited production Shiraz from blocks of old vines in the Barossa Valley; Brown Brothers released its deliciously juicy red Tarrango (a crossing of Touriga Nacional and Sultana grapes) for the first time in Britain; and the first two fully EC-accredited organic Australian wines, including a Chardonnay/Sauvignon blend, are coming into Safeway from Penfolds.

Delicious dry Rieslings are popping up everywhere (although not always under that name); and, assuming that the EC ban on third country botrytized wines is finally lifted in 1993, we could all be drinking some gorgeous sweet Sémillons and Rieslings this Christmas – and maybe even the odd bottle of botrytized Chardonnay. I can think of worse ways to celebrate. **Joanna Simon**

WHITE GRAPES & FLAVOURS

CHARDONNAY Several leading winemakers admit they haven't yet mastered this – but that merely whets the taste-buds because already some are world-class. Oaking – sometimes by means of oak chips – is the rule for all but the cheapest.

Often the wine is a shockingly bright gold-yellow, and the fruit rich but not too lush; a suggestion of ripe apples, melons, figs or pineapples, with savoury toastiness from the wood. The one major criticism is that acidity levels need to be raised in some of the very warm regions and this is not always done subtly enough, leaving a slight lemon-peel citric flavour. The wines mature quickly – two years is often enough – but don't fade too fast. Best: *Arrowfield* (Hunter), *Basedow* (SA), *Capel Vale* (Capel Vale, WA), *Coldstream Hills* (Yarra), *Dalwhinnie* (Victoria), *Dromana* (Mornington), *Eden Ridge* (Adelaide Hills), *Evans Family* (Hunter), *Evans & Tate* (Margaret & Swan Rivers), *Hardy's* (Padthaway), *Tim Knappstein* (Lenswood), *Krondorf Show Chardonnay* (Barossa), *Lake's Folly* (Hunter), *Leeuwin Estate* (Margaret River), *Lindemans* (Padthaway), *Moss Wood* (Margaret River), *Mountadam* (Adelaide Hills), *Nicholson River* (Gippsland), *Penfolds* (Padthaway), *Penley Estate* (Coonawarra), *Petaluma* (Adelaide Hills), *Pierro* (Margaret River), *Piper's Brook & Tasmanian Wine Co* (Tasmania), *Rosemount Show Reserve* and *Roxburgh* (Hunter), *Rouge Homme* (SA), *Orlando St Hilary* (Barossa), *St Huberts* (Yarra), *St Leonards* (NE Victoria), *Shaw & Smith* (Adelaide Hills), *Stafford Ridge* (Adelaide Hills), *Stoniers Merricks* (Mornington), *Tarrawarra* (Yarra), *Tyrrell* (Hunter Valley), *Wynns* (Coonawarra), *Yarra Yering* (Yarra Valley).

CHENIN BLANC This ripens to a much fuller, fruitier and blander style than its steelier Loire counterpart. *Moondah Brook* (Swan Valley) do a good example.

GEWÜRZTRAMINER Called Traminer, this is planted mostly in South Australia and New South Wales. Blowsy and spicy, it is often added to Riesling for a tasty, commercial blend. In cool parts of Victoria, it can be sublimely scented and delicate. *Delatite* and *Lillydale* are excellent, but the best yet is from *Brown Bros'* new high-altitude vineyard at Whitlands. In South Australia *Orlando* does well in the Eden Valley, as does *Tolley* in the Barossa.

MARSANNE In Central Victoria, both *Chateau Tahbilk* and *Mitchelton* have made big, broad, ripe Marsanne.

MUSCAT There are two types of Australian Muscat: first, the 'bladder pack' *Fruity Gordo*, which in English becomes bag-in-box Muscat of Alexandria – fruity, sweetish, swigging wine, from a heavy-cropping lowish-quality grape grown in irrigated vineyards along the Murray River; second, Liqueur Muscat, made from the Brown Muscat, a strain of the top quality Muscat à Petits Grains, grown in north-east Victoria. It is a sensation: dark, treacly even, with a perfume of strawberry and honeyed raisins. Best producers include *All Saints, Bailey's, Bullers, Campbells, Yalumba, Chambers, Morris* and *Stanton & Killeen*.

RIESLING The true German Riesling is always called Rhine Riesling in Australia, where it is the most widely-planted noble white grape. In the Barossa Valley of South Australia it usually makes off-dry wine, with appley fruit and a decent lick of lemony acidity. But Australia also makes some of the world's greatest dry Riesling – a steely, slaty wine, full, but flecked with limey acidity, which after a few years develops strong, petrolly aromas. This comes from the hills above Adelaide and the Barossa – at Springton, Eden Valley, Clare (especially good) and Pewsey Vale. The Coonawarra, Western Australia and cool-climate areas of Victoria make equally exciting dry Riesling. There are also some sweet, botrytis-affected Rieslings from the Barossa and Adelaide Hills. Top names: *Leo Buring, Orlando, Yalumba/Hill-Smith* (Barossa); *Leconfield, Wynns* (Coonawarra); *Petaluma* (with Clare fruit), *Jim Barry, Tim Knappstein, Mitchell, Pike* (Clare); *Brown Bros* (Whitlands); *Delatite, Diamond Valley, Lillydale* (Victoria); *Moorilla Estate* and *Pipers Brook* (Tasmania).

SAUVIGNON BLANC Sauvignon Blanc has caught on in a big way – mostly in South Australia, with one or two bright spots in Victoria. It overripens quickly, though, becoming oily, flat and fruitless. Nonetheless, there is some good stuff from *Jim Barry* (Clare), *Saltram* (Barossa Valley), *Hardy's Collection, Lindemans* (Padthaway), *Hill-Smith* (Adelaide Hills), *Primo Estate* and *Wirra Wirra* (McLaren Vale), *Yalumba* (Oxford Landing) and *Stafford Ridge*, all in South Australia; *Taltarni* and *Tisdall* in Victoria, *Katnook* (Coonawarra) and *Alkoomi, Cullens* and *Goundrey* in Western Australia.

SÉMILLON At its finest in Australia. An excellent blender – fattening up the lean flavours of Sauvignon, and broadening a less than top Chardonnay. By itself, the greatest examples are from the Hunter Valley and Western Australia, where it starts slowly, building into a magnificent strong white full of mineral, toasted nut, herb and honey flavours. South Australia makes a less majestic, more modern style. Best: *Lindemans, McWilliams, Peterson, Rothbury, Sutherland, Tyrrell* (NSW), *Tim Adams, Basedow, Grosset, Hamilton, Hardy's, Hill-Smith, Mount Horrocks, Penfolds, Yalumba* (SA), *Brown Bros, Morris, Yarra Ridge* (Victoria), *Cape Mentelle, Chateau Xanadu, Moss Wood, Sandstone* (WA). It also makes a sweet, noble-rot-affected wine: *De Bortoli, Rosemount* (NSW), *Basedow, Wolf Blass, Peter Lehmann* (SA) and *Rumbalara* (Granite Belt).

RED GRAPES & FLAVOURS

CABERNET SAUVIGNON A top quality variety here, but can be grown well even in the irrigated riverlands where high yields produce an attractive, gently blackcurranty wine. Blackcurrant is the key to Australian Cabernet, and it is at its most splendid in Western Australia, SA's Southern Vales and cooler parts of Victoria, and at its most delicately balanced in South Australia's Coonawarra. Top producers: *Bowen Estate* (Coonawarra), *Brown Bros, Chateau Le Amon, Chateau Tahbilk, Coldstream Hills, Dromana Estate, Delatite, Hollick, Mildara* (Coonawarra), *Mount Langi-Ghiran, Parker Estate, Penley Estate* (Coonawarra), *Plantagenet* (Margaret River), *Seppelt's Drumborg, Seville Estate, St Huberts, Tisdall Mount Helen, Yarra Yering* (Victoria), *Capel Vale Cape Mentelle, Leeuwin Estate, Moss Wood, Vasse Felix* (WA), *Chateau Reynella, Grosset, Katnook, Leconfield, Lindeman's St George* and *Pyrus, Geoff Merrill, Orlando, Penfolds, Petaluma, Pike, Pirramimma, Rosemount, Shottesbrooke, Wirra Wirra, Wolf Blass, Wynns Coonawarra* and *John Riddoch, Brokenwood, Lake's Folly, Peterson, Moorilla Estate, Pipers Brook* (Tasmania), *Basedow* (SA), *Peter Lehmann* (SA), *Mitchelton* (Vic), *Goundrey* (WA).

PINOT NOIR As in the rest of the world, a thoroughly troublesome variety. However, there are signs that a distinctly Australian flavour is starting to emerge which is quite different from the overworked Burgundian model. At its best, it is remarkably perfumed, and has big, soft, rather glyceriny flavours of plum and cherry, mint and even honey. We may not see *many* great Australian Pinot Noirs, but those that we do see will be among the finest in the world. Top producers: *Moss Wood* (WA), *Bannockburn, Coldstream Hills, Delatite, Dromana Estate, Giaconda, Mount Mary, St Huberts, Yarra Yering* (Victoria), *Rothbury, Tyrrells* (NSW), *Moorilla Estate, Pipers Brook, Heemskerk* (Tasmania) and *Wignalls* (Mount Barker), *Mountadam* (SA) and *Tarrawarra* (Victoria).

SHIRAZ This marvellous grape (the Syrah of France) can make sensational wine in Australia, and yet is generally used as a bulk-producing makeweight. Yet even at its most basic level, it will produce juicy, chunky reds in enormous quantities. Often blended with Cabernet Sauvignon for richness. *Penfolds' Grange Hermitage* shows just how successful this blend can be. Also good is *Lindemans' Coonawarra Limestone Ridge*. By itself, Shiraz has a brilliant array of flavours from leathery, deep wines, full of dark chocolate, liquorice and prunes intensity to a rich, spicy, plums and coconut, blackcurrant lusciousness that is most unusual in a dry red wine – and delicious! Top producers: *Bailey's, Best's, Cathcart Ridge, Chateau Le Amon, Chateau Tahbilk, Dalwhinnie, Hanging Rock, Montara, Mount Langi-Ghiran, Redbank, Wynns Coonawarra, Yarra Yering* (Victoria), *Cape Mentelle, Plantagenet* (WA), *Tim Adams, Basedow, Bowen, Coriole, Penfolds, Orlando* (SA), *Drayton, Lindemans, Rosemount, Rothbury, Tyrrell* (NSW), *Bannockburn* (Victoria), *Cape Mentelle* (Margaret River), *Capel Vale* (Capel Vale, WA), *Jasper Hill* (Bendigo), *Charles Melton* (Barossa), *Coriole* (Southern Vales), *Jim Barry's The Armagh* (Clare Valley), *St Hallett Old Block* (Barossa Valley), *Penley Estate* (Coonawarra), *Henschke, David Wynn Patriarch, Hardy's Eileen Hardy, Mount Hurtle* (all SA), *De Bortoli* (Yarra) and the *Rockford Basket Press* from the Barossa Valley.

The price guides for this section begin on page 391.

WINES & WINE REGIONS

ADELAIDE HILLS (South Australia) An ill-defined, but top quality, high altitude zone east of Adelaide. First-class vineyards for cool-climate whites include *Orlando*'s *Steingarten*, *Mountadam* and *Yalumba*'s *Heggies*, *Pewsey Vale* and *Petaluma*,whose '*Croser*' fizz is one of Australia's best.

BAROSSA VALLEY (South Australia) A large, well-known zone where various of the greatest companies are established – *Basedow, Leo Buring, Hill-Smith, Orlando, Penfolds, Seppelt, Tollana, Wolf Blass* and *Yalumba*. They process a huge amount of fruit, 75 per cent of it from outside the Barossa. In Australia trucking grapes, juice or wine hundreds of miles for blending is fine – so long as you tell people.

BENDIGO (Victoria) This 19th-century wine region, destroyed by phylloxera, has been re-planted and produces excellent Cabernet Sauvignon, good Shiraz and some Pinot Noir. *Balgownie* is the leader, with *Chateau Le Amon, Craiglee, Harcourt Valley, Heathcote, Mount Ida, Passing Clouds* and *Yellowglen* also important.

CANBERRA DISTRICT (ACT) Within the Australian Capital Territory, Canberra boasts a number of modest wineries producing wines to match.

CENTRAL VICTORIA Goulburn Valley is the most important vineyard area, with *Chateau Tahbilk* producing big old-style Shiraz and Cabernet, and some interesting white Marsanne. *Tisdall* makes superbly fruity Cabernet Sauvignon, Chardonnay and Sauvignon Blanc; *Mitchelton* is also good. The *Delatite* vineyards at Mansfield produce delicate whites and remarkably intense reds in cool-climate conditions.

CLARE VALLEY (South Australia) A warm area north of Adelaide, first planted with red grapes, but now making more fine whites, in particular a deftly fragrant style of Rhine Riesling and soft, attractively grassy Sauvignon; Chardonnay is gentle and good. Best exponents: *Jim Barry, Tim Knappstein, Horrocks, Mitchells* and *Pike* but many Barossa wineries use Clare fruit, and *Petaluma* and *Wolf Blass* have vines there. *Tim Adams, Jeffrey Grosset, Tim Knappstein, Leasingham* and *Wendouree* produce the best reds.

COONAWARRA (South Australia) One of the most carefully defined wine zones in Australia, and perhaps the most famous. Incredibly fertile and planted to the hilt, this streak of red soil is about 14.5km long and between 1.5km and 200 metres wide. Cabernet Sauvignon is the main variety, characterized by a soft, blackcurranty fruit turning cedary with age. Shiraz is good, as are Merlot and Malbec. There are also some beautifully stylish Rhine Rieslings and Chardonnays. Best names: *Bowen Estate, Brand's Laira, Hardy / Chateau Reynella, Hollick, Katnook, Leconfield, Lindemans' Limestone Ridge* and *St George, Mildara, Orlando, Petaluma, Penfolds, Rosemount, Seppelt, Penley Estate* and *Wynns*.

GEELONG (Victoria) The best wines are dark, intensely-flavoured Cabernets from vineyards like *Idyll* and *Bannockburn*, Pinot Noir from *Prince Albert* and *Bannockburn* and whites from *Idyll*.

GLENROWAN (Victoria) Famous for the the great wines produced by *Bailey's* – torrid, palate-blasting reds from Cabernet Sauvignon and Shiraz (called Hermitage locally) and, more importantly, Liqueur Muscats. These are intensely sweet, seeming to distil the very essence of the overripe brown Muscat grape, as well as adding an exotic tangle of orange and honey. At Milawa, *Brown Brothers* makes a wide range of good table wines and fortifieds, but its best wines are from the Koombahla vineyard in King Valley, and the high altitude Whitlands site.

GRANITE BELT (Queensland) The Granite Belt sits on a plateau about 1000 metres up: altitude and southern latitude allow grapes to be grown in a banana, pineapple and mango belt. Most wines serve the captive local markets and some (*Ballandean, Koninos Wines, Rumbalara, Robinsons Family* and *Stone Ridge*) are good. *Ironbark Ridge* is one to watch.

GREAT WESTERN (Victoria) Historic area best known as the original source of base wine for Australia's celebrated fizz – *Seppelt's Great Western* – but more exciting for the quality of its reds. The Shiraz is outstanding, full of chocolate, coconut and cream flavours as at *Cathcart Ridge*, or dry, liquoricy and with impressive pepperiness as at *Mount Langi-Ghiran*. *Best's, Montara* and *Seppelt* are other top producers. There is also excellent Chardonnay from *Best's* and *Seppelt,* and good Cabernet Sauvignon from *Mount Langi-Ghiran* and 'Vintage port' from *Montara*.

HUNTER VALLEY (New South Wales) Leading NSW wine region, making great wines. Hunter reds are traditionally based on Shiraz (Hermitage) and whites on Sémillon. Both can age better than almost any other Australian wines. The Shiraz used to be notorious for a 'sweaty saddle' sulphurous flavour when young which disappeared with time to give a gentle, buttery, smoky flavour. The Sémillon often ages even better, starting out crisp and straightforward but over 10 to 15 years developing a luscious, honeyed nuttiness, tempered by a vaguely old-Riesling, oily, herby character. Nowadays riper Sémillon grapes are giving a more immediately attractive style. Cabernet and Chardonnay are both successful here. Pinot Noir, especially from *Rothbury* and *Tyrrell* can be very fine, and there's even some good Traminer and some sweet wine, from botrytis-affected Sémillon.

The valley is in two halves. Upper Hunter is a recent, irrigated development, dominated by *Rosemount*, but *Arrowfield Simon Whitlam* and *Simon Gilbert* labels can also be good. The region is basically a white wine producer, but on the whole Cabernet Sauvignon has fared much better than Shiraz. Lower Hunter is the traditional quality area. Best producers: *Allandale, Brokenwood, Evans Family, Hungerford Hill, Lake's Folly, Lindeman, McWilliams, Peterson, Rothbury Estate, Saxonvale, Sutherland, Tyrrell*.

LOWER GREAT SOUTHERN (Western Australia) A vast, rambling area dotted with vineyards of considerable promise, especially in the zone round Mount Barker. *Alkoomi, Forest Hill, Goundrey, Howard*

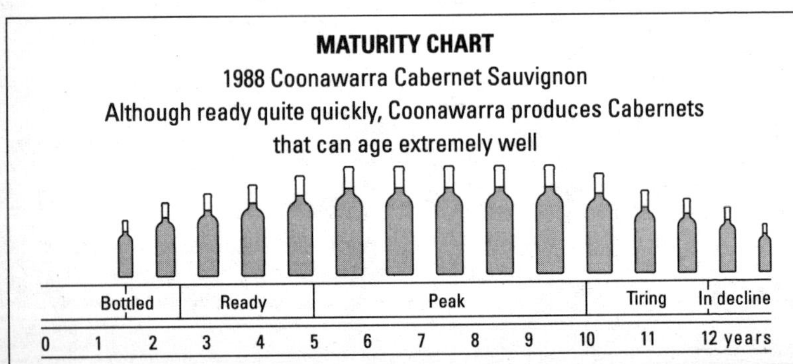

Park and *Plantagenet* are good. The whites are fragrant and appetizing, with zesty Riesling and Sauvignon Blanc, but the reds are even more exciting, with particularly spicy, tobaccoey Cabernet Sauvignons.

MARGARET RIVER (Western Australia) There has been an astonishing number of superb wines from this area. Foremost among them are *Cape Mentelle, Cullens, Leeuwin Estate, Moss Wood, Sandalford, Redgate* and *Vasse Felix*. At their best, the Margaret River Cabernets exhibit magnificent fruit with a streak of grassy acidity and are as good as top-line Classed Growths in Bordeaux. Pinot Noir also does well sometimes. Chardonnay is increasingly barrel-fermented and shows enormously rich flavours, balanced by acidity and toasty oak. Sémillon is frequently now made in an apple-fresh, but weighty style – though old-style Sémillons age superbly. There is also some port-style wine and *Happ's* have planted traditional Portuguese varieties which are looking interesting.

MCLAREN VALE (South Australia) Important area just south of Adelaide. Originally known for thick, heavy reds, it has recently begun to make beautifully balanced reds and whites of positively cool-climate style. Great Cabernet, Shiraz and Chardonnay have already been produced, and much fine Sauvignon Blanc and Sémillon, too. Good producers: *Blewitt Springs, Chateau Reynella, Coriole, Hardy's, Richard Hamilton, Geoff Merrill, Middlebrook, Pirramimma, Ryecroft, Shottesbrooke, Wirra Wirra, Woodstock*.

MORNINGTON PENINSULA (Victoria) One of the coolest wine zones of Australia, Mornington Peninsula is a weekend playground for the rich of Melbourne. It has a patchwork of 80 vineyards and relatively small wineries, among the best of which are *Dromana, Stoniers Merricks* and *Moorooduc Estate*.

MUDGEE (New South Wales) Capable of producing good table wines owing to a late spring and cold nights. Though established on Shiraz (*Montrose* is outstanding) the best reds have been deep, tarry, plummy Cabernets. But Chardonnay is even more successful, usually made rich, soft and full of fruit-salad flavours. Look for *Montrose, Craigmoor, Huntington, Miramar*.

MURRUMBIDGEE IRRIGATION AREA (New South Wales) Known as the MIA, this vast irrigated area centred round Griffith provides between 15 and 20 per cent of the total Australian crop. Most of it is bulk wine blended by various companies in various states, but *McWilliams* makes some attractive wines, as does *de Bortoli*, including a Sauternes-style Sémillon.

PADTHAWAY (South Australia) An increasingly important high-quality area, especially for whites, notably Chardonnay, Rhine Riesling and Sauvignon Blanc. Established in the 1960s when pressure on land in Coonawarra forced major wineries to look elsewhere. Padthaway was chosen because it also had some of the 'terra rossa' soil which makes Coonawarra so special. Grapes are grown here for sparkling wine, and there is some exceedingly good sweet Riesling. Best: *Hardy's, Lindemans, Seppelt*; major producers such as *Orlando* and *Penfolds* also use the grapes.

'PORT' Shiraz and other Rhône-type grapes are often used to make exceptionally high-quality 'port'. The 'Vintage ports' are wonderful. Top names include: *Lindemans, Montara, Penfolds, Saltram, Seppelt, Stanton & Killeen, Yalumba*.

PYRENEES (Victoria) An area north-west of Melbourne, producing very dry Shiraz and Cabernet reds, and primarily Sauvignon whites. Top names: *Dalwhinnie, Mount Avoca, Redbank, Taltarni, Warrenmang*, and for sparkling wines, *Chateau Remy* and *Taltarni*.

RIVERLAND (South Australia) The grape basket of Australia – a vast irrigation project on the river Murray providing 38 per cent of the national crop. Dominated by the three highly efficient *Berri, Renmano* and *Angoves* wineries, it makes enormous amounts of bag-in-box wines of consistently good quality. But it also yields fresh, fruity Rhine Riesling, Chardonnay, Sauvignon, Colombard, Chenin, Cabernet and Shiraz.

RUTHERGLEN (Victoria) The centre of the fortified wine tradition. The white table wines are generally dull, except for some consistently fine wines from *St Leonards*. The reds are rich and robust. The fortified wines, either as *solera*-method 'sherries', as 'Vintage ports', or as intense, brown sugar-sweet Tokays, are all memorable. The true heights are achieved by Liqueur Muscats, unbearably rich but irresistible with it. Good producers: *Bullers, Campbells, Chambers, Morris, Stanton & Killeen*.

SPARKLING WINES Along with Pinot Noir, quality sparkling wine is a Holy Grail in Australia. Leading the pack are *Croser, Domaine Chandon* (known as *Green Point* in the UK), *Yalumba D, Salinger* and *Jansz*. Cheaper are *Seaview, Angas Brut* and *Orlando Carrington*; going upmarket, look for *Seppelt's Blanc de Blancs* and *Pinot Noir / Chardonnay*. For a change try *Yalumba's Cabernet* and *Seppelt's Shiraz* (two sparkling reds).

SWAN VALLEY (Western Australia) One of the hottest wine regions in the world, the Swan Valley made its reputation on big, rich reds and whites, but even the famous *Houghton's Supreme* is now much lighter and fresher. Good names: *Bassendean, Evans and Tate, Houghton, Moondah Brook, Sandalford*.

TASMANIA Only tiny amounts so far, but there is some remarkable Chardonnay from *Pipers Brook* and *Tasmanian Wine Co*, and Cabernet from *Pipers Brook, Heemskerk, Moorilla Estate*. Pinot Noir from here can be very good.

YARRA VALLEY (Victoria) The Yarra Valley could be emerging as Victoria's table wine superstar. It is cooler than any other mainland Australian area, with a variety of soil types suitable for different grapes' needs. Successes are equally divided between red and white, with exciting 'Bordeaux blends' of Cabernet Sauvignon, Cabernet Franc and Merlot, arguably Australia's finest Pinot Noirs and great sparkling wine from Domaine Chandon. Whites, too; the scented flavours of Gewürztraminer, Rhine Riesling and Chardonnay are a revelation. Good producers include: *Coldstream Hills, De Bortoli, Diamond Valley, Lillydale, Mount Mary, Seville Estate* (who also make great sweet wine), *St Huberts, Yarra Burn, Yarra Yering, Yeringberg* and *Tarrawarra*.

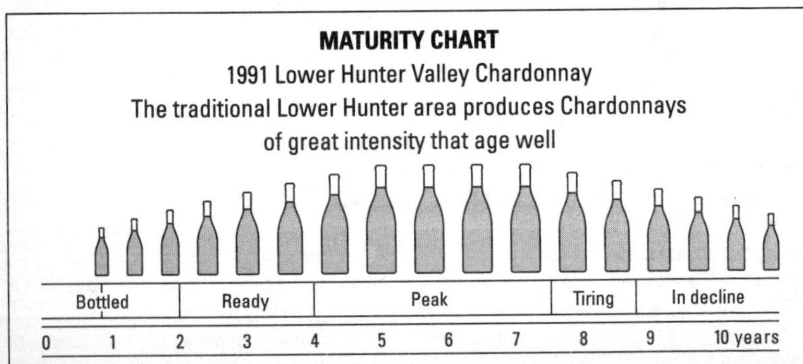

WINERY PROFILES

TIM ADAMS ★★★★ (South Australia) Spectacular early results: spellbinding Sémillon and a dense, full-flavoured Shiraz. Tiny amounts but building a cult following.

BAILEY'S OF GLENROWAN ★★★★ (Victoria) Greatest of Australia's fortified winemakers, its 'Founder' Liqueur Muscat is an unbearably delicious concentration of sweet, dark flavours. Also reassuringly traditional Cabernet and Shiraz.

BANNOCKBURN ★★★★ (Victoria) Gary Farr, wine-maker at Domaine Dujac in Burgundy, produces some of cool-climate Geelong's best wines: a rich Pinot Noir, full-bodied Chardonnay and Shiraz.

BAROSSA VALLEY ESTATES ★★(★) (South Australia) Berri-Renmano-Hardy-owned, this specializes in high-quality cheap wine.

JIM BARRY ★★★★ (South Australia) Clare Valley winery producing outstanding Chardonnay, Rhine Riesling, Sauvignon Blanc and a splendid Shiraz, The Armagh.

BASEDOW ★★★★ (South Australia) Old Barossa winery now surging ahead with big, oaky Chardonnay, fine Watervale Riesling, hearty, chocolaty Shiraz and Cabernet.

BERRI-RENMANO and HARDY★★★(★) (South Australia) This public company, which crushes 25% of all Australian wine, is the result of last year's merger of Berri-Renmano and the family company of Hardy's. It's a powerful combination, with Berri's high standard, cheap own-labels and Hardy's impressive quality across the range from the Bird Series and Nottage Hill to Chateau Reynella and Eileen Hardy.

WOLF BLASS ★★★(★) (South Australia) Though now owned by Mildara, Wolf Blass still has a knack of producing what people like: wines of tremendous fruit and well-judged oak. Good Riesling, voluptuous Chardonnay and five styles of red which are, in rising price order, red, yellow, grey, brown and black label.

DE BORTOLI ★★★(★) (New South Wales) Shot to fame with an astonishing sweet 1982 botrytis Sémillon, and has since put together a string of well-priced basics. De Bortoli's new Yarra property makes some of the region's best Chardonnay, Cabernet and Shiraz.

BROKENWOOD ★★★★(★) (New South Wales) Small, high-class Hunter Valley winery noted for eclectic blends such as Hunter/Coonawarra Cabernet and latterly Hunter/McLaren Vale Sémillon/Sauvignon Blanc. Low-yielding Graveyard vineyard produces one of Australia's best Shiraz: concentrated, profound and long-living.

BOWEN ESTATE ★★★★ (South Australia) The best value in Coonawarra: elegant Cabernet/Merlot and razor-fine Shiraz renowned for consistency and quality. Very good Riesling, Chardonnay.

BROWN BROTHERS ★★★(★) (Victoria) Family firm, and a huge range of good wine. The best vineyards are the cool Koombahla and even cooler Whitlands; look for Muscat, Sémillon, Chardonnay, Koombahla Cabernet, Whitlands Gewürz and Riesling.

CAPE MENTELLE ★★★★(★) (Western Australia) Important Margaret River winery now part-owned by Veuve Clicquot with founder David Hohnen; also owns New Zealand's buzz winery Cloudy Bay. Excellent Cabernet and variations on the Sémillon/Sauvignon theme as well as Shiraz – and Zinfandel, of all things to find in Australia.

CHATEAU TAHBILK ★★★★ (Victoria) Historic Goulburn Valley winery with great traditional reds.

COLDSTREAM HILLS ★★★★(★) (Victoria) Aussie wine writer James Halliday opted for practising what he preached. World class Pinot Noir, exciting Chardonnay and Cabernet.

DELATITE ★★★★(★) (Victoria) 'A magic piece of dirt, it could grow anything' is how the owners describe the Delatite vineyard. The wines have an individuality of fruit plus superb wine-making which puts them in the top class. Dry Riesling is delicious, the sweet version superb, while Pinot Noir, Gewürz, Cabernet and Shiraz are brilliant.

DOMAINE CHANDON ★★★★ (South Australia) Moët & Chandon's Green Point Estate in the Yarra Valley released its second Champagne method sparkler in the UK in 1993. Outstanding quality.

DROMANA ★★★★ (Victoria) Excellent Chardonnay, promising Pinot Noir and Cabernet/Merlot in the Mornington Peninsula, as well as the good-value Schinus Molle label.

HENSCHKE ★★★★★ (South Australia) Old red vines, some of them 100 years old, that yield deep, dark, curranty wines of top class. Whites equally stunning – Riesling, Sémillon and Chardonnay.

HILL-SMITH/YALUMBA ★★★★ (South Australia) A large Barossa company producing good wines under the Yalumba and Hill Smith labels, and exceptional ones under the Signature, Heggies and Pewsey Vale Vineyard labels, where dry and sweet Rieslings are some of the finest in Australia. Yalumba D is very good fizz.

HOLLICK ★★★★ (South Australia) With vineyards on the best soils of Coonawarra, Ian Hollick and winemaker Pat Tocaciu harvest some of the region's suavest reds; a soft and tobaccoey Cabernet/Merlot and an outstanding Cabernet *cuvée*, Ravenswood. They make fine Pinot and Chardonnay fizz and the district's most successful Riesling.

HOWARD PARK ★★★(★) (Western Australia) Expensive but superb, long-living wines. The Riesling is intense, perfumed and austere; the Cabernet deep and structured. Both need cellaring.

LAKE'S FOLLY ★★★★ (New South Wales) Tiny Hunter Valley winery making highly idiosyncratic Chardonnay and Cabernet, very exciting with age.

LEEUWIN ESTATE ★★★★ (Western Australia) Ultra-high profile, ultra-high prices for exciting Chardonnay and Pinot Noir, blackcurrant-and-leather Cabernet Sauvignon, good Riesling and Sauvignon.

LINDEMANS ★★★★ (Victoria) Remarkable firm, now part of Penfolds. Has land in the Hunter, Padthaway, Barossa and Coonawarra. Exceptionally good basic varietals, while Coonawarras, Padthaways and old-style Hunters are among Australia's finest. Coonawarra reds Limestone Ridge and St George are tip-top, as is the claret blend, Pyrus.

MCWILLIAMS ★★(★) (New South Wales) Old-fashioned giant now rapidly improving its quality. Though traditionally a Hunter company, much McWilliams wine now comes from Griffith in the MIA. Blends like the Hillside Colombard/Chardonnay show what can be done with fairly basic fruit.

CHARLES MELTON ★★★★ (South Australia) A 1000-case Barossa winery with Grenache-based Nine Popes and a Shiraz of exceptional concentration and character.

GEOFF MERRILL ★★★(★) (South Australia) Walrus-moustached, charismatic and irreverent Merrill combines an instinct for wine with marketing ability. He makes worthy Cabernet, full Chardonnay, crisp Sauvignon/Sémillon and thirst-quenching Grenache rosé at Mount Hurtle.

MILDARA BLASS★★(★) (South Australia) Based in the irrigated Murray River hinterland, but with large holdings in Coonawarra. Quality is erratic, though price is fair. It also owns Yellowglen and Balgownie in Victoria, Krondorf in SA and Morton Estate in New Zealand.

MITCHELTON ★★★(★) (Victoria) Wide range of styles in the Goulburn Valley, notably fine, full-flavoured Rieslings, good Chardonnay under the Preece label and the speciality of the house, Marsanne.

MOORILLA ESTATE ★★★★ (Tasmania) The first of the new-wave Tasmanian wineries, producing a polished range of crisp cool-climate wines. Pinot Noir is a speciality; aromatic Riesling, Chardonnay and Gewürztraminer are also excellent.

MOSS WOOD ★★★★ (Western Australia) Superbly original wines from one of Margaret River's best. Sémillon, with and without wood-aging, is some of the best in Australia. Pinot Noir is daring and delicious, Chardonnay less daring but just as delicious, Cabernet rich and structured.

MOUNTADAM ★★★★(★) (South Australia) David Wynn established this Adelaide Hills vineyard after selling Wynns in Coonawarra. His son Adam makes complex, Burgundian Chardonnay, substantial Pinot Noir, idiosyncratic Riesling, lean Cabernet.

MOUNT LANGI-GHIRAN ★★★★ (Victoria) Great Western winery making dry, intense Shiraz and long-lived Cabernet.

MOUNT MARY ★★★★ (Victoria) Finely structured Cabernet-based Bordeaux blend and a Pinot Noir improving with age. Tiny production, much sought-after.

ORLANDO ★★★ (South Australia) Barossa winery with fine quality at every level. Its boxed wine is outstanding, its RF Cabernet, Riesling and Chardonnay are usually the best in the price bracket, and St-Helga Riesling, St-Hilary Chardonnay and St-Hugo Cabernet are among the best.

PENFOLDS ★★★★★ (South Australia) The greatest red winemakers in Australia, and now good in whites too. Its basics are clean and tasty, its varietals packed with flavour, and its special selection reds, culminating in the deservedly legendary Grange Hermitage, are superlative, hugely structured wines of world class. If you can't afford Grange, try Bin 28, Bin 128, Bin 389 or the new Bin 407 Cabernet Sauvignon.

PENLEY ESTATE ★★★★ (South Australia) Kym Tolley is a scion of the Penfolds and Tolley families, hence Penley. He planted his Coonawarra estate in 1988, but so far his award-winning Shiraz, Cabernet/Shiraz and Chardonnay come from bought-in grapes.

PETALUMA ★★★★(★) (South Australia) The baby of Brian Croser is hitting its stride. Some of his Rieslings, sweet and dry, (Chardonnays, too) have been tip-top, and his Cabernet-based reds are improving each year. Also 'Croser' fizz.

PIPERS BROOK ★★★★ (Tasmania) Keenly-sought wines which combine classy design, clever marketing and skilful wine-making by Andrew Pirie. Steely aromatic Riesling, classically reserved Chardonnay, serious Pinot Noir and tasty, barrel-fermented Sauvignon Blanc are the best.

PLANTAGENET ★★★(★) (Western Australia) In an unglamorous apple packing shed in chilly Mount Barker, John Wade and Tony Smith make a fine range. Noted for peppery Shiraz, melony/nutty Chardonnay, fine limey Riesling and elegant Cabernet Sauvignon.

ROCKFORD ★★★★ (South Australia) The individuality of Rocky O'Callaghan's wines, especially his Basket Press Shiraz, has made him a Barossa cult.

ROSEMOUNT ★★★(★) (New South Wales) The company which did more than any to help Australia take the UK by storm with Chardonnay, Fumé Blanc and Cabernet. The last two are no longer so good, though Chardonnay is on the way back and the single vineyard Roxburgh and Show Reserve Chardonnays are impressive. Worldwide, the Chardonnays have set new standards for affordable quality. We are seeing surprising Pinot Noir and excellent Sémillon and Shiraz.

ROTHBURY ★★★★ (New South Wales) One of the leading Hunter companies founded by the indomitable Len Evans. Its wines went through a bad patch a few years ago, but are now back on form with classic flavours. The Chardonnay and Sémillon are now some of the Hunter's best and Pinot Noir and Shiraz increasingly good.

ST HALLETT ★★★★ (South Australia) Big Bob McLean (a small winemaker in only one sense), with Stuart Blackwell and the Lindner family in the Barossa, makes full, oaky Sémillon and Chardonnay and a rich Shiraz, Old Block, from old vines.

ST HUBERTS ★★★★ (Victoria) Now owned by Rothbury and back at the top. Brilliant whites and reds; Chardonnay and Cabernet Sauvignon are exceptional.

SEPPELT ★★★★ (Victoria) Leading makers of quality fizz from Champagne grapes, peaking with Salinger. Also fruity, easy-drinking styles. Now part of Penfolds.

SHAW & SMITH ★★★★ (South Australia) Itinerant winemaker Martin Shaw and his cousin, Michael Hill-Smith MW, make fine Sauvignon Blanc and Chardonnay in the Southern Vales. A duo to watch.

STONIERS MERRICKS ★★★★ (Victoria) Fine Chardonnay and Cabernet from this Mornington Peninsula winery.

TALTARNI ★★★ (Victoria) Remarkable bone-dry, grassy-sharp Fumé Blanc; fine Cabernet and Shiraz which soften (after about a decade) into classy, if austere reds. If it sounds rather French – well, the winemaker grew up at Château Lafite.

TISDALL ★★★ (Victoria) Goulburn winery making fresh, easy-to-drink reds and whites and cool-climate, quality classics from its Mount Helen grapes.

TYRRELL ★★★(★) (New South Wales) Eccentrically brilliant Hunter winery which sells 'port' and 'blackberry nip' to tourists through the front door while making some classic wines out the back. There has never been a more exciting Aussie Chardonnay than the Vat 47 of the early '80s, and for years Tyrrell was the only maker of great Pinot Noir. Vat 1 Sémillon is also excellent, as is his 'plonk' – Long Flat Red and White.

VASSE FELIX ★★★★ (Western Australia) One of the original Margaret River wineries. Classic regional style of rich, leafy, curranty Cabernet and spicy, fleshy Shiraz.

WIRRA WIRRA★★★★ (South Australia) Fine, concentrated reds, whites and fizz; exceptional Angelus Cabernet Sauvignon.

WYNNS ★★★(★) (South Australia) Big, oaky Chardonnay, refined Cabernet and Shiraz from this Coonawarra company. Top-line John Riddoch Cabernet is expensive but worth every penny.

YARRA YERING ★★★★★ (Victoria) Wonderful Yarra Valley winery, where Bailey Carrodus labels his Cabernet-based wine Dry Red No.1 and his Shiraz-based wine Dry Red No.2: exceptional, powerful and concentrated yet fragrant reds. Fine Pinot Noir and Chardonnay as well.

NEW ZEALAND

It's easy to be patronizing about New Zealand. Stuck out in the Pacific Ocean with a clear run south to Ranulph Fiennes territory, the place has a curious, time-warp feel to it. There are moments when the visitor feels he's stepped straight onto the set of that sixties series, *Dixon of Dock Green.*

But the quiet exterior conceals one of the most dynamic wine industries in the world. After the cut-throat rationalization of the mid-Eighties, New Zealand's winemakers have emerged with renewed determination to conquer the world.

And conquered it they have. Fortunately for us, the growing export drive has focused on Britain. Led by companies like Montana, Nobilo, Matua Valley, Selaks, Delegats, Babich, Villa Maria and Cooks, Kiwi wines have enjoyed massive success here. Last year's figures were up nearly 80 per cent in volume and (crucially) 120 per cent in value – the latest in a series of increases.

It was the Sauvignon Blancs that seduced us first. The pungent, elderflower and gooseberry character of Marlborough Sauvignon (typified by wineries like Montana, Wairau River, Villa Maria, Oyster Bay and Babich) is difficult to ignore. But, sensibly, New Zealand has realised that it can't rely on a single, often rather simple, flavour as its calling card. Kiwi Sauvignon is wonderful stuff, but my feeling is that Chardonnay has more long-term potential, especially in Marlborough, Martinborough, Hawke's Bay and Canterbury. Unfashionable Riesling could also be a winner in Marlborough and Canterbury. We're beginning to recognize the promise of New Zealand sparkling wines, too. Le Brun, Deutz/Montana and Cloudy Bay are all producing top-notch fizzes.

Green to red

An even bigger transformation has taken place in the quality of the reds. Once dismissed as tasting like Cabernet Franc from a dire vintage in the Loire, Kiwi reds have benefited enormously from new clones, better wine-making and more open vineyard canopies to encourage ripening, and have thrown off their lean and green image. The quality of the Cabernet from producers like Goldwater, Te Mata, Stonyridge, Montana, Vavasour and Matua Valley notwithstanding, it is hard to resist the impression that Merlot and especially Pinot Noir will eventually win through as the varieties most suited to New Zealand's range of climates. Hawkes Bay and Waiheke Island look like Cabernet's best hopes of proving me wrong. Add the handful of sweet white wine styles made at places like Rongapai, Hunters, Giesen, Coopers Creek, Selaks and Grove Mill, and you have a vibrant wine industry producing an enviable variety of wines.

The only dark, potentially damaging, cloud on the horizon is beyond the wineries' control. After the general excellence of the 1991 vintage, 1992 was something of a disappointment. The harvest took place three weeks later than usual and some of the South Island whites, in particular, are a little austere. Many were sweetened up to balance high levels of natural acidity.

More worrying for the Kiwis was the shortfall in quantity last year. The 1992 crop was down 20 per cent, and 1993 was down a further 40 per cent. At a time when New Zealand is producing better wines than ever, it would be unfortunate, to say the least, if the country simply ran out of stock.

TIM ATKIN

WHITE GRAPES & FLAVOURS

CHARDONNAY NZ's vineyards are only a dolphin's leap from the South Pole, and the cool ripening period makes light, intense, high-acid Chardonnay with penetrating apple, peach, pineapple and pear flavours, softened by new oak. Hawke's Bay makes classics, followed by Marlborough, Nelson and Wairarapa. Gisborne's are softer, less intense. Best: *Babich, Cloudy Bay, Collard's (Tolaga, Rothesay), Cooks* (Hawke's Bay and Gisborne), *Coopers Creek, Delegat's, Kumeu River, Hunter's, Morton Estate, Matawhero, Matua Valley (Judd, Yates* and *Egan Estates), Nobilo (Dixon Estate, Te Karaka), de Redcliffe, Selaks, Te Mata, Vidal, Villa Maria.*

CHENIN BLANC This tricky Loire grape is at its most versatile here, ranging from stone-dry to rich. Best with some sweetness. It could make fine Vouvray styles, but is usually too overcropped. *Collard's* is good; *Cooks* and *Matawhero* not bad.

GEWÜRZTRAMINER Can be world class: pungent, reeking of black pepper, mangoes, lychees, yet dry and refreshing. Gisborne is a good region and *Matawhero* can be great. Others: *Coopers Creek, Morton Estate, Nobilo, Pacific Wines, Villa Maria.*

MÜLLER-THURGAU The dominant New Zealand grape. When well made, as by *Montana*, it has a flowering curranty, green tang, or, from *Nobilo*, the grapiness of many German Rheinhessens. Also good: *Collard's, Cooks, Delegat's, Matawhero, Matua Valley* and *Totara.*

RIESLING A lot of Rhine Riesling (as NZ calls it) is made into bland blends, but there are outstanding wines. *Corbans' Stoneleigh* is good, as are *Babich, Collard's, Coopers Creek, Selaks' Brigham Creek, Delegat's, Matua Valley, Millton, Seifried (Redwood Valley Vineyard). Montana* is lean but OK; *Giesen* may make the most classic dry Riesling yet. *Delegat's, Ngatarawa, St Helena, Corbans* and *Seifried* have made rich late-harvest wines. NZ could become a great sweet wine land.

SAUVIGNON BLANC A few top the world already. The best, such as *Montana Marlborough Sauvignon*, or *Selaks* from Hawke's Bay, bring nettly, asparagus-and-gooseberry-fruit to fresh, sharp balance, rounded off with honey and spice. Recent attempts to modify the grassy style and introduce complexity seem successful. Also good: *Cloudy Bay, Babich, Brookfields, Coopers Creek, Corbans' Stoneleigh, Selaks, Hunters, Delegat's, Montana*'s *Brancott Estate, Morton Estate, Vidal, Villa Maria.*

SÉMILLON Steering away from the heavy, oily Aussie tradition to something fresher, like the grassy *Vidal* or the classic beeswax-and-sweet-apples of *Villa Maria, Montana* and *Delegat's*. It is increasingly blended with Sauvignon or Chardonnay as at *Babich, Delegat's* and *Mission.*

RED GRAPES & FLAVOURS

CABERNET SAUVIGNON Weedy and green in the early days, the Cabernets are certainly still dry, but the fruit has developed into a piercing, fresh, grassy, blackcurrant-and-nettles style about as pure as you can get. *Cooks' Hawke's Bay Cabernet* is usually grassy, soft and delicious but there are also many single estates producing outstanding wine. Each successive vintage shows improvements. Top wineries for Cabernet include the great *Te Mata, Cloudy Bay* (from 1987), *Cooks' Fernhill, Goldwater, Kumeu River, Montana, Matua Valley, Neudorf, Ngatarawa, St Nesbit, Selaks, Vidal* and *Villa Maria.*

MERLOT Planted primarily for blending with Cabernet (the *Te Mata Coleraine* is classic), but also made into varietals. *Kumeu River* is full, peppery and plummy and *Esk Valley* is packed with fruit.

PINOT NOIR The record is less than uniform, but there have been shining examples, from wineries like *St Helena* and *Martinborough,* and as the vines (and skills) mature, the wines improve in concentration and quality each vintage. Up-and-coming names to watch are *Waipara Springs* and *Omihi Hills.* Pinot Noir also makes excellent perfumed white – *Matua Valley*'s is first-rate.

WINES & WINE REGIONS

GISBORNE (North Island) They call Gisborne 'carafe' country, because it's a positive grape basket of a region, planted with one-third of the nation's vines. Above all, it is the home of Müller-Thurgau, which can yield 20 to 25 tons per hectare on the Poverty Bay alluvial flats. In general, the wine is light but good, but there are exceptions. Matawhero is a high-quality sub-area, as are Tolaga and Tikitiki further north. From these areas, Chenin and Gewürztraminer and, increasingly, award-winning Chardonnay, can be excellent. Reds on the whole are less exciting in Gisborne, although *Delegat's* have produced some good Cabernet.

HAWKE'S BAY (North Island) Potentially New Zealand's greatest wine region: it is becoming clear that, as well as fine whites, great reds could be made here. Indeed, the deep gravel banks, allied to its being one of the country's sunniest areas, mean that there is potential for Cabernet and Merlot to produce top quality claret-type reds. I believe that if *any* of the world's regions is ever going to produce the flavour equivalent of a Médoc Classed Growth it will be Hawke's Bay, but in the meantime the joyous originality of the fruit flavours is as shocking as it is delightful. Good names: *Brookfields, Cooks, Matua Valley, Vidal, Ngatarawa, Villa Maria* and *Te Mata.*

The price guides for this section begin on page 399.

MARLBOROUGH (South Island) Now one of the biggest vineyard regions in the country – and still growing. The strengths – thanks to a long, slow ripening period – have always been white wines: outstanding Rhine Riesling, Chardonnay and especially Sauvignon. Reds are improving dramatically.

OTHER NORTH ISLAND North of Auckland, there are excellent reds and whites at Waimauku (with *Matua Valley* and *Collards*), Huapai (*Nobilo*) and Kumeu (*Coopers Creek, Kumeu River* and *Selaks*), though they are frequently vinified from grapes grown elsewhere on the island. West of Auckland at Henderson the top producers include *Babich, Collard's, Delegat's* – with award-winning white wines – and *Pacific.* South of Auckland is the impressive *Villa Maria* as well as *St Nesbit* and *de Redcliffe.* On Waiheke Island, *Goldwater Estate* and *Stonyridge Vineyard* are producing excellent wine. *Morton Estate* on Bay of Plenty is also one of New Zealand's best producers.

OTHER SOUTH ISLAND Nelson to the east of Marlborough is a minor area, but has good performers in *Neudorf* and *Seifried.* Canterbury is dominated by the excellent *St Helena* and *Giesen; Larcomb, Omihi Hills* and *Waipara Springs* also look set to produce exciting wines. And at *Gibbston Valley* and *Rippon Vineyard,* good Chardonnay and Pinot Noir are already showing what the world's most southerly vineyards can achieve.

WINERY PROFILES

BABICH ★★★ Fresh Fumé Vert (Sémillon and Chardonnay), oaky Irongate Chardonnay, grassy Hawke's Bay Cabernet.

DANIEL LE BRUN ★★★★(★) NZ's finest fizz producer is now one of the three top producers outside Champagne.

CLOUDY BAY ★★★★★ Excellent Sauvignon, fattened with a little Sémillon, sells out within days. Chardonnay and, eventually, Cabernet may be even better.

CORBANS ★★★ Includes Cooks and McWilliam's. Cooks' Fernhill is rich Cabernet, Longridge a nice Chardonnay.

DELEGAT'S ★★★ White specialist near Auckland, using mostly Hawke's Bay and Gisborne fruit. Fine Sauvignon, Chardonnay and sweet wine; promising Cabernet.

HUNTER'S★★★★(★) Produce Sauvignon Blanc and Chardonnay of considerable elegance and complexity.

KUMEU RIVER ★★★★(★) Imaginative winery. Merlot/Cabernet, and Chardonnay increasingly exciting.

MARTINBOROUGH ★★★★ Lovely Riesling, Müller-Thurgau, Sauvignon, Chardonnay and outstanding Pinot Noir.

MATUA VALLEY ★★★★(★) Superb single-estate Chardonnays and exciting Cabernet reds. Also delicious Gewürztraminer, Riesling and some of New Zealand's best Müller-Thurgau. Decent rosé Pinot Noir.

MONTANA ★★★(★) Marlborough Sauvignon Blanc from here is regularly one of New Zealand's best. Cabernet is on the up. New sparkling wines, Lindauer and upmarket Deutz (made with French help) are great value.

MORTON ESTATE ★★★★ Award-winning Sauvignon, Chardonnay and Gewürz. Winemaker John Hancock has begun his assault on red wine and makes good fizz.

NGATARAWA ★★★ Newish Hawke's Bay winery likely to make great red and sweet in the near future, and fine Chardonnay.

NOBILO ★★★ Good Chardonnay (oak-aged and single vineyard), barrel-fermented Sauvignon, White Cloud Müller-Thurgau.

PALLISER ★★★ Very promising young Martinborough winery specializing in oaky Chardonnay, off-dry and botrytized Rieslings and Pinot Noir.

C J PASK ★★★★ One of the best red wine growers in New Zealand. Good Pinot Noir; very good Merlot and Cabernet/Merlot.

ST HELENA ★★★(★) Shot to prominence with its 1982 Pinot Noir. It's taken a while to match that peak again but the last few vintages (except 1989) have been superb.

SELAKS ★★★★ Spot-on Sauvignon Blanc and Sauvignon/Sémillon, a 3:2 blend. Top of the range is Founder's Selection.

TE MATA ★★★★★ Te Mata Coleraine is the most consistently impressive and most sought-after of NZ reds. Te Mata Awatea is also a fine red and Elston Chardonnay, is rich, powerful and Burgundian in style.

VAVASOUR★★★★ Producer of fantastic reds: the Reserve Shiraz and the French-style Reserve Cabernet Sauvignon/Franc are superb.

VILLA MARIA ★★★★ Vidal, Esk Valley and Villa Maria Reserve Bin wines from Sauvignon to Merlot. Classic Cabernets and rich, juicy Chardonnays.

UNITED KINGDOM

We have finally done it. In 1992 the English wine harvest passed the magic limit of 25,000 hectolitres, beyond which no EC country can plant any more vines unless it has a quality wine scheme in operation. The 1992 total, 26,500hl, is the largest ever, beating the previous record of 22,500hl in 1989.

Well done, everybody. A pity it coincided with the middle of a force ten recession, but there we are. The trouble was that not all producers had sold – and some had not even bottled – their 1991 harvest because of negligible demand. Where the tanks were still full of '91, people wisely decided not to bother making any '92 at all. If they couldn't sell what they'd got, why make more?

Never mind, there was a compensation. The long-awaited quality wine system would put at least some of our stuff on a par with French *appellation contrôlée* wines. Surely that would be good for business?

The scheme – still officially a pilot one – began in 1991, in anticipation of our joining the big league. At the time when plans were being drawn up a recession was not envisaged, so the idea of planting more vines, especially the very successful Seyval Blanc, made sense.

But then Brussels moved the goal posts. Beyond the 25,000-hl limit it is now forbidden to plant any more vines at all, whether a quality wine scheme is in place or not. You can see the logic. Brussels is determined to drain the Euro wine lake. Even though our entire annual harvest is only about 0.03 per cent of the French, we are not considered a special case.

Scheming bureaucrats

Nevertheless the change has removed, at a stroke, our reason for having a quality wine scheme. But the fact that we don't need it has not stopped us from flinging ourselves enthusiastically into the bureaucratic mess that accompanies such an application. Drinkers are advised that any resemblance between the new regulations and reality are purely coincidental.

In the first place, it is nonsense to exclude some of our best wines from the quality scheme. Seyval Blanc is a hybrid, an inter-specific cross that is not entirely *Vitis vinifera* and therefore doesn't have the right genes to make 'quality wine' as defined by the EC, although it regularly wins gongs and 'Best Wine of the Year' trophies.

We cannot fight the entire EC on this issue by ourselves, especially since the Ministry of Agriculture devotes most of its energy to sheep and fishing. However, the Germans, who never seem to tire of genetic manipulation, are growing Cabernet Sauvignon that has been tweaked with *Vitis amarensis* to make it resistant to disease. How long will it be before the French take an interest in this? When they do, we should not be at all surprised to see the anti-hybrid opposition melt away. English growers who champion Seyval Blanc may just need to bide their time.

Then there is the question of what to call English quality wine. Certainly not English Quality Wine, that's for sure, because under the EC system the quality wine region must be smaller than the table wine region in which it finds itself. The current compromise is to divide the country into two: Northern Counties and

Southern Counties. But since the counties of Lancashire, Yorkshire, Durham, Cleveland, Tyne & Wear, Cumbria and Northumberland don't produce more than a few bucketfuls of wine grapes between them, it is all effectively Southern Counties wine.

When I say all, I mean roughly what's available in Tesco. That seems to be about the top and bottom of this great leap forward. Nobody could (or would) tell me how much of the harvest was officially classified as Quality Wine, possibly because it is such an embarrassingly small volume. But of our 450-odd growers, only 13 producers gained the right in 1991 to the Southern Counties appellation. And then only for some of their wines. And not all of them are going to use it on the label anyway. At the time of writing only Tesco seems to be carrying the good news beyond the cellar door.

Not only each wine, but each bottling, needs a separate application. And at £79 plus VAT (reduced slightly if several wines are entered simultaneously) for each submission, it is not universally considered good value. Unlike the French AC system, Southern Counties has nothing to do with *terroir*: it has more in common with Germany's *amtliche prüfungsnummer* scheme. If analysis, and a tasting panel with at least two Masters of Wine on it, gives the green light, then a given batch is entitled to be called Southern Counties.

Those in favour of the scheme claim that a customer seeing the word 'quality' on the label will prefer that wine to a simple table wine. If that argument holds water, then those who produce both may find their table wine snubbed in favour of a politically correct (but possibly inferior) wine. It is doubtful whether the customer is gaining much by all this.

JIM AINSWORTH

WHITE WINES

BACCHUS In Germany, this new crossing usually produces fat, blowsy, marmalade-Muscatty flavours. In England it is more likely to produce a sharp wine, with strong flavours of gooseberry, elderflower and orange rind. *Barkham, Partridge Vineyard, Three Choirs, Coddington and Shawsgate* are good; *Chiltern Valley*'s *1989 Noble Bacchus* showed that a warm summer can produce lusciously rich wines too.

FABER A crossing of Pinot Blanc and Müller-Thurgau, making fragrant wines with good acidity. One of the few varieties where you can actually taste Riesling characteristics.

HUXELREBE A cross (of Gutedel, alias Chasselas, with Courtillier Musqué) that in Germany beetles to overripeness in no time at all. The wine there is usually rich, flat and grapy. In England it's generally the exact opposite, renowned for a grapefruit pith taste and a greenish bite. For this reason it is often softened up by blending. *Headcorn*'s version is almost as delicate as a German Mosel; *Lamberhurst* and *Biddenden* are fuller; *Staple St James* and *Pilton Manor* more grapefruity and smoky. *Nutbourne Manor*'s is concentrated, *Astley* mixes it with Müller-Thurgau for Huxelvaner while *Three Choirs* late-picks it and tries to make a sweetie.

KERNER A bright, new German crossing of Riesling and Trollinger that has been producing good results. *Astley*'s is light and *Oatley* mixes it successfully with Kernling for a gingery, apple-sweet wine in best Cox's Orange Pippin style.

MADELEINE ANGEVINE Basically this is a table grape, but it performs quite well in England, where its somewhat 'fruit-juicy' character is matched by good acidity, either in the green but refreshing, elderflower perfumed style of *Astley 1985* and *'86*, or the more honeyed but appley style of *Hooksway 1984*. *Sharpham* blends it with Huxelrebe and produces a flinty Loire lookalike.

MÜLLER-THURGAU One of the original German crosses – from Riesling and Silvaner in 1882 – and the English work-horse, taking up over one-third of the acreage. Consequently, there is a fair bit of dull Müller (sometimes called Rivaner) about, needing beefing up with something more aromatic. *Wootton, Bruisyard St Peter, Breaky Bottom, St Nicholas of Ash, Staple St James, Tenterden, St George's* are good. And it can make very attractive, slightly sweet wine (through the addition of *Süssreserve,* or unfermented grape juice, just before bottling), as at *Pulham, Lamberhurst* and *Rowney*.

ORTEGA German cross making fat, rich, grapy wine mostly in the Mosel, of all places, but better suited to England. *Hidden Spring* is concentrated, and *Biddenden,* in particular, makes a delicious, slightly sweet but tremendously fruity elderflower and apricot-tasting example. It is usually blended and rarely seen on its own.

REICHENSTEINER A real 'EC' grape, since it is a crossing of French Madeleine Angevine, German Müller-Thurgau and Italian Calabrese. Does this multi-coloured background make it an exciting, tempestuous grape? Sadly, it's rather more of a Brussels bureaucrat clone. It's usually pretty dull when dry, but made slightly sweet, it can develop a pleasant, smoky, quince-and-peaches taste which ages well.

The price guides for this section begin on page 402.

Carr Taylor and *Rock Lodge* use it for Champagne-method fizz, *Three Choirs '90 'New Release'* was 50/50 Huxelrebe and Reichensteiner and *Nutbourne Manor*'s version is also good.

SCHEUREBE Silvaner crossed with Riesling, capable of producing good grapefruity, curranty wines in good years. *Thames Valley*'s late-harvest version is seductively good.

SCHÖNBURGER A *good,* pink grape. It makes a fat wine by English standards, with a pears-and-lychees flavour and good acidity. Dry versions like *Saxon Valley*'s need ripe fruit to balance the acidity, and it needs expert wine-making or it can end up tasting like bathroom detergent. The best are made by *Lamberhurst, Wootton, Carr Taylor*, *Coxley* and *Three Choirs*.

SEYVAL BLANC A French hybrid with around 15 per cent of UK acreage. *Breaky Bottom* is the most successful – dry and Sauvignon-like when young, honeyed like Burgundy after four to five years – but it is generally best blended with something more exotic like Schönburger or Huxelrebe, or made sweetish. *Hambledon* blends it with Pinot Meunier and Chardonnay, *Three Choirs* with Reichensteiner and *Adgestone* with Reichensteiner and Müller, while *Tenterden* makes a very good oaked Reserve. *Thames Valley*, too, hits it with oak for its *Fumé; Hidden Spring* and *Headcorn* are also good.

OTHER WHITES Numerous other varieties are being tried. The most interesting are Gewürztraminer at *Barton Manor* on the Isle of Wight where it was planted in plastic tunnels in 1984, and Ehrenfelser, aged in a 4000-litre oak barrel, at *Penshurst*; *Wootton*'s Auxerrois is a pungent, salty-sappy wine, while *Tenterden* also achieves lean and nervy results with this variety. *Carr Taylor* has achieved good results with Pinot Blanc for its concentrated *Kemsley Dry*. There are also some efforts with Chardonnay, at, for example, the new, 250-acre *Denbies Estate* at Dorking in Surrey, England's most ambitious vineyard project yet.

RED & ROSÉ WINES

CABERNET SAUVIGNON *Beenleigh* in Devon has been growing this in plastic tunnels, along with Merlot, and the 1989 version is clean and fresh, if light.

PINOT NOIR There are now over 20 hectares of the great Burgundy grape planted. So far, full reds have been difficult to achieve, but Kent has several patches making very good rosé – *Chiddingstone* blends it with Pinot Meunier to make a delicious wine redolent of eucalyptus; *Bodiam Castle* makes a tasty rosé blended with Blauburger, as well as a dry, honeyed Blanc de Pinot Noir white; *Biddenden* mixes it with Dornfelder and Gamay to produce a light, cherryish red; and *Tenterden*'s blend with Dunkelfelder makes a gently honeyed, smoky, mango-flavoured pink. *Three Choirs* rosé from Pinot Noir has earthy raspberry-and-Morello-cherry fruit; *Conghurst* rosé is also good, with grapy, herbaceous flavours. Some estates are now planting Pinot Noir for sparkling wine.

TRIOMPHE D'ALSACE This hybrid, one of whose parents is the Alsace Knipperlé, is proving a popular variety in England's trying climate. The best examples have a fresh, raspberry-and-spice character like *Meon Valley*'s *Meonwara* or *Thames Valley*'s balanced *Dry Red.* The trick, as with all reds in England, is to settle for a light, graceful wine and not to over-extract flavour – the deepest English reds tend to taste of vegetation rather than fruit.

EASTERN EUROPE

This is the part of the world where more hope is being invested in the wine industry than probably anywhere else. Every adventurous winemaker, every wine merchant who sees him or herself as a bit of a pioneer, a bit of a fixer, is out there looking for an opportunity. It may be the chance to buy a share of a famous vineyard, or to transform the wines of a promising co-operative by making them clean their vats out properly and ferment at the right (low) temperature; it may mean bullying and cajoling people who have been making wines all their lives into making them the way you want them to, and then convincing them that they can't expect to sell them in Britain for more than £3.50, and 'Oh, by the way, all the shipments must be identical and if they're not they'll be sent back.' It may mean investing in new winery equipment; it may mean reorganizing the entire picking system of a region. Whatever it means, there are people over here queuing to do it, and to invest serious money, too; and if anybody doubts that it's working, they should taste some of the stuff now appearing in the supermarkets. Clean, fresh flavours are beginning to dislodge the old tired, dirty ones; and winners and losers are already showing.

BULGARIA

This is a winner in the red stakes, but then it has been for some while. Cabernet Sauvignon and Merlot are still generally the best, but the young blends can be terrific, too. The wineries are taking to their new marketing freedom like ducks to water, and competing among themselves like mad; all sorts of new names are popping up as a result. Some of the reds are getting seriously good, but the whites... Well, in trade tastings they often seem pretty good, but they still don't seem reliable enough when picked off the shop shelf. Best (for reds): Suhindol, Assenovgrad Mavrud, Russe; (whites): Preslav, Khan Krum.

THE CZECH STATE

The old Czechoslovakia was never a great exporter of wine, and the split has left the Czech State with two wine regions – Bohemia and Moravia – but only a third of the area under vine of the former, larger country. Bohemia is the coolest, but the grapes are fairly similar in both regions: mostly white, from varieties like Pinot Blanc, Grüner Veltliner, Rhine Riesling, Laski Rizling and Sauvignon Blanc. Slovakia, so far, seems more go-ahead. The Melnik Winery, the country's largest, has just been returned to private ownership. The Lobkowicz family, which bought it, had owned it before Communism and now seem to want to improve the quality of the wines.

SLOVAKIA

This is the part of the old Czechoslovakia where Western investment and management – in the person of Angela Muir of Heart of Europe – have been paying dividends. As a result Slovakia is drawing ahead of the Czech State in quality terms. The flavours are fresh and fruity and improving all the time – and anyone who thinks it's been easy should bear in mind that Angela Muir earned herself the nickname of 'The General' from the Slovaks.

HUNGARY

Hungary's wines have been moving in two different directions in the past year. On the fresh and fruity side, Hugh Ryman's innovations at the Gyöngyös Estate continue to make waves: there is Sauvignon and Chardonnay from here on every high street in Britain, and every other winemaker who wants to export to the West must measure his or her wines against Ryman's. The latest to join the fray is Piero Antinori, one of a group of partners investing in the Bataapatai Estate. But Hungary's traditional flagship is Tokaji, the botrytized dessert wine that has not, in recent years, been all it was cracked up to be. There is investment in Tokaji now from abroad (most recently from Vega Sicilia in Spain) and already quality is looking up: watch this space.

ROMANIA

Plenty of Western investors have investigated Romania's possibilities, and quite a lot of them have then gone elsewhere. But some of the wines are good, albeit more old-fashioned in style. Go for the reds, or the botrytized sweet whites; the latter (look for the Tamaoisa grape) can be superb value. There is also a tiny amount of botrytized Chardonnay.

CIS STATES

Moldova is revealing itself as a source of big, beefy reds (Hugh Ryman is at work here, as well), but wine is produced all along the Black Sea coast. The biggest concentrations of familiar grapes like Cabernet and Chardonnay are in Moldova, and there is also lots of the excellent red Saperavi. The Ukraine makes a lot of white, from Rkatsiteli and Aligoté, and Georgia is fond of tannic, yellow white wines. Yes, tannic.

SLOVENIA

There's more to the countries of the old Yugoslavia than just Slovenia, of course, but the verdict on the others will have to wait awhile yet, sadly. There's plenty of promising private wine-making in Slovenia, but the quantities are small and the prices not that low; the best co-ops (like Vipava) are a better bet. Ljutomer could be good, if it tried harder.

EASTERN EUROPEAN CLASSIFICATIONS

BULGARIA In order of quality there are Country Wines (replacing the old Mehana, or bistro wines), Varietal Wines with Stated Geographic Origin (from 43 regions) and Controliran wines, from 27 zones. Special Reserves and Estate Selections are not official terms but indicate high quality.

HUNGARY 'Minosegi Bor' means 'Quality Wine', and is more or less equivalent to AC.

ROMANIA In order of quality there are VS (Vinul de Calitate Superioara, or Superior Quality); VSO (Vinul de Calitate Superioara & Denumire de Origine, or Superior Quality with Appellation of Origin); VSOC (Vinul Superioara de Origine Controlata) which includes Spätlese, Auslese and TBA lookalike categories.

SLOVENIA All six Yugoslav republics shared a system. Premium (Kvalitetno) Wine is from a specific region. Select Wine (Cuveno or Vrhunsko Vino) can be from a single vineyard.

THE CZECH STATE, SLOVAKIA, CIS STATES No system of classifications.

RED GRAPES & WINES

CABERNET SAUVIGNON Widely grown, and spans the quality scale. Bulgaria has the best; some oak-aged examples from Villanyi in Hungary, Kozhushny in Moldavia, and Dealul Mare and Murfatlar in Romania are rich, ripe and silky.

FRANKOVKA Native Czech grape yielding attractive grassy, peppery wines.

GAMZA Bulgarian grape, meaty, tarry, ripe wines. Often teamed with Merlot.

KADARKA Hungarian vine which yields spicy wine with good body and tannin.

KEKFRANKOS Thought to be the Gamay from Beaujolais. Also called Blaufrankisch.

MAVRUD Bulgarian; rich fruit, but can be rather tannic and unbalanced.

MELNIK Indigenous Bulgarian grape making concentrated, spicy reds.

MERLOT Widely grown. At its best it is full, oaky, soft and blackcurranty. Bulgaria's Stambolovo and Sakar are good for older, oakier ripe Reserves. Romanian Merlots from Murfatlar and Dealul Mare can need about eight years to mellow.

PINOT NOIR Decidedly variable. None of the Pinot Noirs in last year's *Webster's* tasting showed particularly well. It's a difficult grape, and Eastern Europe is not the only place not to have conquered it.

ST LAURENT Muscaty Austrian grape that can be delicious in Slovakia.

VRANAC Montenegran speciality, making robust reds.

WHITE GRAPES & WINES

ALIGOTÉ Light, dry wines in Romania, Bulgaria and Russia. Sometimes blended with Ugni Blanc.

CHARDONNAY Everywhere in all guises. But the success rate is not great so far.

EZERJO Widely grown Hungarian; grassy, light wine, sometimes short on acidity.

FURMINT Hungarian; wines high in alcohol. Very susceptible to noble rot, and is the principal grape in Tokaji.

GEWÜRZTRAMINER Fair examples from Villanyi in Hungary, though balance is not always right.

IRSAY OLIVER Czech grape; gentle fruit and light spice; could use more acidity.

MUSCAT Usually the Ottonel variety, grown for medium-sweet and dessert wines.

PINOT BLANC Elegant from Nagyréde and Dunavár in Hungary; also some from the Czech State and Slovakia.

PINOT GRIS Full from Lake Balaton and smokier and rounder (and called Ruländer) in the Czech State and Slovakia.

RIESLING Seldom exciting, and why bother, when Germany, Alsace and others can do so much better?

SAUVIGNON BLANC Best are from Gyöngyös in Hungary: assertive and spicy.

TRAMINER Some attractive, zingy, aromatic Traminer from Moravenka in the Czech State is starting to appear.

WELSCHRIZLING (Same as Laski-, Olasz- and Riesling Italico.) Produces medium-dry, sometimes fruity, sometimes dirty wines, usually best avoided.

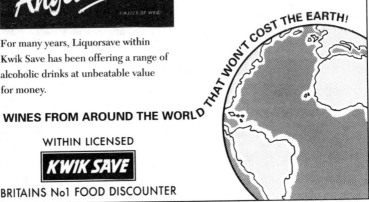

OTHER WINE REGIONS

ARGENTINA

Argentina is still the sort of place that makes people laugh when I mention it as a potential source of highly enjoyable wine – but it is, it is. Potential is, however, the operative word. Nature has done her bit with the right climate, if winemakers choose properly, but until very recently man was doing his best to mess it up by only making cheap and not very cheerful wines, in large quantities.

Slowly things are looking up, though. There are now some producers making good quality everyday wines that are temptingly cheap, and that can offer a change from the ubiquitous Chardonnay and Cabernet Sauvignon.

Some of these, if they are red, are made from Malbec, a grape grown in south-west France but not much regarded elsewhere. In Argentina the quality can vary somewhat but wines from *Trapiche* are worth investigating.

The indigenous white grape to look out for is Torrontes, an aromatic, lime-and-orange scented number especially good from *Michel Torino* or *Etchart* (who labels it *Cafayate*; try also the *Cafayate* Cabernet Sauvignon). The French varieties are out in force in Argentina as well, of course; *Flichman* and *Trapiche* Cabernets are worth a look, as is *Flichman*'s Syrah.

AUSTRIA

Wine-making standards have been transformed here in the last few years, and Austria is revealing itself as a source of highly individual dry whites. And glory be, a few are even finding their way over here.

There are four wine regions: Niederosterreich (or Lower Austria), Burgenland, Steiermark and Vienna itself, which boasts vineyards actually within the city boundaries. Lower Austria's finest area is the Wachau, a place of steep slopes and terraces overlooking the Danube, and of wines from the Grüner Veltliner and Rhine Riesling which can be as good as anything in Austria and, in the case of Riesling, as good as most of Germany too. These Rieslings are serious wines and deserve aging, but the Austrian fashion is for young wines and few of them make it past their second birthday.

It is the Burgenland, though, that is becoming established as Austria's top area. In the north there is a lake, the Neusiedlersee, which is broad and shallow and obligingly spreads humidity over a wide area to the east; it's almost impossible not to make botrytized dessert wines there. On the western bank there is some botrytis but also plenty of dry whites too, and further south there are some decent reds.

The driest of the dry come from Steiermark, or Styria. You want searing acidity? You want lean whites made from barely-ripe grapes and selling for extortionate prices? Then Styria is your sort of place. The Austrians just love them, which explains the prices.

CANADA

Hybrid grapes, which are most easily able to withstand the climate, take up the bulk of Canada's vineyards. But there's a Vintners' Quality Alliance in Ontario, designed to improve quality. The table wines are generally a little dilute, but the sweet Ice Wines (the best are made from the hybrid Vidal grape) can be a delight.

CHILE

Uneven quality is the bugbear here. When the wines are good, they are very, very good, but when they're bad...

As is so often the case when the wines are a little unreliable, the reds are the better bet. The Cabernet Sauvignon at its best has lots of rich blackcurrant fruit but some of the whites are improving: try the Torres Riesling, or the Chardonnay from Concha y Toro or Montes, and the Sauvignon from Errázuriz Panquehue.

Chile has benefited from massive injections of foreign investment (from Torres, Chateau Lafite Rothschild, Franciscan Cellars of California, William Fèvre of Chablis and Bruno Prats of Château Cos d'Estournel, among others) but it has suffered, accordingly, from hype. It was billed as the Next Big Thing long before it was ready for it; and while the wines are improving all the time, they don't have the reliability to compete with Australia at the most basic end, or the thrilling flavours to compete at the top end. Yet.

CYPRUS

To describe many Cyprus wines as 'unexciting' is a compliment; all too often 'undrinkable' is the more appropriate term. There's Cyprus 'sherry' of course, but it's not much good (and not called 'sherry' for much longer, either). The table wines we see over here are frequently tired, flabby and oxidized. One reason is that the growers are paid according to the sugar levels in their grapes, which inevitably leads to too much sugar and not enough acidity; another reason is that the grapes take too long to get to the wineries, and ferment on the way.

Thankfully, a few bright spots are appearing in this otherwise depressing picture. The Xynisteri grape is one of them. When grown in the cooler, mountainous centre of the island it can produce fresh, lively whites – if it is handled properly. At present it accounts for some ten per cent of the vineyards, and is mostly not handled properly. *ETKO* makes a respectable version, called *Nefeli*, and *Keo* have a cool-fermented Xynisteri which is remarkably fragrant.

The other most widely planted native grape variety – in fact the most widely planted of all – is the black Mavro, which so far makes better raisins than it does wine. There is a debate going on as to whether Cyprus should move wholeheartedly towards French varieties like Cabernet Sauvignon and Chardonnay, and the government's research station at Limassol grows these and more. If the pioneering work on grapes and wine-making being done there were taken up by the big producers, then Cyprus would at last begin to fulfil its potential.

GREECE

Greece's wine-making history is rather more glorious than its present, but since the Greeks like their wines oxidized, there are only a handful of companies making wines that are likely to appeal to international tastes. There is a whole raft of appellations, of which the Côtes de Meliton is the best all-round bet; Muscats are also generally sound, and sometimes excellent if from Samos.

Château Carras is a pretty good shot at the classic Bordeaux blend, and is enthusiastically promoted and therefore quite expensive. *Tsantali* reds are also fairly reliable, and cheaper, and *Xinomavro Naoussis* is surprisingly good, with herby, slightly earthy fruit.

For Retsina addicts (yes, they do exist), *Tsantali* and *Metaxa* have the authentic taste, and Sainsbury's own-label is good, with a little more resin.

INDIA

Money can buy you anything if you're a millionaire; even your very own Champagne lookalike. A perfectly good wine it is too, which is astonishing in a country that produces hardly any other wine. But when Bombay millionaire Sham Chougule decided he wanted to produce wine, he asked Piper Heidsieck to come and help; a state-of-the-art winery was built to process the grapes from high-altitude vineyards, and *Omar Khayyam* is the result. It's not cheap, though.

ISRAEL

If a whole country's wine industry specializes in making a particular sort of wine (kosher) for a captive worldwide audience (observant Jews) then two things are likely to happen. First, it will produce that wine admirably well, to kosher standards; Jews the world over will be able to rely on the rabbinical signature on the label and will know that the wine has been produced in accordance with the strictest rules. Second, it will taste awful. That captive audience will be far more interested in the purity (in kosher terms) of the wine than in what it tastes like.

Then, the worldwide wine revolution being what it is, two more things will happen – and indeed have happened. First, California wine-making techniques will be brought in to make kosher wines that taste good enough to tempt non-Jews, too. And second, the biggest wine-making company in Israel (*Carmel*) will be forced to follow suit and invest US$8m in new equipment. The most attractive wines in Israel are however still made by the newcomer, the *Golan Heights* winery, whose *Yarden* wines are the best, followed by the *Golan* range.

LEBANON

Lebanese wine is, to all intents and purposes for us in Britain, *Château Musar*. There are other vineyards, to be sure, but it is *Musar* that is sought-after and admired; it is also Musar that puts the worries of most other winemakers firmly in the shade.

Frost and rot, the causes of most growers' sleepless nights, are not a problem for Serge Hochar of *Musar*. Civil war, on the other hand, is, and in 1984 he was not able to make a wine at all: the front line between Christian and Muslim zones ran between the vineyards and the winery, and the grape-laden lorries were not able to cross it.

In other years the chances of a successful vintage have looked thin, yet the wine has been made. In 1989 the winery, the office and Hochar's apartment were all hit by shelling, yet the wine was good; in 1990 the grapes narrowly missed being caught by the blockade which began on 28 September. In 1991, by contrast, the winery was regarded locally as one of the safest places to be, and many of the villagers took shelter in the cellars. In 1992 it was the grapes that suffered. A long cold winter and frost and hail reduced the crop, but the grapes were healthy although sugar levels are lower than usual and acidity higher. Still, a good vintage, says Hochar.

Musar's style is, typically, big and powerful. For a time in the late sixties Hochar turned to making lighter wines more reminiscent of Médoc, but now the wines are huge again, and age superbly – Hochar in fact reckons they should be drunk at 15 years, and will be even better at 30. The trouble is, they're often so wonderful at seven, when they are released, that keeping them that long requires an awful lot of willpower.

LUXEMBOURG

Luxembourg's wines, from the banks of the Mosel, are of little other than local interest. They lack the body, the interest and the aging potential of the best of their neighbours further down the river in Germany, but are perfectly acceptable, with light, delicate fruit. Most are made from Müller–Thurgau, here called Rivaner, which accounts for half the area under vine. Other grapes grown are Elbling, Riesling, Auxerrois, Gewürztraminer and Pinot Gris, with the last two making some of the most interesting wines.

NORTH AFRICA

Forget all those jokes about Algerian Burgundy: the march of Islamic fundamentalism in North Africa means that the vineyard area is shrinking and output is falling. At this rate, any sort of Algerian wine could eventually be no more than a memory.

It wouldn't, it has to be said, be a particularly fond memory for most people. Algeria, Tunisia and Morocco did a great deal to beef up the weaker, weedier French wines in the years before such things became illegal, and independence from France in the fifties and sixties followed by the tightening up of EC rules in the seventies dealt all three countries a double blow.

The wines are still seen in Britain, however. Morocco makes some decent reds, like *Sidi Brahim*, made only from Cinsaut, and *Tarik*, a hot-climate blend of Cinsaut, Carignan and Grenache. Tunisia might have a name for its Muscats, if they were less generally oxidized, and Algeria, the biggest producer of the three in terms of quantity, can boast the Coteaux de Mascara, which makes heavy, rustic, rather coarse reds. All three countries have *appellation contrôlée* systems based on the French model. The term is *Appellation d'Origine Garantie* in Algeria and Morocco and *Appellation d'Origine Contrôlée* in Tunisia.

SOUTH AFRICA

It must be awfully difficult being a southern hemisphere wine region. Everybody compares you to Australia, where men are men and the Chardonnay is cheap, and then blames you by implication because you are doing things differently.

South Africa emerged blinking on to the world stage only a couple of years ago; and it soon became clear that isolation had done nothing to help her wine industry. A bit of competition, we all said, would work wonders; and, little by little, it is. It is happening gradually: quite rightly, the South African growers are taking the time to discover what the outside world has to offer them. All the time their Chardonnays are becoming more commercial and their reds are softening, and names like Hamilton-Russell, Neil Ellis, Rustenberg, Warwick Farm and Overgaauw are leading the way. At the other end of the market there are inexpensive Colombards perfect for casual glugging.

SWITZERLAND

Swiss wines may be labelled in French, German or Italian, but little is seen in Britain in any language. The most popular grape, the Chasselas, changes its name to Dorin in the Vaud, Perlan in Geneva and Neuchatel and Fendant in the Valais. Pinot Noir can be good, but like all Swiss wines, it is light, clean, fruity and expensive.

TURKEY

Turkey's history of viticulture is rather more impressive than the wine itself. Although only three per cent of the total – huge – grape crop is made into wine, wine-making can be traced back some 4000 years – plenty of time in which to count the 1172 different grape varieties currently registered as being cultivated.

It's hard positively to recommend Turkish wines or even any individual grape varieties, but *Buzbag* (red), *Villa Doluca* and *Doluca* (red and whites), *Hosbag* (red), *Villa Dona* (red and white) are brand names to consider.

ZIMBABWE

There is some wine made here, and some is even exported to Britain, under the name of *Marondera*. You could try it, just to prove to your friends that it exists.

PRICE GUIDES

I suppose it could cross your mind that you don't need price guides – perish the thought, because if nobody wants a Price Guide I shall be back to doing pantomime at Northampton rep by next Christmas. But does that mean that you don't feel the need to know where to find the best price for a wine? That you don't want to find out what alternatives you can expect for the money you wish to spend? That you don't want to know if you're on to a super bargain? Surely not.

On expensive wines the price differences are often dramatic. On cheaper wines, the differences may be small but they're still worth knowing about. And our specially recommended wines may well be in limited distribution: it's of crucial importance to find out *where* the wines are stocked, as well as what the price differences are. By using these price guides judiciously, you should be able to drink *better* and more *cheaply* during the coming year.

• All prices are *per bottle inclusive of VAT*, unless otherwise stated. Remember that many merchants sell only by the case.

• Wines are listed in price bands and by vintage. Price bands run from the lowest to the highest. Vintages run from the most recent to the oldest. Within these categories the wines are listed in alphabetical order to help you find a particular wine more easily.

• Within the price bands, stockists are listed in brackets after each entry in ascending order of price. Occasionally, the same wine will fall into more than one price band, but before you get too agitated about variations in price, remember that wine warehouses, for example, often come out much cheaper because you have to buy by the case, they do not deliver, they do not have smart high street premises, and so on. Equally, there's no getting away from the fact that the price of a given wine sometimes varies wildly for no good reason.

• The claret prices are a special case. Specific prices are shown in ascending order by vintage. There *are* some dramatic price variations here – some are to do with keen pricing and the reverse; more often they will be because claret is now (for better or for worse) an investment medium and responsive to market pressures. A merchant buying wine *en primeur* in Bordeaux on Monday *afternoon* may pay 25 per cent more than the going rate that morning! Replacement stocks over the years will vary in cost and currency movements will also be a factor. So – for the sake of clarity – the prices we list were valid in the late spring/early summer of 1993.

• In the claret guide, all châteaux are listed alphabetically regardless of class. When a wine is quoted EC or IB, it means that the wine is offered on an *en primeur* basis (in Bordeaux or at the châteaux) or in bond (in the UK). All EC and IB prices are per dozen. The EC price simply includes the price of the wine in the bottle and excludes shipping, duties and taxes such as VAT. The EC price is usually payable when the wine is offered in the summer following the vintage.

The other costs (including VAT on both invoices) become payable when the wine is shipped. The *crus classés* and better *bourgeois* are shipped two years later, and the *petits châteaux* and the lesser *bourgeois* after a year. You should check the exact terms of sale with your merchant who will give you a projection of the final 'duty paid delivered' price at current rates of shipping, duty and VAT.

• Where merchants sell only by the case we have divided by 12 the VAT-inclusive price of a single case.

• When clubs (e.g. Les Amis du Vin) have both member and non-member prices we have used the *non-member* prices.

• Stars (★) denote wines that the editors consider particularly good value for money *in their class.*

• To get the most out of the lists in the book, please remember that *Webster's* is a price GUIDE not a price LIST. An invaluable reference whenever you are ordering or buying wine, it is not meant to replace up-to-date merchants' lists. What it *does* do, however, is give you a unique opportunity to compare prices; to develop a sense of what you can reasonably expect to pay for any given wine; to spot a bargain; to work out exactly what you can afford – *and to find it.*

MERCHANT CODES

The following list of abbreviations enables you to identify the merchants from whose lists the wines in the price guides were selected. For more detailed information on each merchant, see the Merchant Directory on page 412.

AD	Adnams
AMI	Les Amis du Vin (also Cullen's)
AS	Ashley Scott
ASD	ASDA
AUG	Augustus Barnett
AUS	Australian Wine Centre
AV	Averys
BAR	Barnes Wine Shop
BE	Bedford Fine Wines
BEK	Berkmann Wine Cellars
BER	Berry Bros & Rudd
BIB	Bibendum
BOD	Bordeaux Direct
BOR	Borg Castel
BOT	Bottoms Up
BR	Broad Street Wine Company
BU	The Butlers Wine Cellar
BUT	Bute Wines
BY	Anthony Byrne
BYR	D. Byrne & Co
CAP	Cape Province Wines
CB	Corney & Barrow
CHA	Châteaux Wines
CV	Celtic Vintner
DAV	Davisons
DI	Direct Wine
EL	Eldridge, Pope & Co
EY	Philip Eyres
FA	Farr Vintners
FIZ	Fine Wines of New Zealand
GA	Gateway Food Markets
GAU	Gauntleys of Nottingham
GE	Gelston Castle Fine Wines
GR	The Grape Shop
GRE	Peter Green
GRG	Grog Blossom
HAL	Halves
HA	John Harvey & Sons
HAC	Harcourt Fine Wine
HAG	Gerard Harris Fine Wines

HAH	Haynes Hanson & Clark
HAW	Roger Harris Wines
HAY	Richard Harvey Wines
HE	Douglas Henn-Macrae
HIC	Hicks & Don
HIG	High Breck Vintners
HOG	J.E. Hogg
HUN	Hungerford Wine Company
JU	Justerini & Brooks
KA	J.C. Karn & Son Ltd
LAY	Lay & Wheeler
LO	London Wine
LOR	Lorne House Vintners
MAJ	Majestic Wine Warehouses
MAR	Marks & Spencer p.l.c.
MOR	Moreno Wines
MV	Morris & Verdin
NA	The Nadder Wine Co Ltd
NI	James Nicholson
OD	Oddbins
PE	Thos. Peatling
PEN	Penistone Court Wine Cellars
PIP	Christopher Piper Wines
RAE	Raeburn Fine Wines
REI	Reid Wines
ROB	Roberson
SAF	Safeway
SAI	Sainsbury
SOM	Sommelier Wine Company
SUM	Summerlee Wines
TAN	Tanners
TES	Tesco
THR	Thresher
TW	T. & W. Wines
UN	Unwins
VA	Valvona & Crolla
VIC	Victoria Wine
VIG	La Vigneronne
VIN	Vintage Wines
WAI	Waitrose
WCL	Winecellars
WHG	Whiclar & Gordon
WHI	Whitesides of Clitheroe
WIC	Sunday Times Wine Club
WIW	Wines of Westhorpe Ltd
WR	Wine Rack
WRI	Wright Wine Company
WS	Wine Society
WW	Windrush Wines
WY	Peter Wylie Fine Wines
YAP	Yapp Brothers

RED BORDEAUX

d'Agassac *cru grand bourgeois exceptionnel Haut-Médoc*
1988 £8.95 (WAI)
1985 £8.45 (PE) £9.50 (WS) £9.95 (GE)
1983 £11.34 (TW)
1982 £11.50 (GE) £11.85 (WHI)

Amiral-de-Beychevelle *St-Julien*
1989 £15.80 (PIP)
1988 £15.80 (PIP) £16.20 (WRI)
1979 £27.50 (ROB)
1975 £38.25 (ROB)

Andron-Blanquet *cru grand bourgeois exceptionnel St-Éstèphe*
1986 £10.20 (PIP)
1985 £10.20 (PIP)
1982 £13.30 (LOR)

l'Angélus *grand cru classé St-Émilion*
1990 £16.81 (BUT)
1989 £21.88 (BUT) £23.97 (CB)
1988 £13.75 (WHG)
1985 £15.54 (AV) £24.85 (PE)
1983 £19.75 (AD)
1982 £29.00 (JU)
1966 £28.20 (REI)
1959 £49.93 (REI)

d'Angludet *cru bourgeois supérieur exceptionnel Margaux*
1991 EC £77.00 (SUM)
★ **1990** £10.73 (BUT) £10.75 (AD) £11.99 (NI)
1990 EC £114.00 (SUM)
1989 £9.95 (BE) £10.50 (LAY) £10.99 (BUT) £11.15 (BEK) £12.60 (PIP) £12.95 (BER)
1988 £10.75 (BE) £11.16 (CV) £11.60 (HAG) £12.25 (DAV) £13.00 (HAY) £14.82 (TAN)
1986 £11.50 (BE) £12.34 (CV) £13.00 (HAY) £14.53 (BUT) £18.86 (TAN)
1985 £13.00 (HAY) £13.95 (AMI) £15.00 (GE)
1983 £10.76 (REI) £11.56 (BUT) £15.00 (HAY)
1982 £16.60 (LOR)
1982 IB £155.00 (BIB)
1978 £18.21 (REI) £18.41 (BUT)

des Annereaux *Lalande-de-Pomerol*
1988 £7.85 (WHG)
1986 £7.85 (WHG)

Archambeau *Graves*
1990 £7.80 (WRI)

Arnauld *cru bourgeois Haut-Médoc*
1985 £8.95 (GE)

l'Arrosée *grand cru classé St-Émilion*
1990 £20.00 (WS)
1989 £21.80 (JU)
1988 £18.50 (GE) £19.50 (HUN) £21.00 (JU)
1986 £16.62 (BUT)
1985 £27.00 (JU)
1983 £26.00 (JU)

Ausone *1er grand cru classé St-Émilion*
1990 £54.00 (AD) £55.97 (BUT)
1989 £61.90 (BUT)
1988 £65.05 (BUT)
1986 £47.14 (AV) £52.54 (BUT) £53.00 (AD)
1986 IB £420.00 (FA)
1985 £49.93 (REI) £49.95 (AD) £57.00 (UN)
1985 IB £425.00 (FA)
1983 £49.95 (LAY) £52.88 (BEK) £55.00 (HAC) £57.37 (HA) £57.50 (BU) £65.28 (BUT)
1981 £65.00 (JU)
1979 £48.47 (FA)
1970 £88.13 (BIB)
1966 IB £600.00 (FA)
1964 £70.50 (REI)

Bahans-Haut-Brion *Graves*
1990 £12.95 (BUT)
1989 £12.95 (BAR) £16.00 (BUT) £18.60 (WS)
1989 EC £120.00 (RAE)
1988 £14.95 (NI)
1986 £15.90 (JU)
1985 £19.80 (JU) £23.09 (CB)

Batailley *5ème cru classé Pauillac*
1992 EC £70.00 (SUM)
1991 EC £88.00 (SUM)
1990 EC £80.00 (HIG) £114.00 (SUM)
1989 £10.75 (BUT) £11.35 (HIG) £13.00 (BER)
1989 imperial £112.00 (HAG)
1988 £9.40 (BEK) £10.58 (HIG)
1986 £9.60 (WS) £14.85 (DAV) £14.95 (BER)
1982 £19.09 (BIB)
1981 £14.68 (REI)
1974 £16.86 (BOR)
1971 £18.50 (REI)
1970 £20.00 (BU) £24.46 (BUT) £25.00 (WY)
1966 £43.90 (GR)

Beau-Rivage *Bordeaux*
Non-vintage £3.64 (EL)

Beau-Site *cru grand bourgeois exceptionnel St-Éstèphe*
1990 £7.49 (OD)
1990 EC £58.00 (HIG)
1989 £7.86 (BUT)
1988 £7.95 (WS)
1986 £8.95 (DAV)
1985 £12.10 (WRI)

Beau-Site-Haut-Vignoble *cru bourgeois St-Éstèphe*
1989 £7.48 (EY)

Beaumont *cru grand bourgeois Haut-Médoc*
1990 £6.24 (BUT)
★ **1989** £6.99 (NA) £7.70 (JU) £7.95 (SUM) £7.99 (UN) £8.85 (GRE) £9.45 (WRI)
1988 £6.58 (BEK) £6.95 (WS) £6.99 (LO) £7.64 (EL) £7.99 (DAV) £8.85 (GRE)
1986 £7.50 (WS) £11.40 (WRI)
1985 £8.35 (WS)

Beauséjour *1er grand cru classé St-Émilion*
1990 £25.00 (JU)
1989 £25.00 (JU)
1988 £22.00 (JU)
1962 £17.50 (BU)

Bel-Air *Puisseguin-St-Émilion*
1989 £7.35 (HAG)

Belair *1er grand cru classé St-Émilion*
1989 £21.25 (BUT)
1987 £19.62 (CB)
1986 £23.56 (CB)
1985 £16.00 (MV) £19.95 (AD) £22.24 (BUT)
1985 IB £112.00 (FA)
1983 £14.68 (REI) £16.95 (AMI) £17.77 (BUT)
1982 £20.04 (BUT)

Beychevelle *4ème cru classé St-Julien*
1989 £16.50 (NA) £16.95 (BAR) £19.50 (BU) £19.95 (WHG) £20.13 (BUT) £23.50 (JU)
1989 IB £155.00 (FA)
1988 £14.75 (GRE) £17.50 (HUN)
1988 magnum £29.50 (BU)
1986 £17.50 (HUN) £18.99 (AUG) £19.65 (PE)
1985 £18.27 (BY) £18.99 (AUG) £22.75 (HAG) £22.90 (UN) £23.25 (LOR) £24.85 (PE)
1984 £15.42 (AV) £18.49 (AUG) £19.50 (UN)
1983 £13.51 (BIB) £19.89 (WHI) £28.34 (AV)
1983 magnum IB £135.00 (FA)
1982 £21.50 (HAY) £21.75 (PE) £24.75 (VIC) £25.04 (TAN) £25.91 (HIC) £25.96 (LAY)

1982 IB £215.00 (FA) £225.00 (BIB)
1981 £18.75 (LOR)
1981 magnum £39.95 (REI)
1978 £19.09 (BIB) £23.50 (EL) £25.61 (GR)
1970 £32.50 (BU) £49.20 (AD) £54.50 (ROB)
1966 £48.47 (BIB) £85.00 (ROB)
1964 £40.00 (VIG)
1964 IB £216.00 (FA)
1961 £135.00 (JU)
1959 £50.00 (VIG)
1928 £183.50 (WHG)

le Bon-Pasteur *Pomerol*
1989 £14.95 (WHG) £18.75 (HUN)
1989 magnum £40.00 (HUN)
1985 £21.43 (BUT)

la Bonnelle *St-Émilion*
1988 £7.95 (WHG)

le Boscq *cru bourgeois supérieur St-Éstèphe*
1989 £7.90 (JU)

le Bourdieu *cru bourgeois Haut-Médoc*
1989 £7.99 (PIP)

Bourgneuf-Vayron *Pomerol*
1989 £13.62 (BUT)
1982 £16.90 (JU)

Bouscaut *cru classé Pessac-Léognan*
1989 EC £93.00 (RAE)
1986 £9.75 (RAE)
1985 £13.90 (JU)
1983 £8.94 (LO)
1962 £22.50 (BU)

Boyd-Cantenac *3ème cru classé Margaux*
1982 £17.03 (REI) £17.14 (BIB)
1976 £16.45 (REI)
1970 £29.75 (HAC)

Branaire-Ducru *4ème cru classé St-Julien*
1990 £13.35 (BUT)
1989 £13.60 (BE) £15.47 (BUT)
1986 £18.90 (LOR)
1985 £16.91 (BUT) £18.00 (DI) £18.50 (ROB)
1983 £15.95 (ROB) £16.95 (NA) £16.96 (HOG)
1982 £19.65 (LAY) £25.95 (BAR) £29.00 (JU)
1982 IB £185.00 (FA)
1981 £17.03 (REI)
1978 £16.00 (WY) £22.50 (BU)
1975 £17.95 (BU) £28.81 (AV)
1970 £29.40 (TAN) £31.13 (REI)
1961 £70.00 (GRE)

Brane-Cantenac *2ème cru classé Margaux*
1989 EC £150.00 (RAE)
1988 £14.99 (RAE)
1985 £14.53 (BY) £21.50 (UN) £21.75 (VIC)
1982 £17.03 (REI) £18.11 (BIB)
1978 £14.69 (BIB) £16.00 (WY)
1976 £14.32 (BUT)
1970 £25.00 (PE) £25.00 (WY) £29.45 (TW)
1966 £29.99 (NI)
1961 £52.88 (BIB)

du Breuil *cru bourgeois Haut-Médoc*
1992 EC £49.50 (SUM)
1990 EC £68.00 (SUM)

Cabannieux *Graves*
1989 £7.32 (SUM)
1988 £8.75 (HAG) £8.95 (GRE)
1986 £7.65 (WHI)

Cadet-Piola *grand cru classé St-Émilion*
1989 £16.80 (JU)
1988 £14.80 (JU)
1983 £16.90 (JU)

Calon-Ségur *3ème cru classé St-Éstèphe*
1989 £13.65 (WHG) £15.60 (BE) £19.22 (AV)
1988 £16.95 (BER) £17.35 (BUT) £18.50 (HUN) £19.45 (CB) £20.23 (AV)
1985 £12.35 (BY) £17.37 (BUT) £18.50 (UN) £18.50 (HUN) £19.53 (AV) £19.75 (HUN)
1983 £23.25 (AMI)
1982 £26.56 (EL) £32.00 (JU)
1982 IB £225.00 (BIB)
1970 £28.00 (WY)
1970 IB £220.00 (FA)
1966 £35.00 (BU) £38.68 (BIB) £55.00 (JU)
1962 £29.96 (REI)
1961 £58.26 (BIB) £75.00 (ROB)
1959 £29.51 (GR)
1947 £65.00 (VIG)
1945 £100.00 (BU)

EC (ex-cellar) price per dozen, excl shipping, duty and VAT. IB (in bond) price per dozen, excl duty and VAT. All other prices, per bottle incl VAT.

de Camensac *5ème cru classé Haut-Médoc*
1986 £11.60 (LOR) £12.75 (WHG)
1985 £13.35 (WRI) £14.95 (ROB)
1983 £11.90 (LOR)
1982 £13.99 (GRE)
1981 £12.75 (GRE)
1978 £14.50 (BU) £16.80 (HAC)
1975 £19.75 (ROB)
1971 £17.50 (BU)
1970 £18.21 (REI)

Canon *1er grand cru classé St-Émilion*
1990 £20.93 (BUT) £26.00 (JU)
1989 £27.50 (AD) £29.64 (BUT) £29.95 (MAJ) £30.69 (AV) £33.00 (JU)
1989 EC £250.00 (RAE)
1988 £21.50 (HAY) £23.50 (RAE) £25.14 (BUT)
1986 £21.95 (RAE) £22.86 (BUT) £23.44 (CB)
1985 £23.50 (HAY) £24.95 (AMI) £26.50 (PIP) £27.51 (BUT) £33.00 (JU)
1983 £24.46 (AV) £29.09 (WHI)
1979 £28.75 (ROB) £32.50 (HUN)
1970 IB £300.00 (FA)

Canon-la-Gaffelière *grand cru classé St-Émilion*
1989 £16.17 (BUT)
1989 EC £125.00 (RAE)
1961 £52.64 (TW)

Cantemerle *5ème cru classé Haut-Médoc*
1990 £12.69 (BUT)
1989 £15.97 (BUT)
1988 £13.95 (ROB) £14.00 (GE) £19.95 (WHG)
1987 £11.55 (PE) £14.99 (TES)
1986 £15.65 (PE)
1985 £12.53 (BEK) £16.45 (EL) £16.65 (PE)
1983 £17.63 (EL) £18.00 (HOG) £27.00 (JU)
1982 £12.24 (BIB) £15.86 (EL) £24.85 (PE)
1981 £9.99 (LO) £14.75 (BU) £14.90 (HOG)

1979 £14.00 (WY) £14.75 (BU)
1978 £19.00 (HAC)
1975 £14.69 (EL) £15.42 (BEK) £18.00 (WS)
1970 £21.73 (REI) £24.68 (EL) £40.00 (ROB)
1966 £23.50 (EL) £25.00 (BU)

Cantenac-Brown *3ème cru classé Margaux*
1990 £13.52 (BUT)
1989 £13.15 (WHG) £13.20 (BE)
1988 £10.52 (LO) £12.50 (LOR)
1970 £22.11 (BUT)
1968 £25.00 (HUN)

Carbonnieux *cru classé Pessac-Léognan*
1985 £14.85 (ROB)
1982 £13.50 (BE)

de Cardaillan *Graves*
1986 £6.95 (DAV)

la Cardonne *cru grand bourgeois Médoc*
1989 £7.63 (AV)
1987 £8.40 (PIP) £8.75 (ROB)

les Carmes-Haut-Brion *Pessac-Léognan*
1989 £15.40 (BUT)
1988 £13.49 (WHG)

Caronne-Ste-Gemme *cru grand bourgeois exceptionnel Haut-Médoc*
1988 £7.95 (AMI)
1986 £8.46 (EL) £11.00 (BE)
1985 £8.60 (WS) £11.44 (BOR)
1983 £9.50 (LOR)
1982 £9.80 (WS) £11.50 (GE)

Carruades de Lafite Rothschild (Moulin des Carruades until 1987) *Pauillac*
1990 EC £110.00 (HIG)
1989 £15.22 (BUT) £15.45 (LAY)
1988 £17.29 (BUT) £17.99 (BOT) £17.99 (WR)
1987 £13.25 (LAY) £13.49 (WR) £13.49 (BOT)
1986 £16.88 (BUT)
1985 £16.99 (BUT)
1983 £9.30 (BIB) £19.95 (AMI)
1981 £20.60 (WHI)
1980 £17.04 (TW)

Certan-de-May *Pomerol*
1990 £36.00 (JU)
1989 £36.19 (BUT) £37.78 (HAH) £42.00 (JU)
1988 £37.90 (GAU) £39.44 (BUT)
1986 £42.95 (CB)
1985 £35.00 (BU) £38.01 (CB) £40.21 (BUT)
1985 IB £295.00 (FA)
1983 £32.95 (LAY)
1983 IB £230.00 (FA)

Certan-Giraud *Pomerol*
1989 £17.00 (BUT)
1985 £17.91 (REI)
1985 IB £120.00 (FA)

de Chantegrive *Graves*
1985 £10.77 (BIB)

Chasse-Spleen *cru grand bourgeois exceptionnel Moulis*
★ **1990** £11.70 (AD) £11.87 (BUT) £12.90 (JU)
1989 £14.03 (BUT) £14.65 (GRE) £16.31 (BY)
1988 £11.95 (GRE) £14.74 (CHA)
1987 £9.85 (GRE) £10.56 (CHA) £11.46 (BY)
1986 £10.10 (HUN) £12.05 (BUT)
1986 magnum £34.70 (HAG)
1985 £12.50 (BE)
1985 magnum £29.90 (GRE)
1983 £14.95 (BAR) £17.75 (AD)
1982 £16.80 (BUT) £17.50 (HAY) £21.75 (PE)
1981 £15.09 (REI)
1976 £18.20 (WRI)
1957 £18.50 (BU)

Chauvin *grand cru classé St-Émilion*
1986 £10.04 (BUT)
1983 £11.50 (RAE)
1982 £13.22 (BIB) £14.50 (BU)
1979 £10.50 (HAY)
1978 £14.20 (BIB)

Cheret-Pitres *Graves*
1989 £8.58 (CHA)

Cheval-Blanc *1er grand cru classé St-Émilion*
1990 £41.98 (BUT)
1989 £55.00 (HUN) £56.79 (BUT) £70.00 (JU)
1989 magnum £110.00 (HUN)
1988 £44.81 (BUT) £58.00 (JU)
1986 £47.18 (CB) £56.00 (JU) £62.85 (DAV)
1985 £44.06 (BEK) £49.50 (PIP) £53.50 (BUT)
1985 IB £425.00 (BIB)
1984 £28.61 (AV) £35.00 (WS) £38.00 (BER)
1983 £48.00 (WS) £54.00 (BER) £65.85 (DAV)
1983 IB £360.00 (FA)
1982 £31.32 (REI) £73.00 (WY) £75.00 (BER)
1982 IB £960.00 (BIB)
1981 £41.34 (AV) £46.00 (BER) £48.00 (GE) £51.45 (NI) £54.71 (VIN) £55.00 (JU)

1978 £65.00 (BU) £68.00 (BER) £85.00 (ROB)
1975 £52.88 (BIB) £79.50 (DAV)
1971 IB £550.00 (FA)
1970 £42.07 (GR) £125.00 (DAV) £135.00 (ROB)
1970 magnum IB £955.00 (BIB)
1966 IB £900.00 (FA)
1953 £217.37 (REI)

Cissac *cru grand bourgeois exceptionnel Haut-Médoc*
1992 EC £64.25 (SUM)
1991 EC £74.50 (SUM)
1990 £8.84 (BUT) £8.99 (OD) £9.66 (TAN) £9.70 (JU) £9.95 (LAY) £9.99 (NA)
1990 EC £84.00 (SUM) £86.35 (HAH)
1989 £8.95 (LAY) £9.40 (MV) £9.95 (HUN) £10.30 (JU) £11.03 (SUM) £11.81 (CB)
1989 magnum £24.50 (HAG)
1988 £8.95 (HAY) £9.50 (HUN) £9.54 (AV) £9.60 (JU) £10.30 (WS) £10.87 (EL)
1986 £8.99 (NA) £9.74 (HA) £11.32 (BUT) £11.40 (HAG) £11.40 (LAY) £11.70 (JU)
1986 IB £85.00 (FA)
1985 £9.75 (HAY) £10.25 (PE) £10.48 (NI) £10.83 (BUT) £10.87 (EL) £11.00 (MV) £11.95 (LAY) £11.99 (OD) £12.50 (HIG)
1983 £9.56 (BUT) £11.36 (EL) £12.20 (PIP) £12.41 (HIC) £12.95 (HIG) £12.99 (LO)
1982 £14.65 (BUT) £14.90 (WRI) £18.95 (ROB)
1981 £12.93 (CV) £14.45 (NI) £15.50 (ROB)
1981 magnum £37.20 (HAG)
1978 £16.61 (BUT)
1978 magnum £33.69 (LO)
1975 £14.63 (EL) £15.86 (REI)
1971 £13.81 (EL)
1970 £20.25 (BUT) £25.26 (EL)

Citran *cru grand bourgeois exceptionnel Haut-Médoc*
1988 £9.67 (BEK) £11.85 (PIP) £14.16 (CB)

Clarke *cru bourgeois Listrac*
1989 £10.79 (NI)
1986 £11.95 (NI)
1985 £14.15 (PE)

Clerc-Milon *5ème cru classé Pauillac*
1989 £15.22 (BUT) £17.80 (JU)
1988 £13.50 (AV)
1986 £12.75 (HUN) £17.44 (BUT)
1985 £14.65 (AUG) £15.95 (GRE) £16.00 (GE)
1983 £13.95 (WS) £14.75 (ROB) £15.45 (AUG)
1982 £15.95 (BU)
1970 £25.26 (REI)

Clinet *Pomerol*
1990 £28.16 (BUT) £30.00 (JU)
1990 IB £259.00 (WY)
1989 £30.13 (BUT)
1985 £25.00 (HAG)
1985 IB £200.00 (FA)
1982 £19.00 (WY) £20.00 (BU)

Clos des Jacobins *grand cru classé St-Émilion*
1989 £20.23 (BUT)
1985 £17.95 (ROB) £20.75 (PE)
1981 £13.16 (LO)

Clos du Clocher *Pomerol*
1989 £15.95 (JU)
1988 £13.90 (JU)

Clos du Marquis *St-Julien*
1990 £10.40 (BUT)
1989 £12.54 (BUT)

1989 EC £102.00 (RAE)
1988 £9.95 (HUN) £10.50 (RAE) £11.20 (JU) £11.41 (BUT) £12.59 (NI) £14.69 (THR)
1986 £11.50 (HUN) £11.81 (BUT) £13.20 (JU) £13.49 (SAI) £21.25 (VIC)
1985 £12.50 (HUN) £20.25 (VIC)
1982 IB £120.00 (FA)

Clos Fourtet *1er grand cru classé St-Émilion*
1989 £24.00 (BER)
1986 £17.90 (BER)
1985 £14.66 (WIC) £20.48 (SUM)
1985 IB £108.00 (BIB)
1949 £85.00 (WY)

Clos l'Eglise *Lalande-de-Pomerol*
1988 £7.52 (EL)
1985 £19.29 (BUT)
1983 £16.26 (BUT)

Clos René *Pomerol*
1989 £14.70 (JU)
1988 £13.50 (JU)
1978 £21.19 (BUT)

la Clotte *grand cru classé St-Émilion*
1989 £17.68 (CB) £19.89 (BUT)
1988 £12.63 (CB)
1986 £14.04 (CB)
1970 £17.62 (REI)

Connétable Talbot *St-Julien*
1988 £9.75 (NI)
1987 £9.69 (AUG) £10.99 (PE)
1985 £11.45 (PE)
983 £11.55 (PE)

la Conseillante *Pomerol*
1990 £31.99 (OD) £33.43 (BUT)
1989 £42.44 (AV) £44.23 (BUT) £45.00 (JU)
1988 £44.79 (AV)
1986 £21.73 (REI) £25.61 (GR) £31.48 (AV)
1985 £27.96 (BUT) £33.04 (AV) £39.06 (PEN)
1984 £20.35 (AV)
1983 £19.50 (GE) £22.11 (LO)
1982 £38.68 (BIB)
1981 IB £210.00 (FA)
1978 £22.90 (BUT)
1970 £52.87 (REI)

Corbin *grand cru classé St-Émilion*
1989 £10.41 (BUT)

Corbin-Michotte *grand cru classé St-Émilion*
1970 £20.00 (BU)

Cormeil-Figeac *grand cru St-Émilion*
1989 £8.35 (BUT)

Cos d'Estournel *2ème cru classé St-Éstèphe*
1990 £21.25 (BUT) £21.40 (AD) £21.99 (OD)
1990 IB £175.00 (WY)
1990 EC £200.00 (HIG)
1989 £23.00 (BE) £26.79 (BUT) £27.20 (AD) £28.34 (AV) £31.00 (JU) £32.00 (BER)
1989 IB £250.00 (BIB)
1989 EC £230.00 (RAE)
1988 £22.11 (BUT) £23.00 (JU) £24.95 (BER)
1986 £18.95 (WHG) £19.50 (HUN) £19.65 (LAY) £22.15 (PE) £22.96 (BUT)
1986 IB £210.00 (FA)
1985 £20.90 (UN) £21.50 (HUN) £24.00 (BER)
1983 £18.15 (REI) £21.68 (BEK) £24.99 (TAN)
1982 £39.68 (BUT)
1981 £20.37 (TAN)
1978 £31.65 (LAY) £45.00 (VIG)
1975 £21.54 (BIB) £24.65 (LAY) £27.50 (BU)
1970 £39.00 (MV) £41.12 (REI) £41.70 (BUT)

1962 £45.00 (BU) £50.00 (WY)
1962 IB £385.00 (FA)
1959 £81.66 (REI)
1957 £25.00 (BU)
1928 £189.00 (WHG)

Cos Labory *5ème cru classé St-Éstèphe*
1990 £14.45 (LAY)
1989 £13.50 (HUN)
1988 £12.50 (HUN)
1986 £9.65 (PE)
1985 £12.50 (HUN) £12.55 (PE) £15.80 (PIP)
1970 £19.50 (BE)

Coufran *cru grand bourgeois Haut-Médoc*
1990 £8.94 (BEK)
1985 £10.50 (GRE)
1978 £9.30 (BIB) £12.88 (BUT)

Couvent-des-Jacobins *grand cru classé St-Émilion*
1986 £13.65 (PE)
1985 £18.70 (PIP)

le Crock *cru grand bourgeois exceptionnel St-Éstèphe*
1989 £10.50 (BER)
1989 EC £72.00 (RAE)
1985 £9.45 (PE)

la Croix *Pomerol*
1985 £14.75 (WHG)
1983 £16.23 (PEN)
1981 £12.95 (WHG)

la Croix-de-Gay *Pomerol*
1990 £13.90 (BUT)
1989 £14.50 (BE) £14.97 (BUT)
1985 £15.95 (ROB)

la Croix-du-Casse *Pomerol*
1989 £12.58 (BEK)
1985 £15.73 (GR)
1982 £19.85 (HAG)

Croizet-Bages *5ème cru classé Pauillac*
1970 £17.05 (BUT)
1961 £75.00 (ROB)

la Dame de Montrose *St-Éstèphe*
1989 £10.88 (BUT)
1985 £18.35 (BUT)

Dassault *grand cru classé St-Émilion*
1983 £19.20 (BE)

Dauzac *5ème cru classé Margaux*
1988 £15.50 (WRI)

Desmirail *3ème cru classé Margaux*
1990 EC £110.00 (HIG)
1989 £13.31 (HIG)
1989 EC £99.00 (RAE)
1988 £11.75 (RAE)

Deyrem-Valentin *cru bourgeois Margaux*
1988 £8.57 (EY)

Domaine de Chevalier *cru classé Pessac-Léognan*
1991 EC £138.00 (RAE)
1990 EC £168.00 (RAE)
1989 £27.04 (BUT) £27.75 (AD) £29.50 (HUN)
1989 EC £235.00 (RAE)
1988 £28.00 (JU)
1986 £22.87 (BUT)
1985 £28.00 (BER) £28.34 (AV) £33.25 (WHI)
1983 £18.22 (BEK) £18.25 (HAY) £19.79 (REI) £23.50 (CV) £24.00 (GE) £25.00 (BE)
1983 IB £160.00 (FA)
1982 £20.56 (BEK) £25.00 (BU) £32.00 (BE) £37.95 (AD) £38.90 (BUT) £42.30 (TW)
1982 IB £210.00 (FA)
1979 £24.95 (BAR)
1978 £24.50 (HAC) £25.40 (BUT)
1975 £25.11 (EY)
1970 IB £495.00 (FA)

Domaine de l'Eglise *Pomerol*
1992 EC £81.00 (SUM)
1991 EC £106.00 (SUM)
1990 EC £100.00 (HIG) £140.00 (SUM)
1989 £13.31 (HIG) £14.30 (BER) £16.15 (BUT)
1988 £12.33 (HIG)
1986 £15.85 (DAV)
1985 £15.35 (WS)
1983 £12.93 (HIG)
1982 £13.22 (BIB)

Domaine la Grave *Graves*
1990 £6.25 (GE)
1990 EC £60.00 (HIG)
1989 £8.81 (HIG)
1988 £7.99 (HIG)
1986 £8.52 (TW)

la Dominique *grand cru classé St-Émilion*
1989 £16.59 (BUT) £18.50 (HUN) £19.50 (JU)
1986 £16.50 (BER) £17.95 (ROB)
1985 £14.95 (AMI) £17.08 (BUT) £22.00 (JU)

Ducru-Beaucaillou *2ème cru classé St-Julien*
1990 £21.34 (BUT) £21.49 (OD) £26.00 (JU)
1990 EC £220.00 (HIG)
1990 double magnum £106.00 (JU)
1989 £25.00 (BE) £26.00 (MV) £26.95 (LAY) £28.68 (BUT) £32.00 (JU) £32.50 (BER)
1989 EC £256.00 (RAE)

1989 double magnum £135.00 (JU)
1989 jeroboam £220.00 (JU)
1989 imperial £266.00 (JU)
1988 £21.50 (RAE) £23.33 (BUT) £23.50 (HAY) £25.65 (LAY) £26.00 (JU) £26.44 (EL)
1988 double magnum £106.00 (JU)
1988 jeroboam £172.00 (JU)
1988 imperial £205.00 (JU)
1986 £23.01 (BUT) £24.95 (AMI) £24.99 (PE) £29.00 (BER) £34.00 (VIC)
1986 IB £243.00 (BIB) £248.00 (WY)
1985 £23.50 (HAY) £26.86 (BUT) £27.99 (OD) £28.50 (BER) £29.20 (UN) £29.95 (AD)
1984 £17.00 (WS) £18.24 (AV) £18.99 (PE) £21.00 (BER) £25.00 (UN)
1983 £18.80 (EL) £20.00 (WS) £20.56 (BEK) £23.62 (BUT) £23.65 (PIP) £24.69 (VIC) £25.96 (LAY) £27.10 (GAU) £28.50 (CB)
1983 IB £175.00 (FA)
1982 £37.50 (BU) £38.50 (LOR) £38.78 (EL)
1981 £23.79 (TAN) £24.67 (REI) £28.95 (DAV)
1981 IB £180.00 (FA)
1981 magnum £73.00 (SOM)
1979 £17.14 (BIB) £29.95 (PE)
1978 £24.48 (BIB) £29.95 (AMI) £36.05 (SUM) £36.65 (LAY) £45.00 (JU)
1976 £25.85 (EL) £29.95 (BAR) £33.78 (TAN)
1975 £24.68 (EL) £26.00 (BU) £31.28 (AV) £35.00 (WS) £43.00 (DI) £45.00 (ROB)
1975 jeroboam £350.00 (DI)
1971 £23.50 (BIB)
1970 £63.52 (TAN) £65.00 (JU) £69.00 (AD)
1966 £55.81 (REI) £65.00 (JU)
1964 IB £228.00 (FA)
1962 £19.51 (GR) £32.90 (BIB)
1961 £105.75 (BIB) £146.87 (REI)
1943 £125.00 (ROB)

Duhart-Milon-Rothschild *4ème cru classé Pauillac*
1990 £13.86 (BUT) £14.95 (LAY)
1989 £14.95 (LAY) £16.53 (BUT) £18.24 (AV)
1986 £15.00 (BUT) £17.80 (JU) £22.70 (AV)
1985 £17.95 (ROB) £18.72 (PIP) £20.00 (JU)
1983 £15.00 (GE) £18.50 (LOR)
1982 £19.50 (ROB) £20.00 (WS) £22.95 (AMI)

Durfort-Vivens *2ème cru classé Margaux*
1985 £17.95 (ROB)
1982 £18.11 (BIB) £22.38 (HA)
1970 £25.26 (LO)

l'Église-Clinet *Pomerol*
1990 £19.44 (BUT) £21.00 (JU)
1990 EC £140.00 (RAE)
1989 £21.82 (BUT) £22.50 (JU)
1988 £19.00 (GE)
1986 £17.56 (BUT)

l'Enclos *Pomerol*
1989 £13.44 (BOR) £13.70 (JU)
1988 £12.80 (LOR)
1986 £14.69 (CV) £15.75 (PIP)
1985 £17.25 (BUT)
1982 £20.00 (BUT)

l'Évangile *Pomerol*
1990 £34.00 (BE) £35.40 (BUT) £39.00 (JU)
1988 £35.00 (BU) £45.00 (HUN)
1985 £39.25 (BUT) £41.54 (CB)
1983 £36.00 (HAG)
1983 IB £210.00 (FA)

Feytit-Clinet *Pomerol*
1990 £11.75 (AD) £12.53 (TAN)
1989 £17.80 (CB)
1988 £12.20 (AD)
1986 £14.20 (AD)
1985 £20.50 (BE)
1983 £15.00 (WS)
1959 £40.00 (ROB)

Les Fiefs-de-Lagrange *St-Julien*
1990 £7.91 (TAN) £9.00 (WS)
1989 £7.99 (OD) £10.63 (HAH)
1988 £10.35 (WS) £10.69 (HOG)
1986 £11.80 (JU)
1985 £18.09 (BUT)

de Fieuzal *cru classé Pessac-Léognan*
1990 £13.81 (BUT) £14.99 (OD) £15.70 (JU)
1989 £15.22 (TAN) £15.99 (OD) £16.01 (BUT) £16.65 (BER) £16.71 (HAH)

1989 IB £146.00 (WY)
1988 £12.99 (NI) £14.75 (BER)
1986 £13.65 (PE) £14.95 (AMI)
1985 £12.99 (BEK) £14.15 (PE) £14.50 (HUN) £14.76 (GR) £15.86 (TAN) £15.94 (BUT)
1983 £13.50 (WS) £14.95 (AD) £15.95 (ROB)
1982 £14.76 (GR) £21.75 (PE)
1981 £15.86 (REI)

Figeac *1er grand cru classé St-Émilion*
1990 £20.93 (BUT) £26.00 (JU)
1989 £26.75 (BUT) £29.05 (AV) £32.00 (JU)
1989 EC £245.00 (RAE)
1986 £25.78 (BUT) £27.52 (AV) £27.70 (LOR)
1985 £28.93 (AV) £30.16 (BY) £30.29 (VIC) £30.50 (UN) £31.77 (BUT) £36.00 (JU)
1985 IB £213.00 (BIB)
1983 £28.00 (WS) £32.00 (ROB) £37.69 (VIC)
1983 magnum £48.15 (HAG)
1982 IB £330.00 (FA) £354.00 (WY)
1978 £33.54 (BUT)
1975 £30.55 (BEK) £35.10 (PIP)

la Fleur-Pétrus *Pomerol*
1990 £29.65 (BUT) £33.65 (LAY) £35.08 (CB)
1989 £40.38 (BUT)
1988 £28.06 (TAN) £31.92 (BUT)
1986 £39.50 (ROB) £41.19 (CB)
1985 £39.55 (BUT)
1983 £28.95 (LAY)
1983 IB £210.00 (FA)
1970 £49.93 (REI)
1970 IB £500.00 (FA)
1947 £225.00 (ROB)

Fombrauge *grand cru St-Émilion*
1989 £11.05 (BER)
1988 £7.81 (EL) £8.24 (BOR) £10.30 (BER)
1986 £7.53 (HA) £8.18 (EL) £11.75 (BER)
1985 £13.00 (BUT)
1961 £55.00 (ROB)

Fonbadet *cru bourgeois supérieur Pauillac*
1985 £12.34 (BUT)
1983 £11.56 (HOG)

Fonroque *grand cru classé St-Émilion*
1990 IB £90.00 (MV)
1989 £15.80 (AV) £16.74 (CB)
1988 £19.68 (CB)
1986 £13.81 (CB)
1985 £14.94 (BUT)
1982 £12.34 (BUT)
1981 £14.95 (VIG)

les Forts-de-Latour *Pauillac*
1990 £17.30 (BUT) £19.65 (LAY)
1985 £24.21 (HA) £24.95 (LAY) £25.50 (AD)
1985 IB £180.00 (FA)
1983 £19.65 (WHI)
1982 £23.95 (AMI) £28.07 (BUT)
1982 IB £250.00 (FA)
1978 £30.40 (AD) £31.65 (LAY) £36.25 (VIC)
1970 £44.06 (REI)
1970 IB £280.00 (FA)

Fourcas-Dupré *cru grand bourgeois exceptionnel Listrac*
1988 £7.20 (GR) £10.11 (HAH) £10.12 (PIP)
1986 £9.50 (GE) £9.60 (BE)
1985 £9.87 (PIP) £9.99 (CV)
1983 £13.80 (HAG)

Fourcas-Hosten *cru grand bourgeois exceptionnel Listrac*
1989 £9.75 (BER)
★ **1988** £8.42 (HIG) £10.50 (GRE)
1986 £9.40 (HIG) £9.75 (GRE)
1985 £11.95 (DI) £12.50 (ROB)
1982 £18.85 (AV)
1978 £11.75 (BU)
1949 £76.37 (REI)

Franc-Mayne *grand cru classé St-Émilion*
1986 £9.78 (HOG)
1983 £12.22 (BY)

la Gaffelière *1er grand cru classé St-Émilion*
1989 £23.00 (JU)
1985 £20.41 (AV)
1970 £30.00 (HOG)
1961 £56.98 (REI)

la Garde *Pessac-Léognan*
1989 £8.03 (BEK)
1988 £6.99 (NA)
1985 £8.95 (LOR)
1983 £7.95 (BU)
1982 £11.95 (BU)
1961 £9.76 (GR)

le Gay *Pomerol*
1989 £22.91 (BUT)
1989 IB £214.00 (WY)
1985 £18.00 (WY) £20.93 (BUT)
1983 £15.39 (BY)
1982 £29.00 (JU)
1982 IB £180.00 (FA)

Gazin *Pomerol*
1989 £18.71 (BUT) £20.98 (HAH) £22.50 (JU)
1989 IB £146.00 (WY)
1989 magnum £42.38 (HAH)
1988 £27.91 (CB)
1983 £23.95 (AMI)
1981 magnum £37.50 (ROB)

Giscours *3ème cru classé Margaux*
1990 £16.61 (BUT)
1989 £14.50 (BE) £14.95 (BU)
1988 £13.70 (NI) £14.99 (THR) £14.99 (WR) £14.99 (BOT) £16.64 (HIG)
1985 £19.50 (ROB) £27.00 (JU)
1985 IB £130.00 (FA)
1983 £21.10 (LOR) £25.00 (JU)
1982 £22.20 (LOR) £23.50 (BIB) £37.00 (ROB)
1982 IB £200.00 (FA)
1978 £25.26 (REI) £26.95 (AMI) £35.00 (JU)
1970 £31.82 (BIB) £35.00 (WY) £55.00 (ROB)
1966 £30.45 (NI)
1961 £52.88 (BIB) £64.03 (REI)

du Glana *cru grand bourgeois exceptionnel St-Julien*
1988 £8.99 (MAJ) £10.50 (BER)
1982 £11.50 (HAY)

Gloria *cru bourgeois St-Julien*
1990 £11.57 (BUT) £12.96 (BEK)
1989 £12.50 (BE) £12.95 (GRE) £13.02 (BUT) £13.95 (BU) £14.38 (AV) £14.69 (PEN)
1988 £11.99 (UN) £13.50 (BER) £15.72 (PIP)
1985 £16.29 (NA) £17.35 (NI) £17.95 (AMI)
1985 IB £90.00 (FA)
1983 £17.00 (BUT) £17.20 (LOR)
1978 £19.24 (BUT)
1970 £27.75 (ROB)

Grand-Barrail-Lamarzelle-Figeac *grand cru classé St-Émilion*
1985 £6.31 (LO)
1982 £12.60 (WS)

Grand-Mayne *grand cru classé St-Émilion*
1990 £11.99 (OD) £16.58 (BEK)
1989 £12.26 (BUT) £12.49 (OD)

Grand-Pontet *grand cru classé St-Émilion*
1990 £10.49 (OD)
1989 £9.99 (OD)
1988 £10.99 (OD)
1985 £10.99 (OD) £12.30 (BEK) £14.92 (HAH)

Grand-Puy-Ducasse *5ème cru classé Pauillac*
1989 £11.50 (DI) £13.63 (CB) £15.70 (WRI)
1988 £11.95 (GRE)

1985 £15.65 (PE) £17.50 (ROB) £19.95 (AMI)
1982 £14.12 (BUT)

Grand-Puy-Lacoste *5ème cru classé Pauillac*
1990 £13.69 (BUT) £15.65 (LAY)
1989 £16.00 (MV) £16.31 (BUT) £19.50 (JU)
1989 EC £141.00 (RAE)
1988 £14.99 (RAE) £17.50 (JU) £19.10 (HAG)
1986 £14.95 (HUN) £16.72 (BUT)
1985 £16.76 (BEK) £19.41 (TAN) £19.75 (AD) £19.95 (HUN) £21.26 (BUT) £22.50 (JU)
1983 £11.75 (REI) £13.06 (BUT) £17.45 (WHI)
1983 IB £130.00 (FA)
1982 £25.20 (REI) £26.95 (LAY) £30.35 (WHI)
1981 £17.32 (BUT) £17.95 (LAY) £18.14 (HIC)
1978 £24.00 (GE) £26.97 (TAN) £27.95 (AD)
1970 £32.21 (TAN) £35.65 (LAY) £45.00 (VIG)
1961 £61.68 (REI)

Grangeneuve de Figeac *grand cru St-Émilion*
1988 £10.99 (BOT) £10.99 (WR)

la Grave-Trigant-de-Boisset *Pomerol*
1989 £20.61 (CB) £21.91 (BUT)
1988 £14.98 (CB)
1986 £16.86 (CB)
1985 IB £110.00 (FA)

Gressier-Grand-Poujeaux *cru bourgeois supérieur Moulis*
1988 £10.98 (NI)
1985 £9.99 (TAN) £10.25 (PE) £10.95 (BAR)
1983 £7.36 (LO)
1981 £6.50 (GE) £8.34 (BEK) £9.73 (PIP)
1979 £10.95 (WHG) £12.15 (ROB)
1970 £24.27 (BUT)

Greysac *cru grand bourgeois Médoc*
1989 £8.95 (ROB)
1985 £8.25 (PE)

Gros-Caillou *St-Éstèphe*
1989 £6.90 (BUT)

Gruaud-Larose *2ème cru classé St-Julien*
1990 £21.26 (BUT)
1989 £19.95 (WHG) £25.36 (BUT) £29.00 (JU) £29.50 (HUN) £30.02 (CB)
1988 £15.78 (LO) £16.00 (HAY) £21.50 (JU) £21.64 (BUT) £23.05 (AV) £23.36 (BER)
1986 £19.50 (HUN) £20.00 (HAY) £24.85 (PE) £26.35 (WHI) £27.50 (GAU)
1986 IB £155.00 (FA)
1985 £13.95 (DAV) £18.50 (HUN) £18.99 (NI) £19.01 (BUT) £19.50 (ROB) £19.90 (UN)
1983 £17.90 (BUT) £18.50 (GE) £19.00 (WY) £22.75 (PE) £23.55 (HA) £24.00 (JU)
1983 IB £140.00 (FA)
1983 ½bottle £14.00 (HAG)
1982 £25.95 (BIB) £27.85 (PE) £32.31 (BEK)
1982 IB £275.00 (FA)
1981 £14.20 (FA) £20.00 (HAY) £20.75 (PE) £22.00 (WS) £22.95 (BAR) £27.65 (HAG)
1978 £28.95 (PE) £29.95 (LAY) £32.60 (HAG)
1975 £23.79 (TAN) £24.00 (BIB) £25.26 (REI)
1973 £13.59 (BOR)
1971 magnum £56.98 (REI)
1970 £44.95 (AMI)
1970 IB £350.00 (BIB) £366.00 (WY)
1966 £60.00 (ROB) £60.00 (WHI)
1961 magnum IB £1,295.00 (FA)
1953 magnum IB £1,120.00 (FA)
1934 £110.00 (ROB)

Guillot *Pomerol*
1985 £12.50 (GE)
1983 £12.50 (GE)

la Gurgue *cru bourgeois supérieur Margaux*
1989 £10.95 (BE) £12.73 (BUT)
1988 £9.99 (GRE) £10.20 (BE) £11.00 (GE)

Hanteillan *cru grand bourgeois Haut-Médoc*
1990 £8.80 (TAN)
1989 £5.30 (GR) £6.95 (ASD) £8.08 (HAH)
1988 £7.00 (WS) £7.95 (TAN)
1986 £9.32 (PIP) £9.50 (WHI)

Haut-Badon *grand cru St-Émilion*
1989 £8.50 (AS)

Haut-Bages-Avérous *cru bourgeois Pauillac*
1989 £12.15 (BUT) £14.58 (BER)
1988 £12.36 (HA) £14.99 (THR) £14.99 (BOT) £14.99 (WR) £17.78 (BY)
1985 £14.99 (SAF)
1985 IB £108.00 (BIB)
1983 £13.50 (ROB)

Haut-Bages-Libéral *5ème cru classé Pauillac*
★ **1990** £9.85 (BUT) £11.75 (GRE) £12.65 (LAY)
1989 £11.80 (BE) £12.54 (TAN) £12.80 (JU)
1988 £10.95 (BE) £11.50 (GRE) £13.97 (TAN)
1986 £10.50 (WS) £10.94 (BUT) £12.50 (BER)
1985 £13.60 (WS) £15.50 (GRE)
1983 £15.84 (AV) £19.00 (WRI)
1970 £18.74 (BUT)

Haut-Bailly *cru classé Pessac-Léognan*
1989 £18.00 (HUN) £18.94 (AV)
1989 EC £132.00 (RAE)
1989 magnum £38.00 (HUN)
1988 £12.95 (RAE) £14.50 (HAY) £15.00 (JU)
1982 £16.50 (HAY) £20.85 (AD)
1982 magnum £26.44 (BIB)
1981 £15.00 (GE) £17.03 (REI) £21.50 (ROB)
1978 £19.99 (OD)
1970 £19.09 (BIB)
1966 £95.05 (HUN)

Haut-Batailley *5ème cru classé Pauillac*
1990 £11.25 (BUT) £12.90 (JU)
1990 IB £98.00 (MV)
1989 £13.00 (MV) £13.55 (BUT)
1989 IB £107.00 (WY)
1986 £11.54 (BUT) £12.53 (BIB) £12.83 (HOG) £13.34 (CB) £14.73 (LO)
1985 £14.99 (WR) £14.99 (BOT) £14.99 (THR) £15.50 (UN) £16.39 (CV) £16.90 (JU)
1983 magnum £26.44 (BIB)
1982 £19.09 (BIB) £23.50 (GRE)
1970 £25.11 (AV) £28.00 (GE)

Haut-Brion *1er cru classé Pessac-Léognan*
1990 £43.56 (BUT) £47.99 (OD) £48.00 (JU)
1990 IB £370.00 (BIB)
1990 EC £377.00 (RAE) £450.00 (HIG)
1989 £62.15 (BUT) £80.00 (JU)
1988 £37.50 (NI) £47.29 (VIC) £49.00 (JU)
1988 imperial £780.00 (HUN)
1986 £43.84 (BUT) £43.87 (CB) £45.00 (PE)
1986 IB £345.00 (FA)
1985 £43.83 (BY) £49.50 (BU) £50.02 (BUT)
1985 double magnum £240.00 (JU)

1985 imperial £460.00 (JU)
1984 £26.95 (RAE) £38.00 (BER) £38.50 (UN)
1983 £39.50 (HUN) £40.00 (HOG) £40.00 (WS)
1983 IB £315.00 (FA)
1983 magnum £67.56 (BIB)
1982 £48.95 (REI) £55.32 (BIB) £58.75 (NA) £66.08 (BUT) £69.99 (OD) £72.00 (BER)
1982 IB £575.00 (FA)
1981 £36.43 (BEK) £42.95 (HUN) £43.20 (PIP) £47.00 (BER) £55.00 (JU)
1981 imperial £460.00 (JU)
1978 £50.76 (EY) £53.85 (BIB) £62.00 (BER) £65.14 (BUT) £70.00 (JU) £99.99 (VIC)
1975 £53.42 (BUT) £53.85 (BIB) £60.00 (TAN)
1970 £49.00 (NI) £61.20 (BIB) £68.00 (WY) £75.00 (NA) £110.00 (ROB)
1970 magnum £231.71 (GR)
1966 £87.64 (BIB) £90.60 (BUT) £98.00 (GE)
1964 £80.00 (GE)
1960 £59.00 (VIG)
1955 £117.50 (BIB) £150.15 (BUT)
1929 £470.00 (REI)
1928 £395.00 (ROB)

Haut-Gardère *Pessac-Léognan*
1989 £7.79 (BUT)

Haut-Marbuzet *cru grand bourgeois exceptionnel St-Éstèphe*
1990 £15.17 (BUT)
1988 £13.50 (WRI) £14.05 (GA) £15.25 (GRE)
1985 £15.85 (WHI)
1985 ½bottle £8.25 (GRE) £8.25 (WHI)
1982 £14.75 (LOR)

Haut-Sarpe *grand cru classé St-Émilion*
1985 £14.95 (WHG) £17.04 (CV)

Hortevie *cru bourgeois St-Julien*
1988 £13.10 (HAG)

Houissant *cru bourgeois supérieur St-Éstèphe*
1989 £7.99 (NA)
1988 £7.05 (EL)

d'Issan *3ème cru classé Margaux*
1990 £13.75 (CHA)
1990 IB £108.00 (MV)
1989 £16.05 (BER) £16.70 (JU) £17.95 (HUN)
1988 £12.75 (BU) £12.95 (RAE) £14.40 (JU)
1986 £12.91 (BUT) £15.95 (AMI) £20.00 (VIG)
1985 £12.95 (BU) £15.51 (BUT) £19.00 (WS)
1985 IB £138.00 (BIB)
1985 magnum £30.00 (MV)
1983 £18.75 (BU) £19.05 (AV)
1982 £18.50 (BU) £21.85 (NI)

Kirwan *3ème cru classé Margaux*
1989 £12.95 (DI) £16.00 (HAG)
1981 £17.54 (PEN)
1964 £17.63 (BIB)
1959 £45.00 (VIG)

Labadie *cru bourgeois Médoc*
1990 £6.95 (GA)
1988 £7.64 (PIP)

Labégorce *cru bourgeois supérieur Margaux*
1989 £9.70 (BE)

Labégorce-Zédé *cru bourgeois supérieur Margaux*
1990 £11.14 (BUT)
1989 £11.50 (TAN) £12.20 (AD) £12.59 (BUT)
1988 £9.99 (PE) £12.50 (JU)
1986 £10.72 (BUT) £10.75 (PE) £12.95 (DAV)
1985 £11.65 (BUT)
1982 £18.95 (DI)

Lacoste-Borie *Pauillac*
1988 £9.54 (AV) £19.55 (DAV)
1986 £7.95 (PE) £8.95 (WS)
1985 £16.69 (BUT)

Laffitte-Carcasset *cru bourgeois St-Éstèphe*
1988 £8.49 (TES)

Lafite-Rothschild *1er cru classé Pauillac*
1990 £47.00 (BE) £50.72 (BUT)
1990 EC £450.00 (HIG)
1989 £55.97 (BUT) £59.50 (BU) £65.45 (PEN)
1988 £49.22 (BUT) £59.29 (VIC) £62.00 (JU)
1986 £55.00 (MV) £58.85 (CB) £60.15 (PE)
1985 £45.00 (WY) £45.63 (BY) £49.06 (BUT)
1985 IB £420.00 (FA) £450.00 (BIB)
1984 £29.00 (JU) £34.00 (PE) £37.50 (HUN)
1984 IB £210.00 (FA)
1983 £49.00 (BER) £49.99 (OD) £52.88 (EL) £52.99 (HA) £55.00 (JU)
1983 IB £375.00 (FA)
1982 £83.23 (BIB) £83.50 (HUN) £95.00 (BER) £110.00 (WS) £110.00 (JU) £111.63 (EL)
1981 £49.00 (HUN) £49.99 (OD) £58.49 (BY)
1978 £80.00 (AMI)
1976 £57.50 (BU) £100.00 (HAC)
1970 £87.64 (BIB) £111.84 (AV) £130.00 (ROB)
1970 magnum £237.80 (GR) £275.00 (ROB)

1962 £99.87 (REI) £124.00 (PE)
1961 £286.00 (OD) £399.00 (PE)
1959 £235.00 (BIB)
1955 £105.75 (BIB)
1953 £188.00 (BIB) £205.62 (REI)
1948 £170.37 (REI)
1945 ½ bottle £225.00 (FA)
1943 £293.00 (WY)
1923 £338.00 (WY)

Lafleur *Pomerol*
1990 £125.16 (BUT)
1989 £43.31 (BUT) £93.10 (BUT)
1988 £36.86 (BUT) £68.88 (BUT)
1970 £55.00 (ROB)
1961 IB £2,400.00 (FA)

Lafleur-Gazin *Pomerol*
1983 £18.61 (AV)
1982 £20.19 (AV)
1981 £17.00 (WS)

Lafon-Rochet *4ème cru classé St-Éstèphe*
1990 £9.99 (OD)
1989 £12.20 (LOR) £12.49 (OD) £13.50 (JU)
1986 £11.85 (HOG) £14.40 (LOR)
1985 £14.50 (LOR)
1982 £14.50 (BU) £16.50 (HOG)

Lagrange *Pomerol*
1989 £14.09 (BUT) £19.23 (AV)
1988 £13.50 (JU)
1985 £15.02 (BUT) £19.25 (BUT)
1983 £13.50 (WS)
1978 £16.00 (WY)
1964 £25.26 (REI)

Lagrange *3ème cru classé St-Julien*
1990 £11.88 (BUT) £14.95 (LAY)
1989 £13.50 (BE) £17.95 (BER)
1986 IB £125.00 (BIB)
1985 £16.61 (BUT)
1983 £14.50 (HOG) £20.30 (LOR)
1982 £23.00 (ROB)
1970 £32.00 (ROB)
1966 £41.12 (TW)

la Lagune *3ème cru classé Haut-Médoc*
1990 £12.19 (BUT)
1989 £15.94 (LAY) £16.80 (JU) £16.95 (NI) £17.50 (HUN) £17.95 (MAJ) £18.75 (ROB)
1989 IB £150.00 (BIB)
1989 EC £122.00 (RAE)
1988 £12.93 (CV) £13.70 (HIG) £15.05 (BEK)
1987 £11.59 (SAF) £11.74 (HOG) £13.00 (LOR)
1986 £13.67 (CB) £13.96 (BUT) £14.15 (PE) £14.50 (HUN) £14.69 (HIG) £17.20 (LAY)
1985 £16.96 (LAY) £18.75 (ROB) £19.16 (BUT) £19.25 (NI) £19.50 (UN) £19.95 (AMI)
1985 IB £130.00 (FA)
1985 imperial £180.00 (JU)
1983 £18.50 (BE) £18.85 (DAV) £19.28 (BEK) £19.30 (NI) £24.63 (PIP)
1982 £24.00 (SOM) £25.96 (LAY)
1982 IB £200.00 (FA) £255.00 (BIB)
1981 £14.20 (LO) £19.50 (HAC)
1979 £24.75 (GRE)
1978 £25.85 (REI) £29.00 (BE) £30.38 (BUT)
1978 IB £180.00 (FA)
1975 £23.40 (BUT) £29.00 (JU) £30.00 (ROB)
1975 magnum £42.30 (REI)
1970 £50.00 (HUN)
1966 £35.00 (BU)

Lalande-Borie *cru bourgeois St-Julien*
1990 IB £83.00 (MV)
1989 £9.95 (TAN) £11.80 (JU)
1988 £9.90 (MV) £10.80 (JU)
1986 £10.44 (BUT) £10.87 (CB) £13.00 (MV)
1985 £11.50 (WS) £14.72 (BUT)

de Lamarque *cru grand bourgeois Haut-Médoc*
1988 £10.16 (CB)
1986 £9.81 (CB)
1985 £10.40 (CB)

Lamothe-Cissac *cru grand bourgeois Haut-Médoc*
1989 £7.50 (DI)
1988 £8.65 (DI)
1987 £6.43 (BUT) £7.50 (DI)
1986 £8.70 (DI)

Lanessan *cru bourgeois supérieur Haut-Médoc*
★ **1990** £7.91 (BUT)
1989 £9.20 (MV) £9.80 (BUT)
1988 £9.17 (EL)
1985 £9.86 (BUT) £12.83 (BEK) £15.52 (PIP)
1983 £12.65 (NI)
1981 £9.78 (CHA)

Langoa-Barton *3ème cru classé St-Julien*
1990 £13.20 (BUT) £16.95 (TAN)
1990 IB £99.00 (BIB)
1989 £12.50 (BE) £14.44 (SUM) £14.95 (NA) £14.95 (BU) £16.50 (JU) £16.98 (CB)
1988 £13.99 (NA) £14.50 (JU)
1986 £13.92 (BUT) £15.66 (WIC)
1986 IB £133.00 (BIB)
1985 £17.39 (NA)
1985 IB £143.00 (BIB)
1983 £12.90 (LO) £17.50 (BE)
1982 £25.00 (WS)
1982 IB £173.00 (BIB)

Larcis-Ducasse *grand cru classé St-Émilion*
1990 £14.16 (BOR)
1985 £9.50 (GE)

Larmande *grand cru classé St-Émilion*
1989 £14.00 (MV) £14.72 (BUT) £16.44 (AV) £16.50 (JU) £17.48 (BER) £17.50 (BU)
1988 £14.20 (JU)
1986 £14.80 (JU) £15.60 (WS)
1985 £13.97 (BUT) £15.50 (JU)

Laroque *grand cru St-Émilion*
1988 £9.99 (AUG)

Larose-Trintaudon *cru grand bourgeois Haut-Médoc*
1989 £7.95 (DI)
1985 £7.09 (BEK) £8.14 (HA) £8.72 (PIP)

Laroze *grand cru classé St-Émilion*
1986 £10.39 (SAF) £11.75 (HIG)
1985 £12.50 (HIG)

Larrivet-Haut-Brion *Pessac-Léognan*
1989 £13.30 (BUT)
1985 £12.34 (BUT)
1966 £25.00 (BU)

Lartigue-de-Brochon *cru bourgeois Haut-Médoc*
1988 £5.95 (HAY)
1986 £6.45 (PE) £8.20 (JU)

Lascombes *2ème cru classé Margaux*
1990 £15.49 (AUG)
1989 £12.05 (WHG) £12.07 (GR) £14.44 (SUM)
1988 £12.00 (WY) £13.99 (PE) £17.99 (AUG)
1986 £17.91 (WIC) £17.95 (ROB)
1982 £18.15 (REI) £23.85 (GRE)
1981 £20.99 (VIN)
1966 £32.00 (WY)
1955 £50.00 (VIG) £55.00 (ROB)

Latour *1er cru classé Pauillac*
1991 EC £315.00 (RAE)
1990 £45.82 (BUT)
1990 IB £450.00 (BIB)
1989 £47.00 (PEN) £50.59 (BUT) £53.94 (LAY) £65.00 (DI) £66.31 (TAN) £70.00 (JU)
1989 IB £420.00 (FA)
1988 £39.50 (RAE) £39.95 (AMI) £39.95 (NI) £41.70 (BY) £45.55 (BUT) £47.50 (BU)
1988 imperial £795.00 (HUN)
1986 £39.00 (MV) £45.00 (HUN) £59.00 (JU)
1986 IB £360.00 (FA) £438.00 (BIB)
1985 £43.99 (OD) £58.30 (UN) £60.00 (ROB) £65.00 (HUN) £65.15 (PE)
1984 £29.50 (VIG) £33.50 (ROB) £39.00 (BER)
1983 £25.45 (REI) £39.95 (NI) £43.00 (HOG) £49.00 (HUN) £49.00 (JU) £50.94 (HA)
1983 IB £355.00 (FA)
1983 magnum £67.56 (BIB) £94.88 (GR) £120.00 (ROB)
1982 £85.00 (BER) £99.88 (PEN) £99.99 (VIC)
1982 IB £838.00 (WY)
1982 imperial IB £620.00 (FA)
1981 £36.16 (BUT) £38.78 (EL) £58.00 (JU) £60.00 (ROB) £61.50 (GRE) £61.65 (PE)
1981 imperial IB £330.00 (FA)
1978 £39.20 (BUT) £85.00 (AMI) £88.00 (HOG)
1978 magnum £175.00 (JU)
1978 imperial £41.13 (FA)
1976 £44.06 (BIB) £65.00 (HUN) £68.00 (JU)
1975 £63.65 (BIB) £70.30 (BUT) £75.00 (HUN)
1972 ½ bottle £14.75 (BU)
1971 £66.17 (BUT)
1970 £105.47 (BUT) £109.00 (PE)
1970 magnum IB £1,050.00 (BIB)
1970 double magnum £881.25 (CB)
1969 £35.63 (BUT)
1967 £50.00 (GE)
1966 £126.80 (BIB)
1964 magnum IB £900.00 (FA)
1961 £587.56 (CB) £595.00 (ROB)
1961 magnum £979.16 (FA)
1955 £79.27 (GR) £105.75 (BIB)
1953 magnum IB £2,400.00 (FA)
1945 magnum £1,100.00 (FA)

Latour-à-Pomerol *Pomerol*
1990 £23.33 (BUT) £27.65 (LAY)
1989 £38.83 (CB)
1988 £24.62 (CB) £28.69 (TAN) £28.72 (BUT)
1985 £32.95 (LAY)
1982 £28.00 (WY)
1981 £28.38 (BUT)
1978 IB £240.00 (FA)
1970 £55.00 (HAC)
1970 IB £520.00 (FA)

Laujac *cru grand bourgeois Médoc*
1989 £7.78 (AV)
1985 £10.00 (HAG)

Lavillotte *cru bourgeois Médoc*
1988 £8.95 (GE)
1986 £8.95 (GE)
1983 £9.95 (GE) £10.95 (WHG)
1981 £9.95 (GE)

Léoville-Barton *2ème cru classé St-Julien*
1992 EC £97.00 (SUM)
1990 £14.25 (AD) £14.75 (BUT) £14.99 (OD) £15.31 (SUM) £16.20 (JU) £16.50 (SOM)
1990 IB £120.00 (MV)
1990 EC £140.00 (HIG) £157.75 (HAH)
1989 £14.38 (BUT) £15.94 (LAY) £15.95 (AD) £16.34 (SUM) £16.45 (NA) £17.45 (BER)
1989 IB £130.00 (FA) £153.00 (BIB)
1989 EC £139.00 (RAE)
1988 £14.25 (SUM) £14.28 (BY) £14.75 (GRE)
1986 £14.10 (BUT) £14.90 (LOR) £15.39 (NA) £16.50 (HAY) £16.77 (HOG) £16.95 (GRE)
1986 IB £135.00 (FA) £153.00 (BIB)
1985 £15.85 (BY) £15.90 (UN) £16.00 (WY) £16.95 (GRE) £17.29 (BUT) £19.00 (BE)
1983 £14.90 (WS) £17.07 (BUT) £17.29 (WHI) £18.95 (LO) £19.00 (BE) £19.95 (LAY)
1983 IB £130.00 (FA)
1982 £23.99 (BIB) £25.60 (TAN) £27.95 (LAY)
1981 £14.30 (BUT) £21.22 (HAH)
1978 £27.95 (LAY) £31.80 (AD) £32.00 (WS)
1975 £18.29 (GR) £20.56 (BIB) £29.50 (HUN)
1966 £47.00 (REI)
1961 £95.00 (ROB) £110.50 (AD)
1960 £20.00 (BU)

All châteaux are listed alphabetically regardless of class.

Léoville-Las-Cases *2ème cru classé St-Julien*
1990 £22.41 (BUT)
1989 £32.24 (BUT) £34.00 (BER) £34.22 (AV)
1989 IB £253.00 (WY)
1989 double magnum £82.00 (JU)
1988 £37.74 (AV)
1986 £19.95 (WHG) £25.46 (FA) £27.41 (BUT) £30.95 (PE) £31.48 (AV)
1985 £25.43 (BY) £29.00 (BER) £29.45 (BUT) £33.04 (AV) £35.60 (VIC) £36.00 (JU)
1985 IB £253.00 (BIB)
1983 £22.03 (TAN) £22.50 (BU) £25.96 (LAY) £26.41 (PIP) £27.70 (LOR) £28.50 (CB) £29.02 (WHI) £29.50 (AD) £33.00 (JU)
1983 IB £175.00 (FA)
1983 ½ bottle £15.36 (HAL)
1982 £60.00 (PE)
1981 £23.17 (TAN) £29.63 (BY) £30.00 (ROB)
1981 magnum £47.32 (GR)
1978 £36.49 (BUT) £39.00 (MV) £45.00 (ROB)
1976 £25.97 (TAN)
1975 £33.49 (BEK) £39.96 (PIP) £44.50 (ROB) £49.00 (JU) £49.95 (AMI)
1971 £20.56 (BIB) £39.00 (MV)
1970 £40.00 (WS) £41.12 (REI) £43.28 (TAN) £45.00 (SOM) £50.00 (OD) £53.49 (AV)
1970 IB £330.00 (FA)
1966 £79.29 (NI) £85.00 (JU)
1964 £25.00 (BU)
1957 £25.00 (BU)
1955 £105.00 (ROB)

Léoville-Poyferré *2ème cru classé St-Julien*
1990 £15.34 (BUT)
1990 EC £117.00 (RAE)
1989 £19.80 (JU) £20.07 (HAH) £23.32 (CB)
1988 £14.95 (RAE)
1986 £17.45 (BER)
1985 £15.37 (BY) £17.50 (HUN) £17.80 (UN) £19.92 (EL) £24.70 (HAG) £34.25 (VIC)
1985 magnum £30.00 (HAY)
1983 £17.00 (GE) £17.59 (BEK) £19.50 (BE)
1982 £24.00 (GE) £24.82 (TAN) £25.00 (MV) £26.20 (HAG) £26.95 (GRE)
1982 IB £135.00 (FA)
1981 £16.58 (LO) £18.00 (HUN) £19.95 (LOR)
1978 £21.57 (LO) £26.00 (JU) £40.60 (VIC)
1978 IB £173.00 (BIB)
1970 £25.00 (WY)
1964 £35.35 (HUN)
1961 £70.50 (BIB)
1959 £49.00 (GE)
1952 £49.00 (VIG)

Lestage *cru bourgeois Listrac*
1989 £5.98 (BER)
1964 £6.95 (WHG)

Liversan *cru grand bourgeois Haut-Médoc*
1990 £8.49 (OD)
1989 £8.99 (OD) £10.50 (JU) £11.54 (NI)
1988 £8.15 (PE) £8.95 (JU) £9.20 (BER) £10.29 (AV) £10.42 (HAH) £11.54 (NI)
1986 £9.80 (BER) £10.49 (NI) £10.90 (JU)
1983 £11.34 (CB)

Livran *cru bourgeois Médoc*
1989 £8.10 (HAG)

Loudenne *cru grand bourgeois Médoc*
★ **1990** £7.25 (JU)
1989 £7.55 (NA)
1988 £5.89 (BOT) £5.89 (THR) £5.89 (WR)

la Louvière *Pessac-Léognan*
1990 £10.31 (BUT) £10.49 (OD)
1989 £11.66 (BUT) £11.99 (OD) £12.99 (TES)
1983 £12.48 (NI)

Lynch-Bages *5ème cru classé Pauillac*
1990 £19.69 (BUT) £25.00 (JU)
1990 IB £208.00 (WY)
1989 £24.95 (LAY) £25.44 (BUT) £28.50 (HUN) £29.00 (JU) £30.00 (BER)
1989 jeroboam £198.00 (JU)
1988 £18.47 (BUT) £18.50 (RAE) £21.00 (JU) £22.95 (DAV) £24.50 (WHG)
1987 £17.50 (LOR) £18.67 (BY) £20.50 (ROB)
1986 £14.50 (HUN) £19.87 (BUT) £19.99 (PE) £20.15 (HA) £21.66 (LAY) £22.70 (AV)
1986 IB £180.00 (FA) £183.00 (BIB)
1985 £18.86 (BY) £23.69 (WHI) £24.50 (HUN) £24.78 (BUT) £25.25 (VIC) £25.50 (NA)
1985 IB £240.00 (FA)

All châteaux are listed alphabetically regardless of class.

1984 £14.65 (PE) £14.95 (RAE) £15.70 (BY) £18.00 (UN) £18.50 (BER)
1983 £20.00 (HAY) £21.15 (PEN) £22.91 (REI) £24.10 (HAG) £24.40 (LOR) £24.82 (AV)
1982 £34.00 (WY) £34.95 (AMI) £35.00 (HUN)
1981 £18.99 (OD) £28.00 (ROB)
1978 £26.00 (WY) £31.99 (OD)
1978 IB £278.00 (WY)
1978 magnum £85.00 (JU)
1976 £19.79 (REI) £23.50 (EL)
1976 jeroboam £210.00 (DI)
1975 £35.00 (JU) £45.00 (ROB)
1975 IB £240.00 (FA)
1970 £49.95 (AMI) £59.50 (DI) £68.07 (BUT)
1961 £170.00 (JU)

Lynch-Moussas *5ème cru classé Pauillac*
1990 £9.99 (OD)
1989 £9.99 (NA) £10.99 (NI)
1978 £12.24 (BIB) £17.50 (HAG)

Magdelaine *1er grand cru classé St-Émilion*
1990 £24.95 (LAY)
1989 £26.50 (CB) £29.01 (BUT)
1988 £21.03 (CB) £21.93 (TAN) £23.67 (BUT)
1985 IB £150.00 (FA)
1982 £48.00 (ROB)
1981 £20.47 (BUT) £24.00 (WY)
1970 £60.00 (JU)

Malartic-Lagravière *cru classé Pessac-Léognan*
1985 £14.57 (BUT)
1973 £13.49 (BOR)
1971 £16.86 (BOR)

Malescasse *cru bourgeois Haut-Médoc*
1986 £6.64 (BUT) £7.50 (WS)

Malescot-St-Exupéry *3ème cru classé Margaux*
1986 £14.80 (WRI) £14.95 (VIG)
1985 £17.15 (TW) £19.60 (BE)
1983 £16.50 (DI)
1982 £21.60 (DI)
1978 £15.84 (BOR)
1970 £25.00 (BU) £29.96 (REI)
1966 £35.00 (VIG)

de Marbuzet *cru grand bourgeois exceptionnel St-Éstèphe*
1990 £9.36 (BUT)
1989 £12.80 (JU)
1988 £11.80 (JU)

Margaux *1er cru classé Margaux*
1990 £46.89 (BUT) £53.50 (OD)
1990 IB £495.00 (WY)
1989 £56.81 (BUT) £59.00 (HUN) £59.65 (AD)
1989 IB £495.00 (FA)
1988 £46.99 (OD) £49.65 (LAY) £55.25 (VIC)
1986 £48.35 (BUT) £55.00 (VIG) £58.95 (LAY)
1985 £42.68 (BUT) £54.20 (UN) £54.50 (GRE) £58.00 (BE) £58.75 (CV) £59.00 (HUN) £64.85 (VIC) £65.15 (PE)
1984 £39.00 (HUN) £40.50 (UN) £43.00 (BER)
1983 £48.00 (HUN) £49.00 (UN) £49.95 (LAY) £53.85 (BIB) £55.00 (NA) £55.00 (OD) £56.33 (BUT) £58.00 (BER) £64.63 (EL)
1983 IB £420.00 (FA)
1982 £77.84 (BIB) £84.50 (GRE) £85.00 (JU)
1981 £41.13 (BEK) £42.31 (BUT) £46.50 (BE) £49.93 (REI) £50.53 (PEN) £55.95 (LAY) £58.00 (JU) £60.73 (PIP) £65.00 (ROB)
1981 IB £395.00 (FA)
1975 £49.50 (BU) £87.44 (BUT)
1971 £51.46 (GR)
1970 £53.85 (BIB) £78.50 (TAN) £105.00 (PE)
1966 £75.00 (BU) £140.00 (ROB)
1962 £65.00 (BU) £82.00 (WHG)
1961 £323.12 (REI)
1959 £176.25 (BIB)
1950 magnum £293.75 (REI)
1934 £175.00 (ROB)

Marquis d'Alesme-Becker *3ème cru classé Margaux*
1988 £9.99 (MAJ)
1986 £11.65 (PE)
1983 £15.75 (BU)
1982 £16.50 (BU)
1966 £29.50 (BU)

Marquis de Ségur *St-Éstèphe*
1985 £18.09 (BUT)

Marquis-de-Terme *4ème cru classé Margaux*
1989 £12.00 (MV) £13.90 (JU)
1988 £11.00 (MV) £12.62 (PEN) £12.99 (TES)
1985 £15.31 (BUT)
1983 £13.75 (BEK) £14.90 (HOG)
1976 £14.50 (BU)

Stars (★) indicate wines selected by the editors as particularly good value in their class.

Martinet *grand cru St-Émilion*
1989 £8.66 (AV) £8.75 (GE)
1988 £7.50 (GE)

Maucaillou *cru bourgeois Moulis*
1989 £12.29 (BEK)
1988 £11.45 (SAI) £11.85 (NI)
1986 £12.80 (JU) £12.95 (DAV)
1985 £9.39 (WHI) £10.95 (AMI)
1970 £19.50 (ROB)

le Menaudat *1ères Côtes de Blaye*
1989 £5.86 (AV)

Meyney *cru grand bourgeois exceptionnel St-Éstèphe*
1990 £10.50 (JU) £10.55 (BUT)
1989 £11.85 (HUN) £11.95 (BUT) £11.99 (UN)
1988 £9.75 (HUN) £9.95 (BU) £9.99 (UN)
1986 £9.75 (HUN) £11.65 (PE) £13.00 (WS) £16.00 (HAG) £16.25 (GRE)
1985 £10.95 (HUN) £10.99 (UN) £11.25 (PE) £12.75 (ROB) £13.15 (BUT) £13.15 (LO)
1983 £12.99 (WHI) £14.50 (HOG) £14.65 (PE)
1982 £18.49 (WHI) £21.46 (GR)
1979 £13.50 (HOG)
1978 £22.10 (LO)
1970 £19.50 (BU)
1967 £14.69 (BIB)
1961 £48.47 (BIB)

Millet *Graves*
1988 £8.77 (HOG)

la Mission-Haut-Brion *cru classé Pessac-Léognan*
1990 £35.98 (BUT) £42.00 (JU)
1990 EC £295.00 (RAE)
1989 £49.00 (JU) £50.26 (BUT)
1988 £40.00 (JU)
1986 £34.45 (AV) £35.22 (BUT) £39.99 (PE)
1985 £43.24 (EL) £44.62 (BUT) £48.65 (HUN)
1985 IB £275.00 (FA)
1984 £25.05 (AV) £35.00 (BER) £36.20 (UN)
1983 £28.00 (WY) £34.00 (HOG) £35.50 (GRE)
1983 IB £260.00 (FA)
1982 £58.00 (BER) £68.00 (JU) £70.00 (ROB)
1981 £32.31 (BEK) £38.95 (PIP) £39.95 (BER)
1980 £25.50 (ROB) £45.00 (VIG)
1979 £42.50 (BER)
1979 IB £320.00 (FA)
1978 £44.06 (BIB)
1976 £46.95 (AMI) £55.00 (JU)
1966 £78.00 (SOM) £87.64 (BIB)
1962 £65.00 (BU)

Monbousquet *grand cru St-Émilion*
1983 £9.85 (LOR)
1982 £9.85 (LOR)
1959 £48.00 (ROB)

Monbrison *cru grand bourgeois exceptionnel Margaux*
1990 £15.50 (JU) £19.12 (BUT)
1989 £16.80 (JU) £16.87 (BUT)
1988 £20.00 (VIG)
1985 £11.32 (BUT)

Monlot-Capet *St-Émilion*
1988 £9.20 (BE) £9.65 (LAY)

Montbrun *cru bourgeois Margaux*
1985 £9.99 (DAV)

Montgrand-Milon *Pauillac*
1989 £7.95 (WHG) £8.78 (GR)

Montrose *2ème cru classé St-Éstèphe*
1990 £29.63 (BUT)
1990 IB £175.00 (WY)
1989 £19.98 (PEN) £23.20 (HAG) £23.50 (JU) £23.80 (BUT) £25.20 (CB) £25.45 (BER)
1988 £16.35 (WHG) £18.80 (EL)
1985 £16.58 (BY) £17.63 (EL) £22.00 (HUN)
1985 IB £145.00 (FA)
1983 £23.69 (VIC) £23.88 (AV)
1982 £21.05 (BEK) £21.10 (LOR) £22.00 (WY) £23.50 (EL) £25.70 (PIP) £26.95 (GRE)
1982 IB £215.00 (BIB)
1981 £12.92 (EL) £18.86 (PIP)
1978 £20.90 (HAC) £21.15 (EL)
1978 IB £190.00 (FA)
1977 £12.35 (BUT)
1976 £14.57 (BUT)
1970 £45.00 (WY) £55.00 (JU)
1966 £47.00 (PEN)
1964 £40.00 (VIG)
1961 £57.75 (NI)
1959 IB £500.00 (FA)

Moulin-du-Cadet *grand cru classé St-Émilion*
1985 £14.19 (HAH)
1962 £18.00 (BU)

Moulinet *Pomerol*
1989 £14.50 (HAG)
1986 £14.79 (BOT) £14.79 (THR) £14.79 (WR)
1985 £13.50 (UN) £14.73 (LO) £16.57 (TW)
1983 £18.68 (TW)
1973 £18.68 (TW)

Mouton-Baronne-Philippe
1990 £11.99 (OD) £12.37 (BUT)
1989 £12.79 (BUT) £14.49 (OD)
1989 EC £115.00 (RAE)
1988 £11.85 (GRE) £12.95 (BU) £14.49 (OD)
1986 £13.55 (PE) £14.73 (BUT) £14.95 (HUN)
1985 £14.95 (AUG) £17.10 (EL) £17.16 (TW) £17.50 (UN) £18.95 (ROB)
1983 £11.99 (AUG) £12.89 (LO) £12.99 (GRE)
1982 £15.90 (GRE) £19.97 (REI)
1981 £11.57 (LO) £17.50 (ROB)
1978 £20.26 (REI)
1975 £17.33 (REI)
1966 £25.00 (BU) £29.51 (GR)

Mouton-Rothschild *1er cru classé Pauillac*
1991 IB £285.00 (BIB)
1990 £43.65 (BUT) £53.50 (OD)
1990 IB £395.00 (BIB)
1990 EC £450.00 (HIG)
1989 £57.91 (BUT)
1988 £46.99 (OD)
1986 £64.57 (BUT) £87.50 (VIC)
1985 £45.99 (OD) £49.16 (BUT) £55.00 (UN) £55.00 (HUN) £58.75 (CV) £64.80 (VIC)
1985 IB £420.00 (FA)
1984 £31.00 (DI) £35.00 (WS) £35.80 (HAH) £37.50 (ROB) £38.50 (UN) £39.00 (BER)
1984 ½ bottle £29.08 (TW)
1983 £36.89 (AUG) £39.99 (OD) £41.12 (BEK) £43.00 (HOG) £44.00 (HUN) £45.00 (UN) £47.36 (PIP) £48.00 (WS) £50.25 (BUT) £52.00 (JU) £52.00 (WHI) £55.00 (NA)
1983 IB £385.00 (FA)

1982 £107.71 (FA) £129.00 (DAV)
1981 £38.26 (HOG) £45.00 (HUN) £46.25 (WHI) £47.00 (BIB) £52.95 (AMI) £58.00 (JU)
1979 £44.65 (EL) £65.80 (NI) £75.00 (DI)
1979 IB £394.00 (WY)

1978 £58.26 (BIB) £69.00 (HUN) £70.00 (BER) £71.50 (OD) £85.00 (JU) £90.00 (ROB)
1975 £63.65 (BIB) £70.21 (BUT) £89.00 (GAU)
1975 magnum £155.63 (REI)
1975 imperial £63.65 (FA)
1970 £91.06 (BIB) £105.64 (LAY) £115.00 (JU)
1970 magnum £237.80 (GR)
1966 magnum £254.38 (REI)
1964 £94.00 (HUN)
1964 magnum IB £900.00 (FA)
1962 £82.00 (WHG) £115.85 (GR)
1961 £411.25 (BIB)
1959 £445.00 (ROB)
1959 magnum IB £3,500.00 (FA)
1955 £176.25 (BIB)
1953 magnum IB £4,500.00 (FA)
1945 £998.75 (FA)
1945 magnum £2,400.00 (FA)
1936 £191.87 (BUT)
1929 magnum £1,000.00 (FA)
1921 magnum IB £4,000.00 (FA)

Nenin *Pomerol*
1990 £13.49 (OD)
1989 £16.49 (OD)
1985 £16.90 (UN) £17.70 (BE) £18.04 (EL)
1983 £22.31 (HA)
1982 £14.00 (WY)
1970 £22.91 (REI)

Notton *Margaux*
1988 £8.90 (HA) £9.37 (HOG) £9.99 (MAR)
1980 £7.99 (RAE)

les Ormes-de-Pez *cru grand bourgeois St-Éstèphe*
1990 £10.99 (OD) £11.14 (BUT) £14.26 (BY)
1989 £12.04 (BUT) £14.50 (HUN)
1988 £11.49 (UN) £12.85 (BER)
1986 £8.82 (SUM) £9.99 (PE) £10.07 (BUT) £11.50 (BER) £18.39 (BY)
1985 £9.99 (UN) £14.81 (BEK) £19.87 (PIP)
1981 £13.61 (HA) £15.93 (PIP)

Palmer *3ème cru classé Margaux*
1992 EC £122.00 (SUM)
1991 EC £184.00 (SUM)
1990 £24.22 (BUT) £24.51 (TAN) £30.00 (JU)
1990 EC £275.00 (SUM)
1989 £24.50 (BE) £28.19 (TAN) £30.02 (BUT) £30.35 (NI) £31.48 (AV) £33.00 (BER)
1989 IB £240.00 (FA)
1988 £23.50 (HAY) £23.74 (TAN) £28.75 (BE)
1987 £17.30 (BE) £17.60 (HAG) £17.63 (CV)
1987 magnum £39.95 (BAR)
1986 £24.99 (PE) £25.00 (HAY) £26.95 (DI) £29.00 (BE) £29.38 (CV) £30.00 (BER)
1985 £27.04 (BUT) £28.95 (AMI) £30.00 (BER) £30.00 (BE) £30.95 (PE) £32.32 (CV)
1985 IB £228.00 (FA)
1983 £28.33 (NI) £35.00 (BER) £39.00 (BE)
1982 £28.00 (WY) £29.50 (BU) £39.50 (BER) £39.85 (WHG) £43.20 (HAG) £43.50 (ROB)
1982 IB £275.00 (FA) £350.00 (BIB)
1981 £26.43 (REI) £27.31 (BUT) £39.00 (ROB)
1979 £29.37 (FA) £38.00 (JU)
1978 £39.64 (LAY)
1976 £33.84 (BUT) £45.00 (ROB)
1975 £95.00 (ROB)
1975 magnum £96.94 (BIB)
1971 £34.27 (BIB)
1970 £75.00 (WS) £99.87 (REI) £105.00 (ROB)
1966 £195.00 (ROB)
1961 £334.87 (REI)
1960 £45.00 (VIG)
1959 £210.00 (ROB)
1940 £57.50 (BU)

Panigon *cru bourgeois Médoc*
1987 £5.18 (GR)
1985 £5.98 (GR)

Pape-Clément *cru classé Pessac-Léognan*
1990 £17.23 (BUT)
1989 £21.13 (TAN) £24.50 (JU)
1989 EC £172.00 (RAE)
1988 £19.21 (BUT) £22.00 (BER)
1985 £14.65 (WHG) £20.27 (BUT)
1982 £20.75 (HAC)
1982 IB £175.00 (BIB)
1981 £29.38 (CV)
1970 £28.00 (WY) £30.39 (NI)
1966 £35.00 (VIG)
1962 £27.50 (BU)

Patache d'Aux *cru grand bourgeois Médoc*
★ **1990** £7.77 (BUT)
1989 £7.49 (NA) £8.49 (TES) £8.50 (HUN)
1988 £7.95 (HUN)
1985 £9.25 (WHI)
1982 £10.20 (BUT) £11.10 (LOR)
1981 £9.82 (BUT)

Paveil-de-Luze *cru grand bourgeois Margaux*
1989 £10.46 (EL)
1988 £8.45 (GRE)
1985 £9.85 (GRE)
1973 £7.50 (BU)

Pavie *1er grand cru classé St-Émilion*
1990 £18.95 (BUT)
1990 EC £142.00 (RAE)
1989 £16.75 (WHG) £21.00 (MV) £21.58 (BUT)
1989 IB £185.00 (BIB)
1986 £19.99 (PE)
1985 £19.99 (OD) £21.01 (BUT)
1985 IB £150.00 (FA)
1983 £17.50 (HAC) £18.73 (BUT)
1982 £25.23 (PIP) £25.85 (BUT) £29.95 (AMI)
1982 IB £200.00 (FA) £283.00 (BIB)
1975 £25.52 (BUT) £29.00 (JU)
1970 £30.32 (BUT)
1959 £50.00 (VIG)
1924 £95.00 (ROB)

Pavie-Decesse *grand cru classé St-Émilion*
1990 EC £84.00 (RAE)
1989 £13.04 (BUT) £14.68 (AV)
1988 £12.75 (GE) £13.20 (JU)
1985 £14.20 (PIP)

Pavie-Macquin *grand cru classé St-Émilion*
1989 £11.54 (BUT)

Pavillon-Rouge-du-Château Margaux *Margaux*
1990 £14.68 (BUT) £15.49 (OD)
1989 £17.49 (OD) £19.50 (JU) £20.80 (LOR)
1988 £14.99 (OD) £20.80 (LOR) £22.99 (TES)
1986 £18.75 (DAV) £18.80 (JU) £19.00 (WY)
1985 £19.27 (BUT) £27.28 (NI)
1983 £24.25 (AD)

Pédesclaux *5ème cru classé Pauillac*
1985 £18.47 (BUT)

Petit-Village *Pomerol*
1990 £23.88 (BUT)
1989 £27.11 (BUT) £29.75 (HUN) £33.00 (JU)
1988 £21.82 (BUT) £25.00 (JU)
1952 £65.00 (HUN)

Pétrus *Pomerol*
1990 £235.55 (BUT)
1990 IB £1,900.00 (WY)
1989 £270.31 (CB)
1989 IB £2,550.00 (BIB)
1988 £164.56 (CB)
1987 £176.25 (TW)
1987 magnum IB £1,000.00 (FA)
1986 IB £1,500.00 (FA)
1986 magnum £303.54 (BIB)
1985 £251.25 (BUT) £260.00 (PE)
1983 £170.00 (HUN) £190.02 (CB) £195.00 (AMI) £230.00 (PE)
1983 magnum £368.15 (REI)
1982 £344.55 (BUT) £399.00 (PE)
1981 £206.00 (DAV)
1981 IB £1,500.00 (FA)
1979 £181.13 (REI)
1970 £283.96 (BIB) £350.00 (JU)
1958 £195.00 (BU)
1955 ½ bottle £270.25 (TW)
1948 £140.24 (GR)

de Pez *cru bourgeois supérieur St-Éstèphe*
1990 £12.20 (JU)
1989 £14.95 (VIG)
1988 £12.50 (WRI)
1986 £10.92 (HOG) £15.55 (WRI)
1985 £13.89 (BUT) £15.95 (VIG)
1983 £17.13 (BUT)
1979 £12.75 (BU)
1978 £15.18 (BIB) £27.78 (BUT)
1975 £18.21 (REI)
1970 £22.50 (BU) £28.78 (REI) £30.00 (VIG)

Phélan-Ségur *cru grand bourgeois exceptionnel St-Éstèphe*
1990 £9.74 (BUT) £9.99 (OD)
1989 £12.20 (LOR)
1988 £11.49 (UN) £14.48 (BEK) £19.52 (PIP)
1982 £13.95 (BU) £19.95 (HOG)
1981 £11.89 (PEN) £15.70 (WRI)

Pibran *cru bourgeois Pauillac*
1990 £11.49 (OD) £11.71 (BUT)
1989 £12.00 (BUT) £15.95 (MAJ) £17.45 (CB)
1988 £12.00 (GE)

Pichon-Longueville (Pichon-Baron until 1988) *2ème cru classé Pauillac*
1990 £20.59 (BUT) £26.00 (JU)
1990 EC £190.65 (HAH)
1989 £21.00 (GE) £27.13 (BUT) £28.50 (HUN)

1989 IB £230.00 (BIB)
1989 EC £222.00 (RAE)
1988 £17.00 (HUN) £19.23 (BUT) £21.00 (JU) £22.50 (HUN) £23.64 (AV) £29.90 (BER)
1986 £20.00 (GE) £21.90 (GAU) £36.41 (TAN)
1985 £19.50 (HUN) £21.00 (PIP) £22.00 (UN)
1983 £25.10 (BEK) £32.50 (ROB)
1982 £16.00 (WY) £27.26 (PIP)
1982 IB £140.00 (FA)
1981 £19.83 (PIP) £20.75 (ROB)
1979 £16.75 (LOR) £21.61 (GR)
1975 £14.20 (BIB) £18.99 (OD) £32.00 (BE)
1970 £65.80 (NI)
1970 IB £240.00 (FA)
1964 £22.50 (BU)

Pichon-Longueville-Lalande (Pichon-Lalande until 1993) *2ème cru classé Pauillac*
1990 £19.85 (AD) £20.51 (BUT) £22.99 (OD)
1989 £26.00 (MV) £29.55 (BUT) £31.00 (HUN)
1989 IB £225.00 (FA) £276.00 (WY)
1989 EC £252.00 (RAE)
1988 £22.95 (BAR) £23.50 (CV) £23.50 (HAY)
1988 imperial £375.00 (HUN)
1986 £28.61 (BUT) £34.00 (VIC) £39.00 (JU)
1986 IB £275.00 (BIB)
1986 jeroboam £266.00 (JU)
1985 £22.75 (PE) £27.60 (GAU) £29.95 (AD)
1985 IB £225.00 (FA) £235.00 (BIB)
1985 jeroboam £245.00 (JU)
1985 imperial £290.00 (JU) £300.00 (HUN)
1983 £25.10 (BEK) £27.50 (BU) £29.20 (PIP)
1983 IB £225.00 (FA) £253.00 (BIB)
1983 magnum IB £240.00 (FA)
1983 jeroboam IB £160.00 (FA)
1982 £46.86 (BUT) £56.25 (VIC)
1982 imperial IB £435.00 (FA)
1981 £22.68 (BUT) £28.00 (WS) £29.00 (BE)
1979 £40.00 (WS)
1978 £38.00 (EY) £43.93 (BUT) £50.00 (HAG)
1976 £28.66 (GR)
1975 £28.89 (BIB) £40.80 (BE)
1970 £59.65 (LAY) £64.62 (REI) £75.00 (JU)
1964 £29.38 (BIB)

EC (ex-cellar) price per dozen, excl shipping, duty and VAT. IB (in bond) price per dozen, excl duty and VAT. All other prices, per bottle incl VAT.

le Pin *Pomerol*
1991 £66.00 (JU)
1991 EC £625.00 (RAE)
1990 £77.21 (BUT)
1989 £135.60 (BUT)
1988 £95.89 (BUT)
1986 £94.12 (BUT)
1983 £122.40 (BIB)
1982 IB £1,950.00 (BIB)

Pique-Caillou *Graves*
1988 £7.83 (TAN)
1985 £11.70 (HAG)

Plagnac *cru bourgeois Médoc*
1989 £6.99 (UN)
1988 £6.99 (UN)
1987 £5.85 (PE) £7.69 (WHI)
1986 £7.05 (EL)

la Pointe *Pomerol*
1989 £12.50 (BE)
1988 £15.65 (HAG)
1981 £14.68 (REI) £16.80 (TW)
1980 £15.21 (TW)
1978 £21.73 (REI)
1966 £25.00 (VIG)
1945 £107.00 (WY)

Pontet-Canet *5ème cru classé Pauillac*
1990 £13.86 (BUT)
1989 £13.77 (BUT) £16.25 (HIG)
1988 £14.68 (HIG)
1986 £12.95 (BER) £13.64 (HOG)
1985 £19.50 (ROB)
1983 £11.57 (LO) £14.00 (HOG) £17.10 (WRI)
1982 £14.00 (WS) £22.61 (AV)
1959 £45.00 (VIG)
1945 £73.00 (WY)

Potensac *cru grand bourgeois Médoc*
1990 £7.77 (BUT) £8.85 (WS) £8.95 (LAY)
1990 EC £65.30 (HAH)
1989 £8.12 (BUT) £9.10 (JU)
1989 EC £62.00 (RAE)
1988 £7.95 (HAY) £8.50 (RAE) £8.95 (JU)
1986 £8.25 (HAY) £8.65 (PE) £9.74 (CHA) £10.13 (BUT) £10.74 (CHA) £10.90 (JU)
1986 IB £73.00 (FA)
1985 £9.95 (AMI) £11.89 (BUT) £12.33 (REI)
1983 £6.85 (HAC)
1982 £13.22 (FA) £14.95 (BAR) £15.95 (BU) £15.95 (DI) £16.00 (JU) £17.99 (MAJ)
1982 IB £143.00 (BIB)
1978 £15.42 (BUT)

Poujeaux *cru grand bourgeois exceptionnel Moulis*
1990 £9.99 (OD)
1989 £10.77 (TAN) £10.82 (BUT) £11.99 (NI) £12.80 (JU) £12.95 (MAJ)
1989 IB £85.00 (FA)
1988 £10.80 (JU) £12.34 (EL)
1986 £10.34 (NI) £11.00 (HAY)
1985 £9.02 (BEK) £10.50 (HAY) £11.10 (PIP)
1985 IB £90.00 (FA)
1983 £9.61 (BEK) £11.90 (PIP) £14.67 (CHA)

la Prade *Côtes de Francs*
1989 £6.95 (WS) £7.34 (WW)

Prieur de Meyney *St-Estèphe*
1988 £8.75 (WHI) £9.10 (WRI)
1987 £8.45 (PE)
1985 £8.95 (PE)

Prieuré-Lichine *4ème cru classé Margaux*
1989 £16.40 (AV)
1988 £14.74 (CHA)
1986 £13.42 (BUT)
1985 £16.40 (LOR)
1983 £15.20 (BEK) £17.75 (WRI) £19.60 (PIP)
1982 £13.22 (BIB) £18.37 (BUT) £18.90 (LOR)
1975 £25.00 (ROB)

Rahoul *Graves*
1985 £8.97 (BUT) £15.95 (AMI)
1982 £13.16 (TW)

Ramage-la-Bâtisse *cru bourgeois Haut-Médoc*
1989 £9.99 (THR) £9.99 (WR) £9.99 (BOT)
1988 £9.69 (WR) £9.69 (THR) £9.69 (BOT)
1986 £9.99 (CV)

Rausan-Ségla *2ème cru classé Margaux*
1990 £20.99 (OD)
1989 £22.95 (NA) £26.99 (OD)
1988 £17.79 (NA) £25.90 (HAG) £43.21 (BUT)
1986 £30.00 (HAG)
1985 £15.86 (REI) £15.90 (UN) £17.00 (GE)
1983 £22.11 (AV)
1982 £16.50 (BU) £26.90 (LOR)

All châteaux are listed alphabetically regardless of class.

1981 £20.20 (WRI)
1978 £18.00 (BU)
1976 £18.95 (ROB)
1975 £15.18 (BIB) £22.93 (GR)
1970 magnum £50.00 (BU)
1962 £27.50 (BU)
1952 £49.00 (VIG)
1949 £85.00 (ROB)
1947 £79.00 (WY)
1937 £55.00 (VIG)
1934 £75.00 (VIG)

Rauzan-Gassies *2ème cru classé Margaux*
1988 £16.85 (DAV)
1985 £16.90 (LOR)
1983 £16.95 (ROB)
1978 £16.40 (BOR)
1970 £22.50 (BU) £39.50 (ROB)
1961 £52.88 (BIB) £90.00 (AMI)
1960 £22.50 (BU)
1959 £45.00 (VIG)
1945 £62.00 (WY)

Réserve de la Comtesse *Pauillac*
1989 £11.64 (LAY)
1988 £10.61 (BUT) £12.46 (LAY) £12.89 (SAI) £12.95 (JU) £13.79 (AV) £14.49 (WR)
1986 £12.95 (LAY)
1985 £14.15 (PE)
1984 £12.45 (VIC) £13.45 (BY) £13.85 (ROB)
1983 £13.95 (WS)

Respide *Graves*
1988 £5.75 (GRE)
1986 £11.63 (TW)
1985 £10.46 (TW)
1959 £35.00 (VIG)

Roc-St-Bernard *Fronsac*
1989 £4.95 (WHG)

du Rocher *grand cru St-Émilion*
1989 £10.75 (HAG)

de Roquetaillade-la-Grange *Graves*
1990 £7.65 (LAY)
1988 £6.90 (BE)
1986 £6.99 (DAV) £8.23 (SUM) £8.26 (HOG)
1985 £8.75 (AMI)

Rouget *Pomerol*
1990 £13.98 (CB)
1985 £15.24 (BUT)
1981 £17.50 (ROB) £18.95 (AMI)
1961 £52.87 (REI)

Rozier *grand cru St-Émilion*
1989 £9.45 (SAI)
1988 £6.77 (EY)

St-Bonnet *cru bourgeois Médoc*
1989 £7.74 (LAY)
1985 £8.43 (BUT)

St-Pierre *4ème cru classé St-Julien*
1990 £12.99 (OD)
1989 £16.50 (BUT) £16.99 (OD)
1987 £12.83 (BY)
1986 £13.79 (HA) £13.99 (OD) £16.95 (VIG)
1985 £13.99 (TAN) £19.80 (JU)
1985 IB £110.00 (FA)
1983 £18.00 (LOR)
1982 £19.15 (HAH) £22.80 (LOR) £24.50 (AD)
1981 £23.60 (WRI)
1979 £12.95 (BU) £15.00 (GE) £16.46 (GR) £19.09 (REI) £22.40 (HAG)
1970 £34.75 (AD)
1961 £67.56 (REI)

de Sales *Pomerol*
1988 £12.03 (AV)
1985 £12.00 (WY) £13.73 (BUT)
1983 £13.97 (BEK) £16.20 (BUT) £16.97 (PIP)
1975 £29.38 (TW)

Sarget de Gruaud-Larose *St-Julien*
1987 £10.55 (PE) £10.79 (BOT) £10.79 (THR) £10.79 (WR) £11.09 (TAN)
1986 £8.41 (LO) £11.99 (WHI) £15.25 (HAG)
1985 £11.95 (LAY) £13.95 (DAV)
1983 £11.50 (LOR) £13.99 (PE)

Sénéjac *cru bourgeois supérieur Haut-Médoc*
★ **1990** £6.78 (TAN) £7.90 (MV) £8.75 (GE)
1990 IB £60.00 (MV)
1989 £7.90 (MV) £8.10 (JU) £8.50 (BER)
1988 £9.60 (PIP)
1987 £7.60 (LOR) £7.67 (EL)
1986 £9.60 (MV)

la Serre *grand cru classé St-Émilion*
1989 £14.85 (HAG)
1989 EC £99.00 (RAE)
1986 £10.75 (PE)
1985 £12.65 (PE)

Stars (★) indicate wines selected by the editors as particularly good value in their class.

Siran *cru bourgeois supérieur Margaux*
1989 £12.01 (GR) £12.33 (NI)
1988 £12.80 (NI)
1987 £9.40 (CV)
1986 £10.75 (PE) £16.95 (SOM) £19.80 (PIP)
1985 £16.95 (SOM) £20.10 (PIP)
1984 £7.25 (HAY)
1983 £16.95 (SOM) £21.00 (PIP)
1981 £19.32 (NI)
1979 £20.95 (NI)

Smith-Haut-Lafitte *cru classé Pessac-Léognan*
1989 £11.69 (NA)
1988 £10.25 (NA) £10.58 (EL)
1985 £11.90 (UN) £16.25 (NA)
1983 £13.75 (LOR)
1975 £10.77 (BIB)

Sociando-Mallet *cru grand bourgeois Haut-Médoc*
1991 EC £89.00 (RAE)
1990 £12.09 (BUT)
1989 £14.19 (BUT) £14.95 (MAJ) £15.30 (JU)
1989 IB £133.00 (BIB)
1989 EC £104.00 (RAE)
1988 £10.99 (RAE) £12.80 (JU) £13.50 (HAY)
1986 £14.50 (HAY)
1984 £9.25 (HAY)

Soutard *grand cru classé St-Émilion*
1987 £9.40 (MV) £9.45 (JU)
1985 £16.00 (GE)
1981 £13.00 (GE)
1964 £28.00 (GE)
1962 £22.50 (BU)

Talbot *4ème cru classé St-Julien*
1990 £16.49 (OD)
1989 £18.31 (TAN) £18.56 (BUT) £22.00 (BER)
1989 ½ bottle £9.00 (WY)
1988 £12.62 (LO) £15.95 (ROB) £15.95 (WHG) £16.80 (JU) £17.50 (HUN) £18.65 (PE)
1987 £11.99 (NI) £12.50 (BU) £14.95 (VIG)
1986 £12.62 (LO) £16.00 (HUN) £16.85 (DI) £18.80 (JU) £19.90 (BER) £20.60 (WHI)
1985 £17.03 (BUT) £17.50 (UN) £18.06 (BEK) £18.50 (BER) £19.95 (AMI) £19.95 (LAY) £20.75 (GRE) £20.75 (PE) £21.00 (PIP)

1984 £12.55 (PE) £16.20 (UN)
1983 £15.07 (BUT) £15.50 (DI) £19.85 (DAV) £19.99 (PE) £22.50 (ROB)
1983 IB £145.00 (FA) £173.00 (BIB)
1982 £21.00 (WY) £21.50 (LOR) £24.85 (PE)
1982 IB £250.00 (BIB)
1981 £17.42 (BUT) £19.15 (PE) £25.00 (ROB) £25.00 (VIG) £25.55 (HAG)

1979 £29.50 (LOR)
1978 £22.38 (BUT) £26.85 (PE) £26.97 (TAN)
1978 IB £185.00 (BIB)
1975 £21.54 (BIB)
1970 £25.00 (MV) £33.72 (BOR) £37.81 (AV)
1962 double magnum £246.75 (REI)
1961 £56.30 (BIB) £95.00 (JU)
1947 £140.00 (ROB)

Terre Rouge *Médoc*
1988 £6.93 (BUT)

Terrey-Gros-Caillou *St-Julien*
1989 £10.06 (EY)
1988 £9.76 (BEK) £11.90 (PIP)
1986 £9.20 (HOG) £10.80 (JU)
1985 £10.50 (LOR)

du Tertre *5ème cru classé Margaux*
1989 £17.50 (BER)
1986 £15.80 (LOR)
1983 £15.95 (ROB)

le Tertre Rôteboeuf *grand cru St-Émilion*
1990 £22.08 (BUT) £23.09 (CB)
1989 £22.84 (BUT)
1988 £18.81 (BUT)
1986 £19.36 (BUT)

la Tour-Carnet *4ème cru classé Haut-Médoc*
1985 £12.95 (GRE)

la Tour-de-By *cru grand bourgeois Médoc*
1990 £9.22 (TAN)
1990 EC £60.00 (HIG)
1989 £5.79 (GR) £8.42 (HIG) £8.49 (UN)
1988 £7.48 (BOR) £7.49 (UN) £7.63 (HIG) £7.85 (HUN) £8.37 (TAN) £8.50 (GRE)
1986 £7.95 (AMI) £7.95 (PE) £9.45 (GRE) £9.50 (WRI) £9.95 (PIP)
1983 £9.09 (WHI)
1981 £8.75 (BU)
1978 £13.17 (BUT)

la Tour-de-Grenet *Lussac-St-Émilion*
1990 £7.65 (TAN)
1989 £7.45 (LAY)
1988 £5.30 (SOM)

la Tour-de-Mons *cru bourgeois supérieur Margaux*
1990 £9.49 (OD)
1988 £9.89 (SAF) £10.80 (JU)
1985 £10.99 (WR) £10.99 (THR) £10.99 (BOT)
1966 £40.72 (BUT)

Tour-du-Haut-Moulin *cru grand bourgeois Haut-Médoc*
1989 £8.90 (JU)
1986 £8.68 (BEK) £8.95 (LOR) £10.23 (PIP)
1985 £9.03 (BUT)

la Tour-Figeac *grand cru classé St-Émilion*
1990 £12.00 (BOR)
1985 £14.65 (PE) £14.70 (UN)

la Tour-Haut-Brion *cru classé Pessac-Léognan*
1985 £30.00 (WS)

la Tour-St-Bonnet *cru bourgeois Médoc*
1991 £4.99 (OD)
1990 £6.49 (BUT) £6.95 (JU)
1989 £5.99 (NA) £7.49 (UN) £7.75 (BER)
1988 £6.25 (HAC) £6.46 (EL) £7.05 (REI) £7.20 (BER) £7.60 (WRI)
1986 £6.83 (HOG) £8.25 (GRE)
1985 £7.60 (WS) £7.95 (HAC)
1982 £11.00 (GE)

All châteaux are listed alphabetically regardless of class.

Les Tourelles de Longueville *Pauillac*
1990 £11.14 (BUT) £15.20 (HAH)
1989 £15.99 (BOT) £15.99 (THR) £15.99 (WR)
1989 EC £93.00 (RAE)
1988 £10.60 (RAE) £20.16 (BY)
1987 £14.61 (BY)

Tronquoy-Lalande *cru grand bourgeois St-Éstèphe*
1990 £8.06 (BEK)
1988 £9.40 (EL)
1985 £8.50 (LOR)
1962 £21.95 (GR)
1961 £22.50 (BU)

Troplong-Mondot *grand cru classé St-Émilion*
1990 £14.01 (BUT)
1989 £15.45 (BUT) £15.80 (JU) £15.95 (MAJ)
1988 £14.00 (JU)
1986 £13.95 (DAV) £15.00 (LOR)
1959 £19.00 (MV)
1947 £35.00 (MV)

Trotanoy *Pomerol*
1990 £33.75 (BUT)
1989 £49.76 (BUT)
1988 £34.92 (BUT) £35.36 (CB)
1986 £36.48 (CB) £37.09 (BUT) £37.50 (BU)
1985 £54.23 (CB)
1983 £32.95 (LAY) £37.63 (BUT)
1983 IB £220.00 (FA)
1982 IB £850.00 (BIB)
1979 IB £395.00 (BIB)
1972 £22.50 (BU)
1970 £79.00 (WY)
1970 IB £850.00 (FA)
1959 IB £1,400.00 (FA)
1957 £60.00 (ROB)
1955 £90.00 (ROB)

Trottevieille *1er grand cru classé St-Émilion*
1992 EC £120.00 (SUM)
1991 EC £162.00 (SUM)
1990 EC £150.00 (HIG) £215.00 (SUM)
1989 £14.95 (WHG) £18.73 (BUT) £18.80 (HIG) £21.00 (BER) £22.33 (PEN)
1988 £18.90 (BER)
1986 £19.00 (WS) £23.50 (PEN)
1985 £19.50 (HUN)
1983 £17.95 (DAV)
1970 £49.00 (HUN)
1947 £125.00 (ROB)

Verdignan *cru grand bourgeois Médoc*
1985 £8.09 (BEK) £9.73 (PIP)
1983 £9.99 (GRE)
1978 £13.89 (BUT)
1976 £10.73 (BOR)

Vieux-Château-Certan *Pomerol*
1990 £26.02 (BUT) £29.95 (LAY)
1990 EC £220.00 (RAE)
1989 £30.63 (BUT) £31.71 (TAN) £36.44 (AV) £36.50 (BER) £39.00 (JU)
1989 EC £290.00 (RAE)
1988 £26.82 (BUT) £28.00 (HUN)
1988 magnum £50.00 (HAY)
1987 £16.65 (PE) £17.00 (WS) £19.90 (JU)
1986 £26.15 (PE) £27.02 (BUT) £29.50 (BER) £35.00 (TAN) £39.00 (JU)
1986 IB £240.00 (FA)
1986 double magnum £160.00 (JU)
1986 jeroboam £266.00 (JU)
1985 £20.00 (HAY) £30.00 (BER) £32.00 (PIP) £32.00 (PE) £35.30 (UN) £36.00 (JU)
1985 IB £195.00 (BIB)
1983 £26.50 (BER) £30.00 (ROB)
1982 £30.00 (HAY) £34.00 (DI) £35.50 (NI)
1982 IB £275.00 (FA)
1978 £33.00 (PE)
1976 £23.00 (WY)
1970 IB £330.00 (FA)
1964 magnum IB £720.00 (FA)

Villegeorge *cru bourgeois supérieur exceptionnel Haut-Médoc*
1987 £7.26 (EY) £7.45 (JU)
1986 £9.75 (RAE)

Villeneuve de Cantemerle *Haut-Médoc*
1988 £10.99 (BOT) £10.99 (THR) £10.99 (WR)
1987 £7.99 (BOT) £7.99 (WR) £7.99 (THR)
1986 £8.99 (WHI) £9.95 (VIG) £10.75 (PE)

Vraye-Croix-de-Gay *Pomerol*
1989 £16.15 (BUT)
1982 £13.14 (BUT)

EC (ex-cellar) price per dozen, excl shipping, duty and VAT. IB (in bond) price per dozen, excl duty and VAT. All other prices, per bottle incl VAT.

PETITS CHÂTEAUX

de Barbe *Côtes de Bourg*
1989 £3.99 (SAF) £5.59 (DAV)
1988 £5.29 (EL)

Bédats-Bois-Montet *1ères Côtes de Bordeaux*
1987 £4.70 (LOR)
1986 £5.30 (LOR)

de Belcier *Côtes de Castillon*
1988 £7.23 (CV)
1986 £6.25 (DAV)

Bertin *Montagne-St-Émilion*
1988 £6.49 (BUT)
1986 £6.33 (BUT)

Bonnet *Bordeaux Supérieur*
1990 £5.01 (EL) £5.99 (NI) £6.29 (BOT) £6.29 (THR)

du Bousquet *Côtes de Bourg*
1990 £5.65 (SAI)

Calon *Montagne-St-Émilion*
1989 £19.22 (AV)
1988 £20.23 (AV)
1955 £41.71 (TW)

Canon de Brem *Canon-Fronsac*
★ **1990** £7.64 (MV) £10.69 (CB) £10.69 (CB)
1989 £9.40 (MV) £9.99 (BUT)
1988 £8.50 (MV)
1986 £9.30 (MV) £9.75 (CB) £9.75 (CB)

la Claverie *Côtes de Francs*
1986 £6.57 (BEK) £7.90 (PIP)

la Croix-des-Moines *Lalande-de-Pomerol*
1990 £9.90 (JU) £10.99 (RAE)
1987 £9.49 (AUG)

de la Dauphine *Fronsac*
1990 £9.23 (CB)
1989 £7.70 (MV) £8.71 (BUT) £9.10 (JU) £9.46 (CB)
1988 £7.80 (JU) £9.09 (AV) £12.28 (CB)

l'Éperon *Bordeaux*
1992 EC £22.50 (SUM)
1991 EC £23.50 (SUM)
1990 EC £26.00 (SUM)

l'Escadre *1ères Côtes de Blaye*
1990 £4.70 (JU)

le Gardera *1ères Côtes de Bordeaux*
1990 £5.75 (AUG)
1988 £5.95 (PE) £6.85 (HAG)
1987 £5.45 (PE)
1986 £5.65 (PE)
1975 £12.30 (BUT)

Grand-Mazerolles *1ères Côtes de Blaye*
1990 £5.34 (REI)
1985 £5.99 (PE)

Gros-Moulin *Côtes de Bourg*
1990 £4.54 (BEK)

Guionne *Côtes de Bourg*
1990 £4.46 (HOG)
1988 £4.85 (PE)
1986 £5.65 (PE)

Haut-Gillet *Montagne-St-Émilion*
1985 £6.17 (EL)

de Haut-Sociondo *1ères Côtes de Blaye*
★ **1989** £4.95 (SUM)
1988 £7.35 (HAG)
1986 £5.99 (GRE)

du Juge *1ères Côtes de Bordeaux*
1990 £4.99 (AUG) £5.30 (LOR)
1989 £6.41 (AV)
1988 £4.92 (BY)

Lamothe *1ères Côtes de Bordeaux*
1987 £8.60 (HAG)

du Lyonnat *Lussac-St-Émilion*
1989 £5.49 (GR)
1988 £6.95 (WHG) £7.84 (BY) £7.87 (CV) £7.95 (AMI) £8.95 (ROB)
1962 £24.00 (BU)

Macquin-St-Georges *St-Georges-St-Émilion*
1990 £6.20 (AD) £6.74 (TAN) £6.88 (HAH) £7.34 (CB)
1989 £6.49 (TAN) £6.87 (CB)
1988 £6.25 (DAV) £6.75 (CB)

Mazeris *Canon-Fronsac*
1990 £8.10 (JU)
1989 £10.20 (JU) £11.57 (CB)
1988 £8.00 (MV) £9.55 (BUT) £9.60 (JU)
1986 £10.05 (CB) £11.70 (JU)
1985 £14.00 (JU)

Méaume *Bordeaux Supérieur*
★ **1990** £5.10 (JU)
1989 £4.95 (BE) £5.10 (JU) £5.29 (MAJ)
1988 £5.50 (BE)

Mendoce *Côtes de Bourg*
1990 £5.49 (DAV)
1989 £5.29 (SAF) £5.49 (DAV)

Montaiguillon *Montagne-St-Émilion*
1989 £7.03 (BEK)

Péconnet *Bordeaux Supérieur*
1986 £4.99 (PE)

Pérenne *1ères Côtes de Blaye*
1989 £5.31 (BEK) £5.95 (PIP)

les Petits Arnauds *Côtes de Blaye*
1989 £5.25 (HOG) £5.65 (GRE)
1988 £5.99 (VIC)

Pitray *Bordeaux Supérieur Côtes de Castillon*
1990 £5.40 (JU)
1990 IB £38.00 (BIB)
1989 £5.60 (JU) £6.52 (CB) £6.75 (PIP)
1988 £5.49 (PE)

Plaisance *Montagne-St-Émilion*
1989 £5.95 (WS)
1988 £5.95 (JU)

de Prade *Bordeaux Supérieur*
1986 £6.95 (BAR)

Puygueraud *Côtes de Francs*
★ **1990** £7.16 (TAN)
1989 £7.88 (BUT)
1988 £9.22 (TAN)
1987 £8.16 (REI)
1985 £8.96 (BUT)

Richotey *Fronsac*
★ **1990** £5.55 (AD) £5.75 (TAN) £6.17 (CB)
1989 £6.05 (CB)
1987 £4.92 (CB)
1985 £5.15 (RAE)

la Rivière *Fronsac*
1989 £8.60 (BE)
1988 £10.20 (BE)
1986 £8.95 (BE) £10.50 (DI)
1985 £14.04 (TW)
1983 £9.50 (BE)
1981 £12.87 (TW)

Roquevieille *Côtes de Castillon*
1988 £5.58 (PEN)

Rouet *Fronsac*
1989 £5.95 (HAY) £5.99 (RAE)
1988 £5.50 (HAY)
1986 £6.45 (PE)
1985 £7.65 (PE)

Sirius *Bordeaux*
1989 £5.95 (GE) £5.95 (BE) £5.95 (HAY) £5.99 (WR) £5.99 (THR) £5.99 (BOT)
1988 £5.95 (GE)
1986 £4.99 (NA)

de Sours *Bordeaux Supérieur*
1990 £7.17 (CB)
★ **1989** £5.39 (NI) £6.07 (BUT) £6.70 (CB)
1988 £6.35 (CB)

Tanesse *1ères Côtes de Bordeaux*
1989 £5.99 (WHI)
1986 £4.82 (EL)
1985 £6.45 (PE)

Thieuley *Bordeaux Supérieur*
1990 £4.40 (SOM) £5.80 (JU)
1989 £5.95 (PIP)
1988 £5.70 (WS)

Timberlay *Bordeaux Supérieur*
1990 £5.29 (AUG) £5.35 (DAV) £5.63 (HAH)

Toumalin *Canon-Fronsac*
1988 £6.47 (EY) £6.95 (GE)

Tour de l'Espérance *Bordeaux Supérieur*
1990 £4.62 (BY)
1989 £3.95 (HOG) £4.62 (BY)

Tour-Musset *Montagne-St-Émilion*
1988 £7.85 (PIP)

Villars *Fronsac*
1989 £7.70 (MV) £8.10 (LOR)
1988 £7.39 (EY) £8.50 (MV)
1986 £8.30 (LAY) £8.95 (DAV) £8.95 (LOR)

WHITE BORDEAUX

DRY

Under £5.00

Non-vintage
Asda Bordeaux Blanc (ASD)
Tertre de Launay (DAV)
1992
Baudac (CV)
Bonnet (THR, BOT, NI, WR)
Carriole Barton Sauvignon (BIB)
Moulin de Launay (AD)
Thieuley (SOM)
1991
Carriole Barton Sauvignon (BIB)
Fondarzac (ASD)
Safeway Château Canet (SAF)
1990
Moulin de Launay (TAN)

£5.00 to £5.99

1992
Baudac (HUN)
★ de Sours (MAJ, CB)
Thieuley (MAJ, JU, WS, HAH, BIB)
1991
Baudac (SUM)
Maitre d'Estournel (AD)
de Sours (NI)
Thieuley (HIC)
1990
Coucheroy (NI)
Reynon (GR)
de Sours (MAJ)
1989
Sirius (BE, BOT, WR, THR)
1988
Cabannieux (WHI)
Sirius (GE)

£6.00 to £6.99

1992
de l'Étoile (AD)
1991
de l'Étoile (TAN)
Reynon Vieilles Vignes (OD)
1990
Baudac les Trois Hectares (SUM)
Cabannieux (OD)
Coucheroy (BOT, WR, THR)
Loudenne (JU)
1989
Roquetaillade-la-Grange (BEK, BE, DAV)

£7.00 to £8.99

1992
Reynon Vieilles Vignes (WS)
1990
Cruzeau (EL)
★ Doisy-Daëne Grand Vin Sec (OD)
la Grave (GE)
de Rochemorin (WAI)
1989
Cabannieux (ROB)
Guiraud 'G' (BUT)

★ de Landiras (EY)
de Ricaud (ROB)
1988
Château Talbot Caillou Blanc (WHI)
1986
Rieussec 'R' (HA)
1979
de Rochemorin (RAE)

£9.00 to £11.99

1990
Couhins-Lurton (JU)
la Louvière (BUT)
Montalivet (AD)
1989
Bouscaut (RAE)
Doisy-Daëne Grand Vin Sec (AD)
Montalivet (TAN)
Rieussec 'R' (CB)
1988
Bouscaut (RAE)
la Grave (BUT)
Rahoul (GR)
1986
Larrivet-Haut-Brion (REI)
1985
Carbonnieux (BER)
Rieussec 'R' (ROB, BUT)
1983
Olivier (DI)
1982
Carbonnieux (WY)

£12.00 to £14.99

1990
Carbonnieux (GE)
1989
Bouscaut (BIB, BER)
Carbonnieux (GE, HAH)
Couhins-Lurton (RAE, REI, AD, TAN, BIB)
la Louvière (BUT)
la Tour Martillac (NI)
1988
la Louvière (JU)
1986
la Louvière (WS)
Smith-Haut-Lafitte (BUT)
1981
Couhins-Lurton (RAE)

£15.00 to £19.99

1990
Smith-Haut-Lafitte (OD)
1989
Pavillon Blanc du Château Margaux (LAY)
1988
Pavillon Blanc du Château Margaux (WY)
la Tour Martillac (BUT)
1987
de Fieuzal (BEK, BER)
'L' de la Louvière (RAE, AD)
Laville-Haut-Brion (BEK)
1985
Smith-Haut-Lafitte (BUT)
1982
Malartic-Lagravière (BUT)
1976
Roumieu (WY)

£20.00 to £29.99

1990
de Fieuzal (PIP, BUT, OD, AD)
1989
de Fieuzal (TAN, OD)
1988
de Fieuzal (OD)
Pavillon Blanc du Château Margaux (JU)
1985
'Y' d'Yquem (FA)

£30.00 to £39.99

1988
Haut-Brion Blanc (BIB)
Laville-Haut-Brion (BUT)
Pavillon Blanc du Château Margaux (ROB)
'Y' d'Yquem (BUT)
1987
Haut-Brion Blanc (JU)
1986
Domaine de Chevalier (BUT)
1985
Haut-Brion Blanc (HA)
'Y' d'Yquem (REI, VIG)
1983
Domaine de Chevalier (BER)
1982
Laville-Haut-Brion (ROB)
1979
'Y' d'Yquem (REI)

£40.00 to £59.99

1991
Domaine de Chevalier (JU)
1990
Laville-Haut-Brion (JU)
1989
Domaine de Chevalier (BUT, JU)
1988
Domaine de Chevalier (JU)
Haut-Brion Blanc (RAE, BUT, JU)
1985
Laville-Haut-Brion (JU)
1983
Haut-Brion Blanc (WY)
Laville-Haut-Brion (JU, BER)
1982
Haut-Brion Blanc (WY)
1967
Laville-Haut-Brion (WY)
1947
Olivier (WY)
1926
Pavillon Blanc du Château Margaux (WY)

£60.00 to £79.99

1990
Haut-Brion Blanc (JU)
1989
Haut-Brion Blanc (JU)
1982
Domaine de Chevalier (TW)
1981
Pavillon Blanc du Château Margaux (TW)
1967
Laville-Haut-Brion (VIG)
1949
Carbonnieux (WY)

£85.00 to £95.00

1990
Haut-Brion Blanc (BUT)
1947
Laville-Haut-Brion (WY)

SWEET

Under £5.00

Non-vintage
Asda 1ères Côtes de Bordeaux (ASD)

£5.00 to £5.99

1989
★ de Berbec (WHG, OD)
★ Mayne des Carmes (OD)

£6.00 to £6.99

1990
Bastor-Lamontagne ½ bottle (WHG)
1989
Bastor-Lamontagne ½ bottle (WAI)
Cantegril (ROB)
★ Liot ½ bottle (HAL)
★ Loupiac Gaudiet (HOG)
1988
Bastor-Lamontagne ½ bottle (WHI, BUT)
de Berbec (CV)
Loupiac Gaudiet (WAI)
Mayne des Carmes (OD)

£7.00 to £8.99

1990
★ Clos St-Georges (SAI)
Fayau (MV)
Laurette (SUM)
★ Loupiac Gaudiet (HAH)
Rayne-Vigneau ½ bottle (BUT)
du Tich (PE)
des Tours (JU)
1989
Domaine de Noble (BIB, HIC)
★ Lousteau-Vieil (PIP)
des Tours (AD)
1988
★ Broustet (BUT)
la Chartreuse ½ bottle (EY)
Coutet ½ bottle (WY)
Filhot (OD)
Liot ½ bottle (HAL)
la Nère (EL)
Rabaud-Promis ½ bottle (BUT, RAE)
Rayne-Vigneau ½ bottle (WY)
1987
Guiteronde du Hayot (ROB)
1986
Rabaud-Promis ½ bottle (BUT)
1985
Coutet ½ bottle (DAV, HA)
1983
Liot ½ bottle (HAL)

£9.00 to £11.99

1990
des Arroucats (CB)
Guiraud ½ bottle (BUT)
Lamothe-Guignard (NI)
Liot (TAN)
1989
Coutet ½ bottle (SUM, BUT)
Liot (WS)
Rabaud-Promis ½ bottle (BIB)
1988
Bastor-Lamontagne (JU, WHI)
★ Caillou (HAY)
Guiteronde du Hayot (HOG)
les Justices ½ bottle (TW)
Liot (BIB, HAY, EL, JU)
Menota (SOM)
1986
Climens ½ bottle (BUT)
Coutet (FA)
Coutet ½ bottle (ROB)
Filhot ½ bottle (HAL)
les Justices ½ bottle (TW)
de Malle (DAV)
Rieussec ½ bottle (BIB)
de Veyres (JU)
1985
Doisy-Dubroca (WHG)
de Malle (BU)
1984
Les Cyprès de Climens (VIC)
1983
Doisy-Dubroca ½ bottle (HAL)
Suduiraut ½ bottle (WY)
de Veyres (BUT)
1981
Nairac ½ bottle (TW)
1979
Coutet ½ bottle (WY)
1978
Doisy-Daëne (WY)
1977
Climens ½ bottle (RAE)
1975
d'Arricaud (RAE)

£12.00 to £14.99

1990
Climens ½ bottle (BUT)
Rayne-Vigneau (NI)
1989
Bastor-Lamontagne (WHG, JU)
Broustet (BUT)
Coutet (WHG)
Rieussec ½ bottle (BUT)

1988
Cantegril (AD)
Climens ½ bottle (BUT)
Filhot (BIB, RAE)
Guiraud ½ bottle (BUT, EL)
Lamothe-Guignard (LAY, AD, GE)
Rieussec (OD)
St-Amand (BE)
1987
Lafaurie-Peyraguey (PE)
Rieussec ½ bottle (VIG)
1986
Filhot (GRG)
Rabaud-Promis (BUT)
Rieussec ½ bottle (WY, BAR, WHI)
St-Amand (GE)
Suduiraut ½ bottle (HAG)
1985
Climens ½ bottle (REI)
Coutet (DAV)
Filhot (DAV)
Lamothe-Guignard (PIP)
1984
Coutet (ROB)
Rieussec (DAV)
1983
de Malle (DAV)
Suduiraut ½ bottle (BIB, HAL)
1982
la Tour Blanche (HOG)
1981
la Tour Blanche (WY)
1979
Doisy-Védrines (WY)
1966
Doisy-Daëne (WY)

£15.00 to £19.99

1990
Bastor-Lamontagne (JU, BUT)
Coutet (TAN)
Doisy-Daëne (BUT)
de Malle (BUT)
la Tour Blanche (NI)
1989
Coutet (BIB, BUT, SUM)
Doisy-Daëne (GE, TAN, AD, BER)
Filhot (BER)
Lafaurie-Peyraguey (BAR)
Lamothe-Guignard (PIP)
Mayne des Carmes (SAI)
Nairac (BE)
Rabaud-Promis (BIB)
Rayne-Vigneau (AD)
Romer du Hayot (AD)
1988
la Chartreuse (TAN)
Climens (NI)
Coutet (PE, HOG, BER, CB)
Filhot (HUN, EL, CB)
Rabaud-Promis (RAE, JU)
Rayne-Vigneau (EL)
Rieussec ½ bottle (WY, REI)
Suduiraut (WHG)
1986
d'Arche (GE)
Broustet (PIP)
les Justices (TW)
Lamothe-Guignard (EY)
Nairac (BUT)
Rabaud-Promis (WS)
Rayne-Vigneau (AD)
Rieussec (WY)
Sigalas-Rabaud (PIP)
1985
Climens (BIB)
Coutet (ROB)
Guiraud (HA)
Lamothe-Guignard (LAY)
Suduiraut (TAN, AD)
1983
Climens ½ bottle (WY)
Coutet (BIB)
Filhot (DAV, WY, ROB)
Lafaurie-Peyraguey (HOG)
Lamothe-Guignard (GE, BE)
Rabaud-Promis (HOG)
Rayne-Vigneau (HOG)
Rieussec ½ bottle (WY, DAV)
la Tour Blanche (HOG)
1982
Rieussec (DAV)
1981
Coutet (NI)
Rieussec (DAV)
1979
Rieussec (WY)
1978
Coutet (BU)
Rayne-Vigneau (ROB)
Suduiraut (BU)
1972
Suduiraut (WY)

In each price band wines are listed in vintage order. Within each vintage they are listed in A–Z order.

£20.00 to £29.99

1990
Climens (NI, BUT)
Guiraud (BUT)
Rabaud-Promis (JU)
Rieussec (NI, JU)
1989
la Tour Blanche (JU, BER)
1988
Doisy-Daëne (TAN)
Guiraud (BUT, JU)
de Malle (PIP)
la Tour Blanche (BUT, PIP)
1986
Climens (BUT)
Guiraud (HAG)
1985
Lafaurie-Peyraguey (PE)
Rieussec (DAV)
1983
Climens (WY, REI, BIB)
Coutet (BE, PIP, ROB, HA, AD, TAN)
Rieussec (GR, WY)
Suduiraut (BIB, BUT)
1981
de Malle (DI)
1980
Guiraud (HAG)
1979
Rayne-Vigneau (DI)
1976
Guiraud (HAG)
1975
Coutet (REI)
Rieussec (BAR)
1971
Romer du Hayot (VIG)
1964
Guiraud (REI)
1924
Guiraud ½ bottle (WY)

£30.00 to £39.99

1989
Climens (TAN, JU)
Raymond Lafon (MV)
Rieussec (TAN, JU)
Sigalas-Rabaud (BER)
Suduiraut (TAN)
1988
Rieussec (BUT)
1983
Climens (MV, BUT)
de Fargues (FA)
Rieussec (BIB, BUT, BUT, DAV, NI)
1976
Climens (WY)
1975
Filhot (WY)
1969
Guiraud (VIG)
1961
Doisy-Daëne (WY)
1939
Coutet (WY)
1919
Rayne-Vigneau (WY)

£40.00 to £49.99

1988
Raymond Lafon (JU)
1980
de Fargues (VIG)
1970
Rieussec (ROB)
Suduiraut (VIG)
1961
Coutet (WY)
1949
d'Arche (WY)
1935
la Tour Blanche (WY)
1919
Sigalas-Rabaud (WY)
1918
Rabaud-Promis (WY)

£50.00 to £59.99

1985
de Fargues (BUT)
1966
Climens (TW)
1962
Sigalas-Rabaud (WY)
1961
Guiraud (BIB)
1947
Rayne-Vigneau (WY)
1940
Lafaurie-Peyraguey (WY)

£60.00 to £89.99

1986
d'Yquem ½ bottle (WY, BIB)
1985
d'Yquem ½ bottle (TW)
1984
d'Yquem (WY, BIB, DI)
1983
d'Yquem ½ bottle (BUT, WY)

1970
Gilette Crème de Tête (CB)
1961
Rieussec (WY)
1948
Filhot (WY)
Rayne-Vigneau (WY)
1945
Rayne-Vigneau (WY)
1940
la Tour Blanche (WY)
1926
Lafaurie-Peyraguey (WY)
1924
Coutet (WY)
Filhot (WY)
1918
Rayne-Vigneau (WY)
1914
Suduiraut (WY)

£90.00 to £119.99

1988
d'Yquem (FA)
1986
d'Yquem (WY)
1985
d'Yquem (LAY)
1983
d'Yquem (WY)
1982
d'Yquem (WY)
1981
d'Yquem (WY, UN)
1980
d'Yquem (WY)
1979
d'Yquem ½ bottle (EL)
1971
de Fargues (WY)
1961
Gilette Crème de Tête (TW)
1955
Gilette Crème de Tête (TW)
1937
Coutet (WY)
Filhot (WY)
1926
Rieussec (WY)
1923
Lafaurie-Peyraguey (ROB)
1921
Guiraud (WY)
1919
Climens (WY)

£120.00 to £149.99

1986
d'Yquem (BUT, BIB, WS, TAN, AD)
1985
d'Yquem (BUT, DI, JU)
1983
d'Yquem (BUT, HA)
1975
d'Yquem (BUT)
1949
Filhot (HUN)
1947
Climens (WY)
1928
Climens (WY)
1921
Filhot (WY)

£150.00 to £199.99

1986
d'Yquem (EL, JU, BER, TW, CB)
1947
Rieussec (ROB)
1934
Filhot (ROB)

£200.00 to £299.99

1976
d'Yquem (ROB)
1965
de Ricaud ½ bottle (BIB)
1961
d'Yquem (TW)
1949
Gilette Crème de Tête (TW)

£300.00 to £350.00

1962
d'Yquem (ROB)
1954
de Ricaud ½ bottle (BIB)

£400.00 to £499.99

1955
d'Yquem (ROB)
1953
d'Yquem (WY)

£600.00 to £630.00

1953
d'Yquem (ROB)
1949
d'Yquem (WY)
1918
d'Yquem (WY)

BASIC BURGUNDY

RED

Under £5.00

Non-vintage
Asda Bourgogne Rouge (ASD)
Tesco Red Burgundy (TES)
1990
★ Bourgogne Pinot Noir Fûts de Chêne, Cave de Buxy (WHG)
1988
Bourgogne Pinot Noir Cave de Buxy (WHG)
Bourgogne Rouge Boisson-Vadot (BEK)

£5.00 to £5.99

1990
Bourgogne Pinot Noir Cave de Buxy (WAI)
Bourgogne Rouge Tastevinė, Bichot (DAV)

£6.00 to £6.99

1990
Bourgogne Passe-Tout-Grain, Rion (MV)
1988
Bourgogne Pinot Noir Domaine de la Combe (BIB)
1986
Bourgogne Passe-Tout-Grain, Vallet (BOR)
Bourgogne Rouge Tastevinė, Bichot (UN)

£7.00 to £7.99

1990
Bourgogne Passe-Tout-Grain, Jayer (JU)
Bourgogne Pinot Noir Jadot (WR, THR, BOT)
1989
Bourgogne Pinot Noir Jadot (VIC)
Bourgogne Pinot Noir Parent (EY, WHG)
1988
Bourgogne Passe-Tout-Grain, Jayer (RAE)
★ Bourgogne Pinot Noir Parent (CV)

£8.00 to £10.99

1990
Bourgogne Pinot Noir Michel Lafarge (HAH)
Bourgogne Pinot Noir Parent (HAG)
Bourgogne Rouge Coche-Dury (BEK)
1988
Bourgogne Passe-Tout-Grain, Jayer (JU)
1987
Bourgogne Rouge Jayer (RAE)

c. £19.00

1988
Bourgogne Rouge Jayer (BUT)

WHITE

Under £5.00

1990
★ Bourgogne Aligoté Brocard (WAI)

£5.00 to £5.99

Non-vintage
Sainsbury's Burgundy Chardonnay (SAI)
1990
Bourgogne Aligoté Sorin-Defrance (SUM, WHI)
Bourgogne Chardonnay Sorin (HOG)

£6.00 to £7.99

1991
Bourgogne Aligoté de Bouzeron, Villaine (BY, AD)
Bourgogne Blanc Latour (PEN)
1989
Bourgogne Aligoté Diconne (BEK)

£8.00 to £9.99

1992
Bourgogne Chardonnay Jadot (VIC)
1990
Bourgogne Chardonnay les Champs Perriers, Clerc (TAN)
1988
Bourgogne Blanc Jobard (RAE)

£10.00 to £16.00

1989
Bourgogne Blanc Leflaive (CB, DI)
1986
Bourgogne Blanc Jobard (BUT)

SPARKLING

Under £7.00

Non-vintage
★ Crémant de Bourgogne Cave de Lugny (WAI, GA, MAR, OD)
★ Sainsbury's Crémant de Bourgogne Rosé (SAI)
1989
★ Crémant de Bourgogne Rosé, Cave de Bailly (WHG)

c. £8.00

1989
Crémant de Bourgogne Cave de Viré (CV)

CÔTE D'OR

RED

Under £6.00

1990
Hautes-Côtes de Beaune, Caves des Hautes-Côtes (DI)
Hautes-Côtes de Nuits, Caves des Hautes-Côtes (OD)
1988
Hautes-Côtes de Beaune, Caves des Hautes-Côtes (OD, DI)

£7.00 to £7.99

1990
Hautes-Côtes de Beaune, Mazilly (MV)
Savigny-lès-Beaune Latour (LOR)

£8.00 to £8.99

Non-vintage
Côte de Beaune-Villages Germain (AUG)
1990
Côte de Beaune-Villages Drouhin (NI)
Hautes-Côtes de Nuits, Michel Gros (BY)
1989
Savigny-lès-Beaune Latour (TAN, PEN)
Savigny-lès-Beaune Pavelot (GE)
1988
★ Marsannay Fougeray (GRG)

£9.00 to £9.99

1991
★ Chorey-lès-Beaune Tollot-Beaut (JU)
1990
Chassagne-Montrachet Henri Germain (AD)
Santenay la Maladière, Jaffelin (OD)
Savigny-lès-Beaune Faiveley (WAI)
1989
Côte de Beaune la Grande Châtelaine, Lescure (PIP)
St-Aubin les Frionnes, Prudhon (JU, HAY)
1988
Pernand-Vergelesses Rollin (RAE)
★ St-Aubin Sentier du Clou, Prudhon (BIB)
1987
Savigny-lès-Beaune Henri de Villamont (ROB)
1986
Santenay Clos Tavannes, Domaine de la Pousse d'Or (DAV)
1983
Pernand-Vergelesses Île de Vergelesses, Chanson (BUT)

£10.00 to £10.99

Non-vintage
Beaune du Château, Domaine du Château de Beaune (PEN)
1990
★ Chorey-lès-Beaune Tollot-Beaut (BEK, AD)
Monthélie Garaudet (PIP)
1989
Chorey-lès-Beaune Tollot-Beaut (JU)
Meursault les Forges, Prieur-Brunet (EL)
1988
★ St-Romain Domaine Gras (ROB)
Savigny-lès-Beaune Pavelot (DAV)

1986
Chorey-lès-Beaune Tollot-Beaut (GRE)
1985
★ St-Aubin les Castets, Lamy (PE)
1983
Beaune Clos du Roi, Chanson (BUT)

£11.00 to £11.99

1990
Marsannay Charlopin (WCL)
Santenay Drouhin (NI)
Savigny-lès-Beaune les Serpentières, Drouhin (OD)
1988
Monthélie Monthélie-Douhairet (MV, WCL)
Morey-St-Denis Regis Bouvier (BEK)
Santenay Latour (PEN)
1986
Auxey-Duresses Roulot (BUT)
Pommard les Argillières, Lejeune (HAY)
Santenay la Maladière, Prieur (CV)
1985
Hautes-Côtes de Nuits, Michel Gros (BUT)
Santenay Latour (WHI)
1983
Beaune Clos des Fèves, Chanson (BUT)
1982
★ Beaune Teurons, Rossignol (CHA)

£12.00 to £12.99

1990
Fixin Alain Guyard (NI)
1989
★ Gevrey-Chambertin Rossignol-Trapet (BEK)
Savigny-lès-Beaune Aux Grands Liards, Bize (AD)
1988
Beaune Vignes Franches, Mazilly (MV)
Fixin Fougeray (GRG)
Gevrey-Chambertin Rodet (EL)
★ Pernand-Vergelesses Île de Vergelesses, Chandon de Briailles (BEK)
Santenay Drouhin (ROB)
Savigny-lès-Beaune Latour (DAV)
Savigny Peuillets, Capron-Manieux (MV)
1987
Chassagne-Montrachet Champs-Gains, Jean Marc Morey (DAV)
Gevrey-Chambertin Trapet (BY)
Vosne-Romanée les Violettes, Georges Clerget (BY)
1986
Santenay les Gravières, Domaine de la Pousse d'Or (BY)
1985
Beaune Montée Rouge, Voarick (WRI)
1983
Aloxe-Corton les Chaillots, Latour (WHI)
Beaune Marconnets, Chanson (BUT)

£13.00 to £13.99

1990
★ Beaune Bressandes, Henri Germain (TAN)
Chambolle-Musigny Lignier (SOM)
1989
Côte de Nuits-Villages Jayer-Gilles (AD)
Gevrey-Chambertin Lignier (SOM)
1988
Beaune Grèves, Moillard (BE)
Monthélie Parent (TAN)
Nuits-St-Georges Labouré-Roi (PIP)
Pernand-Vergelesses Rollin (JU)
1986
Aloxe-Corton Rollin (RAE)
Beaune Teurons, Jadot (GRE)
Chambolle-Musigny Faiveley (HOG)
Morey-St-Denis Clos des Ormes, Faiveley (HOG)
Morey-St-Denis Olivier Leflaive (TW)
1985
Chorey-lès-Beaune Tollot-Beaut (BUT)
Côte de Nuits-Villages Jayer-Gilles (PE)

£14.00 to £14.99

1989
Aloxe-Corton Rollin (NI)
Beaune Bressandes, Henri Germain (AD)
Beaune Vignes Franches, Latour (VIG)
★ Nuits-St-Georges Michelot (BEK)
Savigny-lès-Beaune les Lavières, Tollot-Beaut (JU)
1988
Gevrey-Chambertin Trapet (BY)
Savigny-lès-Beaune les Lavières, Tollot-Beaut (AD)
1987
Beaune Clos du Roi, Tollot-Beaut (BEK)
Gevrey-Chambertin Domaine des Varoilles (AUG)
Nuits-St-Georges Faiveley (GRE)
Volnay Lafarge (BEK)
Vosne-Romanée Engel (ROB)
1986
★ Nuits-St-Georges Clos de la Maréchale, Faiveley (HOG)
Nuits-St-Georges Faiveley (ROB)
1985
Pommard la Platière, Coche (RAE)
1983
Chambolle-Musigny Roumier (RAE)
Meursault Clos de la Baronne, Manuel (CV)
1982
★ Auxey-Duresses Ampeau (CHA)

£15.00 to £15.99

1990
Nuits-St-Georges Champy (HOG)
1989
Gevrey-Chambertin Armand Rousseau (TAN)
Gevrey-Chambertin Latour (PEN)
Pernand-Vergelesses Île de Vergelesses, Chandon de Briailles (HAH)
1988
Beaune Épenottes, Parent (CV)
★ Beaune Teurons, Rossignol-Trapet (BY)
1987
Volnay 1er Cru Lafarge (BEK)
Volnay les Caillerets, Marquis d'Angerville (OD)
Vosne-Romanée les Suchots, Noëllat (BEK)

In each price band wines are listed in vintage order. Within each vintage they are listed in A–Z order.

1986
Beaune Grèves, Tollot-Beaut (HAY)
Chambolle-Musigny Faiveley (DI)
Chambolle-Musigny la Combe d'Orvaux, Grivot (LAY)
Chapelle-Chambertin Trapet (GRE)
Morey-St-Denis Monts Luisants, Pernin-Rossin (RAE)
Nuits-St-Georges les Vaucrains, Michelot (BEK)
1985
Beaune Grèves, Moillard (VIC)
Gevrey-Chambertin Faiveley (HOG)
1983
Aloxe-Corton Latour (PEN)
Volnay Chanson (BUT)

£16.00 to £16.99

1990
Gevrey-Chambertin Armand Rousseau (EL)
1989
Gevrey-Chambertin Rossignol-Trapet (TW)
Morey-St-Denis Clos de la Bussière, Roumier (TAN)
Nuits-St-Georges Gouges (BE)
Nuits-St-Georges les Hauts Pruliers, Machard de Gramont (LOR)
Nuits-St-Georges Rodet (WHI)
Pommard Clos Blanc, Machard de Gramont (AD)
Vosne-Romanée les Violettes, Georges Clerget (SUM)
1988
Beaune 1er Cru, Domaine du Château de Meursault (LO)
Chambolle-Musigny Dujac (BUT, BY)
★ Chambolle-Musigny Noëllat (BEK)
Chambolle-Musigny Roumier (TAN)
Santenay Clos Tavannes, Domaine de la Pousse d'Or (HAG)
1986
Beaune Bressandes, Henri Germain (AD)
Beaune Grèves, Moillard (WRI)
Clos de la Roche Dujac (BY)
Gevrey-Chambertin Vieille Vigne, Domaine des Varoilles (CHA)
★ Latricières-Chambertin Trapet (BEK)
Nuits-St-Georges Rion (MV)
Santenay Clos Tavannes, Domaine de la Pousse d'Or (HAG)
Volnay Santenots Matrot (CB)
1983
Beaune Teurons, Domaine du Château de Beaune (PEN)
Corton Chanson (BUT)

£17.00 to £19.99

1990
Chambolle-Musigny Dujac (BUT)
Corton Latour (LOR)
Gevrey-Chambertin Bachelet (GAU)
Gevrey-Chambertin Rossignol-Trapet (HAH)
Morey-St-Denis Clos des Ormes, Lignier (JU)
Nuits-St-Georges Robert Chevillon (GAU)
1989
Aloxe-Corton Tollot-Beaut (JU, LAY, AD)
Beaune Grèves, Tollot-Beaut (JU)
Gevrey-Chambertin Cazetiers, Armand Rousseau (AD)
Morey-St-Denis Dujac (AD)
Nuits-St-Georges Faiveley (GRE)
Volnay Frémiets, Marquis d'Angerville (GE)
Volnay Lafarge (WS)
1988
Beaune Chouacheux, Machard de Gramont (JU)
Beaune Épenottes, Machard de Gramont (JU)
Chambolle-Musigny Beaux Bruns, Rion (MV)
Gevrey-Chambertin Bachelet (GAU)
Gevrey-Chambertin Drouhin (NI)
Morey-St-Denis Dujac (HAG)
Nuits-St-Georges Faiveley (TAN)
Savigny-lès-Beaune les Lavières, Tollot-Beaut (JU)
Savigny-lès-Beaune les Vergelesses, Bize (HAH)
Volnay Champans, Gagnard-Delagrange (BY)
Volnay Lafarge (RAE)
Vosne-Romanée Rion (MV)
1987
Beaune 1er Cru, Domaine du Château de Meursault (VIN)
Beaune Teurons, Jacques Germain (WHI)
Chambolle-Musigny Lignier (JU)
Corton-Bressandes Tollot-Beaut (BEK)
Corton Tollot-Beaut (BEK)
Gevrey-Chambertin Bachelet (ROB)
Gevrey-Chambertin Faiveley (DI)
Mazis-Chambertin Armand Rousseau (EL)
Morey-St-Denis Clos de la Bussière, Roumier (ROB)
Morey-St-Denis Clos des Ormes, Lignier (BIB)
Nuits-St-Georges Clos de la Maréchale, Faiveley (GRG)
Nuits-St-Georges les Damodes, Machard de Gramont (JU)

Pommard Clos Blanc, Machard de Gramont (JU)
Pommard Lejeune (RAE)
Volnay Clos des Chênes, Lafarge (BEK)
Volnay les Caillerets, Domaine de la Pousse d'Or (ROB)
Volnay Santenots Lafon (MV)
Volnay Santenots Matrot (CB)

1986

Beaune Clos des Fèves, Chanson (HAG)
Clos de la Roche Armand Rousseau (EL)
Morey-St-Denis Dujac (VIG)
Nuits-St-Georges Clos de la Maréchale, Faiveley (DI)
Nuits-St-Georges Jadot (VIC)
Nuits-St-Georges les Pruliers, Grivot (LAY)
Nuits-St-Georges les Vaucrains, Gouges (ROB)
Pommard les Chaponniers, Parent (EY)
Savigny-lès-Beaune Marconnets, Bize (TW)

1985

Aloxe-Corton Voarick (BUT)
Corton Latour (VIC)
Nuits-St-Georges Faiveley (HOG)
Savigny-lès-Beaune Aux Grands Liards, Bize (WS)
Savigny-lès-Beaune les Vergelesses, Bize (BUT)
Volnay Santenots Rougeot (PE)

1983

Beaune Grèves, Tollot-Beaut (BUT)
Clos de la Roche Armand Rousseau (ROB)
Morey-St-Denis Clos des Ormes, Lignier (BUT)

1982

Beaune Clos du Roi, Ampeau (CHA)
Volnay Santenots Ampeau (CHA)

1978

Santenay Remoissenet (GRE)

£20.00 to £24.99

1991

Volnay Santenots Boillot (WW)
Volnay Santenots Lafon (JU)

1990

Gevrey-Chambertin Cazetiers, Armand Rousseau (EL)
Morey-St-Denis Dujac (TAN)
Pommard les Argillières, Lejeune (JU)

1989

Morey-St-Denis Clos des Ormes, Faiveley (GRE)
Pommard les Argillières, Lejeune (JU)
Volnay Clos des Ducs, Marquis d'Angerville (EL)
Volnay les Caillerets, Clos des 60 Ouvrées, Domaine de la Pousse d'Or (LAY)
Volnay Santenots-du-Millieu, Tête de Cuvée, Lafon (TAN)
Vosne-Romanée Jean Gros (BOT)

1988

Aloxe-Corton Tollot-Beaut (JU)
Chambolle-Musigny Faiveley (GRE, WRI)
Gevrey-Chambertin Clos des Varoilles, Domaine des Varoilles (TAN)
★ Mazis-Chambertin Armand Rousseau (TAN)
Nuits-St-Georges Clos de la Maréchale, Faiveley (BE)
Pommard les Argillières, Lejeune (JU)
Volnay Clos des Chênes, Lafarge (BEK, PIP)
Volnay les Caillerets, Clos des 60 Ouvrées, Domaine de la Pousse d'Or (BY)
Volnay les Caillerets, Marquis d'Angerville (OD)
Volnay Santenots Lafon (MV)
Vosne-Romanée les Beaumonts, Domaine Rion (OD)

1987

Beaune Clos des Mouches, Drouhin (GRE)
Échézeaux Mugneret (BEK)
Gevrey-Chambertin Lavaux-St-Jacques, Maume (PE)
Nuits-St-Georges Clos de Forets St-Georges, Domaine de l'Arlot (LAY)
Nuits-St-Georges Richemone, Pernin-Rossin (RAE)
Vosne-Romanée les Chaumes, Rion (MV)

1986

Chambertin Clos-de-Bèze, Armand Rousseau (BUT)
★ Chambertin Trapet (BEK, BY)
Chambolle-Musigny les Charmes, Michel Clerget (JU)
Charmes-Chambertin Armand Rousseau (VIG)
Clos de Vougeot Grivot (PIP, BUT)
Clos de Vougeot Noëllat (BEK)
Corton Tollot-Beaut (JU)
Latricières-Chambertin Trapet (PIP)
Musigny Vieilles Vignes, de Vogüé (FA)
Nuits-St-Georges Vignes Rondes, Rion (GRE)
Volnay Caillerets Cuvée Carnot, Bouchard Père (VIC)
Volnay Clos des Ducs, Marquis d'Angerville (CB)
Vosne-Romanée Beaux Monts, Thomas-Moillard (AUG)
Vosne-Romanée les Beaumonts, Domaine Rion (GAU)

1985
Chambolle-Musigny la Combe d'Orvaux, Grivot (BUT)
Gevrey-Chambertin Clos des Varoilles, Domaine des Varoilles (ROB)
Latricières-Chambertin Trapet (HA)
Pommard Parent (TW)
Vosne-Romanée Confuron-Cotetidot (ROB)
Vosne-Romanée Jean Gros (BUT)
1983
Aloxe-Corton Tollot-Beaut (BUT)
Beaune Clos des Ursules, Jadot (BUT)
Corton-Grancey Latour (WY)
Latricières-Chambertin Trapet (BY)
Nuits-St-Georges Clos de Thorey, Moillard (PEN)
Pommard les Argillières, Lejeune (BUT)
1976
Beaune Faiveley (TW)
Beaune Grèves, Moillard (BUT)
★ Gevrey-Chambertin Clos St-Jacques, Clair-Daü (BUT)

£25.00 to £29.99

1990
Mazis-Chambertin Armand Rousseau (EL)
Nuits-St-Georges les Vaucrains, Robert Chevillon (GAU)
Volnay Santenots Lafon (JU)
Vosne-Romanée les Chaumes, Rion (GAU)
1989
Charmes-Chambertin Armand Rousseau (EL)
Clos de la Roche Armand Rousseau (BUT)
Corton-Bressandes Tollot-Beaut (JU)
Nuits-St-Georges Jayer-Gilles, Robert Jayer (WS)
1988
Beaune Clos des Mouches, Drouhin (TW)
Chapelle-Chambertin Trapet (BEK)
Clos St-Denis Lignier (JU)
Corton-Bressandes Voarick (HAG)
Corton Pougets, Jadot (BOT, THR, WR)
Nuits-St-Georges Clos des Argillières, Rion (GAU)
Nuits-St-Georges Vignes Rondes, Rion (GAU)
Pommard Pezerolles Domaine de Montille (HAH)

Stars (★) indicate wines selected by the editors as particularly good value in their class.

1986
Bonnes-Mares Bertheau (BEK)
Chambertin Clos-de-Bèze, Faiveley (GRE)
Chambolle-Musigny les Amoureuses, de Vogüé (EL)
Gevrey-Chambertin Combottes, Dujac (BY)
Pommard Rugiens Domaine Courcel (EL)
1985
Charmes-Chambertin Armand Rousseau (BUT)
Corton Bonneau du Martray (ROB)
Morey-St-Denis Clos des Ormes, Lignier (BUT)
Nuits-St-Georges Clos de Thorey, Moillard (JU)
Volnay les Caillerets, Domaine de la Pousse d'Or (WS)
Volnay Santenots Lafon (BUT)
1983
Chambertin Clos-de-Bèze, Damoy (BUT)
Clos de la Roche Dujac (CB)
Clos St-Denis Dujac (CB)
Clos St-Denis Lignier (BUT)
Grands-Échézeaux Mongeard-Mugneret (RAE)
Pommard Clos de la Commaraine, Jaboulet-Vercherre (WRI)
1982
Clos de la Roche Armand Rousseau (VIG)
Corton Bonneau du Martray (BUT)
Corton Clos des Cortons, Faiveley (DI)
1979
Clos de Vougeot Ponnelle (WHI)

£30.00 to £39.99

1990
Gevrey-Chambertin Clos St-Jacques, Armand Rousseau (EL, BUT)
1989
Bonnes-Mares Lignier (JU)
Chambertin Armand Rousseau (AD)
Chambolle-Musigny les Amoureuses, Roumier (TAN)
Clos de Vougeot Mongeard-Mugneret (AD)
Clos St-Denis Dujac (BUT, TAN)
1988
Charmes-Chambertin Dujac (BUT, AD)
Clos de Vougeot Grivot (BUT)
Corton-Bressandes Tollot-Beaut (AD)
Latricières-Chambertin Trapet (BY)
Musigny Prieur (EL)
Ruchottes-Chambertin Armand Rousseau (ROB)
Volnay Clos de la Bousse d'Or, Domaine de la Pousse d'Or (THR, WR, BOT)

1987
Bonnes-Mares Roumier (BUT)
Chambertin Armand Rousseau (BUT)
Charmes-Chambertin Bachelet (GAU)
Clos de Vougeot Arnoux (WHI)
Corton Clos des Cortons, Faiveley (JU)
Échézeaux Jacqueline Jayer (BUT)
Nuits-St-Georges Henri Jayer (JU)
Nuits-St-Georges les Boudots, Méo-Camuzet (BIB)
1986
Chambertin Clos-de-Bèze, Armand Rousseau (EL)
Clos de la Roche Ponsot (MV)
Clos de Vougeot Grivot (DAV)
Clos de Vougeot Méo-Camuzet (PE)
Clos St-Denis Dujac (BY)
Musigny de Vogüé (EL)
1985
Charmes-Chambertin Dujac (BIB)
Clos de la Roche Armand Rousseau (BUT)
Corton-Bressandes Voarick (BUT)
Corton Clos des Cortons, Faiveley (BIB)

Corton-Grancey Latour (WY)
Corton les Renardes, Voarick (BUT)
Échézeaux Mongeard-Mugneret (BUT)
Grands-Échézeaux Mongeard-Mugneret (BIB)
Volnay Clos des Chênes, Lafarge (BUT)
1983
Beaune Hospices de Beaune, Rolin (HA)
Clos de Vougeot Moillard (PEN)
Échézeaux Domaine de la Romanée-Conti (FA, WY)
Pommard Hospices de Beaune, Domaine de la Charité, Mommessin (EL)
1982
Latricières-Chambertin Faiveley (TW)
Romanée-St-Vivant Domaine de la Romanée-Conti (BIB)
1980
Musigny Vieilles Vignes, de Vogüé (BIB)
1978
Gevrey-Chambertin Faiveley (BUT)
Nuits-St-Georges Faiveley (BUT)
1976
Gevrey-Chambertin Faiveley (TW)
Nuits-St-Georges Clos de la Maréchale, Faiveley (TW)
Nuits-St-Georges Faiveley (TW)
1959
Morey-St-Denis Chanson (VIG)

£40.00 to £49.99

1989
Chambertin Clos-de-Bèze, Armand Rousseau (TAN)
Clos de Vougeot Méo-Camuzet (BUT)
Échézeaux Dujac (VIG)
Échézeaux Georges Jayer (JU)
1988
Bonnes-Mares Dujac (BUT)
Bonnes-Mares Lignier (JU)
Chambertin Trapet (BY)
Chambertin Vieilles Vignes, Trapet (PIP)
Clos St-Denis Dujac (BUT)
Corton Clos des Cortons, Faiveley (JU)
Échézeaux Faiveley (WS)
Mazis-Chambertin Faiveley (JU)
1986
Chambertin Armand Rousseau (VIG)
Échézeaux Domaine de la Romanée-Conti (BUT)
1985
Bonnes-Mares Domaine des Varoilles (JU)
Nuits-St-Georges Henri Jayer (BUT)
1978
Chambertin Clos-de-Bèze, Clair-Daü (BUT)
Corton-Grancey Latour (BIB)
Mazis-Chambertin Faiveley (TW)

£50.00 to £59.99

1990
Chambertin Clos-de-Bèze, Faiveley (JU)
Clos de la Roche Dujac (BUT)
Échézeaux Domaine de la Romanée-Conti (EL)
1989
Chambertin Armand Rousseau (BUT)
Romanée-St-Vivant Domaine de la Romanée-Conti (FA)
1987
Échézeaux Henri Jayer (JU)
Vosne-Romanée Cros Parantoux, Henri Jayer (JU)
Vosne-Romanée les Brulées, Henri Jayer (JU)
1983
Grands-Échézeaux Domaine de la Romanée-Conti (WY)

£60.00 to £79.99

1989

Richebourg Domaine de la Romanée-Conti (FA)

Richebourg Domaine Gros (BY)

1988

Échézeaux Domaine de la Romanée-Conti (CB)

Musigny Vieilles Vignes, de Vogüé (TW)

1986

Grands-Échézeaux Domaine de la Romanée-Conti (TW)

Romanée-St-Vivant Domaine de la Romanée-Conti (BUT)

1985

Échézeaux Domaine de la Romanée-Conti (BUT, WY)

1976

Échézeaux Domaine de la Romanée-Conti (VIG)

Musigny Faiveley (TW)

1972

Bonnes-Mares de Vogüé (REI)

£80.00 to £99.99

1990

Grands-Échézeaux Domaine de la Romanée-Conti (EL, CB)

Romanée-St-Vivant Domaine de la Romanée-Conti (EL, CB)

1988

Richebourg Domaine Gros (JU)

1985

Chambertin Ponsot (BIB)

Romanée-St-Vivant Cuvée Marey Monge, Domaine de la Romanée-Conti (BUT)

1982

La Tâche Domaine de la Romanée-Conti (VIN, TW)

1928

Beaune Marconnets, Chanson (ROB)

£100.00 to £139.99

1990

Richebourg Domaine de la Romanée-Conti (EL, CB)

1988

Romanée-St-Vivant Domaine de la Romanée-Conti (JU)

1987

Richebourg Domaine de la Romanée-Conti (BUT, TW)

1985

Richebourg Domaine de la Romanée-Conti (BUT)

£155.00 to £199.99

1990

La Tâche Domaine de la Romanée-Conti (EL, TAN, CB)

1988

Richebourg Domaine de la Romanée-Conti (JU)

1985

La Tâche Domaine de la Romanée-Conti (BUT)

c. £350.00

1986

Romanée-Conti Domaine de la Romanée-Conti (BUT)

c. £472.00

1990

Romanée-Conti Domaine de la Romanée-Conti (EL)

c. £705.00

1988

Romanée-Conti Domaine de la Romanée-Conti (TW)

WHITE

Under £10.00

1991

Marsannay Jadot (THR, WR, BOT)

Pernand-Vergelesses Leflaive (AD)

St-Aubin 1er Cru, Leflaive (AD)

St-Romain Domaine Leflaive (AD)

1988

★ St-Romain Prieur-Brunet (EL)

1987

Santenay Blanc Lequin-Roussot (RAE)

£10.00 to £11.99

1991

Pernand-Vergelesses Rollin (NI)

1990

Monthélie le Champ Fulliot, Garaudet (PIP)

St-Aubin la Chatenière, Roux Père et Fils (EL)

1989
Auxey-Duresses Diconne (BEK)
Pernand-Vergelesses Leflaive (WS)
St-Aubin Prudhon (HAY)
St-Romain Clos Sous le Château, Jean Germain (TAN)
1988
Pernand-Vergelesses Chanson (TAN, HAG)
★ Savigny-lès-Beaune Capron-Manieux (MV)
1986
Pernand-Vergelesses Guyon (HOG)
1984
Corton-Charlemagne Bonneau du Martray (FA)

£12.00 to £13.99

1990
Puligny-Montrachet Labouré-Roi (EL)
St-Romain Clos Sous le Château, Jean Germain (JU)
1989
Chassagne-Montrachet Latour (WHI)
Meursault Boisson-Vadot (BEK)
Meursault Latour (WHI, LOR, HOG)
Puligny-Montrachet Latour (HOG)
1988
★ Pernand-Vergelesses Dubreuil-Fontaine (BY)
Pernand-Vergelesses Rollin (RAE, BIB)
1987
Meursault Ropiteau (HOG)
Pernand-Vergelesses Rollin (RAE)
Puligny-Montrachet Grands Champs, Jean Germain (GE)

£14.00 to £15.99

1991
Meursault Drouhin (OD)
Meursault Henri Germain (TAN)
1990
Meursault Clos des Meix-Chavaux, Jean Germain (HAH)
Meursault Jaffelin (GA)
Pernand-Vergelesses Rollin (JU)
Puligny-Montrachet Latour (PEN)
1989
Meursault Blagny, Latour (HOG)
St-Aubin Albert Morey (DAV)
1988
★ Chassagne-Montrachet les Embrazées, Albert Morey (BEK)
Meursault Clos du Château, Château de Meursault (LO)
Puligny-Montrachet Carillon (ASD)
1987
Meursault les Luchets, Roulot (BUT)
Meursault l'Ormeau, Coche (RAE)
Puligny-Montrachet Ropiteau (HOG)
1985
★ Puligny-Montrachet Jean Germain (GE)

£16.00 to £17.99

1990
Chassagne-Montrachet les Champs Gains, Albert Morey (BEK)
Clos du Château de Meursault Bourgogne Chardonnay (VIN)
Meursault Genevrières, Latour (EY)
Meursault Henri de Villamont (ROB)
Puligny-Montrachet Grands Champs, Jean Germain (HAH)
1989
Chassagne-Montrachet les Caillerets, Albert Morey (BEK)
Meursault Jean Germain (JU)
Puligny-Montrachet les Folatières, Boisson-Vadot (BEK)
★ Puligny-Montrachet les Folatières, Latour (WY)
1988
Chassagne-Montrachet Albert Morey (DAV)
Meursault Jobard (RAE)
Meursault l'Ormeau, Coche (BIB)
Meursault Matrot (CB)
Puligny-Montrachet Grands Champs, Jean Germain (DAV)
1987
Chassagne-Montrachet Albert Morey (DAV)
Meursault Chanson (TW)
Meursault Genevrières, Jobard (RAE)
1986
Meursault Labouré-Roi (CV)
Puligny-Montrachet Carillon (GE)
1983
Auxey-Duresses-Ecussaux, Ampeau (REI)

£18.00 to £19.99

1990
Meursault Charmes, Henri Germain (TAN)
Puligny-Montrachet Carillon (AD)
Puligny-Montrachet Leflaive (LAY)
Puligny-Montrachet Olivier Leflaive (AMI)
Puligny-Montrachet Sauzet (BEK, PE, EL)
1989
Chassagne-Montrachet Albert Morey (PIP)
Chassagne-Montrachet les Vergers, Colin (EY)
Meursault les Tillets, Chouet-Clivet (VIG)
Meursault les Vireuils, Roulot (HAY)

Meursault Santenots, Monthélie-Douhairet (MV)
Puligny-Montrachet Carillon (MV, LAY)
Puligny-Montrachet Drouhin (NI)
Puligny-Montrachet Sauzet (PE)

1988

Chassagne-Montrachet les Embrazées, Albert Morey (PIP)
Chassagne-Montrachet Morgeot, Gagnard Delagrange (BY)
Meursault Blagny, Latour (WY)
Meursault Drouhin (NI)
Meursault Michelot-Buisson (BY, HAG)
Puligny-Montrachet Clerc (BY)
Puligny-Montrachet Latour (PEN)
Puligny-Montrachet Olivier Leflaive (DI)

1987

Puligny-Montrachet Clerc (TW)

1986

Chassagne-Montrachet Javillier (VIN)
Meursault Jadot (VIC)
Meursault Jobard (BUT)
Meursault l'Ormeau, Coche (BIB)

1985

Meursault Jaffelin (PEN)

£20.00 to £24.99

1991

Meursault Charmes, Boillot (WW)

1990

Chassagne-Montrachet la Boudriotte, Gagnard-Delagrange (HAH)
Meursault Jobard (LAY)
Puligny-Montrachet les Folatières, Clerc (BY)
Puligny-Montrachet les Referts, Sauzet (HAG)

1989

Chassagne-Montrachet Jadot (WR, BOT, THR)
Chassagne-Montrachet Latour (VIG)
Chassagne-Montrachet les Caillerets, Bachelet-Ramonet (BIB)
Meursault Blagny, Matrot (CB)
Meursault Clos de Mazeray, Prieur (WHI)
Meursault Jobard (RAE, HAH)
Puligny-Montrachet Jean Germain (JU)
Puligny-Montrachet Leflaive (CB)
Puligny-Montrachet les Folatières, Latour (EY, VIG)

1988

Chassagne-Montrachet Clos de Chapelle, Duc de Magenta (HA)
Chassagne-Montrachet les Chaumes, Jean-Marc Morey (DAV)
Meursault Clos de la Barre, Lafon (JU)
Meursault Henri Germain (AD)
Meursault Poruzots, Jobard (BIB)
Puligny-Montrachet Clos de la Garenne, Drouhin (WY)
Puligny-Montrachet Clos de la Mouchère, Boillot (DAV)
Puligny-Montrachet Leflaive (TW, BIB, AD)
Puligny-Montrachet les Folatières, Drouhin (BR)

1987

Puligny-Montrachet les Folatières, Chartron (JU)
Puligny-Montrachet les Perrières, Sauzet (PE)

1986

Meursault Clos du Cromin, Leflaive (BUT)
Meursault Genevrières, Latour (BUT)
Puligny-Montrachet Clos de la Mouchère, Boillot (DAV)
Puligny-Montrachet Jadot (VIC)
Puligny-Montrachet Labouré-Roi (CV)
Puligny-Montrachet les Champs Gains, Clerc (PE)
Puligny-Montrachet les Folatières, Clerc (HAG)

1985

Puligny-Montrachet Clerc (TW)

1983

Puligny-Montrachet les Folatières, Latour (BUT)

£25.00 to £29.99

1991

Meursault Clos de la Barre, Lafon (JU)
Puligny-Montrachet les Perrières, Sauzet (TAN)
Puligny-Montrachet les Referts, Sauzet (JU)

1990

Corton-Charlemagne Latour (FA)
Meursault Clos de la Barre, Lafon (JU, GAU)
Puligny-Montrachet Champs Canet, Sauzet (BEK)
Puligny-Montrachet Clavoillon, Leflaive (PE)

1989

Meursault Charmes, Leflaive (TW)
Puligny-Montrachet Clos de la Garenne, Drouhin (WY)
Puligny-Montrachet les Folatières, Chartron (JU)
Puligny-Montrachet les Referts, Sauzet (BEK)

1988
Beaune Clos des Mouches, Drouhin (RAE)
Chassagne-Montrachet les Chenevottes, Niellon (GAU)
Chassagne-Montrachet Sauzet (ROB)
Corton-Charlemagne Bonneau du Martray (BEK)
Puligny-Montrachet Champs Canet, Sauzet (ROB, WS)
Puligny-Montrachet Clavoillon, Leflaive (CB)
Puligny-Montrachet les Perrières, Sauzet (TW)
Puligny-Montrachet les Referts, Sauzet (TW)
1987
Corton-Charlemagne Drouhin (WY)
Meursault Charmes, Lafon (JU)
1986
Corton-Charlemagne Jadot (HA)
Meursault Genevrières, Jobard (BUT)
Puligny-Montrachet les Folatières, Bouchard Père (PEN)
1985
Chassagne-Montrachet Morgeot, Henri Germain (AD)
1983
Meursault Ampeau (CHA)
1981
Puligny-Montrachet les Combettes, Ampeau (REI)
1976
Meursault Charmes, Ampeau (CHA)

£30.00 to £39.99

1991
Meursault Charmes, Lafon (JU)
Meursault Perrières, Lafon (JU)
Puligny-Montrachet les Combettes, Sauzet (TAN, JU)
1990
Corton-Charlemagne Bonneau du Martray (JU)
Corton-Charlemagne Rollin (JU)
Puligny-Montrachet les Combettes, Sauzet (EL)

*Please remember that **Webster's** is a price GUIDE and not a price LIST. It is not meant to replace up-to-date merchants' lists.*

Puligny-Montrachet les Perrières, Sauzet (EL)
Puligny-Montrachet les Pucelles, Leflaive (AD)
1989
Bâtard-Montrachet Albert Morey (BEK)
Chassagne-Montrachet Marquis de Laguiche (LAY)
Corton-Charlemagne Bonneau du Martray (LAY)
Puligny-Montrachet Clavoillon, Leflaive (CB, BIB, AD, DI, PE)
Puligny-Montrachet les Caillerets, Domaine Chartron (JU)
1988
Corton-Charlemagne Ancien Domaine des Comtes de Grancey (HAG)
Corton-Charlemagne Drouhin (WY)
Corton-Charlemagne Latour (WY, EY, LOR)
Corton-Charlemagne Leflaive (AD, HAH)
Corton-Charlemagne Rollin (RAE, BIB)
Meursault Clos de la Barre, Lafon (VIG)
Puligny-Montrachet Leflaive (BUT)
Puligny-Montrachet les Pucelles, Clerc (TW)
Puligny-Montrachet les Pucelles, Leflaive (MV)
1987
Bâtard-Montrachet Clerc (PIP)
Bienvenues-Bâtard-Montrachet Bachelet (BIB)
Bienvenues-Bâtard-Montrachet Leflaive (TAN)
Chassagne-Montrachet Marquis de Laguiche (TW)
Corton-Charlemagne Leflaive (AMI)
Corton-Charlemagne Tollot-Beaut (JU)
1986
Bâtard-Montrachet Albert Morey (EY)
Corton-Charlemagne Bouchard Père (PEN)
Corton-Charlemagne Latour (BUT)
Corton-Charlemagne Thévenot (EL)
1985
Puligny-Montrachet Clavoillon, Leflaive (HAY)
Puligny-Montrachet Sauzet (WS)
1983
Chassagne-Montrachet Marquis de Laguiche (WY)
Corton-Charlemagne Tollot-Beaut (BUT)
Puligny-Montrachet les Folatières, Drouhin (WY)
1980
Corton-Charlemagne Bonneau du Martray (GR)

£40.00 to £49.99

1990
Corton-Charlemagne Latour (VIG)
Meursault Charmes, Lafon (GAU)
Meursault Perrières, Lafon (GAU)
1989
Bienvenues-Bâtard-Montrachet Leflaive (CB)
Puligny-Montrachet les Pucelles, Leflaive (BIB, DI, JU, BUT)
1988
Bâtard-Montrachet Gagnard-Delagrange (BY)
Bienvenues-Bâtard-Montrachet Clerc (TW)
Bienvenues-Bâtard-Montrachet Leflaive (JU)
Corton-Charlemagne Tollot-Beaut (JU)
1987
Bâtard-Montrachet Olivier Leflaive (TW)
Chevalier-Montrachet Chartron (ROB)
1986
Criots-Bâtard-Montrachet Olivier Leflaive (TW)
1985
Chassagne-Montrachet Marquis de Laguiche (WY)
Corton-Charlemagne Labouré-Roi (GR)
Corton-Charlemagne Latour (VIC, BUT, JU)

£50.00 to £69.99

1990
Beaune Clos des Mouches, Drouhin (WY)
Chevalier-Montrachet Leflaive (AD)
1989
Bâtard-Montrachet Leflaive (HAY, DI, BIB)
Chevalier-Montrachet Chartron (JU)
Corton-Charlemagne Latour (AMI)
1988
Bâtard-Montrachet Leflaive (JU)
Chevalier-Montrachet Leflaive (HAY, CB)
Criots-Bâtard-Montrachet Blain-Gagnard (BIB)
1986
Bâtard-Montrachet Latour (WY, BUT)
Bienvenues-Bâtard-Montrachet Leflaive (BUT)
Chevalier-Montrachet Bouchard Père (PEN)
Corton-Charlemagne Jadot (JU)
le Montrachet Thénard (BUT)
1983
Bâtard-Montrachet Remoissenet (WS)
Corton-Charlemagne Latour (PE)
le Montrachet Château Herbeux (BUT)
1981
le Montrachet Latour (WY)
1978
Chevalier-Montrachet Bouchard Père (BU)
1976
Corton-Charlemagne Bonneau du Martray (GR)
1971
Corton-Vergennes Hospices de Beaune, Chanson (VIG)

£70.00 to £99.99

1989
le Montrachet Latour (WY)
le Montrachet Thénard (WS)
1988
Chevalier-Montrachet Leflaive (JU)
le Montrachet Marquis de Laguiche (WY)
1986
Chevalier-Montrachet Leflaive (BUT)
1985
Bâtard-Montrachet Leflaive (BUT)
le Montrachet Latour (WY, BUT)
1982
Bâtard-Montrachet Leflaive (ROB)
1973
Bâtard-Montrachet Latour (REI)

£100.00 to £125.00

1987
le Montrachet Marquis de Laguiche (TW)
1986
le Montrachet Marquis de Laguiche (WY, BUT)
1971
Corton-Charlemagne Latour (WY)

£300.00 to £355.00

1990
le Montrachet Domaine de la Romanée-Conti (EL)
1983
le Montrachet Domaine de la Romanée-Conti (WY)
1982
le Montrachet Domaine de la Romanée-Conti (TW)

c. £491.00

1978
le Montrachet Domaine de la Romanée-Conti (FA)

c. £565.00

1986
le Montrachet Domaine de la Romanée-Conti (BUT)

CÔTE CHALONNAISE

RED

Under £9.00

1991
Mercurey Domaine de la Croix, Jacquelet-Faiveley (NA)
Rully Drouhin (OD)
1989
Givry Voarick (WRI)
Mercurey Latour (PEN)
1988
Givry Chanson (AS)
★ Mercurey Domaine du Meix-Foulot (CV)
1987
Mercurey Domaine du Meix-Foulot (ROB)
Rully Bouchard Père (PEN)
Rully Clos de Bellecroix, Domaine de la Folie (BUT)

£9.00 to £10.99

1990
Mercurey Domaine de la Croix, Jacquelet-Faiveley (NA)
Mercurey les Mauvarennes, Faiveley (DI)
1989
Mercurey Domaine de la Croix, Jacquelet-Faiveley (BE, WRI)
1988
Givry Remmoissenet (GRG)
Mercurey Domaine de la Croix, Jacquelet-Faiveley (BE, HUN)
Mercurey Latour (PEN)
1986
Mercurey Château de Chamirey (EL)
Mercurey les Veleys, de Launay (GE)
1985
Mercurey Domaine de la Croix, Jacquelet-Faiveley (AUG)
1983
Mercurey Château de Chamirey (GRG)
Mercurey Clos l'Évêque, Juillot (RAE)
1982
Mercurey Château de Chamirey (EL)

£12.00 to £15.00

1988
Rully Clos de Bellecroix, Domaine de la Folie (BUT)
1985
★ Mercurey Clos des Barraults, Juillot (BUT)
Mercurey Juillot (BUT)

WHITE

Under £9.00

1991
★ Montagny 1er Cru, Leflaive (AD)
1990
Montagny 1er Cru Alain Roy, Cave des Vignerons de Mancey (BEK)
Montagny 1er Cru, Cave de Buxy (CV, PIP)
Montagny Latour (PEN, LOR)
★ Rully la Chaume, Dury (JU, RAE)
1989
Montagny 1er Cru, Cave de Buxy (GA)
Montagny Latour (HOG)
Rully la Chaume, Dury (EY, HAY)
1988
★ Montagny 1er Cru, Cave de Buxy (CV)

£9.00 to £10.99

1991
Montagny 1er Cru, Leflaive (LAY)
Montagny Latour (HAG)
Rully Faiveley (NA)
1990
Mercurey Château de Chamirey, Rodet (WHI)
Montagny 1er Cru les Loges, Sarjeant (DAV, TAN)
Rully Faiveley (GRG)
Rully Marissou, Dury (RAE, JU)
1989
Givry Ragot (ROB)
Mercurey Voarick (WRI)
Montagny Leflaive (BUT)
Rully la Chaume, Dury (JU)
Rully Marissou, Dury (JU)
1988
Rully Clos St-Jacques, Domaine de la Folie (BUT)
Rully Varot, Delorme (HAG)
1986
Montagny Latour (BUT)

£11.00 to £13.99

1990
Montagny Clos de la Saule (WIC, BOD)
Mercurey Clos Rochette, Faiveley (NA, GRG, GRE)
Rully, Faiveley (JU)
1989
Mercurey Clos Rochette, Faiveley (DI)
Rully Faiveley (JU)

MÂCONNAIS

RED

Under £5.00

1992
Mâcon-Supérieur Rouge, Cave de Buxy (CV)
1991
Mâcon Rouge Loron (UN, EL)
1990
Mâcon Rouge Pasquier-Desvignes (AUG)

WHITE

Under £5.00

1992
Mâcon-Villages Cave Co-op. de Viré (WHG)
Mâcon-Viré les Grands Plantes, Cave Co-op. de Viré (WHG)
1991
Mâcon-Villages Cave Co-op. de Viré (GA)
Mâcon-Viré les Grands Plantes, Cave Co-op. de Viré (WHG)
1990
★ Mâcon-Villages Cave Co-op. de Viré (SAF)

£5.00 to £5.99

1992
Mâcon-Villages Cave Co-op. de Viré (CV)
Mâcon-Villages Cave Co-op. Prissé (JU)
1991
Mâcon-Prissé Duboeuf (BEK)
Mâcon-Villages Duboeuf (NI)
Mâcon-Villages Rodet (MAR)
★ St-Véran Domaine St-Martin, Duboeuf (BEK)
1990
Mâcon-Lugny Duboeuf (BEK)
Mâcon-Prissé Duboeuf (NI)
Mâcon-Villages Loron (TAN)

£6.00 to £6.99

1992
Mâcon la Roche Vineuse, Merlin (BIB)
St-Véran Domaine de la Batie, Duboeuf (DAV)
St-Véran Duboeuf (BOT, THR, WR)
1991
Mâcon Chardonnay Talmard (AD, TAN)
Mâcon-Lugny les Genièvres, Latour (HOG, PEN, LOR, TAN)
Mâcon-Prissé Cave Co-op. Prissé (HAH)
St-Véran Domaine de la Batie, Duboeuf (DAV)
St-Véran Domaine de Vignemont (PEN)
St-Véran Duboeuf (WR, BOT, THR)
1990
Mâcon-Lugny les Genièvres, Latour (WHI)
St-Véran Duboeuf (NI)
1989
Mâcon-Peronne Domaine de Mortier, Josserand (PE)
Mâcon-Viré Domaine des Chazelles (ASD)

£7.00 to £7.99

1992
Mâcon-Charnay Blanc Manciat-Poncet (HAW)
Mâcon-Lugny les Genièvres, Latour (DAV)
St-Véran Domaine Deux Roches (HAH)
1991
Mâcon Chardonnay Talmard (HAH)
Mâcon-Clessé Signoret (HAW)
Mâcon la Roche Vineuse, Merlin (MV)
Mâcon-Lugny les Genièvres, Latour (HIG, HAG, DAV)
Mâcon-Viré Cuvée Spéciale, Bonhomme (GE)
Pouilly-Fuissé Latour (WHI)
Pouilly-Loché Cave des Crus Blancs (HAW)
Pouilly-Vinzelles Mathias (PIP)
St-Véran Domaine de Vignemont (HAG)
St-Véran Domaine les Colombiers (PIP)
1990
Mâcon Blanc Clos de Condemine, Luquet (ROB)
Mâcon-Lugny les Genièvres, Latour (HUN, VIN)
Pouilly-Fuissé Labouré-Roi (NA)
St-Véran Depardon (VIN)
St-Véran Latour (HOG)
1989
Mâcon-Clessé Guillemot (TAN)
Mâcon-Villages Domaine d'Azenay (BR)
1988
St-Véran Cave Co-op. Prissé (CV)

£8.00 to £9.99

1992
Pouilly-Fuissé Dépagneux (WCL)
1991
Mâcon la Roche Vineuse, Merlin (WCL)
Mâcon Monbellet, Goyard (WS, BIB)
Mâcon-Viré Goyard (RAE)
St-Véran Château Fuissé, Vincent (WS, EL)
St-Véran Corsin (AD)
St-Véran Domaine Deux Roches (BAR)

1990
Mâcon Monbellet, Goyard (BIB)
Mâcon-Viré Goyard (RAE)
Pouilly-Fuissé Domaine Béranger, Duboeuf (NI)
Pouilly-Fuissé Latour (HOG)
Pouilly-Fuissé Loron (DI)
St-Véran Château Fuissé, Vincent (TAN, AD)
St-Véran Latour (VIG)
1989
Pouilly-Fuissé Domaine Béranger, Duboeuf (BEK)
★ Pouilly-Fuissé la Mure, Depardon (HIG)
Pouilly-Fuissé les Vieux Murs, Loron (WRI)
1988
St-Véran Château Fuissé, Vincent (HAG)
1986
St-Véran Latour (BUT)

£10.00 to £15.99

1991
Mâcon-Villages Domaine de la Bon Gran, Thévenet (AD)
Pouilly-Fuissé Château Fuissé, Vincent (WS)
Pouilly-Fuissé Château Pouilly, Mommessin (HAG)
1990
Mâcon-Clessé Domaine de la Bon Gran, Thévenet (JU, TAN)
Mâcon-Clessé Thévenet (WW)
Mâcon-Villages Domaine de la Bon Gran, Thévenet (AD)
Pouilly-Fuissé les Crays, Forest (NA)
Pouilly-Fuissé Manciat-Poncet (HAW)
1989
Mâcon-Clessé Domaine de la Bon Gran, Thévenet (JU)
Pouilly-Fuissé Château Fuissé, Vincent (VIG)
St-Véran Château Fuissé, Vincent (JU)
1988
Pouilly-Fuissé Château Fuissé, Vincent (VIG)
1987
Pouilly-Fuissé Château Fuissé, Vincent (TW)

In each price band wines are listed in vintage order. Within each vintage they are listed in A–Z order.

1986
Pouilly-Fuissé Domaine de l'Arillière (BUT)
Pouilly-Fuissé Latour (BUT)
St-Véran Château Fuissé, Vincent (BUT)
St-Véran Corsin (BUT)

£16.00 to £19.99

1990
Pouilly-Fuissé Château Fuissé, Vincent (TAN, AD)
1989
Pouilly-Fuissé Château Fuissé, Vincent (AD)
1988
Pouilly-Fuissé Château Fuissé, Vincent (RAE, TW)
Pouilly-Fuissé Château Fuissé Vieilles Vignes, Vincent (SOM)
1986
Pouilly-Fuissé Corsin (BUT)

£20.00 to £25.00

1991
Pouilly-Fuissé Château Fuissé Vieilles Vignes, Vincent (EL)
1990
Pouilly-Fuissé Château Fuissé Vieilles Vignes, Vincent (AD)
1989
Pouilly-Fuissé Château Fuissé Vieilles Vignes, Vincent (JU)
1988
Pouilly-Fuissé Château Fuissé Vieilles Vignes, Vincent (EY, JU)

c. £26.00

1985
Pouilly-Fuissé Château Fuissé Vieilles Vignes, Vincent (BUT)
1982
Pouilly-Fuissé Château Fuissé Vieilles Vignes, Vincent (BUT)

c. £30.00

1986
Mâcon-Clessé Thévenet botrytized (BR)

CHABLIS

WHITE

Under £6.00

1992
Sauvignon de St-Bris, Brocard (JU)
1991
Sauvignon de St-Bris, Domaine des Remparts (HOG)
1990
Chablis Domaine Servin (GR)
1989
Sauvignon de St-Bris, Brocard (HIC)
Sauvignon de St-Bris, Sorin (WHI)

£6.00 to £6.99

1992
Chablis la Chablisienne (VIC, WAI)
Sauvignon de St-Bris, Goisot (NA)
1991
Asda Chablis (ASD)
Chablis la Chablisienne (WAI, MAR)
Chablis Simmonet-Febvre (CHA)
Sainsbury's Chablis (SAI)
1990
Chablis Domaine de Biéville, Moreau (HOG)
★ Chablis Durup (EL)
Sauvignon de St-Bris, Defrance (VIG)

£7.00 to £7.99

1992
Chablis Moreau (DAV)
1991
Chablis Brocard (OD)
Chablis Domaine de Biéville, Moreau (WHI)
Chablis Domaine des Manants, Brocard (AD)
Chablis Domaine Ste-Claire, Brocard (CV)
Chablis Drouhin (NI)
Chablis Durup (HAH)
Chablis Latour (WHI, EY, LOR)
★ Chablis Légland (BIB)
Chablis Louis Michel (NI)
Chablis Moreau (DAV)
1990
Chablis Château de Maligny, Durup (BY)
Chablis Domaine du Valéry, Durúp (TAN)
★ Chablis Droin (PIP)
Chablis Gautheron (SOM)
Chablis Tremblay (BOT, THR, WR)
Sauvignon de St-Bris, Renard (WRI)
1989
Chablis Domaine de l'Églantière (PE)
Chablis Domaine Rottiers-Clotilde (AS)

£8.00 to £9.99

1992
Chablis Brocard (HIC)
Chablis Drouhin (HIC)
Chablis Laroche (AUG)
1991
Chablis Bernard Defaix (PE)
Chablis Domaine de l'Églantière (PE)
Chablis Droin (RAE)
Chablis Fûts de Chêne, Grossot (LAY)
Chablis Gautheron (UN)
Chablis Grossot (LAY)
★ Chablis Montmains, Louis Michel (NI)
Chablis Vocoret (BIB)
1990
Chablis 1er Cru, Laroche (DI)
Chablis Bacheroy-Josselin (DI)
Chablis Brocard (HIC)
Chablis Château de Maligny, Durup (BOT, THR, WR)
Chablis Domaine de l'Églantière (PE)
Chablis Domaine Servin (NA, WRI, WHG)
Chablis Fèvre (BAR)
Chablis Fourchaume, Durup (EL)
Chablis Laroche (DI)
Chablis Mont de Milieu, Couperot (WHG)
Chablis Moreau (BOT, THR, WR)
Chablis Pautré (HIG)
Chablis Vaillons, Simmonet-Febvre (CHA)
Chablis Vau Ligneau, Hamelin (BEK)
Chablis Vocoret (BUT)
1989
Chablis Château de Maligny, Durup (BY)
Chablis Fourchaume, Domaine de Colombier, Mothe (ASD)
Chablis Montmains, Moreau (HA)
Chablis Pautré (HIG)

£10.00 to £11.99

1991
Chablis la Forêt, Vocoret (BIB)
Chablis Montmains, Légland (BIB)
1990
★ Chablis la Forêt, René Dauvissat (BUT)
Chablis la Forêt, Vocoret (BIB)
Chablis Montée de Tonnerre, Domaine Servin (WRI)
Chablis Montée de Tonnerre, Louis Michel (OD, WHI)
Chablis Montmains, Domaine de la Tour Vaubourg (LOR, JU)
Chablis Montmains, Louis Michel (OD)

1989
Chablis Daniel Defaix (VIG)
Chablis la Forêt, Pinson (BIB)
Chablis Montmains, Brocard (CV)
Chablis Vaillons, Bernard Defaix (RAE)
Chablis Vaillons, Simmonet-Febvre (CHA)
Chablis Vaucoupin, J. Moreau (BER)
Chablis Vaudevey, Laroche (GRE)
1988
Chablis Fourchaume, Durup (BY)
Chablis la Forêt, Pinson (BIB)
Chablis Mont de Milieu, Pinson (BIB)
Chablis Montmains, Louis Michel (GAU)
1987
Chablis 1er Cru Grand Cuvée, la Chablisienne (WHG, GA)
Chablis Defaix (ROB)
Chablis Mont de Milieu, Pinson (WCL)
1986
Chablis Régnard (BUT)
Chablis Vaillons, Bernard Defaix (EY)
1985
Chablis Domaine Ste-Claire, Brocard (BUT)

£12.00 to £13.99

1991
Chablis 1er Cru, Drouhin (NI)
Chablis la Forêt, René Dauvissat (TAN)
★ Chablis Vaillons, Raveneau (HAH)
1990
Chablis Fourchaume, Laroche (HAG)
Chablis Séchet, Louis Michel (BER)
Chablis Vaillons, Bernard Defaix (BER)
Chablis Vaillons, Defaix (DAV)
Chablis Vaillons, Droin (PIP)
1989
Chablis Montée de Tonnerre, Louis Michel (GAU)
Chablis Montmains, Domaine de la Tour Vaubourg (JU)
Chablis Vaillons, Laroche (AUG)
1988
Chablis Montée de Tonnerre, Regnard (HUN)
Chablis Vaudevey, Laroche (DI)
1986
Chablis Montée de Tonnerre, Louis Michel (BUT)

£14.00 to £16.99

1990
Chablis Montée de Tonnerre, Droin (JU)
1989
Chablis Mont de Milieu, Pic (BER)
1988
Chablis Valmur, Moreau (HOG)
1987
Chablis Vaillons, Defaix (VIG)
Chablis Vaudésir, Droin (RAE)
1986
Chablis Valmur, Moreau (HOG)
1985
Chablis Vaillons, Étienne Defaix (ROB)
★ Chablis Vaillons, Vocoret (BUT)

£17.00 to £19.99

1991
Chablis Grenouilles, Droin (TAN)
1990
Chablis les Clos, Droin (RAE, HAY)
★ Chablis les Clos, René Dauvissat (BUT)
1989
Chablis les Clos, Louis Michel (GAU)
Chablis les Clos, Pinson (BIB)
Chablis Valmur, Droin (RAE)
1988
Chablis les Clos, Pinson (BIB)
Chablis les Preuses, René Dauvissat (BUT)
Chablis Vaudésir, Droin (PIP)
★ Chablis Vaudésir, Louis Michel (GAU)
Chablis Vaudésir, Robin (BEK)

£20.00 to £24.99

1990
Chablis Blanchots, Laroche (GRE)
Chablis Grenouilles, Droin (HAY, JU)
1989
Chablis Vaudésir, Droin (JU)
1988
Chablis Blanchots, Laroche (DI)
Chablis Bougros, Fèvre (HA)
Chablis les Clos, René Dauvissat (BUT)
1987
Chablis les Preuses, Pic (BER)
1986
Chablis Vaudésir, Fèvre (BUT)

£25.00 to £35.00

1990
Chablis les Clos, Laroche (DI)
1989
Chablis les Clos, Pic (BER)

RED

£5.50 to £6.50

1991
Pinot Noir de St-Bris, Brocard (AD)
1988
★ Bourgogne Irancy Ste-Claire, Brocard (BEK)

BEAUJOLAIS

RED

Under £4.50

Non-vintage
Asda Beaujolais (ASD)
Sainsbury's Beaujolais (SAI)
1992
★ Beaujolais-Villages Cellier des Samsons (WAI)
Waitrose Beaujolais (WAI)
1991
Beaujolais-Villages Cellier des Samsons (WAI)
Beaujolais-Villages Domaine de la Ronze (ASD)
Waitrose Beaujolais (WAI)
1990
Beaujolais Loron (DI)

£4.50 to £4.99

1992
Beaujolais Duboeuf (NI)
Beaujolais-Villages Cellier des Samsons (BY)
Beaujolais-Villages Château de Néty (EL)
★ Beaujolais-Villages Duboeuf (WR, MAR, NI, BOT, THR)
1991
Beaujolais-Villages Château du Basty (OD)
Beaujolais-Villages Château du Bluizard (TES)
Beaujolais-Villages Duboeuf (TES)

£5.00 to £5.49

1992
Beaujolais Château de Tanay (HAW)
Juliénas Pelletier (EL)
Morgon le Clachet, Brun (EL)
1991
Beaujolais-Villages Domaine de la Ronze (JU)
Brouilly Château de Nevers, Duboeuf (BEK)
Chénas Château de Chénas (WHI)
Juliénas Domaine des Mouilles, Duboeuf (BEK)
1990
Morgon Jambon (ASD)

£5.50 to £5.99

1992
Beaujolais Cave Beaujolais de St-Verand (HAW)
Beaujolais-Villages Château des Vierres, Duboeuf (DAV)
Brouilly Duboeuf (MAR)
Côte de Brouilly Domaine de Chavannes (EL)
1991
Beaujolais Lantignié, Domaine Joubert (AD)
Beaujolais-Villages Château des Vierres, Duboeuf (DAV)

Beaujolais-Villages Château Lacarelle (CV, WCL)
Beaujolais-Villages les Champs Bouthier, Sapin (PEN)
Beaujolais-Villages Rochette (HAY)
Brouilly Large (CHA)
Brouilly Loron (TAN)
Chénas Duboeuf (LO)
Chiroubles Domaine de la Grosse Pierre (WHI)
Côte de Brouilly Duboeuf (NI)
Juliénas Duboeuf (NI)
Juliénas les Envaux, Pelletier (CHA)
Juliénas Loron (UN)
Morgon Bouchard Père (HOG)
★ Morgon Domaine des Versauds, Dépagneux (EY)
Morgon le Clachet, Brun (CHA)
Morgon Loron (UN)
Regnié Braillon (VIG)
1990
Juliénas les Envaux, Pelletier (CHA)
Morgon Domaine Jean Descombes, Duboeuf (BEK)
1989
Juliénas Domaine de Beauvernay, Piat (JU)

£6.00 to £6.49

1992
Beaujolais-Villages Cave des Producteurs Juliénas (HAW)

Brouilly Château de Nevers, Duboeuf (DAV)
Morgon Domaine Jean Descombes, Duboeuf (WR, BOT, THR, NI)
Moulin-à-Vent le Vivier, Brugne (EL)

1991

Brouilly Château de St-Lager, Dépagneux (AUG)
Chénas Château de Chénas (HAW)
Chiroubles Méziat (OD)
Fleurie Domaine des Quatre Vents, Duboeuf (BEK)
Fleurie la Madone, Duboeuf (BEK)
Juliénas Domaine du Grand Cuvage, Duboeuf (DAV)
Juliénas Domaine Joubert (AD, TAN)
Morgon Domaine des Vieux Cèdres, Loron (WRI)
Moulin-à-Vent le Vivier, Brugne (WHI)
Regnié Château de Basty (OD)
Regnié Château de la Pierre, Loron (WRI)
★ St-Amour Domaine du Paradis (BEK)

1990

Beaujolais-Villages Latour (AMI)
Juliénas Domaine de la Vieille Église, Loron (DI)
Morgon Domaine des Versauds, Duboeuf (LO)

1989

Chénas Château Bonnet (HOG)
Juliénas Clos des Poulettes, Loron (GRE)

1988

Moulin-à-Vent Domaine des Héritiers Tagent, Duboeuf (BEK)

1987

Morgon Chanson (PEN)

£6.50 to £6.99

1992

Beaujolais Blaise Carron (HAW)
Beaujolais Garlon (HAW)
Beaujolais-Villages Château du Grand Vernay (HAW)
Brouilly Château de Nevers, Duboeuf (NI)
Brouilly Château des Tours (PIP)
Chénas Léspinasse (HAW)
Chiroubles la Maison des Vignerons (AD)
Chiroubles Passot (WW)
Fleurie Duboeuf (THR, WR, BOT)
Juliénas Léspinasse (HAW)
Juliénas Pelletier (WRI)
Regnié Roux (HAW)

1991

Brouilly Château des Tours (PIP)
Brouilly Château Thivin (AD)
Brouilly Grand Clos de Briante, Loron (WRI)
Brouilly Latour (HOG)
Chiroubles Château de Javernand, Duboeuf (GRE)
Chiroubles Château de Raousset (JU)
Côte de Brouilly Joubert (TAN)
Fleurie Château de Fleurie, Loron (EL)
★ Fleurie Sélection Éventail, Domaine de Montgénas (EY, CHA)
Fleurie Verpoix (ASD)
Juliénas Domaine de la Vieille Église, Loron (WRI)
Morgon Château de Raousset, Duboeuf (JU)
Morgon le Clachet, Brun (VIG)
Moulin-à-Vent Loron (UN)

1990

Brouilly Domaine Franchet (SUM)
Morgon Aucoeur (AD)
★ Morgon Côte de Py, Savoye (HIC)
Moulin-à-Vent Brugne (CHA)

1989

Beaujolais-Villages Jadot (VIC)
Chénas Duboeuf (ROB)
Côte de Brouilly Château Thivin (RAE)
Juliénas Aujas (GRG)
Morgon Château Gaillard (RAE)
Morgon Fontcraine, Loron (GRE)
St-Amour les Bonnets, Bernard Patissier (PE)

£7.00 to £7.49

1992

Chiroubles la Maison des Vignerons (HAW)

1991

Chénas Léspinasse (HAG)
Fleurie Château de Raousset, Duboeuf (JU)
Fleurie Domaine des Quatre Vents, Duboeuf (LO)
Juliénas les Capitains, Louis Tête (HOG)
Juliénas Pelletier (WIC)
Morgon Aucoeur (HAW)
Morgon Janodet (MV)
★ Moulin-à-Vent Domaine Lemonon, Loron (WRI)

1990

Morgon Janodet (MV)
Moulin-à-Vent le Vivier, Brugne (HIG)

1989

Fleurie Collin-Bourisset (BOR)

In each price band wines are listed in vintage order. Within each vintage they are listed in A–Z order.

£7.50 to £7.99

1992
Beaujolais Cuvée Centenaire, Charmet (HAW)
Brouilly Geoffray (HAW)
Côte de Brouilly Château Thivin (HAW)
Fleurie Cave Co-op. de Fleurie (HAW)
Fleurie Domaine des Quatre Vents, Duboeuf (DAV)

Moulin-à-Vent le Vivier, Brugne (WRI)
Regnié Noël (HAW)
1991
Brouilly Château des Tours (SOM, BIB)
Brouilly Jean Lathuilière (WCL)
Brouilly Michaud (MV)
Chiroubles Loron (BU, TAN)
Fleurie Cave Co-op. de Fleurie (CV, HAW)
Fleurie Château de Fleurie, Loron (WRI, GRE)
Fleurie Colonge (BIB)
Fleurie la Madone, Duboeuf (GRE)
Juliénas Benon (HAW)
Juliénas Domaine de Berthets, Dépagneux (ROB)
Moulin-à-Vent Domaine Bruyère (OD)
Moulin-à-Vent Domaine de la Tour du Bief, Duboeuf (NI, THR, BOT, WR)
Moulin-à-Vent Duboeuf (LO)
1990
Chénas Benon (HAW)
Côte de Brouilly Château du Grand Vernay (HAW)
Fleurie Château de Fleurie, Loron (TAN, DI)
Fleurie Sélection Éventail, Domaine de Montgénas (CHA)
Moulin-à-Vent Janin (HAY)
1989
Côte de Brouilly Château Thivin (GRE)
Regnié Duboeuf (ROB)
St-Amour Domaine des Billards, Loron (GRE)
1988
Moulin-à-Vent Château des Jacques (AS)
Moulin-à-Vent Domaine de la Tour du Bief, Duboeuf (DAV)
Regnié Duboeuf (TW)

£8.00 to £8.99

1992
Brouilly Jean Lathuilière (HAW)
1991
Fleurie la Madone, Louis Tête (HOG)
Fleurie Michel Chignard (MV)
Juliénas Condemine (HAW)
Moulin-à-Vent Janin (PIP)
1990
Brouilly Château des Tours (ROB)
Juliénas Aujas (HAW)
Morgon Château Gaillard (BIB)
Morgon Genillon (BOD, WIC)
1989
Brouilly Domaine de Saburin (PEN)
St-Amour Domaine des Pins, Duboeuf (PIP)

£9.00 to £11.50

1991
Fleurie Colonge (ROB)
Juliénas Aujas (HAG)
1990
Moulin-à-Vent Château du Moulin-à-Vent (HAW, HAG)
Moulin-à-Vent Domaine Charvet (TAN)
1985
Beaujolais-Villages Duboeuf (BUT)

c. £17.00

1978
Moulin-à-Vent Duboeuf (BUT)

WHITE

Under £6.00

1992
Beaujolais Blanc Bully (WHG)
1991
Beaujolais Blanc Bully (TES)
Beaujolais Blanc Duboeuf (BEK)

c. £7.00

1991
Beaujolais Blanc Château des Tours (PIP)

c. £9.00

1992
Beaujolais Blanc Charmet (HAW)

ROSÉ

Under £6.50

1992
Beaujolais Supérieur Rosé, Cave Beaujolais du Bois d'Oingt (HAW)

CHAMPAGNE

SPARKLING WHITE

Under £10.00

Non-vintage

★ Bruno Paillard ½bottle (HAL)
Moët & Chandon ½bottle (TAN, AUG)

£10.00 to £11.99

Non-vintage

★ Adnams Champagne (AD)
Alfred Gratien ½bottle (WCL)
Asda Champagne (ASD)
Bollinger ½bottle (BUT)
★ Descombes (THR, WR, BOT)
Duchâtel (UN)
Georges Gardet (GR)
Matthieu (GR)
Moët & Chandon ½ bottle (TES, WHG, SUM, WHI, OD, HAG)
Sainsbury's Champagne (SAI)
Tanners Reserve (TAN)
★ de Telmont (MAJ)
Tesco Champagne (TES, TES)
Veuve Clicquot ½bottle (GRG, ROB)
★ Waitrose Champagne (WAI)

£12.00 to £14.99

Non-vintage

Alexandre Bonnet Prestige (HAY)
Ayala (MAJ)
Beerens (BIB)
★ Blin (OD)
Boizel (AUG)
Boizel Rich (AUG)
Bollinger ½ bottle (DI)
Canard-Duchêne (HOG, MAJ, GRE)
Drappier Carte d'Or (BOT, WR, THR, BY)
Ellner (DAV, LAY)
George Goulet (SOM)
Heidsieck Dry Monopole (LO, OD)
Jacquart Tradition (MV, ASD, BOT)
Joseph Perrier (GRG)
Joseph Perrier Cuvée Royal (CV)
Laurent-Perrier (BIB)
Mercier (WHI, ASD, WAI, TES, LAY, THR, WR, VIC, BOT, UN, SAF, DAV)
Michel Gonet (BU)
★ Pierre Vaudon 1er Cru (HAH)
Piper Heidsieck (TES, HOG, ASD, NI, AUG, GA,)
Pol Roger (GR, SOM)
Pol Roger White Foil (SOM)
Pommery (HOG)
★ Salon (EY, SOM, HAY, THR, WR, BOT, JU)

1988

Matthieu (GR)
Sainsbury's Champagne (SAI)

1986

★ Pol Roger (SOM)

1985

de Telmont (MAJ)
Veuve Clicquot ½bottle (GRG)

£15.00 to £19.99

Non-vintage

★ Alfred Gratien (WCL)
Besserat de Bellefon Crémant (GRE)
★ Billecart-Salmon (WW, SAF, OD, BAR)
Bollinger (HOG)
Bricout Carte Noire (WR, THR, BOT, BOR)
Bricout d'Or (WCL)
Bruno Paillard (BUT, ROB)
Bruno Paillard Blanc de Blancs (BEK)
Canard-Duchêne (ROB, GE, MV, HUN)
Charles Heidsieck (TES)
Comte de Robart (VIG)
Deutz (ROB)
Dom Ruinart (BAR)
Drappier (BOT, THR, WR)
Ellner (LAY)
George Goulet (PIP)
Heidsieck Dry Monopole (HUN, DI)
Henriot Blanc de Blancs (VIC)
Jacquart Tradition (GAU)
Jacquesson Blanc de Blancs (YAP)
Jacquesson Perfection (YAP)
Joseph Perrier (PE, HIC, HAG, TAN)
Joseph Perrier Cuvée Royal (ROB, HAG)
Lanson (HOG, HA, ASD, TES, AUG, GA, VIC, SAF, JU, WAI, PE, BOT, THR, WR, WHI, UN, DAV, EL, WRI)
Laurent-Perrier (GRG, LAY, OD, AMI, PE, BOT, WR, THR, MAJ, UN, EL, VIC, WHG, PEN, CHA, JU, MV, AD, BAR, WHI, CB, GAU)
★ Louis Roederer (HOG, NI, DAV, TAN, GRE, TES, MAJ)
Louis Roederer Rich (NI)
Mercier (PE, SUM, ROB)
Moët & Chandon Brut Impérial (HOG, ASD, TAN, SAF, SAI, AUG, LAY, UN, TES, WAI, WRI, WHI, WR, SUM, SUM, GRE, JU, DAV, PE, VIC, EL, HUN, WHG)
Mumm Cordon Rouge (LO, VIC, THR, WR, BOT, OD)

Perrier-Jouët (LO, GRG, WHI, OD, JU, REI)
Piper Heidsieck (OD, GRE)

Pol Roger (BOR, HOG, GRE, PEN, JU, TES, REI, WRI, THR, BOT, WR, UN, OD)
Pommery (HAH, NA, GRE)
The Society's Champagne (WS)
Taittinger (GRG, BIB, TES, UN)
Thienot (AMI)
Veuve Clicquot (HOG, GRE, HAY, WY, LO, WHI, HUN, LAY, GRG, GA, OD, DAV, TES, MAJ)

1988

Perrier-Jouët (GRG, OD)

1987

Heidsieck Dry Monopole (OD)

1986

Drappier Carte d'Or (BY)
Duval Leroy Fleur de Champagne (TAN)
Ellner (DAV)
Jacquesson Perfection (YAP)
Waitrose Champagne (WAI)

1985

Ayala (ASD)
Bollinger ½bottle (HAL)
Bruno Paillard (BEK)
Descombes (BOT, WR, THR)
Duchâtel (UN)
Joseph Perrier (HIC)
Piper Heidsieck (NI)
Pol Roger Blanc de Chardonnay (SOM)
★ Salon (AD)

1983

Bauget-Jouette (HIG)
Canard-Duchêne (ROB)
Georges Gardet (GR)
Lanson (WHI)
de Venoge Blanc de Blancs (WHI)
Veuve Clicquot ½bottle (BAR)

1982

Georges Gardet (GR)
★ Pommery (ROB)

£20.00 to £24.99

Non-vintage

Besserat de Bellefon Cuvée des Moines (GRE)
Bollinger (PIP, GRE, WHI, TAN, LAY, JU, JU, WRI, BE, WCL, HUN, WAI, SAF, ASD, SUM, SUM, BUT, TES, OD, DAV, GRG, MAJ, PE, HA, CB, UN, EL, AUG, DI, WR, AD, THR, BOT, VIC, MV, HAH, HAG)
Bruno Paillard Blanc de Blancs (GAU)
Charles Heidsieck (UN, HUN, GAU)
Dom Ruinart (REI)
Gosset Brut Reserve (AMI)
Laurent-Perrier (HAG)
Laurent-Perrier Ultra Brut (ROB, AD)
Louis Roederer (HAY, WR, BOT, THR, UN, OD, WRI, WCL, LAY, WHI, WAI, JU, CV, AMI, BIB, SUM, AD, PE, WS, CB, HA, HAH, EL, MV, HIC, BAR, HAG)
Louis Roederer Rich (PEN)
Moët & Chandon Brut Impérial (CB, HAG, VIN, BUT)
Mumm Cordon Rouge (TES, GA, UN)
Mumm Crémant de Cramant Blanc de Blancs (ROB)
Perrier-Jouët (PIP)
Pol Roger (HAY, GE, TAN, HAH, WS, AMI, VIN)
Taittinger (WHI, LAY, WRI, HAG)
Veuve Clicquot (WAI, JU, UN, THR, BOT, WR, BIB, WCL, TAN, AUG, WRI, WHG, ROB, MV, CB, VIC, HAH, HAG, VIN)
Veuve Clicquot White Label Demi-Sec (WCL, HAG)

1988

Perrier-Jouët (PIP)

1986

Billecart-Salmon Cuvée N.F. Billecart (WW)
Moët & Chandon (WHI, TES, DAV, EL, HAG)
Pol Roger (HOG, JU, REI)

1985

Bollinger (WHI)
Bruno Paillard (WIC)
George Goulet (PIP)
George Goulet Crémant Blanc de Blancs (PIP)
Joseph Perrier Cuvée Royal (HAG)
Lanson (HOG, GA)
Laurent-Perrier (CHA, CB, BAR, AD)
Moët & Chandon (WHI, TAN, PE, UN, OD, WRI, HUN, VIC, JU, HAG)
Mumm Cordon Rouge (OD)
Perrier-Jouët (AMI)
Pol Roger (PEN, GRE)
Salon (BIB)
Thienot (AMI)
Veuve Clicquot (GRE, LO, GRG, WCL)

1983
Lanson (WAI, PE, HA, VIC, BOT, THR, WR)
Moët & Chandon (AUG, WHG)
Taittinger (WHI)
★ Veuve Clicquot (HOG, WHI)
1982
Canard-Duchêne (BUT)
Perrier-Jouët (PEN)
1975
★ Veuve Clicquot (FA)

£25.00 to £29.99

Non-vintage
Bollinger (VIN)
Krug Grande Cuvée ½bottle (HAL)
Louis Roederer (VIN)
Perrier-Jouët Blason de France (PIP, AMI)
1986
Billecart-Salmon (BAR, OD)
Pol Roger (TAN)
Taittinger (JU, HAG)
1985
Billecart-Salmon (OD)
Bollinger (HOG, WCL, PIP, GRE, GRG, JU, MV, TAN, WRI, PE, AD)
Bollinger Année Rare RD (PEN, ROB)
Jacquesson Signature Cuvée de Prestige (YAP)
Louis Roederer (WCL, BIB, MV, JU, ROB, TAN)
Louis Roederer Blanc de Blancs (NI)
Pol Roger (SOM)
Taittinger (GRG, VIG)
Veuve Clicquot (PE, UN, THR, BOT, WR, JU, MV, LAY, PIP, WS, EL, HIC, HAH)
1983
Alfred Gratien (WS)
Dom Ruinart (MAJ)
Louis Roederer (PEN)
Louis Roederer Blanc de Blancs (GRE)
Veuve Clicquot (PE, CB, HUN, WRI, BIB)
1982
Alfred Gratien Crémant (HAY)
Georges Gardet (HIC)
Pol Roger Blanc de Chardonnay (GRE)
Veuve Clicquot (GE)
1979
Pol Roger (BIB)
1978
Moët & Chandon (GRG)
1966
Bollinger ½ bottle (BUT)

£30.00 to £39.99

Non-vintage
Lanson magnum (LAY, WHI, WRI)
Laurent-Perrier magnum (CHA)
Moët & Chandon magnum (TAN, LAY, TES, WAI, WRI, WHI, AUG)
Pol Roger White Foil magnum (WRI, PEN)
Veuve Clicquot magnum (GRG)
1986
Bollinger (DAV)
1985
Billecart-Salmon Blanc de Blancs (WW)
Bollinger (THR, WR, BOT, CB, BE, EL, TW, DI, BAR, VIC, HAH, HAG, VIN)
Bollinger Année Rare RD (BUT)
Heidsieck Diamant Bleu (OD)
Louis Roederer (CB, MAJ)
Louis Roederer Blanc de Blancs (LAY)
Pol Roger (VIN)
Pol Roger Blanc de Chardonnay (REI, PEN, AMI, VIN)
1983
Alfred Gratien (WCL)
Bollinger (AUG)
Dom Ruinart Blanc de Blancs (BAR)
Louis Roederer Blanc de Blancs (PEN)
Perrier-Jouët Belle Époque (BE)
1982
Pol Roger Blanc de Chardonnay (GE, WRI, ROB)
1981
Dom Ruinart Blanc de Blancs (VIC)
1979
Bruno Paillard (BUT)
Pol Roger (BUT)
Pol Roger Cuvée Sir Winston Churchill (GRE)
1976
Bruno Paillard (BUT)
Laurent-Perrier Millésime Rare (CHA)
1975
Bruno Paillard (BUT)
1969
★ Bruno Paillard (BUT)

£40.00 to £49.99

Non-vintage
Bollinger magnum (LAY, GRG, TAN, DI)
Moët & Chandon magnum (HAG)
Pol Roger magnum (ROB)
Veuve Clicquot magnum (GAU)
1986
Perrier-Jouët Belle Époque (PIP)
1985
Dom Pérignon (HOG)

Louis Roederer Cristal (WHI)
Perrier-Jouët Belle Époque (BY, WRI, WHI, OD, HAG, GRE, BE)
Taittinger Comtes de Champagne Blanc de Blancs (LAY)
Veuve Clicquot la Grande Dame (GRE, GE)
1983
Dom Ruinart Blanc de Blancs (PE)
Perrier-Jouët Belle Époque (AD, GRG, PEN, WHI, JU)
Veuve Clicquot magnum (GRG)
1982
Bollinger RD (WCL, PIP, GRE, TAN, GRG, ROB)
Pol Roger Cuvée Sir Winston Churchill (PEN, GE)
Pol Roger Cuvée Sir Winston Churchill magnum (REI)
Taittinger Comtes de Champagne Blanc de Blancs (DI, BUT)
1979
Bollinger Année Rare RD (BUT)
Bollinger RD (DI, AD)
Lanson magnum (BOT, WR)
1976
Bollinger Année Rare RD (BUT)
Krug (BUT)
1971
Charles Heidsieck (BUT)

1983
Dom Pérignon (BIB, WY, LAY, PE, WHI, ROB, CB, WRI, PEN, HAH, GRG)
Louis Roederer Cristal (WHG)
1982
Bollinger RD (HAG, BIB)
Dom Pérignon (FA, TES, AUG)
George Goulet Cuvée de Centenaire (PIP)
Pol Roger Cuvée Sir Winston Churchill (TAN)
1981
Taittinger Comtes de Champagne Blanc de Blancs (WHI)
1979
Bollinger RD (VIN)
1976
Taittinger Comtes de Champagne Blanc de Blancs (BUT)
1971
Piper Heidsieck (BUT)

£50.00 to £59.99

Non-vintage
Bollinger magnum (AD)
Krug Grande Cuvée (AMI, VIC, REI, GRG, BUT, AD, JU, HUN, EL, WHI, BAR, LAY)
Laurent-Perrier Cuvée Grande Siècle (AD, CB, CHA, EL)
1986
Louis Roederer Cristal (LAY)
Taittinger Comtes de Champagne Blanc de Blancs (HAG, JU)
1985
Bollinger magnum (TAN)
Dom Pérignon (BY, HA, LO, TAN, PE, BOT, WR, THR, EL, OD, UN, DAV, AMI, JU)
Louis Roederer Cristal (WCL, NI, GRE, BIB, HAH, PEN, AD, WHG, CV, JU, WRI, TAN, OD, MAJ)
Moët & Chandon magnum (UN)
Perrier-Jouët Belle Époque (VIN)
Pol Roger Cuvée Sir Winston Churchill (ROB)
Taittinger Comtes de Champagne Blanc de Blancs (ROB)
Veuve Clicquot la Grande Dame (ROB)

£60.00 to £74.99

Non-vintage
Krug Grande Cuvée (PE, PEN, TAN, AUG, CB, BIB, HAH, HAG, ROB, VIN)
Louis Roederer Cristal (WS)
1985
Dom Pérignon (HAG)
Louis Roederer Cristal (PE, EL, CB, ROB, AMI, GRG, LO, HAG, BAR)
1983
Dom Pérignon (VIC, HAG, VIG, VIN)
Louis Roederer Cristal (AUG, VIN)
1982
Dom Pérignon (GRG)
Krug (AUG, JU, BUT, AD, WHI, LAY, VIC, OD, TAN, CB)
Salon (CB)
1981
Krug (JU)
1979
Krug (REI, GRE)
1978
Dom Pérignon (WY)
1975
Bollinger Année Rare RD (TAN, BUT)

1973
Dom Pérignon (WY)
1970
Bollinger magnum (BUT)

£75.00 to £99.99

Non-vintage
Bollinger jeroboam (LAY, TAN)
Pol Roger jeroboam (WRI)
1985
Taittinger Collection Artist's Label Vasarely (ROB)

1982
Bollinger Vieilles Vignes Françaises, Blanc de Noirs (GRE)
Krug (BIB, DAV, TW, HAH, ROB, GRG, VIN)
Taittinger Collection Artist's Label Vasarely (ROB)
1981
Krug (BAR)
1978
Dom Pérignon (BIB)
1975
Dom Pérignon (TW, ROB)
1973
Bollinger Année Rare RD (AD)
1971
Dom Pérignon (WY)
1966
Krug (BIB)
1964
Dom Pérignon (WY)
1947
Pommery (WY)
1929
Mumm Cordon Rouge (BUT)

£100.00 to £125.00

Non-vintage
Krug magnum (BUT)
Lanson jeroboam (WRI)
Laurent-Perrier Cuvée Grande Siècle magnum (CHA)
1983
Dom Pérignon magnum (ROB)
1982
Krug Clos du Mesnil Blanc de Blancs (VIG)
1979
Pol Roger Cuvée Sir Winston Churchill magnum (VIN)
1959
Krug (FA)
1955
Dom Pérignon (WY)

£130.00 to £165.00

1982
Krug Clos du Mesnil Blanc de Blancs (ROB)
Krug magnum (BUT)
1980
Krug Clos du Mesnil Blanc de Blancs (GRE)
1979
Krug Clos du Mesnil Blanc de Blancs (HUN, VIG)
1971
Taittinger Comtes de Champagne Blanc de Blancs (ROB)
1955
Dom Pérignon (BIB)

£195.00 to £205.00

Non-vintage
Pol Roger methuselah (WRI, PEN)
1973
Krug Collection (ROB)

c. £280.00

Non-vintage
Pol Roger salmanazar (PEN, WRI)

c. £340.00

1982
Dom Pérignon magnum (ROB)

SPARKLING ROSÉ

Under £15.00

Non-vintage
Alexandre Bonnet Prestige (HAY)
★ Bruno Paillard (BEK)
Bruno Paillard ½ bottle (HAL)
Charbaut (BR)
Matthieu (GR)
Sainsbury's Champagne Rosé (SAI)
de Telmont (MAJ)
Waitrose Champagne Rosé (WAI)

£15.00 to £19.99

Non-vintage
Alexandre Bonnet Prestige (WCL)
Ayala (AMI)
Bauget-Jouette (HIG)
Canard-Duchêne (HOG, MAJ, ROB)
Jacquart (MV)
Jacquesson (YAP)
Lanson (BOT, THR, WR, HA)
Mercier (UN, ROB)
Piper Heidsieck (NI)
Pommery (ROB)
Tanners Reserve (TAN)
1985
Moët & Chandon (WHI)
Pol Roger (SOM)

£20.00 to £29.99

Non-vintage
Billecart-Salmon (WW, OD, BAR)
Bricout (WCL)
Canard-Duchêne (BUT)
Lanson (PE, WHI, LAY, VIC, UN)
Laurent-Perrier (REI, HOG, GRG, LO, WHG, HUN, AMI, WHI, LAY, OD, CHA, UN, TAN, BOT, WR, THR, MAJ, CB, EL, PEN, JU, BIB, ROB, GRE, BAR, MV, WRI, AUG, HAG)
Louis Roederer (NI, BIB)
Joseph Perrier Cuvée Royale (HAG)
1986
Louis Roederer (WHI, AMI)
1985
Bollinger (TAN)
George Goulet (SOM, PIP)
Moët & Chandon (UN)
Pol Roger (WRI, ROB)
1983
Veuve Clicquot (GRE, GRG)
1982
Pol Roger (PEN)

£30.00 to £39.99

1986
Louis Roederer (JU)
1985
Bollinger (BE, GRG, DI)
1983
Bollinger (BE)
Veuve Clicquot (ROB)
1982
Perrier-Jouët Belle Époque (PIP)

£40.00 to £49.99

Non-vintage
Laurent-Perrier magnum (GRG, CHA)
1985
Perrier-Jouët Belle Époque (GRG, ROB)
1982
Perrier-Jouët Belle Époque (PEN)
1981
Dom Ruinart (GE, DI)

£50.00 to £59.99

1986
Taittinger Comtes de Champagne (JU)
1985
Taittinger Comtes de Champagne (WHI)
1983
Taittinger Comtes de Champagne (WHI, BIB)

c.£115.00

Non-vintage
Krug (WHI)

c.£141.00

1982
Dom Pérignon (LO, BIB)

STILL WHITE

£15.00 to £17.99

Non-vintage
Laurent-Perrier Blanc de Chardonnay Coteaux Champenois (CHA)
Ruinart Coteaux Champenois Chardonnay (VIC)

STILL RED

£15.00 to £17.00

Non-vintage
Laurent-Perrier Pinot Franc, Cuvée de Pinot Noir, Coteaux Champenois (CHA)
1982
Bollinger Ay Rouge la Côte aux Enfants Coteaux Champenois (GRE)

*Please remember that **Webster's** is a price GUIDE and not a price LIST. It is not meant to replace up-to-date merchants' lists.*

NORTHERN RHÔNE

RED

Under £5.00

Non-vintage
Sainsbury's Crozes-Hermitage (SAI)
1988
St-Joseph Gripa (GE)

£5.00 to £6.99

1990
Crozes-Hermitage Cave des Clairmonts (WAI, MV)
★ Crozes-Hermitage Domaine de Thalabert, Jaboulet (NI)
Crozes-Hermitage Domaine des Entrefaux (BY, SUM)
St-Joseph Cave Co-op. Agricole de St Désirat-Champagne (YAP)
1989
Crozes-Hermitage Cave de Vins Fins à Tain-Hermitage (ROB)
Crozes-Hermitage Delas (AUG, CV)
Crozes-Hermitage Domaine des Remizières, Desmeure (RAE)
Crozes-Hermitage Jaboulet (HOG, OD)
1988
Crozes-Hermitage Delas (PEN)
★ Crozes-Hermitage Domaine de Thalabert, Jaboulet (HAY)
Crozes-Hermitage Jaboulet (HOG, REI)

£7.00 to £8.99

1991
Crozes-Hermitage Graillot (BY, YAP, OD)
St-Joseph Coursodon (WR, THR, BOT)
1990
Crozes-Hermitage Chapoutier (TAN)
Crozes-Hermitage Desmeure (PE)
Crozes-Hermitage Domaine des Clairmonts, Borja (HIC)
Crozes-Hermitage Graillot (BOT, WR, BUT)
Crozes-Hermitage les Meysonniers, Chapoutier (OD, GAU)
St-Joseph Deschants, Chapoutier (DI)
St-Joseph le Grand Pompée, Jaboulet (HOG, OD, LAY)
1989
Crozes-Hermitage Domaine de Thalabert, Jaboulet (NI, WHI)
St-Joseph Cave Co-op. Agricole de St Désirat-Champagne (WAI)
St-Joseph le Grand Pompée, Jaboulet (HA)
1988
Crozes-Hermitage Pascal (LO)
St-Joseph Cave Co-op. Agricole de St Désirat-Champagne (CV)
St-Joseph le Grand Pompée, Jaboulet (VIC)
1986
★ Cornas Michel (YAP)
St-Joseph Deschants, Chapoutier (BOT)
1985
Crozes-Hermitage Domaine de Thalabert, Jaboulet (HOG)
Crozes-Hermitage les Meysonniers, Chapoutier (BUT)
1984
Hermitage la Chapelle, Jaboulet (OD)
1983
★ Crozes-Hermitage Domaine des Remizières, Desmeure (BUT)

£9.00 to £11.99

1991
Crozes-Hermitage Domaine de Thalabert, Jaboulet (GRE)
St-Joseph Grippat (YAP)
1990
Cornas Coteau, Michel (THR, BOT, WR)
1989
★ Cornas Noel Verset (BUT)
St-Joseph Deschants, Chapoutier (GAU, JU)
1988
Crozes-Hermitage Jaboulet (VIN)
St-Joseph Clos de l'Arbalestrier, Florentin (AD)
1987
Cornas Noel Verset (WCL, RAE, BIB)
Côte-Rôtie Delas (AUG, PEN)
St-Joseph Clos de l'Arbalestrier, Florentin (RAE, BIB)
1986
Cornas Jaboulet (HOG, GR, GRE)
Cornas Noel Verset (HAY)
Hermitage le Gréal, Sorrel (BIB)
1985
St-Joseph Deschants, Chapoutier (BUT)
St-Joseph Jaboulet (PE)
1983
★ Côte-Rôtie les Jumelles, Jaboulet (BUT)
Crozes-Hermitage Domaine de Thalabert, Jaboulet (HOG)
1982
Cornas Jaboulet (BU)
Hermitage Domaine des Remizières (RAE)

£12.00 to £14.99

1991
Côte-Rôtie Champet (YAP)
1990
Cornas Rochepertuis, Jean Lionnet (AD, JU)
Côte-Rôtie Seigneur de Maugiron, Delas (OD)
1989
Cornas Clape (YAP)
Cornas de Barjac (JU, LAY)
Côte-Rôtie Burgaud (BUT, YAP)
Côte-Rôtie Delas (PEN)
Hermitage Desmeure (JU)
1988
Cornas Clape (OD)
Cornas Noel Verset (RAE)
1987
Côte-Rôtie Barge (GE)
Côte-Rôtie Burgaud (YAP)
Côte-Rôtie Jamet (BIB)
Hermitage Chave (YAP, ROB)
Hermitage la Chapelle, Jaboulet (EY, BOT)
Hermitage Marquise de la Tourette, Delas (PEN)
1986
Cornas Clape (BUT)
Côte-Rôtie Barge (RAE)
Côte-Rôtie Champet (OD)
Côte-Rôtie Côte Blonde la Garde, Dervieux-Thaize (WCL)
Côte-Rôtie Guigal (GR)
★ Côte-Rôtie Jasmin (FA)
Côte-Rôtie les Jumelles, Jaboulet (HOG, GRE)
Hermitage Domaine des Remizières (RAE, WCL, BUT)
1985
Cornas de Barjac (JU, BUT)
★ Côte-Rôtie Brune et Blonde, Guigal (FA)
Côte-Rôtie les Jumelles, Jaboulet (BU)
Hermitage Cuvée des Miaux, Ferraton (BUT)
Hermitage Desmeure (BIB)
Hermitage Domaine des Remizières (WCL)
Hermitage Guigal (FA)
Hermitage la Sizeranne, Chapoutier (JU)
1983
Côte-Rôtie Chapoutier (BU)
Hermitage Jaboulet (HOG, WHI)
Hermitage la Sizeranne, Chapoutier (BU)
1982
Côte-Rôtie les Jumelles, Jaboulet (HOG)
1980
Crozes-Hermitage Domaine de Thalabert, Jaboulet (BUT)

£15.00 to £19.99

1990
Côte-Rôtie Chapoutier (DI)
Côte-Rôtie Côte Blonde, René Rostaing (BUT)
Côte-Rôtie Gérin (THR, WR, BOT)
Côte-Rôtie Jasmin (YAP)
Côte-Rôtie René Rostaing (BUT, JU, HAH, VIG)
Hermitage Grippat (YAP)
Hermitage la Sizeranne, Chapoutier (DI)
1989
Cornas les Ruchottes, Colombo (GAU)
Côte-Rôtie Brune et Blonde, Guigal (BY, EL)
Côte-Rôtie Jamet (GAU, BUT)
Côte-Rôtie Seigneur de Maugiron, Delas (PEN)
Hermitage la Sizeranne, Chapoutier (TAN, GAU, AD, VIG)
1988
Côte-Rôtie Barge (MV)
Côte-Rôtie Brune et Blonde, Guigal (AD, JU, GAU, NI, OD)

Côte-Rôtie Brune et Blonde, Vidal-Fleury (GRE, GRG)
Côte-Rôtie Chapoutier (MV)
Côte-Rôtie Delas (CV)
Côte-Rôtie les Jumelles, Jaboulet (HOG, JU)
Hermitage Chave (FA, YAP)
Hermitage Guigal (OD, JU, AD)
Hermitage la Chapelle, Jaboulet (HOG, VIC)
Hermitage la Sizeranne, Chapoutier (AD, HUN)
Hermitage le Gréal, Sorrel (GE)
1987
Côte-Rôtie Brune et Blonde, Guigal (GAU)
Côte-Rôtie Côte Brune, Gentaz-Dervieux (EY, RAE)
Côte-Rôtie Guigal (BE, TAN)
1986
Côte-Rôtie Côte Blonde, René Rostaing (JU)
Côte-Rôtie Côte Brune, Gentaz-Dervieux (RAE, BUT)
Crozes-Hermitage Domaine de Thalabert, Jaboulet (VIC)

Hermitage Chave (OD)
Hermitage Guigal (BE)
Hermitage la Chapelle, Jaboulet (HOG, MV, HAY, WHI, JU, AD)
Hermitage la Sizeranne, Chapoutier (GRE)
1985
Côte-Rôtie Champet (LAY)
Côte-Rôtie Chapoutier (BUT)
Hermitage la Chapelle, Jaboulet (FA, RAE)
Hermitage Sorrel (BUT)
1984
Côte-Rôtie Brune et Blonde, Guigal (JU)
Hermitage Chave (WS)
1983
Côte-Rôtie Brune et Blonde, Guigal (FA, GE)
Côte-Rôtie les Jumelles, Jaboulet (GAU, WS)
Hermitage Desmeure (BIB)
Hermitage Guigal (JU)
Hermitage la Chapelle, Jaboulet (WS)
1981
Hermitage Chave (REI)
Hermitage Guigal (BUT)
1980
Côte-Rôtie les Jumelles, Jaboulet (WHI)

£20.00 to £29.99

1991
Hermitage Chave (YAP)
1990
Cornas les Ruchottes, Colombo (VIG)
1989
Côte-Rôtie Côte Brune, Gentaz-Dervieux (FA)
Côte-Rôtie la Viallere, Dervieux-Thaize (VIG)
Hermitage Chave (AD)
1988
Côte-Rôtie Burgaud (GAU)
Côte-Rôtie Jamet (BUT)
1986
Côte-Rôtie Guigal (WS)
Côte-Rôtie Jasmin (AD)
1985
Cornas Clape (BUT)
Côte-Rôtie Burgaud (BUT)
1983
Côte-Rôtie Gentaz-Dervieux (GAU)
1982
Hermitage Chave (BIB, GAU)
Hermitage la Chapelle, Jaboulet (GAU)
1980
Hermitage la Chapelle, Jaboulet (ROB)
1979
Hermitage Guigal (BUT)

£30.00 to £39.99

1990
Hermitage la Chapelle, Jaboulet (NI)
1985
Hermitage Chave (VIG, BUT, AD)
1983
Côte-Rôtie Jasmin (ROB)
Hermitage la Chapelle, Jaboulet (FA)
1979
Côte-Rôtie Brune et Blonde, Guigal (VIG)
Hermitage la Chapelle, Jaboulet (GAU, PIP)

£40.00 to £60.00

1978
Côte-Rôtie Brune et Blonde, Guigal (VIG)
1976
Hermitage la Chapelle, Jaboulet (HOG)
1971
Côte-Rôtie les Jumelles, Jaboulet (VIG)
1964
Cornas Jaboulet (WS)

£70.00 to £89.99

1987
Côte-Rôtie la Mouline Côte Blonde, Guigal (GAU)
1982
Côte-Rôtie la Landonne Côte Brune, Guigal (BUT)
Côte-Rôtie la Mouline Côte Blonde, Guigal (BUT)
1978
Hermitage Chave (BUT)
Hermitage la Chapelle, Jaboulet (MV, FA)
1972
Hermitage la Chapelle, Jaboulet (BIB)

£90.00 to £120.00

1986
Côte-Rôtie la Mouline Côte Blonde, Guigal (BUT, TW)

£130.00 to £150.00

1983
Côte-Rôtie la Mouline Côte Blonde, Guigal (BUT)
1955
Côte-Rôtie les Jumelles, Jaboulet (TW)

£170.00 to £180.00

1985
Côte-Rôtie la Landonne Côte Brune, Guigal (BUT)
Côte-Rôtie la Mouline Côte Blonde, Guigal (BUT)

WHITE

Under £7.00

1991
★ Crozes-Hermitage Domaine des Clairmonts (YAP)
Crozes-Hermitage la Mule Blanche, Jaboulet (HA)
1989
Crozes-Hermitage Domaine des Entrefaux (BY)
Crozes-Hermitage la Mule Blanche, Jaboulet (HOG, GAU)
St-Joseph Courbis (BUT)

£7.00 to £11.99

1991
★ St-Joseph Grippat (YAP)
1989
Hermitage la Tourette Delas (PEN)
1988
Crozes-Hermitage Domaine des Remizières (RAE)
Hermitage Chante-Alouette, Chapoutier (BER)
1986
St-Joseph Clos de l'Arbalestrier, Florentin (RAE)

£12.00 to £15.99

1991
Hermitage Grippat (YAP)
1990
Hermitage Chante-Alouette, Chapoutier (TAN)
Hermitage Chevalier de Stérimberg, Jaboulet (TAN)
1989
Hermitage Guigal (JU)
1988
Hermitage Guigal (BE)
Hermitage les Rocoules, Sorrel (BY)
1987
Hermitage Chave (YAP)
Hermitage Chevalier de Stérimberg, Jaboulet (WHI, VIG)
1986
Hermitage Chevalier de Stérimberg, Jaboulet (GRE)
Hermitage Domaine des Remizières (PE, RAE)

£16.00 to £19.99

1992
Condrieu Vernay (YAP)
1991
Condrieu Barge (MV)
Condrieu Château du Rozay Cuvée Ordinaire (YAP)
Condrieu Coteaux de Chéry, Perret (AD, JU)
1990
Condrieu Guigal (MV, AD, BE)
Condrieu les Cepes du Nebadon, Paret (PE)
1989
Condrieu Barge (EY, RAE)
Condrieu Coteaux de Chéry, Perret (JU)
Condrieu Delas (PEN)
Condrieu Dumazet (WCL)
Condrieu Guigal (BUT)
1988
Hermitage Chave (YAP, WS, ROB)
Hermitage Chevalier de Stérimberg, Jaboulet (VIG)
1987
Condrieu Vernay (VIG)
1985
Condrieu Dumazet (BUT)
Hermitage Chante-Alouette, Chapoutier (BUT, AD)
Hermitage les Rocoules, Sorrel (BUT)

£20.00 to £24.99

1991
Condrieu Vernay (YAP)
Hermitage Chave (YAP)
Hermitage les Rocoules, Sorrel (BIB)
1990
Condrieu Dumazet (BIB)
Hermitage Chave (YAP)
1989
Condrieu Jurie des Camiers (REI)
Condrieu Vernay (EL)
1988
Condrieu Guigal (BUT)
1985
Hermitage Chave (BUT)
1983
Hermitage Guigal (VIG)

£25.00 to £35.00

1991
Château Grillet (YAP)
Condrieu Coteau de Vernon, Vernay (YAP)
1989
Château Grillet (YAP)
Condrieu Château du Rozay (WS)

c. £66.00

1971
Château Grillet (REI)

SOUTHERN RHÔNE

RED

Under £3.00

Non-vintage
Asda Coteaux du Tricastin (ASD)
Asda Côtes du Rhône (ASD)
Sainsbury's Vin de Pays de l'Ardèche (SAI)
Tesco Côtes du Rhône (TES)
1991
Vin de Pays des Coteaux de l'Ardèche, Duboeuf (BEK)

£3.00 to £3.99

Non-vintage
Côtes du Rhône Meffre (VIC)
1992
Vin de Pays de Vaucluse, Domaine de l'Ameillaud (AUG)
1991
Côtes du Rhône Guigal (GR)
Waitrose Côtes du Rhône (WAI)
1990
Coteaux du Tricastin Domaine de Grangeneuve (ASD)
Côtes du Rhône Château du Bois de la Garde, Mousset (ASD)
Côtes du Ventoux Jaboulet (HOG, OD)
1989
Côtes du Ventoux Pascal (LO)
1988
★ Côtes du Ventoux Pascal (LO)

£4.00 to £4.99

1992
★ Côtes du Rhône Caves des Vignerons de Vacqueyras (TAN)
Côtes du Rhône Château du Grand Moulas (AD)
Lirac Domaine les Garrigues (CHA)
1991
Vin de Pays des Coteaux de l'Ardèche, Duboeuf (DAV)
1990
Côtes du Rhône Domaine St-Gayan (YAP)
Côtes du Rhône la Haie aux Grives, Domaine Vieux Chêne (JU)
★ Côtes du Rhône Parallèle 45, Jaboulet (NI, HOG, OD)
Côtes du Ventoux Domaine des Anges (GRG)
Côtes du Ventoux la Vieille Ferme (JU, GRE, MV, AMI, WCL, ROB)
1989
Côtes du Rhône Domaine Pélaquié (BUT)
Côtes du Ventoux Domaine des Anges (JU)
Côtes du Ventoux Jaboulet (MAJ)
1988
★ Côtes du Rhône Guigal (GR, HAY)

£5.00 to £6.99

Non-vintage
Châteauneuf-du-Pape Domaine Avril (BUT)
1992
Côtes du Rhône-Villages Château du Grand Moulas (AD)
1991
Côtes du Rhône Château du Grand Moulas (CV)
Côtes du Rhône Coudoulet de Beaucastel (GR)
Côtes du Rhône Valréas, Bouchard (WS)
Côtes du Rhône-Villages Château du Grand Moulas (TAN)
1990
★ Côtes du Rhône Coudelet de Beaucastel (OD)
Côtes du Rhône Guigal (OD, HIC)
Côtes du Rhône-Villages Jaboulet (EY)
★ Gigondas Domaine Raspail (HA)
Lirac Sabon (PIP)
Vacqueyras Jaboulet (HOG, EY)
1989
Côtes du Rhône Guigal (MV, ROB, AD)
Côtes du Rhône Puyméras (YAP)
Côtes du Rhône-Villages Rasteau, Cave des Vignerons de Rasteau (CV)
Côtes du Rhône-Villages Rasteau Domaine la Soumade (WHI, PIP)
Lirac les Queyrades, Méjan (AD, TAN, HAH)
Côtes du Rhône-Villages Sablet Château du Trignon (LOR)
Vacqueyras Caves Bessac (EL)
Vacqueyras Domaine la Garrigue (HIC)
Vacqueyras Jaboulet (NI)
Vacqueyras Pascal (DAV)
1988
Côtes du Rhône Cuvée Personnelle, Pascal (LO, YAP, HAG)
Côtes du Rhône Guigal (BE, NI, BUT, JU, BY, LAY)
Lirac la Fermade, Domaine Maby (LOR, YAP)
Vacqueyras Jaboulet (WHI)
Vacqueyras Pascal (LO, YAP)

1986
Côtes du Rhône-Villages Château la Couranconne (BIB)
1985
★ Côtes du Rhône Cuvée Personnelle, Pascal (LO, LOR, HAG)

£7.00 to £8.99

1992
Côtes du Rhône-Villages Cuvée de l'Ecu, Château du Grand Moulas (AD)
1991
Châteauneuf-du-Pape Quiot (MAR)
1990
Châteauneuf-du-Pape Domaine Grand Tinel (JU)
Châteauneuf-du-Pape Domaine la Roquette (BEK)
Côtes du Rhône Coudoulet de Beaucastel (MV, BAR)
Côtes du Rhône-Villages Domaine Ste-Anne (TAN)
Gigondas Domaine de Gour de Chaulé (JU)
Gigondas Jaboulet (HOG)
Lirac Domaine de Castel Oualou (GRE)
1989
Châteauneuf-du-Pape Domaine Brunel (SAI)
★ Châteauneuf-du-Pape Domaine de Nalys (WW)
Châteauneuf-du-Pape Domaine du Père Caboche (OD)
Côtes du Rhône Coudelet de Beaucastel (WCL)
Gigondas Domaine de Gour de Chaulé (EL, JU)
Gigondas Domaine du Cayron (BUT)
Gigondas Guigal (NI)
Gigondas Jaboulet (HOG, NI, WHI)
Vacqueyras Domaine la Fourmone, Combe (TAN)
1988
Cairanne Rabasse-Charavin (PIP)
Gigondas Domaine du Grand Montmirail (YAP)
Gigondas Domaine St-Gayan, Roger Meffre (OD, YAP)
Gigondas Guigal (BE, GR)
Vacqueyras Cuvée Spéciale, Pascal (VIN)
1987
Châteauneuf-du-Pape Domaine du Vieux Télégraphe (JU)
Gigondas Domaine Raspail (ROB)
Gigondas Domaine St-Gayan, Roger Meffre (YAP)

1986
Côtes du Rhône Guigal (TW)
Gigondas Domaine du Grand Montmirail (DAV, HAG)
Vacqueyras Domaine de la Couroulu (HUN)
1985
★ Châteauneuf-du-Pape Domaine de Mont-Redon (BR)
1983
Gigondas Jaboulet (BUT)

£9.00 to £11.99

1991
Châteauneuf-du-Pape Domaine du Vieux Télégraphe (AD)
Châteauneuf-du-Pape Domaine Font de Michelle (CB)

1990
Châteauneuf-du-Pape Chante-Cigale (CV)
Châteauneuf-du-Pape Château la Nerthe (OD)
Châteauneuf-du-Pape Domaine de Montpertuis (EL)
★ Châteauneuf-du-Pape Domaine du Vieux Télégraphe (AD, HAH, TAN, JU)
Châteauneuf-du-Pape Domaine Font de Michelle (THR, WR, BOT)
Châteauneuf-du-Pape la Bernardine, Chapoutier (DI, OD)
Châteauneuf-du-Pape les Cèdres, Jaboulet (HOG, GRE)
Châteauneuf-du-Pape Vieux Donjon (YAP)
Gigondas Domaine du Cayron (AD, JU, LAY)
1989
★ Châteauneuf-du-Pape Château du Mont-Redon (GAU)
Châteauneuf-du-Pape Delas (AUG)
Châteauneuf-du-Pape Domaine du Vieux Télégraphe (LAY, TAN, SOM, PIP, AD, GAU, BUT, JU, CV)
Châteauneuf-du-Pape Domaine Grand Tinel (HAH)
Châteauneuf-du-Pape Vieux Donjon (YAP)

1988
Châteauneuf-du-Pape Chante-Cigale (YAP, BAR)
Châteauneuf-du-Pape Clos des Papes, Avril (HAY, RAE, BUT)
★ Châteauneuf-du-Pape Domaine de Nalys (GRE)
Châteauneuf-du-Pape Domaine du Père Caboche (YAP)
Châteauneuf-du-Pape Domaine du Vieux Télégraphe (JU)
Châteauneuf-du-Pape Domaine Font de Michelle (JU)
Châteauneuf-du-Pape Vieux Donjcn (YAP)
Côtes du Rhône Château de Fonsalette (HOG, BUT)
Gigondas Domaine les Pallières (WHI, BIB, PIP)
1987
Châteauneuf-du-Pape Clos des Papes, Avril (EY, BIB, HAY, RAE)
1986
Châteauneuf-du-Pape Château la Nerthe (HOG)
Châteauneuf-du-Pape Domaine du Vieux Télégraphe (REI)
Châteauneuf-du-Pape Vieux Donjon (GE)
1985
Châteauneuf-du-Pape Château de la Font du Loup (HOG)
Châteauneuf-du-Pape Domaine du Père Caboche (YAP)
Châteauneuf-du-Pape Vieux Donjon (GE, BUT)
Côtes du Rhône Château de Fonsalette (BUT)
1983
Châteauneuf-du-Pape Clos des Papes, Avril (BUT)
Châteauneuf-du-Pape les Cèdres, Jaboulet (BUT)

£12.00 to £14.99

1990
Châteauneuf-du-Pape Château de Beaucastel (FA, TAN, JU)
Châteauneuf-du-Pape Clos des Papes, Avril (GAU)
1989
Châteauneuf-du-Pape Château de Beaucastel (NI)
Châteauneuf-du-Pape Clos Pignan, Reynaud (BUT, VIG)
Côtes du Rhône Château de Fonsalette (BUT, VIG, GAU, HOG)
1988
Châteauneuf-du-Pape Château de Beaucastel (FA, WCL, AD, GR, MAJ, NI)
Châteauneuf-du-Pape Clos Pignan, Reynaud (HOG)
1987
Châteauneuf-du-Pape Château de Beaucastel (ROB)
Hermitage Bernard Faurie (HAH)
1986
Châteauneuf-du-Pape Château de Beaucastel (FA)
Châteauneuf-du-Pape Clos des Papes, Avril (BUT)
Côtes du Rhône Château de Fonsalette (BUT)
1985
Châteauneuf-du-Pape Clos des Papes, Avril (BUT)
Châteauneuf-du-Pape la Bernardine, Chapoutier (GRE, DI)

£15.00 to £19.99

1990
Châteauneuf-du-Pape Château de Beaucastel (BUT, OD, LAY, AD, GAU, VIG)
Hermitage Bernard Faurie (HAH, JU)
1989
Hermitage Bernard Faurie (PIP, JU)
1986
Châteauneuf-du-Pape Château de Beaucastel (HAG, ROB)
Châteauneuf-du-Pape Château Rayas (HOG)
1985
Châteauneuf-du-Pape Château de Beaucastel (ROB)
Châteauneuf-du-Pape Domaine du Vieux Télégraphe (REI)
1983
Châteauneuf-du-Pape Château de Beaucastel (AD, GAU)
1981
Châteauneuf-du-Pape Château de Beaucastel (BR)
Châteauneuf-du-Pape les Cèdres, Jaboulet (WS)

£20.00 to £30.00

1989
Châteauneuf-du-Pape Château Rayas (BUT, VIG)
1988
Châteauneuf-du-Pape Château Rayas (BUT, AD)

1983
Châteauneuf-du-Pape Château de Beaucastel (BUT, ROB)
1978
Châteauneuf-du-Pape les Cèdres, Jaboulet (WS)

£35.00 to £40.00

1966
Châteauneuf-du-Pape la Grappe des Papes, Jaboulet (REI)
1962
Châteauneuf-du-Pape Clos de l'Oratoire des Papes (REI)

WHITE

Under £6.00

1992
Côtes du Rhône Domaine Pélaquié (BIB)
1991
Côte du Rhône Laudun Blanc, Domaine Pélaquié (SUM, LAY)
Côtes du Rhône Domaine St-Gayan (YAP)
Vin de Pays des Coteaux de l'Ardèche Chardonnay, Latour (EY, REI)
1990
Côtes du Rhône Domaine Pélaquié (BUT)
Côtes du Rhône Puyméras (YAP)
Lirac la Fermade, Domaine Maby (YAP)
Vin de Pays des Coteaux de l'Ardèche Chardonnay, Latour (HOG)
1989
Côtes du Rhône Domaine Pélaquié (BUT)
Côtes du Rhône Guigal (BE, NI)
Vin de Pays des Coteaux de l'Ardèche Chardonnay, Latour (HAG)

£6.00 to £9.99

1990
Côtes du Rhône Guigal (GAU)
1989
Châteauneuf-du-Pape Domaine de Nalys (HOG)
1988
Côtes du Rhône Guigal (TW)

*Please remember that **Webster's** is a price GUIDE and not a price LIST. It is not meant to replace up-to-date merchants' lists.*

£10.00 to £12.99

1992
Châteauneuf-du-Pape Domaine du Père Caboche (YAP)
Châteauneuf-du-Pape Domaine du Vieux Télégraphe (AD)
Côtes du Rhône Coudelet de Beaucastel (JU)
1991
Châteauneuf-du-Pape Domaine de Nalys (WW)
Châteauneuf-du-Pape Domaine du Vieux Télégraphe (LAY)
1990
Châteauneuf-du-Pape Domaine du Vieux Télégraphe (SOM, JU)
Viognier Domaine Ste-Anne (TAN)
1989
Châteauneuf-du-Pape Domaine Font de Michelle (JU)
Côtes du Rhône Château de Fonsalette (VIG)
1988
Châteauneuf-du-Pape Domaine de Mont-Redon (WS)

£13.00 to £15.99

1992
Châteauneuf-du-Pape Domaine Font de Michelle (DAV, BOT, THR, WR)
1991
Châteauneuf-du-Pape Domaine Font de Michelle (BOT, WR, THR)
1990
Châteauneuf-du-Pape Domaine du Père Caboche (HAG)
1987
Côtes du Rhône Château de Fonsalette (BUT)
1986
Châteauneuf-du-Pape Clos Pignan (VIG)

£16.00 to £24.99

1991
Châteauneuf-du-Pape Château de Beaucastel (VIG)
1990
Châteauneuf-du-Pape Château de Beaucastel (AD)
Châteauneuf-du-Pape Roussanne Vieilles Vignes, Château de Beaucastel (AD)
1989
Châteauneuf-du-Pape Château de Beaucastel (TAN, JU, VIG)
Châteauneuf-du-Pape Château Rayas (AD)

Châteauneuf-du-Pape Roussanne Vieilles Vignes, Château de Beaucastel (GAU)

1988

Châteauneuf-du-Pape Roussanne Vieilles Vignes, Château de Beaucastel (WCL)

1986

Châteauneuf-du-Pape Liquoreux, Château Rayas (HOG)

£25.00 to £35.00

1991

Châteauneuf-du-Pape Roussanne Vieilles Vignes, Château de Beaucastel (VIG)

1989

Châteauneuf-du-Pape Château Rayas (VIG, GAU)

1988

Châteauneuf-du-Pape Château Rayas (BUT)

1987

Châteauneuf-du-Pape Château Rayas (VIG)

1982

Châteauneuf-du-Pape Château de Beaucastel (VIG)

ROSÉ

Under £6.50

1991

Tavel Château de Trinquevedel (EL)

1990

Lirac Rosé la Fermade, Domaine Maby (YAP)

Tavel Château de Trinquevedel (HOG)

Tavel la Forcadière, Domaine Maby (LOR)

1989

Tavel Domaine de la Genestière (WHI)

£6.50 to £7.99

1992

Tavel Domaine de la Genestière (PIP)

1991

Tavel la Forcadière, Domaine Maby (YAP, PE)

Tavel l'Espiègle, Jaboulet (HOG)

1990

Tavel la Forcadière, Domaine Maby (PE)

SPARKLING

£7.00 to £9.00

Non-vintage

Clairette de Die Brut Archard-Vincent (YAP)

Clairette de Die Tradition Demi-sec Archard-Vincent (YAP)

FORTIFIED

Under £7.00

1990

Muscat de Beaumes-de-Venise Jaboulet ½ bottle (OD)

1989

Muscat de Beaumes-de-Venise Domaine de Coyeux ½ bottle (AD, BOT, THR, WR)

£7.00 to £9.99

Non-vintage

Muscat de Beaumes-de-Venise Cave Co-op. de Beaumes-de-Venise (NA, WHI, AD)

Muscat de Beaumes-de-Venise Cuvée Pontificale, Pascal (YAP, LO, DAV)

1992

Muscat de Beaumes-de-Venise Domaine de Durban (EL)

1991

Muscat de Beaumes-de-Venise Cave Co-op. de Beaumes-de-Venise (OD)

Muscat de Beaumes-de-Venise Domaine de Durban (YAP, SOM)

Muscat de Beaumes-de-Venise Jaboulet (HOG)

1990

Muscat de Beaumes-de-Venise Domaine de Coyeux (HAY)

1988

Muscat de Beaumes-de-Venise Domaine de Coyeux (JU, LAY)

£10.00 to £12.99

Non-vintage

Muscat de Beaumes-de-Venise Cave Co-op. de Beaumes-de-Venise (CV)

Muscat de Beaumes-de-Venise Cuvée Pontificale, Pascal (HAG)

Muscat de Beaumes-de-Venise Perrin (PE)

1990

Muscat de Beaumes-de-Venise Domaine de Durban (PIP)

Muscat de Beaumes-de-Venise Domaine des Bernardins (PIP)

Muscat de Beaumes-de-Venise Jaboulet (GRE)

__Webster's__ is an annual publication. We welcome your suggestions for next year's edition.

LOIRE

DRY WHITE

Under £4.00

Non-vintage

Asda Muscadet de Sèvre-et-Maine (ASD)

Sainsbury's Blanc de Blancs du Val de Loire Saumur (SAI)

Sainsbury's Muscadet de Sèvre-et-Maine (SAI)

Sainsbury's Sauvignon de Touraine (SAI)

1992

Muscadet de Sèvre-et-Maine Château de la Dimerie (SAI)

★ Muscadet de Sèvre-et-Maine sur lie Carte d'Or, Sauvion (BEK)

Sauvignon de Touraine Comte d'Ormont, Saget (WHI)

★ Sauvignon de Touraine Confrérie d'Oisly et Thésée (OD)

★ Sauvignon du Haut Poitou Cave Co-op (WAI)

Waitrose Muscadet (WAI)

1991

Saumur Cave des Vignerons de Saumur (TES, MAJ)

1989

Muscadet de Sèvre-et-Maine sur lie les Découvertes, Sauvion (BEK)

£4.00 to £4.99

1992

Chardonnay du Haut Poitou Cave Co-op (HAY, WAI)

Muscadet de Sèvre-et-Maine Fief de la Brie, Bonhomme (AD)

Muscadet de Sèvre-et-Maine sur lie Château de la Ferronière (EL)

★ Muscadet sur lie Chéreau Domaine de la Mortaine (YAP)

Saumur Cave des Vignerons de Saumur (YAP)

Sauvignon de Touraine Domaine de la Garrelière (KA)

Sauvignon de Touraine Domaine de la Renaudie (KA)

Sauvignon de Touraine Domaine Guenault (LOR)

Sauvignon de Touraine Domaine Guy Mardon (VIC)

Sauvignon de Touraine Plouzeau (KA)

Sauvignon du Haut Poitou Cave Co-op (HAY, MAJ, JU)

1991

Chardonnay du Haut Poitou Cave Co-op (WAI, LO, JU)

Muscadet de Sèvre-et-Maine sur lie, Thuaud (CHA)

Sauvignon de Touraine Langlois-Château (HOG)

Sauvignon du Haut Poitou Cave Co-op (LO)

1990

Chardonnay du Haut Poitou Cave Co-op (DAV)

★ Menetou-Salon Montaloise (TES)

Muscadet de Sèvre-et-Maine sur lie Château de la Jannière (DAV)

Pineau de la Loire Confrérie d'Oisly et Thésée (WS)

★ Quincy Domaine de la Maison Blanche (ASD)

Saumur Blanc Domaine Langlois (HOG)

Sauvignon de Touraine Domaine de la Preslé (NI)

£5.00 to £5.99

1992

Gros Plant sur lie Château du Cleray (PIP)

Muscadet de Sèvre-et-Maine Domaine des Hauts Pemions (CV)

Muscadet de Sèvre-et-Maine Fief de la Brie, Bonhomme (TAN)

Muscadet sur lie Château l'Oiselinière, Carré (WS)

Muscadet sur lie Chéreau-Carré (WW)

St-Pourçain Cuvée Printanière Union des Vignerons (PIP)

Sauvignon de Touraine Domaine de la Charmoise, Marionnet (BIB)

Sauvignon de Touraine Domaine de la Preslé (PIP)

Vin de Thouarsais, Gigon (YAP)

1991
★ Muscadet de Sèvre-et-Maine sur lie Château de Cléray (ROB)
Muscadet de Sèvre-et-Maine sur lie Clos des Bourguignons (HAH)
★ Muscadet de Sèvre-et-Maine sur lie Domaine des Dorices (GRE)
Quincy Domaine de la Maison Blanche (SAI)
Sauvignon de Touraine Confrérie d'Oisly et Thésée (WW, HAH)
1990
Menetou-Salon Domaine de Chatenoy (NI)
Muscadet de Sèvre-et-Maine sur lie Cuvée LM, Louis Métaireau (SOM)
Muscadet de Sèvre-et-Maine sur lie Domaine des Dorices (NA)
Muscadet des Coteaux de la Loire, Guindon (BIB)
Quincy Pierre Mardon (GE)
Saumur Blanc Domaine Langlois (DI)
Sauvignon de Touraine Domaine des Corbillières (BUT)
★ Vouvray Château Moncontour (OD)
Vouvray Domaine de l'Épinay (ASD)
1988
Menetou-Salon Roger (WHI)

£6.00 to £6.99

1992
★ Montlouis Domaine des Liards, Berger (YAP)
Muscadet de Sèvre-et-Maine sur lie Château de Cléray (PIP)
Muscadet de Sèvre-et-Maine sur lie Moulin de la Gravelle (LOR)
★ Pouilly-Fumé Bailly (WS)
Quincy Jaumier (YAP)
Quincy Pierre Mardon (AD)
Reuilly Robert & Gérard Cordier (YAP)
Sancerre Domaine de Fort (WHG)
Sauvignon de Touraine Domaine du Clos St-Georges, Oisly et Thésée (CB)
Vouvray Jarry (YAP)
1991
Azay-le-Rideau la Basse Chevrière (YAP)
Coteaux du Giennois Balland-Chapuis (SUM)
Menetou-Salon la Charniviolle, Foumier (HOG)
Menetou-Salon Morogues, Pellé (WCL)
Muscadet de Sèvre-et-Maine sur lie, Bossard (ROB)
Muscadet de Sèvre-et-Maine sur lie Château de la Ragotière Black Label (VIN)
Muscadet sur lie Domaine de Basseville, Bossard (EY)
Pouilly-Fumé les Loges, Saget (MAJ)
Sancerre Domaine de Fort (WHG)
Sancerre Mellot (TES)
1990
Menetou-Salon la Charniviolle, Foumier (BEK)
Pouilly-Fumé Saget (MAR)
Reuilly Beurdin (WCL)
1989
Muscadet de Sèvre-et-Maine sur lie Premier Jour, Louis Métaireau (SOM)
Vouvray Château Moncontour (NI)
Vouvray Domaine de l'Épinay (CV)
1988
★ Vouvray Domaine de l'Épinay (CV)
1987
Vouvray Clos Naudin, Foreau (HOG)
1980
★ Vouvray Clos Naudin, Foreau (AD)

£7.00 to £7.99

1992
Menetou-Salon Domaine de Chatenoy (VIG)
Menetou-Salon Pellé (EL, WR, BOT, THR)
Menetou-Salon Teiller (YAP)
Muscadet de Sèvre-et-Maine sur lie Cuvée de Millénaire, Marquis de Goulaine (AV)
Muscadet sur lie Domaine de Chasseloir (LOR)
Pouilly-Fumé les Loges, Saget (GRE)
Sancerre Domaine de la Garenne, Reverdy (HAY)
1991
Menetou-Salon Domaine de Chatenoy (GA)
Menetou-Salon la Charnivolle, Fournier (PIP)
Menetou-Salon Morogues, Pellé (CV)
Menetou-Salon Pellé (MV, HAH, LOR)
Menetou-Salon Roger (TAN)
Pouilly-Fumé Seguin Père et Fils (HAY)
Sancerre Château de Thauvenay (ASD)
★ Sancerre Clos de la Crêle, Lucien Thomas (EL)
Sancerre Clos le Grand Chemarin, Migeon (BEK)
Sancerre Domaine du P'tit Roy (SOM)
Sancerre la Reine Blanche (WS)
Sancerre Paul Prieur (HA)
Savennières Baumard (GRE)
Savennières Clos du Papillon, Baumard (GRE, EL)
Vin de Pays du Jardin de la France Cépage Chardonnay, Domaine Couillaud (VIN)

1990
Menetou-Salon les Thureaux, Mellot (GRE, AMI)
Menetou-Salon Morogues, Pellé (CV)
Menetou-Salon, Rat (PE)
Pouilly-Fumé Domaine de Petit Soumard (ROB)
Pouilly-Fumé Domaine des Chailloux, Chatelain (BEK)
Pouilly-Fumé les Loges, Jean-Claude Guyot (YAP)
Quincy Pierre Mardon (ROB)
Sancerre Raimbault-Barrier (BU)
Savennières Clos de Coulaine (RAE)
★ Savennières Clos du Papillon, Baumard (HOG, BEK, EL)
Savennières Domaine de la Bizolière (YAP)
Savennières Domaine du Closel, Mme de Jessey (YAP)
Vouvray Domaine Peu de la Moriette (PIP)
Vouvray le Haut Lieu, Huet (WS)
1989
Savennières Baumard (HOG)
1988
Muscadet sur lie Château de Chasseloir de St-Fiacre Fût de Chêne Neuf (LOR)
Savennières Château de Chamboureau, Soulez (YAP)
Savennières Clos de Coulaine (RAE)
1986
Jasnières Caves aux Tuffières, Pinon (YAP)
1984
Vouvray Clos du Bourg, Huet (BIB)
Vouvray le Haut Lieu, Huet (RAE)

£8.00 to £9.99

1992
Pouilly-Fumé Didier Dageneau (JU)
Pouilly-Fumé Domaine des Berthiers, Jean-Claude Dagueneau (BR)
Pouilly-Fumé Domaine Thibault (HIC)
Pouilly-Fumé Figeat (JU)
Pouilly-Fumé Seguin Père et Fils (BIB, RAE)
Sancerre Balland-Chapuis (HIC)
Sancerre Daulny (HAH)
Sancerre Domaine de Montigny, Natter (BIB)
Sancerre Laporte (PIP)
Sancerre le Grand Chemarin, Balland-Chapuis (CV)
Sancerre les Perriers, Vatan (YAP)
Savennières Château d'Epiré (YAP)
1991
Chinon Blanc Raffault (WS)
Menetou-Salon le Petit Clos, Roger (BER)
Pouilly-Fumé André Dezat (NI)
Pouilly-Fumé Bailly (HUN)
Pouilly-Fumé Château Fauray (BAR)
Pouilly-Fumé Domaine des Berthiers, Jean-Claude Dagueneau (SUM)
Pouilly-Fumé Domaine des Rabichattes (RAE, PE)
Pouilly-Fumé Domaine Thibault (TAN)
Pouilly-Fumé Redde (EL)
Sancerre André Dézat (TAN)
Sancerre Balland-Chapuis (BER, PE)
Sancerre Clos du Roy, Millérioux (HOG, CB)
Sancerre Domaine de Montigny, Natter (LAY)
Sancerre le Chêne Marchand, Roger (TAN)
Sancerre les Crilles, Gitton (HIG)
Sancerre les Tuileries, Redde (EL)
Sancerre Roger (MV)
Sancerre Vacheron (AD, MAJ)

Savennières Clos de Coulaine (BIB)
Savennières Clos du Papillon Domaine du Closel (PIP)
1990
Menetou-Salon Montaloise (ROB)
Pouilly-Fumé Château de Tracy (AD, CV, TAN, LAY)
Pouilly-Fumé Didier Dageneau (WR, BOT, THR)
Pouilly-Fumé Domaine des Rabichattes (BER)
Pouilly-Fumé Domaine Thibault (LAY)
Pouilly-Fumé Jean Pabiot (HAH)
Pouilly-Fumé la Loge aux Moines, Moreux (CB)
Pouilly-Fumé les Loges, Saget (VIN, ROB)
Pouilly-Fumé Redde (HOG)
Sancerre André Dézat (CV, BER)
Sancerre Balland-Chapuis (BER)
Sancerre Clos de la Poussie (BER)
Sancerre Comte Lafond Château du Nozet (HOG)
Sancerre Laporte (DI)
Savennières Clos de Coulaine (BER)
Savennières Clos du Papillon, Baumard (HA, ROB)

1989
Pouilly-Fumé Domaine Thibault (BER)
Sancerre les Galinots, Gitton (HIG)
Vouvray le Haut Lieu, Huet (RAE, JU)
1987
Savennières Roche-aux-Moines, Soulez (YAP)
1985
Vouvray Aigle Blanc, Poniatowski (GRE, VIG, ROB)
1984
Sancerre Clos des Roches, Vacheron (BUT)
1983
Vouvray Aigle Blanc, Poniatowski (VIG)
Vouvray le Haut Lieu, Huet (AV)
Vouvray le Mont, Huet (AD)
1976
★ Vouvray Château de Vaudenuits (UN)

£10.00 to £14.99

1991
Pouilly-Fumé Château de Tracy (HAG)
Pouilly-Fumé de Ladoucette Château du Nozet (VIC)
Pouilly-Fumé Didier Dageneau (TAN)
Pouilly-Fumé les Pechignolles (HIG)
Pouilly-Fumé Vieilles Vignes Caves de Pouilly-sur-Loire (HAG)
Sancerre Clos des Roches, Vacheron (ROB)
1990
Pouilly-Fumé Château de Tracy (LOR, CB)
Pouilly-Fumé de Ladoucette Château du Nozet (HOG, GRE, WHI, ROB, BER, HUN)
Pouilly-Fumé Vieilles Vignes, Didier Dagueneau (BR)
Sancerre les Romains, Gitton (HIG)
Savennières Roche-aux-Moines, Soulez (WS)
1989
Pouilly-Fumé Cuvée Prestige, Châtelain (BEK, MV)
Sancerre Comte Lafond Château du Nozet (GRE)
1988
Savennières Clos St-Yves (AV)
1986
Pouilly-Fumé de Ladoucette Château du Nozet (BUT)

Stars (★) indicate wines selected by the editors as particularly good value in their class.

£15.00 to £19.99

1991
Sancerre Chavignol la Grande Côte, Cotat (GAU)
1990
Pouilly-Fumé Pur Sang, Didier Dagueneau (BOT, WR)
Sancerre Chavignol la Grande Côte, Cotat (AD)

£20.00 to £29.99

1989
Pouilly-Fumé Baron de L Château du Nozet (WRI)
Pouilly-Fumé Silex, Didier Dagueneau (BOT, WR)
1988
Pouilly-Fumé Baron de L Château du Nozet (ROB)
1986
Pouilly-Fumé Baron de L Château du Nozet (WHI)

c. £50.00

1959
Vouvray Brédif (ROB)

SPARKLING

Under £7.00

Non-vintage
Anjou Rosé Gratien & Meyer (HAY)
Cadre Noir Saumur (WHI)
Safeway Saumur (SAF)
Saumur Ackerman 1811 Brut (AUG, DAV)
Saumur Ackerman 1811 Rosé (DAV)
Saumur Brut Gratien & Meyer (HOG, HAY)
Saumur Rosé Gratien & Meyer (HOG)
1990
Saumur Brut Bouvet-Ladubay (MAR)

£7.00 to £7.99

Non-vintage
Château Langlois Crémant de Loire (HOG, HOG)
Crémant de Loire Brut Gratien & Meyer (WS)
Montlouis Mousseux Brut Berger (JU, YAP)
Saumur Brut Bouvet-Ladubay (JU)
Saumur Langlois-Château (GRG)
Saumur Rosé Langlois-Château (GRG)
★ Vouvray Brut Brédif (AUG)
Vouvray Foreau (GE)
1989
★ Saphir Bouvet-Ladubay (NI)

£8.00 to £9.99

Non-vintage
Château Langlois Crémant de Loire (DI)
Montlouis Mousseux Demi-sec, Berger (YAP)
Saphir Bouvet-Ladubay (NI)
Saumur Brut Bouvet-Ladubay (HAG)
Vouvray Brut Brédif (ROB)
Vouvray Foreau (AD)
Vouvray Méthode Champenoise, Huet (RAE)

SWEET WHITE

Under £7.00

1990
Malvoisie Guindon (YAP)
Vouvray Château de Vaudenuits (GRE)
1989
Coteaux du Layon Domaine des Saulaies (TAN)
1988
Coteaux du Layon Clos de Ste-Catherine, Baumard (HOG)
1987
Coteaux du Layon Domaine des Saulaies (BIB)
Vouvray Brédif (GRE)
1986
Coteaux du Layon Leblanc (RAE)
1982
Coteaux du Layon Beaulieu, Chéné (MV)
★ Vouvray Clos du Bourg, Huet (BOR)

£7.00 to £8.99

1990
Coteaux du Layon Château de la Roulerie (YAP)
Coteaux du Layon Château de la Roulerie les Aunis (YAP)
1989
Coteaux du Layon Beaulieu, Chéné (JU)
Coteaux du Layon Leblanc (RAE)
Vouvray Domaine Peu de la Moriette (TAN)
1988
★ Coteaux du Layon Clos de Ste-Catherine, Baumard (GAU)
1987
Vouvray Clos du Bourg, Huet (RAE)
1986
Montlouis Moelleux Deletang (RAE)
1985
Montlouis Moelleux Deletang (RAE)
Vouvray Moelleux Bourillon Dorléans (MV)
1978
★ Coteaux du Layon Beaulieu, Chéné (MV)

£9.00 to £12.99

1990
Vouvray Moelleux Jarry (YAP)
1989
Coteaux du Layon Clos de Ste-Catherine, Baumard (HOG, GRE, EL)
Vouvray Aigle Blanc Réserve, Poniatowski (GRE)
Vouvray le Haut Lieu, Moelleux, Huet (RAE)
1988
Quarts-de-Chaume Baumard (GRE)
Vouvray Clos Baudoin, Poniatowski (GRE)
1986
Quarts-de-Chaume Baumard (HOG)
1985
Vouvray Clos Naudin, Foreau (HOG)
1983
Anjou Moulin Touchais (EL)
Coteaux du Layon Clos de Ste-Catherine, Baumard (HOG)
1982
Quarts-de-Chaume Baumard (HOG)
1976
Coteaux du Layon Beaulieu, Chéné (MV)
1973
Coteaux du Layon Beaulieu, Chéné (MV)

£13.00 to £15.99

1990
Vouvray le Haut Lieu, Moelleux, Huet (LAY, AD)
1989
Coteaux de l'Aubance Domaine de Bablut (AD)
Montlouis Moelleux Deletang (WS)
Quarts-de-Chaume Baumard (HOG)
Quarts-de-Chaume Château de Bellerive (WS)
Vouvray Moelleux Bourillon Dorléans (MV)
1988
Vouvray Clos du Bourg, Huet (WS, AD, JU)
Vouvray Moelleux Huet (LAY)
1981
Anjou Moulin Touchais (EL)
1979
Anjou Moulin Touchais (EL)
1970
Coteaux du Layon Ravouin-Gesbron (RAE)

£16.00 to £19.99

1990
Bonnezeaux Château de Fesles (TAN)
Quarts-de-Chaume Baumard (GRE, EL)
Quarts-de-Chaume Château de Bellerive (JU)

1989
Coteaux du Layon Clos de Ste-Catherine, Baumard (VIG)
Quarts-de-Chaume Baumard (GRE)
Quarts-de-Chaume Château de Bellerive (JU)
Quarts-de-Chaume Château de l'Echarderie (YAP)
Vouvray Moelleux Bourillon Dorléans (VIG)
Vouvray Moelleux Huet (RAE)
1988
Bonnezeaux la Chapelle Château de Fesles (MV)
1986
Vouvray Clos du Bourg, Huet (BIB)
1981
Anjou Moulin Touchais (ROB)
1979
Anjou Moulin Touchais (WRI)
1975
Anjou Moulin Touchais (EL)
1971
Coteaux du Layon Ravouin-Gesbron (AD)
1964
Vouvray Moelleux Bourillon Dorléans (MV)

£20.00 to £29.99

1989
Bonnezeaux la Chapelle Château de Fesles (GAU)
Vouvray Clos du Bourg, Huet (JU, LAY, AD)

£30.00 to £39.99

1980
Vouvray Cuvée Constance, Huet (BIB)
Vouvray le Haut Lieu, Moelleux, Huet (JU)
1970
Anjou Moulin Touchais (EL)
1969
Anjou Moulin Touchais (EL)
1961
Vouvray Moelleux Huet (WS)

£40.00 to £49.99

1989
Vouvray Cuvée Constance, Huet (BUT, JU)
1969
Vouvray Clos du Bourg, Huet (AD)
1967
Quarts-de-Chaume Baumard (VIG)

c. £65.00

1935
Bonnezeaux Château des Gauliers, Mme Fourlinnie (YAP)

c. £80.00

1959
Vouvray Clos du Bourg, Huet (AD)

ROSÉ

Under £5.00

Non-vintage
Tesco Rosé d'Anjou (TES)
1992
Anjou Rosé Cellier de la Loire (NI)
Cabernet d'Anjou Château Perray-Jouannet (YAP)
★ Rosé de Cabernet du Haut Poitou Cave Co-op (WAI)
★ Touraine Rosé Noble Jouée, Clos de la Dorée (AD)
Waitrose Rosé d'Anjou (WAI)
1991
Coteaux d'Ancenis Guindon (YAP)
1989
Vin de Thouarsais, Gigon (YAP)

£5.00 to £7.99

1992
Reuilly Pinot Noir, Beurdin (AD)
1991
Azay-le-Rideau la Basse Chevrière, Pavy (YAP)
Reuilly Pinot Gris, Cordier (YAP)
1990
★ Sancerre Rosé les Romains, Vacheron (WHI)

£8.00 to £10.00

1992
Sancerre Rosé Dezat (PIP)
1991
Sancerre Rosé Dezat (LAY, AD)
1990
Sancerre Rosé les Romains, Gitton (CV)

c. £24.00

1961
Cabernet d'Anjou Domaine de Bablut Demi-Sec (AD)

*Please remember that **Webster's** is a price GUIDE and not a price LIST. It is not meant to replace up-to-date merchants' lists.*

RED

Under £4.00

1991
★ Gamay du Haut Poitou Cave Co-op (WAI, LO)

£4.00 to £4.99

1992
Gamay de Touraine Domaine de la Renaudie (KA)
1991
Cabernet de Touraine Domaine de la Renaudie (KA)
Gamay de Touraine Domaine de la Charmoise, Marionnet (RAE)
St-Pourçain Union des Vignerons (YAP)
Saumur Cave des Vignerons de Saumur (AD)
1990
Anjou Rouge Logis de la Giraudière, Baumard (EL, GRE)
Vin de Thouarsais Gigon (YAP)
1989
★ Bourgueil la Hurolaie, Caslot-Galbrun (TES)

£5.00 to £6.99

1992
Chinon l'Arpenty Desbourdes (YAP)
Gamay de Touraine Domaine de la Charmoise, Marionnet (BIB)
1991
Anjou Rouge Tijou (HIG)
1990
Anjou Cabernet Clos de Coulaine (JU, RAE)
Bourgueil Clos de la Henry, Morin (AV)
Bourgueil Domaine des Ouches (WHI)
Chinon Château de Ligre (HAY)
★ Chinon Langlois-Château (HOG)
St-Nicolas de Bourgueil Clos du Vigneau (HAY)
St-Nicolas-de-Bourgueil Domaine du Fondis (TAN)
1989
★ Bourgueil Domaine de Raguenières (CV, WCL, HIG)
Chinon Domaine Morin (AV)
1986
Chinon Domaine de la Chapellerie, Olek (RAE)
★ Chinon Domaine de Turpenay, Couly (EL)

£7.00 to £9.99

1992
Chinon Vieilles Vignes, Angelliaume (PIP)
1991
Sancerre André Dezat (PIP)
Sancerre Domaine du P'tit Roy (NI)
Saumur-Champigny Domaine de Villeneuve (PIP)
1990
Bourgueil Domaine des Ouches (PIP)
Chinon Cuvée Prestige, Gouron (KA)
Chinon les Gravières (LAY)
Menetou-Salon Rouge, Pellé (WCL)
Sancerre Reverdy (HAY)
Saumur-Champigny Filliatreau (YAP)
St-Nicolas-de-Bourgueil Clos de la Contrie, Ammeux (YAP)
1989
Anjou Cabernet Clos de Coulaine (BIB)
Bourgueil Domaine du Grand Clos, Audebert (LAY)
★ Bourgueil Vieilles Vignes, Lamé-Delille-Boucard (VIG)
Chinon Cuvée Prestige, Gouron (KA)
Samur-Champigny Lavigne (TAN)
Sancerre Clos du Roi, Crochet (JU)
Sancerre Clos du Roy, Millerioux (HOG)
Saumur-Champigny Vieilles Vignes, Filliatreau (YAP)
1988
Anjou Cabernet Clos de Coulaine (BIB)
★ Chinon les Grezeaux, Baudry (MV)
Sancerre Domaine de Montigny, Natter (BIB)
1987
Bourgueil Beauvais, Druet (BY)
Bourgueil Grand Mont, Druet (BY, YAP)
1986
Bourgueil Domaine du Grand Clos, Audebert (BER)
Bourgueil Grand Mont, Druet (BY)
Chinon Domaine de Turpenay, Couly (TAN)
1984
Bourgueil Grand Mont, Druet (BY)

£10.00 to £15.00

1992
Chinon Clos de la Dioterie, Joguet (AD)
1990
Bourgueil Beauvais, Druet (AD, JU)
Chinon Clos de l'Echo, Couly-Dutheil (LAY)
1989
Chinon Clos de la Dioterie, Joguet (JU)

c. £19.00

1988
Bourgueil Cuvée Vaumoreau, Druet (AD)

ALSACE

WHITE

Under £4.50

Non-vintage
Sainsbury's Pinot Blanc (SAI)
1992
★ Pinot Blanc Cave Co-op. Turckheim (BOT, WR, THR)
1991
Pinot Blanc Cave Co-op. Turckheim (BOT, THR, WR, VIC)

£4.50 to £4.99

1992
Pinot Blanc Cave Co-op. de Ribeauvillé (AUG)
Pinot Blanc Tradition, Cave Co-op. Turckheim (BR, CV, WCL)
1991
★ Riesling Cave Co-op. Turckheim (VIC)
Sylvaner Hugel (HOG)
1990
Sylvaner Trimbach (GRG)
1989
Pinot Blanc Dopff & Irion (HOG)
Sylvaner Dopff & Irion (EL, GRE)
1988
Riesling Louis Gisselbrecht (SOM)
★ Tokay-Pinot Gris Sipp (GRG)

£5.00 to £5.99

1992
Gewürztraminer Cave Co-op. Turckheim (BR, WR, THR, BOT)
Pinot Blanc Louis Gisselbrecht (PIP, HIC)
Pinot Blanc Producteurs de Beblenheim (HAH)
Riesling Seigneur d'Alsace, Dopff & Irion (EL)
Sylvaner Louis Gisselbrecht (PIP)
Tokay-Pinot Gris Dopff & Irion (EL)
1991
Gewürztraminer Cave Co-op. Turckheim (WR, BOT, THR, GA)
Muscat Réserve, Cave Co-op. Turckheim (OD)
Pinot Blanc Muré (BEK)
Pinot Blanc Schlumberger (NI)
★ Sylvaner Vieilles Vignes, Ostertag (MV)
Tesco Gewürztraminer (TES)
Tokay-Pinot Gris Cave Co-op. Turckheim (LO, OD)
1990
Flambeau d'Alsace Hugel (DI)
★ Gewürztraminer Réserve Prestige, Cave Co-op. Turckheim (NI)
Gewürztraminer Sipp (WHI)
Pinot Blanc Hugel (HOG)
Pinot Blanc Muré (ROB)
Pinot Blanc Schlumberger (HOG)
★ Pinot Blanc Trimbach (GRG)
Tokay-Pinot Gris Dopff & Irion (HOG)
Waitrose Gewürztraminer (WAI)
1989
Pinot Blanc Trimbach (HOG)
Riesling Dopff & Irion (GRE)
Riesling Louis Gisselbrecht (PE)
1988
Edelzwicker Rolly Gassmann (RAE, HAY)
Riesling Réserve Cave Co-op. Turckheim (VIN)
Sylvaner Schleret (YAP)
Sylvaner Trimbach (HOG)

£6.00 to £6.99

Non-vintage
Sainsbury's Gewürztraminer (SAI)
1992
Gewürztraminer Seigneur d'Alsace, Dopff & Irion (EL)
Tokay-Pinot Gris Louis Gisselbrecht (PIP)
1991
Gewürztraminer Cave Co-op. de Ribeauvillé (AUG)
Gewürztraminer Muré (BEK)
Muscat Louis Gisselbrecht (PIP)
Pinot Blanc Rolly Gassmann (BIB)
Pinot Blanc Tradition, Kuentz-Bas (JU)
Riesling Rolly Gassmann (BIB)
Sylvaner Zind-Humbrecht (BY)
1990
Gewürztraminer Dopff au Moulin (GRG)
Muscat Wiederhirn (HIG)
Pinot Blanc Willy Gisselbrecht (ROB)
Riesling Louis Gisselbrecht (PIP, HIC)
★ Riesling Tradition, Kuentz-Bas (WS)
Sylvaner Hugel (BER, HUN)
Sylvaner Vieilles Vignes, Ostertag (GAU)
Sylvaner Zind-Humbrecht (WR)
1989
Gewürztraminer Dopff & Irion (HOG)
Gewürztraminer Schléret (YAP)
★ Gewürztraminer Trimbach (GRG)

Pinot Blanc Cattin (CB)
Riesling Blanck (AV)
Riesling Hugel (HOG)
★ Riesling Princes Abbés, Schlumberger (HOG, GRE)
Riesling Schleret (YAP)
Riesling Trimbach (GRG)
Sylvaner Vieilles Vignes, Ostertag (GAU)
Tokay-Pinot Gris Wiederhirn (HIG)

1988

Pinot Blanc les Amours, Hugel (BUT)
Pinot Blanc Trimbach (BUT)
Riesling Hugel (WS)
Riesling les Faitières (CHA)
Riesling Trimbach (HOG)
Tokay-Pinot Gris les Maquisards, Dopff & Irion (HOG)

1986

Sporen Hugel (HOG)

1985

Riesling les Murailles, Dopff & Irion (HOG)
Sylvaner Hugel (TW)

£7.00 to £8.99

Non-vintage

Muscat Schlumberger (BAR)

1992

Gewürztraminer Ingersheim (DAV)
Gewürztraminer Louis Gisselbrecht (HIC)

1991

Gewürztraminer Altenbourg, Blanck (AD)
Gewürztraminer Blanck (HAH)
Gewürztraminer Louis Gisselbrecht (SOM)
Gewürztraminer Rolly Gassmann (BIB, BIB)
Muscat Réserve, Trimbach (WS)
Muscat Schlumberger (EY)
Riesling les Murailles, Dopff & Irion (EL)

Riesling Turkheim, Zind-Humbrecht (BY)
Tokay-Pinot Gris Schlumberger (EY, NI)

1990

Auxerrois Rolly Gassmann (BIB)
Gewürztraminer Caves de Bennwihr (PE)
Gewürztraminer Hugel (HOG)
Gewürztraminer les Faitières (CHA)
Gewürztraminer Réserve, Cave Co-op. Turckheim (WCL)
Riesling Réserve, Dopff & Irion (ROB)
Tokay-Pinot Gris Tradition, Kuentz-Bas (JU)

1989

Gewürztraminer des Princes Abbés, Schlumberger (TAN)
Gewürztraminer Hugel (AD, DAV)
Gewürztraminer les Sorcières Dopff & Irion (GRE)
Gewürztraminer Rolly Gassmann (HAY)
Gewürztraminer Tradition, Kuentz-Bas (BER, JU)
Gewürztraminer Trimbach (HOG)

Muscat les Amandiers, Dopff & Irion (HOG)
Muscat Réserve, Trimbach (GAU, ROB)
Pinot Blanc Rolly Gassmann (TAN)
★ Riesling Turkheim, Zind-Humbrecht (FA)
Tokay-Pinot Gris Hatschbourg, Cattin (CB)
Tokay-Pinot Gris les Maquisards, Dopff & Irion (EL, GRE)
★ Tokay-Pinot Gris Réserve, Trimbach (GRG, GAU)

1988

Auxerrois Rolly Gassmann (RAE, PE, BIB)
Gewürztraminer Trimbach (BUT)
Muscat Réserve, Heydt (CB)
Muscat Schleret (YAP)
Muscat Zind-Humbrecht (BY)
Pinot Blanc Rolly Gassmann (RAE)
Riesling Schoenenberg, René Schmidt (BER)
Sporen Hugel (GRE)

1987

Gewürztraminer Réserve Rolly Gassmann (BIB)
Riesling Hugel (HUN)
Riesling Rolly Gassmann (HAY)
Sporen Hugel (VIN)

1985

Gewürztraminer Trimbach (BUT)
Pinot Blanc Hugel (TW)
Riesling Hugel (TW)

1983

Pinot Blanc Hugel (BUT)

£9.00 to £11.99

Non-vintage
Riesling Saering, Schlumberger (BAR)
1991
Gewürztraminer Bollenberg, Cattin (CB)
Gewürztraminer Tradition, Kuentz-Bas (HAG)
Muscat Schleret (LAY)
Riesling Herrenweg, Zind-Humbrecht (BY)
Tokay-Pinot Gris Schleret (YAP)
1990
Muscat Réserve, Trimbach (BER, HAG)
Riesling Heimbourg Cave Co-op. Turckheim (WCL)
Riesling Herrenweg, Zind-Humbrecht (WR)
★ Riesling Saering, Schlumberger (HIC)
Riesling Turkheim, Zind-Humbrecht (WR)
Tokay-Pinot Gris Schlumberger (HIC)
1989
Gewürztraminer Brand Grand Cru de Turckheim (OD)
Gewürztraminer Réserve Particulière, Faller (BUT)
Gewürztraminer Réserve, Trimbach (GAU)
Gewürztraminer Tradition, Hugel (WS)
Riesling Kappelweg, Rolly Gassmann (JU)
★ Riesling Réserve Particulière, Faller (BUT)
★ Riesling Schlossberg, Blanck (AD)
Riesling Tradition, Hugel (AD)
Tokay-Pinot Gris Dopff au Moulin (BE)
Tokay-Pinot Gris Tradition, Hugel (DI)
1988
Gewürztraminer Hugel (TW, HUN)
Gewürztraminer Jubilee, Hugel (HOG)
Muscat Rolly Gassmann (JU)
Riesling Frédéric Emile, Trimbach (GRG)
Riesling Réserve, Trimbach (TW)
Riesling Rolly Gassmann (TAN)
Riesling Schoenenberg, Dopff au Moulin (HOG)
Tokay-Pinot Gris Rolly Gassmann (JU)
1986
Gewürztraminer Réserve Particulière, Faller (BUT)
Gewürztraminer Seigneurs de Ribeaupierre, Trimbach (HOG)
Riesling Frédéric Emile, Trimbach (HOG)
Riesling Saering, Schlumberger (HOG, NI)
1985
Gewürztraminer Osterberg, Sipp (WHI)
★ Gewürztraminer Seigneurs de Ribeaupierre, Trimbach (GRG)
Gewürztraminer Tradition, Hugel (TW)
Riesling Réserve Personnelle, Hugel (DI)
Riesling Tradition, Hugel (BUT)
Tokay-Pinot Gris Réserve, Trimbach (BUT)
Tokay-Pinot Gris Tradition, Hugel (BUT)
1983
Gewürztraminer Hugel (BUT)

£12.00 to £14.99

1990
Gewürztraminer Herrenweg, Zind-Humbrecht (WR)
Muscat Goldert, Zind-Humbrecht (WR)
Riesling Jubilee, Hugel (WS)
1989
Gewürztraminer Jubilee, Hugel (WS, JU)
Gewürztraminer Kitterlé, Schlumberger (NI)
Muscat Moench Reben, Rolly Gassmann (BIB)
Riesling Schlossberg, Faller (LAY)
Tokay-Pinot Gris Kitterlé, Schlumberger (AMI)
Tokay-Pinot Gris Millesime, Rolly Gassmann (JU)
1988
Gewürztraminer Brand Grand Cru de Turckheim (HUN)
Gewürztraminer Goldert, Zind-Humbrecht (BY)
Gewürztraminer Réserve Personnelle, Hugel (AV)
Gewürztraminer Réserve, Trimbach (BUT)
Gewürztraminer Turckheim, Dopff (WR)
Riesling Brand, Zind-Humbrecht (BY)
Riesling Muenchberg, Ostertag (MV, WCL)
Riesling Réserve Personnelle, Hugel (DAV)
1987
Gewürztraminer Rangen, Zind-Humbrecht (BY)
1986
Gewürztraminer Réserve Personnelle, Hugel (TAN)
Riesling Kitterlé, Schlumberger (HOG)
1985
Riesling Frédéric Emile, Trimbach (GRE, TW)
1983
Gewürztraminer Réserve Personnelle, Hugel (BUT, DI, WRI)
Riesling Réserve Personnelle, Hugel (BUT, DI)
Riesling Trimbach (GAU)
Tokay-Pinot Gris Réserve, Rolly Gassmann (RAE)

£15.00 to £19.99

1991

Gewürztraminer Clos Windsbuhl, Zind-Humbrecht (GAU)

Gewürztraminer Herrenweg, Zind-Humbrecht (GAU)

Riesling Brand, Zind-Humbrecht (GAU)

1989

Gewürztraminer Herrenweg Vendange Tardive, Zind-Humbrecht (BY, FA)

Gewürztraminer Vendange Tardive, Wiederhirn (HIG)

Riesling Altenberg de Bergheim, Koehly (BUT)

Tokay-Pinot Gris Schlumberger (BER)

1988

Gewürztraminer Seigneurs de Ribeaupierre, Trimbach (GAU)

Tokay-Pinot Gris Réserve Personnelle, Trimbach (WS)

1985

Gewürztraminer Fronholz Vendange Tardive, Ostertag (MV)

Gewürztraminer Kitterlé, Schlumberger (GRE, HOG)

1983

Gewürztraminer Vendange Tardive, Muré (WRI)

Gewürztraminer Vendange Tardive, Ostertag (MV)

Gewürztraminer Vendange Tardive, Wiederhirn (HIG)

Riesling Bergheim Burg Vendange Tardive, Deiss (REI)

Riesling Vendange Tardive, Dopff & Irion (HOG)

Tokay-Pinot Gris Réserve Personnelle, Hugel (BUT)

Tokay-Pinot Gris Vendange Tardive, Dopff & Irion (HOG)

1981

Riesling Frédéric Emile, Trimbach (TW)

Riesling Réserve Personnelle, Hugel (VIG)

Riesling Schoenenberg Vendange Tardive, Dopff au Moulin (HOG)

1979

★ Riesling Frédéric Emile, Trimbach (TW)

In each price band wines are listed in vintage order. Within each vintage they are listed in A–Z order.

£20.00 to £24.99

1989

Gewürztraminer Cuvée Exceptionelle, Schléret (YAP)

Gewürztraminer Vendange Tardive, Zind-Humbrecht (ROB)

1988

Gewürztraminer Sélection de Grains Nobles, Cave Co-op. de Turckheim (CV)

1985

Gewürztraminer Vendange Tardive, Hugel (WS, DI)

Riesling Clos Ste-Hune, Trimbach (AD)

1983

Gewürztraminer Vendange Tardive, Dopff & Irion (HOG, GRE)

Gewürztraminer Vendange Tardive, Hugel (HOG, DI)

Riesling Frédéric Emile, Trimbach (TW)

1982

Riesling Clos Ste-Hune, Trimbach (BUT)

1976

Gewürztraminer Seigneurs de Ribeaupierre, Trimbach (RAE)

£25.00 to £29.99

1990

Gewürztraminer Herrenweg, Zind-Humbrecht (BY)

1988

Tokay-Pinot Gris Vendange Tardive, Hugel (WS)

1986

Gewürztraminer Cuvée Christine, Schlumberger (GRE, NI)

1985

Gewürztraminer Cuvée Anne Vendange Tardive, Rolly Gassmann (BIB, RAE)

Gewürztraminer Cuvée Christine, Schlumberger (REI)

1983

Gewürztraminer Cuvée Christine, Schlumberger (BUT)

Gewürztraminer Sélection de Grains Nobles, Dopff & Irion (HOG)

£30.00 to £39.99

1989

Gewürztraminer Cuvée Anne, Schlumberger (GRE, AMI)

1986

Gewürztraminer Hengst Vendange Tardive, Zind-Humbrecht (BY)

Gewürztraminer Sélection de Grains Nobles, Dopff & Irion (EL)

1985
Gewürztraminer Vendange Tardive, Faller (BUT)
Riesling Vendange Tardive, Faller (BUT)
1983
Gewürztraminer Vendange Tardive, Hugel (TW)
Gewürztraminer Vendange Tardive, Trimbach (BUT)
Riesling Sélection de Grains Nobles, Dopff & Irion (EL)
1981
Gewürztraminer Vendange Tardive, Hugel (AV, VIG)
1976
Gewürztraminer Vendange Tardive, Hugel (FA)
1975
Riesling Frédéric Emile, Trimbach (VIG)

£40.00 to £49.99

1989
Gewürztraminer Vendange Tardive, Anne Schlumberger (REI)
1983
Riesling Frédéric Emile Vendange Tardive, Trimbach (TW)
1976
Gewürztraminer Cuvée Christine, Schlumberger (VIG)
Riesling Frédéric Emile Vendange Tardive, Trimbach (VIG)

£50.00 to £65.00

1988
Tokay-Pinot Gris Sélection de Grains Nobles, Dopff au Moulin (BER, VIG)
1986
Gewürztraminer Sélection de Grains Nobles, Hugel (WS)
1983
Tokay-Pinot Gris Sélection de Grains Nobles, Beyer (REI)
Gewürztraminer Sélection de Grains Nobles, Heydt (CB)
1976
Tokay-Pinot Gris Vendange Tardive, Hugel (TW)

£85.00 to £90.00

1976
Gewürztraminer Sélection de Grains Nobles, Hugel (VIG)
Tokay-Pinot Gris Sélection de Grains Nobles, Hugel (REI)

c. £100.00

1989
Gewürztraminer Rangen Sélection de Grains Nobles, Zind-Humbrecht (BY)

RED

Under £8.00

1992
Pinot Noir Louis Gisselbrecht (PIP)
1990
Pinot Noir Schleret (YAP)

£8.00 to £9.99

1990
Pinot Noir Hugel (DI)
1989
Pinot Noir Hugel (DI)

£10.00 to £12.99

1989
Pinot Noir Herrenweg, Zind-Humbrecht (WR)
1988
Pinot Noir Réserve Personnelle, Hugel (DAV)
Pinot Noir Réserve, Rolly Gassmann (RAE)
Pinot Noir Rolly Gassmann (BIB)
1985
Pinot Noir Réserve, Rolly Gassmann (BIB)

£16.00 to £17.99

1988
Pinot Noir Réserve Personnelle, Hugel (DI, VIG)
1985
Pinot Noir Réserve Personnelle, Hugel (TW)

SPARKLING

Under £9.00

Non-vintage
★ Crémant d'Alsace Cuvée Julien, Dopff au Moulin (GRG, HOG, WHI, GRE)

£9.00 to £10.00

Non-vintage
Crémant d'Alsace Dopff & Irion (EL)
Crémant d'Alsace Dopff au Moulin (LAY)

Stars (★) indicate wines selected by the editors as particularly good value in their class.

SOUTH-EAST FRANCE

RED

Under £3.00

Non-vintage
Asda Corbières (ASD)
★ Asda Côtes de Roussillon (ASD)
Asda Minervois (ASD)
Sainsbury's Corbières (SAI)
Sainsbury's Côtes du Roussillon (SAI)
Sainsbury's Minervois (SAI)
St-Chinian Rouanet (WAI)
Tesco Corbières (TES)
1991
Côtes Catalanes Château de Jau (OD)
★ Vin de Pays de l'Aude Cabernet Sauvignon, Foncalieu (WAI)

£3.00 to £3.49

Non-vintage
★ Fitou Mme Claude Parmentier (VIC)
1992
Sainsbury's Vin de Pays de la Cité de Carcassonne, Domaine Sautès le Bas (SAI)
1991
Costières de Nîmes Château de Nages (WAI)
Vin de Pays de l'Hérault, Domaine de Chapître (MV)
1990
★ Côtes de la Malpère Château Malvies (AUG)
Côtes du Lubéron Cellier de Marrenon (LOR)
Faugères l'Estagnon (BOT, THR, WR)
1989
★ Fitou Caves du Mont Tauch (HOG)

£3.50 to £3.99

Non-vintage
Coteaux d'Aix-en-Provence Château la Coste (WHI)
1992
Côtes de Thongue Domaine Comte de Margon (AD)
★ Côtes de Thongue Cépage Syrah, la Condamine l'Évêque (WS)
Vin de Pays du Vaucluse Domaine Vieux Chêne (JU)
1991
Cabardès Château Ventenac (MAJ)
Cabardès Domaine de Cannettes-Hautes (HAY)
★ Corbières Château de Cabriac (EL)
Côtes du Roussillon-Villages, Vignerons Catalans (GE)
Sainsbury's Vin de Pays du Vaucluse Syrah, Domaine Chancel (SAI)
Vin de Pays des Maures, Domaine d'Astros (SUM)
Vin de Pays du Gard Domaine de Valescure (BIB)
1990
Corbières Château de Jonquières (BE)
★ Coteaux de Murviel, Domaine de Limbardie (DAV)
Côtes de Thongue, Clos Ferdinand (WCL)
Fitou Caves du Mont Tauch (AUG, MAR)
Minervois Domaine de l'Abbaye de Tholomies (SAF)
St-Chinian Domaine des Soulié (SAF)
Vin de Pays des Bouches-du-Rhône Domaine du Temps Perdu (GRE)
Vin de Pays du Gard Domaine Mas de Montel (BEK)
1989
Corbières Château de Cabriac (DAV)
★ Costières de Nîmes Grand Bourry (SAI)
★ Minervois Château de Fabas (GE)
St-Chinian Rouanet (HIG)
1988
★ Faugères Château de Grézan (PEN)
Fitou Caves du Mont Tauch (GRE)

£4.00 to £4.99

Non-vintage
Vin de Pays des Sables du Golfe du Lion, Listel (PE)
1992
Coteaux de Murviel, Domaine de Limbardie (JU, AD)
Minervois Cuvée Émilie, Russol (BER)
1991
Corbières Château de Mandourelle (TAN)
Coteaux d'Aix-en-Provence Château de Fonscolombe (LAY)

Coteaux de Murviel, Domaine de Limbardie (MV, TAN)
Côtes du Roussillon Château de Jau (OD)
Côtes du Vivarais Domaine de Belvezet (LAY, TAN)
Fitou Caves du Mont Tauch (NI)
Minervois Château de Paraza (OD, NA)
★ Mont Baudile, Domaine d'Aupilhac (AD)

1990

★ La Clape Château de Pech-Celeyran (AD)
Coteaux d'Aix-en-Provence Château de la Gaude (YAP)
Coteaux du Languedoc Domaine de l'Abbaye de Valmagne (EL, GRE)
Coteaux du Lyonnais, Duboeuf (PIP)
Côtes du Lubéron Château Val Joanis (ASD)
Côtes du Vivarais Domaine de Belvezet (MV)
Minervois Château de Gourgazaud (REI)
★ Minervois Domaine de Ste-Eulalie (DAV, AD, TAN)
★ Safeway Corbières, Château de Caraguilhes (SAF)

1989

★ La Clape Château de Pech-Celeyran (BER)
Corbières Château les Ollieux (RAE)
★ Corbières Chatellerie de Lastours (CV)
Coteaux d'Aix-en-Provence Château de Fonscolombe (GRE)
★ Coteaux du Languedoc Château de Pech-Celeyran (TAN)
Côtes de la Malpère Château Malvies (HAG)
Côtes du Lubéron Château Val Joanis (BE)
Minervois Domaine de Ste-Eulalie (BOT, THR, WR)

1988

Corbières Château les Ollieux (JU)
Côtes de Provence Château de Pampelonne, les Maîtres Vignerons de St-Tropez (BEK)

1987

Faugères Domaine de Fraisse (WHI)
Vin de Pays des Sables du Golfe du Lion, Domaine du Bosquet (PEN)

£5.00 to £6.99

1991

Costières de Nîmes Château de la Tuilerie (AV)
Côtes du Lubéron Château de Canorgue (YAP)
★ Vin de Pays d'Oc Syrah, la Fadèze (LAY)

1990

★ Collioure Domaine du Mas Blanc (WW)
Corbières Château de Lastours (WCL, BU)
Minervois Daniel Domergue (CB)
★ Vin de Pays d'Oc La Cuvée Mythique, Dubernet/Vign. de Val d'Orbieu (NI)

1988

Corbières Château de Lastours (PEN)
Minervois Domaine de l'Abbaye de Tholomies (BER)

1987

Bandol Mas de la Rouvière, Bunan (NI)

£7.00 to £8.99

1990

Côtes de Provence Domaine Richeaume (SAF)
Côtes du Roussillon Black Label, Domaine Sarda Malet (BIB)

1989

★ Faugères Cuvée Spéciale, Gilbert Alquier (SUM)

1988

★ Bandol Mas de la Rouvière, Bunan (YAP)

1987

Bandol Domaine de Pibarnon (BEK)

1984

Bandol Domaine Tempier (GE)

£9.00 to £10.99

1991

Vin de Pays de l'Hérault, Mas de Daumas Gassac (NI)

1990

Bandol Domaine Tempier (WW)
Vin de Pays de l'Hérault, Mas de Daumas Gassac (SUM, OD, AD)

1989

Coteaux du Languedoc Prieuré de St-Jean de Bébian (AD)
Vin de Pays de l'Hérault, Mas de Daumas Gassac (SOM, GRE)

1988

Coteaux d'Aix-en-Provence Domaine de Trévallon (SOM)

1987

Bandol Château de la Rouvière, Bunan (YAP)

£11.00 to £14.99

1990

Bandol Cuvée Migoua (WW)
Bandol Cuvée Tourtine (WW)

1989

Palette Château Simone (YAP)

1988
Palette Château Simone (VIG)
Vin de Pays de l'Hérault, Mas de Daumas Gassac (BUT, JU, AMI)
1987
Vin de Pays de l'Hérault, Mas de Daumas Gassac (AMI)

£15.00 to £20.00

1989
Côtes de Provence Domaines Ott (PEN)
1985
Vin de Pays de l'Hérault, Mas de Daumas Gassac (BUT)
1980
Palette Château Simone (VIG)

£25.00 to £30.00

1983
Vin de Pays de l'Hérault, Mas de Daumas Gassac (VIG)
1982
Vin de Pays de l'Hérault, Mas de Daumas Gassac (VIG)
1981
Vin de Pays de l'Hérault, Mas de Daumas Gassac (VIG)

WHITE

Under £4.00

Non-vintage
Tesco Vin de Pays de l'Aude (TES)
1992
Corbières les Producteurs du Mont Tauch (AUG)
★ Vin de Pays d'Oc Chardonnay, Fortant de France (WAI)
1991
Vin de Pays d'Oc Chardonnay, Philippe de Baudin (also Chais Baumière) (SAI)

£4.00 to £4.99

Non-vintage
Vin de Pays des Sables du Golfe du Lion, Listel Blanc (PE)
1992
Côtes du Lubéron la Vieille Ferme (MV, GRE)
★ Vin de Pays d'Oc Cépage Chardonnay, Ryman (SAI)
★ Vin de Pays d'Oc Chardonnay, Philippe de Baudin (also Chais Baumière) (EY, CV)
★ Vin de Pays d'Oc Sauvignon, Virginie (LAY, NA)
1991
Coteaux d'Aix-en-Provence Château de Fonscolombe (LAY)
★ Vin de Pays de l'Hérault Cépage Muscat Sec, du Bosc (WS)
1990
Vin de Pays des Sables du Golfe du Lion, Domaine de Villeroy Blanc de Blancs (PEN)
Vin de Pays d'Oc Cépage Chardonnay, Ryman (VIC)
1989
Côtes du Lubéron Château Val Joanis (WHI)
1988
Côtes du Lubéron la Vieille Ferme (GRG)

£5.00 to £6.99

1992
Côtes de Provence Mas de Cadenet (WW)
Mauzac Primaire Cave de Blanquette de Limoux (WIC)
Mauzac Sec, Cave de Blanquette de Limoux (WIC)
1991
★ Vin de Pays d'Oc Chardonnay, des Rives de l'Argent Double (OD)
1990
Côtes du Lubéron la Vieille Ferme (GRG)

£7.00 to £8.99

1991
Cassis Clos Ste-Magdeleine, Sack (YAP)
1990
Bandol Mas de la Rouvière, Bunan (YAP)

£10.50 to £13.99

1991
Vin de Pays de l'Hérault, Mas de Daumas Gassac (SUM)
1990
Bellet Château de Crémat, Jean Bagnis (YAP)

Cassis Clos Ste-Magdeleine, Sack (VIG)
Palette Château Simone (YAP)
Vin de Pays de l'Hérault, Mas de Daumas Gassac (SOM)

£14.00 to £17.99

1992
Vin de Pays de l'Hérault, Mas de Daumas Gassac (NI)
1990
Côtes de Provence Domaines Ott (ROB)
1989
Côtes de Provence Domaines Ott (PEN)
Côtes de Provence Clos Mireille Blanc de Blancs, Domaines Ott (ROB)
Palette Château Simone (VIG)
Vin de Pays de l'Hérault, Mas de Daumas Gassac (BUT, AMI)

ROSÉ

Under £4.00

1988
Côtes du Lubéron Château Val Joanis (WHI)

£4.00 to £4.99

Non-vintage
Vin de Pays des Sables du Golfe du Lion Gris de Gris, Domaine de Jarras (PE)
1992
Coteaux d'Aix-en-Provence Château de Fonscolombe (AD)

£5.00 to £6.99

1991
Côtes de Provence Carte Noire, Vignerons de St-Tropez (WHI)
Côtes du Lubéron Château Val Joanis (ROB)

£7.00 to £9.99

1992
Bandol Mas de la Rouvière (YAP)
1991
Coteaux des Baux-en-Provence Terres Blanches (VIG)
1989
Vin de Pays de l'Hérault, Mas de Daumas Gassac (BUT)
1987
Vin de Pays de l'Hérault, Mas de Daumas Gassac (BUT)

£12.50 to £15.00

1990
Côtes de Provence Château de Selle, Domaines Ott (GRG)
Palette Château Simone (VIG)

SPARKLING

Under £7.00

1989
Blanquette de Limoux Brut Cave Co-op. de Limoux (UN, BOT, THR)
1985
★ Blanquette de Limoux Aimery (HOG)

£8.00 to £8.99

Non-vintage
Blanquette de Limoux Brut Cave Co-op. de Limoux (AV)
1983
Blanquette de Limoux Sieur d'Arques (BER)

FORTIFIED

Under £3.00

Non-vintage
★ Sainsbury's Muscat de St-Jean de Minervois ½ bottle (SAI)

£7.50 to £9.99

Non-vintage
Rasteau Vin Doux Naturel, Domaine la Soumade (PIP)
1991
Muscat de Rivesaltes Château de Jau (GE)
Muscat de Rivesaltes Domaine Cazes (WW)
1990
Muscat de Rivesaltes Domaine Cazes (ROB)

£10.00 to £12.99

1989
Muscat de Rivesaltes Domaine Cazes (VIG)
1978
Vieux Rivesaltes Domaine Cazes (ROB)

c. £23.00

1969
Maury Mas Amiel (VIG)

SOUTH-WEST FRANCE

RED

Under £3.00

Non-vintage
Asda Bergerac (ASD)
1991
Côtes de Duras Seigneuret (WAI)
★ Côtes de St-Mont, Producteurs Plaimont (SOM)

£3.00 to £3.99

Non-vintage
Asda Cahors (ASD)
Sainsbury's Bergerac (SAI)
Vin de Pays du Comté Tolosan Domaine de Callary (PE)
1991
Côtes de St-Mont, Producteurs Plaimont (PIP, AD, TAN)
1990
Côtes de Duras les Producteurs Réunis (AUG)
Côtes de St-Mont Les Hauts de Bergelle (SOM)
Côtes de St-Mont, Producteurs Plaimont (AUG)
★ Côtes du Frontonnais Château Bellevue-la-Forêt (OD)
Côtes du Marmandais Cave de Cocumont (GA)
Côtes du Marmandais Château Marseau (WAI)
1989
★ Cahors Château St-Didier-Parnac, Rigal (OD)

£4.00 to £4.99

1991
Gaillac Château Clement Termes (BOT, WR, THR)
Gaillac Domaine de Labarthe (SOM)
1990
Côtes de St-Mont Les Hauts de Bergelle (TAN)
Côtes du Frontonnais Carte Blanche Château Montauriol (OD)
Côtes du Frontonnais Château Bellevue-la-Forêt (SAI, NI)
Côtes du Frontonnais Château Ferran (BEK, CV)
★ Gaillac Château Clement Termes (BOT, WR, THR, BAR)
1989
★ Bergerac Château la Jaubertie (NI)
Cahors Château de Gaudou (SOM)
★ Cahors Château d'Eugénie (EY)
Gaillac Château Larroze (BE)
★ Marcillac Cave de Valady (WIC, BOD)
Vin de Pays du Comté Tolosan Domaine de Baudare (ROB)

1988
Gaillac Domaine Jean Cros (BE)
Vin de Pays du Comté Tolosan Domaine de Baudare (ROB)

£5.00 to £5.99

1992
★ Marcillac Domaine du Cros, Teulier (AD)
1991
Madiran Domaine Damiens (BIB)
1990
Bergerac Domaine de la Raze (BOD)
Cahors Château de Gaudou (WCL)
Cahors Château d'Eugénie (HIC)
★ Cahors Domaine Pierre Sèche (CV, BU)
Côtes de Bergerac Château Court-les-Mûts (BIB)
Côtes du Frontonnais Château Ferran (PIP, WCL)
Madiran Domaine Damiens (BIB)
1989
Cahors Château de Gaudou (GRG)
Côtes du Frontonnais Château Ferran (ROB)
1988
★ Buzet Tradition les Vignerons de Buzet (PE)

*Please remember that **Webster's** is a price GUIDE and not a price LIST. It is not meant to replace up-to-date merchants' lists.*

Cahors Château d'Eugénie (PIP)
Cahors Château Lagrezette (BEK)
★ Côtes de Bergerac Château Court-les-Mûts (BIB)

£6.00 to £7.99

1990
Cahors Château de Grezels, Rigal (AUG)
Cahors Clos la Coutale (WW)
Pécharmant Château de Tiregand (TAN)
1989
Cahors Domaine de la Pineraie (CV)
1988
Cahors Château St-Didier-Parnac, Rigal (LAY)
Cahors Prieuré de Senac (WR, BOT, THR)
Côtes de St-Mont, Château de Sabazan (LAY)
1986
★ Madiran Château de Peyros (HIC)

£8.00 to 8.99

1988
Cahors Château Lagrezette (ROB)
Madiran Château d'Aydie (PIP)
1985
Cahors Château du Cayrou, Jouffreau (TAN)

c. £12.00

1990
Madiran Château Montus (VIG)

DRY WHITE

Under £3.00

Non-vintage
Asda Vin de Pays des Côtes de Gascogne (ASD)
Sainsbury's Bergerac (SAI)
1992
Côtes de Duras Croix du Beurrier (WAI)

£3.00 to £3.99

Non-vintage
Asda Côtes de Duras (ASD)
1992
Bergerac Sauvignon Foncaussade (SAF)
Côtes de Duras Sauvignon, les Vignerons des Coteaux de Duras (BEK)
Côtes de Gascogne Domaine de Planterieu (WAI)
★ Côtes de Gascogne Domaine San de Guilhem (MV)
Côtes de Gascogne Domaine de Tariquet (THR, WR, BOT)
Côtes de Gascogne Producteurs Plaimont (MAR, JU)
Côtes de St-Mont Producteurs Plaimont (AD, LAY)
Vin de Pays des Landes, Domaine du Comte (SUM)
1991
Bergerac Château du Chayne (GA)
Côtes de Gascogne Domaine de Rieux (PE)
Côtes de Gascogne Domaine San de Guilhem (HOG)
Côtes de Gascogne Domaine de Tariquet (BAR)
Côtes de Gascogne Domaine le Puts (CV, MAJ)
Côtes de St-Mont Les Hauts de Bergelle (SOM)
Côtes de St-Mont Producteurs Plaimont (AUG)
Vin de Pays Charentais Cave St-André (ROB)

£4.00 to £4.99

1992
Bergerac Sec Château de Tiregand (TAN)
Côtes de Gascogne Domaine de Rieux (AD, TAN, HAG)
Côtes de St-Mont Producteurs Plaimont (TAN)
1991
★ Bergerac Château la Jaubertie (NI)
Chardonnay Ryman (MAJ)
Côtes de Gascogne Domaine de Rieux (REI, EY, BER)
Côtes de St-Mont Les Hauts de Bergelle (TAN, BER)
Vin de Pays des Terroirs Landais, Domaine de Laballe (JU)
1989
Bergerac Château la Jaubertie (NI)

£5.00 to £5.99

1992
Bergerac Château le Fagé (BER)
Côtes de Gascogne Domaine des Cassagnoles (WIC)
Côtes de Saussignac Château Court-les-Mûts (BIB)

Webster's is an annual publication. We welcome your suggestions for next year's edition.

Pacherenc du Vic-Bilh Domaine Damiens (BIB, AD)

1991

Bergerac Château le Fagé (NA)

Côtes de Saussignac Château Court-les-Mûts (BIB)

Pacherenc du Vic-Bilh Domaine Damiens (BIB)

1990

Bergerac Château la Jaubertie Cépage Sauvignon (NI)

Côtes de Gascogne Cuvée Bois Domaine de Tariquet (WR, BOT, THR)

Côtes de Gascogne Domaine de Tariquet (MAJ)

£6.00 to £6.99

1992

Bergerac Domaine de Grandchamp (SAI)

1991

Bergerac Château la Jaubertie (HIG)

1990

Bergerac Château la Jaubertie Cépage Sauvignon (REI)

Côtes de Gascogne Domaine des Cassagnoles (BOD)

1989

Bergerac Château la Jaubertie Cépage Sauvignon (WHI)

£7.00 to £8.99

1991

Jurançon Sec Domaine Cauhapé (MV)

Pacherenc du Vic-Bilh Domaine Boucassé (VIG)

1990

★ Jurançon Sec Domaine Cauhapé (MV, AD)

£9.00 to £11.00

1991

Jurançon Sec Domaine Cauhapé (WCL, TAN)

1990

Jurançon Sec Domaine Cauhapé (VIG)

c. £16.00

1988

Jurançon Sec Domaine Cauhapé (WCL)

SWEET WHITE

Under £7.00

1990

★ Jurançon Moelleux Château Jolys (WHI)

Monbazillac Château Theulet (BAR)

1988

★ Monbazillac Château la Brie (AUG)

£7.00 to £7.99

1989

Jurançon Clos Guirouilh (ROB)

1986

Jurançon Cru Lamouroux (HAY)

c. £16.00

1989

Jurançon Grains Nobles, Cave de Gan (REI)

ROSÉ

Under £5.00

1992

★ Bergerac Château la Jaubertie (NI)

1991

Bergerac Château la Jaubertie (NI)

£5.00 to £5.99

1992

Bergerac Château la Jaubertie (VIC)

Bergerac Château Court-les-Mûts (BIB)

1991

Bergerac Château Court-les-Mûts (BIB)

1989

Bergerac Château la Jaubertie (WHI)

Stars (★) indicate wines selected by the editors as particularly good value in their class.

JURA & SAVOIE

JURA RED

Under £4.50

Non-vintage
Bonchalaz Maire (GRG, ROB)

£6.00 to £7.50

1988
Côtes du Jura Pinot Noir/Trousseau, Boilley (CV, WCL)
Côtes du Jura Rouge Bourdy (AD)

JURA WHITE

Under £4.00

Non-vintage
Bonchalaz Maire (GRG)

£6.00 to £9.99

1990
Chardonnay-Savagnin Château d'Arlay, Laguiche (SUM)
1989
Côtes du Jura Cépage Chardonnay, Boilley (CV)
Côtes du Jura Cépage Savagnin, Boilley (CV, WCL, ROB)
1988
Côtes du Jura Blanc Bourdy (WS)
1986
Côtes du Jura Cépage Savagnin, Boilley (PEN)

£18.00 to £24.99

Non-vintage
Vin de Paille La Vignière, Maire ½ bottle (ROB, VIG)
1983
Vin Jaune Château-Chalon, Bourdy (WS)
1978
Vin Jaune Château-Chalon, Maire (ROB)

£26.00 to £28.99

1985
Vin Jaune Château-Chalon, Bourdy (AD)
Vin Jaune Côtes du Jura Château d'Arlay, Laguiche (SUM)
1982
Vin Jaune Côtes du Jura Château d'Arlay, Laguiche (REI)

c. £35.00

1979
Vin Jaune Château-Chalon, Bourdy (WS)

c. £45.00

1967
Vin Jaune Château-Chalon, Bourdy (VIG)

c. £82.00

1959
Vin Jaune Château-Chalon, Bourdy (WS)

JURA ROSÉ

c. £4.50

Non-vintage
Vin Gris Cendré de Novembre Maire (HOG)

SAVOIE RED

c. £5.50

1991
Mondeuse St-Jean de la Porte, J Perrier & Fils (AD)

SAVOIE WHITE

Under £5.00

1991
Vin de Savoie Abymes (EL)

£5.00 to £6.99

1992
Apremont les Rocailles, Pierre Boniface (TAN)
Seyssel Tacounière, Mollex (WS)
1991
Apremont les Rocailles, Pierre Boniface (PE)
1990
Apremont les Rocailles, Pierre Boniface (PE)

*Please remember that **Webster's** is a price GUIDE and not a price LIST. It is not meant to replace up-to-date merchants' lists.*

RHINE

Kab.	=	Kabinett
Spät.	=	Spätlese
Aus.	=	Auslese
BA	=	Beerenauslese
TBA	=	Trockenbeerenauslese

WHITE

Under £3.00

Non-vintage

Asda Liebfraumilch (ASD)

Asda Mainzer Domherr Spät. (ASD)

★ Asda Niersteiner Spiegelberg Kab. (ASD)

Sainsbury's Liebfraumilch (SAI)

Sainsbury's Trocken QbA, Rheinhessen (SAI)

Tesco Hock (TES)

Tesco Niersteiner Gutes Domtal (TES)

Victoria Wine Liebfraumilch (VIC)

Waitrose Bereich Nierstein (WAI)

Waitrose Liebfraumilch (WAI)

£3.00 to £3.99

Non-vintage

Liebfraumilch Black Tower (THR, SAF, GA, WR, BOT)

Liebfraumilch Blue Nun (GA, SAF, WR, THR, BOT)

Liebfraumilch Crown of Crowns (WHI, PE)

Rheingau Riesling, Schloss Reinhartshausen (GA)

1992

Liebfraumilch Blue Nun (AUG)

Niersteiner Gutes Domtal, Langenbach (BOT, WR, THR)

1991

Liebfraumilch Blue Nun (WAI)

Niersteiner Gutes Domtal, Rudolf Müller (CB)

Oppenheimer Krötenbrunnen, Rudolf Müller (CB)

Rüdesheimer Rosengarten, Rudolf Müller (TAN)

Sainsbury's Oppenheimer Krötenbrunnen Kab. (SAI)

1990

Niersteiner Gutes Domtal, Rudolf Müller (HAH)

1988

Niersteiner Gutes Domtal, Deinhard (HOG)

£4.00 to £4.99

Non-vintage

Liebfraumilch Black Tower (WHI)

Liebfraumilch Blue Nun (WHI, UN)

1991

Liebfraumilch Blue Nun (DAV)

Niersteiner Spiegelberg Riesling Kab., Rudolf Müller (TAN)

1990

★ Wachenheimer Mandelgarten Müller-Thurgau Kab., Bürklin-Wolf (DI)

1988

Niersteiner Gutes Domtal, Deinhard (HUN)

£5.00 to £5.99

1992

Niersteiner Spiegelberg Kab., Guntrum (DAV)

1991

Kreuznacher Riesling Spät., Paul Anheuser (TES)

Mainzer Domherr Bacchus Kab., Guntrum (PIP)

1990

★ Binger Scharlachberg Riesling Kab., Villa Sachsen (TES)

Niederhauser Pfingstweide Riesling, Anheuser (SUM)

1989

Altenbamberger Rotenberg Riesling Kab., Staatliche Weinbaudomäne (EY)

Mainzer Domherr Bacchus Kab., Guntrum (WRI)

★ Niersteiner Pettenthal Riesling Spät., Balbach (TES)

Oppenheimer Schloss Müller-Thurgau Trocken, Guntrum (WRI)

★Wachenheimer Rechbächel Riesling Kab., Bürklin-Wolf (ASD)

1988

Dexheimer Doktor Spät., Guntrum (AS)

1987

Geisenheimer Kläuserweg Scheurebe Kab., Ress (WW)

1986

Wallhäuser Muehlenberg Riesling Trocken, Prinz zu Salm-Dalberg'sches Weingut (HAC)

1985

★ Eltviller Sonnenberg Riesling Kab., Simmern (RAE)

1983

★ Oestricher Doosberg Riesling Kab., Schönborn (GA)

£6.00 to £6.99

1990

Kreuznacher Kahlenberg Riesling Kab., August Anheuser (BER)

Niersteiner Klostergarten Riesling Kab., Balbach (AD)

Niersteiner Oelberg Spät., Gessert (NI)

Niersteiner Spiegelberg Kab., Guntrum (HAG)

1989

Binger Scharlachberg Riesling Spät., Villa Sachsen (SAF)

Deidesheimer Leinhöhle Kab., Bassermann-Jordan (HAG, RAE)

★ Freinsheimer Goldberg Riesling Spät., Lingenfelder (OD)

Johannisberger Klaus Riesling Kab., Schönborn (JU)

Schloss Böckelheimer Kupfergrube Riesling Kab., Staatliche Weinbaudomäne (EY)

★ Schloss Vollrads Grün-Gold, Matuschka-Greiffenclau (EL)

1988

Deidesheimer Kieselberg Riesling Kab., Basserman-Jordan (WCL)

Johannisberger Erntebringer Riesling Kab., Hessisches Weingut (WCL)

Johannisberger Erntebringer Riesling Kab., Sichel (HUN)

★ Kiedricher Sandgrub Riesling Kab., Schloss Groenesteyn (VIC)

1987

Wallhäuser Johannisberg Riesling Aus., Prinz zu Salm-Dalberg'sches Weingut (WCL)

1985

Deidesheimer Hohenmorgen Riesling Kab., Bassermann-Jordan (LAY)

1983

Norheimer Dellchen Riesling Spät., August Anheuser (HOG)

★ Oestricher Doosberg Riesling Kab., Schönborn (EL)

£7.00 to £7.99

1991

Schloss Vollrads Grün-Gold, Matuschka-Greiffenclau (EL)

1990

Eltviller Sonnenberg Riesling Kab., Simmern (AD)

★ Kiedricher Sandgrub Riesling Kab., Schloss Groenesteyn (HOG)

Kreuznacher Kahlenberg Riesling Spät., Paul Anheuser (ROB)

Schloss Böckelheimer Kupfergrube Riesling Kab., Staatliche Weinbaudomäne (TAN)

★ Wachenheimer Luginsland Riesling Kab., Bürklin-Wolf (JU)

1989

Deidesheimer Leinhöhle Kab., Bassermann-Jordan (JU)

Freinsheimer Goldberg Riesling Spät., Lingenfelder (EY)

Johannisberg Deinhard Heritage Selection (WR, BOT, THR)

★ Johannisberger Erntebringer Riesling Kab., Balthasar Ress (SUM)

Kreuznacher St-Martin Riesling Kab., Anheuser (PE)

Niederhauser Hermannsberg Riesling Spät., Staatliche Weinbaudomäne (EY)

Niersteiner Pettenthal Riesling Spät., Balbach (JU)

1988

★ Forster Jesuitengarten Riesling Kab., Bassermann-Jordan (EY)

Kreuznacher Kahlenberg Riesling Spät., Paul Anheuser (CV)

Kreuznacher St-Martin Riesling Kab., Anheuser (PE)
Niersteiner Oelberg Riesling Kab., Herrnsheim (HAC)
Niersteiner Pettenthal Riesling Spät., Balbach (VIC)
Schloss Vollrads Blau-Gold, Matuschka-Greiffenclau (EL)
Wachenheimer Rechbächel Riesling Kab., Bürklin-Wolf (DI)

1987

Grosskarlbacher Burgweg Scheurebe Kab., Lingenfelder (HAC)

1986

Erbacher Marcobrunnen Riesling Kab., Simmern (LAY)
Ruppertsberger Gaisböhl Riesling Kab., Bürklin-Wolf (DI)

1985

Hochheimer Domdechaney Riesling Spät., Domdechaney Werner'sches (VIC)
★ Schloss Böckelheimer Kupfergrube Riesling Spät., Staatliche Weinbaudomäne (RAE)

1983

Traisener Rotenfels Riesling Spät., Crusius (HOG)

£8.00 to £9.99

1990

Oppenheimer Herrenberg Scheurebe Spät., Guntrum (WRI)
Schloss Vollrads Blau-Silber, Matuschka-Greiffenclau (EL)
Wachenheimer Böhlig Riesling Spät., Bürklin-Wolf (JU)

1989

Forster Kirchenstuck Riesling Kab., Bassermann-Jordan (BIB, JU)
Hochheimer Königin Victoria Berg Riesling Kab., Deinhard (WHI)
Johannisberger Erntebringer Riesling Kab., Deinhard (BER)
Riesling Spät. Trocken, Weingut Lingenfelder (NI)
Schloss Böckelheimer Kupfergrube Riesling Spät., Staatliche Weinbaudomäne (HOG)

Stars (★) indicate wines selected by the editors as particularly good value in their class.

★ Steinberger Riesling Kab., Staatsweingüter Eltville (HOG)

1988

Deidesheimer Hohenmorgen Riesling Spät., Basser-Jordan (EY, RAE)
Forster Jesuitengarten Riesling Kab., Bürklin-Wolf (JU)
Forster Jesuitengarten Riesling Spät., Bassermann-Jordan (VIC)
★ Forster Ungeheuer Riesling Spät., Deinhard (PEN)
Hochheimer Hölle Riesling Kab., Aschrott (AV)
Niederhauser Hermannsberg Riesling Spät., Staatliche Weinbaudomäne (EY)

1987

Rüdesheimer Berg Roseneck Riesling Kab., Deinhard (PEN)

1986

Niersteiner Oelberg Riesling Aus., Senfter (HOG)
Rauenthaler Baiken Riesling QbA Charta, Verwaltung der Staatsweingüter Eltville (HAC)

1985

★ Erbacher Siegelsberg Riesling Kab., Schloss Reinhartshausen (HAC)

Niederhauser Hermannshöhle Riesling Spät., Staatliche Weinbaudomäne (HOG)
Winkeler Hasensprung Riesling Spät., Deinhard (BER)
1983
Hochheimer Hölle Riesling Spät., Aschrott (BER)
★ Wachenheimer Gerümpel Riesling Spät., Bürklin-Wolf (GRE)

£10.00 to £11.99

1992
Freinsheimer Goldberg Riesling Spät., Lingenfelder (HAC)
Freinsheimer Goldberg Scheurebe Spät., Lingenfelder (HAC)
1990
Freinsheimer Goldberg Riesling Spät., Lingenfelder (ROB)
Scheurebe Spät. Trocken, Lingenfelder (WCL)
1989
Freinsheimer Goldberg Riesling Spät., Lingenfelder (WCL)
1988
Forster Ungeheuer Riesling Spät., Deinhard (BER)
Hochheimer Königin Victoria Berg Riesling Spät., Deinhard (PEN)
Niersteiner Rehbach Riesling Spät., Heyl zu Herrnsheim (HAC)
Scheurebe Spät. Trocken, Lingenfelder (AD)
1985
Hochheimer Hölle Riesling Spät., Aschrott (BER)
1983
Hochheimer Herrenberg Riesling Aus., Nagler (HOG)
Hochheimer Königin Victoria Berg Riesling Spät., Deinhard (PEN)
Rauenthaler Baiken Riesling Spät., Staatsweingüter Eltville (HOG, GRE)

£12.00 to £14.99

1983
Wachenheimer Gerümpel Riesling Spät., Bürklin-Wolf (WS)
Wachenheimer Mandelgarten Scheurebe Aus., Bürklin-Wolf (PE)
1976
Erbacher Siegelsberg Riesling Spät., Schloss Reinhartshausen (BER)

£15.00 to £19.99

1989
Geisenheimer Rothenberg Riesling Aus., Deinhard (JU)
1985
Wachenheimer Rechbächel Riesling Aus., Bürklin-Wolf (AD)
1983
Wachenheimer Böhlig Riesling Aus., Bürklin-Wolf (BER)
1979
Erbacher Marcobrunnen Riesling Spät., Staatsweingüter Eltville (HAC)
1976
Johannisberger Hölle Riesling Aus., Deinhard (BER)

£20.00 to £29.99

1976
Oppenheimer Krötenbrunnen, Deinhard (PEN)
Niersteiner Oelberg Riesling BA, Herrnsheim (HAC)

c. £38.00

1985
Grosskarlbacher Burgweg Scheurebe TBA ½ bottle, Lingenfelder (HAC)

RED

£9.00 to £12.00

1990
Spätburgunder QbA, Lingenfelder (HAC)
1989
Spätburgunder QbA, Lingenfelder (VIG, ROB)

Webster's *is an annual publication. We welcome your suggestions for next year's edition.*

MOSEL/FRANKEN/BADEN

Kab.	=	Kabinett
Spät.	=	Spätlese
Aus.	=	Auslese
BA	=	Beerenauslese
TBA	=	Trockenbeerenauslese

MOSEL WHITE

Under £3.00

Non-vintage
Sainsbury's Mosel (SAI)
Sainsbury's Piesporter Michelsberg (SAI)
1991
Waitrose Piesporter Michelsberg (WAI)
1990
Waitrose Bereich Bernkastel (WAI)

£3.00 to £3.99

1992
Piesporter Michelsberg Schneider (EL)
1991
Bereich Bernkastel Riesling, Schneider (WHI, EL)
Piesporter Michelsberg Reh (BIB)
Piesporter Michelsberg Rudolf Müller (CB)
1990
Wiltinger Scharzberg Riesling Kab., Zentralkellerei (TES)
1988
Deinhard Green Label (VIC)

£4.00 to £4.99

1991
Bereich Bernkastel, Rudolf Müller (CB)
1990
Deinhard Green Label (AUG)
★ Falkensteiner Hofberg Riesling Kab., F-W-Gymnasium (WS)
1989
Deinhard Green Label (WHI)
1987
Deinhard Green Label (PEN)

£5.00 to £5.99

1992
★ Graacher Himmelreich Riesling Kab., Kesselstatt (ASD)
1991
Bernkasteler Badstube Riesling, Lauerberg (WAI)
1990
Reiler Mullay Hofberg Riesling Kab., Rudolf Müller (TAN)
1988
Falkensteiner Hofberg Riesling Kab., F-W-Gymnasium (VIC)
★ Scharzhofberger Riesling Kab., Kesselstatt (EL)
1987
Neefer Frauenberg Riesling Kab. (BOR)
1986
Erdener Treppchen Riesling Spät., Monchhof (WAI)

£6.00 to £6.99

1989
Brauneberger Juffer Riesling Kab., Kesselstatt (BY)
Graacher Himmelreich Riesling Kab., F-W-Gymnasium (WHI, LOR)
Waldracher Krone Riesling Kab., Scherf (BER)
★ Wehlener Sonnenuhr Riesling Kab., Richter (SUM)
1988
Bernkasteler Badstube Riesling Kab., Loosen (EY)
Ockfener Bockstein Riesling Spät., Dr Fischer (ASD)
Scharzhofberger Riesling Kab., Kesselstatt (NI)
★ Serriger Antoniusberg Riesling Kab., Simon (HOG)
Wehlener Nonnenberg Riesling, S.A. Prüm (DI)

£7.00 to £7.99

1991
Serriger Schloss Saarsteiner Riesling Kab., Schloss Saarstein (BIB)
1990
Bernkasteler Lay Riesling Kab., Loosen (GE)
Graacher Himmelreich Riesling Spät., F-W-Gymnasium (EY, CV, WS)
★ Oberemmeler Hutte Riesling Spät., Hövel (EY)
Serriger Schloss Saarsteiner Riesling Kab., Schloss Saarstein (BAR)
1989
Josephshofer Riesling Spät., Kesselstatt (NI)
★ Kaseler Nies'chen Riesling Spät., Bischöfliches Priesterseminar (JU)

Scharzhofberger Riesling Kab., Hövel (BOT, WR, THR)
Serriger Schloss Saarsteiner Riesling Kab., Schloss Saarstein (SUM)

1988
Graacher Himmelreich Riesling Spät., F-W-Gymnasium (LOR)
Kaseler Nies'chen Riesling Kab., Deinhard (PEN)

1983
★ Bernkasteler Badstube Riesling Spät., Heidemanns-Bergweiler (HOG)
Ockfener Bockstein Riesling Spät., Rheinart (GRE)

£8.00 to £9.99

1990
Bernkasteler Bratenhöfchen Riesling Spät., Lauerburg (BE)
Erdener Treppchen Riesling Spät., Monchhof (WS, JU)
Scharzhofberger Riesling Spät., Hövel (WW)
Serriger Schloss Saarsteiner Riesling Spät., Schloss Saarstein (BAR)
★ Trittenheimer Apotheke Riesling Aus., F-W-Gymnasium (EY)

1989
Bernkasteler Lay Riesling Kab., Loosen (BER, ROB)
Eitelsbacher Marienholz Riesling Spät., Bischöfliches Konvikt (PE)
Enkircher Steffensberg Riesling Spät., Immich (GE)
Josephshof Riesling Spät., Kesselstatt (JU)
★ Ockfener Bockstein Riesling Spät., Dr Fischer (JU)
Scharzhofberger Riesling Spät., Hohe Domkirche (HOG)
Wehlener Sonnenuhr Riesling Kab., J.J. Prüm (NI, HOG)

1988
Bernkasteler Badstube Riesling Spät., Heidemanns-Bergweiler (GRE)
Graacher Himmelreich Riesling Aus., F-W-Gymnasium (TES)
Wehlener Sonnenuhr Kab., J.J. Prüm (GAU)
Wehlener Sonnenuhr Riesling Spät., Weins Prüm (WR, BOT, THR)

In each price band wines are listed in vintage order. Within each vintage they are listed in A–Z order.

1985
Josephshof Riesling Spät., Kesselstatt (JU)
Maximin-Grünhäuser Abtsberg Riesling Kab., Schubert (GRE)
★ Urziger Würzgarten Riesling Aus., Bischöfliches Priesterseminar (JU)

1983
Falkensteiner Hofberg Riesling Spät., F-W-Gymnasium (GRE)

£10.00 to £11.99

1990
Graacher Himmelreich Riesling Aus., F-W-Gymnasium (LOR)
Maximin-Grünhäuser Herrenberg Riesling Kab., Schubert (JU)

1989
Maximin-Grünhäuser Abtsberg Riesling Kab., Schubert (JU)
Scharzhofberger Riesling Kab., Egon Müller (JU)

1988
Trittenheimer Apotheke Riesling Aus., F-W-Gymnasium (VIC)

1983
Kaseler Nies'chen Riesling Aus., Bischöfliches Priesterseminar (GRE, PE)
★ Serriger Vogelsang Riesling Aus., Staatlichen Weinbaudomänen (HAC)

£12.00 to £14.99

1990
Oberemmeler Hutte Riesling Aus., Hövel (EY, WW)

1989
Maximin-Grünhäuser Abtsberg Riesling Spät., Schubert (JU)
Wehlener Sonnenuhr Riesling Kab., Deinhard (TAN)

1983
Bernkasteler Bratenhöfchen Riesling Aus., Deinhard (PEN)
Graacher Himmelreich Riesling Spät., Prüm (WS)
Josephshofer Riesling Aus., Kesselstatt (JU)

Oberemmeler Hutte Riesling Aus., Hövel (WS)
Wehlener Sonnenuhr Riesling Aus., F.W. Prüm (PE)

£15.00 to £19.99

1990
Brauneberger Juffer Sonnenuhr Riesling Aus., Fritz Haag (JU)
Graacher Himmelreich Riesling Aus., J.J. Prüm (NI)
1989
Brauneberger Juffer Sonnenuhr Riesling Aus., Fritz Haag (VIG)
Scharzhofberger Riesling Spät., Egon Müller (JU)
1988
Wehlener Sonnenuhr Aus., J.J. Prüm (GAU)
1986
Josephshofer Riesling Aus., Kesselstatt (HAG)
1983
Bernkasteler Graben Riesling Spät., Deinhard (AD)
Kaseler Kehrnagel Riesling Aus., Simon (HUN)
Wehlener Abtei Eiswein, Schneider ½ bottle (WHI)

£20.00 to £29.99

1990
Maximin-Grünhäuser Abtsberg Riesling Aus., Schubert (JU)
1989
Maximin-Grünhäuser Abtsberg Riesling Aus., Schubert (JU)
Mulheimer Helenkloster Riesling Eiswein, Richter ½bottle (SUM)

£30.00 to £39.99

1990
Mulheimer Helenkloster Riesling Eiswein, Richter ½bottle (BER, SUM)
1983
Bernkasteler Doctor Riesling Aus., Deinhard (BER)

£45.00 to £55.00

1983
Bernkasteler Graben Riesling Eiswein, Deinhard ½bottle (AD)
1975
Bernkasteler Bratenhöfchen Riesling BA. Eiswein, Deinhard (WRI)

c. £77.00

1976
Serriger Würzberg TBA, Simon (BOR)

FRANKEN WHITE

£8.00 to £9.50

1991
Schloss Castell Silvaner Trocken, Fürstlich Castell'sches Domänenamt (HAG)
1988
Casteller Kirchberg Müller-Thurgau, Fürstlich Castell'sches Domänenamt (HAC, WCL)

BADEN WHITE

Under £4.50

Nonvintage
Baden Dry, Zentralkellerei (BAR)
Sainsbury's Baden (SAI)

c. £7.00

1988
Rivaner, Karl Heinz Johner (HAC)

c. £11.00

1988
Pinot Blanc, Karl Heinz Johner (HAC)

BADEN RED

c £16.00

1987
Pinot Noir, Karl Heinz Johner (HAC)

GERMAN SPARKLING

Under £6.00

Non-vintage
Henkell Trocken (TES, SAF, VIC)

£6.00 to £7.99

Non-vintage
Henkell Trocken (AUG, WHI, UN, WRI)

*Please remember that **Webster's** is a price GUIDE and not a price LIST. It is not meant to replace up-to-date merchants' lists.*

ITALY

NORTH-WEST RED

Under £4.00

1990
★ Dolcetto d'Acqui Viticoltori dell'Acquese (VIC)

£4.00 to £4.99

1992
Barbera d'Asti Viticoltori dell'Acquese (AD)
Dolcetto d'Acqui Viticoltori dell'Acquese (AD)
1991
Barbera d'Asti Viticoltori dell'Acquese (EL)
1989
Barbera d'Alba Fontanafredda (PEN)

£5.00 to £5.99

1988
★ Barbaresco Ascheri (WCL)
Barbera Oltrepò Pavese, Fugazza (WHI)
★ Inferno Nino Negri (HOG, GRE)
Sassella Nino Negri (HOG)
1987
Barolo Terre del Barolo (SAF, MAR)
1983
Gattinara Berteletti (HOG)

£6.00 to £6.99

1991
Dolcetto d'Alba Corsini, Mascarello (BOT)
Dolcetto d'Alba Priavino, Voerzio (OD)
1990
Dolcetto d'Alba Ascheri (WCL)
1989
★ Ronco de Mompiano Pasolini (WCL)
1988
Barbera d'Asti Guasti Clemente (HOG)
Barolo Aliberti (BY)
Barolo Fontanafredda (AUG)
Dolcetto d'Alba Bruno Giacosa (JU)
1987
Barolo Giacosa Fratelli (TES)
Gattinara Travaglini (EL)
1982
★ Barolo Riserva Fontanafredda (OD)

£7.00 to £7.99

1990
Dolcetta d'Alba Clerico (BIB)
Dolcetto d'Alba Bruno Giacosa (AD)
Nebbiolo d'Alba San Rocco, Mascarello (GRE)
Ronco de Mompiano Pasolini (WCL, GRG)
1989
Barbaresco Ascheri (OD)
Barbera d'Alba Altare (WCL)
Barolo Ascheri (OD)
1988
Barolo Fontanafredda (WHI, DAV, BOT, WR)
Ronco de Mompiano Pasolini (VA, BAR)
1986
Barolo Riserva Borgogno (ASD)
1985
Barbaresco Fontanafredda (PEN)

£8.00 to £9.99

1991
Dolcetto d'Alba Aldo Conterno (WCL)
Nebbiolo d'Alba San Rocco, Mascarello (WCL)
1990
Barbera d'Alba Aldo Conterno (VA, WCL)
Barbera d'Alba Conca Tre Pile, Aldo Conterno (SOM, EY, WCL)
Nebbiolo d'Alba San Rocco, Mascarello (WCL, JU)
1989
Barolo Ascheri (WCL, VA)
Freisa delle Langhe Vajra (GRE, WCL)
Nebbiolo d'Alba San Rocco, Mascarello (ROB)
1988
Barbaresco Santo Stefano, Castello di Neive (VA)
Barolo Ascheri (GRE, LAY)
Barolo Oddero (ROB)
Freisa delle Langhe Vajra (GAU)
Nebbiolo d'Alba San Rocco, Mascarello (BER)
Nebbiolo delle Langhe Vajra (WCL)
1987
Barbaresco Fontanafredda (VIG)
Barbaresco Riserva Borgogno (LAY)
Barbaresco Sori Paytin, Pasquero (WCL)
Barolo Fontanafredda (HUN)
Barolo Terre del Barolo (HAH)
Franciacorta Rosso Cá del Bosco (WCL)
1983
★ Barbaresco Gallina di Neive, Bruno Giacosa (RAE)
Gattinara Travaglini (WHI)
1982
Barolo Riserva Fontanafredda (NI)
1976
Barbaresco Sori Paytin, Pasquero (WCL)

£10.00 to £12.49

1989
Sfursat Nino Negri (GRE)
Vignaserra Voerzio (OD)
1988
Barolo Zonchera Ceretto (TAN)
1987
Barolo la Serra di la Morra, Voerzio (OD)
1985
Barolo Montanello, Monchiero (WCL)
Barolo Riserva Borgogno (ROB, PE)
Sfursat Nino Negri (GRE)
1980
★ Barolo Montanello, Monchiero (WCL)
1978
Barolo Fontanafredda (HOG)

£12.50 to £14.99

1988
Barbaresco Sori Paytin, Pasquero (WS)
Barolo Monprivato, Mascarello (REI)
Barolo Prunotto (WS)
Dolcetto d'Alba Vignabajla, Gaja (OD)
Sfursat Nino Negri (VIG)
1987
Barolo Bussia Soprana, Aldo Conterno (PIP)
Maurizio Zanella, Ca' del Bosco (WCL)
Nebbiolo Il Favot, Aldo Conterno (WCL, PIP)
1986
Barolo Marcenasco, Renato Ratti (PE)
Barolo Pio Cesare (DI)
Nebbiolo Il Favot, Aldo Conterno (WCL)
1985
★ Barolo Pio Cesare (GRE)
Barolo Soriginestra, Fantino (WCL)
Nebbiolo Il Favot, Aldo Conterno (WCL)
1983
Barolo Bruno Giacosa (RAE)
1982
Barbaresco Bruno Giacosa (HOG)
Barolo Riserva Fontanafredda (VIG)
Carema Ferrando (WCL)
1979
Barolo Montanello, Monchiero (WCL)
Barbaresco Bruno Giacosa (HOG)
Barolo Riserva Fontanafredda (VIG)
Carema Ferrando (WCL)

Stars (★) indicate wines selected by the editors as particularly good value in their class.

£15.00 to £19.99

1990
Nebbiolo Il Favot, Aldo Conterno (WCL)
1988
Barolo Monprivato, Mascarello (GE, WCL)
1987
Barbera d'Alba Vignarey, Gaja (VA, TW)
Barolo Bussia Soprana, Aldo Conterno (WCL)
Barolo Monprivato, Mascarello (WCL)
1986
Barolo Bussia Soprana, Aldo Conterno (ROB, TAN, WCL)
1985
Barbaresco Marcarini, Mascarello (WCL)
Barolo Bricco Rocche Brunate, Ceretto (NI)
Barolo Bussia Soprana, Aldo Conterno (WCL)
Barolo Pio Cesare (DI)
1982
Barolo Gattinera, Fontanafredda (VA)
Barolo Lazzarito, Fontanafredda (GRE, VA)
Barolo Montanello, Monchiero (WCL)
Barolo Riserva Giacomo Conterno (VA)
1978
Barolo Gattinera, Fontanafredda (HOG)
Barolo Montanello, Monchiero (WCL)
1967
Barolo Borgogno (WCL)
1964
Barolo Borgogno (WCL)

£20.00 to £29.99

1988
Barolo Bricco Rocche Brunate, Ceretto (BOT, WR)
Maurizio Zanella, Ca' del Bosco (VA)
1986
Barolo Monprivato, Mascarello (JU)
1985
Barolo Bricco Rocche Brunate, Ceretto (TAN)
Barolo Giacomo Conterno (VA)
Barolo Monprivato, Mascarello (GRE, WCL, GAU)
1983
Maurizio Zanella, Ca' del Bosco (VA)
1982
Barolo Conca, Renato Ratti (AD)
1978
Barbaresco Cantina del Barbaresco (GRG)
Barbaresco Vigneto Monticchio, Produttori (WCL)
Barolo Borgogno (VA)
Barolo Pio Cesare (WCL)

1976
Barolo Vigneto Villero, Ceretto (WCL)
1974
Barbaresco Bricco Asili, Ceretto (WCL)
Barolo Montanello, Monchiero (WCL)
1971
Barolo Borgogno (VA)
Barolo Mascarello (WCL)
Barolo Montanello, Monchiero (WCL)
Barolo Riserva Borgogno (GRE)
1970
Barolo Ceretto (WCL)
Barolo Montanello, Monchiero (WCL)
1969
Barolo Mascarello (WCL)
Barolo Montanello, Monchiero (WCL)
1967
Barolo Ceretto (WCL)

£30.00 to £39.99

1988
Pinero Ca' del Bosco (WCL)
1987
Pinero Ca' del Bosco (WCL)
1986
Darmagi Gaja (VA)
1983
Darmagi Gaja (VA)
1979
Barolo Monfortino, Giacomo Conterno (WCL)
1971
Barolo Ceretto (WCL)
Barolo Pio Cesare (WCL)
Barolo Riserva Borgogno (ROB)
1970
Barbaresco Vigneto Montefico, Ceretto (WCL)
Barolo Zonchetta, Ceretto (WCL)

1967
Barolo Borgogno (VA)
Barolo Mascarello (WCL)
1961
Barolo Borgogno (VA)
Barolo Riserva Borgogno (BU)

£40.00 to £49.99

1970
Barolo Monfortino, Giacomo Conterno (WCL)
1968
Barolo Giacomo Conterno (WCL)
1964
Barolo Prunotto (WCL)
Barolo Bussia, Prunotto (WCL)
1961
Barolo Pio Cesare (WCL)

£50.00 to £69.99

1986
Barbaresco Sori San Lorenzo, Gaja (TW)
1983
Barbaresco Sori Tildin, Gaja (VA)
1982
Barbaresco Gaja (WCL)
1978
Barbaresco Gaja (VA, TW)
1964
Barbaresco Gaja (WCL)

c. £150.00

1961
Barbaresco Gaja (VA)

NORTH-WEST WHITE

Under £6.00

1992
★ Moscato d'Asti Ascheri (WCL)
1991
Moscato d'Asti Chiarlo (NI)
1990
Moscato d'Asti Chiarlo (WAI)

£6.00 to £7.99

1992
★ Favorita Deltetto (WCL)
Gavi Fontanafredda (HAG)
1991
Favorita Deltetto (WCL)
★ Gavi dei Gavi, la Scolca (DI)
1990
Favorita Malvira (AD)
Gavi Fontanafredda (ROB)
Mompiano Bianco Pasolini (WCL, VA)
1987
Gavi Fontanafredda (HUN)

£8.00 to £9.99

1992
Arneis del Piemonte San Michel, Deltetto (WCL)

1991
Arneis del Piemonte Renesio, Damonte (AD)
Arneis del Piemonte San Michel, Deltetto (WCL)

£10.00 to £20.00

1991
Arneis Blange Ceretto (ROB)
1989
Pio di Lei, Pio Cesare (VA)

£20.00 to £30.00

1989
Chardonnay Ca' del Bosco (ROB, VA, WCL)
1988
Chardonnay Rossj Bass, Gaja (TW)

c. £31.00

1989
Chardonnay Rossj Bass, Gaja (VA)

NORTH-WEST SPARKLING

Under £5.00

Non-vintage
Asda Asti Spumante (ASD)
Asda Moscato Spumante (ASD)
Sainsbury's Asti Spumante (SAI)
Tesco Asti Spumante (TES)

£5.00 to £5.99

Non-vintage
Asti Spumante Martini (HOG, WAI, TES, GA)
Gancia Pinot di Pinot (VA)
Gancia Spumante (VA)

£6.00 to £6.99

Non-vintage
Asti Spumante Fontanafredda (VA)
Asti Spumante Martini (WRI, AUG, VIC, VIN, WR, BOT, THR, DAV, UN, OD)

7.00 to 7.99

Non-vintage
Asti Spumante Martini (EL, TAN, HAG)

c. £14.00

1988
Mompiano Spumante Brut Pasolini (WCL)

c. £20.00

Non-vintage
Franciacorta Brut, Ca' del Bosco (VA)

NORTH-EAST RED

Under £3.00

Non-vintage
Asda Valpolicella (ASD)
Sainsbury's Bardolino Classico (SAI)
Sainsbury's Valpolicella Classico (SAI)
1991
Waitrose Valpolicella Classico (WAI)

£3.00 to £3.99

1992
Victoria Wine Valpolicella (VIC)
1990
★ Bardolino Classico Superiore Boscaini (WHI)
Valpolicella Classico Negarine (SAI)
1989
Valpolicella Classico Boscaini (SAF, WHI)

£4.00 to £4.99

1992
Bardolino Portalupi (VA)
Valpolicella Classico Superiore Zenato (DAV)
1991
Valpolicella Classico Superiore Masi (PIP)
Valpolicella Classico Superiore Zenato (DAV)
1990
Bardolino Classico Superiore Masi (PIP, DI)
Teroldego Rotaliano Gaierhof (WAI)
Valpolicella Classico Masi (AUG, OD)
★ Valpolicella Classico Superiore Masi (DI)
Valpolicella Classico Superiore Rizzardi (GRE)
Valpolicella Classico Superiore Villa Girardi (NI)
Valpolicella Classico Superiore Zenato (WR, THR, BOT)
1989
Bardolino Classico Superiore Rizzardi (HOG, GRE)
Valpolicella Classico Castello d'Illasi, Santi (HOG)
Valpolicella Classico Superiore Masi (BY)
Valpolicella Classico Superiore Rizzardi (HOG)
1988
Valpolicella Classico Tedeschi (LAY)

£5.00 to £5.99

1992
★ Molinara Quintarelli (BIB)
1991
Bardolino Classico Ca' Bordenis (TAN)
Valpolicella Classico Allegrini (WCL, GRG)

1990
Cabernet Grave del Friuli, Collavini (VA)
Maso Lodron Letrari (WS)
1989
Lagrein Dunkel Viticoltori Alto Adige (VA)
1988
Valpolicella Classico Superiore Tommasi (LOR)
Valpolicella Classico Superiore Valverde, Tedeschi (AD)

£6.00 to £7.99

1991
Molinara Quintarelli (AD)
1988
Cabernet Riserva, Lageder (WCL)
Campo Fiorin Masi (PIP, VA, DI)
Refosco Grave del Friuli Collavini (VA)
1986
Merlot Collio Collavini (VIC)

£8.00 to £9.99

1990
Valpolicella Classico Palazzo della Torre, Allegrini (LAY)
1988
Castello Guerrieri (NA)
Palazzo della Torre, Allegrini (GRG, VA)
Valpolicella Classico la Grola, Allegrini (VA, WCL)
Valpolicella Classico Palazzo della Torre, Allegrini (WCL, GAU)
Valpolicella Classico Superiore La Grola, Allegrini (WS)
Venegazzù della Casa Loredan-Gasparini (GRE, VIC)
1987
Castello Guerrieri (HOG)
Recioto Amarone Montresor (HOG)
Valpolicella Classico Quintarelli (BIB)
Venegazzù della Casa Loredan-Gasparini (VA, ROB)
1986
Recioto Amarone Santi (HUN)
Valpolicella Classico Superiore Quintarelli (AD)
Valpolicella Monte Cà Paletta, Quintarelli (RAE)
1985
Recioto Amarone Negrar (EL)
★ Recioto Amarone Tommasi (LOR)
Valpolicella Monte Cà Paletta, Quintarelli (RAE)

£10.00 to £12.99

1988
Cabernet Grai (BIB)
Recioto Amarone Tedeschi (ROB, LAY)
Recioto Classico della Valpolicella Allegrini (WCL)
1986
Cabernet Grai (BIB)
1985
Recioto Amarone Bolla (VA)

Recioto Amarone della Valpolicella Allegrini (TAN, WS, GRG)
Recioto Amarone Fabiano (GRE)

£13.00 to £14.99

1989
Cabernet Sauvignon Puiatti (WCL)
Pinot Nero Puiatti (WCL)
1988
Venegazzù della Casa Black Label, Loredan-Gasparini (GRE)
1986
Venegazzù della Casa Black Label, Loredan-Gasparini (VA)
1978
★ Recioto Amarone Quintarelli (AS)

£15.00 to £20.00

1990
Recioto Classico della Valpolicella Allegrini (JU)
1988
Recioto Amarone Mezzanella, Masi (PIP)
1986
Recioto Amarone Mezzanella, Masi (WCL)
1983
Recioto Amarone Fieramonte, Allegrini (VA, WCL)
1980
Recioto Amarone Masi (DI)

£20.00 to £29.99

1986
La Poja, Allegrini (AD, WCL, VA)
1980
Recioto Amandorlato Monte Ca' Paletta (AD)

c. £35.00

1983
Recioto della Valpolicella Quintarelli (WCL)
1979
Nebbiolo Recioto della Valpolicella Classico Quintarelli (AD)

NORTH-EAST WHITE

Under £3.00

Non-vintage
Asda Soave (ASD)
Sainsbury's Soave (SAI)
Sainsbury's Verduzzo del Piave (SAI)
Tesco Soave (TES)
1991
Waitrose Soave (WAI)

£3.00 to £3.99

1992
Bianco di Custoza Pasqua (SAI)
Chardonnay Ca' Donini (WHI, AUG)
Pinot Grigio Ca' Donini (VIC, AUG)
1991
Chardonnay Ca' Donini (WHI)
Soave Classico Boscaini (SAF, WHI)
Tocai Friulano di Aquileia, Ca' Bolani (SAI)
1990
★ Bianco di Custoza Tommasi (LOR)
Lugana Tommasi (LOR)
Pinot Grigio Ca' Donini (WHI)
Pinot Grigio Ca'vit (ROB)
Soave Classico Boscaini (SAF)
Soave Classico Superiore Tommasi (LOR)

£4.00 to £4.99

1992
Soave Classico di Monteforte Santi (WHG)
Soave Classico Masi (AUG)
Soave Classico Superiore Masi (PIP)
Soave Classico Tedeschi (LAY)
★ Soave Classico Zenato (ASD, DAV)
1991
Asda Chardonnay Alto Adige (ASD)
Pinot Grigio Ca' Donini (BAR)
Pinot Grigio Ca'vit (TAN, LO)
Sainsbury's Chardonnay Alto Adige (SAI)
Soave Classico di Monteforte Santi (WHG)
Soave Classico Superiore Masi (DI)
1990
★ Pinot Grigio Tiefenbrunner (TES)
Soave Classico di Monteforte Santi (ROB)
Soave Classico Zenato (WAI)
Tocai di San Martino, Zenato (WAI)

£5.00 to £5.99

1992
Lugana di San Benedetto, Zenato (DAV)
1991
Lugana Cà dei Frati (SOM)
Pinot Grigio Tiefenbrunner (WHI)
Soave Classico Pieropan (GRE)
Tocai di San Martino della Battaglia, Zenato (JU)
1990
Chardonnay di Appiano Viticoltori Alto Adige (VA)
Chardonnay Tiefenbrunner (WHI, AD)
Pinot Bianco Tiefenbrunner (AD)
Soave Classico Anselmi (OD)
Soave Classico Monte Tenda, Tedeschi (AD)

£6.00 to £7.99

1992
Chardonnay EnoFriulia (PIP)
Lugana Cà dei Frati, Dal Cero (TAN)
Pinot Grigio EnoFriulia (WCL)
Pinot Grigio Santa Margherita (VA)
Soave Classico Col Baraca, Masi (PIP)
Soave Classico Monte Carbonare, Di Suavia (BIB)
Soave Classico Pieropan (WCL)
1991
Chardonnay EnoFriulia (WCL)
Gewürztraminer Tiefenbrunner (VA, TAN)
Lugana Cà dei Frati, Dal Cero (VA, LAY)
Pinot Grigio Lageder (BY, WHG, GRG, HIC, BER)
Soave Classico Superiore Anselmi (VA)
Soave Classico Superiore Pieropan (SUM, TAN)
★ Soave Classico Vigneto Calvarino, Pieropan (EY, LAY, WCL, GRG)
Soave Classico Vigneto la Rocca, Pieropan (GRE)
Tocai EnoFriulia (WCL)
Vinattieri Bianco (BIB)
1990
Chardonnay Tiefenbrunner (TAN)
Chardonnay Vinattieri (BY)
Gewürztraminer Tiefenbrunner (AD)
Lugana Cà dei Frati (BAR)

Lugana Cà dei Frati, Dal Cero (LOR, WCL)
Pinot Bianco Grai (BIB)
Pinot Grigio Lageder (WCL)
Soave Classico Monte Carbonara, Tessari (AD)
Soave Classico Superiore Pieropan (LOR, BAR)
Soave Classico Vigneto Calvarino, Pieropan (GAU)
Vinattieri Bianco (BIB)
1989
Lugana Cà dei Frati, Dal Cero (GAU)
Pinot Bianco Grai (BIB)

£8.00 to £9.99

1991
Pinot Grigio Collio, Puiatti (SOM)
Soave Classico Capitel Foscarino, Anselmi (VA)
Soave Classico Superiore Masi (REI)
1990
Soave Classico Superiore Pieropan (BY)
Soave Classico Vigneto la Rocca, Pieropan (WCL, GAU)
1989
★ Recioto di Soave Capitelli, Anselmi (OD)
1979
Pinot Bianco Collio, Puiatti (SOM)

£10.00 to £11.99

1991
Chardonnay Collio, Puiatti (WCL)
Pinot Bianco Jermann (VA)
Pinot Grigio Collio, Felluga (VA)
Riesling Renano Collio, Puiatti (WCL)
1990
Chardonnay Collio, Puiatti (WCL)
Pinot Bianco Collio, Puiatti (WCL, GAU)
Pinot Grigio Collio, Puiatti (GAU, BAR, JU)
Ribolla Collio, Puiatti (WCL)
1989
Pinot Bianco Collio, Puiatti (WCL)
1988
Vendemmia Tardiva Pojer e Sandri 1/2 Bottle (WCL)
1987
Chardonnay Vinattieri (BIB)

£12.00 to £14.99

1991
Pinot Grigio Jermann (BAR)
1990
Chardonnay Jermann (REI)
1988
Chardonnay Löwengang, Lageder (WCL)

£15.00 to £25.00

1990
Recioto di Soave Capitelli, Anselmi (VA)
1989
Torcolato Vino Liquoroso Maculan (VA)
1988
Torcolato Vino Liquoroso Maculan (AD)
1987
Recioto di Soave Capitelli, Anselmi (BY)
1983
Vin de la Fabriseria Tedeschi (AD)

c. £41.00

1991
Pinot Grigio Collio, Puiatti (GRG)

NORTH-EAST ROSÉ

c. £4.50

1992
Bardolino Chiaretto, Portalupi (VA)

NORTH-EAST SPARKLING

Under £4.50

Non-vintage
Alionza Frizzante di Castelfranco (BOD, WIC)

£6.50 to £8.00

Non-vintage
Prosecco di Conegliano Carpenè Malvolti (HOG, VA, GRG)

£11.50 to £16.00

Non-vintage
Berlucchi Brut (VA)
Ferrari Brut (VA)
1987
Brut Metodo Classico Carpene Malvolti (GRG)

CENTRAL RED

Under £4.00

1991
Chianti Rufina Villa di Vetrice (GRE)
★ Rosso Cònero San Lorenzo, Umani Ronchi (NI)
Victoria Wine Chianti (VIC)
1990
★ Chianti Rufina Villa di Vetrice (SOM)
Rosso Cònero San Lorenzo, Umani Ronchi (WAI)
Tesco Chianti Classico (TES)
Waitrose Chianti (WAI)

£4.00 to £4.99

1991

Chianti Classico Ruffino (VA)
Chianti Rufina Riserva Tenuta di Remole, Frescobaldi (AMI)
Santa Cristina, Antinori (GRE, VIC)

1990

Chianti Classico Aziano, Ruffino (HOG)
Chianti Classico Rocca delle Macie (NI, SAF, WAI, AUG, DAV)
Chianti Rufina Tenuta di Remole, Frescobaldi (HOG)
Chianti Rufina Villa di Vetrice (PIP, GRG, WCL, VA, AD, ROB, HAH)
★ Parrina Rosso La Parrina (OD, EY, WCL, BAR, VA)
★ Santa Cristina, Antinori (MAJ, WR, BOT, THR)

1989

Chianti Classico Rocca delle Macie (MAJ)
Sainsbury's Chianti Classico (SAI)

1988

Chianti Rufina Riserva Villa di Vetrice (BOT, WR, THR, WCL, BAR)
Chianti Rufina Tenuta di Remole, Frescobaldi (CV)
★ Montefalco Rosso d'Arquata Adanti (OD)

1985

Chianti Rufina Riserva Villa di Monte (TES)

£5.00 to £5.99

1991

★ Carmignano Barco Reale, Capezzana (SOM)
Chianti Fattoria di Gracciano (BIB)

1990

Chianti Classico la Lellera, Matta (WHI, EL)
Chianti Classico San Felice (HOG)
Chianti Fattoria di Gracciano (BIB)
Chianti Rufina Riserva Tenuta di Remole, Frescobaldi (VA)
★ Chianti Rufina Selvapiana (THR, WR, BOT)
Rosso Cònero San Lorenzo, Umani Ronchi (VA, NI)
★ Rosso di Montalcino Campo ai Sassi, Frescobaldi (AMI)

1989

Chianti Classico Felsina Berardenga (SOM)
Chianti Classico Viticcio Landini (LOR)
Chianti Rufina Selvapiana (THR, WR, BOT, WCL)
Montefalco Rosso d'Arquata Adanti (VA)
Morellino di Scansano Poggio Valente (GAU)
Rosso di Montalcino Campo ai Sassi, Frescobaldi (WAI, HOG)

1988

Rosso Cònero Marchetti (WCL)
Rosso Cònero San Lorenzo, Umani Ronchi (GRE, SAI, WR, THR, BOT)

1983

★ Chianti Classico Monsanto (RAE)

£6.00 to £6.99

1991

Carmignano Barco Reale, Capezzana (AD, ROB)
Chianti Classico San Felice (VA)

1990

Carmignano Barco Reale, Capezzana (WCL, REI)
★ Chianti Classico Castello di Volpaia (WS)
Chianti Classico Castello Vicchiomaggio (VIC)
Chianti Classico Rocca delle Macie (AV)
Santa Cristina, Antinori (BUT)

1989

Chianti Classico Castello di Volpaia (AD)
Chianti Classico Isole e Olena (GRG, WCL)
Rosso di Montalcino Altesino (SOM)

1988

★ Chianti Classico Isole e Olena (SOM)

Chianti Classico Riserva Castello di Nipozzano, Frescobaldi (HOG)
Chianti Classico Riserva Rocca delle Macie (WAI)
Chianti Classico Riserva Villa Antinori (GRE, SAI, VA, LAY)
Chianti Classico Villa Antinori (HOG, MAJ)
Rubesco Torgiano Lungarotti (ROB)
★ Vino Nobile di Montepulciano di Casale (SAI)

1987

Chianti Classico Riserva Ducale, Ruffino (HOG)

1986

Vino Nobile di Montepulciano Cerro (HOG)

1985

Chianti Rufina Riserva Villa di Vetrice (EY, AD, WCL, GAU, LOR)

1980

★ Chianti Rufina Riserva Selvapiana (WCL)

£7.00 to £7.99

1991
Chianti Classico Felsina Berardenga (WCL)
Chianti Classico Fontodi (BOT, WR)
1990
Chianti Classico Castello di Fonterutoli (WS)
Chianti Classico Felsina Berardenga (PIP, GRG, WCL, WW)
Chianti Classico Fontodi (WS)
Rosso di Montalcino Altesino (WCL)
★ Rosso di Montalcino il Poggione (AD)
1989
Chianti Classico Castello di Cacchiano (WCL)
Pomino Rosso Frescobaldi (VIC)
Ser Gioveto, Rocca delle Macie (GRE, VA)
Vino Nobile di Montepulciano le Casalte (SOM)
1988
Chianti Classico Castello di Cacchiano (GAU)
Chianti Classico Riserva Antinori (LO)
Chianti Classico Riserva Rocca delle Macie (BAR)
Chianti Rufina Riserva Castello di Nipozzano (AUG, ROB)
Chianti Rufina Riserva Selvapiana (GRG)
Vino Nobile di Montepulciano Bigi (VA)
1987
Chianti Classico Felsina Berardenga (WR, BOT)
Chianti Classico Riserva Rocca delle Macie (VIG)
Chianti Rufina Castello di Nipozzano (VA)
Chianti Rufina Riserva Castello di Nipozzano (WHI)
Grifi Avignonesi (WAI)
★ Vino Nobile di Montepulciano Poliziano (ROB)
Vino Nobile di Montepulciano Riserva, Bigi (GRE)
1986
★ Pomino Rosso Frescobaldi (CV)
Vino Nobile di Montepulciano Bigi (PEN)

£8.00 to £8.99

1991
★ Ornellaia Le Volte, Ludovico Antinori (PIP, NA, REI, WCL, VA)
1990
Brusco dei Barbi Fattoria dei Barbi (VIG)
Chianti Classico Castello di Ama (WS)
Chianti Classico Isole e Olena (VA, WCL)
Ser Gioveto, Rocca delle Macie (VIC)
1989
Chianti Classico Peppoli, Antinori (GRE, VA)
Rosso di Montalcino Talenti (BIB)
Ser Gioveti Toscana (AUG)
Vino Nobile di Montepulciano Cerro (PE)
1988
★ Carmignano Villa Capezzana (WCL)
Chianti Classico Isole e Olena (WCL, GAU, HIC, ROB)
Chianti Classico Riserva Castello di Volpaia (AD)
Chianti Classico Villa Cafaggio (WRI)
Ser Gioveto, Rocca delle Macie (NI, BAR)
Vino Nobile di Montepulciano Baiocchi (WRI)
Vino Nobile di Montepulciano le Casalte (GAU)
1987
Chianti Classico Riserva di Fizzano, Rocca delle Macie (VA, GRE)
Chianti Rufina Riserva Castello di Nipozzano (UN)
Sagrantino di Montefalco, Adanti (VA)
Vino Nobile di Montepulciano Bigi (VIG)
1986
Chianti Classico Riserva di Fizzano, Rocca delle Macie (GA)
Vino Nobile di Montepulciano Cerro (PE)

£9.00 to £9.99

1990
Chianti Classico Peppoli, Antinori (LAY)
1989
Chianti Classico Peppoli, Antinori (WCL, BOT, WR, THR)
Chianti Classico Riserva Peppoli (TAN)
Pomino Rosso Frescobaldi (ROB)
Vino Nobile di Montepulciano Bindella (BIB)
1988
Palazzo Altesi, Altesino (SOM)
Pomino Rosso Frescobaldi (ROB)
Vino Nobile di Montepulciano Bindella (BIB)
★ Vino Nobile di Montepulciano Trerose (LAY)
1987
Ghiaie della Furba, Capezzana (OD)
1986
Chianti Classico Riserva Badia a Coltibuono (AD)
Chianti Classico Riserva Monsanto (RAE)
Vinattieri Rosso Secondo (BY)
★ Vino Nobile di Montepulciano Avignonesi (VA)

1985
Cabernet Sauvignon di Miralduolo, Lungarotti (VA)
1977
★ Chianti Rufina Riserva Villa di Vetrice (GAU)

£10.00 to £11.99

1988
Chianti Classico Riserva Felsina Berardenga (BER)
Chianti Classico Riserva Fontodi (WCL)
Morellino di Scansano Riserva, le Pupille (VA)
Prunaio di Viticcio Landini (LOR)
1987
Chianti Classico Riserva Castello di Cacchiano (WCL)
Chianti Classico Riserva Castello di Volpaia (ROB)
Chianti Classico Riserva Fontodi (WCL)
Grifi Avignonesi (WCL)
1986
Brunello di Montalcino Castelgiocondo (CV, HOG)
Chianti Classico Riserva Castello di Cacchiano (GAU)
Chianti Classico Riserva Felsina Berardenga (WCL)
Chianti Classico Riserva Marchese Antinori (DI)
Chianti Rufina Riserva Selvapiana (GRG)
Vino Nobile di Montepulciano Avignonesi (WCL)
1985
★ Brunello di Montalcino il Poggione (AD)
Ca' del Pazzo Caparzo (GRE)
Chianti Classico Riserva Ducale, Ruffino (HOG)
Chianti Classico Riserva Felsina Berardenga (WCL)
Chianti Classico Riserva Fontodi (WCL)
Vinattieri Rosso (BIB)
1983
Chianti Classico Riserva del Barone, Brolio (WHG)
1980
Chianti Classico Riserva Castello Vicchiomaggio (WRI)

£12.00 to £14.99

1990
Chianti Classico Riecine (WCL)
1989
Cepparello, Isole e Olena (VA, WCL)
1988
Brunello di Montalcino Talenti (BIB)
Ca' del Pazzo Caparzo (VA)
Ghiaie della Furba, Capezzana (WCL)
Grifi Avignonesi (REI)
Palazzo Altesi, Altesino (GAU)
Quercia Grande, Capaccia (OD)
1987
Balifico Castello di Volpaia (AD)
Brunello di Montalcino Altesino (BY, GRG)
Brunello di Montalcino Val di Suga (DI)
Chianti Classico Riserva Vigneto Rancia, Felsina Berardenga (WCL)
Chianti Classico Riserva Vina del Sorbo, Fontodi (WCL)
Coltassala Castello di Volpaia (AD)
Fontalloro, Felsina Berardenga (WCL)
Ghiaie della Furba, Capezzana (TAN)
Quercia Grande, Capaccia (VA)
1986
Brunello di Montalcino Villa Banfi (PIP)
Cepparello, Isole e Olena (GAU)
★ Coltassala Castello di Volpaia (REI)
Fontalloro, Felsina Berardenga (WCL)
Sangioveto Badia a Coltibuono (AD)
1985
★ Balifico Castello di Volpaia (BUT)
Brunello di Montalcino Altesino (SOM)
Brunello di Montalcino Castelgiocondo (GRE, UN)
Brunello di Montalcino Fattoria dei Barbi (HOG)
Carmignano Riserva Villa Capezzana (WCL, TAN)
1983
★ Brunello di Montalcino Castelgiocondo (GRE)
Chianti Classico Riserva Rocca delle Macie (BUT)
1981
Chianti Classico Riserva Monsanto (RAE)
1980
Brunello di Montalcino Fattoria dei Barbi (GRE)
Rubesco Torgiano Riserva Lungarotti (VA)
1977
★ Brunello di Montalcino Fattoria dei Barbi (HOG)

In each price band wines are listed in vintage order. Within each vintage they are listed in A–Z order.

£15.00 to £19.99

1990

Syrah Isole e Olena (WCL)

1989

Ornellaia Ludovico Antinori (BAR, REI, GRG)

1988

Cabernet Sauvignon Isole e Olena (WCL)
★ Cepparello, Isole e Olena (GAU, CB)
Chianti Classico Riecine (WCL)
Chianti Classico Riserva Riecine (WCL)
Flaccianello della Pieve, Fontodi (WR, BOT, WCL)
I Sodi di San Niccolò, Castellare (AD, VA)
Solatio Basilica Villa Cafaggio (GE)
★ Tignanello Antinori (TAN)

1987

Brunello di Montalcino Barbi (VIG)
Grifi Avignonesi (JU)
Tignanello Antinori (GR, WCL)

1986

Balifico Castello di Volpaia (REI)
Brunello di Montalcino Altesino (JU)
Brunello di Montalcino Poggio Antico (ROB)
Chianti Rufina Montesodi, Frescobaldi (WCL)
Flaccianello della Pieve, Fontodi (WCL)
Mormoreto Predicato di Biturica, Frescobaldi (WCL, AMI)
Nipozzano Cuvée Montesodi, Frescobaldi (CV)
Tignanello Antinori (GAU, BER)

1985

Brunello di Montalcino Poggio Antico (OD)
★ Chianti Rufina Montesodi, Frescobaldi (WHI, VA, HAG)
Chianti Rufina Riserva Montesodi, Frescobaldi (AMI)
Sangioveto Grosso, Monsanto (RAE)
Tignanello Antinori (HOG)

1981

San Giorgio Lungarotti (REI)

1974

Chianti Classico Riserva Monsanto (RAE)

£20.00 to £24.99

1990

Ornellaia Ludovico Antinori (PIP, NA, VA)

1988

Le Pergole Torte, Monte Vertine (VA)
Tignanello Antinori (BOT, THR, WR, LAY, VA, HAH, ROB)

1981

Tignanello Antinori (BUT)

£25.00 to £29.99

1989

Sassicaia Incisa della Rocchetta (VA, VIG, LAY)

1987

Sassicaia Incisa della Rocchetta (GR, TAN, WCL, REI)

1986

Sammarco Castello dei Rampolla (WCL)

£30.00 to £39.99

1989

Sassicaia Incisa della Rocchetta (JU)

1988

Sassicaia Incisa della Rocchetta (WS)

1987

Sassicaia Incisa della Rocchetta (DI, CB, BUT)

1986

Sassicaia Incisa della Rocchetta (GRE, GAU)
Solaia Antinori (GR)

1984

Sassicaia Incisa della Rocchetta (AD, VA)

1982

Tignanello Antinori (BUT)

1973

Brunello di Montalcino Barbi (VIG)

1962

Chianti Classico Riserva Montagliari (WS)

£40.00 to £49.99

1988

Sassicaia Incisa della Rocchetta (BUT, ROB)
Solaia Antinori (LAY)

1987

Solaia Antinori (DI)

1986

Solaia Antinori (WCL, ROB, CB)

1985

Sassicaia Incisa della Rocchetta (BUT)
Solaia Antinori (BUT)

1980

Sassicaia Incisa della Rocchetta (BUT)

1971

Brunello di Montalcino Barbi (VIG)

£60.00 to £70.00

1982

Solaia Antinori (BUT)

1976

Sassicaia Incisa della Rocchetta (BUT)

c. £74.00

1977

Brunello di Montalcino Biondi-Santi (VA)

c. £110.00

1975
Brunello di Montalcino Biondi-Santi (VA)

c. £125.00

1971
Brunello di Montalcino Biondi-Santi (VA)

CENTRAL WHITE

Under £4.50

Non-vintage
Sainsbury's Frascati Secco (SAI)
Sainsbury's Orvieto Secco (SAI)
1992
Orvieto Classico Amabile Bigi (VA)
Orvieto Classico Secco Bigi (WHG)
Orvieto Secco Bigi (VA)
Verdicchio dei Castelli di Jesi Classico, Umani Ronchi (VA)
1991
Frascati Superiore Colli di Catone (OD)
Frascati Superiore Monteporzio (HOG)
Orvieto Classico Abboccato Antinori (HOG)
Orvieto Classico Secco Antinori (HOG)
Orvieto Classico Secco Bigi (WHG)
Orvieto Secco Ruffino (HOG)
Tesco Frascati (TES)

£4.50 to £4.99

1992
Frascati Superiore Colli di Catone (AUG)
Frascati Superiore Fontana Candida (WHG)
Frascati Superiore Gotto d'Oro (LAY, WR, THR, BOT)
Frascati Superiore Monteporzio (VA)
Galestro Antinori (BOT, WR, VA, THR)
Orvieto Classico Abboccato Antinori (THR, LAY, WR, BOT)
Orvieto Classico Antinori (DAV)
Orvieto Classico Secco Antinori (WS, WR, THR, LAY, BOT)
Verdicchio dei Castelli di Jesi, Brunori (BIB)
1991
Bianco d'Arquata Adanti (VA)
Frascati Superiore Fontana Candida (WHG)
Frascati Superiore Gotto d'Oro (PEN)
Orvieto Classico Amabile Bigi (WHI)
Orvieto Classico Antinori (DAV)
Orvieto Secco Antinori (LO)
Verdicchio dei Castelli di Jesi, Brunori (BIB)
1990
Orvieto Classico Abboccato Antinori (ROB)

£5.00 to £6.99

Non-vintage
Vin Santo Antinori (HOG, GRE)
1992
Bianco Villa Antinori (LAY)
Orvieto Classico Vigneto Torricella, Bigi (HAG)
Orvieto Secco Antinori (PIP)
★ Pomino Frescobaldi (VA)
Verdicchio dei Castelli di Jesi Classico, Casal di Serra (VA)
★ Vernaccia di San Gimignano Montenidoli (BIB)
★ Vernaccia di San Gimignano Teruzzi e Puthod (PIP, EY, HIC)
1991
Bianco Villa Antinori (TAN, JU, WR, THR, BOT, DI, HAH, BER)
Frascati Superiore Satinata, Colle di Catone (EY, WCL)
Galestro Antinori (DI)
Orvieto Classico Vigneto Torricella, Bigi (VA, OD, AD)
Verdicchio dei Castelli di Jesi Classico, Casal di Serra (SAI, EL, NI)
Vernaccia di San Gimignano Teruzzi e Puthod (GRG, WCL, ROB)
1990
Verdicchio dei Castelli di Jesi Classico, Casal di Serra (BAR, VIC)
Vernaccia di San Gimignano la Torre (WRI)
Vernaccia di San Gimignano San Quirico (GRE, AMI)
Vernaccia di San Gimignano Teruzzi e Puthod (BAR)
1989
Galestro Frescobaldi (CV)

£7.00 to £8.99

1992
Borro Lastricato Selvapiana (WCL)
1991
Borro della Sala, Antinori (WCL, TAN)
Chardonnay Villa di Capezzana (WCL)
Pomino Frescobaldi (UN)
1990
Borro della Sala, Antinori (GRE, PIP, DI)
Orvieto Classico Terre Vineate, Il Palazzone (WCL)
1989
Chardonnay di Miralduolo, Lungarotti (BER)

£9.00 to £10.99

1990
Pomino il Benefizio, Frescobaldi (CV)
Vergena Sauvignon Blanc, Frescobaldi (CV)
1989
Pomino il Benefizio, Frescobaldi (AMI)
1985
Pomino il Benefizio, Frescobaldi (GRE)

£11.00 to £12.99

1991
Chardonnay I Sistri, Felsina Berardenga (LAY, HIC, WCL)
Chardonnay Isole e Olena (WCL)
Vernaccia di San Gimignano Terre di Tufo, Teruzzi e Puthod (WCL, GRG)
Vernaccia di San Gimignano Teruzzi e Puthod (VA)
1990
Chardonnay I Sistri, Felsina Berardenga (GRG)
Chardonnay le Grance, Caparzo (AMI)
Frascati Colle Gaio, Colli di Catone (WCL)
1988
Pomino il Benefizio, Frescobaldi (PIP)
1987
Pomino il Benefizio, Frescobaldi (WCL)
1985
Vin Santo Antinori (GRE)

£13.00 to £14.99

1986
Orvieto Classico Muffa Nobile, Berberani (WCL)
1987
Cabreo La Pietra Ruffino (HOG)
Pomino il Benefizio, Frescobaldi (HAG)
1985
Vin Santo Selvapiana (WCL)
1979
Vin Santo Villa di Vetrice (WCL)

£18.00 to £19.99

1990
Cervaro della Sala, Antinori (LAY, VA, WCL)
1983
Orvieto Classico Pourriture Noble, Decugnano dei Barbi (VIG)

CENTRAL ROSÉ

Under £7.00

1991
Carmignano Vinruspo Rosato, Capezzana (WCL)

CENTRAL SPARKLING

Under £4.00

Non-vintage
Lambrusco Amabile Luigi Gavioli (HOG, VA)
Lambrusco Bianco Ca' de Medici (WAI)
Lambrusco Bianco San Prospero (AUG)
Lambrusco Ca' de Medici (WAI)
Lambrusco di Sorbara Cavicchioli (OD)
Lambrusco di Sorbara Cesari (PEN)
Lambrusco San Prospero (GRE)

SOUTHERN RED

Under £4.00

1992
Montepulciano d'Abruzzo Umani Ronchi (WHG)
1991
Montepulciano d'Abruzzo Bianchi (VA)
Montepulciano d'Abruzzo Umani Ronchi (WHG, VIC, NI)
1990
Cellaro Rosso C.S. di Sambuca (GRG, BAR, WCL)
★ Cirò Classico Librandi (ASD)
Monica di Sardegna, C.S. di Dolianova (WCL)
★ Montepulciano d'Abruzzo Tollo (AUG)

£4.00 to £5.99

1992
Montepulciano d'Abruzzo Bianchi (HAG)
1990
Corvo Rosso Duca di Salaparuta (HOG, TAN, UN)
Montepulciano d'Abruzzo Illuminati (HOG)
1989
Copertino Riserva, Cantina Copertino (VA, WCL, BAR, GRG)
Corvo Rosso Duca di Salaparuta (GRE, PIP)
Salice Salentino Riserva Candido (PIP)
1988
Salice Salentino Candido (OD, BAR, NA)
★ Salice Salentino Riserva Candido (GE, GRG, WCL)

£6.00 to £8.99

1989
Regaleali Rosso (DI, TAN)
1987
Aglianico del Vulture, Fratelli d'Angelo (ROB, TAN, VA)
Ramitello Di Majo Norante (WCL)

1989
Regaleali Rosso (DI, TAN)
1987
Aglianico del Vulture, Fratelli d'Angelo (ROB, TAN, VA)
Ramitello Di Majo Norante (WCL)

£10.00 to £15.00

1986
Regaleali Rosso del Conte (GE)
1977
Rosso Brindisi Patriglione, Taurino (WCL)

c. £20.00

1985
Montepulciano d'Abruzzo Valentini (WCL)

SOUTHERN WHITE

Under £4.00

1992
Cellaro Bianco C.S. di Sambuca (GRG, WCL)
1991
Settesoli Bianco (HOG, VA)
★ Vermentino di Sardegna C.S. di Dolianova (WCL)
1990
Settesoli Bianco (ROB)

£4.00 to £5.99

1992
Locorotondo (WCL)
Terre di Ginestra vdt (VA)
1991
Corvo Bianco Duca di Salaparuta (HOG, UN, VA)
★ Corvo Colomba Platino Bianco (HOG)
Locorotondo (GRG, WCL, VA)
Pinot Bianco di Puglia, Vigna al Monte (HOG)
Sauvignon di Puglia, Vigna al Monte (GRE)
Terre di Ginestra vdt (TES, UN)
1990
Cellaro Bianco C.S. di Sambuca (JU)
Preludio No. 1 Torrebianco (GRE)
Sauvignon di Puglia, Vigna al Monte (HOG)
Terre di Ginestra vdt (ROB)
1989
Preludio No. 1 Torrebianco (HOG)

£6.00 to £7.99

1991
Regaleali Bianco (DI)
1990
Regaleali Bianco (ROB)

£10.00 to £15.00

1991
Lacryma Christi del Vesuvio, Mastroberardino (DI)
1987
Trebbiano d'Abruzzo Valentini (WCL)

c. £18.00

1988
Corvo Bianco di Valguarnera Duca di Salaparuta (ROB)

SOUTHERN ROSÉ

c. £4.00

1992
Cellaro Rosato C.S. di Sambuca (GRG)

SOUTHERN SPARKLING

c. £9.00

1989
Corvo Brut Cuve Close (VA)

SOUTHERN FORTIFIED

Under £11.00

Non-vintage
Josephine Dore de Bartoli (WCL)
★ Vecchio Samperi 10-year-old, de Bartoli (WCL)

£11.00 to £12.99

Non-vintage
Marsala Vigna la Miccia, de Bartoli (VA, WCL, TAN)

£17.00 to £19.99

Non-vintage
Il Marsala 20-year-old de Bartoli (VA)
Moscato Passito di Pantelleria Bukkuram, de Bartoli (VA)
Vecchio Samperi 20-year-old, de Bartoli (VA)

£20.00 to £25.00

Non-vintage
Vecchio Samperi 30-year-old, de Bartoli (WCL)

Stars (★) indicate wines selected by the editors as particularly good value in their class.

RIOJA

RED

Under £5.00

Non-vintage
Siglo Gran Reserva (GR)
1990
★ CVNE (CV, BAR)
El Coto (DAV)
★ El Coto Crianza (GRG)
Rivarey (VIC)
1989
CVNE (WHI, WHG)
Marqués de Cáceres (LO, WHI, CV, WS)
1988
Campo Viejo (AUG, WHI)
CVNE Viña Real (CV, WHI, MOR, TES)
★ Marqués de Cáceres (AUG)
★ Montecillo Viña Cumbrero (BOT, THR, WR)
Sainsbury's Rioja (SAI)
1987
CVNE Viña Real (WHI)
Marqués de Cáceres (HOG, BE, GRE, LAY)
1986
★ Campo Viejo Reserva (AUG)
1985
★ Domecq Domain (HOG)

£5.00 to £5.99

1990
CVNE (BEK, BEK, LAY, HUN)
1989
Beronia (BIB)
El Coto Crianza (HAG)
Marqués de Cáceres (EL, WCL, TAN, MOR, JU)
1988
Berberana Carta de Oro (MOR, UN)
Berón (WHI)
★ Beronia (PE)
Faustino V Reserva (GRE, WHI)
★ La Rioja Alta Viña Alberdi (WAI, SOM)
Siglo Saco (GRE)
1987
Campo Viejo Reserva (WR, THR, BOT)
Marqués de Cáceres (HAH, DAV)
1986
Berberana Reserva (GRG, MAJ)
El Coto Crianza (ROB)
Lagunilla Valle Tinto (JU)
Marqués de Cáceres (DI)
1985
Beronia Reserva (HOG)
Campo Viejo Reserva (WHI)

£6.00 to £6.99

Non-vintage
Domecq Domain (UN)
1989
Marqués de Cáceres (VIN)
1988
CVNE Viña Real (VIG)
La Rioja Alta Viña Alberdi (JU)
Marqués de Riscal (GRE)
Marqués de Riscal Reserva (HAG, MOR, VIC)
1987
Baron de Ley (BOT, THR)
Faustino V Reserva (HUN, MOR)
La Rioja Alta Viña Alberdi (ROB, ROB)
Marqués de Cáceres (BER)
1986
Baron de Ley (WR, BOT)
Berberana Reserva (GR)
Coto de Imaz Reserva (DAV)
CVNE Reserva (CV)
Marqués de Murrieta (HOG)
Marqués de Riscal Reserva (PEN)
1985
Beronia Reserva (OD, GRE, RAE)
★ Bodegas Riojanas Monte Real Reserva (BY)
Coto de Imaz Reserva (DAV)
Marqués de Cáceres Reserva (LO)
Viña Berceo Reserva (WHG)
1982
Lagunilla Viña Herminia (GE)
1981
★ Campo Viejo Gran Reserva (AUG, OD)

£7.00 to £7.99

1988
Marqués de Murrieta (GRE)
★ Marqués de Murrieta Reserva (WR, THR, BOT, MOR)
Marqués de Riscal (PE)
1987
Muga (MOR)
1986
Baron de Ley (BAR)
Beronia Reserva (BIB)
★ Contino Reserva (PIP)
La Rioja Alta Viña Alberdi (BER)
1985
Beronia Reserva (BIB)
CVNE Imperial Reserva (PIP)
CVNE Viña Real Reserva (PIP, CV)
Marqués de Cáceres Reserva (HAH, WHI, DI)

1984
Bodegas Riojanas Monte Real Reserva (MOR)
Contino Reserva (CV)
1983
Marqués de Riscal (UN)
1981
Campo Viejo Gran Reserva (GA)
1980
Siglo Saco Gran Reserva (GRE)

£8.00 to £8.99

1989
Remelluri (BIB, TAN)
1988
Marqués de Murrieta (WCL, DAV, TAN)
★ Marqués de Murrieta Castillo Ygay Gran Reserva (LAY)
Marqués de Murrieta Reserva (AD, WRI, MAJ)
1987
★ Contino Reserva (CV)
Marqués de Murrieta (DAV)
1986
Contino Reserva (AD)
★ CVNE Imperial Gran Reserva (LAY)
CVNE Imperial Reserva (AD)
CVNE Viña Real Reserva (LAY)
Marqués de Murrieta (DAV)
1985
Contino Reserva (PEN, CV, LOR, AMI)
★ Coto de Imaz Gran Reserva (DAV)
★ CVNE Imperial Gran Reserva (PIP)
CVNE Imperial Reserva (CV, BEK, LOR, WS, ROB)
★ CVNE Viña Real Gran Reserva (PIP, CV)
Faustino I Gran Reserva (WHI, GRE)
★ La Rioja Alta Viña Ardanza Reserva (SOM, HOG)
★ Remelluri (WS)
1984
Bodegas Riojanas Monte Real Reserva (GAU)
Bodegas Riojanas Viña Albina Reserva (GAU)
1983
Berberana Gran Reserva (BU)
1982
★ Faustino I Gran Reserva (HOG)
1981
CVNE Viña Real Reserva (PEN, CV, WS)
La Rioja Alta Viña Arana (HOG)
Marqués de Cáceres Reserva (PEN, CV)
1980
Campo Viejo Gran Reserva (WHI, MOR)

£9.00 to £9.99

1989
Remelluri Reserva (WW, MOR)
1988
Marqués de Murrieta Reserva (BIB, HAH, JU)
1987
Contino Reserva (LAY)
Marqués de Murrieta Reserva (BIB)
1986
Contino Reserva (EL, VIC, WR, BOT, BIB, MOR)
Marqués de Murrieta (AMI)
Marqués de Murrieta Reserva (NI, HAG, ROB)
1985
CVNE Imperial Gran Reserva (CV, PEN, MOR)
CVNE Imperial Reserva (HUN)
CVNE Viña Real Gran Reserva (MOR)
CVNE Viña Real Reserva (BER)
La Rioja Alta Viña Ardanza Reserva (EY, LAY, AD, AMI, SAF, MOR)
Marqués de Murrieta (WHI)
Marqués de Murrieta Reserva (WRI, ROB)
1984
Marqués de Murrieta Castillo Ygay Gran Reserva (BUT)
1983
Berberana Gran Reserva (DAV, GR)
1982
CVNE Viña Real Gran Reserva (CV)
Lagunilla Gran Reserva (JU)
1981
Contino Reserva (CV)
CVNE Viña Real Gran Reserva (CV)
1980
Berberana Gran Reserva (GRG)

£10.00 to £12.99

1986
CVNE Imperial Gran Reserva (BIB)
CVNE Imperial Reserva (HAG)
1985
Conde de la Salceda Gran Reserva (TAN)
Contino Reserva (BER, REI)
CVNE Imperial Gran Reserva (REI, TAN, BIB, VIG)
CVNE Imperial Reserva (BER)
CVNE Viña Real Gran Reserva (VIG)
Faustino I Gran Reserva (MOR)
La Rioja Alta Viña Ardanza Reserva (WR, BOT, THR, REI, JU)
López de Heredia Viña Tondonia (TAN)
1983
Marqués de Murrieta (GRE)
Marqués de Murrieta Gran Reserva (HOG)

1982
CVNE Imperial Gran Reserva (PIP, CV, LOR)
CVNE Imperial Reserva (LOR, CB, VIN)
CVNE Viña Real Gran Reserva (ROB, LOR, VIG)
Marqués de Cáceres Reserva (DI)
1981
CVNE Viña Real Reserva (BER, VIG)
★ La Rioja Alta Reserva 904 Gran Reserva (SOM, HOG)
Marqués de Cáceres Gran Reserva (VIN)
1980
Beronia Gran Reserva (GRE)
1978
Berberana Gran Reserva (PEN)
Marqués de Cáceres Gran Reserva (LO, WHI)
Marqués de Cáceres Reserva (MOR)
1975
Berberana Gran Reserva (PEN, BE, MOR)
Bodegas Riojanas Monte Real Gran Reserva (BY, MOR)
Bodegas Riojanas Viña Albina Gran Reserva (MOR)
Marqués de Cáceres Gran Reserva (CV)

£13.00 to £19.99

1983
Marqués de Murrieta Gran Reserva (MAJ, JU, AD, BIB)
1982
CVNE Imperial Reserva (VIG)
La Rioja Alta Reserva 904 Gran Reserva (BOT, THR, WR, LAY)
1981
La Rioja Alta Reserva 904 (JU, AMI)
La Rioja Alta Reserva 904 Gran Reserva (MOR, EY, PE, GAU, HAG, CB)
1980
Beronia Gran Reserva (BIB)
1978
Beronia Gran Reserva (BIB)
Marqués de Murrieta Gran Reserva (WCL)
1976
López de Heredia Viña Tondonia Gran Reserva (MOR)
1975
CVNE Imperial Gran Reserva (CV)
Marqués de Murrieta Gran Reserva (MOR)
Montecillo Gran Reserva (BAR)
1973
Lagunilla Gran Reserva (BUT)

£20.00 to £22.99

1978
Marqués de Murrieta Gran Reserva (CB)
1976
López de Heredia Viña Tondonia Gran Reserva (TAN)
1970
Bodegas Riojanas Monte Real Gran Reserva (GAU)

£30.00 to £39.99

1973
La Rioja Alta Reserva 890 Gran Reserva (GAU)
1970
Marqués de Murrieta Gran Reserva (CB)
Solar de Samaniego Gran Reserva (VIG)
1964
Bodegas Riojanas Monte Real Gran Reserva (GAU)

£49.00 to £59.99

1968
Marqués de Murrieta Gran Reserva (MOR, ROB)
Marqués de Murrieta Castillo Ygay Gran Reserva (ROB, AD, JU)
1964
Bodegas Riojanas Monte Real Gran Reserva (VIG)
1950
Bodegas Riojanas Monte Real Gran Reserva (VIG)
1942
Marqués de Murrieta Castillo Ygay Gran Reserva (BUT)

£75.00 to £99.99

1952
Marqués de Murrieta Castillo Ygay Gran Reserva (AD, MOR)
1951
CVNE Viña Real Gran Reserva (VIG)
1942
Marqués de Murrieta Castillo Ygay Gran Reserva (AMI)

WHITE

Under £4.00

Non-vintage
Tesco White Rioja (TES)
1992
★ Marqués de Cáceres (LO, EY)
Viña Ramon Balada Xarel-lo (BIB)
1991
Marqués de Cáceres (HOG, WHI, VIC)

£4.00 to £4.99

1992
El Coto (DAV)
Marqués de Cáceres (CV, AUG, GRE, WCL, AD, JU)
1991
El Coto (DAV)
Marqués de Cáceres (ROB, EL, LAY, HAH, DI, TAN)
1990
★ CVNE Monopole (PIP)
El Coto (UN)
Viña Berceo (WHG)
1989
CVNE Monopole (HAG)
Viña Berceo (WHG)

£5.00 to £5.99

1992
Marqués de Cáceres (MOR)
1991
Faustino V (MOR)
Marqués de Cáceres (AV, VIN)
1990
CVNE Monopole (CV, HUN, LAY)
Marqués de Cáceres (BER)
1989
Berberana Carta de Plata (TW)
CVNE Monopole (MOR, PE, BEK)
1988
CVNE Monopole (PEN, PE)
La Rioja Alta Viña Ardanza Reserva (SAF)
1987
★ CVNE Reserva (PIP, CV)
1985
CVNE Reserva (PEN)

£6.00 to £7.99

1992
Muga (EL)
1991
Muga (MOR)
1989
CVNE Monopole (TAN, CB)
1987
CVNE Reserva (MOR, WS)
Marqués de Murrieta (GRE, MOR)
Marqués de Murrieta Reserva (BOT, WR, THR, AD, VIC)
1986
Bodegas Riojanas Monte Real (MOR)
Marqués de Murrieta (HOG, WCL, DAV)
Marqués de Murrieta Reserva (HAG, MAJ)
1985
La Rioja Alta Viña Ardanza Reserva (ROB)

£8.00 to £10.99

1988
Marqués de Murrieta Reserva (BIB)
1987
CVNE Reserva (VIG)
Marqués de Murrieta Reserva (JU, BIB, AMI)
1986
Marqués de Murrieta (TAN, WHI, NI)
Marqués de Murrieta Reserva (WRI, PEN, ROB)
1985
Marqués de Murrieta Reserva (WRI, AV)
1984
Marqués de Murrieta (TW)
1983
Marqués de Murrieta Ygay Gran Reserva (BUT)

£11.00 to £13.99

1985
López de Heredia Tondonia Reserva (MOR)
1980
Marqués de Murrieta (TW)
1976
Marqués de Murrieta Reserva (BE)

£25.00 to £34.99

1974
Bodegas Riojanas Monte Real (VIG)
1970
Marqués de Murrieta Ygay Gran Reserva (GRE, AD)
1966
Bodegas Riojanas Monte Real (VIG)

£50.00 to £59.99

1962
Marqués de Murrieta Ygay Gran Reserva (MOR)
1948
Marqués de Murrieta (VIG)

ROSÉ

Under £5.00

1991
Marqués de Cáceres Rosado (CV, DI)

£5.00 to £8.00

1991
Marqués de Cáceres Rosado (MOR)
Faustino V Rosado (MOR)
1985
Marqués de Murrieta Rosado (MOR)

OTHER SPANISH TABLE WINES

RED

Under £3.00

Non-vintage
★ Don Darias (TES, SAF, WR, THR, BOT)
Don Hugo, Alto Ebro (WAI)
Sainsbury's Navarra (SAI)

£3.00 to £3.99

1992
Sainsbury's La Mancha (SAI)
1990
★ Fariña Colegiata (MAJ)
1989
★ Chivite Gran Feudo (DI)
Condé de Caralt (MOR)
René Barbier (CV)
1988
Chivite Gran Feudo (HOG)
Sainsbury's Valdepeñas (SAI)
Señorio de los Llanos (SOM)
1987
★ Felix Solis Viña Albali Reserva (BOT, THR)
Señorio de los Llanos Reserva (HOG, LOR)
1986
Felix Solis Viña Albali Reserva (AUG)
Palacio de León (VIC)

£4.00 to £4.99

1992
Monte Ory (AD)
1991
Ochoa (EL)
1990
Ochoa (HAG, BIB)
Torres Tres Torres (WHI)
1989
Fariña Colegiata (EL, LOR)
Fariña Gran Colegiata (OD)
★ Raimat Abadia (TES, SAI)
Torres Coronas (HOG, TES, EY, GRE, LO, WHI, PEN, CV, DI, PE)
Torres Gran Sangredetoro (DI)
Torres Tres Torres (WHI, BOT, WR, THR, MOR)
1988
★ Ochoa Tempranillo (HOG)
Raimat Merlot (SAF)
René Barbier Reserva (CV)
★ Señorio de los Llanos Reserva (JU, LAY)
Señorio de Sarria (GRE)
Torres Tres Torres (GRE, PEN)
1987
Condé de Caralt Tinto Reserva (SOM)
Señorio de los Llanos Reserva (ROB)
1986
Chivite Gran Feudo Reserva (HOG, DI)
Felix Solis Viña Albali Reserva (GRE)
Marius Tinto Reserva Almansa, Piqueras (JU, TAN)
1985
Palacio de León (SUM)
1984
★ Señorio de los Llanos Gran Reserva (MAJ)

£5.00 to £5.99

1990
Ochoa Tempranillo (CV)
Torres Coronas (DAV)
1989
Ochoa Tempranillo (MOR, MAJ)
Raimat Abadia Reserva (HIC)
Torres Las Torres (CV, BE, DI)
1988
Ochoa Tempranillo (WCL)
Raimat Tempranillo (SAF)
★ Scala Dei Priorato (SOM, MOR)
Torres Coronas (UN)
Torres Gran Sangredetoro (WHI, BE)
1987
Chivite Gran Fuedo Reserva (GRG)
Ochoa Cabernet Sauvignon (HOG)
Torres Gran Sangredetoro (WHI, WR, BOT)
Torres Viña Magdala (GRE)
1986
Fariña Colegiata (GRE)
Fariña Gran Colegiata Reserva (TAN)
Raimat Abadia (GAU)
Torres Gran Sangredetoro (HOG, GRE)
1985
Condé de Caralt Reserva (WRI)
Vall Reserva Masía Vallformosa (BAR)
1984
René Barbier Reserva (ROB, VIG)
Señorio de los Llanos Gran Reserva (PE, MOR, JU)
1983
Señorio de los Llanos Gran Reserva (PEN)
1980
★ Felix Solis Viña Albali Gran Reserva (GA)
1975
Castillo de Tiebas Reserva (PEN)

£6.00 to £6.99

1989
Ochoa Tempranillo (AD, WR, BOT, THR, REI, TAN)
Raimat Cabernet Sauvignon (TES)
Raimat Tempranillo (GA, GRE, VIC)
Torres Las Torres (ROB, PEN, MOR)
Torres Viña Magdala (WHI, BE, PEN)
1988
Ochoa Tempranillo (VIG)
Scala Dei Priorato (GRG)
Torres Gran Sangredetoro (MOR, ROB)
1987
Ochoa Cabernet Sauvignon (CV)
Senoro de Lazán Reserva Montesierra, Somontano (EL)
★ Torres Gran Coronas (HOG, GRE, RAE)
Torres Gran Sangredetoro (WRI)
Torres Viña Magdala (WHI)
1986
Fariña Colegiata (GAU)
Ochoa Reserva (CV)
Torres Gran Coronas (RAE)
Torres Gran Sangredetoro (GAU)
Torres Viña Magdala (MOR)
1985
Ochoa Reserva (HOG)
1982
Ochoa Reserva (PE)

£7.00 to £7.99

1989
Ochoa Tempranillo (HAG)
Raimat Cabernet Sauvignon (BOT, WR, THR, VIC)
Raimat Tempranillo (MOR)
1988
Priorato Extra, Barril (WS)
Raimat Cabernet Sauvignon (GRE)
Raimat Merlot (GRE)
Torres Gran Coronas (DAV)
1987
Torres Gran Coronas (LO, BE, EY, CV, WHI, SAI, BOT, WR, ROB, MOR, DAV)
1986
Torres Gran Coronas (GAU)
1985
Raimat Cabernet Sauvignon (GAU)
Torres Gran Coronas (PEN, GAU)
1984
Jean León Cabernet Sauvignon (TAN, AMI)
1982
Ochoa Reserva (TAN)
1978
Castillo de Tiebas Reserva (SUM)

£8.00 to £9.99

1989
Pesquera, Fernandez (NI, OD)
1988
Torres Gran Coronas (HIC)
1987
Priorato Extra, Barril (WCL)
Torres Gran Coronas (HAG)
1986
Marqués de Griñon Cabernet Sauvignon (CB, GRE)
1985
★ Mauro (DAV)
1984
Jean León Cabernet Sauvignon (VIG)

£10.00 to £14.99

1989
Pesquera Cosecha Especial, Fernandez (CB)
Torres Mas Borras Pinot Noir (DI)
1988
Pesquera Cosecha Especial, Fernandez (VIG)
Pesquera, Fernandez (JU, TAN, AMI, PE)
Torres Mas La Plana (VIG)
Torres Mas Borras Pinot Noir (HOG, MOR, EY, GRE, PEN, CV, WHI, GAU)
1987
Marqués de Griñon Crianza (BOT)
Pesquera Cosecha Especial, Fernandez (GAU)
1986
Marqués de Griñon Crianza (MOR)
1985
Chivite Gran Fuedo Reserva (MOR)
Pesquera, Fernandez (NI, BE)
Raimat Cabernet Sauvignon (WR, BOT)
1983
Jean León Cabernet Sauvignon (ROB)
1982
Jean León Cabernet Sauvignon (PE)
1981
Jean León Cabernet Sauvignon (LAY, MOR)
1979
Jean León Cabernet Sauvignon (REI)

£15.00 to £19.99

1987
Torres Mas La Plana (MOR)
Torres Mas la Plana Reserva (EY)
Vega Sicilia 3rd year (LAY)
1986
Vega Sicilia Valbuena 3rd year (DI)

1985
Torres Mas La Plana (HOG, GRE, DI, CV, WRI, LO)
Vega Sicilia 3rd year (NI)
Vega Sicilia Valbuena 3rd year (PEN)
1984
Pesquera Reserva, Fernandez (VIG)
1983
Torres Mas La Plana (RAE, GRE, DI)
1981
Torres Mas La Plana (OD)

£20.00 to £29.99

1985
Torres Mas La Plana (HAG)
Vega Sicilia Valbuena 5th year (DI)
1975
Torres Mas La Plana (DI)

£30.00 to £39.99

1984
Vega Sicilia Valbuena 5th year (VIG)
1976
Torres Mas La Plana (VIG)

£40.00 to £49.99

1982
Vega Sicilia Unico (GRE)
1980
Vega Sicilia Unico (TAN)
Vega Sicilia Valbuena 5th year (MOR)
1979
Vega Sicilia Unico (DI)
1975
Vega Sicilia Unico (FA, AMI)

£50.00 to £59.99

1980
Vega Sicilia Unico (GAU)
1975
Vega Sicilia Unico (DI, GAU, JU, MOR)
1962
Vega Sicilia Unico (DI)

£60.00 to £74.99

1968
Vega Sicilia Unico (FA, GAU, ROB)
1962
Vega Sicilia Unico (FA, GAU)

c. £89.00

1970
Torres Mas La Plana (VIG)
1966
Vega Sicilia Unico (REI)

WHITE

Under £3.00

Non-vintage
Castillo de Liria (WAI)
Tesco Spanish Dry White Wine (TES)
Tesco Spanish Sweet White Wine (TES)
1992
Castillo de Liria (VIC)

£3.00 to £3.99

Non-vintage
★ Co-op. del Ribeiro Pazo, Ribeiro Blanco (WCL)
★ Moscatel de Valencia Castillo de Liria (WAI, AUG, TAN)
Safeway Moscatel de Valencia (SAF)
Sainsbury's Moscatel de Valencia (SAI)
1992
Castillo de Alhambra (AUG)
1991
Condé de Caralt (WCL)
★ Torres Gran Viña Sol (TES)
1990
Torres Viña Sol (HOG)

£4.00 to £4.99

Non-vintage
Barbadillo Castillo de San Diego (CV, WCL)
Los Llanos Armonioso (TAN, MOR)
Torres Moscatel Malvasia de Oro (HOG)
1992
Torres Viña Esmeralda (EY)
Torres Viña Sol (DAV, MOR, LAY)
1991
Scala Dei Priorato (MOR)
Torres San Valentin (DI, WHI)
Torres Viña Esmeralda (HOG, LO, BE, WHI)
Torres Viña Sol (DI, GRE, LO, WHI, BE, PE, TAN, BOT, THR, WR)
1990
Barbadillo Castillo de San Diego (PE)
Torres San Valentin (WHI)
Torres Viña Esmeralda (WHI)

£5.00 to £6.99

1992
Torres Viña Esmeralda (DAV)
1991
Marqués de Alella (MOR, TAN)
Marqués de Riscal Blanco Rueda (MOR)
Torres Gran Viña Sol (LO, WHI, BE, DI, EY, MOR, GRE, PE, TAN, LAY, HAG)
Torres Viña Esmeralda (CV, GRE, MOR, WRI, WR, BOT, THR, PE, TAN, ROB)

1990
Marqués de Griñon (MOR, WRI)
Torres Gran Viña Sol (WHI, CV, BOT)
Torres Fransola (DI)
1989
Torres Gran Viña Sol (CV)

£7.00 to £9.99

1991
Lagar de Cervera Hermanos (BOT, WR, TAN, ROB, ROB)
Torres Gran Viña Sol (RAE, VIG)
Torres Fransola (MOR, WHI, EY)
1990
Lagar de Cervera Hermanos (GAU)
Torres Gran Viña Sol (RAE, VIG)
Torres Fransola (GRE, WHI, ROB)
1989
Raimat Chardonnay (MOR)

£15.00 to £19.99

1990
Torres Milmanda Chardonnay (CV, WHI)
1989
Torres Milmanda Chardonnay (DI, GRE)
1988
Torres Milmanda Chardonnay (WHI)
Jean León Chardonnay (REI)
1984
Jean León Chardonnay (MOR)

£20.00 to £24.99

1990
Torres Milmanda Chardonnay (PE)
1988
Torres Milmanda Chardonnay (BE, REI)

SPARKLING

Under £6.00

Non-vintage
Castellblanch Brut Zero (HOG)
Castellblanch Cristal Seco (WAI)
★ Condé de Caralt Brut (MOR)
Condé de Caralt Semi-seco (MOR)
Freixenet Brut Rosé (PIP)
Freixenet Carta Nevada (PIP, CV, WHI)
★ Freixenet Cordon Negro Brut (HOG)
Jean Perico Brut (HOG)
Sainsbury's Cava Spanish Sparkling Wine (SAI)
Segura Viudas Brut (HOG, DI, OD)

£6.00 to £6.99

Non-vintage
Codorníu Brut Première Cuvée (VIC)
Condé de Caralt Blanc de Blancs (MOR, OD)
Freixenet Cordon Negro Brut (CV, SAF, WHI, LAY, VIC, AUG, WR, BOT, THR, EL, DAV, PE)
Marqués de Monistrol Brut (AUG, PE)
Marqués de Monistrol Rosé Brut (AUG, THR, BOT, WR, PE)
Mont Marçal Brut (GRG)
1989
Freixenet Cordon Negro Brut (WHG, ROB)
1988
Castellblanch Brut Zero (MOR)
Freixenet Brut Nature (LOR, MAJ)
Freixenet Cordon Negro Brut (PIP, MOR)

£7.00 to £7.99

Non-vintage
Raimat Chardonnay Brut (BOT, THR, WR)
1990
Codorníu Brut (HUN)
Codorníu Brut Première Cuvée (MOR)
Freixenet Cordon Negro Brut (HAG)
1988
Freixenet Cordon Negro Brut (HUN)

£8.00 to £8.99

Non-vintage
Raimat Chardonnay Brut (VIC)
1988
Codorníu Chardonnay Brut (VIC)
1987
Codorníu Chardonnay Brut (AUG)

£9.00 to £10.99

1988
Codorníu Chardonnay Brut (MOR)
Condé de Caralt Brut (MOR)

FORTIFIED

Under £4.00

Non-vintage
Bodegas Alvear Montilla Cream (LAY)
Bodegas Alvear Montilla Medium Dry (LAY, TAN)
Bodegas Alvear Montilla Pale Dry (LAY, TAN)
Sainsbury's Moscatel de Málaga ½ bottle (SAI)

£8.00 to £9.99

Non-vintage
Málaga Lagrima 10 años Scholtz (GRE, TAN)
★ Málaga Solera 1885 Scholtz (GRE, PE)

SHERRY

DRY

Under £5.00

Double Century Fino, Domecq (BOT, THR)
★ Elegante, Gonzalez Byass (HOG, WHI)
Fino Bertola (HOG)
Fino Hidalgo (BIB)
la Gitana Manzanilla, Hidalgo ½ bottle (HAL)
Harvey's Luncheon Dry (HOG, WHI)
★ Lustau Fino (DI, MAJ)
★ Manzanilla de Sanlúcar, Barbadillo (OD)
Valdespino Fino (PEN, AS, WCL)
Waitrose Fino (WAI)

£5.00 to £6.99

Amontillado Napoleon, Hidalgo (EY, NI, AD, WS, WW)
Elegante, Gonzalez Byass (AUG, TES, THR, WR, BOT, WAI, DAV, UN)
★ Fino de Balbaina, Barbadillo (BAR, PIP, HIC)
★ Fino de Sanlúcar, Barbadillo (SUM, PIP, HAY, BIB)
Fino Hidalgo (VIN, NI, HAH)
★ la Gitana Manzanilla, Hidalgo (EY, EL, OD, HOG, WS, WAI, WW, BIB, HAH)
Harvey's Luncheon Dry (HA, THR, BOT, WR, WRI, HAG)
la Ina, Domecq (HOG, WHI, WRI, UN, HAH)
★ Inocente Fino, Valdespino (VIN, HOG, WS, WCL)
★ Lustau Dry Oloroso (DI)
★ Lustau Palo Cortado (HIG)
Manzanilla de Sanlúcar, Barbadillo (SUM, PIP, HAY, PEN, BAR, ROB, GE, BIB, HIC, CB)
★ Manzanilla Pasada Solear, Barbadillo (SUM, PIP, CV, ROB, JU)
Manzanilla Pastora, Barbadillo (HAY)
Ostra Manzanilla (LAY)
San Patricio Fino, Garvey (CV, HOG, PEN, ROB, WS, HAG)
Tio Pepe, Gonzalez Byass (WHI, HOG, WRI, ROB, GRG)

£7.00 to £8.99

Don Zoilo Finest Fino (HOG)
Don Zoilo Pale Dry Manzanilla (HOG)
Don Zoilo Very Old Fino (GRG)
Fino Especial, Hidalgo (BIB, TAN, LAY)
la Guita Manzanilla, Hidalgo (HOG)
Harvey's Palo Cortado (HOG, HA)
Inocente Fino, Valdespino (WRI, AS, ROB)
Jerez Cortado, Hidalgo (WW, AD)
Manzanilla Pasada Almacenista, Lustau (DI, HAG)
Manzanilla Pasada de Sanlúcar, Hidalgo (TAN)
Manzanilla Pasada Solear, Barbadillo (WS, BIB, HIC)
Oloroso Dry, Hidalgo (AD, TAN)
Oloroso Especial, Hidalgo (WW, LAY)
Oloroso Seco Barbadillo (PIP)
★ Tio Diego Amontillado, Valdespino (WCL, WS)
Tio Guillermo Amontillado, Garvey (CV)
Tio Pepe, Gonzalez Byass (TES, AUG, DAV, WAI, OD, JU, EL, UN, HAH, HAG, THR, BOT, WR)
Valdespino Manzanilla (TW)

£9.00 to £9.99

Don Zoilo Old Dry Oloroso (BAR)
Don Zoilo Pale Dry Manzanilla (BAR, REI)
Don Zoilo Very Old Fino (BAR)
Dos Cortados Old Dry Oloroso, Williams & Humbert (BOT, THR, WR, HOG)
la Ina, Domecq (HA)
Jerez Cortado, Hidalgo (LAY)
Manzanilla Pasada Almacenista, Lustau (HOG)
★ Palo Cortado del Carrascal, Valdespino (ROB)
Palo Cortado, Valdespino (WS)

£10.00 to £11.99

Don Zoilo Pale Dry Manzanilla (VIG)
Don Zoilo Palo Cortado (HOG)
Don Zoilo Very Old Fino (VIG)
★ Oloroso Seco Barbadillo (BIB)

Palo Cortado del Carrascal, Valdespino (BIB)
Palo Cortado, Valdespino (WCL)
Principe Manzanilla, Barbadillo (GAU)

£12.00 to £14.99

Don Zoilo Palo Cortado (GRG, REI)
Palo Cortado, Don Beningo (HIC)

MEDIUM

Under £5.00

Amontillado Lustau (DI, MAJ)
Amontillado Martial, Valdespino (HAH)
Amontillado Valdespino (AS, ROB)
Caballero Amontillado, Gonzalez Byass (TES)
Concha Amontillado, Gonzalez Byass (HOG, WHI)
Harvey's Club Amontillado (HOG, WHI)
Waitrose Amontillado Sherry (WAI)

£5.00 to £6.99

Amontillado de Sanlúcar, Barbadillo (SUM, PIP, HAY, BAR, BIB, HIC, WHG)
Amontillado Lustau (OD)
Amontillado Tomás Abad (WIC)
Concha Amontillado, Gonzalez Byass (AUG, WAI)
Dry Fly Amontillado, Findlater (WAI)
Dry Sack, Williams & Humbert (HOG, WRI)
Harvey's Club Amontillado (TES, BOT, WR, THR, HA, WAI, AUG, WRI, DAV, HAG, HAH, OD)
Sandeman Amontillado (ROB)
Tanners Medium Sherry (TAN)

£7.00 to £10.99

Amontillado Almacenista, Lustau (DI, HOG)
Don Zoilo Amontillado (HOG)
★ Don Zoilo Finest Old Amontillado (ROB)
Harvey's Fine Old Amontillado (HA)
Oloroso de Jerez, Almacenista Viuda de Antonio Borrego (DI)
Oloroso Muy Viejo Almacenista, Lustau (HOG)
★ Palo Cortado, Barbadillo (HAG, SUM)
Viejo Oloroso, Valdespino (WS)

£11.00 to £12.99

Amontillado Almacenista, Lustau (PEN, GAU)
★ Oloroso Muy Viejo Almacenista, Lustau (PEN, GAU)
Palo Cortado, Barbadillo (PIP)
Sandeman Royal Corregidor Oloroso (HOG)
Sandeman Royal Esmeralda (HOG)

£15.00 to £17.99

Amontillado del Duque, Gonzalez Byass (BOT, THR, WR, HOG, GRG, RAE)
★ Apostoles Oloroso, Gonzalez Byass (HOG, GRG, RAE)
Coliseo Amontillado, Valdespino (HOG, WCL)

£19.00 to £20.99

Amontillado del Duque, Gonzalez Byass (PE, VIN)
Apostoles Oloroso, Gonzalez Byass (PE, VIN)

SWEET

Under £5.00

The Society's Cream (WS)

£5.00 to £6.99

Non-vintage
Bertola Cream (HOG)
Croft Original Pale Cream (WHI, TES, HOG, WAI, UN, BOT, THR, WR, WRI, AUG, OD, DAV, JU, EL, VIN)
Harvey's Bristol Cream (WHI, TES, UN, WAI, THR, BOT, WR, HOG, HA, AUG, OD, WRI, DAV)
Harvey's Bristol Milk (HA)
Harvey's Copper Beech (HA)
Sanlúcar Cream, Barbadillo (HIC)
Tanners Cream Sherry (TAN)
Tanners Mariscal Cream (TAN)

£7.00 to £9.99

Don Zoilo Rich Old Cream (HOG)
Harvey's Bristol Cream (HAH, EL)
★ Lustau's Old East India (HOG)
Pedro Ximenez, Barbadillo (PIP)

£15.00 to £17.99

★ Matusalem Oloroso, Gonzalez Byass (BOT, THR, WR, HOG, RAE)

£18.00 to £20.99

Matusalem Oloroso, Gonzalez Byass (OD, PE, ROB, VIN)

PORTUGUESE TABLE WINES

RED

Under £3.00

Non-vintage
Quinta de Cardiga Ribatejo (TES)
★ Sainsbury's Arruda (SAI)
1989
Tesco Bairrada (TES)
Tesco Dão (TES)

£3.00 to £3.99

1992
Alentejo Borba Adega Co-operativa (AUG)
1990
Alentejo Borba Adega Co-operativa (VIC, UN)
★ Dão Grão Vasco (DAV)
1989
Bairrada Dom Ferraz (AUG, WCL)
Bairrada Reserva Caves Aliança (DI)
Bairrada Reserva Dom Ferraz (BOT, WR, THR)
Dão Caves Velhas (GRG)
Dão Dom Ferraz (AUG, UN)
Dão Grão Vasco (PE, GRE)
Dão Reserva Dom Ferraz (WR, BOT, THR)
★ Periquita J.M. da Fonseca (OD, MAJ)
1988
Dão Terras Altas, J.M. da Fonseca (WHI)
1987
Bairrada Dom Ferraz (WAI)
Bairrada Reserva Caves Aliança (MAJ)
Dão Reserva, Caves Aliança (DI)
Dão Reserva Dom Ferraz (WCL)
1986
★ Pasmados J.M. da Fonseca (WAI)
Quinta de Santo Amaro, João Pires (WHI)
1985
Quinta de Santo Amaro, João Pires (WHI)
Tesco Douro (TES)

£4.00 to £4.99

1992
★ Douro Quinta de la Rosa (GE)
1990
Periquita J.M. da Fonseca (BOT, WR)
1989
Dão Terras Altas, J.M. da Fonseca (TAN, PIP, HAG)
Periquita J.M. da Fonseca (WHI, TAN)
★ Tinto da Anfora João Pires (WAI, OD)
1988
Dão Grão Vasco (AV)
João Pires Meia Pipa (OD, THR, WR, BOT)
Pasmados J.M. da Fonseca (BOT)
Periquita J.M. da Fonseca (WHI, GRE, PE, ROB)
Tinto da Anfora João Pires (WAI)
1986
Dão Terras Altas, J.M. da Fonseca (GRE)
Tinto Velho Reguengos (TES)
1985
Bairrada Reserva Caves Aliança (PEN)
Beira Mar Reserva, da Silva (GRG)
Dão Garrafeira Grão Vasco (PE, GRE)
1984
Pasmados J.M. da Fonseca (GRE)
1983
Beira Mar Reserva, da Silva (WCL)
1980
★ Bairrada Frei João (GE)

£5.00 to £5.99

1991
Douro Quinta de la Rosa (VIN)
1990
★ Quinta da Bacalhoa (SAI)
1989
Quinta da Bacalhoa (SAI)
Tinto da Anfora João Pires (WR, THR, BOT, MAJ, WCL)
1988
Pasmados J.M. da Fonseca (PIP)
Tinto da Anfora João Pires (WRI)
1987
Quinta da Camarate, J.M. da Fonseca (WRI, AD, PIP)
Tinto da Anfora João Pires (WRI)
1986
Quinta da Camarate, J.M. da Fonseca (WHI, GRE, WCL, PE)
Tinto Velho J.M. da Fonseca (ROB)
Tinto Velho Reguengos (ROB, WRI)
1985
Beira Mar Reserva, da Silva (AD)
Dão Garrafeira Grão Vasco (ROB)
Pasmados J.M. da Fonseca (HAG)
Quinta da Camarate, J.M. da Fonseca (WHI)
1984
★ Garrafeira Particular Caves Aliança (DI)
1983
Bairrada Frei João (WRI)

1982
Casal da Azenha, da Silva (GRG)
Garrafeira J.M. da Fonseca (WHI)
1980
Garrafeira Caves Velhas (WCL)
1979
Garrafeira da Silva (GRG, UN)

£6.00 to £6.99

1989
Tinto da Anfora João Pires (WHI, LAY)
1983
Beira Mar Reserva, da Silva (VIN)
1980
Casal da Azenha, da Silva (VIN)

£7.00 to £9.99

1988
Bairrada Luis Pato (BOT)
Tinto da Anfora João Pires (HAG)
1979
Garrafeira Particular da Silva (VIN)

£10.00 to £11.99

1990
Quinta da Côtto Grande Escolha, Champalimaud (AD)
1985
Quinta da Côtto Grande Escolha, Champalimaud (ROB)

c. £19.00

1983
Barca Velha, Ferreira (OD)

WHITE

Under £4.00

Non-vintage
Sainsbury's Vinho Verde (SAI)
Vinho Verde Aveleda (HOG)
Vinho Verde Casal Garcia (PEN, AUG)
Vinho Verde Casal Mendes Caves Aliança (DI)
Vinho Verde Gazela (OD, DAV, GRE)
★ Vinho Verde Quinta de Aveleda (HOG)
1992
Bairrada Caves Aliança (GA, MAJ)
1991
Dão Dom Ferraz (WCL)
Dão Grão Vasco (OD, PE)
Dão Terras Altas J.M. da Fonseca (MAJ)
1990
Bairrada Terra Franca (GRE)
Dão Dom Ferraz (GRG)

£4.00 to £4.99

Non-vintage
Vinho Verde Aveleda (HUN, WHI, HAG)
Vinho Verde Dom Ferraz (VIN)
Vinho Verde Gazela (TAN, EL)
1992
Dão Terras Altas J.M. da Fonseca (PIP)
Vinho Verde Aveleda (PIP)
1991
Dry Palmela Moscato, João Pires (OD)
★ João Pires Branco (SAI, GRE)
1990
Dão Grão Vasco (AV)
1989
João Pires Catarina (OD)

£5.00 to £5.99

Non-vintage
Vinho Verde Aveleda (AV)
1992
João Pires Branco (PIP)
1991
João Pires Branco (WHI, JU, HUN)
1990
★ Planalto Reserva (GRE)

c. £7.00

1989
João Pires Branco (VIN)

ROSÉ

Under £4.00

Non-vintage
Mateus Rosé (SAI)

£4.00 to £4.99

Non-vintage
Mateus Rosé (GA, TES, WAI, HOG, AUG, VIC, WHI, DAV)

5.00 to 5.99

Non-vintage
Mateus Rosé (PE, UN, VIN)

FORTIFIED

Under £7.00

1984
Moscatel de Setúbal J.M. da Fonseca (GRE)

c. £16.00

Non-vintage
Moscatel de Setúbal 20-year-old J.M. da Fonseca (TAN)

PORT

Under £6.00

Non-vintage
Waitrose Fine Ruby (WAI)
★ Waitrose Fine Tawny (WAI)

£6.00 to £6.99

Non-vintage
Cockburn's Fine Ruby (HOG, WHI, HA, VIC)
Cockburn's Fine Tawny (HOG, HA)
Sandeman Fine Old Ruby (THR, BOT, WR)
Sandeman Tawny (BOT, THR, WR)
Smith Woodhouse Fine Tawny (UN, WCL)
Smith Woodhouse Ruby (UN, WCL, DAV)
Warre's Ruby (AUG, WHI)

£7.00 to £8.99

Non-vintage
Churchill Dry White (CV, WW)
Cockburn's Fine Ruby (UN, EL, DAV)
Cockburn's Fine Tawny (UN, VIC)
Cockburn's Fine White (UN)
Cockburn's Special Reserve (HOG, WHI, HA, AUG, WAI, VIC, THR, WR, BOT, UN, OD)
Delaforce Special White Port (BOT, WR, THR)
Dow's Fine Ruby (ROB)
Dow's Fine Tawny (ROB)
Dow's No. 1 White (PEN)
Fonseca Bin 27 (HOG, GRG, GRE, WCL, BE, LO)
Graham Ruby (HAG)
Graham Tawny (HAG)
Offley Boa Vista (OD)
Quinta do Noval Late Bottled (HOG, WHI, EY, PEN, WAI, AUG, GRE, DI, HUN, WRI, TAN)
Ramos-Pinto Vintage Character (HAH)
Sandeman Fine Old White (EL)
Sandeman Founder's Reserve (OD)
Taylor Late Bottled (VIC)
Taylor Special Ruby (HAH)
Taylor Special Tawny (HAH)
Warre's Warrior (WHI, AUG, THR, WR, BOT)
1986
Cockburn's Late Bottled (HA, WHI, VIC)
Croft Late Bottled (JU)
★ Dow's Late Bottled (MAJ)
Graham Late Bottled (NI)
1985
Dow's Late Bottled (SUM, WAI)
★ Taylor Late Bottled (HOG)

£9.00 to £11.99

Non-vintage
Churchill Dry White (TAN)
Churchill's Finest Vintage Character (HAY, LOR, HIC, BAR)
★ Cockburn's 10-year-old Tawny (HA, HOG)
Croft Late Bottled (THR, WR, BOT)
Delaforce His Eminence's Choice (JU)
Dow's Vintage Character (HOG, PEN, WRI)
Fonseca 10-year-old Tawny (HOG)
Graham 10-year-old Tawny (NI, BIB)
Graham Late Bottled (BOT, WR, THR)
Sandeman Late Bottled (WR, BOT, THR)
Taylor Chip Dry White Port (GRE, DAV)
Taylor Late Bottled (WR, THR, BOT)
Warre's 10-year-old Tawny (WHI)
★ Warre's Nimrod Old Tawny (AUG)
Wellington Wood Port (BER)
1987
Ramos-Pinto Late Bottled (BEK, HAH)
Smith Woodhouse Fine Crusted (WCL)
1986
Graham Late Bottled (LO, GRE, HAH, HUN)
Taylor Late Bottled (TES, ROB, WHG)
1985
Graham Late Bottled (HOG, HAG, REI, JU)
Quinta do Noval (FA)
1982
Graham Late Bottled (BIB)
Quinta da Eira Velha (ROB)
1981
Smith Woodhouse (WCL)
Warre's Late Bottled (WHI)
1980
Royal Oporto (TES)
Taylor ½ bottle (HAL)

£12.00 to £14.99

Non-vintage
Dow's 10-year-old Tawny (ROB)
Dow's Vintage Character (WIC)
Fonseca 10-year-old Tawny (GRG, PIP, WCL)
Graham 10-year-old Tawny (HUN, GRE, MAJ)
Taylor 10-year-old Tawny (WHI, LAY, GRE, WR, THR, BOT, PEN, HUN, UN, WRI, DAV)
Warre's Nimrod Old Tawny (WHI)
1983
Churchill's Quinta do Agua Alta (HAY)
★ Fonseca (SUM)
Royal Oporto (DI, WRI)
Warre (BAR, HA)
1982
Churchill (HAH)
Delaforce (TAN)
Sandeman (THR, WR, BOT)

1981
Smith Woodhouse Late Bottled (GAU, ROB)
Warre's Late Bottled (PIP, WCL, GE, HAH)
1980
Fonseca (BIB, WY)
Smith Woodhouse (EL)
Warre (WY, BIB)
1979
Dow Quinta do Bomfim (OD)
Warre's Late Bottled (WAI, PEN, DI, GAU)
Warre's Quinta da Cavadinha (AUG, GE)
1970
★ Martinez (BUT)

£15.00 to £19.99

Non-vintage
Cockburn's 20-year-old Tawny (HOG, HA)
Graham 20-year-old Tawny (NI)
★ Sandeman 20-year-old Tawny (OD)
1985
Churchill (LAY, BUT)
Dow (BIB, LAY, BUT, BOT, WR, THR)
Fonseca (BIB, WHG)
Graham (WY, BUT, GRE)
Taylor (BUT, WHG)
Warre (MV, BIB, GR, EL)
1983
Dow (LAY, THR, WR, BOT, TAN, HOG, BUT, EL)
Fonseca (BIB, HOG, BUT)
Gould Campbell (HAG, JU)
Graham (BIB, GR, MAJ)
Offley Boa Vista (THR, WR, BOT, VIG)
Royal Oporto (TW, VIN, UN)
Smith Woodhouse (DI, HAG, WR, BOT, THR)
Taylor (GR, TAN, NA, EL, HOG)
Warre (BIB, HOG, LAY, TAN, EL, BUT, ROB)
1982
Churchill (LAY, BER, WW, TW)
Quinta do Noval (HOG, HA, WR, THR, BOT, AD)
Sandeman (HOG, AD)
Warre's Quinta da Cavadinha (WAI, CV, PIP, WHI, WCL, OD, DI, LAY, TAN, ROB)
1980
Dow (ROB, HOG, WHG, DAV, BER)
Fonseca (HOG, GRE, ROB)
Gould Campbell (BER, JU)
Graham (EL, BAR, DAV, NI, ROB)
Taylor (WY, EL, HOG, CV, WHI, GRE, DAV)
Warre (LAY, CV, ROB, PEN, GRG, DAV, BER)
1978
Fonseca Guimaraens (GRE, NA, GRG)
Graham Malvedos (WHI, GAU)
Quinta do Noval (PEN, DAV, VIC)
Taylor Quinta de Vargellas (GRE, LAY, WRI, HAH, ROB, THR, WR, BOT, VIC, TAN, HAG)
1977
Delaforce (OD)
Dow (SUM)
Gould Campbell (EL)
Royal Oporto (GRG)
Smith Woodhouse (EL)
★ Warre (BIB)
1976
Fonseca Guimaraens (GRE, WCL, GRG, BOT)
Taylor Quinta de Vargellas (WR, BOT)
1975
Croft (BIB)
Dow (BUT)
Fonseca (BUT)
Graham (BIB)
Warre (BUT)
1970
★ Cockburn (FA)
Gould Campbell (JU)
Royal Oporto (BIB)
Sandeman (FA)
Smith Woodhouse (BIB)
Taylor ½ bottle (HAL)
Warre (BUT, FA)

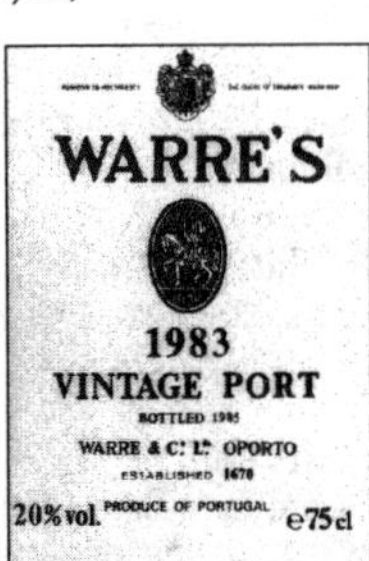

WARRE'S
1983
VINTAGE PORT
BOTTLED 1985
WARRE & C.° L.° OPORTO
ESTABLISHED 1670
20% vol.
PRODUCE OF PORTUGAL
e75cl

£20.00 to £24.99

Non-vintage
Fonseca 20-year-old (PIP, GRG)
Martinez 20-year-old Tawny (HIC)
Quinta do Noval 20-year-old Tawny (DI)
Sandeman 20-year-old Tawny (WAI, BOT)
Taylor 20-year-old Tawny (WHI, LAY, ROB, UN, HUN, GRE, PEN, EL, BOT, WR, THR)
1985
Cockburn (DAV, JU)
Graham (GE, VIC, GAU, HAG, DAV)
Smith Woodhouse (HUN, JU)
Warre (HAG, ROB, DAV)
1983
Cockburn (BUT, DAV)
Fonseca (HAG, JU, LOR, DAV, VIC, BOT, WR)
Graham (VIG, ROB, UN, DAV, BOT, WR, THR)
Warre (HAG, JU, UN, DAV, GAU, AUG, VIC)

1982
Croft (VIG, DAV, UN)
Sandeman (TAN, UN)
1980
Dow (WAI, HAG, GAU, JU)
Fonseca (BER, JU, VIC)
Graham (BER, VIC, JU)
Taylor (GRG, BER, ROB, HAG)
Warre (HAG, GAU, JU, AUG, VIC)
1978
Fonseca Guimaraens (VIG)
Taylor Quinta de Vargellas (VIG)
1977
Gould Campbell (BER, WHI)
Graham (EL, FA, BIB)
Quarles Harris (BUT, BER, AD)
Warre (GR, EL, WCL)
1975
Cockburn (BU, BER, GRG)
Croft (BU, BER)
Dow (TAN, BER, PEN, LAY)
Graham (NI, DAV, BER, TAN, HA)
Quinta do Noval (VIC, ROB)
Warre (CV, NI, AD, DAV, BER, PEN, VIC, WHI)
1970
Croft (FA)
Dow (FA)
Graham (BIB)
Martinez (WHG)
Offley Boa Vista (JU)
Quinta do Noval (BIB)
1966
Dow (FA)
Gould Campbell (JU)
Sandeman (FA)
1958
Quinta do Noval (FA)

£25.00 to £29.99

Non-vintage
Taylor 20-year-old Tawny (TAN, VIN)
1985
Croft (JU)
Fonseca (ROB)
Graham (JU)
Taylor (HAG, WHI, DAV)
Warre (JU)
1977
Dow (DI, LAY, BUT)
Fonseca (HA, HOG, LOR)
Graham (WS, WHI, GRE, WHG)
Sandeman (HOG, BER, JU)
Smith Woodhouse (WHI)
Taylor (BIB, WY)
Warre (BU, LAY, TAN, GE, NI, WHG)
1975
Graham (ROB, GAU, AUG)
Quinta do Noval (AUG)
Taylor (DAV, AUG)
1970
Cockburn (JU, DAV)
Croft (BIB, WHI, DAV)
Dow (BIB, BUT)
Fonseca (WHG, FA, BIB, HUN)
Rebello Valente (VIC)
Taylor (BIB, FA, WY)
Warre (BIB, TAN)
1966
Croft (WY)
Delaforce (BER)
Offley Boa Vista (BER)
Rebello Valente (BUT)
Smith Woodhouse (REI)
1960
Croft (FA)
Warre (FA)

£30.00 to £39.99

1977
Croft (BER, JU, CB, HAG, DAV)
Dow (PEN, BER, DAV, GAU, VIC)
Graham (HUN, JU, DAV)
Taylor (TAN, AD, DAV)
Warre (JU, PEN, AUG, ROB, BER, UN, HAG)
1970
Dow (BER, DI, DAV, ROB)
Fonseca (DAV, AD, BER, LOR, HOG, GRE)
Graham (AUG, LAY, JU, GRG, GAU, BUT, DAV)
Quinta do Noval (BER, EY)
Taylor (TAN, BAR, DI, DAV, HUN, WHI)
Warre (CV, LAY, BER, JU, DAV, CB, ROB)
1966
Dow (BUT, DAV)
Fonseca (BIB, WS, FA)
Graham (WS, DAV)
Taylor (BUT, FA, EY, BU, DAV)
Warre (AD, GR)
1963
Cockburn (WY, TAN)
Croft (GR, WY, MV)
Quinta do Noval (FA, MV)
1960
Cockburn (BUT, DAV)
Dow (BUT, BAR, DI)
Sandeman (DAV, JU)
Taylor (WY, DAV)
1958
Fonseca (BU)
1950
Cockburn (FA)

£40.00 to £49.99

1977
Taylor (UN, ROB)
1970
Fonseca (ROB)
Fonseca Guimaraens (GAU)
Graham (ROB, NI)
Quinta do Noval (VIN)
Warre (THR, BOT, WR)
1966
Dow (EL)
Fonseca (JU)
Sandeman (ROB)
Taylor (WS, TAN, HAG)
1963
Cockburn (BIB, HA)
Quinta do Noval (BU, EY)
Warre (BIB, NI, WS, BAR)
1960
Croft (JU, ROB)
Fonseca (JU)
Graham (JU, BUT)
1955
Cockburn (FA)
Gould Campbell (TW)
Quinta do Noval (FA)
1944
Royal Oporto (TW)

£50.00 to £74.99

Non-vintage
Fonseca 40-year-old (GRG)
Quinta do Noval 40-year-old Tawny (DI)
Taylor 40-year-old Tawny (GRE, PEN, UN)
1966
Graham (ROB)
1963
Croft (WHG, HAG, WS, ROB, DAV)
Dow (HAG, JU, DAV)
Fonseca (FA, BIB, EL, BUT)
Graham (FA, DAV, WS)
Quinta do Noval (WHG, NI)
Taylor (FA, BIB, DAV, REI)
Warre (HAG, ROB, DAV)
1955
Martinez (HUN, WHI)
Quinta do Noval (HUN)
1952
Calem (ROB)
1950
Croft (WY)
1924
Rebello Valente (WY)
1915
Gould Campbell (VIG)

£75.00 to £99.99

1963
Dow (ROB)
Fonseca (JU)
Taylor (JU, ROB)
1955
Taylor (WY, FA)
1920
Sandeman (FA)

£100.00 to £139.99

1955
Graham (JU)
1948
Taylor (FA)
1935
Cockburn (WY)
Graham (WY)
1927
Warre (WY)
1920
Dow (WY)
Warre (WY)
1908
Mackenzie (FA)

£140.00 to £179.99

1948
Graham (FA)
1945
Quinta do Noval (BUT)
1927
Cockburn (WY)
Croft (WY)
1920
Taylor (WY)
Warre (BIB)
1912
Cockburn (WY)

£180.00 to £220.00

1948
Graham (BIB)
1935
Taylor (FA)
1927
Taylor (TW)
1920
Taylor (BIB)

c. £400.00

1945
Fonseca (ROB)
1931
Quinta do Noval (TW)

MADEIRA

Under £8.00

Non-vintage

Bual Blandy (HOG, NI)
Bual Old Trinity House Rutherford & Miles (HAH, ROB, GRG)
Malmsey Blandy (HOG, NI)
Malmsey Cossart Gordon (CV)
Rainwater Good Company Cossart Gordon (DI)
Sercial Blandy (HOG, NI)
Sercial Cossart Gordon (CV)
Sercial Old Custom House Rutherford & Miles (ROB, GRG)
Verdelho Blandy (HOG)

£8.00 to £9.99

Non-vintage

5-year-old Bual Cossart Gordon (DI, CV)
★ 5-year-old Malmsey Cossart Gordon (DI)
Bual Blandy (VIN, THR, WR, BOT, TAN, OD)
Bual Cossart Gordon (BAR, WCL)
Bual Old Trinity House Rutherford & Miles (BE)
Finest Old Malmsey Cossart Gordon (HAY)
Malmsey Blandy (HAH, GRE, VIN, DAV)
Malmsey Cossart Gordon (WCL)
Rainwater Good Company Cossart Gordon (JU, PEN)
Sercial Blandy (GRE, VIN, BOT, THR, WR, TAN, OD)
Sercial Cossart Gordon (HAH, BAR, JU, WCL)
Verdelho Blandy (GRE, VIN)

£10.00 to £14.99

Non-vintage

10-year-old Malmsey Blandy (HOG, WAI, NI, GRE, ROB)
10-year-old Malmsey Cossart Gordon (GRE)
5-year-old Bual Cossart Gordon (SUM, JU, GRE, HIC)
5-year-old Malmsey Cossart Gordon (SUM, GRE, AD)
5-year-old Sercial Cossart Gordon (SUM, JU, GRE)
Finest Old Bual Cossart Gordon (PIP)
Finest Old Malmsey Cossart Gordon (PIP)
Finest Old Sercial Cossart Gordon (PIP)
Malmsey Cossart Gordon (AV)
Rainwater Good Company Cossart Gordon (AV, AD)
Sercial Cossart Gordon (AV)

£15.00 to £19.99

Non-vintage

10-year-old Malmsey Cossart Gordon (CV, HIC, JU)
10-year-old Verdelho Cossart Gordon (CV, HIC)
★ Very Old Sercial Duo Centenary Celebration Cossart Gordon (HAH)

£20.00 to £49.99

1954

Bual Henriques & Henriques (BU, GRE)

1950

Sercial Rutherford & Miles (GRE)

1934

Verdelho Henriques & Henriques (GRE)

£50.00 to £79.99

1952

Verdelho Cossart Gordon (DI)
Malmsey Rutherford & Miles (HAG)

1950

Sercial Leacock (VIG)

1920

Malmsey Cossart Gordon (WHG)

£89.00 to £95.00

1934

Verdelho Henriques & Henriques (VIG)

1931

Verdelho Blandy (VIG)

1920

Malmsey Cossart Gordon (DI)

1914

Bual Cossart Gordon (DI)

c. £115.00

1920

Bual Blandy (VIG)

£140.00 to £160.00

1930

Malmsey Quinta do Serrado (AD)

1927

Bual Quinta do Serrado (AD)

Stars (★) indicate wines selected by the editors as particularly good value in their class.

UNITED STATES

CALIFORNIA RED

Under £4.00

Non-vintage
E&J Gallo Dry Reserve (SAF, BOT, THR, AUG, GA, PE)
1989
Mountain View Pinot Noir (WAI)
1988
★ Glen Ellen Cabernet Sauvignon (GA)

£4.00 to £5.99

Non-vintage
Franzia Cabernet Sauvignon (VIC)
Trefethen Eshcol Red (WHI)
1990
Fetzer Zinfandel (SOM, OD, SAF)
Glen Ellen Cabernet Sauvignon (AUG, GRE)
Quady Elysium Black Muscat ½ bottle (GRG)
Robert Mondavi Cabernet Sauvignon (HAH)
Robert Mondavi Woodbridge Cabernet Sauvignon (THR, BOT, WR, WHI)
1989
Fetzer Zinfandel (CV, WHI)
Glen Ellen Cabernet Sauvignon (HOG)
La Crema Pinot Noir (SAI)
★ Robert Mondavi Cabernet Sauvignon (VIC)
Robert Mondavi Woodbridge Cabernet Sauvignon (HUN)
1988
Inglenook Petite Sirah (WRI)
Inglenook Zinfandel (VIC)

£6.00 to £7.99

1992
★ Cá del Solo Big House Red (MV, AD)
1991
★ Cá del Solo Big House Red (WCL)
★ Saintsbury Garnet Pinot Noir (GE)
1990
★ Cá del Solo Big House Red (REI)
Fetzer Zinfandel (JU)
Hawk Crest Cabernet Sauvignon (WW)
Quady Elysium Black Muscat (NI, HAG)
1989
★ Carneros Creek Pinot Noir (WCL, ROB)
Quady Elysium Black Muscat ½ bottle (HAL)
Robert Mondavi Woodbridge Cabernet Sauvignon (BER)
1988
Beaulieu Beautour Cabernet Sauvignon (GRG, SAI)
Buena Vista Zinfandel (WCL, WCL)
Clos du Bois Cabernet Sauvignon (WHI)
Clos du Bois Merlot (AMI)
Firestone Cabernet Sauvignon (HOG, PIP)
Firestone Merlot (WHI, HOG, AMI)
Franciscan Cabernet Sauvignon (BAR)
Pedroncelli Cabernet Sauvignon (LAY)
★ Ridge Paso Robles Zinfandel (HOG)
1987
Beringer Cabernet Sauvignon (GA)
Clos du Bois Cabernet Sauvignon (WHI)
1986
Dry Creek Cabernet Sauvignon (HOG)
Firestone Pinot Noir (HOG)
Sterling Cabernet Sauvignon (OD)

£8.00 to £9.99

1992
Saintsbury Garnet Pinot Noir (BIB)
1990
Il Podere dell'Olivos Nebbiolo (MV)
★ Jade Mountain Mourvèdre (MV)
Joseph Phelps Le Mistral (AMI)
Ridge Paso Robles Zinfandel (AMI, AD)
★ Sanford Pinot Noir (SOM)
1989
Clos du Bois Merlot (WCL, PE)
Firestone Cabernet Sauvignon (BOT, WR, THR)
Laurel Glen Cabernet Sauvignon (WW)

Ridge Geyserville Zinfandel (GRE)
Ridge Paso Robles Zinfandel (SAF, GE)
1988
Buena Vista Cabernet Sauvignon (WCL)
Dry Creek Cabernet Sauvignon (NI)
★ Saintsbury Pinot Noir (RAE)
1987
Franciscan Cabernet Sauvignon (PEN)
Renaissance Cabernet Sauvignon (AD)

1986
Clos du Val Zinfandel (CHA)
★ Sanford Pinot Noir (HOG)
Schug Cellars Pinot Noir (VIG)
1985
Rutherford Hill Cabernet Sauvignon (HOG)
1984
Clos du Val Pinot Noir (CHA)
1982
Clos du Val Cabernet Sauvignon (CHA)

£10.00 to £11.99

1991
Saintsbury Pinot Noir (JU, AD)
1990
★ Au Bon Climat Pinot Noir (MV)
Cá del Solo Barbera (WCL)
Calera Jensen Pinot Noir (PIP)
Jade Mountain La Provençale (WCL, MAJ)
Ojai Syrah (AD)
Ridge Geyserville Zinfandel (WS)
Saintsbury Pinot Noir (WS, GE, HAH, WR, BOT)
Sanford Pinot Noir (AMI, ROB)
Shafer Merlot (AD)
1989
★ Bonny Doon Le Cigare Volant (RAE, WCL)
Cuvaison Merlot/Zinfandel (BY)
Newton Merlot (WCL)
Ridge Geyserville Zinfandel (GE, PIP, ROB, HAH)
Robert Mondavi Pinot Noir (TAN, WS)
Saintsbury Pinot Noir (HAH)
1988
Dry Creek Zinfandel (HAH)
Ridge Geyserville Zinfandel (GAU)
Sanford Pinot Noir (WHI, NI, WCL)
Shafer Cabernet Sauvignon (WS)
★ Simi Cabernet Sauvignon (LAY)
1987
Clos du Val Merlot (CHA)
Robert Mondavi Cabernet Sauvignon (ROB, VIG)
Rutherford Hill Merlot (AV)
Shafer Merlot (ROB)
Simi Cabernet Sauvignon (CB)
1986
Newton Cabernet Sauvignon (WCL)
Renaissance Cabernet Sauvignon (PEN)
Ridge York Creek Cabernet Sauvignon (GRE)
Robert Mondavi Cabernet Sauvignon (HOG)
Sanford Pinot Noir (WHI)
Simi Cabernet Sauvignon (TAN, LAY)
Trefethen Cabernet Sauvignon (AMI)
1985
Clos du Val Cabernet Sauvignon (CHA)
Ridge York Creek Cabernet Sauvignon (HOG)
1984
Ridge York Creek Cabernet Sauvignon (GAU)
Robert Mondavi Oakville Cabernet Sauvignon (WHI)

£12.00 to £14.99

1990
Bonny Doon Le Cigare Volant (MV)
Calera Jensen Pinot Noir (JU)
★ Qupe Syrah Bien Nacido (MV)
Saintsbury Pinot Noir (BIB, BER)
1989
Au Bon Climat Pinot Noir (MV, ROB)
Carneros Creek Pinot Noir (BER)
Joseph Phelps Cabernet Sauvignon (AMI)
Qupe Syrah Bien Nacido (MV)
Ridge Geyserville Zinfandel (VIG)
Robert Mondavi Pinot Noir (HAG)
Stag's Leap Cabernet Sauvignon (ROB)
1988
Clos du Val Cabernet Sauvignon (WS)
Cuvaison Cabernet Sauvignon (BY)
Trefethen Cabernet Sauvignon (BER)
1987
Bonny Doon Le Cigare Volant (BUT)
Cuvaison Cabernet Sauvignon (HUN)
Joseph Phelps Cabernet Sauvignon (WCL)
Laurel Glen Cabernet Sauvignon (BAR)
Robert Mondavi Oakville Cabernet Sauvignon (NI)
1986
Calera Jensen Pinot Noir (HOG)
Carmenet Cabernet Sauvignon (SOM)
Iron Horse Cabernet Sauvignon (AMI)
Newton Merlot (BER)
1985
Clos du Val Cabernet Sauvignon (BER)
1984
Renaissance Cabernet Sauvignon (WHI)
1982
★ Beaulieu Vineyards Georges de Latour Private Reserve Cabernet Sauvignon (JU)
Simi Reserve Cabernet Sauvignon (CB)

£15.00 to £19.99

1990
Saintsbury Pinot Noir Reserve (WS, GE)
1989
Matanzas Creek Merlot (HAH)

1988
Au Bon Climat Pinot Noir (BUT)
Matanzas Creek Merlot (BAR)
Qupe Syrah Bien Nacido (GAU)
Robert Mondavi Pinot Noir Reserve (WHI, VIG)
Stag's Leap Cabernet Sauvignon (BER, VIG)
1987
Sterling Cabernet Sauvignon Reserve (OD)
1986
Chalone Pinot Noir (AMI)
Jordan Cabernet Sauvignon (LAY)
Robert Mondavi Pinot Noir Reserve (WHI)
1985
Jordan Cabernet Sauvignon (PEN)
1984
Mayacamas Cabernet Sauvignon (GAU)
1983
Freemark Abbey Cabernet Bosche (VIG)
1982
Acacia St Clair Pinot Noir (BUT)
1980
Ridge York Creek Cabernet Sauvignon (AD)
Robert Mondavi Cabernet Sauvignon Reserve (HOG, WHI, GRE)
1976
Firestone Pinot Noir (BUT)

£20.00 to £29.99

1992
Saintsbury Pinot Noir Reserve (BIB)
1990
Calera Jensen Pinot Noir (AMI)
1988
Dominus Christian Moueix (MV)
Robert Mondavi Cabernet Sauvignon Reserve (BER)
1987
Beringer Cabernet Sauvignon (ROB)
Robert Mondavi Cabernet Sauvignon Reserve (NI, JU)
1986
Dominus Christian Moueix (MV, HAH, LAY)
1984
Alexander Valley Cabernet Sauvignon (BUT)
1982
Jekel Cabernet Sauvignon Private Reserve (BUT)
1980
Ridge Monte Bello Cabernet Sauvignon (VIG)
1979
Robert Mondavi Cabernet Sauvignon (ROB)
1977
Robert Mondavi Cabernet Sauvignon Reserve (VIG, GAU)

£30.00 to £39.99

1987
Mondavi/Rothschild Opus One (GRE, PE)
Robert Mondavi Cabernet Sauvignon Reserve (GAU)
1986
Heitz Martha's Vineyard Cabernet Sauvignon (AMI)
1983
Mondavi/Rothschild Opus One (RAE)
1982
Heitz Martha's Vineyard Cabernet Sauvignon (GRE)
1981
Mondavi/Rothschild Opus One (HOG)
1980
Ridge Monte Bello Cabernet Sauvignon (BUT)
1978
Jekel Cabernet Sauvignon (BUT)
Ridge Monte Bello Cabernet Sauvignon (AD)

£40.00 to £49.99

1988
Mondavi/Rothschild Opus One (BUT, BOT, WR)
1987
Mondavi/Rothschild Opus One (PIP, TAN, BUT, BOT, WR, ROB, NI)
1986
Mondavi/Rothschild Opus One (CV, GRE, BUT, NI)
1985
Mondavi/Rothschild Opus One (HAH, WHI)
1977
Heitz Bella Oaks Cabernet Sauvignon (GRG)
Heitz Martha's Vineyard Cabernet Sauvignon (GRG)
1976
Heitz Martha's Vineyard Cabernet Sauvignon (AD)

£50.00 to £55.00

1987
Mondavi/Rothschild Opus One (AMI)
1985
Mondavi/Rothschild Opus One (BUT)

c. £63.00

1985
Heitz Martha's Vineyard Cabernet Sauvignon (BUT)

CALIFORNIA WHITE

Under £4.00

Non-vintage
E&J Gallo Chenin Blanc (THR, BOT, PE)
E&J Gallo French Colombard (SAF, BOT, THR, WR, GA, PE)
E&J Gallo Sauvignon Blanc (SAF, WR, VIC, BOT, THR, PE)
1991
E&J Gallo Chenin Blanc (AUG, DAV)
E&J Gallo French Colombard (AUG, DAV)
E&J Gallo Sauvignon Blanc (AUG)
1990
E&J Gallo Chenin Blanc (UN)
E&J Gallo Sauvignon Blanc (SAI)

£4.00 to £5.99

Non-vintage
Sainsbury's Chardonnay (SAI)
Trefethen Eshcol (WHI)
1991
Dry Creek Chenin Blanc (EY)
Glen Ellen Chardonnay (AUG, GRE)
Hawk Crest Chardonnay (SAF)
Robert Mondavi Woodbridge Sauvignon Blanc (WHI)
Stratford Winery Chardonnay (WS)
1990
★ Dry Creek Chenin Blanc (GRE)
Glen Ellen Chardonnay (WHI)
Quady Essensia Orange Muscat ½ bottle (GRG)
Robert Mondavi Sauvignon Blanc (HAH)
Sterling Chardonnay (OD)
Sterling Sauvignon Blanc (OD)
1989
Dry Creek Chenin Blanc (RAE)
Robert Mondavi Woodbridge Sauvignon Blanc (HUN)
1988
Firestone Selected Harvest Johannisberg Riesling ½ bottle (GRE)
★ Joseph Phelps Johannisberg Riesling Selected Late Harvest ½ bottle (VIC)
Quady Essensia Orange Muscat ½ bottle (PEN)
★ Robert Mondavi Moscato d'Oro (WHI)

Stars (★) indicate wines selected by the editors as particularly good value in their class.

£6.00 to £7.99

1991
Cá del Solo Malvasia Bianca (WCL)
Dry Creek Fumé Blanc (CV)
Firestone Chardonnay (SAI)
Hawk Crest Chardonnay (WW)
★ Murphy Goode Fumé Blanc (AD)
Stag's Leap Sauvignon Blanc (WW)
1990
Clos du Bois Sauvignon Blanc (GRE)
Dry Creek Chenin Blanc (ROB)
Firestone Chardonnay (HOG)
Pedroncelli Chardonnay (LAY)
Preston Cuvée de Fumé (WS)
Quady Essensia Orange Muscat (NI, HAG)
Quady Essensia ½ bottle (WR, THR, BOT)
Sanford Sauvignon Blanc (SOM)
1989
Clos du Bois Sauvignon Blanc (PE)
Dry Creek Chardonnay (HOG)
Quady Essensia Orange Muscat ½ bottle (WHI, ROB, BY)
★ Renaissance Riesling (AD)
Sanford Sauvignon Blanc (AMI)
Stratford Winery Chardonnay (MAJ)
Wente Bros Chardonnay (HOG, PEN, GRE, GA, UN)

1988
Clos du Bois Sauvignon Blanc (PE)
Dry Creek Fumé Blanc (HOG)
★ Renaissance Riesling (PEN, ROB)
Robert Mondavi Moscato d'Oro (AD)
Sanford Sauvignon Blanc (HOG)

£8.00 to £9.99

1992
Il Podere dell'Olivos Arioso (MV)
1991
Cá del Solo Il Pescatore (WCL, MV)
Murphy Goode Fumé Blanc (HAH)
★ Saintsbury Chardonnay (GE)
1990
Alexander Valley Chardonnay (HAH)
Buena Vista Chardonnay (WCL)
Chateau St-Jean Fumé Blanc (PIP)
★ Edna Valley Chardonnay (PIP)
Il Podere dell'Olivos Arioso (WCL)
Simi Sauvignon Blanc (LAY)
1989
Acacia Chardonnay (BOT, WR, THR)
Clos du Bois Chardonnay (WHI, BOT, WR, THR)
Edna Valley Chardonnay (CV)
Sanford Chardonnay (SOM)
Simi Sauvignon Blanc (TAN)
1988
Clos du Bois Chardonnay (WHI)
Clos du Val Chardonnay (CHA)
Edna Valley Chardonnay (HOG)
Robert Mondavi Fumé Blanc (HAG)
Robert Mondavi Oakville Chardonnay (WHI)
Saintsbury Chardonnay (GE)
Swanson Chardonnay (HOG, PEN)
1987
Robert Mondavi Oakville Chardonnay (WHI)
Robert Mondavi Oakville Fumé Blanc Reserve (WHI)
Rutherford Hill Chardonnay (AV)
Sanford Chardonnay (HOG)
Shafer Chardonnay (WRI)
1986
Saintsbury Chardonnay (AV)
1985
Renaissance Riesling Select Late Harvest ½ bottle (GAU)
Robert Mondavi Oakville Fumé Blanc Reserve (WHI)
1983
Renaissance Botrytis Sauvignon ½ bottle (AD)

£10.00 to £11.99

1991
★ Frogs Leap Chardonnay (MV)
Saintsbury Chardonnay (JU, AD, WR, BOT, BIB)
Stag's Leap Chardonnay (WW)
1990
Clos du Bois Chardonnay (AD)
Grgich Hills Fumé Blanc (EL)
Matanzas Creek Sauvignon Blanc (HAH)
Philip Togni Sauvignon Blanc (WW)
Qupe Chardonnay (OD)
Saintsbury Chardonnay (HAH)
★ Simi Chardonnay (CB)
1989
Cuvaison Chardonnay (BY)
Edna Valley Chardonnay (WCL, ROB)
Simi Chardonnay (LAY)
Stag's Leap Sauvignon Blanc (VIG)
1988
Cuvaison Chardonnay (BY)
Edna Valley Chardonnay (EY)
Rutherford Hill Jaeger Chardonnay (AV)
Simi Chardonnay (TAN)
★ Sonoma-Cutrer Chardonnay (WRI)
1987
Robert Mondavi Chardonnay (TAN)

£12.00 to £14.99

1991
Au Bon Climat Chardonnay (MV)
Saintsbury Reserve Chardonnay (JU)
1990
Au Bon Climat Chardonnay (MV, WCL, ROB)
Saintsbury Reserve Chardonnay (AD)
1989
Edna Valley Chardonnay (AMI)
★ Kistler Chardonnay Dutton Ranch (HAH)
Swanson Chardonnay (AV)
1988
Acacia Chardonnay (AMI)
Au Bon Climat Chardonnay (BUT)
Cuvaison Chardonnay (ROB)
Robert Mondavi Oakville Reserve Chardonnay (WHI)
Sanford Chardonnay (NI)
Sonoma-Cutrer les Pierres Chardonnay (HOG)

In each price band wines are listed in vintage order. Within each vintage they are listed in A–Z order.

1987
Cuvaison Chardonnay (HUN)
Robert Mondavi Oakville Reserve Chardonnay (WHI)
Simi Reserve Chardonnay (LAY)
Sonoma-Cutrer les Pierres Chardonnay (PEN)
1986
Iron Horse Chardonnay (BER)
Robert Mondavi Chardonnay Reserve (GAU)
1983
Robert Mondavi Sauvignon Blanc Botrytis ½ bottle (HAL)

£15.00 to £19.99

1991
Bonny Doon Le Sophiste (MV, WCL)
Kistler Chardonnay Dutton Ranch (AD)
1990
Grgich Hills Chardonnay (EL)
Kistler Chardonnay Dutton Ranch (BIB)
1989
Chalone Chardonnay (AMI)
Jordan Chardonnay (LAY)
Stag's Leap Chardonnay (ROB, CB)
1988
Matanzas Creek Chardonnay (BAR)
Robert Mondavi Chardonnay Reserve (VIG)
1987
Robert Mondavi Chardonnay Reserve (AD)
1986
Alexander Valley Chardonnay (PEN)
1984
Acacia Chardonnay (BUT)
1983
Joseph Phelps Johannisberg Riesling Selected Late Harvest ½ bottle (HAL)

c. £24.00

1989
Far Niente Chardonnay (AV)

c. £35.00

1983
Robert Mondavi Sauvignon Blanc Botrytis (VIG)

CALIFORNIA ROSÉ

Under £5.00

Non-vintage
E&J Gallo White Grenache (SAF, VIC)
E&J Gallo White Zinfandel (PE)
1991
E&J Gallo White Grenache (AUG)

£5.00 to £5.99

1991
Robert Mondavi White Zinfandel (WHI, NI)
1990
Robert Mondavi White Zinfandel (WHI, ROB)

CALIFORNIA SPARKLING

Under £9.00

Non-vintage
★ Cuvée Napa Brut Mumm (OD, ROB)

£13.00 to £16.00

1987
Iron Horse Brut (AD)
1986
Schramsberg Blanc de Blancs (ROB, VIG)
1985
Schramsberg Blanc de Blancs (AD)

c. £17.50

1983
Schramsberg Blanc de Noirs (AD)

OTHER USA RED

Under £7.00

Non-vintage
Cameron Pinot Noir (BIB)
1989
Columbia Pinot Noir (ASD)
1988
Covey Run Lemberger (HE)

£7.00 to £8.99

1988
Columbia Pinot Noir (NA, BAR)
1986
Columbia Pinot Noir (PEN)

£9.00 to £13.99

1990
Adelsheim Pinot Noir (WW)

1989
Adelsheim Pinot Noir (ROB)
Cameron Pinot Noir Reserve (BIB)
1988
Cameron Pinot Noir Reserve (BIB)
Château Ste-Michelle Cabernet Sauvignon (WRI)
Eyrie Vineyard Pinot Meunier (WW)
Eyrie Vineyard Pinot Noir (WW)
1987
Llano Estacado Cabernet Sauvignon (HE)
Ponzi Pinot Noir (ROB)
1986
Elk Cove Estate Pinot Noir (HE)

c. £21.00

1989
Domaine Drouhin Pinot Noir (VIG, REI)

OTHER USA WHITE

Under £6.00

1991
Columbia Gewurztraminer (NA)
1988
Columbia Gewurztraminer (PEN)
Fall Creek Emerald Riesling (HE)
1987
Covey Run Aligoté (HE)
Eyrie Muscat Ottonel (WW)

£6.00 to £7.99

1990
Hogue Cellars Fumé Blanc (ROB)
Snoqualmie Semillon (ROB)
1989
Columbia Chardonnay (NA)
Snoqualmie Semillon (WCL)
Stewart Chardonnay (WW)
1988
Columbia Chardonnay (PEN)
Snoqualmie Muscat Canelli (WCL)

£8.00 to £9.99

1988
Llano Estacado Chardonnay (HE)
1987
Elk Cove Estate Chardonnay Estate (HE)
1986
Salishan Chardonnay (WCL)

£10.00 to £13.99

1989
Cameron Chardonnay (BIB)
1988
Cameron Chardonnay (BIB)
1987
Eyrie Vineyard Chardonnay (ROB)

AUSTRALIA

RED

Under £4.00

Non-vintage
Sainsbury's Shiraz/Cabernet Sauvignon (SAI)
1991
Berri Cabernet Sauvignon/Shiraz (WAI)
Orlando Jacob's Creek Red (HOG, NA, THR, BOT, WR, AUS, LO)
★ Penfolds Dalwood Shiraz/Cabernet Sauvignon (HOG, ROB, WCL, BY, GRE)
Penfolds Shiraz/Mataro Bin 2 (SAF)
Tollana Cabernet Sauvignon/Shiraz (BOT, WR, THR)
1990
Hardy Collection Cabernet Sauvignon/Shiraz (PEN)
Lindeman Shiraz Bin 50 (WAI)
Orlando Jacob's Creek Red (KA, GA, SAF)
Seaview Cabernet Sauvignon (GA)
Tollana Cabernet Sauvignon/Shiraz (UN)
Wyndham's Shiraz Bin 555 (MAJ)
Yalumba Oxford Landing Cabernet Sauvignon/Shiraz (ASD)
1989
Krondorf Shiraz/Cabernet Sauvignon (HOG)
Orlando Cabernet Sauvignon (GRE)
Orlando RF Cabernet Sauvignon (WHI, SAF)
Penfolds Coonawarra Shiraz Bin 128 (SOM)
Penfolds Koonunga Hill Cabernet Sauvignon/Shiraz (DAV, AUG, AUS)
Rosemount Diamond Reserve Cabernet Sauvignon/Shiraz (CHA)
Rosemount Diamond Reserve Dry Red (CV)
1988
Brown Bros Shiraz (GRG)
Lindeman Shiraz Bin 50 (WHI)
Nottage Hill Cabernet Sauvignon Limited Reserve (PEN)
★ Rouge Homme Shiraz/Cabernet Sauvignon (GRG)

£4.00 to £4.99

1992
★ David Wynn Cabernet Sauvignon (SOM)
1991
Orlando Cabernet Sauvignon (DAV)
Penfolds Koonunga Hill Cabernet Sauvignon/Shiraz (HOG, OD, VIC, WHI)
★ Rosemount Diamond Reserve Cabernet Sauvignon/Shiraz (NI)
Rosemount Diamond Reserve Dry Red (WHI)
Tyrrells Long Flat Red (PIP)
Yalumba Oxford Landing Cabernet Sauvignon/Shiraz (NI)
1990
Baileys Bundarra Shiraz (OD)
David Wynn Pinot Noir (SOM)
Krondorf Shiraz/Cabernet Sauvignon (GRG)
Leasingham Cabernet Sauvignon/Malbec Bin 56 (MAJ)
Lindeman Cabernet Sauvignon Bin 45 (UN)
Orlando Cabernet Sauvignon (HOG, SAI, DAV)
Orlando RF Cabernet Sauvignon (AUS, VIC)
★ Penfolds Koonunga Hill Cabernet Sauvignon/Shiraz (SOM, MAJ, SAF, DAV)
Peter Lehmann Shiraz (GRE)

£5.00 to £5.99

1993
David Wynn Cabernet Sauvignon (WCL)
David Wynn Pinot Noir (WCL)
1992
Tyrrells Long Flat Red (AV)
Wynns Shiraz (WCL)
1991
David Wynn Cabernet Sauvignon (NA)
David Wynn Pinot Noir (NA)
Rosemount Cabernet Sauvignon (WR, THR, BOT, NI, NA, WHI)
Rosemount Pinot Noir (NI)
Rothbury Estate Syrah (CV)
Rothbury Shiraz (SOM)
Tyrrells Pinot Noir (SAF)
Wyndham's Shiraz Bin 555 (WHI)
1990
Brown Bros Shiraz (GRE)
Penfolds Coonawarra Shiraz Bin 128 (THR, WR, WHI, BOT)
★ Penfolds Kalimna Shiraz Bin 28 (PIP, OD)
Rosemount Cabernet Sauvignon (SAF, GRE)
Rosemount Pinot Noir (GRE, WHI, NA)
Tisdall Cabernet Sauvignon/Merlot (NA)
Wolf Blass Yellow Label Cabernet Sauvignon (HOG)
Wyndham's Cabernet Sauvignon Bin 444 (WHI)

1989
Basedow Shiraz (BIB)
Berri Cabernet Sauvignon (UN)
Brown Bros Shiraz (PIP)
Lindeman Shiraz Bin 50 (HUN)
Mildara Shiraz (GRG)
Penfolds Kalimna Shiraz Bin 28 (HOG, MAJ)
★ Rosemount Hunter Valley Shiraz (WCL)
Rothbury Estate Syrah (GRE)
Taltarni Shiraz (WHI, SOM)
1988
Brown Bros Cabernet Sauvignon (DI)
Brown Bros Shiraz/Cabernet Sauvignon (DI)
Rosemount Cabernet Sauvignon (CHA)
Rosemount Pinot Noir (CHA)
Rosemount Shiraz (CV, CHA)
Rouge Homme Shiraz/Cabernet Sauvignon (EY, GRE, BR, WHI, AV, ROB, WRI)
1984
★ Idyll Cabernet Sauvignon/Shiraz (HOG)

£6.00 to £6.99

Non-vintage
Penfolds Cabernet Sauvignon/Shiraz Bin 389 (GA)
1991
Mitchell Peppertree Shiraz (AD)
Rothbury Shiraz (AMI)
★ Schinus Molle Pinot Noir (NA)
Wyndham's Pinot Noir Bin 333 (WHI)
1990
Brown Bros Shiraz (WHI, MAJ, PE, TAN)
Brown Bros Shiraz/Cabernet Sauvignon (HAG)
Coriole Sangiovese (WS)
Coriole Shiraz (BAR)
De Bortoli Cabernet Sauvignon (OD)
Jamiesons Run Coonawarra Red (BE, DAV)
Mitchell Peppertree Shiraz (LAY, TAN)
Mount Langi Ghiran Shiraz (SOM)
Schinus Molle Cabernet Sauvignon (NA)
Schinus Molle Pinot Noir (WCL)
Thomas Mitchell Cabernet Sauvignon/Shiraz (WRI)
Wolf Blass Cabernet Sauvignon (GRE)

*Please remember that **Webster's** is a price GUIDE and not a price LIST. It is not meant to replace up-to-date merchants' lists.*

1989
★ Baileys Bundarra Shiraz (WRI)
Brown Bros Cabernet Sauvignon (BY, PIP, WHI, PE, AD)
★ Chateau Tahbilk Cabernet Sauvignon (GRE)
Jamiesons Run Coonawarra Red (WHI, DAV)
Mildara Cabernet Sauvignon (BE)
Penfolds Cabernet Sauvignon/Shiraz Bin 389 (MAJ, OD, THR, GRG, BOT, WR)
Rosemount Pinot Noir (ROB)
Rosemount Shiraz (BEK)
Rothbury Shiraz (WCL)
Wolf Blass Cabernet Sauvignon (WHI, LO)
Wolf Blass Yellow Label Cabernet Sauvignon (BY)
1988
Basedow Cabernet Sauvignon (TAN, BIB)
Knappstein Cabernet Sauvignon (OD)
Penfolds Cabernet Sauvignon/Shiraz Bin 389 (HOG, WHI, SAI, MAJ)
Penfolds Coonawarra Shiraz Bin 128 (WCL)
Rosemount Hunter Valley Shiraz (BUT)
Schinus Molle Cabernet Sauvignon (WCL)
Wolf Blass Cabernet Sauvignon (AUS)
★ Wolf Blass Yellow Label Cabernet Sauvignon (SAF)
1987
Hunter Estate Cabernet Sauvignon (PEN)
Lindeman Shiraz Bin 50 (BUT)
1986
Brown Bros Shiraz/Cabernet Sauvignon (WHI)
Taltarni Cabernet Sauvignon (WHI)
Taltarni Merlot (WHI)

£7.00 to £7.99

1991
★ Charles Melton Nine Popes (SOM)
Charles Melton Shiraz (OD)
Mount Langi Ghiran Shiraz (WCL)
Wolf Blass Yellow Label Cabernet Sauvignon (HUN)
1990
Brown Bros Cabernet Sauvignon (JU)
Charles Melton Shiraz (SOM)
Coldstream Hills Cabernet Sauvignon (BEK)
Coriole Cabernet Sauvignon (BAR)
Hollick Coonawarra Cabernet Sauvignon/Merlot (AUS)
Hunter Estate Cabernet Sauvignon (HAG)
★ St Halletts Old Block Shiraz (SOM)
Tim Adams Shiraz (AUS)

1989
Cape Mentelle Shiraz (CV)
★ Coldstream Hills Pinot Noir (SAF)
Rosemount Show Reserve Cabernet Sauvignon (BOT, WR, THR)
Taltarni Cabernet Sauvignon (SAF)
Tim Adams Shiraz (BAR)
1988
Brown Bros Koombahla Cabernet Sauvignon (WHI)
Brown Bros Meadow Creek Cabernet Sauvignon/Shiraz (BY, GRG)
Chateau Tahbilk Cabernet Sauvignon (WCL)
Coriole Cabernet Sauvignon (WS)
Jim Barry Cabernet Sauvignon (TAN)
★ Orlando St Hugo Cabernet Sauvignon (SAI)
Taltarni Shiraz (BR)
Wynns Coonawarra Cabernet Sauvignon (THR, WR, BOT)
1987
Brown Bros Koombahla Shiraz (BY)
Cape Mentelle Zinfandel (CV)
★ Orlando St Hugo Cabernet Sauvignon (HOG)
1986
★ Orlando St Hugo Cabernet Sauvignon (CV)
Penfolds Eden Valley Cabernet Sauvignon (SOM)
Seppelt Cabernet Sauvignon Black Label (GAU)

£8.00 to £8.99

1992
Charles Melton Nine Popes (WCL)
1991
Coldstream Hills Pinot Noir (CV)
1990
Cape Mentelle Shiraz (AD)
Cape Mentelle Zinfandel (RAE)
Katnook Cabernet Sauvignon (BIB)
1989
Bannockburn Pinot Noir (AMI, ROB)
Mount Edelstone Shiraz (WCL)
Pike Cabernet Sauvignon (ROB)
Plantagenet Shiraz (GRG)
Rouge Homme Cabernet Sauvignon (AV)
Tim Adams Shiraz (JU)
1988
Baileys Bundarra Shiraz (GAU)
Cape Mentelle Shiraz (BUT)
Plantagenet Shiraz (KA)
★ Vasse Felix Cabernet Sauvignon (SOM)

1987
Brown Bros Cabernet Sauvignon (BER)
Capel Vale Cabernet Sauvignon (PE)
Knappstein Cabernet Sauvignon (GAU)
Rosemount Show Reserve Cabernet Sauvignon (CHA)
Taltarni Cabernet Sauvignon (HAG)
Taltarni Shiraz (TW)
1986
Cape Mentelle Cabernet Sauvignon (BR)
Penfolds Cabernet Sauvignon/Shiraz Bin 389 (AV)
Rosemount Show Reserve Cabernet Sauvignon (BUT)
1985

Geoff Merrill Cabernet Sauvignon (WRI)
★ Rouge Homme Cabernet Sauvignon (WHI)
1984
Redgate Cabernet Sauvignon (RAE)

£9.00 to £9.99

1991
Cape Mentelle Cabernet Sauvignon (NI)
Mountadam Pinot Noir (WR, BOT)
1990
Moss Wood Cabernet Sauvignon (CV)
Mount Edelstone Shiraz (LAY, AUS)
Mountadam Pinot Noir (SOM)
1989
Cape Mentelle Cabernet Sauvignon (GRE)
Rockford Basket Press Shiraz (GAU, AUS)
1988
Cape Mentelle Cabernet Sauvignon (CV)
Dromana Estate Cabernet/Merlot (BEK)
★ Dromana Estate Pinot Noir (WCL)
Geoff Merrill Cabernet Sauvignon (AUS)
Lindeman Limestone Ridge Shiraz (OD)
Lindeman Limestone Ridge Shiraz/Cabernet Sauvignon (WR, AUS, BOT, UN)
★ Lindeman Pyrus (SAI, AUS, OD)
Lindeman St George Cabernet Sauvignon (WR, OD, AUS, THR, BOT)
Mountadam Cabernet Sauvignon (BOT, WR)

Penfolds St-Henri Cabernet Sauvignon/Shiraz (HOG)
Petaluma Coonawarra Cabernet Sauvignon (OD, BOT, THR, WR)
Rockford Basket Press Shiraz (WCL)
Vasse Felix Cabernet Sauvignon (AMI)
Wolf Blass President's Selection Cabernet Sauvignon (GRE)

1987
Eileen Hardy Shiraz (CV)
Lindeman Limestone Ridge Shiraz/Cabernet Sauvignon (GRG)
Rosemount Giants Creek Pinot Noir (WHI)
Tyrrells Pinot Noir (AV)
Wolf Blass President's Selection Cabernet Sauvignon (AUS)

1986
Lindeman Pyrus (GRG)
Mount Edelstone Shiraz (GE)
Wolf Blass President's Selection Cabernet Sauvignon (WHI)

£10.00 to £11.99

1991
Lake's Folly Cabernet Sauvignon (LAY)
Moss Wood Cabernet Sauvignon (LOR)
Moss Wood Pinot Noir (BR)

1990
Moss Wood Pinot Noir (AD, LOR)
Tarrawarra Pinot Noir (GRG)

1989
Cyril Henschke Cabernet Sauvignon (AUS)
Moss Wood Cabernet Sauvignon (DAV)

1988
Cyril Henschke Cabernet Sauvignon (LAY)
Petaluma Cabernet Sauvignon/Merlot (ROB)

1987
Lake's Folly Cabernet Sauvignon (AUS)
Petaluma Coonawarra Cabernet Sauvignon (WCL)

1986
Moss Wood Cabernet Sauvignon (WCL)
Penfolds Magill Shiraz (WHI)
Rosemount Kirri Billi Merlot (CHA)
Wynns Cabernet Sauvignon (TAN)

1985
Lindeman Pyrus (AV)

£12.00 to £13.99

1991
Pipers Brook Pinot Noir (GRE)

1990
Cape Mentelle Cabernet Sauvignon (JU)
Penley Estate Coonawarra Cabernet Sauvignon (BAR)

1989
Hollick Ravenswood Cabernet Sauvignon (TW)
Yarra Yering Dry Red No.2 (Shiraz) (ROB)

1988
Penfolds Magill Shiraz (BOT, THR, WR, SAF)
Tarrawarra Pinot Noir (BER)
★ Yarra Yering Cabernet Sauvignon (WCL)

1987
Rosemount Kirri Billi Merlot (BOT, WR)
Vasse Felix Cabernet Sauvignon (GRE)

1986
Chateau Xanadu Cabernet Sauvignon (BR)
Yarra Yering Dry Red No.1 (Cabernet) (BER)

1985
Lindeman St George Cabernet Sauvignon (WHI)

£14.00 to £15.99

1990
Penfolds Cabernet Sauvignon Bin 707 (WR, THR, BOT)

1989
Penfolds Cabernet Sauvignon Bin 707 (BOT, WR, THR, GRG, OD, UN)

1986
Wolf Blass Black Label Cabernet Sauvignon (OD)

1985
Lindeman Limestone Ridge Shiraz/Cabernet Sauvignon (RAE)
Wolf Blass Black Label Cabernet Sauvignon (GRE)

£16.00 to £19.99

1989
Yarra Yering Cabernet Sauvignon (ROB, VIG)

1986
Penfolds Cabernet Sauvignon Bin 707 (HOG)

1982
Vasse Felix Cabernet Sauvignon (VIG)

1976
Baileys Bundarra Shiraz (GAU)
Rouge Homme Shiraz/Cabernet Sauvignon (BR)

Stars (★) indicate wines selected by the editors as particularly good value in their class.

£20.00 to £29.99

1989
Jim Barry The Armagh Shiraz (TAN)
1987
Penfolds Grange (SOM, THR, WR, OD, BOT)
1986
Penfolds Grange (WCL)
1985
Penfolds Grange (GRG, HOG)
1981
Penfolds Grange (HA)
1980
Lindeman St George Cabernet Sauvignon (GAU)

£30.00 to £39.99

1984
Penfolds Grange (FA)
1983
Penfolds Grange (FA, BER)

£40.00 to £50.00

1983
Penfolds Grange (GRG)
1982
Penfolds Grange (BER)

c. £86.00

1978
Penfolds Grange (BUT)

WHITE

Under £4.00

1992
★ Hill-Smith Old Triangle Riesling (ASD)
Nottage Hill Chardonnay (AUG, DAV)
Orlando Jacob's Creek Semillon/Chardonnay (HOG, TES, NA, THR)
1991
Orlando Jacob's Creek Semillon/Chardonnay (SAF, AUS, DAV, LO)
Orlando Jacob's Creek White (GA, DAV)

£4.00 to £4.99

Non-vintage
Rosemount Semillon/Chardonnay (VIC)
1992
Hardy Bird Series Gewurztraminer/Riesling (AUG, WHG)
Lindeman Chardonnay Bin 65 (BOT, THR, WR, AUG, OD, SOM, WHI, MAR, UN, SAI)
Mitchelton Un-oaked Marsanne (OD, ASD)
Orlando RF Chardonnay (DAV)
Penfolds Koonunga Hill Semillon/Chardonnay (WCL, OD, THR, BOT)
Penfolds Semillon/Chardonnay (HOG, WHI)
Rosemount Diamond Reserve Semillon/Sauvignon Blanc (CV, WHI, NI)
Seaview Chardonnay (WR, BOT, THR)
Tyrrells Long Flat White (GRG)
Wynns Chardonnay (SOM)
Wynns Rhine Riesling (THR, BOT, WR, SOM)
Yalumba Oxford Landing Chardonnay (NI)
1991
Hardy Bird Series Gewurztraminer/Riesling (SAF)
Hill-Smith Chardonnay (MAJ)
Hill-Smith Old Triangle Riesling (TAN)
★ Orlando RF Chardonnay (HOG, AUS, DAV)
Penfolds Koonunga Hill Semillon/Chardonnay (DAV)
Penfolds Semillon/Chardonnay (GRG)
Rosemount Semillon/Chardonnay (NA)
★ Rothbury Brokenback Semillon (SOM)
Tyrrells Long Flat White (PIP)
★ Yalumba Oxford Landing Chardonnay (ASD)
1990
Basedow Semillon (AUS, WCL)
Lindeman Sauvignon Blanc Bin 95 (WHI)
Nottage Hill Chardonnay (PEN)
Penfolds Chardonnay (WCL)
Peter Lehmann Semillon (GRE)
Rosemount Diamond Reserve Semillon/Sauvignon Blanc (LO, WHI)
Tyrrells Long Flat White (AUS)
1989
Brown Bros Dry Muscat (DI)
Krondorf Sauvignon Blanc (GRG)
Lindeman Semillon/Chardonnay Bin 77 (WHI, UN)
Orlando RF Chardonnay (CV, SAF)
Rosemount Diamond Reserve Semillon/Sauvignon Blanc (CHA)

£5.00 to £5.99

1993
David Wynn Chardonnay (WCL)
David Wynn Riesling (WCL)
Tyrrells Long Flat White (AV)
1992
Brown Bros Dry Muscat (PIP)
David Wynn Chardonnay (NA, HIC)
★ Rosemount Chardonnay (BOT, THR, OD, NI)
Rosemount Fumé Blanc (BOT, WR, THR, NA)
Rothbury Chardonnay (DAV)
Tisdall Chardonnay (NA)

1991
Basedow Semillon (BIB)
Brown Bros Dry Muscat (GRE, BY, WHI, MAJ)
Hardy Collection Chardonnay (WHG, SAI)
Leasingham Chardonnay (MAJ)
★ Pewsey Vale Riesling (ROB)
Rosemount Chardonnay (CV, LO, WHI, DAV)
Rosemount Fumé Blanc (NI, GRE, WHI)
Rothbury Brokenback Chardonnay (SOM)
Rothbury Chardonnay (HOG, EY, GRE, MAJ)
Tisdall Chardonnay (GRG, PIP)
Wyndham's Chardonnay Bin 222 (MAJ)
1990
Brown Bros Sauvignon Blanc (DI)
Krondorf Semillon (AUS)
Mitchelton Wood-Matured Marsanne (WAI)
Peter Lehmann Semillon/Chardonnay (AUS)
Pewsey Vale Riesling (AUS)
Rosemount Chardonnay (SAF)
1989
Brown Bros Sauvignon Blanc (WHI)
Brown Bros Semillon (DI)
Rosemount Chardonnay (CHA)
Rosemount Semillon (DAV)
Rosemount Wood-Matured Semillon (WHI)
1988
Houghton Gold Reserve Verdelho (CV, PEN)
Rosemount Semillon/Chardonnay (CHA)
1986
★ Petersons Semillon (BEK)

£6.00 to £6.99

1992
Brown Bros Sauvignon Blanc (PIP, BY)
Jamiesons Run Chardonnay (NA)
Rosemount Hunter Valley Chardonnay (JU)
★ Shaw & Smith Sauvignon Blanc (OD)
Wolf Blass Chardonnay (GRE, WHI, BY)
1991
Brown Bros Sauvignon Blanc (BOT, THR)
Geoff Merrill Chardonnay (OD)
Hunter Estate Wood-Matured Chardonnay (ASD)
Jamiesons Run Chardonnay (BE)
Katnook Chardonnay (BIB)
Len Evans Chardonnay (MAR)
Penfolds Chardonnay (BOT, OD, WR, WHI)
Pewsey Vale Riesling (WCL)
Shaw & Smith Sauvignon Blanc (SOM)
Wirra Wirra Sauvignon Blanc (AUS)
Wolf Blass Chardonnay (WHI, PIP, VIC, HUN)
Wyndham Estate Oak-Aged Chardonnay (WHI)
1990
Balgownie Chardonnay (GRG)
Basedow Chardonnay (BIB)
Brown Bros Finest Reserve Victorian Muscat (TAN)
Brown Bros Semillon (PIP)
Leasingham Semillon (ROB)
Lindeman Chardonnay Bin 65 (BUT)
Montrose Show Reserve Chardonnay (PIP)
★ Schinus Molle Chardonnay (WCL)
Wirra Wirra Chardonnay (OD)
Wolf Blass Chardonnay (LO, AUS, AUG)
1989
Brown Bros Semillon (BY, AD, PE, GRE)
Mitchelton Wood-Matured Marsanne (WRI)
Pewsey Vale Riesling (BER)
Wolf Blass Chardonnay (SAF)
1988
Brown Bros Semillon (GRG)
Hunter Estate Chardonnay (PEN)
Mitchelton Wood-Matured Marsanne (GRG)
1987
Wolf Blass Gold Label Riesling (HUN)
1984
McWilliams Mount Pleasant Elizabeth Semillon (WCL)
Redgate Riesling (RAE)

£7.00 to £7.99

1992
Cape Mentelle Semillon/Sauvignon Blanc (EY)
1991
Brown Bros Chardonnay (PIP)
Cape Mentelle Semillon/Sauvignon Blanc (WCL, NI)
★ Coldstream Hills Chardonnay (WHG)
Henschke Semillon (LAY)
Hunter Valley Semillon (TAN)
Lindeman Padthaway Chardonnay (WR, BOT, THR, TES)
Mildara Chardonnay (TAN)
★ Petaluma Rhine Riesling (SOM)
Rosemount Show Reserve Chardonnay (WAI, SAI, WR, GRE, WHI, THR, BOT)
Simon Whitlam Chardonnay (WAI)
Tim Adams Semillon (BAR)
Wirra Wirra Chardonnay (AUS, GRG)

In each price band wines are listed in vintage order. Within each vintage they are listed in A–Z order.

1990
Brown Bros Chardonnay (PEN, GRG, PE)
Henschke Semillon (WCL, AUS)
Hunter Estate Chardonnay (HAG)
Knappstein Chardonnay (OD)
Krondorf Chardonnay (AUS)
Rosemount Show Reserve Chardonnay (OD, SAF, WHI)

Shaw & Smith Chardonnay (SOM)
Wynns Chardonnay (BOT, THR, WR)
1989
Cape Mentelle Semillon/Sauvignon Blanc (CV)
1988
Rockford Semillon (AUS)
Rosemount Show Reserve Semillon (WHI)
Rouge Homme Chardonnay (WHI)

£8.00 to £9.99

1992
Moss Wood Semillon (LOR, ROB)
1991
Cape Mentelle Chardonnay (GRE, NI, EY)
Eileen Hardy Reserve Chardonnay (WHG)
Krondorf Chardonnay (VIC)
Moss Wood Semillon (RAE, AD)
Moss Wood Wooded Semillon (RAE, MV)
Plantagenet Chardonnay (KA, GRG)
Shaw & Smith Chardonnay (GE, WCL, GRG)
1990
Cape Mentelle Semillon/Sauvignon Blanc (AD, JU)
Dromana Estate Chardonnay (OD, WCL)
Eileen Hardy Reserve Chardonnay (WHG)
Moss Wood Wooded Semillon (DAV)
Mountadam Chardonnay (SOM, OD, WR)
Petaluma Chardonnay (OD)
Plantagenet Chardonnay (WCL)
1989
Cape Mentelle Chardonnay (RAE)
Eileen Hardy Reserve Chardonnay (CV)
Jamiesons Run Chardonnay (BER)
Rosemount Show Reserve Chardonnay (CHA, WRI)
Schinus Molle Sauvignon (BUT)
Simon Whitlam Chardonnay (GAU)
1986
Rosemount Show Reserve Semillon (BUT)
1985
Quelltaler Estate Wood-Aged Semillon (BER)

£10.00 to £12.99

1991
Moss Wood Chardonnay (BAR, AD, BR)
Petaluma Chardonnay (PIP)
Pipers Brook Chardonnay (GRE, WW)
Tyrrells Vat 47 Chardonnay (AV)
1990
Moss Wood Semillon (VIG)
Pipers Brook Chardonnay (PEN, AD, ROB)
Tyrrells Vat 47 Chardonnay (AUS)
1989
Best's Chardonnay (VIG)
Cullens Chardonnay (PIP)
Lakes Folly Chardonnay (LAY)
Mountadam Chardonnay (GAU)
Petaluma Chardonnay (NI, WCL, AUS)
Tarrawarra Chardonnay (GRG)
1988
Eileen Hardy Reserve Chardonnay (SAF)
Pokolbin Chardonnay (WRI)
Rosemount Giants Creek Chardonnay (WR, BOT, THR)
1987
Lindeman Padthaway Chardonnay (BUT)
Rosemount Giants Creek Chardonnay (CHA)
1986
Rosemount Whites Creek Semillon (CHA)

£13.00 to £15.99

1990
Rosemount Roxburgh Chardonnay (WHI)
1989
Yeringburg Marsanne (VIG)
1988
Rosemount Roxburgh Chardonnay (GRE, CHA, SAF)

£16.00 to £16.99

1990
Rosemount Roxburgh Chardonnay (WR, THR, BOT, NI, BAR)
1989
Rosemount Roxburgh Chardonnay (WCL)
1986
Chateau Xanadu Chardonnay (BR)

c. £20.00

1990
Yarra Yering Chardonnay (VIG)

SPARKLING

Under £6.00

Non-vintage
★ Angas Brut (SOM, SAI, THR, BOT, AUS, WR, NI, MAJ, BAR, OD)
★ Angas Brut Rosé (WR, BOT, THR, SAI, TES, AUS, EY, MAJ, WAI, OD, AUG)
Seaview (GR, WAI, AUS, GRG, LO, WHI, AUG)
Taltarni Brut Taché (SOM)
Yellowglen Brut (GR)

£6.00 to £7.99

Non-vintage
Taltarni Brut (HOG, AD, AUS)
Yalumba D (NI)
1989
Taltarni Brut (WHI)
Taltarni Brut Taché (WHI)
Yellowglen Brut (PEN)

£8.00 to £9.99

1991
★ Green Point Brut Moët & Chandon (SAI)
1990
Croser (SOM)
Green Point Brut Moët & Chandon (AUG)
Seppelt Salinger Brut (BOT, OD, THR)
Yalumba D (OD)
1989
Green Point Brut Moët & Chandon (HOG, WAI, MAJ)
Seppelt Salinger Brut (TES)
1987
Seppelt Sparkling Shiraz (OD, GRG, ROB)

£10.00 to £13.99

Non-vintage
Mountadam Chardonnay/Pinot Noir (SOM)
Schinus Molle Chardonnay/Pinot Noir (BUT)
1990
Croser (OD, NI)
1989
Yalumba D (SOM)
1988
Croser (ROB)
1987
Yalumba D (AD)
1982
Seppelt Sparkling Shiraz (WCL)

c. £17.00

1989
Mountadam Chardonnay/Pinot Noir (NA)

SWEET & FORTIFIED

Under £7.00

1992
Brown Bros Muscat Late Picked (PIP, HAG)
Brown Bros Orange Muscat & Flora ½ bottle (GRE, BY, PIP, WHI, AD, PE, WRI, TAN)
1991
Brown Bros Orange Muscat & Flora (AUS)
Brown Bros Orange Muscat & Flora ½ bottle (DI, BOT, GRG, WR, THR, PE)
1990
Brown Bros Liqueur Muscat (GRG)
Brown Bros Muscat Late Picked (DI, GRE, BY, WHI, WRI, PE)
Brown Bros Orange Muscat & Flora ½ bottle (HAL)
1989
Brown Bros Muscat Late Picked (PEN, MAJ)
1988
Brown Bros Orange Muscat & Flora ½ bottle (PEN)
1985
Brown Bros Noble Late Harvest Riesling ½ bottle (PIP)
1982
Brown Bros Noble Late Harvest Riesling (MAJ)
Brown Bros Noble Late Harvest Riesling ½ bottle (GRE, BY, WHI, PEN, WRI, AUS)

£7.00 to £9.99

Non-vintage
Bleasedale 6-year-old Verdello (BAR)
Chambers Rosewood Liqueur Muscat (AD)
Chateau Reynella 10-year-old Tawny (WR)
Morris Liqueur Muscat (CV, GRE, WCL, KA)
★ Stanton & Killeen Liqueur Muscat (AUS)
Yalumba Museum Release Rutherglen Muscat (AUS)

£10.00 to £12.99

Non-vintage
All Saints Rutherglen Liqueur Muscat (GAU)
★ Baileys Founder Liqueur Muscat (AUS)
Brown Bros Liqueur Muscat (PIP)
Campbells Rutherglen Liqueur Muscat (GRG, ROB, AUS)
Chambers Old Liqueur Muscat (VIG)

c. £16.00

Non-vintage
Bleasedale 16-year-old Verdello (BAR)

NEW ZEALAND

RED

Under £5.50

1991
Cooks Tolaga Bay (AUG)
Montana Marlborough Cabernet Sauvignon (BOT, VIC, KA, AUG, TES, WR)
1990
Cooks Cabernet Sauvignon (WHI, KA, DAV)
Cooks Hawke's Bay Cabernet Sauvignon (AS)
Montana Marlborough Cabernet Sauvignon (GRE, ASD)
1989
Cooks Cabernet Sauvignon (WHI)
Montana Marlborough Cabernet Sauvignon (LO)
1988
Cooks Cabernet Sauvignon (GRE)

£5.50 to £6.99

1992
★ C J Pask Roy's Hill Red (TAN, LAY)
1990
Babich Henderson Valley Pinot Noir (HOG, WHI)
Stoneleigh Marlborough Cabernet Sauvignon (WHI, TES, KA)
Villa Maria Cabernet Sauvignon (GRE, VIC)
1989
Babich Henderson Valley Pinot Noir (WHI)
Redwood Valley Estate Cabernet Sauvignon (HOG)
Stoneleigh Marlborough Cabernet Sauvignon (WHI)
1988
Stoneleigh Marlborough Cabernet Sauvignon (GRE)
1987
Nobilo Pinotage (GRE, WHI, AV, WRI, GRG)
Villa Maria Cabernet Sauvignon (GAU)
1986
Stoneleigh Marlborough Cabernet Sauvignon (PEN)

£7.00 to £8.99

1991
C J Pask Cabernet Sauvignon (LAY)
★ Martinborough Pinot Noir (WCL, SOM)
Redwood Valley Estate Cabernet Sauvignon (FIZ)
St-Helena Pinot Noir (LAY)
1990
Morton Estate Black Label Cabernet Sauvignon/Merlot (BEK)
Redwood Valley Estate Cabernet Sauvignon (GRE)
1989
Cloudy Bay Cabernet Sauvignon/Merlot (NI)
Matua Valley Cabernet Sauvignon (NI, FIZ)
Villa Maria Cabernet Sauvignon (ROB)
1988
Nobilo Cabernet Sauvignon (AV)
1987
St-Nesbit Cabernet Sauvignon/Cabernet Franc/Merlot (FIZ)

£9.00 to £10.99

1991
Cloudy Bay Cabernet Sauvignon/Merlot (RAE, JU)
★ Palliser Estate Martinborough Pinot Noir (WCL)
Palliser Estate Pinot Noir (THR, OD, WR)
1990
Cloudy Bay Cabernet Sauvignon/Merlot (WRI, RAE, AD, WCL)
Hunter Pinot Noir (NA, KA)
1989
Hunter Pinot Noir (DI)
1988
Cloudy Bay Cabernet Sauvignon/Merlot (EY, CV)
Coopers Creek Cabernet Sauvignon/Merlot (HAG)
1987
Cloudy Bay Cabernet Sauvignon/Merlot (CV)
Matua Valley Cabernet Sauvignon (GAU)
1984
Nobilo Concept One (AV)

£11.00 to £14.99

1990
★ Stonyridge Larose Cabernet (FIZ)
★ Te Mata Coleraine Cabernet Sauvignon/Merlot (GRG)
1988
Martinborough Pinot Noir (GAU, BUT)

c. £20.00

1989
Te Mata Coleraine Cabernet Sauvignon/Merlot (VIG)

WHITE

Under £5.00

1992

★ Collards Chenin Blanc (WR, BOT, THR)
Cooks Hawke's Bay Chardonnay (LO, WHI, BOT, WAI, THR, WR)
Cooks Riesling/Chenin Blanc (WR, THR)
Cooks Sauvignon Blanc (LO, WHI, BOT, THR)
Montana Marlborough Chardonnay (OD, WHI, DAV, AUG, VIC, SAF, GRE, ASD)
★ Montana Marlborough Sauvignon Blanc (HOG, SAI, WHI, DAV, OD, AUG, VIC, BOT, KA)

Nobilo Marlborough Sauvignon Blanc (GE, OD)
Nobilo White Cloud (VIC, GRE, AV, TAN)

1991

Cooks Hawke's Bay Chardonnay (KA, TES)
Cooks Sauvignon Blanc (GRE, WHI, KA)
Delegat's Sauvignon Blanc (HOG)
Matua Valley Late Harvest Gewürztraminer ½ bottle (NI)
Montana Marlborough Chardonnay (HOG, WHI, DAV, THR, KA, BOT, WR, TES)
Montana Marlborough Sauvignon Blanc (GRE, WHI)
Nobilo Marlborough Sauvignon Blanc (GRE)

1990

Cooks Chenin Blanc (TES, KA, WHI)
Cooks Semillon (WHI, KA)
Delegat's Sauvignon Blanc (CV)

£5.00 to £5.99

1992

★ Aotea Sauvignon Blanc (KA, FIZ, MV, ROB)
Babich Gisborne Semillon/Chardonnay (WHI, DAV, AUG)
Babich Hawke's Bay Sauvignon Blanc (WHI)
Delegat's Hawke's Bay Sauvignon Blanc (WHG)
Hawke's Bay Chardonnay (EL)
Nobilo Sauvignon Blanc (GRG)
★ Stoneleigh Marlborough Sauvignon Blanc (WHI, BOT, KA, THR, WR)

1991

Babich Gisborne Semillon/Chardonnay (WHI, PEN, WRI, AUG)
Babich Hawke's Bay Sauvignon Blanc (HOG, WHI, CV)
C J Pask Roy's Hill White (TAN)
Collards Marlborough Sauvignon Blanc (WCL)
Delegat's Chardonnay (HOG)
★ Matua Valley Chardonnay (NI)
Morton Estate Sauvignon Blanc (BEK)
Neudorf Dovedale (BOT, THR, WR)
★ Redwood Valley Late Harvest Rhine Riesling ½ bottle (FIZ)
Stoneleigh Marlborough Sauvignon Blanc (WHI)

1990

Babich Hawke's Bay Chardonnay (HOG)
Matua Valley Brownlie Sauvignon (OD)
Morton Estate Chardonnay (BEK)

1989

Delegat's Chardonnay (CV)
Nobilo Gewürztraminer (WHI, GRE)
Redwood Valley Late Harvest Rhine Riesling ½ bottle (WCL)

1988

Nobilo Gewürztraminer (WHI)
Stoneleigh Marlborough Sauvignon Blanc (GA)

1986

Matua Valley Late Harvest Muscat ½ bottle (HAL)

£6.00 to £6.99

1992

Coopers Creek Marlborough Sauvignon Blanc (VIC)
★ Jackson Estate Marlborough Sauvignon Blanc (WHI, CV, JU, WAI, THR, BOT, WR)
Nobilo Gisborne Chardonnay (AV)
Selaks Sauvignon Blanc (EY)
Wairau River Sauvignon Blanc (SOM, FA)

1991

★ Collards Gisborne Chardonnay (WCL, BIB)
Delegat's Hawke's Bay Chardonnay (WHG)
Mills Reef Gewürztraminer (FIZ)
Millton Gisborne Chardonnay (SAF)
Morton Estate Chardonnay (WR, BOT, THR)
Ngatarawa Sauvignon Blanc (HOG, FIZ)
Redwood Valley Sauvignon Blanc (HOG)
Selaks Chardonnay (RAE)
Selaks Sauvignon Blanc (CV, SUM, GRG, WS)
Stoneleigh Chardonnay (WHI, KA)
Vidal Sauvignon Blanc (HOG, KA)

1990
Aotea Sauvignon Blanc (CB)
Mills Reef Dry Riesling (FIZ)
Montana Marlborough Sauvignon Blanc (VIN)
Nobilo Gewürztraminer (AV)
Selaks Sauvignon Blanc (PE)
1989
Nobilo Sauvignon Blanc (PEN)
Stoneleigh Chardonnay (GRE)
1988
Stoneleigh Chardonnay (PEN)

£7.00 to £8.99

1992
Cloudy Bay Sauvignon Blanc (NI, CV, KA)
Hunters Sauvignon Blanc (LO, PIP, NA)
Palliser Estate Sauvignon Blanc (WR, BO)
Selaks Kumeu Estate Sauvignon Blanc (AD)
★ Te Mata Castle Hill Sauvignon Blanc (WS, BOT, WR, HAG)
Wairau River Chardonnay (FA)
1991
★ Collards Rothesay Chardonnay (BIB)
Coopers Creek Marlborough Sauvignon Blanc (WRI)
Dashwood Chardonnay (HAH)
Esk Valley Sauvignon Blanc (KA, GRG)
Hunters Rhine Riesling (NA)
Martinborough Vineyards Chardonnay (SOM)
Morton Estate Chardonnay Reserve (BEK)
Redwood Valley Chardonnay (HOG, FIZ)
Redwood Valley Wood-Aged Sauvignon Blanc (FIZ, ROB)
Te Mata Castle Hill Sauvignon Blanc (GRG, WR, LAY, BOT, WRI)
Vidal Chardonnay (FIZ)
1990
Babich Irongate Chardonnay (WHI)
Collards Hawke's Bay Chardonnay (BIB)
Hunters Gewürztraminer (NA)
Matua Valley Late Harvest Gewürztraminer ½ bottle (BER)
Ngatarawa Chardonnay (HOG, FIZ)
★ Nobilo Dixon Chardonnay (AV)
Rongopai Te Kauwhata Chardonnay (PIP)
1989
Babich Hawke's Bay Chardonnay (HUN)
Babich Hawke's Bay Sauvignon Blanc (HUN)
Brookfield's Sauvignon Blanc (KA)
Mission Chardonnay (FIZ, KA)
Nobilo Dixon Chardonnay (GRE)
Redwood Valley Sauvignon Blanc (KA)
Vidal Chardonnay (KA)

£9.00 to £10.99

1991
Cloudy Bay Chardonnay (NI, EY, JU, AD)
Cloudy Bay Sauvignon Blanc (BUT, BR)
Hunters Sauvignon Blanc (DI)
Hunters Wood-Aged Sauvignon Blanc (TAN)
Kumeu River Chardonnay (FA)
Mills Reef Chardonnay (FIZ)
Palliser Estate Chardonnay (LOR, HAH, JU)
Palliser Estate Martinborough Chardonnay (BOT, WR)
1990
Babich Irongate Chardonnay (HOG)
Hunters Chardonnay (PIP, LO, NA, DAV)
Redwood Valley Chardonnay (KA)
Te Mata Castle Hill Sauvignon Blanc (VIG)
Vidal Chardonnay (ROB)
1989
Babich Irongate Chardonnay (PEN)
Giesen Chardonnay (KA)
Hunters Wood-Aged Sauvignon Blanc (DI)
1988
Nobilo Dixon Chardonnay (GAU)

£11.00 to £13.99

1992
Te Mata Elston Chardonnay (WR, BOT)
1991
Te Mata Elston Chardonnay (GRG, LAY, WR)
1990
Cloudy Bay Chardonnay (BR, BUT, ROB, CB)
1989
Vidal Reserve Chardonnay (FIZ, HOG)
Villa Maria Reserve Chardonnay (HA)
1988
Martinborough Vineyards Chardonnay (GAU, BUT)

£14.00 to £15.99

1990
Kumeu River Chardonnay (UN)
1989
Kumeu River Chardonnay (GRG)

SPARKLING

Under £7.00

Non-vintage
★ Lindauer Brut (WHI, WR, BOT, THR, AUG)

£7.00 to £9.99

Non-vintage
★ Daniel Le Brun Brut (AUG)
Lindauer Brut (ROB, BAR, HAG, SAI)
★ Deutz Marlborough Cuvee (BOT, THR, WR)

UNITED KINGDOM

WHITE

Under £4.50

Non-vintage
Lamberhurst Sovereign (DAV, GRE, PEN)
1990
Hambledon (HAC)
1989
Biddenden Huxelrebe (HAC)
New Hall Müller-Thurgau (GRG)
1987
Lamberhurst Priory Reichensteiner (PEN)

£4.50 to £4.99

1991
Denbies Surrey Gold (WHG, TES)
1990
Lamberhurst Priory Seyval Blanc (VIC)
1989
Lamberhurst Priory Seyval Blanc (PEN)
Pilton Manor Vintage Selection (HAC)
Three Choirs Seyval Blanc/Reichensteiner Dry (TES)
Wake Court (EL)

£5.00 to £5.99

Non-vintage
Three Choirs Medium Dry (BAR)
1990
Astley Severn Vale (TAN)
Bruisyard St Peter Müller-Thurgau (BER)
Carr Taylor Reichensteiner (WHI)
Denbies Surrey Gold (VIC)
1989
Biddenden Ortega (HAC)
Croffta (CV)
Pilton Manor Müller-Thurgau (AV)
★ Staple St-James Müller-Thurgau (BER)
Wraxall Müller-Thurgau/Seyval Blanc (AV)
1988
Lamberhurst Priory Seyval Blanc (WRI)

£6.00 to £7.99

1991
Elmham Park Madeleine Angevine (HIC)
1990
Breaky Bottom Müller-Thurgau (HAC)
Pilton Manor Müller-Thurgau (WRI)
★ Thames Valley Fumé Blanc (THR, BOT, WR)
1989
Cane End (JU)
Chiddingstone Seyval/Kerner (BER)
Lamberhurst Priory Müller-Thurgau (WRI)
Lamberhurst Schönburger (BER)
Pilton Manor Seyval Blanc (HAC)
Staple St-James Huxelrebe (BER)
Wootton Schönburger (AV)
1988
Berwick Glebe (CB)
Pilton Manor Huxelrebe (HAC)

£8.00 to £9.99

1991
Thames Valley Fumé Blanc (BIB)
1989
Thames Valley Fumé Blanc (HAC)

RED

Under £6.00

1989
Biddenden Red (HAC)
1988
Westbury Light Red (HAC)
1986
Meonwara (HAC)
Westbury Pinot Noir (HAC)

ROSÉ

Under £7.00

1990
Conghurst Rosé (HAC)
1989
Conghurst Rosé (HAC)

c. £7.50

1991
Denbies Pinot Noir Rosé (WHG)

SPARKLING

Under £9.00

Non-vintage
Meon Valley Sparkling (HAC)
1989
Rock Lodge Impressario Brut (HAC)

c. £10.50

Non-vintage
Carr Taylor (HAC)

BULGARIA

RED

Under £3.00

Non-vintage
★ Bulgarian Cabernet Sauvignon (SAI, PE)
Bulgarian Cabernet Sauvignon/Merlot (DAV, UN)
Bulgarian Merlot (SAI)
Pavlikeni Cabernet Sauvignon/Merlot (BOT, GRE, VIC, THR, WR, PE)
Petrich Cabernet Sauvignon/Melnik (MAJ)
Russe Cabernet Sauvignon/Cinsaut (WIW)
★ Suhindol Cabernet Sauvignon/Merlot (WIW)
Suhindol Merlot/Gamza (WIW)
1992
Assenovgrad Mavrud (SAF)
1990
Haskovo Merlot (WIW)
Suhindol Gamza (WIW)
1989
Bulgarian Merlot (WHI)
Domaine Boyar Cabernet Sauvignon (OD)
Haskovo Merlot (ASD)
★ Oriahovitza Cabernet Sauvignon Reserve (WIW)
Russe Cabernet Sauvignon/Cinsaut (WR)
Stambolovo Merlot Reserve (WIW)
Suhindol Cabernet Sauvignon (WIW, OD)
Svischtov Cabernet Sauvignon (ASD)
1988
★ Assenovgrad Mavrud (WIW)
Bulgarian Cabernet Sauvignon (MAJ, WAI)
Suhindol Cabernet Sauvignon (AUG)
Suhindol Cabernet Sauvignon Reserve (WIW)

£3.00 to £3.99

Non-vintage
Russe Cabernet Sauvignon Reserve (LAY)
1990
Bulgarian Cabernet Sauvignon (CV)
1988
Bulgarian Merlot (GRE, UN)
Haskovo Merlot (AUG, WR, BOT, THR)
Plovdiv Cabernet Sauvignon (CV, DAV)
Stambolovo Merlot Special Reserve (WIW)
1987
Domaine Boyar Merlot Reserve (OD)
Haskovo Merlot (TAN)
Oriahovitza Cabernet Sauvignon (PE, TAN)
Russe Cabernet Sauvignon Reserve (ASD)
1986
Assenovgrad Mavrud (GRE)
Sakar Mountain Cabernet Sauvignon (TES, WHI, DAV, GRE)
1985
Assenovgrad Mavrud (WAI)
Stambolovo Merlot Reserve (GA, WR, BOT)
★ Suhindol Cabernet Sauvignon Reserve (SAF)

£4.00 to £4.99

1985
Svischtov Cabernet Sauvignon (GRE)
1982
Svischtov Cabernet Sauvignon (WHI)

£5.00 to £6.99

1986
Stambolovo Merlot Special Reserve (CV)
1982
Svischtov Estate Selection Cabernet Sauvignon (AV)

WHITE

Under £3.00

Non-vintage
Bulgarian Muscat/Ugni Blanc (WAI, DAV)
Bulgarian Riesling/Misket (GA, SAI)
Bulgarian Sauvignon Blanc (WHI)
Burgas Muscat/Ugni Blanc (WIW, OD, MAJ)
Russe Welsch-Rizling/Misket (VIC)
1991
Preslav Chardonnay (OD)
1989
★ Khan Krum Chardonnay (WIW, TES)

£3.00 to £3.99

1991
Novi Pazar Chardonnay (WIW)
1990
Khan Krum Special Reserve Chardonnay (WIW)
1989
Khan Krum Special Reserve Chardonnay (THR, WR, BOT)

£4.00 to £4.99

Non-vintage
Balkan Crown Brut (BU)
1989
Novi Pazar Chardonnay (CV, WHI)

SOUTH AFRICA

RED

Under £4.00

1991
Pinotage Culemborg Paarl (WAI)
1990
KWV Cabernet Sauvignon (DAV, PE, UN)
KWV Pinotage (UN, DAV)
KWV Roodeberg (WAI, PE)
1989
★ Backsberg Pinotage (HOG)
KWV Cabernet Sauvignon (HOG, PEN, THR)
KWV Pinotage (HOG, PEN, BOT, DI, WR, WHI)
KWV Roodeberg (HOG, WHI, DAV, UN, WR, BOT, VIC, DI, THR)
KWV Shiraz (HOG)
1988
KWV Cabernet Sauvignon (DI)
KWV Roodeberg (GRE)
KWV Shiraz (PEN)
1986
KWV Roodeberg (PEN)

£4.00 to £4.99

1991
Fairview Pinotage (CAP)
1990
Fairview Pinotage (CAP)
★ Rustenberg Dry Red (HOG, GRG)
1988
Backsberg Cabernet Sauvignon (HOG)
Nederburg Edelrood (CAP)
Nederburg Paarl Cabernet Sauvignon (CAP, HOG, KA)
1987
Klein Constantia Shiraz (HOG)
Nederburg Edelrood (HOG)
Nederburg Pinotage (CAP, KA, HOG)
1983
Diemersdal (PEN, GAU)

£5.00 to £5.99

1992
Rustenberg Dry Red (TAN)
1991
Diemersdal (CAP)
1990
Backsberg Klein Babylonstoren (CAP)
Zonnebloem Pinotage (CAP)
Zonnebloem Shiraz (CAP)
1989
Backsberg Cabernet Sauvignon (CAP)
Fairview Pinotage (WRI, KA)
Groot Constantia Pinotage (CAP)
Hamilton Russell Pinot Noir (HOG)
Zonnebloem Cabernet Sauvignon (CAP)
Zonnebloem Pinotage (CAP)
Zonnebloem Shiraz (CAP)
1988
Diemersdal (CAP, KA, AUG)
Groot Constantia Pinotage (CAP)
Groot Constantia Shiraz (CAP)
Zonnebloem Cabernet Sauvignon (GRE)
1987
Groot Constantia Shiraz (CAP)
KWV Laborie (DAV)
Stellenryk Cabernet Sauvignon (WAI)
Zandvliet Shiraz (TES)
1983
Fairview Pinotage (PEN)

£6.00 to £7.99

1991
★ Hamilton Russell Pinot Noir (WHI, AV)
1990
Hamilton Russell Pinot Noir (GRE, EY, WHI, TAN)
★ Kanonkop Pinotage (EY)
1989
Allesverloren Tinta Barocca (CAP)
Groot Constantia Cabernet Sauvignon (DAV)
Groot Constantia Heerenrood (CAP)
Kanonkop Pinotage (DAV)
1988
Allesverloren Tinta Barocca (CAP)
Delheim Pinotage (PIP)
Fleur du Cap Roodebloem (CAP)
Groot Constantia Cabernet Sauvignon (CAP)
Groot Constantia Heerenrood (CAP)
Hamilton Russell Pinot Noir (GRG, GAU)
Meerendal Pinotage (DI, CAP)
Nederburg Paarl Cabernet Sauvignon (TAN)
Rustenberg Cabernet Sauvignon (HOG, GRE)
1987
Fleur du Cap Roodebloem (CAP)
Hamilton Russell Pinot Noir (LOR)
★ Klein Constantia Cabernet Sauvignon (HOG, AV, TAN, AD, CAP)

£8.00 to £9.99

1991
Kanonkop Pinotage (JU)
1990
Neil Ellis Cabernet Sauvignon (AD, BAR)
1989
Backsberg Klein Babylonstoren (VIG)
Rustenberg Gold (GRE)
1987
Stellenryk Cabernet Sauvignon (CAP)
1986
Meerlust Rubicon (GRE, NA)
1985
Meerlust Rubicon (HOG)
1982
Backsberg Cabernet Sauvignon (PEN)
Uitkyk Carlonet (HOG)

£10.00 to £11.99

1986
Meerlust Cabernet Sauvignon (CAP)

c. £12.50

1986
Warwick Farm Cabernet Sauvignon (VIG)
1982
Rustenberg Cabernet Sauvignon (GRG)

WHITE

Under £4.00

Non-vintage
KWV Muscat de Montac (CAP)
1992
Backsberg Sauvignon Blanc (HOG)
★ KWV Chenin Blanc (MAR, HOG, WAI, WHI, DAV, VIC, WR, UN, THR, AUG, BOT, PE)
KWV Sauvignon Blanc (WAI, UN, THR, DAV, VIC, WR, BOT, AUG, PE)
1991
KWV Chenin Blanc (GRE, DI)
KWV Riesling (HOG, GRE, WHI, UN)
KWV Sauvignon Blanc (MAR, HOG, PEN)
KWV Steen (HOG, WHI)
KWV Steen Special Late Harvest (HOG)
1990
KWV Cape Bouquet (HOG, WHI)
KWV Pinotage (MAR)
KWV Riesling (DI)
1989
KWV Cape Foret (PEN)
KWV Roodeberg (AUG)
KWV Steen (PEN)
1986
KWV Steen Special Late Harvest (PEN)

£4.00 to £5.99

1992
Nederburg Stein (CAP)
1991
Backsberg Sauvignon Blanc (CAP)
★ Hamilton Russell Chardonnay (HOG)
★ Klein Constantia Sauvignon Blanc (CAP, BAR, AV)
KWV Cape Foret (HUN)
Rustenberg Chardonnay (HOG, GRE)
1990
Klein Constantia Sauvignon Blanc (GRE, HOG, CV, CAP)
KWV Cape Foret (CAP)
KWV Chenin Blanc (CAP, GAU)
KWV Laborie (CAP)
de Wetshof Rhine Riesling (CAP)
1989
Koopmanskloof Blanc de Marbonne (CAP)
l'Ormarins Sauvignon Blanc (DI)
de Wetshof Rhine Riesling (CAP)
Zonnenbloem Gewürztraminer (CAP)

£6.00 to £7.99

1992
Hamilton Russell Chardonnay (EY, TAN)
1991
Backsberg Chardonnay (WRI)
Neil Ellis Sauvignon Blanc (ROB)
1990
Klein Constantia Chardonnay (AV, BAR)
le Bonheur Sauvignon Blanc (CAP)
l'Ormarins Sauvignon Blanc (WRI)
Uitkyk Carlsheim (CAP)
1989
Backsberg Sauvignon Blanc (BUT)
Hamilton Russell Chardonnay (LOR, WHI, GAU)
1988
Klein Constantia Sauvignon Blanc (BUT)

£8.00 to £9.99

1990
Backsberg Chardonnay (VIG)
de Wetshof Chardonnay (CAP)
Hamilton Russell Chardonnay (DI)
1989
de Wetshof Chardonnay (HOG)
Rustenberg Chardonnay (GAU)
1988
de Wetshof Chardonnay (DI)
★ Klein Constantia Vin de Constance ½ litre (HOG, GRE)

£11.00 to £13.99

1989
Nederburg Edelkeur ½ bottle (CAP)
1987
Klein Constantia Vin de Constance ½ litre (AD)

c. £15.50

1985
Nederburg Edelkeur ½ bottle (PEN)

ROSÉ

Under £4.50

1991
KWV Cabernet Sauvignon Blanc de Noir (DI, CAP, WHI)
Nederburg Cabernet Sauvignon Blanc de Noir (CAP)
Nederburg Rosé (CAP)
1988
KWV Cabernet Sauvignon Blanc de Noir (PEN)

SPARKLING

£5.50 to £6.49

Non-vintage
KWV Mousseux Blanc Cuvée Brut (CAP)
Laborie Blanc de Noir (CAP)
Nederburg Premiere Cuvée Brut (CAP, HOG)

c. £10.00

Non-vintage
JC Le Roux Sauvignon Blanc (CAP)

FORTIFIED

£4.00 to £4.99

Non-vintage
Cavendish Fine Old Ruby (HOG)
Mymering Pale Extra Dry (HOG, CAP, DI)
Onzerust Medium (HOG, CAP)
Renasans Pale Dry (CAP, DI)

£5.00 to £6.99

1963
Cavendish Vintage (HOG, CAP)

Stars (★) indicate wines selected by the editors as particularly good value in their class.

OTHER WINE REGIONS

ARGENTINA

Under £6.00

1989
Trapiche Cabernet Sauvignon Reserve (JU)

£7.00 to £8.50

1985
Cavas de Weinert Cabernet Sauvignon (HAG)
1983
Cavas de Weinert Cabernet Sauvignon (BUT, JU, CV)

AUSTRIA

Under £5.00

1990
★ Grüner Veltliner Lenz Moser Selection (WAI, PEN, ROB)

CANADA

Under £7.00

1989
Inniskillin Chardonnay (GRE)
1988
Inniskillin Maréchal Foch Red (GRE, AV)
Inniskillin Riesling (ROB)

£10.00 to £10.99

1987
Inniskillin Pinot Noir Reserve (AV)
Inniskillin Chardonnay Reserve (VIG)

CHILE RED

Under £4.00

1991
Concha y Toro Cabernet Sauvignon/Merlot (EY)
1990
Caliterra Cabernet Sauvignon (SAI, SAF)
Concha y Toro Cabernet Sauvignon (GR)
Undurraga Cabernet Sauvignon (GE, GRE)
★ Villa Montes Cabernet Sauvignon (SAF)
1989
Concha y Toro Cabernet Sauvignon (WAI, NI)
Concha y Toro Cabernet Sauvignon/Merlot (NI)
★ Santa Rita 120 Cabernet Sauvignon (BIB, VIC, GRG, AUG)

£4.00 to £4.99

1991
Caliterra Cabernet Sauvignon (WHG)
1990
Concha y Toro Cabernet Sauvignon (EY)
Errázuriz Cabernet Sauvignon (GRE, VIC)
★ Los Vascos Cabernet Sauvignon (WHI, LAY)
Santa Rita Cabernet Sauvignon Reserva (TES)
Torres Cabernet Sauvignon (GRE)
Torres Santa Digna Cabernet Sauvignon (DI)
Undurraga Pinot Noir (GRE, TES)
1989
Caliterra Cabernet Sauvignon (CV)
Cousiño Macul Don Luis Red (NI)
Santa Rita Cabernet Sauvignon Reserva (LAY, BIB)
Undurraga Cabernet Sauvignon (BU, UN)
Villa Montes Cabernet Sauvignon (BAR)
Viña Carmen Cabernet Sauvignon (WAI)
1988
Concha y Toro Merlot (TAN)
Montes Cabernet Sauvignon (ASD)
Santa Rita Cabernet Sauvignon Reserva (GRG)
Undurraga Cabernet Sauvignon (SUM)
Undurraga Cabernet Sauvignon Reserve Selection (GRE)
1987
Concha y Toro Cabernet Sauvignon (VIC)
Concha y Toro Merlot (UN)

£5.00 to £5.99

1991
Domaine Caperana Cabernet Sauvignon (BOD)
1990
Concha y Toro Merlot (OD)
Cousiño Macul Cabernet Sauvignon (HIC)
Montes Cabernet Sauvignon (DAV)
Santa Helena Merlot (DAV)
1989
Los Vascos Cabernet Sauvignon (HUN)
1988
Cousiño Macul Antiguas Reservas Cabernet Sauvignon (EY, GRE)
Viña Linderos Cabernet Sauvignon (BER)
1987
Cousiño Macul Antiguas Reservas Cabernet Sauvignon (NI)

£6.00 to £7.99

1990
Canepa Estate Oak-Aged Cabernet Sauvignon (WIC)
1989
Cousiño Macul Antiguas Reservas Cabernet Sauvignon (TAN)
Santa Rita Cabernet Sauvignon Medalla Real (BIB, SAF, AD)
1988
Marqués de Casa Concha Cabernet Sauvignon (GRE, TAN)
Montes Alpha Cabernet Sauvignon (TES, OD)
Santa Rita Cabernet Sauvignon Medalla Real (BIB)
1987
Montes Alpha Cabernet Sauvignon (BAR)
Santa Helena Seleccion del Directorio Cabernet Sauvignon (WRI)
Santa Rita Cabernet Sauvignon Medalla Real (MOR)
1986
Cousiño Macul Antiguas Reservas Cabernet Sauvignon (MOR)
Cousiño Macul Cabernet Sauvignon (SOM)
Santa Rita Cabernet Sauvignon Medalla Real (MOR)

c. £10.00

1984
Santa Rita Cabernet Sauvignon Medalla Real (MOR)

c. £13.50

1978
Cousiño Macul Cabernet Sauvignon (BUT)

CHILE WHITE

Under £4.00

1993
★ Caliterra Sauvignon Blanc (WHG)
★ Villa Montes Sauvignon Blanc (VIC)
1992
Caliterra Sauvignon Blanc (OD)
Concha y Toro Chardonnay (NI)
Concha y Toro Sauvignon Blanc/Semillon (NI)
Santa Rita 120 Sauvignon Blanc (GRG)
Undurraga Sauvignon Blanc (GRE)
1991
Concha y Toro Chardonnay (NI)
Concha y Toro Sauvignon Blanc/Semillon (NI)
Santa Rita 120 Sauvignon Blanc (BIB, AUG)
Undurraga Sauvignon Blanc (PEN)

£4.00 to £4.99

1992
Caliterra Chardonnay (WHG, ASD, OD, CV)
Torres Sauvignon Blanc (TAN, AD)
Undurraga Chardonnay (GRE)
Villa Montes Sauvignon Blanc (DAV, GRE)
1991
Cousiño Macul Chardonnay (GRE)
★ Errázuriz Chardonnay (VIC, GRE)
Santa Rita Sauvignon Blanc Reserva (BIB, GRG)
1990
Concha y Toro Chardonnay (UN)
Torres Bellaterra Sauvignon Blanc (DI)
1989
Undurraga Sauvignon Blanc (SUM)

£5.00 to £5.99

1992
Cousiño Macul Chardonnay (HAG)
Montes Chardonnay (DAV, LAY, ROB)
Torres Santa Digna Sauvignon Blanc (HAG)
1991
Montes Chardonnay (HUN)
1990
Cousiño Macul Chardonnay (NI)
Santa Rita Chardonnay Medalla Real (SAI)
Santa Rita Sauvignon Blanc Reserva (MOR)

£6.00 to £7.99

1991
Marqués de Casa Concha Chardonnay (GRE, BAR)
Santa Rita Chardonnay Medalla Real (BIB, DI)
1990
Caperana Chardonnay (BOD)
Santa Rita Sauvignon Blanc Medalla Real (MOR, BIB)

c. £8.50

1991
William Fèvre Chardonnay, Santa Rosa del Pera (HIC)

CHILE ROSÉ

Under £5.00

1991
★ Torres Santa Digna Cabernet Sauvignon Rosado (CV)
1989
Torres Santa Digna Cabernet Sauvignon Rosado (GRE)

CYPRUS TABLE WINES

Under £4.00

Non-vintage
Aphrodite Keo White (TES, WHI)
Othello Keo Red (WHI)
Thisbe Keo White (WHI)

CYPRUS FORTIFIED

c. £4.00

Non-vintage
Emva Cream (DAV)

GREECE RED

Under £4.00

Non-vintage
Demestica Achaia Clauss (GRG)
Mavrodaphne Patras, Kourtaki (WAI)
1990
★ Nemea, Boutari (OD)

£4.00 to £5.99

1986
Nemea, Kouros (UN)
1985
★ Château Carras Côtes de Meliton (CV)

£6.00 to £6.99

1987
Château Carras Côtes de Meliton (WS)
1985
Château Carras Côtes de Meliton (DI, VIG)

GREECE WHITE

Under £4.00

Non-vintage
Demestica Achaia Clauss (GRG)
Retsina Kourtaki (WAI, AUG, THR, WR, BOT)
Retsina Metaxas (DAV, AD, PE)
Retsina Tsantali (TAN)
1991
★ Patras, Kouros (AUG)

£4.00 to £5.99

Non-vintage
Samos Muscat (OD)
Samos Nectar 10-year-old (WCL)
1990
Domaine Port Carras Blanc des Blancs Côtes de Meliton (WCL)
1985
Domaine Carras (BOT, THR, WR)

HUNGARY WHITE

Under £3.00

Non-vintage
Hungarian Chardonnay (WHI)
Hungarian Sauvignon Blanc (WHI)
Safeway Nagyrède Dry Muscat (SAF)
1992
Hungarian Chardonnay (WIW)
Hungarian Gewürztraminer (WIW)
Hungarian Sauvignon Blanc (WIW)
Nagyréde Pinot Blanc (AUG)

£3.00 to £5.99

1988
Tokay Szamorodni Dry ½ litre (WIW, AD)
Tokay Szamorodni Sweet ½ litre (WIW)
1986
Tokay Aszú 3 Putts ½ litre (WIW)
Tokay Szamorodni Sweet ½ litre (WIW)
1983
Tokay Szamorodni Dry ½ litre (WIW, ROB)
1982
★ Tokay Aszú 5 Putts ½ litre (OD)

£6.00 to £8.99

Non-vintage
Tokay Szamorodni Sweet ½ litre (UN)
1988
Tokay Aszú 3 Putts ½ litre (GRE)
1986
Tokay Szamorodni Dry ½ litre (BU)
1983
Tokay Aszú 5 Putts ½ litre (WIW, DI)
1981
Tokay Aszú 3 Putts ½ litre (AD, PE, HAG)

£45.00 to £70.00

1964
Tokay Aszú 6 Putts ½ litre (VIG)
1963
Tokay Aszú Muskotalyos ½ litre (AD)
1957
Tokay Aszú 6 Putts ½ litre (AD,JU)
Tokay Aszú Essencia ½ litre (GRE)
1956
Tokay Aszú 4 Putts ½ litre (AD)
Tokay Aszú 5 Putts ½ litre (AD)

£115.00 to £120.00

1963
Tokay Aszú Essencia ½ litre (JU)
1957
Tokay Aszú Essencia ½ litre (VIG)

HUNGARY RED

Under £3.00

Non-vintage
Hungarian Cabernet Sauvignon (WHI)
Hungarian Merlot (WHI)
1992
★ Hungarian Merlot (AUG)
Villany Cabernet Sauvignon (ASD)
1991
Hungarian Cabernet Sauvignon (WIW)
Villany Cabernet Sauvignon (SAF)

£3.00 to £5.99

Non-vintage
Eger Bull's Blood (GA, PE)
1991
Palkonya Cabernet Sauvignon (BOD)
1983
Hungarian Merlot (WIW)
Hungarian Pinot Noir (WIW)

ISRAEL

Under £5.00

Non-vintage
Carmel Cabernet Sauvignon (TES, SAF)
Palwin No. 10 (TES, SAF)
Palwin No. 4 (TES)

£5.00 to £8.99

Non-vintage
Palwin No. 4 (SAF)
1992
Yarden Cabernet Sauvignon White Harvest (WRI)
1991
Yarden Chardonnay (SAF, WRI)
1990
Golan Mount Hermon Dry White (WRI)
Yarden Chardonnay (WRI, ROB)
1988
Gamla Galilee Cabernet Sauvignon (WRI)
1987
Gamla Galilee Cabernet Sauvignon (ROB)

LEBANON RED

Under £7.50

1986
Château Musar (CV, GRE, TAN, BUT, BOT, WR)
1985
Château Musar (PEN, VIC, CV)
1982
★ Château Musar (CV)

£7.50 to £8.00

1986
Château Musar (GE, CHA, WHI, NI, AUG, LO)
1985
Château Musar (BUT, CHA, GRE, GA)
1983
Château Musar (DI)

£8.00 to £9.99

1983
Château Musar (CHA, GRE)
1982
Château Musar (BUT, GRE, WHI)
1981
Château Musar (CV, GE, BUT)

£10.00 to £11.99

1980
Château Musar (AMI, GRE, CHA)
1978
Château Musar (GE)

£12.00 to £17.99

1979
Château Musar (CHA, VIG)
1978
Château Musar (ROB, AMI, CHA, GRE)
1977
Château Musar (NI)

£20.00 to £29.99

1975
Château Musar (GAU, AMI, CHA, WRI)

£35.00 to £39.99

1972
Château Musar (NI, ROB)
1970
Château Musar (GAU)

c. £61.00

1970
Château Musar (CHA)

LEBANON WHITE

Under £7.50

1989
Château Musar Blanc (GRE, GE, AD)

LUXEMBOURG

c. £7.00

Non-vintage
Cuvée de l'Ecusson Brut (EL)

MEXICO

Under £3.00

Non-vintage
L A Cetto Cabernet Sauvignon (GR)
L A Cetto Petit Sirah (GR)

£3.00 to 4.99

Non-vintage
L A Cetto Cabernet Sauvignon (CV)
L A Cetto Petit Sirah (CV)
1988
L A Cetto Cabernet Sauvignon (TES)

MOLDOVA

Under £4.00

1987
★ Negru de Purkar (BU)

£5.00 to £7.99

1988
Negru de Purkar (BU, VIG)
1986
Negru de Purkar (BU)
1987
Directors' Reserve Cuvée Kamrat, Kozhushny Winery (BU, AD, VIG)

£9.00 to £10.99

1979
Negru de Purkar (AD, VIG)
1978
Negru de Purkar (BAR)
1975
Negru de Purkar (BU)

ROMANIA

Under £3.50

Non-vintage
★ Sainsbury's Romanian Pinot Noir (SAI)
1991
Romanian Sauvignon Blanc (GRE)
1986
Classic Pinot Noir (GRE)
★ Tamaioasa (TES)

£3.50 to £4.49

Non-vintage
Pinot Noir Dealul Mare (PE)
1986
Romanian Pinot Noir (BU)
1984
Romanian Cabernet Sauvignon (BU)

MERCHANT DIRECTORY

Abbreviations used in the Merchant Directory are as follows. **Credit cards** Access (AC), American Express (AE), Diners Club (DC), Visa/Barclaycard (V). The following services are available where indicated: **C** cellarage, **EP** *en primeur* offers, **G** glass hire/loan, **M** mail order, **T** tastings and talks.

ADNAMS (AD)

(Head office & mail order) The Crown, High St, Southwold, Suffolk IP18 6DP, (0502) 724222;
The Cellar & Kitchen Store (Southwold collection), Victoria St, Southwold, Suffolk IP18 6JW;
The Wine Shop, South Green, Southwold, Suffolk IP18 6EW, (0502) 722138;
The Grapevine, 109 Unthank Rd, Norwich NR2 2PE, (0603) 613998
Hours Mail order: Mon–Fri 9–5. Cellar & Kitchen Store: Mon–Sat 10–6.30. The Wine Shop: Mon–Sat 10–7.15. The Grapevine: Mon–Sat 9–9.
Credit cards AC V.
Discounts £3 per case if collected (off mail order price).
Delivery £5 1 case, free 2 or more cases mainland UK.
Minimum order 1 mixed case.
C EP G M T
There's hardly an interesting wine that Adnams doesn't have. Pretty well every region is represented, too, including China, should you want to risk it. Brilliant on Australia, New Zealand, California, Germany, Italy, Bordeaux, Burgundy, Rhône, Alsace, Loire, French country – well, everything really. Excellent spirits, too, plus olive oils, vinegars (including the fabulous Valdespino sherry vinegar), ties and tasting blazers. All this, plus Adnams-owned The Crown, The Swan and The Cricketers, makes Southwold worth a detour. Adnams now owns Cheshire merchant Haughton Fine Wines, too.

LES AMIS DU VIN (AMI)

51 Chiltern St, London W1M 1HQ, 071-487 3419;
The Winery, 4 Clifton Rd, London W9 1SS, 071-286 6475
Mail order: 081-451 0469 (24 hour).
Hours Chiltern St: Mon–Fri 10.30–7, closed bank hols. Clifton Rd: Mon–Fri 10.30–8.30, Sat 10–6.30.
Credit cards AC AE DC V.
Discounts 5% unsplit cases for non-members, 10% for members (5% per bottle).
Delivery Free 3 or more cases, otherwise £3.75 London, £5.50 nationally.
C EP G M T
Long on French wine, especially Champagne, Bordeaux, Rhône and Languedoc-Roussillon, though the New World section is strong thanks to sister wholesale company Geoffrey Roberts Associates, which imports a huge range of top names from California and elsewhere. Classic names feature in the list: Guigal, Château de Beaucastel, Opus One; and wines from the south of France often have equally immaculate pedigrees – good names like Château de Fabas and Roger Vergé's Côtes de Provence.

The codes given in brackets on these pages beside the merchants' names are those by which the merchants are listed in the price guides (pages 254-411). They are also listed on page 255.

The mainly French list is augmented by a small selection of wines from Italy, Spain, Germany, Australia, England, Chile and Bulgaria. This is a club, not a shop, with a 24-hour answering machine.

ASDA (ASD)

(Head office) Asda House, Southbank, Great Wilson Street, Leeds LS11 5AD, (0532) 435435, fax (0532) 418666
Hours Mon–Fri 9–8, Sat 8.30–8, open most bank hols.
Credit cards AC V.
T
Well worth investigating: lots of good cheapies and also an adventurous fine wine section.

ASHLEY SCOTT (AS)

PO Box 28, The Highway, Hawarden, Deeside, Clwyd CH5 3RY, (0244) 520655
Hours 24-hr answerphone.
Discounts 5% unsplit case.
Delivery Free in north Wales, Cheshire, Merseyside.
Minimum order 1 mixed case.
G M T

AUGUSTUS BARNETT (AUG)

(Head office) 3 The Maltings, Wetmore Road, Burton-on-Trent, Staffs DE14 1SE, (0283) 512550, fax (0283) 67544
Hours Variable, most 10–10 daily.
Credit cards AC AE V.
Discounts For large orders.
Delivery By arrangement at some branches.
G M T
A much-improved chain. Wines from all corners of the world, including Chile, Portugal, USA, Australia, New Zealand, Spain, Italy and regional France. Augustus Barnett has 544 branches throughout the UK.

AUSTRALIAN WINE CENTRE (AUS)

'Down Under', South Australia House, 50 Strand, London WC2N 5LW, 071-925 0751, fax 071-839 9021
Hours Mon–Fri 10–7, Sat 10–4.
Credit cards AC AE V.
Discounts 5% 1 case cash, collected.
Delivery Free anywhere in UK for orders over £75, otherwise £5.
G M T
A vast range of Australian wines, and an outlet for the Australian Wine Club mail order service. Look here for smaller wineries and older Grange vintages.

AVERY'S (AV)

7 Park St, Bristol BS1 5NG, (0272) 214141, fax (0272) 221729
Hours Mon–Sat 9–7, Sun & bank hols 12–3.
Credit cards AC V.
Discounts By negotiation.
Delivery Free 2 or more cases or within 5 mile radius of central Bristol, otherwise £5.50 per consignment.
C EP G M T
Long-established, and with a strong mail order side. Avery's was a New World pioneer, but the Old World is strong, too. Good house Champagne.

BARNES WINE SHOP (BAR)

51 High St, Barnes, London SW13 9LN, 081-878 8643
Hours Mon–Sat 9.30–8.30, Sun 12–2.
Credit cards AC V.
Discounts 5% mixed case, larger discounts negotiable.
Delivery Free in London.
Minimum order 1 mixed case or magnum (for delivery).
C EP G M T
A well-chosen range from pretty well everywhere, with no reliance on famous names for the sake of it. Quality is high, prices are pretty good.

BEDFORD FINE WINES (BE)

Faulkner's Farm, The Marsh, Carlton, Bedford MK43 7JU, (0234) 721153, fax (0234) 721145
Hours Office hours or by arrangement.
Discounts On preferred wines.
Delivery Free in Bedford, Luton and St Albans areas, £80 minimum order.
Minimum order 1 mixed case.
EP G M T
Claret (back to 1979) is the biggest single section here; other regions are less well represented, though French country wines, Rhône and Burgundy look distinctly interesting. Some good Germans, too. The New World doesn't seem to be exactly a passion, though what's there is good, and there are all those clarets to make up for it.

BERKMANN WINE CELLARS (BEK)

12 Brewery Rd, London N7 9NH, 071-609 4711
Hours Mon–Fri 9–5.30, Sat 10–2. Closed bank holiday weekends.
Credit cards AC V.
Discounts £1 per case collected.
Delivery £3 less than 3 cases or £200 in value (excl vat) for all areas within M25, or £6 for Home Counties.
Minimum order 1 mixed case.
C EP G M T
Berkmann is the wholesale side, Le Nez Rouge the retail side. It's a very strong list that looks mostly towards France: excellent in most areas, and Burgundy lovers will think they've gone to Heaven. There they'll meet some Bordeaux fans and some enthusiasts for Argentinian wines. Australians include Coldstream Hills, there's terrific Pineau des Charentes from Château de Beaulon, Champagne from Bruno Paillard, Beaujolais from Georges Duboeuf (they're Duboeuf's British shippers) and Muscadets from Sauvion, which they also ship.

BERRY BROS & RUDD (BER)

3 St James's St, London SW1A 1EG, 071-396 9600, fax 071-396 9611; The Wine Shop, Hamilton Close, Houndmills, Basingstoke, Hants RG21 2YB, (0256) 23566, fax (0256) 479558
Hours St James's St: Mon–Fri 9.30–5. The Wine Shop: Mon–Fri 9–5, Sat 9–1.
Credit cards AC DC V.
Discounts 3–7.5% according to quantity.
Delivery Free 1 case or more.
C EP G M T
Over 250 years at the same St James's address where there are no wines actually on show – that would not suit this eighteenth-century shop interior. Classic areas are strong, and the whole place is so pointedly fogeyish that you might think they'd never heard of the New World, England or Iberia – and gosh, you'd be wrong.

BIBENDUM (BIB)

113 Regents Park Rd, London NW1 8UR, 071-722 5577
Hours Mon–Sat 10–8.
Credit cards AC AE V.
Delivery Free London, northern England, otherwise £5.45 up to 5 cases.
Minimum order 1 mixed case.
C EP G M T
A top class list, and a merchant that inspires confidence: if a wine's here, you can be sure that it's good. There's more everyday stuff at around a fiver than there used to be, but the glories of the list are the fine wines. There's the best of California, Australia, France, Italy and Spain. Last year Bibendum took over the ailing Yorkshire Fine Wines, and now the two lists are identical, which explains the apparently quirky delivery arrangements. Good prices.

BORDEAUX DIRECT (BOD)

(Head office & mail order) New Aquitaine House, Paddock Rd, Reading, Berks RG4 0JY, (0734) 481718, fax (0734) 461493
Hours Mon–Fri 10.30–7 (Thu till 8), Sat 9–6; 24-hr answerphone. Mail order: Mon–Fri 9–7, Sat & Sun 10–4.
Credit cards AC AE DC V.
Discounts Special offers.
Delivery Free for orders over £50.
G EP M T
The original 'direct from the vineyard' company. Mostly mail order, but there are also five shops in the Thames Valley. Bordeaux Direct offers a particularly good range of French country wines, also well-priced drinking from Chile, Eastern Europe and Spain. Sister company to the Sunday Times Wine Club.

BORG CASTEL (BOR)

Samlesbury Mill, Goosefoot Lane, Samlesbury Bottoms, Preston, Lancs PR5 0RN, phone & fax (025 485) 2128
Hours Mon–Fri 10–5, Thu 7–9.30pm, first Sun of month 12–4.
Discounts 6 or more cases.
Delivery Free 1 case or more within 30 mile radius.
C G M T
On this fairly-priced list most is from France and Germany. A good range from the Rhône and the Loire, and Alsace is represented by the reliable co-op at Turckheim.

BOTTOMS UP (BOT)

(Head office) Sefton House, 42 Church Rd, Welwyn Garden City, Herts AL8 6PJ, (0707) 328244, fax (0707) 371398
Hours Mon–Sat 9–10 (some 10.30), Sun 12–3, 7–10.

Credit cards AC AE V.
Discounts 10% mixed cases wine, 17.5% mixed cases Champagne.
Delivery Free locally (all shops).
G T
Now owned by Thresher, Bottoms Up shops are intended to be the largest outlets of the chain, with the most comprehensive range.

BROAD STREET WINE CO (BR)

Emscote Mill, Wharf Street, Warwick CV34 5LB, (0926) 493951, fax (0926) 495345
Hours Mon–Fri 9–6, Sat 9–1.
Credit cards AC V.
Delivery Free 6 or more cases.
Minimum order 1 mixed case.
C G M T
Largest collection in the UK of vintage Cognacs. Older vintages of Burgundy, Claret and Loire. There are wines from Cloudy Bay and Rongopai from New Zealand, and also good Rhônes.

BUTE WINES (BUT)

Mount Stuart, Rothesay, Isle of Bute PA20 9LR (0700) 502730, fax (0700) 505313.
2 Cottesmore Gardens, London W8 5PR, 071-937 1629.
Delivery (per case) £8.50 for 1, £10.50 for 2, £12.50 for 3, £13.50 for 4, free 5 or more.
Minimum order 1 mixed case, or £250 for delivery outside Central London, Glasgow, Edinburgh, Bute.
EP M T
No shop at either address, but stock is held on Bute, and in London, Glasgow and Corsham. Much emphasis on classic names. Half a dozen top Alsace producers are here in depth,and a few famous names from Italy. There's also a decent sprinkling of New World, while Bordeaux and Burgundy are strongest of all.

BUTLERS WINE CELLAR (BU)

247 Queens Park Rd, Brighton BN2 2XJ, (0273) 698724, fax (0273) 622761
Hours Tue–Wed 9–5.30, Thu–Sat 9–7.
Credit cards AC V.
Delivery Free locally 1 case or more, free mainland England and Wales, some parts of Scotland 3 or more cases; otherwise (per bottle) £4.50 for 1, £5.50 for 2–3, £6.50 for 4–6, £7.50 for 7–12, £10 for 25–35.
G M T
Bin-ends are the mainstay of this shop – and what bin ends. Lots are very old indeed – Geoffrey and Henry Butler make a speciality of anniversary years – but not all are terrifically expensive. There's a rapid turnover, and a new list comes out every six weeks. They also have the sort of wine that's for drinking, not just giving – with a quirky, always good, and often excellent range of wines from just about everywhere. Plenty are priced at under a tenner.

ANTHONY BYRNE (BY)

88 High St, Ramsey, Huntingdon, Cambs PE17 1BS, (0487) 814555, fax (0487) 814962
Hours Mon–Sat 9–5.30.
Credit cards AC V.
Discounts 5% mixed case, 10% unsplit case.
Delivery £6 less than 5 cases, free 5 or more cases.
C EP M T
A list packed with well-selected wines from Burgundy, Alsace, the Loire, the south of France, Italy, Australia, New Zealand... Pudding wines are a passion, and this is one of the few places to sell the extraordinary Château Gilette from Sauternes. There's also some sweet Pacherenc from Gascony – go on, surprise your friends.

D. BYRNE (BYR)

Victoria Buildings, 12 King St, Clitheroe, Lancashire BB7 2EP, (0200) 23152
Hours Mon–Sat 8.30–6 (Thu–Fri till 8).
Discounts £1 mixed case, £1.20 unmixed case, 5% orders over £300.
Delivery Free locally.
C EP G T
It's hard to think of anything that this shop doesn't have. You want demi-sec Veuve Clicquot in halves? You want a choice of six Amarone? You want Trousseau from the Jura? It's all here, alongside hundreds of others. Unfortunately, what this merchant also had this year was a flood, which is why it was unable to supply any information in time for our price guides. But give it a ring or pay it a visit, because its prices are keen and the selection is always enough to make one drool.

CAPE PROVINCE WINES (CAP)

1 The Broadway, Kingston Rd, Staines, Middx TW18 1AT, (0784) 451860/455244, fax (0784) 469267
Hours Mon–Sat 9–9, Sun 12–1.
Credit cards AC V.
Delivery £5.90 locally and London, UK mainland varies with quantity.
Minimum order 6 bottles. **M T**

South African wines, as you might guess, are the be all and end all of this list. There are Nederburg auction wines and rare vintages as well as plenty of others.

CELTIC VINTNER (CV)

73 Derwen Fawr Road, Sketty, Swansea SA2 8DR, (0792) 206661, fax (0792) 296671
Hours Mon–Fri 9–6, other times by arrangement.
Discounts Negotiable.
Delivery Free South Wales, elsewhere at cost.
Minimum order 1 mixed case.
C EP G T
An informative and stimulating list. Balance is the key; with Spain, for instance, you don't just get Torres (which would be no hardship), you get CVNE and Réné Barbier as well. Burgundy looks interesting, and there are quite a few half bottles for the abstemious (or possibly the greedy who want to try everything).

CHÂTEAUX WINES (CHA)

11 Church St, Bishop's Lydeard, Taunton, Somerset TA4 3AT, phone & fax (0454) 613959
Hours Mon–Fri 9–5.30, Sat 9–12.30.
Credit cards AC V.
Discounts Negotiable.
Delivery Free UK mainland 1 case or more.
Minimum order 1 case (usually mixed).
C EP M T
A short list of decent producers without much variety, but there are oddities like red and white Coteaux Champenois from Laurent Perrier. Laurent Perrier Champagne also comes in big sizes, up to the 16-bottle balthazar. Châteaux Wines have no shop; everything is mail order.

CORNEY & BARROW (CB)

12 Helmet Row, London EC1V 3QJ, 071-251 4051;
194 Kensington Park Rd, London W11, 071-221 5122;
31 Rutland Sq, Edinburgh EH1 2BW, 031-228 2233;
Belvoir House, High St, Newmarket CB8 8OH, (0638) 662068
Hours Mon–Fri 9–5.30; 24-hr answerphone.
Credit cards AC V.
Delivery Free London 2 or more cases, elsewhere free 3 or more cases.
C EP G M T
Importer of Château Pétrus and the Domaine de la Romanée Conti, which gives you some clue to the rest of the list. All the Moueix wines are here, plus a range of petits châteaux. *There's also a glittering cast of Burgundy producers and Australia is represented by Penfolds Grange, Italy by the super-Tuscan Sassicaia. At the quirkier end there are a couple of Canadians, and Israelis from Baron Wine Cellars. C&B say they are not pricy. Well, wines like Pétrus don't come cheap, and if you have to ask the price you can't afford it. Don't expect bargains.*

DAVISONS (DAV)

7 Aberdeen Road, Croydon, Surrey CR0 1EQ, 081-681 3222, fax 081-760 0390
Hours Mon–Sat 10–2, 5–10.
Credit cards AC V.
Discounts 8.5% mixed case.
Delivery Free locally.
EP G T
Strong on claret, petits châteaux, *Burgundy and vintage ports bought* en primeur. *The strengths have always been in the classic areas, but these are now joined by wines from Australia, Chile, Spain and Portugal. Often very good prices.*

DIRECT WINE (DI)

5–7 Corporation Square, Belfast, Northern Ireland BT1 3AJ, (0232) 243906, fax (0232) 240202
Hours Mon–Fri 9.30–5.45 (Thu till 8), Sat 10–5.
Credit cards AC V.
Discounts 5% 6 unmixed bottles, 5% 1 mixed case, 7.5% 1 unmixed case.
Delivery Free in Northern Ireland 2 or more cases.
C EP M T
This list specializes in Europe, with a nice balance of good everyday wines and some seriously fine ones from Bordeaux, Burgundy, the Rhône and Alsace. Good Germans and Italians can be found here, too.

ELDRIDGE, POPE (EL)

(Head office) Weymouth Ave, Dorchester, Dorset DT1 1QT, (0305) 251251
Mail order: (0800) 378757.
Hours Mon–Sat 9–5.30.
Credit cards AC V.
Discounts On application.
Delivery £5 less than 2 cases, free 2 or more cases.
C G M T
Oodles of mouth-watering wines from the classic to the rare, from Bordeaux to Mexico. There are now nine shops plus four J.B. Reynier Wine Libraries which turn into wine bars at midday – a great way to taste before you buy, and very good value indeed.

PHILIP EYRES (EY)

The Cellars, Coleshill, Amersham, Bucks HP7 0LS, (0494) 433823, fax (0494) 431349
Hours Usually Mon–Fri 8–10, Sat variable; answerphone out of hours.
Delivery Free within south Bucks, Windsor & Ascot, Berkhamsted, Bicester, Highgate & Hampstead areas, £6.50 central London 1 case, free 2 or more; otherwise £10 UK mainland 1 case, £6.50 2–3 or free 4 or more. Delivery on special offers charged separately.
Minimum order 1 case.
EP
There's no shop, so write or telephone for access to Philip Eyres' well-chosen list. Germany is a passion; look also for clarets, French country and Rhône.

FARR VINTNERS (FA)

19 Sussex St, London SW1V 4RR, 071-828 1960, fax 071-828 3500
Credit cards AC V.
Discounts 10 or more cases.
Delivery £8.50 London; (per case) £3.50 Home Counties, minimum £10.50; £3.75 rest of England and Wales, minimum £11.25; £5.60 Scotland, minimum £16.80 or give 48 hours notice of collection.
Minimum order £200 plus vat.
Farr Vintners are fine wine brokers; they have no shop. This is not the place to come for a bottle of Aussie Chardonnay for supper. It is, however, the place for a splendid selection of serious wines at competitive prices.

FINE WINES OF NEW ZEALAND (FIZ)

PO Box 476, London NW5 2NZ, 071-482 0093, fax 071-267 8400
Hours Mon–Sat 9–5.
Discounts 2 or more cases.
Delivery £9 mixed case except for special offers.
Minimum order 1 mixed case.
M T
Small, quality-minded outfit that pioneered many successful names here. Look for Redwood Valley, Vidal, Matua Valley, Ngatarawa, Ata Rangi... one could go on. Lovely pudding wines in half bottles.

GATEWAY (GA)

(Head office) Gateway House, Hawkfield Business Park, Whitchurch Lane, Bristol BS14 0TJ, (0272) 359359
Hours Mon–Sat 9–6, variable late opening Friday all stores.
Credit cards AC V.
Delivery from Keynsham and Bath stores only, £1 on orders of £20–£50, free over £50.
T
675 stores throughout the UK, about 40 of which have the full list. A further 60–70 have the full list excluding the finer Wine Rack range. Quality is patchy, but there are goodies like Burgundies from the Buxy co-op and some very good southern French wines. Gateway has a good list of clarets, too.

GAUNTLEYS (GAU)

4 High St, Exchange Arcade, Nottingham NG1 2ET, (0602) 417973, fax (0602) 509519
Hours Mon–Sat 9–5.30.
Credit cards AC V.
Delivery Free within Nottingham area, otherwise £6.50 per case + vat.
Minimum order 1 case.
C EP (not Bordeaux) **G M T**
A class list of all the wines you'd most like to have: excellent French, Italian, Spanish, Australian (including four liqueur Muscats), New Zealand, South African, port and sherry. Prices are fair, but not rock-bottom.

GELSTON CASTLE (GE)

Castle Douglas, Scotland DG7 1QE, (0556) 503012, fax (0556) 504183
Hours Mon–Fri 9–7.
Delivery Free within 25 miles of Castle Douglas 1 case or more, £7 rest of mainland UK; free for orders over £150.
Minimum order None, but mixed cases carry a surcharge of £4 per case, unless they comprise two unmixed half dozens.
C EP G M T
A traditional, knowledgeable list from which it would be all too tempting to spend a great deal of money. Lots of brilliant German wines, everyday and fine clarets, plus Rhônes and Burgundies. There's more from Italy and the New World this year, and a small but varied list of half bottles.

THE GRAPE SHOP (GR)

135 Northcote Rd, London SW11 6PX, 071-924 3638, fax 071-924 3670; 85–87 rue Victor Hugo, 62200 Boulogne sur mer, France, (010 33) 2133 9230, fax (010 33) 2133 9231
Hours London: Mon–Fri 10–2 & 5–9.30; Sat 10–9.30, Sun 12–3 & 7–9. Boulogne: Mon–Sun 10–7.30.

Credit cards AC V
Discounts Negotiable.
Delivery 1 case free in Greater London, negotiable elsewhere (including France).
Minimum order 1 bottle.
G M T
An individual list with a high turnover. Lots of good French, including older wines.Prices in our Guides are those obtaining in the Boulogne shop (there is no printed list for London) so should not be directly compared with other prices.

PETER GREEN (GRE)

37A-B Warrender Park Rd, Edinburgh EH9 1HJ, 031-229 5925
Hours Mon–Fri 9.30–6.30, Sat 9.30–7.
Discounts 5% most unsplit cases.
Delivery Free in Edinburgh, elsewhere £6 1 case, £4 each additional case. **G M T**

If you're planning a visit here, go early in the day, because you'll need plenty of time for browsing. Everything looks terrific: Italy, Spain, France, New World and, yes, appropriately for Scotland, malt whiskies, too...

GROG BLOSSOM (GRG)

(Head office) 48 King St, Royston, Herts SG8 9BA, (0763) 247201, fax (0763) 244601;
66 Notting Hill Gate, London W11 3HT, 071-792 3834;
253 West End Lane, London NW6 1XN, 071-794 7808
Hours Mon–Thu 11–10, Fri–Sat 10–10, Sun 12–3, 7–10.
Credit cards AC V.
Discounts 5% mixed case.
G T
This is a small chain of London shops – they boast 450 different wines and a constantly changing selection of bin-ends. There are over 250 beers as well, and the staff are knowledgeable.

HALVES (HAL)

Wood Yard, off Corve St, Ludlow, Shropshire SY8 2PX, (0584) 877866, fax (0584) 877677;
7 Western Road Industrial Estate, Stratford-upon-Avon, Warks CV37 0AH, (0789) 297777
Credit cards AC AE V.
Discounts £2.35 per delivery of 2 or more cases to a single address; 4% on all unmixed cases.
Delivery Free to mainland UK.
Minimum order 1 case of 24 half bottles.
C G M T
Tim Jackson stocks over 200 different wines in half bottles and has just about everything from Alsace to New Zealand, via various unpredictable stops in Cahors and Sicily. He's particularly strong on dessert wines.

HARCOURT FINE WINE (HAC)

3 Harcourt St, London W1H 1DS, 071-723 7202, fax 071-723 8085, answerphone 071-724 5009
Hours Mon–Fri 9.30–6, Sat 11–4.30.
Credit cards AC AE DC V.
Discounts 5% mixed case, additional for larger quantities.
Delivery Free in London 3 or more cases.
G M T
Once known as the English Wine Shop and still stockists of wines from over 45 English vineyards. There is plenty of French and German, too, and French brandy from vintages in the last century.

GERARD HARRIS (HAG)

2 Green End St, Aston Clinton, Aylesbury, Bucks HP22 5HP, (0296) 631041, fax (0296) 631250
Hours Mon–Wed 9.30–6.30, Thu–Sat 9.30–8. Closed bank hols.
Credit cards AC V.
Delivery Free locally 1 case or more.
Minimum order 1 mixed case for delivery, no minimum in shop.
EP G M T
This is owned by The Bell Inn (Aston Clinton) Ltd. Bordeaux and Burgundy are good, particularly the latter; other areas are smaller but avoid being obvious – the Quady dessert wines from California, for example, or Spanish wines that are not just Torres.

All the companies listed in the Merchant Directory have wines featured in the Price Guides (pages 254–411).
*Abbreviations used in the Directory are as follows: **Credit Cards** Access (AC), American Express (AE), Diners Club (DC), Visa/Barclaycard (V).*
*The following services are available where indicated: **C** cellarage, **EP** en primeur offers, **G** glass hire/loan, **M** mail order, **T** tastings and talks.*

ROGER HARRIS (HAW)

Loke Farm, Weston Longville, Norfolk NR9 5LG, (0603) 880171/2, fax (0603) 880291
Hours Mon–Fri 9–5.
Credit cards AC AE DC V.
Discounts (per case) £2 for 2, £2.50 for 3, £3 for 5, £4 for 10.
Delivery Free UK mainland.
Minimum order 1 mixed case.
M T
What the Sunday colour supplements would call 'the Specialists' Specialist' – Beaujolais utterly dominates the list and the working life of Roger Harris. Only Champagne, some Mâconnais and a little Coteaux du Lyonnais get a look-in besides. A high-quality list.

JOHN HARVEY (HA)

31 Denmark St, Bristol BS1 5DQ, (0272) 268882, fax (0272) 253380
Hours Mon–Fri 9.30–6, Sat 9.30–1.
Credit cards AC AE DC V.
Discounts 10% for unbroken case.
Delivery Free 1 case or more UK mainland, no mixed cases.
C EP T
Sherry (Harvey's), port (Cockburn's), and claret (close association with Château Latour) are the strengths. There are regular en primeur *offers for claret and Burgundy, as well as wines from other parts of the world to vary the classic British sideboard tray.*

RICHARD HARVEY (HAY)

Bucknowle House, Bucknowle, Wareham, Dorset BH20 5PQ, (0929) 480352, fax (0929) 481275
Hours By arrangement.
Discounts 5% 6 or more cases.
Delivery Free within 30 miles 3 or more cases.
Minimum order 1 case.
C EP G M T

It's an appointment-only set-up, but worth it for the wine – every producer listed is good quality. The sherries are Barbadillo, the port Churchill Graham, the Chilean wine Montes. An associated company opened in Cherbourg earlier this year at La Maison du Vin, 71 avenue Caruot, Cherbourg 50100 (tel: 010 33 33 43 37 23; fax: 010 33 33 43 98 48). Much of the Richard Harvey list is available at duty-free prices there. Order through the UK office.

HAYNES HANSON & CLARK (HAH)

17 Lettice St, London SW6 4EH, 071-736 787;
36 Kensington Church Street, London W8 4BX, 071-937 4650, fax 071-371 5887
Hours Lettice St: Mon–Thu 9–7, Fri 9–6.
Kensington: Mon–Sat 9.30–7.
Discounts 10% unsplit case.
Delivery Free central London, elsewhere 5 or more cases.
Minimum order Warehouse only 1 case.
EP G M T
An extremely knowledgeable, helpful merchant famous for its Burgundies but with excellent Bordeaux as well. Also go there for Loire, Rhône, delicious house Champagne, a good range of New World and reliable, honest advice.

DOUGLAS HENN-MACRAE (HE)

81 Mackenders Lane, Eccles, Aylesford, Kent ME20 7JA, (0622) 710952, fax (0622) 791203
Hours Mail order & phone enquiries only, Mon–Sat to 10pm.
Credit cards AC V.
Delivery Free UK mainland 10 cases, otherwise £8 plus vat per order.
Minimum order 1 case.
M T
Instead of roaming around the world, concentrates on just two areas – Germany and the US. Some fine-quality drinking – excellent Rieslings and increasingly good Texans. Between publication of this Guide *and Christmas 1993, Douglas Henn-Macrae promises that lots of new wines will be added.*

HICKS & DON (HIC)

(Head office) Blandford St Mary, Dorset DT11 9LS, (0258) 456040, fax (0258) 450147;
Park House, Elmham, Dereham, Norfolk NR20 5JY, (0362) 668571/281;
The Old Bakehouse, Alfred St, Westbury, Wiltshire BA13 3DY, (0373) 864723, fax (0373) 858250
Hours Mon–Fri 8.30–5.
Credit cards AC V.
Discounts Negotiable.
Delivery 1–2 cases £3 per case, 3 or more cases free UK mainland.
Minimum order 1 mixed case.
C EP G M T
Strong on opening offers of claret, Burgundy, cru *Beaujolais, port and the Rhône. Sherries are as strong as ever – all are from that excellent Sanlúcar house, Barbadillo. It's a well-chosen list, and prices are often good. They also have their own English wine, Elmham Park, and they have William Fèvre's Chardonnay from his Chilean venture.*

HIGH BRECK VINTNERS (HIG)

Bentworth House, Bentworth, Nr Alton, Hants GU34 5RB, (0420) 562218, fax (0420) 563827
Hours Mon–Fri 9.30–5.30, other times by arrangement.
Credit cards AC V.
Delivery (south-east) £6 for 1 case, £4 for 2, 3 or more free; (rest of England) £9 for 1, £6 for 2, £4 for 3, 4 or more free.
Minimum order 1 mixed case.
EP G M T
Pretty catholic selection of interesting French names, particularly in Alsace, Bordeaux and the Loire – nice Germans from Deinhard, Italian from Antinori and a reasonable sprinkling of wines specially selected from other areas, including Australia and Spain. There are some new wines from Costières de Nîmes: estates by the names of Château de Campuget and Domaine l'Amarine.

J.E. HOGG (HOG)

61 Cumberland St, Edinburgh EH3 6RA, 031-556 4025
Hours Mon–Tue, Thu–Fri 9–1, 2.30–6; Wed, Sat 9–1.
Delivery Free 12 or more bottles within Edinburgh.
G T
A first-class list of covetable goodies: lots of white Rhônes, top Loires, Germans, Beaujolais, lots of clarets, good Californians (Ridge Zinfandel) and sherries. Good fizz from a wide range of countries.

The codes given in brackets on these pages beside the merchants' names are those by which the merchants are listed in the price guides (pages 254-411). They are also listed on page 255.

HUNGERFORD WINE (HUN)

Unit 3, Station Yard, Hungerford, Berks RG17 0DY, (0488) 683238, fax (0488) 684919;
24 High Street, Hungerford
Hours Mon–Fri 9–5.30, Sat 9–5.
Credit cards AC AE V.
Discounts Negotiable.
Delivery Free within 15 mile radius 1 case, elsewhere varies per offer.
C EP G M T
There's a new baby here called The Claret Club, dealing in just that. Other wines come under the Hungerford banner, as before.

JUSTERINI & BROOKS (JU)

61 St James's St, London SW1A 1LZ, 071-493 8721, fax 071-499 4653;
45 George St, Edinburgh EH2 2HT, 031-226 4202, fax 031-225 2351
Hours London: Mon–Fri 9–5.30 (Thu till 6.30).
Edinburgh: Mon–Fri 9–5.30, Sat till 1.
Credit cards AC AE DC V.
Discounts (per case) £1 for 2–4, £2 for 5–7, £3 for 8 and over.
Delivery Free 2 or more cases, otherwise £9 UK for less than 2 cases, £2.50 within Edinburgh.
C EP G M
Stacks of splendid clarets, Burgundies, Champagnes, Rhônes, Loires, Germans, and even 1947 Tokaji Essencia – a snip at £610 a bottle.

J.C. KARN & SON (KA)

7 Lansdown Place, Cheltenham, Glos GL50 2HU, (0242) 513265
Hours Mon–Fri 9.30–6, Sat 9.30–1.30.
Credit cards AC V.
Discounts 5% mixed case (cash).
Delivery Free in Glos.
G M T
Personally selected list, very good on New Zealand, Australia and the Loire.

LAY & WHEELER (LAY)

(Head office & shop) 6 Culver St West, Colchester, Essex CO1 1JA, (0206) 764446, fax (0206) 560002
Wine Market, Gosbeck's Road, Shrub End, Colchester, Essex CO2 9JT, (0206) 764446
Hours Culver St: Mon–Sat 8.30–5.30. Wine Market: Mon–Sat 8–8.
Credit cards AC V.
Discounts 5% 10 or more mixed cases.
Delivery Free locally 1 case, elsewhere 2 or more cases.
C EP G M T
An informative, well-produced list with lots of information about growers and vintages. L&W are well-established, reputable and knowledgeable and the list is packed with famous names. Very drool-worthy.

LONDON WINE (LO)

Chelsea Wharf, 15 Lots Rd, London SW10 0QF, 071-351 6856; freefone orderline (0800) 581266
Hours Mon–Fri 9–9, Sat 10–7, Sun 12–3.
Credit cards AC AE DC V.
Discounts 5% per case.
Delivery Free locally.
EP G M T
A sound list with plenty of variety. Good on Alsace, and some decent sherries. Prices are competitive.

LORNE HOUSE VINTNERS (LOR)

Gomshall Cellars, The Gallery, Gomshall, Surrey GU5 9LB, (0483) 203795, fax (0483) 203282
Hours Mon–Sat 10–6, (Fri till 8).
Credit cards AC V.
Discounts 10% per case.
Delivery Free 2 or more cases within 25 miles Gomshall, otherwise £5 per consignment.
Minimum order 1 bottle. **C G M T**
Mainly French but also clutches from Germany, Spain and Italy. A 'Shipping Club' offers extra discounts to members.

MAJESTIC (MAJ)

(Head office) Odhams Trading Estate, St Albans Road, Watford, Herts WD2 5RE, (0923) 816999, fax (0923) 819105; 18 London branches plus Acocks Green, Amersham, Birmingham, Bletchley, Bristol, Bushey, Cambridge, Chichester, Croydon, Gloucester, Guildford, Ipswich, Maidenhead, Northampton, Norwich, Oxford, Poole, Reading, St Albans, Salisbury, Stockport, Sunningdale, Swindon, Taunton
Hours Mon–Sat 10–8, Sun 10–6.
Credit cards AC AE DC V.
Delivery Free locally.
Minimum order 1 mixed case.
EP G M T
Still not the force it used to be, with smaller selections despite keen prices. But things may be improving again. Good for Champagne.

MARKS & SPENCER (MAR)

(Head office) Michael House, Baker Street, London W1A 1DN, 071-935 4422; 264 licensed stores all over the country
Hours Variable.
Discounts 12 bottles for the price of 11. **M**

All the companies listed in the Merchant Directory have wines featured in the Price Guides (pages 254–411).
*Abbreviations used in the Directory are as follows: **Credit Cards** Access (AC), American Express (AE), Diners Club (DC), Visa/Barclaycard (V).*
*The following services are available where indicated: **C** cellarage, **EP** en primeur offers, **G** glass hire/loan, **M** mail order, **T** tastings and talks.*

A list that is developing in the direction of the New World and does well within fairly tight parameters. There's plenty of Chardonnay, Sauvignon Blanc and Cabernet Sauvignon, for example, but less and less from less commercial grapes or regions. Southern French wines are good; also a good Winemaker's range.

MORENO WINES (MOR)

11 Marylands Rd, London W9 2DU, 071-286 0678, fax 071-286 0513; 2 Norfolk Place, London W2 1QN, 071-706 3055
Hours Marylands Rd: Mon–Sat 10–9, Sun 12–2.
Norfolk Place: Mon–Fri 10–9, Sat 10–8.
Credit cards AC V.
Discounts 5% mixed case.
Delivery Free locally, elsewhere 5 or more cases. **G M T**

Moreno undoubtedly has the largest range of Spanish wines in the country. There's Toro, Rueda, Somontano, Valencia and others, treats such as Vega Sicilia, Bodegas Riojanas and CVNE; Albariño for when you're feeling rich, plus sherry and brandy.

MORRIS & VERDIN (MV)

28 Churton St, London SW1V 2LP, 071-630 8888
Hours Mon–Fri 8–6. Closed bank hols.
Discounts 5 or more cases.
Delivery Free central London, elsewhere 5 or more cases.
Minimum order 1 mixed case.
C E P G M T
Imaginative list, majoring on Burgundy: names like Rion, Bachelet, Ponsot. Also Ostertag from Alsace, Au Bon Climat, Cá del Solo, Qupé and Bonny Doon from California, some Aussies and NZs and lots of French country wines.

THE NADDER WINE CO (NA)

Hussars House, 2 Netherhampton Road, Harnham, Salisbury, Wiltshire SP2 8HE, (0722) 325418; fax (0722) 421617
Hours Mon–Fri 9–7, Sat 10–3.
Credit cards AC V.
Discounts 5% on orders over £100 (2.5% credit cards), 7.5% over £500 (5% credit cards).
Delivery Free in central London & Salisbury area or for orders of £50 or over; free UK mainland and Isle of Wight min 10 cases; otherwise at cost.
Minimum order 1 case.
G M T
There's quite a lot of scope here if you want mid-level claret, and there's plenty, too, from Australia. Also Columbia Winery from Washington State and some good South African wines. Ports look interesting, if you're feeling in need of fortification.

JAMES NICHOLSON (NI)

27A Killyeagh St, Crossgar, Co. Down, Northern Ireland BT30 9DG, (0396) 830091, fax (0396) 830028
Hours Mon–Sat 10–7.
Credit cards AC DC V.
Discounts 5–10% mixed case.
Delivery Free UK 1 case or more.
Minimum order 1 mixed case.
C EP G M T
A pretty comprehensive list of lots of all the best names. Also lots of good half bottles – Rhône, Burgundy, Musar, claret and dessert wines from New Zealand. What more can you want?

ODDBINS (OD)

(Head office) 31–33 Weir Road, London SW19 8UG, 081-944 4400; 177 shops.
Hours Mon–Sat 9–9, Sun (not Scotland) 12–2, 7–9. Closed Christmas.
Credit cards AC AE V.
Discounts 5% split case wine; 7 bottles Champagne and sparkling wine for the price of 6 (if £5.99 or above).
Delivery Available locally for most shops. Free with reasonable order.
EP G T
How do Oddbins do it? They make a fuss (rightly) about their New World wines but they're good on Bordeaux, Champagne, Germany, Spain, Italy, etc. New this year is a fine wine venture at London's Farringdon Street branch.

THOS. PEATLING (PE)

(Head office) Westgate House, Bury St Edmunds, Suffolk IP33 1QS, (0284) 755948, fax (0284) 705795
Hours Variable.
Credit cards AC AE V.
Discounts 5% mixed case.
Delivery Free in East Anglia, elsewhere 2 or more cases. **C EP G M T**

Strong Peatling points have always been clarets, but the New World wines are getting better all the time. Peatlings also now includes Ostlers, the Australian specialist merchant.

PENISTONE COURT (PEN)

The Railway Station, Penistone, South Yorkshire S30 6HG, (0226) 766037, fax (0226) 767310
Hours Mon–Fri 9–6, Sat 10–3.
Delivery Free locally, UK mainland at cost 1 case or more.
G
A sound list that covers all the major areas, though with a tendency to rely on just one or two major producers in each. They also sell Lamberhurst Vineyards fruit liqueurs – English flavours like plum and pear and raspberry and the rather less English orange.

CHRISTOPHER PIPER (PIP)

1 Silver St, Ottery St Mary, Devon EX11 1DB, (0404) 814139, fax (0404) 812100
Hours Mon–Sat 9–6.
Credit cards AC V.
Discounts 5% mixed case, 10% 3 or more cases.
Delivery Free in South-West 4 or more cases, elsewhere 6 or more cases.
Minimum order 1 mixed case.
C EP G M T
Particularly strong in crus bourgeois *and* petits châteaux *clarets, with very good – though not necessarily the most famous – classed growths. The same policy is followed for Burgundies, with some of the lesser known villages like Saint-Aubin or Marange. The big names are there as well, but this is a thoughtfully put together list with plenty of depth and breadth in the rest of France, besides Germany, Italy and the New World.*

RAEBURN FINE WINES (RAE)

23 Comely Bank Rd, Edinburgh EH4 1DS, phone & fax 031-332 5166
Hours Mon–Sat 9–6.
Credit cards AC V.
Discounts 5% unsplit case, 2.5% mixed case.
Delivery Price negotiable, all areas covered.
C EP G M T
The Scots have always liked their claret, and this is one of the places they come to buy it. Most of this first-class list is French, but there are top producers from Germany, Spain, Italy and particularly California.

REID WINES (1992) LTD (REI)

The Mill, Marsh Lane, Hallatrow, Nr Bristol BS18 5EB, (0761) 452645, fax (0761) 453642
Hours Mon–Fri 9–5.30.
Delivery Free within 25 miles of Hallatrow (Bristol).
C EP G M T
An entertaining list of the best of most regions, including Drouhin Oregon Pinot Noir, Francis Ford Coppola's Rubicon from California and some splendid Tuscans and Loires.

ROBERSON (ROB)

348 Kensington High St, London W14 8NS, 071-371 2121, fax 071-371 4010
Hours Mon–Sat 10–8, Sun 12–3.
Credit cards AC V AE.
Delivery Free locally 1 case or more.
G M T
This new shop (opened November 1991) aims to be the best in London. It stocks around 1000 wines and over 150 spirits and liqueurs, so it can hardly fail to be mouthwatering. A look at our Price Guides makes it apparent that Robersons is not the cheapest; but the range is excellent.

SAFEWAY (SAF)

(Head office) 6 Millington Road, Hayes, Middlesex UB3 4AY, 081-848 8744
Hours Mon–Sat 8–8 (Fri till 9), Sun 10–4 (selected stores).
Credit cards AC V.
G
Safeway is back in the leading pack of High Street outlets. Increasingly good Eastern Europe, New World, French country wines and also sound Italians.

SAINSBURY (SAI)

(Head office) Stamford House, Stamford St, London SE1 9LL, 071-921 6000
Hours Variable, many open late.
Credit cards AC V.
T
The country's largest wine retailer. Sound list enlivened by a vintage selection of fine wines available from 290 main stores with the widest selection of 400 wines available in 60 branches and 9 Savacentres.

SOMMELIER WINE CO (SOM)

23 St George's Esplanade, St Peter Port, Guernsey, Channel Islands, (0481) 721677, fax (0481) 716818; Grapevine, 23 Glategny Esplanade, St Peter Port, Guernsey, Channel Islands, (0481) 721677, fax (0481) 716818
Hours Tue–Thu 10–5.30, Fri 10–6, Sat 9–5.30 (9.30–5.30 Grapevine); answerphone out of hours.
Credit cards AC V (Grapevine only).
Discounts 5% 12 or more bottles.
Delivery Free 12 or more unmixed bottles.
G M (locally) **T**
Interesting, well-chosen list of high quality, like Charlie Melton's Nine Popes or the Yarra Yering wines from Australia.

SUMMERLEE WINES (SUM)

64 High St, Earls Barton, Northants NN6 0JG, phone & fax (0604) 810488; (Office) Freddy Price, 48 Castlebar Rd, London W5 2DD, 081-997 7889, fax 081-991 5178
Hours Mon–Fri 9–2; answerphone out of hours.
Delivery Free England & Wales 5 or more cases, or Northants, Oxford, Cambridge & London 2 or more cases; otherwise £6.50 per case 1–4 cases.
C G
A fairly short, knowledgeable list of excellent clarets and Germans, plus good sherry, port, Faugères and vin jaune. *Freddy Price takes the trouble to seek out wines, and it shows.*

SUNDAY TIMES WINE CLUB (WIC)

New Aquitaine House, Paddock Road, Reading, Berks RG4 0JY, (0734) 481713, fax (0734) 461953
Hours Mail order, 24-hr answerphone.
Credit cards AC AE DC V.
Discounts On special offers.
Delivery Free for orders over £50.
EP M T
Associate company is Bordeaux Direct. Membership fee is £10 per annum. The club also runs tours and tastings and an annual festival in London.

TANNERS (TAN)

26 Wyle Cop, Shrewsbury, Shropshire SY1 1XD, (0743) 232400
Hours Mon–Sat 9–6.
Credit cards AC V.
Discounts 5% 1 mixed case wine (cash & collection), 5% 5 or more cases assorted bottles of wine, 7.5% 10 cases (mail order).
Delivery Free local delivery 1 mixed case or more or nationally for orders under £75, otherwise £6 per order.
C EP G M T

Wide-ranging and adventurously chosen list – good on classic areas like Burgundy (Domaine Dujac, Pousse d'Or, Lafon) and claret, but also the New World. Terrific things from everywhere, in fact – try the excellent Quinta de Agua Alta port from Churchills or Château Carras from Greece.

TESCO (TES)

(Head office) Delamare Road, Cheshunt, Herts EN8 9SL, (0992) 632222, fax (0992) 630794; 401 licensed branches
Hours Variable (open Sunday).
Credit cards AC V.
Wide range, and no longer regarded as runner-up to Sainsbury's in quality terms. Lots of New World wines and good on Italy, Germany and French vins de pays *too. New is an International Winemaker range.*

THRESHER (THR)

(Head office) Sefton House, 42 Church Street, Welwyn Garden City, Herts AL8 6PJ, (0707) 338244, fax (0707) 371398
Hours Mon–Sat 9–10 (some 10.30), Sun (not Scotland) 12–3, 7–10.
Credit cards AC V.
Discounts Available on quantity.
Delivery Free local, selected branches.
G T
Two different shop fascia – **Thresher Wine Shops** *and* **Drink Stores from Threshers.** *Now owns Peter Dominic, Bottoms Up, Wine Rack as well as Thresher shops themselves. Strong on clarets, including a good choice of second wines, an expanding range of Alsace wines (wonderful Zind-Humbrecht), plus an increasingly good selection of French country wines. Australia, New Zealand and California all on the up.*

T. & W. WINES (TW)

51 King St, Thetford, Norfolk IP24 2AU, (0842) 765646
Hours Mon–Fri 9.30–5.30, Sat 9.30–1.00.
Credit cards AC AE DC V.
Delivery Free UK mainland 4 or more cases.
C EP G M
An extraordinary selection of fine, old and rare wines – Burgundies (which are a speciality) dating back to 1949, and half bottles of all sorts back to 1928. Terrific Rhônes, Australians, Californians, Tokaji and most other things as well, including the now hard-to-find Massandra Crimean wines. There is Sauternes from the extraordinary Château Gilette and the same owners' Château les Justices, Willi Opitz's Austrian wines and Hollick from Australia. Lots of anniversary years, too.

UNWINS (UN)

(Head office) Birchwood House, Victoria Road, Dartford, Kent DA1 5AJ, (0322) 272711/7; 300 specialist off-licences throughout the south-east of England
Hours Variable, usually Mon–Sat 10–10, Sun 12–3, 7–10.
Credit cards AC AE DC V.
Discounts 10% mixed case.
G M T
Thorough though not always adventurous list that covers just about everywhere. Quality is rather uneven, so choose carefully.

VALVONA & CROLLA (VA)

19 Elm Row, Edinburgh EH7 4AA, 031-556 6066
Hours Mon–Sat 8.30–6. Closed 1–7 Jan.
Credit cards AC V.
Discounts 5% mixed case.
Delivery Free locally for orders over £25. Mail order £6.90 per case, £3 for orders of more than 4 cases, free for 7 or more.
G M T
Italophiles should instantly move to Edinburgh. V&C have wines from all over Italy, from the cheap to the serious, plus Champagne, port and over 4500 food lines and 35 olive oils.

VICTORIA WINE (VIC)

(Head office) Brook House, Chertsey Road, Woking, Surrey GU21 5BE, (0483) 715066; over 800 branches throughout Great Britain
Hours Variable, usually Mon–Sat 9–6 (high street), 10–10 (local shops), Sun 12–3, 7–10.
Credit cards AC AE V.
Discounts 5% mixed case, 7 bottles for the price of 6 on most Champagnes.
G T
Over 500 wines are available, though many of them need to be ordered in advance through the list, which looks – and is – much better than the shelves in most branches.

LA VIGNERONNE (VIG)

105 Old Brompton Rd, London SW7 3LE, 071-589 6113
Hours Mon–Fri 10–9, Sat 10–7.
Credit cards AC AE DC V.
Discounts 5% mixed case (collected).
Delivery Free locally, £10 mainland England & Wales for orders under £100, £5 for £100–£200, free over £200; mainland Scotland £16 for under £150, £8 for £150–£300, free over £300.
C EP G M T
Fascinating and very personal list, strong on classic and southern French – also the place for exceptional Loire and Alsace, Provençal rarities, top Californians and Aussies. Not cheap.

VINTAGE WINES (VIN)

116 Derby Rd, Nottingham NG1 5FB, (0602) 476565/419614
Hours Mon–Fri 9–5.15, Sat 9–1.
Credit cards AC V.
Discounts 10% mixed case.
Delivery Free within 60 miles.
G M T
Useful merchant with traditional taste who takes particular care with his house wines.

WAITROSE (WAI)

(Head office) Doncastle Rd, Southern Industrial Area, Bracknell, Berks RG12 4YA (0344) 424680; 102 licensed shops.
Hours Mon–Tue 9–6, Wed 9–8, Thu 8.30–8, Fri 8.30–9, Sat 8.30–6.
Discounts 5% for orders over £100 or any whole case of wine.
G
Waitrose is less devoted to own-label wines than some supermarkets and in most areas of its wide-ranging list is remarkably adventurous. Bordeaux and Burgundy, both red and white, are particularly strong – look here for good-value pudding wines. The New World is also good, as is sparkling wine.

WHICLAR & GORDON (WHG)

Glebelands, Vincent Lane, Dorking, Surrey RH4 3YZ, (0306) 885711, fax (0306) 740053
Hours Mon–Fri 9–5.30, Sat 9–4. Closed bank hols; 24-hr answerphone.
Credit Cards AC V.
Discounts 5% unmixed case.
Delivery Free within 10 mile radius, or £1.50 per case for 1–11 cases (minimum charge £6.50).
Minimum order 1 case.
G T

Owned by the Thomas Hardy group of Australia, this merchant is strong on wines made by the Hardy's group. That, however, makes for a fair range. Good clarets and Burgundies, too, including some old vintages. Some countries, notably Spain, seem not to inspire the owners at all.

WHITESIDES OF CLITHEROE (WHI)

Shawbridge St, Clitheroe, Lancs BB7 1NA, (0200) 22281, fax (0200) 27129
Hours Mon–Sat 9–5.30.
Credit cards AC V.
Discounts Dependent on amount, 5% unmixed case.
G M T
Good Loires and a sound though not necessarily imaginative selection from elsewhere, though Bordeaux is good. Don't let the look of the list put you off, though.

WINDRUSH WINES (WW)

The Ox House, Market Square, Northleach, Cheltenham, Glos GL54 3EG, (0451) 860680, fax (0451) 861166; 3 Market Place, Cirencester, Glos GL7 2PE, (0285) 650466
Hours Cheltenham: Mon–Fri 9–6. Cirencester: Mon–Sat 9–5.30.
Credit cards AC V.
Discounts In bond and ex-cellar terms available.
Delivery Free locally, elsewhere £6 for up to 2 cases, free for 3.
Minimum order 1 mixed case.
C EP G M T
Specialists in fine single-estate wines. While the emphasis lies on France, they also have a reputation for the best wines from California and the Pacific North-West. Germany, Italy, Australia and South Africa are also strong. Look out for delicious Billecart Salmon Champagne and The Eyrie Vineyard from Oregon.

WINE RACK (WR)

(Head office) Sefton House, 42 Church Street, Welwyn Garden City, Herts AL8 6PJ, (0707) 328244, fax (0707) 371398
Hours Mon–Sat 9–10 (some 10.30), Sun 12–3, 7–10.
Credit cards AC AE V.
Discounts 5% mixed cases wine, 12.5% mixed cases Champagne.
Delivery Free locally, all shops.
G T
Part of Threshers; but smarter and with a wider, generally more upmarket range. Eighty stores across the country.

WINE SOCIETY (WS)

(Head office) Gunnels Wood Rd, Stevenage, Herts SG1 2BG, (0438) 741177, fax (0438) 741392; Showroom: (0438) 741566
Hours Mon–Fri 9–5; showroom Mon–Fri 9–6, Sat 9–1.
Credit cards AC V.
Discounts (per case) £1 for 5–9, £2 for 10 or more, £3 for collection.
Delivery Free 1 case or more UK mainland and Northern Ireland. Collection facility at Hesdin, France at French rates of duty & vat.
C EP G M T
You have to be a member to buy wines from this non-profit-making co-operative, but lifetime membership is very reasonable at £20. They offer an outstanding range. France is the backbone, but there are also masses of good and adventurous wines from California, Germany, Italy, Spain and Portugal, plus goodies like sun-dried tomatoes and olive oil. In spite of its rather safe image, this is one of the country's more enterprising wine merchants. Quoted prices include delivery, which makes them rather good value.

WINECELLARS (WCL)

153–155 Wandsworth High St, London SW18 4JB, 081-871 2668; The Market, 213–215 Upper St, London N1 1RL, 071-359 5386
Hours Wandsworth High St: Mon–Fri 11.30–8.30, Sat 10–8.30.
Upper St: Daily 9–9.
Credit cards AC V.
Discounts 10% mixed case.
Delivery Free within M25 boundary, or 2 cases UK mainland.
Minimum order 1 mixed case.
C G M T
One of the most exciting ranges of wine in London, and Britain's leading Italian specialist. Each year the list gets bigger and better and includes books, coffee, even pasta flour and wonderful olive oil. But it's not all Italian: Australia is strong, as are – well, most places, really. The California selection is well-chosen and out of the ordinary. Regular tastings are held, including many non-Italian subjects.

WINES OF WESTHORPE (WIW)

Marchington, Staffs ST14 8NX, (0283) 820285, fax (0283) 820631
Hours Mon–Fri and most weekends 8–6.30.
Credit cards AC V.
Discounts (per case) £2.60 for 5–10, £3.20 for 11–15.
Delivery Free UK mainland 2 or more cases.
Minimum order 1 mixed case.
M T
Eastern European specialists: a good range of Bulgarian wines plus Hungarians, a few Chileans, Australians and, new recently, Portuguese. But the Bulgarian wines are still the main point of it all, and have the royal warrant of King Simeon II, exiled king of the Bulgarians. Bet their rivals are really jealous.

WRIGHT WINE CO (WRI)

The Old Smithy, Raikes Rd, Skipton, N. Yorks BD23 1NP, (0756) 700886
Hours Mon–Sat 9–6.
Discounts Wholesale price unsplit case, 5% mixed case.
Delivery Free within 30 miles. **G**
There is a good selection of halves here for the abstemious and plenty of pudding wines (including sweet Champagne) for the seriously greedy. French country wines look good, as do Bordeaux, Burgundy, the Loire Valley, South Africa and the Lebanon (Musar back to 1975).

PETER WYLIE FINE WINES (WY)

Plymtree Manor, Plymtree, Cullompton, Devon EX15 2LE, (0884) 277555, fax (0881) 277556
Hours Mon–Fri 9–6.
Discounts Unsplit cases.
Delivery Free London 3 or more cases, UK mainland £10 1–2 cases, or for 1 case then £6 per case.**C M**
Claret and Sauternes are the specialities, followed by Burgundy, Champagne and port. Madeira features too. There are plenty of older vintages for the buff to wallow in, since mature wines are a speciality.

YAPP BROTHERS (YAP)

The Old Brewery, Mere, Wilts BA12 6DY, (0747) 860423, fax (0747) 860929
Hours Mon–Fri 9–5, Sat 9–1.
Credit cards AC V.
Discounts 6 or more cases.
Delivery £3 for under 2 cases.
C EP G M T
The specialities are the Rhône and the Loire, but there are lots of good French country wine, some Alsace, esoterica like Marc from Château Grillet and very good house Champagne. Also nut oils, olive oil and fish soup.

REGIONAL DIRECTORY

LONDON

Les Amis du Vin AMI
Australian Wine Centre AUS
Barnes Wine Shop BAR
Berkmann Wine Cellars BEK
Berry Bros & Rudd BER
Bibendum BIB
Bottoms Up BOT
Bute Wines BUT
Corney & Barrow CB
Davisons DAV
Farr Vintners FA
Fine Wines of New Zealand FIZ
The Grape Shop GR
Grog Blossom GRG
Harcourt Fine Wines HAC
Haynes Hanson & Clark HAH
Justerini & Brooks JU
London Wine LO
Moreno Wines MOR
Morris & Verdin MV
Roberson ROB
Summerlee Wines SUM
Unwins UN
La Vigneronne VIG
Winecellars WCL

SOUTH-EAST AND HOME COUNTIES

Bedford Fine Wines BE
Berry Bros & Rudd BER
Bordeaux Direct BOD
Bottoms Up BOT
Butlers Wine Cellar BU
Cape Province Wines CAP
Chaplin & Son CH
Philip Eyres EY
Gerard Harris HAG
Douglas Henn-Macrae HE
High Breck Vintners HIG
Hungerford Wine Company HUN
Lorne House Vintners LOR
Unwins UN
Whiclar & Gordon WHG
The Sunday Times Wine Club WIC
Wine Society WS

WEST AND SOUTH-WEST

Averys AV
Bottoms Up BOT
Châteaux Wines CHA
Eldridge, Pope & Co EL
John Harvey & Sons HA
Richard Harvey Wines HAY
Hicks & Don HIC
J.C. Karn KA
Nadder Wine NA
Christopher Piper PIP
Reid Wines REI
Windrush Wines WW
Peter Wylie WYL
Yapp Brothers YAP

EAST ANGLIA

Adnams AD
Anthony Byrne BY
Corney & Barrow CB
Roger Harris Wines HAW
Hicks & Don HIC
Lay & Wheeler LAY
Thos. Peatling PE
T. & W. Wines TW

MIDLANDS

Broad Street Wine Co. BR
Gauntleys GAU
Halves HAL
Summerlee Wines SUM
Tanners TAN
Vintage Wines VIN
Wines of Westhorpe WIW

NORTH

Borg Castel BOR
D Byrne BYR
Penistone Court Fine Wines PEN
Whitesides of Clitheroe WHI
Wright Wine Company WRI

WALES

Ashley Scott AS
Celtic Vintner CV

SCOTLAND

Bute Wines BUT
Corney & Barrow CB
Gelston Castle GE
Peter Green GRE
Justerini & Brooks JU
J.E. Hogg HOG
Raeburn Fine Wines RAE
Valvona & Crolla VA

CHANNEL ISLANDS

Sommelier Wines SOM

NORTHERN IRELAND

Direct Wine DI
James Nicholson NI

COUNTRYWIDE

ASDA ASD
Augustus Barnett AUG
Gateway GA
Majestic MAJ
Marks & Spencer MAR
Oddbins OD
Safeway SAF
Sainsbury SAI
Tesco TES
Thresher THR
Victoria Wine VIC
Waitrose WAI
Wine Rack WR

Oz Clarke's Wine Guide *is an annual publication: we welcome any suggestions you may have for the 1995 edition.* Send them to Webster's, Axe and Bottle Court, 70 Newcomen Street, London SE1 1YT.

INDEX

References to the Price Guide are in *italics*. The Price Guide page numbers refer only to the first entry in each section.

A

B

C

D

M

N

O

P

Q

R

S

ACKNOWLEDGEMENTS

Our thanks go to Wink Lorch for the Cost of a Bottle and the Maturity Charts, and to all those who sent us their wine lists, and everyone who kindly supplied wines for our tasting.